Assessment of Family Violence

Assessment of Family Violence

A Handbook for Researchers and Practitioners

Eva L. Feindler, Jill H. Rathus, and Laura Beth Silver

American Psychological Association

Washington, DC

Published by
American Psychological Association
750 First Street, NE
Washington, DC 20002
www.apa.org

To order
APA Order Department
P.O. Box 92984
Washington, DC 20090-2984

Tel: (800) 374-2721, Direct: (202) 336-5510
Fax: (202) 336-5502, TDD/TTY: (202) 336-6123
Online: www.apa.org/books/
Email: order@apa.org

In the U.K., Europe, Africa, and the Middle East, copies may be ordered from
American Psychological Association
3 Henrietta Street
Covent Garden, London
WC2E 8LU England

Typeset in New Baskerville by EPS Group Inc., Easton, MD

Printer: Phoenix Color Corporation, Hagerstown, MD
Cover designer: NiDesign, Baltimore, MD
Project Manager: Debbie Hardin, Carlsbad, CA

The opinions and statements published are the responsibility of the authors, and such opinions and statements do not necessarily represent the policies of the American Psychological Association.

Library of Congress Cataloging-in-Publication Data
Feindler, Eva L.
   Assessment of family violence : a handbook for researchers and practitioners / Eva L. Feindler, Jill H. Rathus, Laura Beth Silver.— 1st ed.
      p. cm.
Includes bibliographical references and index.
   ISBN 1-55798-900-1 (alk. paper)
   1. Victims of family violence—Psychological testing.   2. Abusive parents—Psychological testing.   3. Abused children—Psychological testing.   4. Family assessment.   I. Rathus, Jill H.   II. Silver, Laura Beth.   III. Title.
   HV6626 .F45 2003
   362.82′6—dc21

2002067563

British Library Cataloguing-in-Publication Data
A CIP record is available from the British Library.

Printed in the United States of America
First Edition

Contents

List of Measures   vii

Preface   xvii

Acknowledgments   xxi

I. Issues in the Assessment of Family Violence   **1**

Chapter 1.   The Assessment of Family Violence: An Overview   3

Chapter 2.   General Issues in the Assessment of Family Violence   11

Chapter 3.   Family Violence Assessment: Test Construction and Psychometrics   39

II. Assessment of Maltreated Children and Adolescents   **51**

Chapter 4.   Interview Methods   63

Chapter 5.   Self-Report Inventories for the Assessment of Children   125

Chapter 6.   Behavioral Observation and Analogue Methods   229

III. Assessment of Parents and Caregivers   **247**

Chapter 7.   Interview Methods   255

Chapter 8.   Self-Report Assessment of Parents and Caregivers   275

Chapter 9.   Behavioral Observation and Analogue Methods   335

IV. Assessment of Family Interaction   **367**

Chapter 10.   Interview Methods   375

Chapter 11.   Self-Report Inventories   387

Chapter 12.   Analogue Methods and Behavioral Coding   433

References   507

Author Index   529

Subject Index   539

About the Authors   579

List of Measures

Chapter 4. Interview Methods

1. Anatomical Doll Questionnaire (ADQ)   63
   Levy, Markovic, Kalinowski, Ahart, and Torres

2. Attributions for Maltreatment Interview (AFMI)   67
   McGee and Wolfe

3. Checklist for Child Abuse Evaluation (CCAE)   69
   Petty

4. Child Abuse and Neglect Interview Schedule–Revised   72
   (CANIS–R)
   Ammerman; Ammerman, Van Hasselt, and Hersen

5. Childhood Experience of Care and Abuse (CECA)   76
   Bifulco, Brown, and Harris

6. Childhood Maltreatment Interview Schedule (CMIS)   80
   Briere

7. Childhood Post-Traumatic Stress Reaction   84
   Index (CPTS–RI)
   Frederick, Pynoos, and Nader

8. Childhood PTSD Interview–Parent Form (CPTSDI)   86
   Fletcher

9. Childhood PTSD Interview–Child Form (CPI–Child)   89
   Fletcher

10. Childhood Trauma Interview (CTI)   93
    Bernstein et al.

11. Children's Attributions and Perceptions Scale (CAPS;   95
    originally Semi-Structured Inventory for Children)
    Mannarino, Cohen, and Berman

12. Children's Perception Questionnaire (CPQ)   98
    Miller-Perrin and Wurtele

13. Clinician Administered PTSD Scale for Children and   101
    Adolescents for the *DSM-IV* (CAPS–CA)
    Nader et al.

14. Parent Impact Questionnaire (PIQ)   105
    Wolfe

15. Self-Report of Childhood Abuse Physical (SRCAP)   107
    Widom and Shepard

16. Structured Interview of Symptoms Associated With   109
    Sexual Abuse (SASA)
    Wells, McCann, Adams, Voris, and Dahl

17. Structured Interview for Disorders of Extreme Stress   111
    (SIDES)
    Pelcovitz et al.

18. Traumatic Antecedents Interview (TAI)   115
    Perry, Herman, and van der Kolk

19. "What If" Situations Test (WIST–III)   118
    Wurtele, Kast, and Kondrick

20. Wyatt Sex History Questionnaire (WSHQ)   122
    Wyatt, Lawrence, Vodounon, and Mickey

Chapter 5. Self-Report Inventories for the Assessment of Children

21. Abusive Sexual Exposure Scale (ASES)   125
    Spaccarelli

22. Adolescent Dissociative Experience Survey (A–DES)   127
    Armstrong, Putnam, and Carlson

23. Angie/Andy Child Rating Scale (A/A CRS)   131
    Praver, Pelcovitz, and DeGuiseppe

24. Assessing Environments Scale (AEIII)   134
    Berger and Knutson

25. Checklist of Sexual Abuse and Related Stressors   138
    (C–SARS)
    Spaccarelli

26. Child Abuse and Trauma Scale (CAT)   142
    Sanders and Becker-Lausen

27. Child Dissociative Checklist (CDC)   145
 Putnam

28. Child Post-Traumatic Stress Reaction Index 148
 (CPTS–RI)
 Frederick, Pynoos, and Nader

29. Child Sexual Behavior Inventory I (CSBI–I) 150
 Friedrich

30. Child's Reaction to Traumatic Events Scale (CRTES) 153
 Jones

31. Child Dissociative Predictor Scale (CDPS) 155
 Branscomb and Fagan

32. Childhood Trauma Questionnaire (CTQ) 158
 Bernstein et al.

33. Children's Impact of Traumatic Events Scale B Revised 161
 (CITES–R)
 Wolfe, Wolfe, Gentile, and LaRose (orig.); Wolfe and
 Gentile (rev.)

34. Conflicts in Relationships Questionnaire (CIRQ) 165
 Wolfe, Reitzal-Jaffe, Gough, and Werkele

35. Emotional and Physical Abuse Questionnaire (EPAB) 169
 Carlin

36. Exposure to Abuse and Supportive Environments– 171
 Parenting Inventory (EASE–PI)
 Nicholas and Bieber

37. Family Environment Questionnaire (FEQ) 175
 Briere and Runtz

38. Feelings and Emotions Experienced During Sexual 177
 Abuse (FEEDSA)
 Wolfe and Birt

39. History of Victimization Form (HVF) 179
 Wolfe, Wolfe, Gentile, and Bourdeau

40. Multidimensional Neglect Scale (MNS) 182
 Straus, Kinard, and Williams

41. Negative Appraisals of Sexual Abuse Scale (NASAS) 185
 Spaccarelli

42. Parent Perception Inventory (PPI)   188
Hazzard, Christensen, and Margolin

43. Parent's Perceptions Questionnaire (PPQ) and   191
Teacher's Perceptions Questionnaire (TPQ)
Wurtele and Miller-Perrin

44. Parent's Report on the Child's Reaction to Stress   194
Scale (PRCS)
Fletcher

45. Personal Safety Questionnaire (PSQ)   197
Wurtele, Kast, Miller-Perrin, and Kondrick

46. Responses to Childhood Incest Questionnaire   199
(RCIQ)
Donaldson and Gardner

47. Sexual Abuse Exposure Questionnaire (SAEQ)   203
Rowan, Foy, Rodriguez, and Ryan

48. Sexual Abuse Fear Evaluation (SAFE)   206
Wolfe and Wolfe

49. Trauma Symptom Checklist for Children (TSCC)   209
Briere

50. Trauma Symptom Checklist 33 and 40   212
(TSC–33 and TSC–40)
Briere and Runtz; Elliot and Briere

51. Trauma Symptom Inventory (TSI)   214
Briere

52. Traumatic Sexualization Survey (TSS)   218
Matorin and Lynn

53. Weekly Behavior Report (WBR)   221
Cohen and Mannarino

54. "When Bad Things Happen" (WBTH)   224
Fletcher

Chapter 6. Behavioral Observation and Analogue Methods
55. Assessment of Physiological Responses to Analogue   229
Audiotaped Scripts
Orr et al.

56. Behavioral Observation of Abused Children 232
   Haskett and Kistner

57. Behavioral Observation of Shelter Children 234
   Copping

58. Behavioral Role-Play in Sex Abuse Prevention (BR–SAP) 236
   Harbeck, Peterson, and Starr

59. Child Abuse Interview Interaction Coding System 239
   (CAIICS)
   Wood, Orsak, and Cross

60. Mock Trial Role-Play (MTRP) 241
   Jaffee, Wilson, and Sas

61. Sexually Anatomically Detailed Dolls 243
   Dawson, Vaughan, and Wagner

Chapter 7. Interview Methods
62. Child Conflict Index (CCI) 255
   Frankel and Weiner

63. Concerns and Constraints Interview (CCI) 258
   Deater, Dodge, Bates, and Pettit

64. Daily Discipline Interview (DDI) 260
   Webster-Stratton

65. Disciplinary Strategies Interview (DSI) 263
   Peterson

66. Parent Discipline Interview (PDI) 266
   Scarr, Pinkerton, and Eisenberg

67. Parental Problem-Solving Measure (PPSM) 268
   Hansen

68. Parent Reaction to Abuse Disclosure Scale (PRADS) 271
   Everson

Chapter 8. Self-Report Assessment of Parents and Caregivers
69. Child Abuse Blame Scale–Physical Abuse (CABS–PA) 275
   Petretic-Jackson

70. Child Abuse Potential Inventory–Form VI (CAPI) 279
   Milner

71. Conflicts and Problem-Solving Scale (CPSS) 281
   Kerig

72. Conflict Tactics Scale: Parent to Child (CTSPC)   284
    Straus

73. Maternal Characteristics Scale (MCS)   288
    Polansky, Gaudin, and Kilpatrick

74. Parent Attribution Scale (PAS)   290
    Celano, Webb, and Hazzard

75. Screening for Problem Parenting (SPP)   293
    Avison, Turner, and Noh

76. Weekly Report of Abuse Indicators (WRAI)   296
    Kolko

77. Intensity of Parental Punishment Scale (IPPS)   298
    Gordon

78. Parent Affect Test (PAT)   301
    Linehan, Paul, and Egan

79. Parent Attribution Test (PAT)   304
    Bugental

80. Parent Behavior Checklist/Parenting Inventory (PBC)   306
    Fox

81. Parent Behavior Inventory (PBI)   309
    Lovejoy, Weis, O'Hara, and Rubin

82. Parent Opinion Questionnaire (POQ)   312
    Azar

83. Parental Anger Inventory (PAI)   315
    MacMillan, Olson, and Hansen

84. Parental Stress Scale (PSS)   318
    Berry and Jones

85. Parenting Alliance Inventory (PAI)   320
    Abidin

86. Parenting Locus of Control Scale (PLCS)   322
    Campis

87. Parenting Scale (PS)   324
    Arnold and O'Leary

88. Parenting Sense of Competence (PSOC)   328
    Gibaud-Wallston and Wandersman

89. Parenting Stress Index (PSI)   330
    Abidin

Chapter 9. Behavioral Observation and Analogue Methods
90. Analogue Parenting Task (APT)   335
    Zaidi

91. Home Simulation Assessment (HSA)   338
    MacMillan

92. Hypothetical Compliance Vignettes (HCV)   340
    Strassberg

93. Judgments in Moments of Anger (JMA)   343
    Dix

94. Maternal Observation Matrix (MOM)   346
    Tutuer, Ewigman, Peterson, and Hosokawa

95. Mother's Responses to Videotapes (MRV)   348
    Smith and O'Leary

96. Parent Behavior Rating Scales (PBRS)   351
    King, Rogers, Walters, and Oldershaw

97. Parent/Child Interaction Observations (PCIO)   353
    Haskett

98. Parent Daily Report (PDR)   356
    Trickett

99. Video Assessment Task (VAT)   359
    Fagot

100. Video Mediated Recall Task (VMRT)   362
    Johnston, Reynolds, Freeman, and Geller

Chapter 10. Interview Methods
101. Children's Marital Conflict Coping Strategies Interview   375
    (CMCCSI)
    O'Brien

102. Child Witness to Violence Interview (CWVI)   378
    Jaffe, Wolfe, and Wilson

103. Family Interaction Interview (FII)   381
    Salzinger

104. Witness to Violence Child Interview   383
     Pynoos and Eth

Chapter 11. Self-Report Inventories
105. Brother–Sister Questionnaire (BSQ)   387
     Graham-Bermann

106. Children's Perceptions of Interparental Conflict Scale   389
     (CPICS)
     Grych, Seid, and Fincham

107. Discord Control and Coping Questionnaire (DCCQ)   392
     Rossman and Rosenberg

108. Family Worries Scale (FWS)   395
     Graham-Bermann

109. Potential Family Conflict Questionnaire (PFCQ)   397
     Margolin

110. Children's Beliefs About Parental Divorce Scale   399
     (CBPDS)
     Berg and Kurdek

111. Family Environment Scale–Children's Version   402
     (FES–CV)
     Pino, Simons, and Slawinowski

112. Conflict Behavior Questionnaire (CBQ)   405
     Prinz, Foster, Kent, and O'Leary

113. Family Adaptability and Cohesion Scale III (FACES III)   408
     Olson, Portner, and Laree

114. Family Assessment Measure III (FAM III)   410
     Skinner, Steinhauer, and Santa-Barbara

115. Family Beliefs Inventory (FBI)   413
     Roehling and Robin

116. Family Crisis Oriented Personal Evaluation Scales   416
     (F–COPES)
     McCubbin, Larsen, and Olson

117. Family Environment Scale (FES)   419
     Moos and Moos

118. Family Inventory of Life Events (FILE)   423
     McCubbin and Patterson

119. Mother–Adolescent Attribution Questionnaire (MAAQ)   425
     Grace, Kelley, and McCain

120. Parent–Adolescent Relationship Questionnaire (PARQ)   429
     Robin, Koepke, and Moye

Chapter 12. Analogue Methods and Behavioral Coding

121. Articulated Thoughts During Simulated Situations   433
     (ATSS)
     O'Brien

122. Audiotaped Interparental Verbal Conflict (AIVC)   437
     Adamson and Thompson

123. Children's Response to Live Interadult Anger (CRLIA)   439
     El-Sheikh and Reiter

124. Checklist for Living Environments to Assess Neglect   442
     (CLEAN)
     Watson-Perczel, Lutzker, Greene, and McGimpsey

125. Cleanup Coding Systems (CCS)   445
     Koenig, Cicchette, and Rogasch

126. Dyadic Parent–Child Interaction Coding System   449
     (DPICS)
     Eyberg and Robinson

127. Exposure to Interadult Anger (EIA)   452
     Hennessey

128. Family Intake Coding System (FICS)   454
     Stormshak and Speltz

129. Family Interaction Task (FIT)   458
     Madonna, Van Scoyle, and Jones

130. Family Interaction Task (FIT)   461
     Silber, Bermann, Handerson, and Lehman

131. Home Accident Prevention Inventory (HAPI)   463
     Tertinger, Greene, and Lutzker

132. Home Interaction Scoring System (HISS)   466
     Jacob, Tennenbaum, Bargiel, and Seilhamer

133. Home Observation for Measurement of the   470
     Environment (HOME)
     Bradley and Caldwell

134. Interaction Behavior Code (IBC)   472
     Prinz and Kent

135. Laboratory Family Interaction Task (LFIT)   476
     Kavanagh, Youngblade, Reid, and Fagot

136. Mother–Child Interaction Task (MCIT)   478
     Shipman and Zeman

137. Mother–Son Interaction Task (MSIT)   481
     Mahoney, Boggio, and Jouriles

138. Observational Coding System for Triadic Interaction   484
     (OCSTI)
     Gordis, Margolin, and John

139. Psychological Maltreatment Scales (PMS)   487
     Brassard, Hart, and Hardy

140. Response-Class Matrix (RCM)   490
     Mash, Johnston, and Kovitz

141. Sibling Conflict Resolution Scale (SCRS)   492
     Roberts

142. Standardized Observation Codes (SOCIII)   495
     Cerezo, Keesler, Dunn, and Wahler

143. Structured Laboratory and Home Observation: 499
     Single Case Study (SLHO)
     Schellenbach, Trickett, and Susman

144. System for Coding Interactions and Family Functioning   501
     (SCIFF)
     Lindahl

Preface

According to Ammerman and Hersen (1999), family violence research has matured considerably, and the core features of clinical assessment have been identified. Indeed, researchers have emphasized an empirically based assessment approach, and numerous measures specifically designed for both victims and perpetrators of family violence have been developed (Ammerman & Hersen, 1999). Most would agree that a multimethod, multibehavioral, multi-informant approach to the assessment of families is ideal. Research in the field of family violence has helped to identify antecedents to child maltreatment (such as difficult child behavior or marital conflict), sequelae of child abuse (both global adjustment problems as well as abuse-specific symptoms), and variables that mediate the occurrence of maltreatment (such as parental reactivity, social support, and parental competence; Wolfe & Birt, 1997; Wolfe & McEachran, 1997).

Although research in the field of family violence has burgeoned and great strides in the development of assessment methods have been made, it is not clear that clinicians and other mental health professionals providing services to families affected by maltreatment have benefited. Often these professionals are called on to help the courts or child protection personnel to make critical decisions. Assessment of parents' caregiving abilities and children's safety helps to inform dispositional decisions such as placement, custody, or visitation arrangements (Budd, 2001). Judgments regarding parental competence help inform termination of parental rights cases so that children do not languish in foster care indefinitely (Azar, Lauretti, & Loding, 1998).

However, despite clinical practice guidelines as well as research on reliable and valid assessment measures, the use of this ideal approach is rarely reported. In 2001, Budd and colleagues reviewed 190 mental health evaluations completed on parents in child protection cases and found several substantive limitations in the content and comprehensiveness of the assessment. The evaluations were predominantly based on a single assessment session, with few sources of information, and they rarely included child–parent observation (Budd, Poindexter, Felix, & Naik-Polan, 2001). More recently, a systematic examination of 207 psychological evaluations of children exposed to abuse or neglect using an extensive coding system was reported (Budd, Felix, Poindexter, Naik-Polan, & Sloss, 2002). Results indicated that in nearly half of the samples, *no* information from parents was obtained, and teachers were rarely contacted. The majority of the evaluations consisted of a single office session with limited use of background information. The researchers found no examples of evaluations that provided a comprehensive assessment of the child's functioning in the actual environments of his or her life (with parents, siblings, peers, at school, etc.). Finally, few cases in which specific referral questions were articulated and in which examiners tailored their assessment approach findings and recommendations to the specific child or family were found (Budd et al., 2002). It is clear that assessment practice has not paralleled advances in either research or treatment.

The usual practices of those who complete psychological evaluations in maltreatment cases still seem to focus on standardized test measures as well as traditional personality assessment. They seem ill-suited for addressing the relational and skills issues involved in parental competence judgments (Azar et al., 1998), for describing clinical sequelae following child sexual abuse (Babiker & Herbert, 1998), or for accurately assessing the variety of developmental and abuse-specific symptoms characteristic of those victimized by family violence. Comprehensive and contextual assessments by the practitioner require not only an understanding of multimodal assessment but also access to various assessment methods and to available, reliable, and valid measures. For these reasons and others, we chose to research the field of clinical assessment of family violence and to collect and organize a compendium of strategies that would help clinicians to achieve this ideal approach to assessment. In addition, as we continue to train new clinicians and to stimulate research on effective prevention and intervention in family violence, this compendium may prove an invaluable resource. This volume may represent one of the only resources available that not only emphasizes a multimethod approach to assessment by a review of interview, self-report, and analogue methods but also describes the exact measure, complete with sample items, administration guidelines, and related research. We also sought to include scale availability information to facilitate practitioners' ability to obtain the assessment device for their own use.

We hope that we have assisted those researchers looking for both global and abuse-specific assessment methods for evaluating intervention and prevention efforts. By creating a user-friendly review of assessments, we likewise hope that practitioners and those involved in the critical decisions made to protect children and restore their families to health will be encouraged to use reliable and valid assessment tools with greater ease.

References

Ammerman, R. T., & Hersen, M. (1999). *Assessment of family violence: A clinical and legal sourcebook* (2nd ed.). New York: John Wiley and Sons.

Azar, S. T., Lauretti, A. F., & Loding, B. V. (1998). The evaluation of parental fitness in termination of parental rights cases: A functional–contextual perspective. *Clinical Child and Family Psychology Review, 1*, 77–100.

Babiker, G., & Herbert, M. (1998). Critical issues in the assessment of child sexual abuse. *Clinical Child and Family Psychology Review, 1*, 231–252.

Budd, K. S. (2001). Assessing parenting competence in child protection cases: A clinical practice model. *Clinical Child and Family Psychology Review, 4*, 1–18.

Budd, K. S., Felix, E. D., Poindexter, L. M., Naik-Polan, A. T., & Sloss, C. F. (2002). Clinical assessment of children in child protection cases: An empirical analysis. *Professional Psychology: Research and Practice, 33*, 3–12.

Budd, K. S., Poindexter, L. M., Felix, E. D., & Naik-Polan, A. T. (2001). Clinical assessment of parents in child protection cases: An empirical analysis. *Law and Human Behavior, 25*, 93–108.

Wolfe, D. A., & McEachran, A. (1997). Child physical abuse and neglect. In E. J. Mash & L. G. Terdal (Eds.), *Assessment of childhood disorders* (pp. 523–568). New York: Guilford Press.

Wolfe, V. V., & Birt, J. (1997). Child sexual abuse. In E. J. Mash & L. G. Terdal (Eds.), *Assessment of childhood disorders* (pp. 569–623). New York: Guilford Press.

Acknowledgments

To begin the acknowledgments, we would like to thank each other (Eva L. Feindler, Jill H. Rathus, and Laura Beth Silver) for collaboration on this volume. None of us fully realized the scope of this project when we initiated it, and it could not have been completed without each author's dedication and hard work. We dedicate this volume to all of the families we have worked with throughout our clinical careers. The critical need for effective prevention and treatment programs for those exposed to violence motivated us to complete this book.

A special note of gratitude goes to Cathy Kudlack from the Psychological Services Center at Long Island University/CW Post Campus. She assisted us with patience, tireless energy, and an unwavering smile. We are eternally indebted to her.

We greatly appreciate the contributions of several current and former graduate students at Long Island University/CW Post Campus in the clinical psychology program: Nick Cavuoto, Anthony Anzalone, Pat Price, Nancy Nichols-Goldstein, Amy Reichstein, Kristan Baker, Glory Blanceagle, and Sharon Spitzer. These students helped with the voluminous research needed for this book, and we cannot imagine completing it without their help. We also thank the many authors of the assessment instruments described in this volume. We contacted many of them requesting copies of their scales or their supporting information, and without their devotion to this field and responsiveness to us, of course, there would be no book.

Anonymous reviewers were also generous with their time, providing detailed and astute feedback that helped us to refine the manuscript and to improve its scope and clarity. In addition, we thank the editorial staff at the American Psychological Association for their patience and guidance from conceptualization to the final stages of production.

Finally, Jill H. Rathus would like to thank her family for continuing to be her greatest source of support and inspiration. Eva L. Feindler would like to dedicate this effort to her mother, who has shown tremendous resiliency during times of illness and who eagerly sought to proofread this volume during her recovery. Laura Beth Silver would like to thank her family and friends for all their support and never-ending belief in her abilities.

Part I

Issues in the Assessment of Family Violence

The Assessement of Family Violence: An Overview

In this volume, we describe and review a wealth of assessment instruments in the field of family violence. Our intention is to furnish practitioners, researchers, and program evaluators with a comprehensive volume that places information concerning a large variety of measurement options at their fingertips.

Scope of the Book

The scope of our volume is narrow in that in the areas in which we chose to focus, we limited our selection of measures primarily to instruments developed for and applied to the assessment of violence, its risk factors, its correlates, and its sequelae as it occurs within the family. As such, we include three major foci of family violence assessment: children, parents, and families (the companion volume to this text, titled *Handbook of Assessment in Partner Violence* [Rathus & Feindler, in press], focuses on partner-directed violence). In addition, we limited our orientation to family violence assessment to a behavioral assessment approach, which we describe later.

Excluded from this volume, then, for the purpose of maintaining our family focus, are sections pertaining to the assessment of such related areas as dating violence, violent crime, school violence, gang violence, general violence–antisocial behavior, and combat-related violence.

The scope of the volume is broad in that we include an exhaustive list of measures within each part, spanning three types of assessment methods: interview assessments, self-report/paper-and-pencil instruments (including rating checklists), and analogue assessments. We include traditional, time-tested instruments as well as those developed in the last years of the twentieth century. We describe measures used widely as well as measures used only in a single study, provided they meet our criteria for inclusion described later. Our hope is to provide readers with a broad sampling of measures in the field so that they can either make use of specific measures we review or perhaps build on the methodology described in a particular area to adapt a measure or develop their own.

Contents

This handbook contains four major parts. Part I, "Issues in the Assessment of Family Violence," provides a general overview of the book and of matters pertaining to the assessment of family violence, and contains three chapters.

Chapter 2 discusses the varying purposes for conducting assessments in family violence, including clinical evaluation (involving standard clinical practice, accountability for the provision of effective treatments, crisis management, and forensic evaluations or other professional consultations), program evaluation, and the stimulation of both quantitative and qualitative research. The chapter then describes assessment approaches, including interviews, self-report measures/rating scales, analogue measures, direct observations in natural settings, and archival records. Advantages and disadvantages of each are discussed. The chapter then moves on to a discussion of assessment targets and then covers ethical, diagnostic, and legal issues (including matters of risk management; subpoenas for client records; reporting requirements; forensic evaluations; and prediction of dangerousness). Finally, discussion of assessment in clinical practice, focusing on assessment objectives, including establishing rapport, obtaining a problem description–definition, setting targets for treatment, measuring pretreatment functioning, measuring treatment progress, and measuring treatment outcome.

Chapter 3 highlights basic principles of test construction and psychometric characteristics of scales, and focuses on a number of research issues relevant to the assessment of family violence. We consider issues involved in developing measures for family violence research, including methods of scale development, scaling, and types of reliability and validity. These sections will provide a review for those trained in assessment but will prove most helpful for readers lacking a background in assessment or psychometrics. We then address difficulties in conducting assessment research in family violence, including difficulties in establishing psychometric properties, issues of "subjecting" victims to research, and placing research participants at risk.

The remaining three parts contain three chapters each, all following a common structure. Part II, "The Assessment of Children," includes measures pertaining to child victims or witnesses of family violence as well as adult survivors of childhood abuse. This part also includes measures filled out by parents, targeting their perceptions or observations of their children's reactions to abusive experiences. Part III, "The Assessment of Parents and Caregivers," includes measures pertaining to maltreating parents or parents at risk for maltreatment. Part IV, "The Assessment of Families," includes measures pertaining to characteristics or dynamics in maltreating or at-risk families (from either the child's or parents' perspective).

The structure of Parts II through IV follows a standard format: an overview of issues relevant to the specific subfield within family violence assessment addressed in that part followed by three chapters: a chapter on interview assessment, a chapter on self-report/paper-and-pencil assessment, and a chapter on analogue assessment. Note that analogue measures take a variety of forms, but all involve some type of direct behavioral observation and some type of recreation or approximation of a natural setting (examples of analogue assessment are use of videotaped conflict scenarios, anatomically detailed dolls, role-play interactions, structured play or discussion tasks for family members, physiological and mechanical assessment methods, and behavioral observation coding systems.)

For quick reference, a table listing all of the instruments follows the table of contents, subdivided by chapter.

Organization and Format

Within each chapter, the measures we describe are included alphabetically by instrument name. Several factors, including assessment target (e.g., assessment of child versus assessment of parent), subtype of assessment device (e.g., observational coding devices), and the specificity of the instruments in measuring violence per se versus related constructs are included.

Within each chapter we present numerous descriptions of instruments, but we do not include the instruments themselves. Instead, we provide the following information for each assessment device:

- *Title and Author:* The title of the assessment device followed by the authors of the assessment device, usually, but not always, corresponding to the authors of the primary reference.
- *Development and Description of Assessment Method:* A brief description of the method, designed for the reader to scan for relevance to his or her purpose before deciding to read the more detailed information that follows. Also this section describes the process of developing the scale. Empirical approaches to scale development are generally described in some detail, and rational–theoretical approaches are also described. This section at times includes the authors' intentions in developing the scale and a prior assessment device the scale is based on or adapted from.
- *Target Population:* This includes the population for whom the scale was intended or on whom the scale was developed or evaluated. Although this section suggests past applications of the scale, it does not necessarily suggest limits on populations to whom the scale might be applied. For paper-and-pencil measures, we include the reading level of the scale, if specified in the measure itself.
- *Equipment Needed:* Some assessment devices within the analogue assessment chapters require specific equipment for their use; these are included if specified by the authors.
- *Format:* The format section includes descriptions of any subscales, the number of items in the scale, as well as sample items.
- *Administration and Scoring:* This section includes the response format (i.e., type of scaling, number of anchor points, etc.), the length of time to complete the instrument (and, when applicable, the length of time required for training in the procedure–training to expertise in the coding system), any particular instructions to the respondent, and scoring information.
- *Psychometric Evaluation:* This section includes information on the scale's norms, reliability, and validity. For norms, when available, we include information on what populations the scale was normed on, means and standard deviations in various popula-

tions, or cut-offs (e.g., for "clinical" levels of the phenomenon of interest). Often, the authors have provided extensive normative information on a variety of subpopulations that are presented in comprehensive tables in the primary article, chapter, or manual accompanying the instrument. In such cases of extensive normative data, for reasons of both economy of space and of obtaining permissions, we refer the reader to the source containing the norms. For reliability, we provide any available reliability information on an instrument, including internal consistency reliability, test–retest reliability, and interrater reliability. We also summarize any available information on a scale's validity, which most often falls within the categories of convergent–discriminant validity and criterion-related validity.

- *Advantages:* We provide advantages of the particular measure described, often including a combination of those noted by the author and our own evaluation of the device's advantages.
- *Limitations:* The discussion of advantages is balanced with mention of limitations inherent in the instrument.
- *Primary Reference:* We provide the original source reference, which typically contains a presentation of the scale development, conceptualization, description, application, and psychometric evaluation. Although these are most often journal articles, the primary scale references are, on occasion, book chapters, professionally published manuals, or unpublished manuscripts.
- *Scale Availability:* Most of the time, complete interview or analogue formats or scales are not included in the primary reference. Thus, we furnish the reader with a source for obtaining the assessment instrument itself (which usually will be accompanied by instructions for scoring). These sources typically comprise the author's direct contact information; an article, chapter, or book containing the scale; or the assessment corporation that currently owns the rights to the assessment device.
- *Related References:* These typically include those that contain related information on the scale's development, psychometric evaluation, or application to a family violence population.
- *General Comments and Recommendations for Practitioners and Researchers:* This section contains a summing up of our review of the scale, final comments on the instrument, or recommendations regarding its use.

Criteria for the Inclusion of Measures

We took a series of steps as we selected the many measures to be included in this volume. We should note that as comprehensive as this volume is, there were numerous additional assessment methodologies that were excluded. First, our orientation in this book favors a behavioral assessment approach to the measurement of family violence.

Behavioral Assessment Approach

Behavioral assessment, as compared to traditional assessment, emphasizes the measurement of observable rather than inferred characteristics, environmentally or contextually determined causes for events over intrapsychic factors or traits, present rather than historical events, ideographic rather than nomothetic assessment, continuous or repeated rather than one-time or pre–post evaluation, multimodal rather than single-method assessment, and the use of psychometrically sound (i.e., reliable and valid) assessment tools. In keeping with this approach, we primarily feature assessment tools using direct observation, analogue methods, physiological assessment, structured interviews, and behavior-rating checklists.[1]

Because we follow a behavioral orientation ourselves, we chose a more in-depth review of this approach rather than what would certainly have been a superficial review of all available relevant assessment methodologies. Although other approaches to research and assessment are certainly valid (e.g., psychodynamic, personality-based, feminist), they simply fall beyond the scope of this book. Moreover, given the multidisciplinary nature of the team approach now common to the investigation and referral process in family violence (i.e., police, judges, child protective case workers, probation officers, case managers, etc.), behavioral assessment approaches offer a detailed account of the most salient variables in the family context, thereby improving communication with personnel from nonclinical fields.

Despite our general tendency to follow a behavioral assessment approach, there are exceptions to this tendency in the measures we include in this volume. Although many of these consist of behavioral rating scales that involve the endorsement of specific behaviors con-

---

[1]Note that although self-monitoring tools (e.g., a daily log of anger outbursts) fall within the domain of behavioral assessment, we do not specifically review such measures because they tend to be highly individualized and not subject to psychometric evaluation.

ducted within a well-defined and recent timeframe (e.g., the Daily Discipline Interview; Webster-Stratton & Spitzer, 1991) or assess contextual stimuli rather than trait-like or intrapsychic phenomena (e.g., measures of family functioning, such as the Family Beliefs Inventory; Roehling & Robin, 1996), we do include several retrospective self-report scales, scales measuring traits or other nonobservable phenomena such as perceptions or automatic thoughts (e.g., the Children's Perceptions of Interparental Conflict Scale; Grych, Seid, & Fincham, 1992), instruments based on nomothetic assessment (i.e., measures with norms for various populations), as well as instruments designed for diagnostic purposes. We included such instruments if they were common enough in the field that we thought by excluding them we would severely limit the utility of this book and misrepresent the assessment strategies most often used in this field. For example, in the area of child abuse, many of the existing measures are retrospective; a strict adherence to including present-focused assessments only would have greatly restricted our coverage of this important area. However, to be included, the minimum requirements of such measures were that they meet at least some, if not all, characteristics of behavioral assessment measures, including meeting psychometric standards of having reasonable reliability and validity.[2]

Additional Criteria

Beyond the behavioral assessment focus, we excluded measures that fell outside of the topical domain of this book (e.g., medical assessment approaches) or fell outside of a family violence focus (e.g., measures relating to violent crime). To obtain the measures reviewed in this volume we embarked on the following process:

1. An exhaustive literature review of measures used in the field of family violence;
2. A supplementary literature review extended to the assessment of family interactions (such that we included methods–scales that have not yet been used in the field of family violence but that we viewed as relevant to assessment in this area);

---

[2]Although we attempted to provide complete descriptions and adequate psychometrics, we were at times limited by insufficient published information on a scale. We decided to include scales with incomplete information available if the scale evidenced other strengths or rounded out a specific area of family violence assessment not well-represented by other devices.

3. A categorization of what we found into "include" and "exclude" groups based on our criteria of behavioral assessment approaches, psychometric support, and other inclusion and exclusion criteria described in the previous paragraphs;

4. A mailing of lists of titles and authors of our selected measures to experts in each subfield (e.g., assessment of children, couples, etc.) for their comments and recommendations regarding any oversights on our part;

5. For the measures we elected to include, we wrote to authors to obtain copies of measures or information that might have been missing from the references we obtained (e.g., additional psychometric development, new adaptations of the scales, etc.).

We then reported what we were able to find; sometimes access to authors or to important information was simply not available.

Conclusion

This chapter has described the scope of this volume, its contents, and its organization and format. It also delineates our criteria for the selection of assessment devices and outlines the multistep process we undertook to arrive at our final group of measures and the information we provide on each of them. Working in the field of family violence in any capacity is difficult; we hope our efforts can facilitate such work by providing the reader with a clear and easy-to-use reference source for learning about and locating relevant assessment tools.

General Issues in the Assessment of Family Violence

The field of assessment of family violence has grown substantially in the past two decades since the problem of family violence has increasingly continued to be the focus of public attention. Historically, targets for assessment of child abuse included (a) parent psychopathology or (b) physical–medical evidence of child physical and sexual abuse. Forensic medical exams are still a large part of the assessment focus for children. Now, however, the focus has come to include psychological sequelae of victimization as the multiple parent behaviors and attitudes. In both the child and family domains, abuse assessment has broadened its scope and has become increasingly sophisticated in both its psychometrics and its understanding of abusive phenomena (e.g., greater focus on context–impact over mere topography of abusive behavior). Evaluators of family violence have traditionally come from a diverse set of mental health fields, and it is important that professionals in each of these fields be familiar with a range of assessment approaches; assessment targets; and ethical, diagnostic, and legal issues.

There are many purposes for assessment in family violence, as well as many broad approaches to assessment. In this book, we primarily adhere to a behavioral assessment approach to the measurement of family violence. This chapter details the objectives of assessment in family violence; discusses issues of cultural diversity in family violence research and assessment; describes specific assessment approaches; outlines ethical, diagnostic, and legal issues in the assessment of family violence; and discusses the use of assessment in clinical practice.

Conduct Assessments: The Varying Purposes for Assessment in Family Violence

Family violence assessment typically involves assessment directed toward clinical evaluation, program evaluation, and research. Next we discuss the use of assessment in each of these areas.

Clinical Evaluation

Conducting assessments in the context of clinical evaluation involves standard clinical practice, accountability for provision of effective treatments, crisis management, and forensic evaluation or other professional consultation (see the later section within this chapter on the use of assessment in clinical practice for elaboration of the objectives of conducting assessments in clinical practice.) As part of standard practice, the primary foci of assessments will include determining the presence, scope, and nature of abuse, as well as its associated features or sequelae. The general purpose is to determine the intervention needed. Often for children, an essential assessment purpose is to determine the veracity of allegations of abuse. The child may or may not be the reporter, but because child abuse is a violation of the law, clinicians are often called on to assess the child and family to substantiate allegations and determine severity.

An additional function of assessment in clinical practice is evaluation of the effectiveness of interventions. Third-party payers require specification of treatment goals and methods and an outcome evaluation documenting the degree to which these goals were obtained. Beyond complying with managed care mandates, however, clinicians ethically seek to provide effective treatments; assessments provide the foundation for such determinations. Particularly in child abuse cases wherein decisions continue to be made in terms of the child's safety and the risk variables, repeated measurement of parent behavior, family environment, and child functioning may be mandated by those in other social services or in criminal justice decisions. For example, an assessment focus might be the determination of when a parent can be considered rehabilitated and able to have the child return home.

Often, a child who is involved in abuse will enter treatment in some type of crisis, or he or she will enter a crisis phase during the course of treatment. The clinician will need to be familiar with crisis assessment and intervention strategies to respond rapidly and appropriately. Such knowledge should include familiarity with assessments of dangerousness, risk factors for imminent danger, statutory abuse reporting and duty-to-warn requirements, suicide assessment, safety planning, and local crisis services.

Finally, the practitioner may be called on to conduct forensic evaluations, to serve as an expert witness, or to serve as a consultant to a professional within another discipline or to someone who has a lesser degree of expertise in the assessment of family violence. Because young children are often determined *not* to be reliable witnesses or reporters of abusive events, forensic evaluations may be necessary to substantiate allegations (see Sattler, 1997, for an excellent discussion of forensic assessment with children and families). When conducting forensic assessments for any purpose, the practitioner will need to be well-versed not only in the various assessment strategies relevant for the particular case but also in the related ethical and legal issues.

Program Evaluation

Another central use for assessment in family violence is program evaluation. Many programs exist for the treatment of diverse aspects of family violence. These programs are typically based in settings such as state or county-based agencies, hospitals, clinics, shelters, university-based counseling centers, or grant-funded clinics. Often, sources of funding for such programs are scarce and frequently threatened. For continued financial support, it has become essential that such programs report program evaluation data. Funding sources have the right to know not only if their programs are working but also how they are working in relation to other possible allocations of their money. Although early family violence program evaluation standards were such that providing data such as annual records of referral, program entry, attrition rates, and recidivism rates would suffice, there is presently a greater demand for more far-reaching outcome assessments.

In the child and family area in particular, there is a strong emphasis on prevention programs, including much focus on sexual abuse prevention as well as parent training to prevent the use of physical violence toward children. These programs would typically include high-risk populations, and evaluation would focus on variables such as knowledge, attitudes, and behaviors, perhaps compared with a matched population that did not receive the prevention program.

Program evaluation also helps determine what works and what

needs to be improved for internal feedback and continued program development. With use of a multimodal assessment battery, one might ascertain that certain programs within a treatment setting are meeting their intended objectives whereas others are not, or that a particular aspect of a program is having the intended effects whereas another aspect is not.

Stimulation of Research

There can be no research without assessment; data collection by definition involves some form of measurement of the research issue at hand. There are many ways that assessment can stimulate research. Assessment can be used to conduct basic research related to family violence in areas such as frustration tolerance or neurotransmitters involved in aggression. It can also be used to conduct correlational or case control studies examining such topics as characteristics of victims or perpetrators of abuse, discrepancies in reporting between perpetrators and victims of abuse, correlates of certain types of abuse, and typologies of abuse or of individuals who abuse. Assessment may be used to identify causal variables in abuse (e.g., are parents with negative attributions and parenting-skill deficits more likely to be physically aggressive?) and potential intervention targets (e.g., cognitive restructuring and parent training). Assessment can also be used in longitudinal research examining predictors of or etiological factors in abuse.

Another avenue of assessment research is the study of assessment methods themselves; Is violence more likely to be detected when relying on spontaneous reports during clinical interview, direct interview questions, or written self-reports? What are the psychometric characteristics of a particular assessment measure? Does a particular assessment strategy discriminate abused from nonabused samples? Can the discrepancies in data collected across multiple informants and with different methodologies be of clinical relevance in our understanding of a family?

Furthermore, assessment is the cornerstone of treatment outcome research. To evaluate the effectiveness of a treatment, assessment devices need to be selected. Such devices commonly include self-report measures or rating scales (e.g., a parent rating scale to determine whether a child exhibits less impulsiveness following treatment). Observational–analogue measures are also useful for assessing treatment outcome (e.g., observation of interactive play to determine whether an abused child exhibits improved social interactions following an intervention). Structured or semistructured interview measures are often used for screening and diagnosis for entering a treatment study but may be used as outcome measures as well (e.g., administration of a diagnostic interview to determine whether a participant no longer meets diagnostic criteria for posttraumatic stress disorder (PTSD) following treatment).

The Role of Culture and Diversity in the Assessment of Family Violence

Research and methodology in family violence has suffered from a lack of attention to issues of culture and diversity; the field of assessment within the family violence field is no exception. Thus, conclusions one draws from assessments may reveal facets of functioning one might assume erroneously to be *etics,* or universal truths, when in fact they may reflect *emics,* or truths that apply to a specific cultural group or segment of the population (Matsumoto, 1994). This issue relates to the lack of attention to external validity, or generalizability, in assessment research in family violence, as discussed in the section on emphasis on internal over external validity in chapter 3. In addition, ethnocentrism, or viewing others through one's own cultural perspectives, may cause us to form stereotypes and biases that limit our ability to view those different from ourselves with objectivity and may lead to damaging conclusions (Matsumoto, 1994).

"Cultural psychology seeks to discover systematic relationships between cultural and behavioral variables, asking whether individuals growing up in culture A tend to develop that culture's psychological qualities" (Berry, 1994, p. 120). Often, researchers are interested in cross-cultural comparisons, examining differences in characteristics between cultures A and B (Berry, 1994). In family violence assessment, we seek to discover relationships between cultural and family violence variables. For example, we might ask what child abuse practices exist within a particular culture, or ask whether individuals from culture A have different attitudes toward child discipline than those from culture B. We discuss central issues pertaining to sensitivity to diversity in the assessment of family violence in this context.

Many issues warrant consideration in attempting to address culture and diversity in research. Some of these pose obstacles that make culture difficult to address in assessment practice in family violence. These issues include problems of defining culture, sampling issues, and measurement issues.

Defining Culture

"Most cross-cultural scholars agree that culture is a shared conglomeration of attitudes, values, behaviors, and beliefs, communicated from one generation to the next through language" (Matsumoto, 1994, p. 21). However, this definition of culture is far from precise. As Matsumoto (1994) argued, there is no clear way to delineate members of a culture. For example, defining culture as race is problematic, because although we might speak of African American or Asian "culture," for example, members of these groups might share some characteristics but vary widely on others. Defining culture as nationality is also flawed, because individuals from particular countries often do not fit their nation's cultural stereotype.

In addition, when looking more broadly than culture and examining the issue of human diversity in general, more definitional issues arise. Not only do we hope that our assessment instruments will provide valid information for the various cultures we might assess, but we hope that this information will be applicable to populations that comprise other forms of diversity as well. Beyond race and nationality, other grouping characteristics of a population that we might characterize as reflecting diversity include religion, sexual orientation, socioeconomic status, age, disability status, and even gender.

Sampling

Often, when we recruit samples designed to represent a culture, we face the problem of representativeness of the sample. That is, are the members of our sample representative of the larger population or culture from which they are drawn? Often, in studying culture we rely on samples of convenience (Lonner, 1994), such as studying a group of people from New York that belong to a particular ethnic group that responds to an advertisement.

Related to sampling is the issue of equivalence. Much cross-cultural research compares cultures by sampling more than one group and comparing them on various measures. Because samples of convenience are much more common than random sampling methods (Lonner, 1994), we run the risk that our sample from one culture may be different in systematic ways than that from the other, on variables other than cultural ones (e.g., socioeconomic status, urban versus city-dwelling, etc.). Thus, our conclusions may reflect as much about these differences, which we may or may not identify, as about cultural differences (Matsumoto, 1994).

Measurement

There are several problems particular to measurement in cross-cultural studies (Hughes, Seidman, & Williams, 1993; Matsumoto, 1994). When a measurement device is applied cross-culturally, problems of culturally based differences in meanings of constructs, meanings of test items, and item intercorrelations (i.e., factor equivalence) must be considered. Language and translation issues also pose potential problems. Moreover, cultural response sets, or systematic tendencies to respond to test items in a particular manner, are also cause for concern. For example, particular groups may have a tendency to acquiesce to a greater extent, to avoid endorsing extreme ratings, or to be less forthcoming in revealing distress. Differences between groups may thus be attributed to culture when in fact they are partly a result of response sets. Task and setting equivalence are relevant measurement issues as well. That is, members of different cultural groups may have different understandings of the assessment situation, which may affect behavior. In summary, "cultural differences in the conceptual definitions of variables and their measurement are very likely, and as consumers of research we need to be aware of these possibilities" (Matsumoto, 1994, p. 31).

Conclusions

The problems identified regarding issues of studying culture affect family violence assessment pervasively. Few of the established measures in the field contain norms for diverse groups or adequately reflect diversity in their development samples. Rarely do investigators conduct comparative studies in an attempt to obtain reliability and validity data cross-culturally. Seldom are standardized measures available in other languages, facilitating use with diverse populations. To improve our sensitivity to issues of cultural diversity, researchers must acquaint themselves with and begin to tackle the many problems outlined herein.

Specific Assessment Approaches

Approaches used in the assessment of family violence include interviews, self-report measures and rating scales, analogue measures, direct observation in natural settings, and archival records. We describe each of these approaches and discuss their strengths and weaknesses.

Interviews

Interviews are the most common form of assessment used in clinical practice. They are not only invaluable for assessing a client's history, the meaning and context of behaviors, and phenomenological experience, but they also form the basis for building rapport. Structured and semistructured interviews also provide the basis for diagnosis of Axis I and Axis II psychopathology (e.g., First, Spitzer, Gibbon, & Williams, 1995; First, Spitzer, Gibbon, Williams, & Benjamin, 1994). Advantages to interviews as an assessment strategy include that they provide face-to-face contact with the client, they allow for follow-up questions and clarifications by both interviewer and interviewee (if not fully structured) that can enhance accuracy of material, and they may allow for insights or observations about the client and the phenomenon of interest that would be unlikely to arise in the absence of direct contact. Flexible formats allow the skilled interviewer to probe or highlight particular areas over others, and the interview content can be broad-based or specific, depending on the needs of the situation. With a more open-ended format, the interview also allows clients to tell their story before imposing a structure on the assessment process, which can begin a therapeutic process while enhancing connection to the interviewer. Advantages for children in particular include reduction of anxiety, desensitization to the assessment process, providing a forum for them to express themselves when they may be too young to respond to paper-and-pencil measures, and obtaining information on cognitive and affective responses not readily observable.

Data yielded from interviews are often, but not always, categorical in nature. For example, a structured interview might reveal that an individual meets diagnostic criteria for two disorders and no others, but will provide little information on the extent of impairment or level of symptomatology. Disadvantages of interviews are that they may be time and labor intensive to administer,[1] they may be subject to unreliable

---

[1] Some standardized diagnostic interviews, however, have now become available in computer-administered formats.

scoring and interpretation, or conversely, may require substantial training to become reliable in their administration and scoring. They also may require a certain level of clinical sophistication and training to administer and interpret. In addition, if they are nonstandardized, they may be subject to inconsistent operationalizations of constructs, such as abusive behavior. In the case of child sexual abuse, interviews with children are especially controversial in that the questions may be leading or suggestive. Thus, interview assessment formats are often supplemented with structured anatomically detailed (SAD) dolls and observations of play.

Self-Report Measures/Rating Scales

Self-report measures and rating scales are the second most common assessment tools. They tend to assess phenomena such as personal characteristics (e.g., attitudes, preferences, beliefs, perceptions, personality characteristics), mood, specific behaviors, and levels of psychiatric symptoms. They typically produce dimensional rather than categorical scores. Rating scales and checklists can be filled out by oneself, by another informant, or even by the assessor him- or herself (e.g., a therapist might fill out a rating scale about a client's behavior in a group therapy session). General advantages include that they tend to be brief, simple, and efficient to administer; they seldom require extensive training procedures for their administration or scoring; and they can be administered to more than one client at once and do not require face-to-face contact with an assessor. Another advantage of rating scales is that most are quantified and yield precise, interpretable scores, which enhances the ease of communication to other professionals. Moreover, a wide variety of highly specific self-report measures–rating scales related to the field of family violence has been developed to date, facilitating the ability for evaluators to assemble a comprehensive paper-and-pencil battery suitable for their assessment needs.

Disadvantages of self-report measures and rating scales include that they may provide overly simplistic information. For example, self-report measures of violent acts have been criticized for failing to provide information about context, meaning, or impact of aggressive behavior (cf., Cascardi & Vivian, 1995). Self-report measures also may be more subject to social desirability or inaccuracies in responding in that the assessor cannot confront inconsistencies or evaluate the respondent's attitude or demeanor as the scale is filled out. For example, parents have shown tendencies to "fake good" on self-report inventories, especially when they know the purpose of the assessment, and adolescents are notoriously inaccurate self-reporters (e.g., Velting, Rathus, & Asnis, 1998). Respondents may also feel that questions on self-report measures are vaguely worded or force response choices that distort the actual nature of their intended responses. In addition, paper–pencil measures depend on the cognitive abilities of the respondent, which limits their use with young children.

Self-monitoring tools, such as daily or weekly logs of specific behaviors or events, also fall under the classification of self-report assessments. These measures are generally fashioned by clinicians for particular treatment programs or for individual clients, and although useful behavioral assessment tools, they are rarely standardized or psychometrically evaluated.

Analogue Measures

Analogue measures have enjoyed increasing use in recent years in the assessment of family violence. Such measures take a variety of forms, and all involve some type of direct behavioral observation. These approaches typically take place in laboratory or clinic–office settings and involve some type of recreation or approximation of a natural setting. The goal is then to assess behaviors in response to such stimuli, with the advantage of a controlled and standardized procedure with established scoring, coding, or other data-collection approaches. Examples of analogue assessment measures are use of videotaped conflict scenarios (used for eliciting some type of response, which is the assessment target), anatomically detailed dolls, role-play interactions, structured play, or discussion tasks for family members. Methods vary widely to include such assessment targets as communication, emotions, frustration tolerance, discipline responses, automatic thoughts, social skills, attributions, anger, and victimization. Home or school environments can also serve as settings for analogue assessments, provided there is a structured task devised for observation (e.g., asking a parent at home to direct a child in play and then in putting toys away).

Analogue assessments of family violence offer situations in which it is difficult to adapt a particular response style (e.g., faking good), and allow for measurement of actual skills or behaviors as opposed to relying on the insight or accuracy of one's self-reports of such attributes. They may be the next best thing to observations in naturalistic settings and may yield the best reflection of particular behaviors. However, some of these procedures may involve lengthy training procedures and high cost for administration, rating, and data coding. Some analogue methods are not portable or practical outside of well-funded laboratory settings, although many are. Another concern is that both the analogue situation and the target of the measurements themselves may not be valid representations of what they are attempting to measure. Perhaps most striking as a disadvantage is the obtrusive and reactive nature of many analogue assessment procedures; the assessment process may be highly salient and may alter responses.

These concerns notwithstanding, it is important to note that analogue assessment is probably the most important type of assessment in parent–child or family interactions, and for these uses tends to be relatively inexpensive and unobtrusive. The most typical paradigm is the observation of parent and child in free play or a structured task and then a forced compliance task. Such a procedure yields a wealth of information about parent discipline style and the patterns of escalating interactions often seen in conflictual families.

Direct Observation in Natural Settings

Another important source of assessment data, particularly with the observation of children, is direct observations in natural settings, such as the school or home. School observations provide for examination of variables related to academic difficulties and conduct problems such as off-task behavior in the classroom or peer interactions on the playground. Especially when evaluating the quality and safety of a child's living situation, a direct observation in the home—observing both naturalistic parent–child interactions as well as the condition of the home —provides extremely important information to supplement that obtained in the evaluator's office. Some direct observations are conducted with children living in shelters (i.e., safe homes for battered women). Such observations can provide important information on children's adjustment or mother–child interactions following traumatic experiences, such as witnessed or experienced family violence and familial dissolution. Note that because observation in natural settings typically involves unstandardized–unstructured assessment, this book does not contain a separate section on natural observation measures. However, several analogue assessments may be applied to or adapted for naturalistic observations (e.g., the observer can be informed by categories from standardized rating systems in terms of variables of interest without applying formal coding systems).

Archival Records

Another source of assessment data important in family violence is the use of archival records. These are records that are used for assessment purposes after-the-fact, sometimes without any face-to-face contact or even knowing the respondents at all. This might be especially likely to occur in the context of research in areas such as sociology or criminology, where large samples are desired and broad patterns and trends are the study targets. However, clinicians working with individuals can sometimes access historical records, and may want to include them as part of a comprehensive clinical assessment or a forensic evaluation. Archival records include such data sources as hospital or medical records, school or employment records, child protective services contacts, criminal records, or police–probation reports. Advantages to such methods include their objectivity, their construct validity (that is, no inference is needed to interpret them), and the often highly informative and corroborating contributions they make to self-reported data. Also, especially when using archival records for large-scale research studies, once such records are obtained, they may be substantially less time-consuming to examine or code than would data obtained from meeting with each individual represented by the records. Finally, archival records provide access to unbiased retrospective data and allow for study of trends in previous years. Potential problems with such sources of assessment data involve difficulty in obtaining access to such records; varying definitions of abuse across states or sites; missing or ambiguous data or data not coded in a way most useful to the present purposes; and samples not under the examiner's control. Because these measures are not standardized, we do not review such approaches.

Assessment Targets

There are many targets of assessment in family violence, whether carried out for clinical or research purposes. Assessment may focus on distal or proximal violence-related variables. Distal variables concern past events and may include targets such as violence witnessed in childhood or childhood familial environment. Proximal variables include recent events (e.g., abuse received within the past six months) as well as ongoing events (e.g., current home environment). Assessment also may focus on the "target" individual (i.e., the person referred to treatment, requesting an evaluation, or participating in a research study); an outside party, such as a parent, teacher, or therapist; or on objective records, such as police, court, or medical records. Assessment may target adults, adolescents, or children; victims–survivors, witnesses, and perpetrators of abuse; individuals or families; abusive behavior itself, associated features, risk factors for, or sequelae of abuse; and a range of types of abuse (e.g., physical, sexual, emotional, neglect).

Although assessment targets and measures themselves have proliferated in the past two decades, there are still severe limitations in assessment within the field of family violence. A major issue is the scale development samples: Almost all of the measures have been developed and validated on highly select samples. Many populations touched by family violence have been overlooked in norming and validation studies, most notably nontraditional family constellations and members of ethnic minority groups. Therefore, when working with these populations one must try to take cultural and socioeconomic variables into account when interpreting these instruments. Because of the many limitations of assessments designed for family violence, we include many well-researched measurement devices not developed for family violence populations but that show promise for use in this field.

Ethical, Diagnostic, and Legal Issues

Regardless of the assessment approach or target, a variety of ethical, diagnostic, and legal issues arise when conducting assessments in family violence.

Ethical Issues

Working in family violence poses several ethical dilemmas with regard to conducting therapeutic activities with clients' best interests and safety in mind. For example, dilemmas that may arise include

1. The right to self-determination and freedom of choice versus mandating treatment (e.g., agency-based programs for perpetrators of family violence; involuntary inpatient psychiatric admission for a patient determined to be a danger to self or others);
2. The right to self-determination in terms of treatment goals versus imposing an agenda onto the client (e.g., in mandated programs with goal of abuse cessation);

3. Maintaining confidentiality versus duty to warn or protect;
4. Respecting privacy versus the obligation to assess in a potentially intrusive manner (e.g., probing questions regarding areas of discomfort for the client; contacting other pertinent individuals in client's life to conduct a fair and thorough evaluation; asking more detailed questions once suspicions of abuse have been aroused).

In addition to these broad ethical dilemmas, the ethical guidelines of the APA include a number of principles that pertain to issues of assessment of family violence (APA, 1997). A list of ethical issues pertaining to the interface of these principles and family violence assessment appears in Exhibit 2.1. Although the published ethical principles by the APA are required for psychologists, evaluators from all disciplines can benefit from following them.

Diagnostic Issues

It often becomes important to assess diagnosis when working with populations involved with family violence, because there are many diagnostic categories that have been associated with both victim and perpetrator roles. The presence of such diagnoses may be clues to assess for abuse and may provide potential intervention targets in identified populations.

For child abuse victims and witnesses to parental violence, diagnostic categories commonly identified include a range of both externalizing and internalizing disorders, including oppositional defiant disorder, conduct disorder, disorders of attention or impulsivity (e.g., attention-deficit hyperactivity disorder), anxiety disorders (e.g., separation anxiety disorder), depressive disorders, and learning disabilities (Fantuzzo, 1990; Hansen, Conway, & Christopher, 1990; Milner & Crouch, 1993; Pelcovitz & Kaplan, 1994). Children who have been sexually abused experience a variety of emotional and behavioral problems. They may meet criteria for any number of diagnostic categories, including anxiety disorders, depressive disorders, hyperactivity and other externalizing disorders, dissociative disorders, and somatoform disorders (Conti, 1993; Green, 1991; Kendall-Tackett, Williams, & Finklehor, 1993). Among the anxiety disorders, PTSD among this population is especially prevalent, with features such as sleep disturbance, fear, phobic avoidance, hypersexualization, and related features such as guilt and anger (Kendall-Tackett et al., 1993; McLeer, Deblinger, Henry, & Or-

Exhibit 2.1

Ethical Considerations Pertaining to the Interface of APA Ethical Principles and Family Violence Assessment

- Psychologists should not carry out roles regarding the assessment of family violence cases for which they do not have specific training/ expertise.
- Psychologists conducting family violence assessments should stay abreast of current research in this field.
- Given the limited state of knowledge regarding recidivism, future dangerousness, and so forth, evaluators should qualify all statements involving prediction.
- When conducting assessments of family violence for research purposes, psychologists must ensure that clients are not harmed and that they provide informed consent.
- When conducting assessments of family violence for research purposes, psychologists also take responsibility for not overgeneralizing results and ensuring that results are reported accurately.
- All mandated reporting laws must be followed when conducting family violence assessments, regardless of the purpose for or context of the assessment.
- Psychologists must notify clients clearly of their roles (e.g., forensic evaluator, therapist, research investigator) and also of when their roles change.
- Psychologists conducting family violence assessments must prevent harm when possible, work to ensure safety, and warn those in danger.
- If a psychologist encounters a family violence assessment situation for which he or she is not properly trained or knowledgeable, he or she should obtain consultation from properly trained professionals or refer the case to an expert in the relevant area.
- When making a determination of risk or danger to others, the assessor must prioritize the concern of prevention or minimization of harm when considering breaking confidentiality.
- In making contact with outside parties (such as family members or court officers) in conducting family violence evaluations, the psychologist must clarify his or her role(s) to those parties and continue to perform within that role.
- The psychologist should communicate and cooperate with outside professional parties (e.g., courts, medical institutions, schools) in a manner that will serve the best interests of their clients when conducting a family violence evaluation.
- In conducting assessments of family violence, psychologists must take care to avoid the abuse of power or the exploitation or misleading of

continued

Exhibit 2.1, continued

others. Assessors must be aware of how their statements or conclusions might be used to the detriment of clients or others, and thus must remain cautious, sensitive, and objective in how they present their findings and what they disclose.

- Psychologists conducting family violence assessments should work toward the mitigation of causes of human suffering as well as toward policy that serves the interests of their clients and the public.
- Psychologists should use tests with which they have training in administration and interpretation of results.
- Psychologists must acknowledge the limitations of their assessment data as well as the limitations of relevant knowledge in the field.

Note: This exhibit was summarized from APA (1997).

vaschel, 1992). In addition, part of the diagnostic presentation with child victims of sexual abuse are features noted by Finklehor and Browne (1985) as characteristic of sexual victimization: symptoms of helplessness, betrayal, stigmatization, and traumatic sexualization.

Adult survivors of child sexual abuse have been found to have enduring problems. A history of sexual abuse has been found to be a significant risk factor for anxiety disorders, most notably chronic or delayed PTSD (e.g., Briere & Runtz, 1993). In addition, they have been found to meet criteria for borderline personality disorder (BPD), dissociative disorders, major depression and other mood disorders, substance abuse disorders, somatoform disorders, sexual disorders, and eating disorders (Briere, 1988; Briere & Runtz, 1993; Green, 1991; cf., Morgan & Cummings, 1999). Also, suicidality may appear alone or as part of other diagnoses such as depression or BPD and other related characteristics include low self-esteem, relationship dysfunction, anger, shame and guilt, cognitive distortions, changes in the meaning made of one's life, and shattered assumptions of safety–invulnerability (e.g., Andrews, 1995; Briere, 1988; Janoff-Bulman, 1989).

Perpetrators of physical and sexual child abuse have a wide range of clinical presentations, but nevertheless may have certain characteristic diagnoses. Perpetrators of child physical abuse have been found to meet criteria for such disorders as depression, substance abuse, and schizophrenia, and often have related characteristics such as child management–parenting skill deficits, severe marital discord, social isolation, poor coping skills, life stress, and inappropriate attributions and expectations regarding children's behavior (e.g., Milner & Crouch, 1993; C. E. Walker, Bonner, & Kaufman, 1988). Perpetrators of child sexual abuse may have forms of psychopathology directly related to their sexually abusive behavior, such as paraphelias, sexual sadism, rape, chronic child molestation, or pedophilia; alternatively, they may meet criteria for diagnoses unrelated to their deviant sexual behavior, such as schizophrenia, antisocial personality, or substance abuse (Becker & Hunter, 1992; Walker et al., 1988). Related characteristics may include deficient heterosocial skills, immaturity and interpersonal–marital difficulties, social isolation and a subjective sense of vulnerability, problems with impulse control, and deviant patterns of sexual arousal (Becker & Hunter, 1992; Walker et al., 1988).

A phenomenon receiving attention within the past decade is the topic of diagnostic issues for the therapist working with trauma victims. The terms "vicarious traumatization" (Pearlman & MacIan, 1995) and "secondary traumatic stress" (Figley & Kleber, 1995) have been applied to therapists who appear to develop symptoms of PTSD as a result of extended work with such populations; it is now recognized that such intensive work does not come without emotional costs.

One issue that is somewhat unique to the field of family violence is the question of whether to assess and treat clients according to diagnostic presentation and symptom level or according to the abusive events experienced or perpetrated (cf., Berliner & Saunders, 1996). Despite a wide array of clinical presentations, treatments for family violence are often generic treatment programs based on the nature of the abuse involved. However, this approach can be problematic, because victims of the same type of abuse may range from presenting as relatively asymptomatic to having full-blown disorders (Kendall-Tackett et al., 1993). Thus, one might argue for the utility of disorder-specific or symptom-specific interventions (e.g., Deblinger, Lippmann, & Steer, 1996).

Legal Issues

A variety of legal issues are relevant to assessment in the field of family violence. Although an in-depth discussion of these issues falls outside of the scope of this book, we briefly address matters of risk management, protection from harm–privacy protection for the family, reporting requirements, forensic evaluations, and prediction of dangerousness.

Risk Management

One way that legal issues may touch family violence professionals is in terms of law suits filed by clients, their families, or outside agencies. Because the outcome of assessment and treatment may have life-and-death consequences, risk management concerns are especially important in this field. According to a report from the Committee on Legal and Ethical Issues in the Treatment of Interpersonal Violence (APA, 1997), good risk management practice includes obtaining consultation or supervision, adhering to ethical practice guidelines, staying current in knowledge of ethical standards as well as legal issues, and meticulously documenting actions regarding cases that pose a high risk. Such documentation involves documentation of risk assessments made, consultation or supervision sought, and an outline of decisions made and on what basis, including actions that were considered but not taken and why. Finally, comprehensive professional liability insurance is essential.

Subpoenas for Client Records

At times, practitioners working in the field of family violence will face subpoenas for client records or subpoena for testimony in court. This poses a potential conflict between the client's right to privacy and the assessor or treating clinician's legal obligations. In this case, immediate consultation with an attorney is recommended. The APA Committee on Legal Issues provides a booklet with guidelines for handling subpoenas (APA, 1997).

Reporting Requirements

Although it is common clinical practice to orient clients regarding informed consent to assessment–treatment and a discussion of the "duty to warn," the essential nature of such practices is highlighted in family violence assessment contexts. Any client or research participant involved in a family violence assessment must grant consent to take part in the process, following a clear explanation by the clinician–assessor of the expected nature of the interaction as well as any policies or obligations. This informed consent must include an explanation of confidentiality and under what circumstances it is upheld, as well as when it must be broken. That is, the practitioner must explain his or her "duty to warn" regarding threat of harm to self, threat of harm to another, or suspicion of ongoing child abuse.

Practitioners conducting assessments will need to be familiar with their state reporting requirements in terms of mandated reporting of child abuse, as well as requirements regarding the duty to warn parties who might be in danger. Although wording varies somewhat from state to state, "When a disclosure of child maltreatment occurs, *the law allows no debate:* state and federal statutes require reporting. Reporting a disclosure of abuse against elders and other adults is also permitted or mandated depending on the state" (APA, 1997, p. 17). The APA provides guidelines on mandated reporting. With cases that are not extremely clearcut, reporting of abuse is most wisely carried out with the consultation of peers who are knowledgeable in this field. In addition, it may be helpful to refer clients for expert assessments in the relevant area, such as a team specializing in the assessment of child sexual abuse (APA, 1997).

Many practitioners who face reporting clients to social service agencies for child abuse express concerns about harming the therapeutic relationship. Some may even feel it may do more harm than good to report a client who is engaged in and making progress in therapy. Although this may be a valid concern, it obviously does not remove the obligation to report when child abuse is suspected. However, certain strategies of reporting may mitigate its negative impact on the patient's trust and connection with the practitioner. First, from the outset of treatment or even a brief assessment–evaluation, it is critical, as mentioned earlier, to begin with informed consent, where that consent includes full understanding of the practitioner's duty to warn. Second, when it is determined that a report must be made, it is advisable not to do this without the client's knowledge but instead inform the client that a report has become necessary and exactly on what basis this decision was made. This is easier when clients have been made aware of reporting requirements at the outset of treatment–assessment. Third, the practitioner can explain to the client exactly what he or she can expect to happen (i.e., usually a visit to the home by a case worker within 24 hours, etc.). The practitioner can validate the client's reactions while asking about specific concerns (e.g., is there danger from a spouse for "saying the wrong thing," losing custody, etc.), and can also act in the role of advocate or problem-solving aid in helping the client to plan for and cope with these concerns. The practitioner can explain that he or she would like to do this as collaboratively as possible with the client, to the extent that this is possible, and that the ultimate goal is to get the family needed help. However, once a decision to report has been made, practitioners must remain firm, and not be swayed by a client's arguments against reporting.

The issue of mandated reporting can also become delicate in

instances in which children disclose abuse, leaving the practitioner with the requirement to report who the abuser is. Young children may not be able to understand the issue and may fear the consequences of reporting; practitioners must then ensure the safety of the child who reports.

Forensic Evaluations: Custody Determination; Legal Implications

Practitioners working in the field of family violence may serve as expert witnesses and testify regarding issues such as the presence and severity level of domestic abuse, the characteristics of abusive relationships, the potential causes or consequences of abuse, the state of current research knowledge in a specific area relating to family violence (e.g., what we know about maternal separation in custody hearings; recovered versus false memories in sexual abuse cases), the likelihood of future dangerousness, or the need for treatment and particular types of treatment needed.

In the role of forensic evaluator, the assessor is careful to serve solely in the role of evaluator, meaning he or she does not also serve as treating clinician or advocate to the client. Instead, he or she

> acts in a neutral and objective manner in order to obtain information concerning a specific case or situation. In this role, the psychologist seeks to help determine whether the client sustained damages, to help evaluate various allegations, or to provide recommendations to a court concerning a disputed situation and/or future actions. (APA, 1997, p. 11)

In doing so, the evaluator reviews all available supporting records–collateral information, remains open to multiple explanations for behaviors, pays heed to present issues of safety, and follows all laws regarding mandated reporting (see Sattler, 1997, for detailed elaboration of forensic assessment).

In conducting forensic evaluations, the therapist should be careful not to ask leading questions, and the client's privacy, whether adult or child, should be protected by interviewing him or her alone (except in the case of small children where this may cause more distress). All issues of mandated reporting and duty to warn apply to forensic evaluations, and the evaluator must attend to issues of assessing risk of harm and dangerousness.

The investigator must be sure not to enter the assessment situation with biases or predetermined conclusions. For example, Richard Gardner's work on parental alienation syndrome (1987, 1989) suggests signs to alert clinicians to potentially false allegations of child sexual abuse.

Finally, conducting forensic evaluations in the area of family violence requires expertise in family violence; this means staying abreast of current research literature, attending relevant conferences and availing oneself of other means of continuing education. It is also necessary to develop expertise in the judicial system and relevant laws.

Prediction of Dangerousness

Clinicians are frequently called on to make predictions about the future violent behavior of clients. This task may come about in the context of evaluating a client's suitability for a particular program; deciding on an involuntary psychiatric commitment; determining whether discharge from a psychiatric or mandated program is warranted; determining parental fitness for retaining custody of children; or making a judgment about needed services at the request of social service agencies, law enforcement workers, or the courts. Of course, violence prediction is an extremely inexact science, largely because violence is a low-frequency and covert event. For example, among mental health workers, the accuracy rate of violence prediction remains no better than 40% (Menzies, Webster, & Sepejak, 1985). However, certain factors lead to maximal power in predicting dangerousness, such as obtaining agreement among multiple evaluators (Werner, Rose, & Yesavage, 1990) and evaluating a series of known general risk factors for violent behavior, such as past violence, being assigned multiple psychiatric diagnoses (particularly substance abuse disorders, along or in combination with another Axis I disorder, and personality disorders [e.g., Borum, 1996; Limandri & Sheridan, 1995]), and consistent display of threatening–hostile mannerisms (cf., Limandri & Sheridan, 1995).

In general, predictions of dangerousness should be made with care and caution, including caution in making overly conclusive statements. Conclusions should be based on review of all relevant information attained through multimodal assessment, including an interview, past history, past records, and when possible other informants. It is also helpful to include standardized measures, and it is extremely important to consider the reliability and validity data concerning instruments chosen; at least a substantial part of the battery must have adequate psychometric properties that will need to be documented in any forensic reports. Also, it must be shown that any measures used are appropriate for the population to which they are applied. For example, a self-report of abuse normed on adolescents will not have the same characteristics when used with children. Following such precautions will help to ensure fairness to clients as well as reduce liability risk to practitioners.

Use of Assessment in Clinical Practice

There are several objectives of conducting assessments in clinical practice. These include establishing rapport, obtaining a problem description–definition, setting targets for treatment, measuring pre-treatment functioning (i.e., obtaining baseline data), measuring treatment progress, and measuring treatment outcome.

Establishing Rapport

An important aspect of the initial assessment process is the need to establish rapport with the client. During this time, roles are clarified (e.g., description and expectations of a mandated treatment program or of a psychodiagnostic evaluation to help in child-placement decisions), and agreement on goals is established.

It is essential to build an alliance with clients during the assessment phase. In the field of family violence, establishing rapport can be difficult. Some clients are mandated and attending treatment against their will; others will have issues with trust that will make it difficult to speak openly with a practitioner. In essence, building a therapeutic alliance involves a collaborative agreement between client and practitioner on therapeutic tasks and goals, as well as an atmosphere of warmth and mutual respect.

When working with mandated or otherwise reluctant clients, building rapport involves validating the frustration and hardship of the client and aligning with the client by asking how the assessment and treatment process can be helpful to him or her. When working with clients who have difficulty with trust, it can be helpful to validate their experience and their hesitancy to self-disclose, to work at a slower than normal pace, and to give the client permission to not answer questions he or she is not ready to discuss. In the case of victimized clients, one must proceed gingerly so as not to retraumatize them during the interview process. Giving the client a sense of control while retaining a warm and nonjudgmental stance can facilitate rapport in such cases. Of course, the assessor must also be mindful of the social desirability of the issues to be assessed. One would expect that parents who are at risk for abuse or neglect, for example, would not be especially forthcoming if in fact their disclosures might substantiate criminal charges or bring about other unwanted consequences.

Establishing rapport with young children, especially those who have witnessed or experienced traumatic events, can be quite challenging. For the most part, they will not understand the purpose for assessment, and the process will require methods that reduce a child's anxiety and allow for spontaneous responding, perhaps in an analogue setting.

Obtaining a Problem Description–Definition

A central aspect of the assessment process is to obtain a description of the presenting problem. This stage of assessment might consist of an initial screening, which would consist of a broad-based assessment to identify need for treatment. The evaluator might use global symptom checklists or comprehensive interviews at this time. In general, obtaining a problem description includes a focus on the *topography* of particular assessment targets such as trauma symptoms or violence, addressing questions such as, What are the presenting symptoms–problematic behaviors? Are various presenting symptoms within a normative level? Are they elevated? Are they in the range of a particular population? Is the symptom picture likely to pose a risk for future danger? Also, many clinical assessments in the field of family violence seek to establish a clinical diagnosis. Establishing a diagnosis is commonplace with individuals presenting with sequelae of abuse, who might be seeking treatment for posttraumatic stress symptoms and other functional impairments. However, assessments for perpetrators of family violence often focus more on identifying behavioral targets for change (i.e., various forms of abusive behaviors as well as skill deficits and other targets) than identifying a diagnosis.

Setting Targets for Treatment

Information gleaned from interviews, self-report questionnaires, or other assessment modes may suggest treatment targets such as specific areas of communication difficulties, problems with anger, assertiveness or parenting-skill deficits, trauma symptoms, or excessive shame and guilt. Functional analysis, a behavioral assessment interviewing method focused on identifying variables that elicit and maintain particular behavior patterns (e.g., internal and external triggers for acting abusively toward a child) will also yield important targets for intervention. Although family violence in its various forms is the treatment priority, the component behaviors reflecting the precursor variables determining risk status or the sequelae will sometimes be the only targets available for intervention.

Measuring Pretreatment Functioning

Pretreatment functioning might be assessed as part of a one-time battery and used as a basis to compare with outcome data as an indication of change resulting from treatment. Alternatively, baseline data might be assessed in a continuous manner, collecting data on one or more aspects of functioning over several days or weeks before the onset of treatment. For example, a parent might monitor a child's oppositional behaviors over time before engaging in a parenting skills program, or a client might fill out a daily questionnaire reflecting the avoidance, intrusion, and arousal symptoms of PTSD for a specified period before beginning a course of exposure therapy. Ongoing, as opposed to one-time, assessment of pretreatment functioning allows for an examination of stability and trends in the phenomena of interest, which permits for more accurate interpretation of change patterns across treatment (Kazdin, 1998).

Measuring Treatment Progress

Some form of assessment is ideally carried out in an ongoing fashion during treatment to provide ongoing feedback to both clients and treatment personnel. For example, it might be a routine part of treatment to fill out a self-report scale, an observer-rated checklist, or a self-monitoring diary. Ongoing assessment can include approaches such as clinical interviews (e.g., beginning each session with questions about disciplining the children over the past week), functional analysis, or a small, select portion of the initial assessment battery.

Those involved in evaluation of child risk situations as well as parental competency will need to periodically report to appropriate agencies (whether Department of Social Services, Child Protective Services, or Family Court-Probation) in terms of treatment progress and outcome. A set of standardized assessment measures, repeatedly administered across time, will assist in the decision making required of those with less contact than the practitioner.

Measuring Treatment Outcome

Another important role of assessment in clinical practice is to measure treatment outcome. Like pretreatment or baseline assessment, treatment outcome might be measured at one point in time (i.e., treatment termination) or, preferably, at continuous intervals for some time after treatment ends, to determine maintenance of behavior change. The posttreatment assessment battery might be the same or very similar to that administered at pretreatment. The aim is to evaluate the overall progress in treatment across a wide variety of domains.

Problems with Pre–Post Evaluation

Although it is beneficial to evaluate one's intervention by assessing clients pre- and posttreatment, there are problems with interpreting changes based on simple pre–post evaluation. Essentially, these problems concern what is known in research methodology as *threats to internal validity* (Kazdin, 1998), which means that one cannot rule out whether factors other than the intervention itself led to the change observed. Included in the list of plausible explanations for the change *other* than the intervention include the statistical tendency for extreme scores at pretreatment to regress toward the mean (i.e., score closer to the average score on a second measurement because of measurement error rather than client improvements); the possibility that clients matured, got wiser, or experienced some other type of internal change that led to the improvement; the possibility that factors outside of the intervention itself led to the change (e.g., a change in family dynamics, legal status, or employment status; a television special on a related topic on family violence); the potential for practice with the assessment measures themselves having produced improved scores; or the chance that changes in the measurement device itself or its scoring led to changes.

In research methodology, one can account for such threats through use of group or single-case experimental designs. However, in typical practice, it is often not feasible to arrange such treatment study designs as part of the evaluation process. Yet, there are some strategies that the practitioner can use to enhance the interpretability of one's treatment evaluations. These include obtaining multiple assessments before treatment, conducting continuous assessments throughout treatment, using follow-up assessments, using a comparison group when possible, and using standardized assessment measures (cf., Briere, 1996c; Kazdin, 1998).

Practicalities of Multimodal Assessment

Although it may be ideal to obtain multiple, multimodal assessments before, during, and after treatment, few researchers or community practitioners have the resources to do so. Thus, small-scale assessments may be a practical alternative and are preferable to a lack of assessment altogether. Such small-scale efforts might be limited to assessments at pre- and posttreatment, include a selection of one or two brief self-report scales able to capture the central treatment targets, a well-defined behavioral rating scale to be filled out by perhaps one observer (e.g., the Child Behavior Checklist; Achenbach, 1991), a clinical-rated checklist, or brief, global measures of functioning that sacrifice detail but provide an efficient way of noting client progress. In addition, one might take a "short-hand" approach to applying resource-intensive measures, such as replacing formal observational measures with elaborate coding systems with making judgments informed by such systems on informal, office-based observations.

Conclusion

When used optimally, assessment not only allows for program evaluation and research stimulation, but it only makes up a rich and ongoing part of clinical practice. The professional working in the field of family violence must consider issues of cultural diversity, as well as a variety of ethical, diagnostic, and legal issues when applying an assessment approach. Regardless of its ultimate application, assessment serves a valuable purpose. Thorough assessment proves crucial not only for purposes of initial screening and obtaining a description of presenting problems, but also for identifying treatment targets and obtaining measures of functioning before, during, and after treatment. Establishing rapport and trust while enhancing disclosure are other important functions of assessment.

Systematic evaluation of treatment outcome using multimodal assessment has become increasingly in demand in the past decade. The clinician might consider many variables in evaluating outcome of clinical practice, including client-related criteria (e.g., level of functioning), service efficiency and cost-related criteria, consumer-related criteria (e.g., client satisfaction), and measures of social impact (cf., Kazdin, 1998). Although a number of problems exist with the interpretation of pre–post evaluation of treatment, many of these can be addressed in clinical practice by obtaining multiple assessments at baseline, conducting repeated assessments over the course of treatment, conducting follow-up assessments, comparing outcome results to untreated groups or groups receiving a different treatment, and using standardized assessment instruments. The effort involved in conducting comprehensive assessments in clinical practice is surely offset by the rewards offered by the accountability, feedback, and communicability that such assessments provide.

Family Violence Assessment: Test Construction and Psychometrics

To interpret the reviews of instruments provided in this volume, it is necessary to understand the central concepts related to the development and psychometrics of the measures reviewed. This chapter reviews essentials of test construction and psychometric characteristics of scales and briefly discusses these issues as they relate to the field of family violence.

Methods of Test Construction

Although an in-depth discussion of test construction falls beyond the scope of this book, we briefly introduce test construction methods. We first present both rational and empirical approaches to scale development and then discuss aspects of test scoring.

Rational and Empirical Approaches to Scale Development

There are two general methods for developing assessment instruments: rational and empirical approaches. The rational approach consists of generating and grouping scale items based on the relevant clinical literature, a priori theoretical notions of constructs, or a combination of the two. The empirical approach essentially involves grouping and retaining scale items based on statistical processes involving conducting some form of factor analysis, evaluating item–scale correlations, and moving or dropping items based on maximizing internal consistency (cf. Jackson, 1970). Another way to develop a scale empirically is to retain items (or assign items to particular scales) based on their ability to discriminate between groups that are differentiated on the construct of interest, a procedure known as *empirical criterion keying* (Golden, Sawicki, & Franzen, 1984). Many scale developers combine both strategies, rationally generating items and then arriving at final scales based on empirical methodology.

Scoring

Another factor in scale construction involves scoring of the instrument. Dimensional scales produce scores that occur on a continuum and represent varying degrees of a construct. Many self-report inventories are scored dimensionally; examples include measures of aggressiveness or depression. Categorical measures produce scores reflecting discrete, all-or-none membership in particular categories and typically reflect the presence or absence of a given variable. Many observational coding systems and interviews are scored categorically; examples of categorically scored variables include clinical diagnosis or communication style.

An additional aspect of scoring involves scaling. Particularly in self-report inventories, but sometimes in other instrument formats as well, noncategorical individual items are rated on some type of continuous scale. The Likert-type scale is the most common of such scales, and represents a range (commonly 1 to 5 or 1 to 7) of anchored choice points that reflect relative agreement or disagreement with the item. Items are then typically summed to yield total scores. The Guttman scale also reflects a range of anchored choice points, but rather than a choice point reflecting a discrimination among items, the highest endorsed item by an individual subsumes all of the item choices that come below it. That is, if a respondent endorses item 4 on a 7-point scale, the assumption is that items 1 through 4 will all be true for the respondent. The Thurstone scale reflects a range of choice points, typically reflecting attitudes that are rated by a group of judges as ranging from reflecting more to less favorable attitudes. Items are retained that reflect good agreement among judges and range evenly from one extreme of the attitude to the other (Nunnally, 1978). Forced-choice scales present the respondent with a set of choices (typically pairs) and ask the respondent to select the more favorable or applicable choice in the set. Many inventories use this format in a "yes/no" or "true/false" format.

An additional consideration involving scoring of assessment devices involves whether scoring is norm-referenced or criterion-referenced. A norm-referenced approach calculates scores according to established normative scoring for a given population. An example of this type of scoring involves a construct such as marital satisfaction, measures of which yield scores that fall within the range of maritally satisfied status or clinically distressed status, based on norms from these groups. Criterion-referenced scoring, in contrast, is a

> method of assessment designed to measure performance and to estimate a person's level of (or in some cases the simple presence or absence of) skill, capability, or achievement in absolute rather than relative terms. The focus is on a person's performance in certain specified content domains. (Linehan, 1980, p. 149)

An example of this type of assessment would be a role-play test to determine a person's performance in assertiveness.

Psychometric Considerations: Reliability and Validity

A central consideration in the development of assessment devices is the reliability and validity of the instrument. Reliability refers to the precision and consistency of measurement, or the extent to which a test score consists of the true score and not measurement error. Validity refers to the extent to which an instrument actually measures the construct it attempts to measure. A test cannot be valid if it is not reliable, because it cannot be said to measure a given construct adequately if it does not do so in an accurate and stable manner. Because we report on assessment devices throughout this volume, we will refer to the following types of reliability and validity that have been established for each instrument.

Types of Reliability

Several types of reliability can attest to the consistency of measurement. The reliability indexes of interest depend on the type of device. For example, if an instrument is purported to measure a stable construct, demonstrating test–retest reliability would be important; if an instrument is purported to measure a single construct, internal consistency reliability would be important. In this section we describe test–retest reliability, interrater reliability, internal consistency reliability, split-half reliability, alternate-forms reliability, and use of the standard error of measurement as a reliability index.

Test–Retest Reliability

Test–retest reliability refers to the degree to which a score remains stable on an instrument from Time 1 to Time 2. This stability will vary according to the target of assessment. For example, certain characteristics are expected to remain stable, such as historical factors (e.g., an abused child's developmental history), basic capabilities in the absence of intervention (e.g., assertiveness skills), or trait-like characteristics such as intelligence and personality. Other characteristics are expected to vary substantially, such as mood ratings. Test–retest reliability is expressed as a simple correlation (i.e., from 0 to 1.0).

Interrater Reliability

Interrater reliability reflects the degree to which multiple raters agree when assigning scores using the same instrument on the same participant within the same time frame. This type of reliability is relevant in assessment situations in which subjective judgments are used, such as in observational or interview assessments. Interrater reliability reflects the degree to which ratings reflect true characteristics of the measured phenomenon, rather than idiosyncratic characteristics or perceptions of particular raters.

Interrater reliability is typically reported in one of four ways. For dimensional data (e.g., total scores on self-report measures), interrater reliability is normally calculated in terms of intraclass correlations (ICCs; Shrout & Fleiss, 1979) or simple Pearson correlations between raters' scores. For categorical data (e.g., types of communication observed in an observational study), interrater reliability is normally calculated using Cohen's (1960) Kappa statistic or by calculating the percentage agreement (number of agreements divided by the number of agreements plus disagreements). Intraclass correlations and kappas are the more conservative estimates of interrater reliability and are preferable to simple correlations and percentage agreement because their calculation takes chance agreement into account. Both ICCs and Kappas range from 0 to 1.0.

Internal Consistency Reliability

Internal consistency reliability, typically measured with Cronbach's coefficient alpha (Cronbach, 1951), reflects the extent to which the content of a scale measures a unidimensional construct. The alpha coefficient averages the intercorrelations among scale items, and ranges from 0 to 1.0. The degree to which internal consistency is desirable depends in part on the nature of the construct measured by the instrument. For example, in a measure of broad personality functioning, we would not expect internal consistency. However, within the subscales of this personality measure (e.g., impulsivity) we would expect more uniform endorsement of characteristics. For tests with dichotomous response choices (e.g., true–false), the Kuder-Richardson 20 Formula (Nannaly & Bernstein, 1994) is used rather than Cronbach's alpha to calculate reliability.

Split Half

Split-half reliability is a form of internal consistency reliability and measures the extent to which two halves of an instrument are intercorrelated. Internal consistency (alpha) is the intercorrelation of all possible split halves of the test.

Alternate Forms

Alternate forms reliability involves the preparing of an equivalent form of the test with nonoverlapping items and calculating the degree to which the two versions are correlated. Alternate form reliability reflects the degree to which the score reflects characteristics of the construct assessed and not the test item content itself. It is useful when there is concern about practice effects of taking the test, which might be particularly likely with some types of tests (e.g., tests of ability) or when the test is repeated within a short enough time frame that items are likely to be remembered.

Standard Error of Measurement

The standard error of measurement (SEM) is an estimate of the standard deviation of error scores of an instrument. Examination of the SEM allows for a direct assessment of the degree of error operating in repeated measurements using the same instrument. Thus, if changes in scores across assessment periods are larger than the SEM, one can conclude that the change that occurred reflects actual change in the level of the variable measured and not merely "noise" in the instrument.

Validity of Constructs

Construct validity refers to the degree to which a test measures the particular construct it purports to measure. Various types of construct validity include convergent and discriminant validity, criterion validity, known-groups validity, and factorial validity.

Convergent and Discriminant Validity

Convergent validity is the correlation of the scale with closely related or overlapping constructs with which it is expected to correlate. Discriminant validity is the lack of correlation (or a modest correlation) with measures of different constructs, with which the measure is expected to be unrelated (or modestly related). For example, a measure of family cohesion might be expected to correlate with measures of family communication and family conflict but not to a measure of job satisfaction.

Criterion-Related Validity

Criterion-related validity refers to correspondence of ratings on an instrument with a relevant specified criterion. There are two types of criterion-related validity: concurrent and predictive validity. Concurrent validity refers to correspondence on an assessment instrument with an outside criterion measure that coincides with the time of measurement. Examples include establishing the criterion-related validity of an interview assessing a recent abuse incident by corroborating the findings with court and medical records concerning that incident. Another example of establishing concurrent validity would include assessment of an additional informant—for example, comparing information obtained on family environment by assessing a child directly with information obtained by assessing the child's parent (when multiple informants fill out the same assessment device regarding the same subject, a high correspondence in scores may also be thought of as supporting interrater reliability). Predictive validity refers to the ability of an instrument to predict an expected future outcome associated with the construct. For example, the predictive validity of an instrument administered at Time 1 designed to measure future dangerousness would be determined by its accuracy in predicting the criterion of dangerous behavior by a designated Time 2.

Known-Groups Validity

Known-groups validity refers to the ability of an assessment device to discriminate between groups already identified as being characterized by varying levels of the construct of interest. For example, if a measure of trauma symptoms yields significantly higher scores in a sample of abused from nonabused children, this would be evidence of the scale's known-groups validity. Known-groups validity may be thought of as a type of criterion validity, because it reflects a correspondence between a particular assessment measure and an established criterion (e.g., an independently determined diagnosis or condition, such as "abused" or "nonabused").

Factorial Validity

Establishing factorial validity involves the statistical technique of factor analysis. Determining validity in this manner can be done in one of two ways. The first involves conducting a factor analysis on scales of interest as well as several other scales that are theoretically related and several that are not. If the scale of interest loads on a factor with the scales with which it is expected to relate (i.e., convergent validity) and not on factors containing the scales with which it is *not* expected to relate (i.e., discriminant validity), than factorial validity has been supported. The second way involves examining individual item loadings. Items on the scales of interest should correlate highly with the factor score of the related construct while not correlating highly with other factors not considered to be representing the same variable.

Content Validity

Content validity refers to the extent to which a measure adequately samples the content domain—that is, the universe of behaviors or attributes that make up a particular construct. For example, an instrument that measures aspects of child abuse including physical abuse, sexual abuse, emotional abuse, and neglect might be said to have good content validity.

Incremental Validity

Not technically a form of validity, incremental validity refers to the extent to which an instrument contributes to the measurement of a construct. High incremental validity means that adding a particular measure to a battery of assessments substantially increases our knowledge about the characteristic measured.

Face Validity

Also not technically a form of validity, face validity refers to the extent to which the purpose of the test can be detected from the item content. High face validity is desirable to the extent that an instrument has credibility; it is undesirable to the extent that the easier it is to determine what a test is measuring, the more susceptible the test will be to both demand characteristics and response biases, such as faking good.

Difficulties in Test Construction and Psychometrics Research in Family Violence

There are many difficulties in conducting adequate scale-development research with assessment measures in family violence. These include problems with definitions of constructs within family violence, difficulties in establishing the psychometric properties of assessment devices, issues of "subjecting" victims to research, placing research participants at risk, and an emphasis on internal over external validity.

Problems With Definitions of Constructs Within Family Violence

There cannot be precise measurement of a phenomenon unless we have a clear understanding of the construct to which we are referring. Yet, there is no gold-standard definition of child abuse or neglect, and variations exist in definitions across states and agencies. Thus, our assessment devices tend to assess variables related to abuse, such as potential for or consequences of abuse, rather than providing clear cutoffs for whether abuse occurred. In addition, we often rely on the use of mandated reporting as an assessment source, because we often conduct research with populations identified by the multiple judgments of multiple professionals [e.g., using inclusion criteria of "physically abused children" as whether the child is in Child Protective Services (CPS) system].

Difficulties in Establishing Psychometric Properties

Although it is desirable to establish family violence assessment instruments with sound psychometric properties, several factors may make it difficult to measure reliability and validity in such instruments. An essential issue is obtaining large enough sample sizes. Large sample sizes are needed to conduct factor analysis (i.e., in obtaining factorial or construct validity), to obtain significance when attempting to discriminate groups or to determine associations among scales (i.e., to determine known-groups validity or convergent and discriminant validity), and to obtain stable calculations of reliability. However, most scale developers do not have ready access to hundreds or even dozens of family violence victims or perpetrators. To obtain large sample sizes, some who develop scales rely on either easily accessible respondents such as college students or "captive" respondents such as those temporarily housed in shelters or mandated to treatment programs—with both types of respondents being not representative of the populations they are presumed to represent.

Another issue pertains to obtaining reliability through use of repeated assessments (i.e., test–retest reliability), multiple raters (i.e., interrater reliability), and lengthy questionnaires (i.e., item length enhances internal consistency ratings). These strategies, although ideal from a scale-development perspective, may not be practical in a treatment setting. For example, one may not wish to ask an abuse victim to fill out multiple measures of similar and dissimilar constructs (to establish convergent and discriminant validity), rather than protect this time for efforts that will be of direct service to the client.

"Subjecting" Victims to Research

Even in nonresearch settings, there may be concern about revictimization through lengthy, intrusive, or structured assessment procedures. In research settings (e.g., scale-development studies), this concern can become exacerbated with methodological requirements such as lengthy procedures and nonflexible protocols. However, most assessment information contributes to case conceptualization and treatment planning, and most research conducted with victims is designed to enhance understanding of their experience and to inform treatment approaches. As long as assessments are carried out in a compassionate manner, there is not an a priori reason to assume that they will be detrimental to clients. In fact, one study found that the majority of women reporting on their history of abuse found the experience to be a positive one (Walker, Newman, Koss, & Bernstein, 1997). Possible benefits of participating in such assessments include relief at expressing one's feelings about past abusive incidents to an accepting listener, validation of one's experiences, providing a sense of purpose or meaning in their experiences, enhancing self-awareness, and empowerment (Hutchinson, Wilson, & Wilson, 1994).

There also may be a hesitancy to expose victimized clients to traumatic cues by asking them to recite their painful stories in an interview or to fill out a measure listing abusive behaviors in efforts to develop or evaluate an assessment device. Similarly, there may be concern about invasion of the client's privacy by asking particularly intrusive or sensitive questions (e.g., questions regarding sexual abuse). In this case, it may be useful to remember that clients likely expect to retell their stories in some format by entering treatment.

In addition, there are a number of ways to protect the rights and well-being of research participants. First, it is essential to ensure that the client's responses will remain confidential and anonymous and to inform the client of these safeguards (Kazdin, 1998). However, in cases of threat of harm to self or another, or suspicion of ongoing child abuse, the assessor's "duty to warn" will preclude maintaining confidentiality. That is one of the places where the notion of informed consent becomes relevant. As part of any research, it is necessary to obtain informed consent from the client. Informing the participant about the nature of the research, the risks and benefits of participating, and the right to withdraw must include an understanding of the conditions under which the researcher must violate confidentiality. Even children, who cannot provide informed consent (this must be provided by a parent or guardian), must still grant assent, and every effort should be made to explain procedures to children in simple terms while giving them the same prerogative to stop participation in the research or refuse to respond to particular questions.

Second, any research protocol, whether in a hospital, clinic, agency, or university setting, must be submitted to and approved by an institutional review board that will have screened the research for its potential harmfulness to the clients. Third, it is crucial to administer assessment procedures with sensitivity, which will require a knowledge of the population that is being assessed and the issues, struggles, and common types of clinical presentation that tend to characterize the particular population of interest. Fourth, it will be important to follow the research procedure immediately with a debriefing, which consists of not only providing more information about the purpose of the research but also gently inquiring about the impact of questions on the participants and assessing how they are feeling at the present moment. Fifth, the research assessor should be knowledgeable about local referrals for clients who need them. These might include the phone numbers of local hotlines or agencies, as well as a list of other local resources such as practitioners and programs specializing in family violence, and sources of advocacy or legal representation. It is helpful to have such resources printed as handouts or pamphlets easily available to clients in need of such information. Similarly, the research assessor will need to be well-versed in crisis strategies and safety planning should it become apparent in the course of the research that such interventions are needed.

Placing Research Participants at Risk

There can be a number of ways that conducting scale-development research in family violence may place participants at risk. The first has to do with conducting the assessments with a family in such a way that issues raised during the assessment process lead to acts of aggression following the session. For example, a child might unwittingly reveal something that angers a parent and may suffer the consequences following the assessment session.

A client may be placed at risk through irresponsible treatment of information, such as calling at home and leaving a message that one is calling from the "child abuse project," sending questionnaires with sensitive questions home, or engaging in telephone interviews without being sure that the respondent is alone, feels unlikely to be interrupted, and feels safe.

Another way the research assessor can place participants at risk is by asking about sensitive material that is subject to laws of mandated reporting (i.e., material that reveals ongoing child abuse or harm intended toward another). This presents a paradox for researchers attempting to study topics such as child abuse or prediction of dangerousness, as some of the very assessment questions needed to conduct the research would seem to set up the participants for being reported. For this reason, many researchers devise research questions in the family violence field that minimize the chance of setting up participants in this way. For example, one might conduct research assessing issues of family violence with populations who are already identified (e.g., assessing outcome of a specialized treatment program for incest perpetrators; assessing symptom levels in children identified by CPS as sexual abuse survivors).

Emphasis on Internal Over External Validity

Throughout this volume, we discuss indexes reflecting attempts to increase the internal validity of the conclusions drawn from the measure. In research methodology, internal validity is primarily concerned with causal inferences and refers to the extent to which we can be confident that our independent variable, and not a confounding variable, accounted for the observed effect on our dependent variable (Kazdin, 1998). In test construction in particular, researchers concern themselves with reliability and validity—that is, whether a test measures precisely and consistently and whether it measures the construct it is purported to measure, usually within the scale-development population. However, the concept of external validity, or the extent to which one can generalize to additional populations and settings, is typically shortchanged or ignored (Sue, 1999). Although internal validity is typically associated with scientific rigor and thus prioritized, "The lack of external validity may render findings meaningless with the actual population of interest" (Sue, 1999, p. 1072). The most classic example of this lack of attention to external validity is the extensive use of college student populations in psychological research. Within the field of family violence assessment, many instruments have norms and psychometric data limited to the scale-development sample, yet may be used with (faulty) assumptions of applicability with other groups. For example, a device might be developed on White, suburban schoolchildren without identified abuse histories but be applied to a multiethnic, urban sample with a history of exposure to violence. The section on cultural diversity in family violence assessment in chapter 2 addressed this problem further, and in particular examined the challenges inherent in addressing issues of external validity.

Conclusion

The development of well-constructed, psychometrically sound instruments would be further enhanced by efforts toward making them comprehensive and relevant to a variety of settings. Toward these ends, Hamby and Finkelhor have outlined a number of recommendations for instrument development regarding the victimization of children:

> Among other things, instruments should (1) allow victimization to be mapped onto conventional crime and child protection system categories; (2) adequately assess victimization by family and other nonstranger perpetrators; (3) ask about crimes specific to childhood, such as nonviolent sexual offenses and neglect; (4) allow for comparisons between juvenile and adult victimizations; (5) collect self-report data with children as young as age 7 years; (6) use simple, behaviorally specific language; (7) protect privacy during data collection; (8) attend to potential ethnic, class, and gender differences; and (9) prepare procedures to assist children in danger. Comprehensive and well-researched instrumentation could greatly advance the study and treatment of juvenile victimization. (2000, p. 829)

Part II

Assessment of Maltreated Children and Adolescents

Introduction: Assessment of Maltreated Children and Adolescents

The assessment of children and adolescents who have been victims of maltreatment requires a sensitive and ethical approach. Clinical concerns in relation to an intrusive process that may further victimize the child often outweigh the need for methodological rigor or the psychometric requirements of research. However, the need for comprehensive and reliable methods for the measurement of antecedents, consequences, and sequelae of child maltreatment is apparent for purposes of screening, designation of at-risk situations, and the evaluation of psychological interventions. This part introduction will review the salient issues as well as obstacles to multimodal assessment of child maltreatment.

Issues in the Assessment of Maltreated Children and Adolescents

Progress in the development of reliable and valid assessment tools has been hampered by the complexity of the child abuse situation. Medical and legal definitions have dominated the determination of occurrence of child physical and sexual abuse, such that reports are made, children are protected, and perpetrators are punished. Early definitions and assessments were narrowly focused on physical harm and endangerment. However, as McGee, Wolfe, Yuen, Wilson, and Carnochan (1995) noted, the heterogeneity and cooccurrence of multiple forms of maltreatment make it difficult to use methods of categorization emphasizing simply occurrence or nonoccurrence. They suggest the use of a subjective approach to measuring maltreatment wherein maltreatment is defined by the victim's self-report of occurrence and severity rather than by "objective" criteria dictated by legal or statutory requirements (McGee et al., 1995). This is sometimes not possible for children to accomplish, either because of age or dynamics embedded within the family situations.

For our purposes, *child maltreatment* as a broad target for assessment and intervention will include physical abuse, sexual abuse, emotional abuse, and neglect using commonly accepted definitions. *Physical abuse* is often defined as an act of commission by the parent–caregiver characterized by nonaccidental injury and infliction of pain, and *neglect* involves chronic pervasive acts of omission wherein the parent–caregiver fails to attend to the child's physical, medical, nutritional, educational, or emotional needs (Hansen & Warner, 1992). The heterogeneous category of *sexual abuse* is best defined as sexual activities involving a child and an adult (or significantly older child), intended for the sexual stimulation of the perpetrator, which constitutes an abusive condition (such as coercion) and a lack of consensuality (Wurtele, 1998). Finally, *emotional abuse* represents inappropriate strategies used by parents–caregivers to control, manipulate, humiliate, shame, and belittle children such that they experience psychological pain. Recently, exposure to partner violence has also been included in the definition of psychological maltreatment of children (Kerig & Fedorowicz, 1999). Clearly, these various forms of child maltreatment differ according to frequency and severity of occurrence, to relationship with the perpetrator, and to acute versus chronic exposure. This variability, coupled with the fact that child maltreatment is most times embedded in a complex and dysfunctional family, makes assessment very difficult.

In addition to the documentation of the occurrence of any form of child maltreatment, there are the antecedent and consequent events that must also be assessed. In terms of antecedents to child maltreatment, the first priority is the assessment of proximal events or direct triggers of abuse. This might require observations of parent–child interactions to determine aspects of child behavior that elicit inappropriate parent response. However, because of both the privacy of most child maltreatment and our mandate to report, it would seem unlikely that observations of direct triggers could be made. Most likely, reliance on child and parent reports in a retrospective fashion would be necessary. Next, the assessment of distal events that have an indirect association to the occurrence of child maltreatment would be in order. This might include the measurement of family interaction, marital functioning, stress, and social support, all of which affect the occurrence of maltreatment (Rittner & Wodarski, 1995). Finally, there is a need to examine at-risk situations in which the child may not have been victimized but may be vulnerable. Although there are many contextual variables that increase the risk for child abuse (e.g., substance use, parental history of abuse), the occurrence of partner abuse clearly emerges as a key risk factor (Salzinger, Feldman, Hammer, & Rosario, 1991). In addition, children who witness family violence are at risk for the development of numerous behavioral and psychological disturbances (Kerig & Fedorowicz, 1999).

When asked to conduct assessments, the usual targets for the clinician as well as the researcher are the consequences and sequelae of child maltreatment. An evaluation of a child victim must be done within a developmental context with consideration given to the child's age, stage-salient tasks, and the developmental processes disrupted by both acute and chronic maltreatment (Kerig & Fedorowicz, 1999). Age of onset of abuse and its duration become important indicators in terms of developmental consequences and associated sequelae. Many victims of child sexual abuse disclose much later in life, which requires retrospective assessment of the abuse and assessment of adult functioning. The development of a maltreated child rarely follows a predictable course because of other negative socialization forces such as family instability, parental dysfunction, and socioeconomic disadvantage and to the interactional processes involved in development (Wolfe & McEachran, 1997).

Comprehensive assessment of the victimized child requires multiple foci across dimensions of functioning. Characteristics of victimized children in the behavioral domain include heightened aggressiveness and hostility toward others and poor social skills, which often lead to peer rejection during latency years (Salzinger, Feldman, Hammer, & Rosario, 1993).

Across the cognitive and socioemotional domains, clinical researchers have noted numerous developmental disturbances in maltreated children. Wolfe and McEachran (1997) reviewed the various developmental delays in language acquisition and the ability to discriminate emotions in others as well as deficits in social information processing that characterize maltreated children and adolescents. In particular, research conducted by Dodge, Pettit, Bates, and Valente (1995) indicated specific patterns of cognitive functioning related to aggressive behaviors of maltreated children as well as adults. These childhood patterns, including a hypervigilance to hostile cues, misperceptions of hostile intention on the part of others, and beliefs supporting the use of responses to interpersonal problems are clearly linked to adult patterns of interpartner violence (Feldman, 1997). Social development may also be compromised by the experience of witnessing domestic abuse as well as being sexually abused. Sexually abused children tend to be less socially skilled and less trusting, and as adults survivors report fears of intimacy, poor relationship choices, and maladaptive interpersonal patterns (Wurtele, 1998). Studies of longer term consequences of childhood sexual abuse indicate a greater risk for revictimization in that adult women are less skilled at self-protection, less sure of their own worth, and more apt to accept victimization as part of being a woman (Messman & Long, 1996). All of these characteristics and developmental delays would require evaluation as part of a comprehensive assessment.

Another critical dimension of the child's early development is attachment security. Substantial research on this aspect of the child–caregiver relationship points out the developmental outcomes of attachment security, including emotion self-regulation, behavioral competence, and self-control, as well as advantages for the creation and maintenance of other close relationships (Thompson, 1999). In the context of the maltreating family, both insecure and disorganized patterns of attachment are characteristic of the parent–child relationship and predict a number of maladaptive and aggressive behavior problems, altered physiological responses to stress, and poor internal representations of relational behavior. Perhaps the core features of a disorganized attachment relationship (difficulties in intimate relationships, unintegrated mental representations, negative self-concepts, and problems with affect regulation) are identifiable in children with abuse histories. Aspects of attachment represent yet another important area for assessment of both child and parent functioning.

Along with the examination of precursors and consequences of child maltreatment, a comprehensive assessment approach should also target protective factors or moderating variables that may account for resiliency often seen in maltreated children. An individual child's strengths may be found in dispositional attributes, such as the ability to adjust to a new situation, high frustration tolerance, or social competence allowing development of healthy relationships with others. Other potential buffers include coping strategies of the victim, cognitive appraisals of the events, as well as contextual variables such as support within and outside the family system (Feldman, 1997).

Issues in the Assessment of Child Maltreatment

A thorough evaluation of child maltreatment would be a multimodel, multicomponent package of assessment methods that would enable the clinician to understand the precursors, consequences, and sequelae of the abuse experience, to identify strengths and protective factors, to evaluate contextual variables, and to determine intervention needs and priorities. Although assessment has typically been focused on the history of maltreatment and the nature and extent of the developmental impairment of the child, we are suggesting that clinicians and researchers broaden their assessment scope beyond general levels of functioning. Targeting individual child strengths and weaknesses across all developmental domains would help to understand age-appropriate behaviors; skill levels in terms of problem solving, safety, and socialization; attitudes and perceptions about maltreatment experiences and about caregiver; peer and romantic relationships; and ability to regulate affect. Because these targets are most likely to become treatment objectives, it is important to adequately assess the child at pretreatment.

An early model for comprehensive assessment was offered by O'Donohue and Elliott (1991), who suggested that a thorough evaluation requires obtaining information from multiple informants (child, parents, siblings, teachers) concerning multiple persons (child, siblings, parents) in diverse settings (home and school) by a variety of assessment measures (self-report, other report, questionnaires, direct observation, role plays, and interviews). This section (chapters 4, 5, and 6) is a review of methods of assessment specifically focused on the child or adolescent who has experienced some form of abuse. Also included are retrospective measures completed by adults who may seek treatment for the abuse experienced during their childhood. Some of the methods, such as semistructured interviews, might be conducted during intake only, and other assessments might be repeatedly administered to assist in monitoring the clinical course of treatment to determine effectiveness (Kolko, 1996a).

Obstacles to Reliable and Comprehensive Assessment

There are several features of the child maltreatment experience that pose challenges to reliable and comprehensive assessment. The interaction sequence in which children are maltreated along various dimensions by specific adults represents behaviors not readily observed by others. Usually child maltreatment occurs in private, and this aspect makes studying it and documenting its occurrence difficult because it often hinges on the report of a young victim, perhaps without any physical evidence (Widom & Shepard, 1996). Children are often pressured or coerced into silence, further compromising their ability to report. Abusive behaviors toward children also exist on a continuum of severity, with the most severe behaviors occurring in a low frequency and covert fashion and the least severe behaviors occurring at a higher frequency. This variability, coupled with the heterogeneity of maltreating families and the wide age range of victims who need to be evaluated, makes assessment especially difficult.

The focus on assessment of parents or adults involved in maltreatment poses other difficulties. Participation in evaluation and treatment may be nonvoluntary or a condition for child custody (Hansen & Warner, 1992). Response biases influence accurate responding on written instruments in that adults recognize and give socially desirable answers (Rittner & Wodarski, 1995) and may underreport occurrences of abusive behaviors because of fear of negative consequences (Kerig & Fedorowicz, 1999).

Recently, researchers have begun to examine the correspondence between respondents. Kolko, Kazdin, and Day (1996) examined child and mother reports of violence and verbal aggression in the home. Their results indicated in part that children reported higher rates of mother-to-child violence than did mothers, but that the opposite occurred for child-to-mother violence—that is, children reported lower rates than mothers. The authors suggest that children and adults may be similarly influenced by family processes influencing reporting but may process and encode aggressive and assaultive interactions quite differently (Kolko et al., 1996).

McGee et al. (1995) examined the correspondence of three reporting sources surrounding maltreatment of adolescents: researchers examining agency files, protection agency social workers, and the maltreated adolescents themselves. Results indicated considerable disagreement with respect to judgments of maltreatment occurrence and severity. In addition, results indicated that subjective estimates of past victimization by the adolescents themselves were more predictive of externalizing and internalizing symptoms related to behavioral adjustment (McGee et al., 1995) than information obtained from other sources.

Retrospective reporting by adults who were victims of child maltreatment presents difficulties as well. Memory deficits because of the passage of time as well as trauma symptomatology (denial, numbing, dissociation) may impede accurate recollection of past events (Kerig & Federowicz, 1999). Some adults, sensitive to issues of social desirability, may even redefine their own behaviors and past experiences in accordance with later life circumstances (Widom & Shepard, 1996). Many researchers and clinicians suggest that the use of multiple sources of information obtained via various methods are the only way to obtain reliable information about maltreatment experiences. In addition, these methods must be sensitive to developmental issues as well as to the contextual factors surrounding the maltreatment.

Legal and Ethical Considerations

Although reporting laws vary according to jurisdiction, the primary ethical concern in the assessment of child maltreatment is the mandate to report both past occurrences and present dangers. Kerig and Federowicz (1999) reviewed the following concerns that arise for the interviewer or assessor: limits of confidentiality, which may affect trust between child and interviewer; legal involvement, which may further traumatize the child; and repercussions of the reporting for the child and other family members. Each of these concerns must be weighed by the interviewer in light of the highest priority, which is always the protection of children from harm.

Often, a clinician is asked to participate in a formal forensic assessment of a child victim and various family members to assist in legal proceedings and child custody decisions. Forensic assessment has specific goals such as substantiation of allegations of abuse, termination of parental rights, child placement, or risk assessment wherein the likelihood of future maltreatment is estimated. The process and requirements of forensic evaluation are certainly beyond the scope of this book (see chapter 3), because our focus is on the clinician and clinical researcher. However, it is hoped that this review of available methods of assessment of child maltreatment will be a resource for those developing protocols for forensic evaluations.

Several controversial issues have emerged as the process of forensic assessment continues to develop and be evaluated. For example, there are a number of concerns about the reliability and validity of information provided by young children during the evaluation process. Because their account of victimization may be the only available source of information, clinicians and researchers have highlighted influential factors and have made suggestions to improve investigatory interview formats. Lamb, Steinberg, and Esplin (1994) provided an excellent review of developmental obstacles in children's accounts of past events. These include their lack of linguistic sophistication, memory distortions related to time and the trauma experienced, susceptibility to suggestion, and a tendency to confuse fantasy with reality. Each of these factors has direct implications for the interview process such that the structure of the interview, the types of questions asked, the interaction between child and interviewer, and the interview content all require careful consideration. Lamb et al. (1994) emphasized the need to elicit children's accounts via free recall and to use more open-ended questions rather than directive or leading questions. Others (e.g., White, 1993) suggest that the interview be accompanied by a free-play session to relax the child, establish rapport, as well as informally observe the child's development. It is hoped that as the need for reliable and valid testimony continues to be emphasized, new interview methods, such as the narrative elaboration technique described by Saywitz and Synder (1996) or statement validity or criterion-based content analysis (Raskin & Esplin, 1991) will help to standardize interview protocols.

There is ongoing research in the application of specific criteria set forth in a criterion-based content analysis (CBCA) of children's statements to evaluate credibility. These criteria focus on general characteristics such as logical structure and quantity of details, specific contents, peculiarities of content such as unusual details and references to unrelated sexual events, and motivation-related content such as assumption of blame or pardoning of the perpetrator (Lamb et al., 1994). Perhaps future research will establish the heuristic value of the CBCA in determining the credibility of children's reports of abuse, because other research continues to indicate that children's suggestibility compromises the accuracy of response to questions.

A recent review by Gordon, Baker-Ward, and Ornstein (2001) of issues related to children's memory for past experiences indicates that even very young children can remember events from some time ago and that children over the age of 3 can provide reasonably accurate accounts of events if interviewed in a nonsuggestive and nonleading manner. However, these authors emphasized that there are significant age differences in children's abilities to provide eyewitness testimony because of specific characteristics of cognitive development. Finally, the review covers research that indicates ways in which children can be influenced to provide complete and elaborated narratives about experiences that did *not* occur. Clearly the substantial amount of research done on children's memories, their suggestibility, and their creditability will have important implications for interview assessments in the areas of child abuse and neglect (DeLoache & Maszolf, 1995; Everson, 1997).

In the case of accuracy and completeness of sexual abuse information recall, communication aids or projective tools such as drawings or anatomically detailed (AD) dolls have often been used during the interview process. In 1995, Koocher and his colleagues (1995) published a review of the scientific and clinical knowledge base to date on the use of AD dolls. In general, their review confirmed that AD dolls can play an important and valid role in the forensic assessment of sexual abuse in that they provide memory cues and means for event reenactments. However, they also summarized the many caveats and concerns associated with the inappropriate or inexperienced use of this assessment format. The lack of standardization of the test apparatus (the dolls themselves), the administration procedures, and the scoring and interpretation procedures are just some of the concerns (Skinner & Giles, 1993). (The reader is referred to Koocher et al., 1995, and Skinner & Berry, 1993, for a complete discussion). Some research with 3-year-olds who had a pediatric examination involving genital touching revealed that the use of anatomically detailed dolls did *not* improve the accurate recall of information (Bruck, Ceci, Francouer, & Renick, 1995). Young children were inaccurate in reporting regardless of how they were questioned or whether they had received a genital exam. These authors concluded that AD dolls are themselves suggestive and elicit behaviors that may be construed as sexual and should not be used as aids to assessment with 3-year-old children (Bruck et al., 1995). Although the controversy surrounding the issue of AD dolls is far from resolved, clinical research on optimal techniques for reliable and valid AD doll use continues. Perhaps some of the instruments and methods described in this section will assist in the development of standardized protocols for sexual abuse assessment. In fact, in a review by Babiker and Herbert

(1998) on direct and indirect methods used in the assessment of child sexual abuse, the study indicated that much clinical research has relied on the use of measurement tools *not* specific to the abuse. The projective methods such as human figure drawings and more general child behavior checklists and self-esteem measures used in many studies seem not to be sensitive to the particular sequalea of sexual abuse. In addition, the absence of normative data on children's sexual behavior and knowledge creates an additional obstacle to the development of reliable and valid measures specific to the area of sexual abuse (Babiker & Herbert, 1998).

In sum, the assessment of children and adolescents who have been victims of maltreatment is a complex process. Documentation of maltreatment occurrence, as well as delineation of antecedent events and the sequelae of maltreatment, are primary tasks. However, assessment of each child's development dysfunctions and their strengths and protective factors are also necessary to fully capture a child's status such that appropriate intervention can be planned. The next three chapters will focus on a variety of methods that can assist both the clinician and the researcher in meeting the goals of assessment.

Interview Methods

Independent of theoretical orientation or assessment situation, the interview continues to be the most widely used method of assessment. The following descriptions of interview methods developed to target specific aspects of family violence will vary according to standardization and psychometric development. However, the flexibility of format and the wide scope of information gathered will help to guide the assessment process. The data obtained from detailed interview methods will lead to other assessment targets and will frame a multimodal assessment approach.

1. Anatomical Doll Questionnaire (ADQ; Levy, Markovic, Kalinowski, Ahart, & Torres)

Development and Description of Assessment Method

Despite their widespread use, no generally accepted protocol exists regarding the clinically or legally preferred manner of using anatomical dolls. Thus, the authors sought to examine interrater reliability of information obtained during a clinical interview protocol that featured anatomical dolls in the assessment of child sexual abuse. A sample of 104 children (74 female, 30 male), ages 2 to 7 (median age = 5) referred for sexual abuse treatment was used.

This semistructured interview method guided by a child's behavior with anatomical dolls is used to record and compare observations and perceptions of the child's statements and behaviors during the interviews.

Target Population

Young children, ages 2 to 7 years, who have been or are suspected to have been sexually abused.

Format

The child interview protocol calls for the use of anatomical dolls to conduct a body parts inventory and act as a facilitative medium. The Anatomical Dolls Questionnaire is used to record and compare interviewers' and observers' observations and perceptions of responses during these interviews. Questions are presented in a dichotomous format and address five areas: statements indicating particular types of abuse (6 items, including penis placed in mouth and rectum penetrated), demonstrations with dolls contingent on the presence of associated statements (11 items, including oral sex and vaginal penetration combinations), observations of children's affective–expressive behaviors (10 items, including cried during interview, aggressive to dolls, withdrew from dolls, and affect changed), perceptions of interview quality (4 items, including maintained eye contact, elaborated on responses regarding abuse, responded immediately to questions, and provided consistent details regarding the abuse), and other general observations (3 items, including stating he or she believed by first person told, asked questions regarding dolls' genitals and manipulated dolls genitals before sex abuse discussed).

Administration and Scoring

Interviewers must have extensive training according to a victim-sensitive, developmentally appropriate interview protocol.

First, the anatomical dolls are used to conduct a body parts inventory, and each child is asked to identify various parts. The behavior of each child generally determines the extent to which the dolls are instrumental to the interview process. Interviewers record any disclosure statements and associated spontaneous doll usage as they occur but respond to the remaining questions regarding other details of the interview and effect on the child immediately after the interview. Only information about doll use associated with a statement of a particular type of sexual activity is elicited. Questions are scored based on dichotomous outcome responses (affirmative/nonaffirmative) that a particular act or verbalization occurred.

Psychometric Evaluation

Norms
None reported.

Reliability
The authors compared questionnaire responses given by trained, experienced child development specialists with those given by inexperienced, unobtrusive observers. The questionnaire addressed various observations and interpretations of statements and behaviors exhibited by children during the interviews. Thirty-four questions were examined for interrater reliability based on dichotomous outcome responses (affirmative/nonaffirmative). Interrater reliability to questionnaires was measured using the Phi statistic, where 1.0 = full agreement (and therefore having high interrater reliability) and 0 = level of agreement no better than chance. Interrater agreement was high for children's verbal reports of abusive acts; however, interrater agreement varied considerably for children's demonstrations of sexual behavior. Some demonstrations yielded perfect agreement (e.g., demonstrating oral sex with two anatomically correct dolls), and others yielded very poor interrater agreement (e.g., touching doll's breast). Interrater agreement for child affective expressions was quite poor.

Reliability statistics for the five substantive areas that were addressed were as follows: statements indicating particular types of abuse (Phi range = 1.0–.572); demonstrations with dolls contingent on the presence of associated statements (Phi range = 1.0–.156); observations of children's affective–expressive behaviors (Phi range = .70–.031); perceptions of interview quality (Phi range = .788–.402); other general observations (Phi range = .793–.402).

Validity
Discriminant validity was demonstrated by differences in doll use: Participants used dolls to demonstrate particular acts of sexual abuse in 44% of cases in which there was a confirmed final diagnosis of sexual abuse and only 14% in which there was no confirmation of sexual abuse.

Statements regarding sexual abuse were made by 53% of participants. 71% of them used dolls to illustrate what they had disclosed and exhibited more than one statement and more than one illustration per child, evidencing a correspondence between what the child was saying and doing.

Advantages

This interview questionnaire format is a nonthreatening, guided method for children to disclose sexual abuse. In addition, the categories of doll interaction can be observed and coded easily to help substantiate verbal disclosure statements. The method does not rely exclusively on verbal reporting–descriptions.

Limitations

There were wide variations in interrater reliability, because some aspects of the interview process are difficult to objectively discern. Relatively few males ($n = 12$) made an associated verbal disclosure of sexual abuse compared to females ($n = 43$), yet nearly all males who had verbally disclosed used dolls for demonstration (92%) compared to their female counterparts (65%), indicating that enactment may vary according to gender, perhaps because doll play is more novel for boys.

Primary Reference

Levy, Markovic, Kalinowski, Ahart, and Torres (1995).

Scale Availability

Available from authors.

Related References

Wolfe and Birt (1997).

General Comments and Recommendations for Practitioners and Researchers

This is a promising method used to quantify children's responses to play with an anatomically detailed doll. It will be necessary to obtain normative information across developmental ages to provide a comparison basis.

2. Attributions for Maltreatment Interview (AFMI; McGee & Wolfe)

Development and Description of Assessment Method

This measure consists of four structured interviews corresponding to hostile maltreatment, including physical and emotional abuse, exposure to family violence, sexual abuse, and neglect that assess a child's attributions for his or her maltreatment. The five subscales were derived from theory and factor analysis.

Target Population

Adolescents who were (or are being) physically, emotionally, or sexually abused, exposed to family violence, or neglected.

Format

Respondents are administered only those interviews that pertain to their experience. After generating a list of all possible causes for their maltreatment, respondents are asked to make agreement ratings in relation to 26 statements read aloud by the interviewer. For each of the maltreatment types, the child's responses are categorized according to five subscales: self-blaming cognition, self-blaming effect, self-excusing, perpetrator blaming, and perpetrator excusing.

Administration and Scoring

After generating the list of all possible causes for their maltreatment, respondents are asked to make agreement ratings from 1 = "do not agree" to 4 = "strongly agree" in relation to 26 statements read aloud by the interviewer.

Psychometric Evaluation

Norms
None reported.

Reliability
Each adolescent was individually interviewed by two researchers, during which time he or she completed the global ratings of his or her maltreatment experiences. Test–retest reliability of adolescent ratings was

evaluated using a subsample of 33 research participants. Times between ratings ranged from 10 to 113 days, with a mean of 31 days. Retest reliability Pearson coefficients were $r = .70$ (emotional), $r = .89$ (neglect), $r = .90$ (physical), $r = 92$ (family violence), and $r = .93$ (sexual) for each of the subscales.

Validity

For ratings of occurrence of various types of maltreatment, adolescent ratings agreed with ratings made by social workers or those found in case files approximately three fourths of the time. This concordance was greatest for sexual abuse (more than 90%) and poorest for neglect (approximately 60%), indicating moderate criterion-related validity. Although adolescents reported more physical maltreatment and less family violence, emotional maltreatment, and neglect relative to official sources, reporting sources were in agreement about whether maltreatment had occurred the majority of the time (McGee et al., 1995). However, on average, adolescents rated their experiences of physical maltreatment as more severe than did official sources, but rated their experiences of emotional maltreatment and neglect as less severe, even when disagreement of occurrence was controlled. Correlations between sources were all low, ranging from .01 (exposure to family violence) to .42 (sexual abuse).

In terms of the reporting source that best predicted concurrent adolescent adjustment problems, adolescent ratings were better predictors of externalizing and internalizing symptoms than were professional ratings (McGee et al., 1995). Although few significant correlations between maltreatment and adjustment resulted from either social workers' or case file ratings, adolescent maltreatment ratings predicted a significant amount of variance in three adjustment measures (self-reported internalizing and externalizing and caretaker-reported internalizing), indicating criterion-related validity.

Advantages

The interview offers comprehensive assessment of five types of maltreatments (physical abuse, sexual abuse, emotional abuse, neglect, and exposure to family violence). It targets adolescents' perceptions of occurrence of these events as well as attributions for each type of maltreatment.

Limitations

The adolescents' report of their maltreatment was based on their individual subjective definition of abuse occurrence and severity and based on retrospective report. Thus, interviewers should not necessarily assume absolute accuracy in adolescents' disclosure, on which the interview about attributions is based.

Primary Reference

McGee and Wolfe (1990).

Scale Availability

>Robin McGee
>Child and Adolescent Mental Health Services
>Valley Regional Hospital
>150 Exhibition St.
>Kentville, Nova Scotia, Canada B4N 5E3

Related References

McGee et al. (1995).

General Comments and Recommendations for Practitioners and Researchers

The different pattern of intercorrelations among maltreatment types found between official sources and adolescents themselves (McGee et al., 1995) suggests that adolescents construct or conceptualize their experience differently than professionals. In any case, assessing adolescents' attributions for maltreatment provides a useful focus for guiding interventions.

---

3. Checklist for Child Abuse Evaluation (CCAE; Petty)

Development and Description of Assessment Method

This is a structured information-gathering checklist used for investigating and evaluating children and adolescents who are or may have been abused or neglected. It was developed to facilitate the evaluation process in child abuse cases.

Target Population

Children and adolescents who were or are or may possibly be abused or neglected.

Format

The structured interview consists of a 264-item checklist that contains 24 sections of varying length. The sections include identification and case description; child's status; accuracy of allegations by the reporter; interview with the child, including physical–behavioral observations, disclosure, emotional abuse, sexual abuse, physical abuse and neglect; events witnessed or reported by others, including emotional abuse, sexual abuse, physical abuse and neglect; the child's psychological status, history and observed–reported characteristics of the accused; credibility of the child observed or reported; competence of the child observed or reported; conclusions, including consistency of other information with evaluation; allegation motives; substantiation of allegations; competence of the child as a witness and level of stress experienced by the child; protection of the child; and treatment recommendations. Sample items include,

> "Possible ulterior motive for reporting abuse/neglect."
> "Child's responsiveness during interview."
> "Claims made by the child about the accused."
> "Frequency/duration of abuse/neglect."
> "Reason for previous lack of disclosure."
> "Presence of others during abuse."
> "History of incarceration (of the accused)."
> "Disclosure consistency of the child."

Administration and Scoring

The checklist is intended for use by professionals with training and experience in the field of child abuse and neglect, and should be used in combination with other sources of case data. Respondents can include any such professional who is familiar with the case. Basic case information should be gathered from the referral source before completing the checklist. The participant is then interviewed to elicit material pertinent to checklist items (interview questions are not provided as part of the CCAE). The interviewer checks off the respondents' answer on the checklist, which provides several options for each question.

If the checklist does not include the answer given, there is space to write it in. The respondent has either the entire checklist or only those sections applicable to the specific situation, although sections I (Identification and Case Description), VI (Interview with the Child—Emotional Abuse), and X (Events Witnessed or Reported by Others—Emotional Abuse) should always be administered. The CCAE contains several highly specific and sophisticated items that should be altered if leading questions are not desirable or the questions are being used to interview children. This measure is not scored.

Psychometric Evaluation

Norms
None reported.

Reliability
None reported.

Validity
None reported.

Advantages
The CCAE is a comprehensive information-gathering tool that obtains and helps organize extensive data for preparing clinical reports. The CCAE can also provide a standard document for the case file, serve as a standardized data-collection tool for research, or serve as a training model for those learning to conduct child abuse evaluations.

Limitations
No psychometric information is available. Because interview questions are not provided, there is limited standardization in how responses to checklist items would be obtained, which may influence results.

Primary Reference

Petty (1990).

Scale Availability

Psychological Assessment Resources, Inc.
P.O. Box 998

Odessa, FL 33556
(800) 331-TEST

Related References

None available.

General Comments and Recommendations for Practitioners and Researchers

Although this is a published protocol that will assist in comprehensive data collection, the lack of a standardized interview and of psychometric development compromises its use in the assessment process.

---

4. Child Abuse and Neglect Interview Schedule—Revised (CANIS—R; Ammerman, 1998; Ammerman, Van Hasselt, & Hersen, 1988; Original)

Development and Description of Assessment Method

Originally the CANIS–R was developed as a research tool for the characterization of type and severity of maltreatment and for the exploration of the interrelationships among etiologic variables and types of maltreatment. However, it has been used more recently as a clinical assessment tool for screening, treatment planning, and outcome evaluation.

This is a semistructured interview administered to parents that collects information about the child's experiences of physical abuse, neglect, psychological abuse and sexual abuse, parental (and others responsible for the child) disciplinary practices, childcare and supervision, as well as parent's history of maltreatment as a child, other forms of family violence, and the child's witnessing family violence.

Target Population

Families where abuse, neglect, or other family violence is occurring, has occurred, or is at risk of occurring.

Format

This semistructured interview is administered to parents. It begins with a section to record demographic information and consists of more than

100 questions categorized into four subsections. Clear and explicit examples of each type of maltreatment are provided for parents to endorse or reject. The interview ends with a summary where the interviewer writes down his or her impressions. The subsections include

- *Child Behavior Problems and Disciplinary Practices:* This section refers to how the parent and other caregivers discipline the child. It includes queries about when and how often incidents occurred. Sample items include
  - "When your child does something that requires punishment or discipline, how do you typically handle the situation?" (choices include verbal threats, slaps, withdrawal of privileges, and behavior modification)
  - "If corporal punishment, thinking of the most severe corporal punishment, did you: (choices include: slap him/her on hands, spank his/her buttocks, shake the infant or young child, throw objects)?"
- *Parental Past and Current History of Family Violence:* In this section the parent describes his or her own childhood experiences of physical abuse, neglect, psychological abuse, and witnessing of family violence as well as current or past experiences with couples violence, including queries about when and how often incidents occurred. Sample items include
  - "How were you disciplined as a child?" (choices include verbal commands, slaps, time out and/or extinction, psychological abuse)
  - "If corporal punishment, outcome of the most severe corporal punishment?" (choices include bruises, burns, cuts)
  - "Was there any form of physical fighting or violence in your home while you were growing up?"
- *Child's Exposure to Violence, Psychological Abuse, and Neglect:* In this section, the parent describes the child's experiences of these phenomena that are perpetrated either by the parent or others. Questions are also asked about the mother's pregnancy and the child's infancy to address neglect or abuse that may have occurred before the child's birth. Sample items include
  - "Do your children observe you and your partner in physical fights?"
  - "Can you remember a time when you caused your child psychological or emotional types of abuse like (choices include screaming mean things at him/her, hurting his/her feelings,

telling him/her you wished he/she was dead or making up mean jokes about him/her?"

- *Sexual Abuse:* This section covers the child's and the parent's childhood experiences of sexual abuse. Sample items include
  - "Has your child ever suggested that someone has inappropriately touched his/her private parts?"
  - "Has your child ever acted in ways which concerned you about this?" (choices include excessive masturbation, flirtations, actually engaging in sexual play)
  - "When you were a child, did any adult or older child have sexual contact with you?"

Administration and Scoring

This scale is administered to parents, although questions can be altered to be administered to adolescents about their own experiences and is intended to be used in conjunction with other sources of information. Interviewers should have mental health or family services training, as well as experience working with maltreating parents and their families. The interview takes about 45 minutes to administer and can be administered at a clinic or home. Questions are posed in different ways to elicit the maximum amount of information, and concrete examples are provided for parents to endorse or reject. Parents should be queried about when and how often the incidents occurred. It is not necessary to read every item verbatim, and items should be rephrased to be consistent with the educational level, intellectual functioning, cultural interpretation, and so forth, of the respondent. Items can be skipped and returned to later if the "flow" of the interview prompts a certain discussion. In addition, the interviewer follows leads provided in the interview to explore more serious forms of abuse.

Because this is essentially a clinical survey, there is no requirement that it be formally scored, although summary scores (based on the CANIS) are possible for research purposes. These include items reflecting maltreating practices that are scored separately for severity and frequency and rated for within the past year and over one year from the interview date. They are rated on a 4-point continuum for both frequency (0 = never and 4 = often) and severity (0 = no physical consequences and 4 = severe). The severity continuum reflects injury, potential for injury, and level of intrusiveness. A total score is then derived for each type of maltreatment for severity and frequency.

Psychometric Evaluation

Norms
None reported.

Reliability
On the CANIS–R, preliminary results showed an interrater agreement that exceeded 85% on all items, summary ratings on physical abuse, neglect, and sexual abuse showing a mean agreement of 84.7% between raters (N = 138), and a Kappa coefficient of .68.

Validity
Construct validity has been established in that a sample of mothers who were divided into groups (according to the CANIS) reflecting severity of physical disciplinary activities differed on a variety of measures of psychosocial functioning, including anger reactivity, social isolation, and depression. Also, reports of physical disciplinary practices on this assessment were not significantly correlated with the Lie Scale of the Child Abuse Potential Inventory (Milner, 1986; r = .09), suggesting that respondents were not systematically biased or withholding in their reporting of information.

Note that additional psychometric evaluation of the CANIS–R is being determined in ongoing research by Ammerman and colleagues.

Advantages
The CANIS–R is unique in that it combines assessment of disciplinary–abusive practices of a parent toward a child or children with assessment of the parent's own background of witnessing–experiencing family violence as well as the parent's past and current experiences of couple violence.

Limitations
In its effort to cover a wide variety of topic areas without being exceedingly long, certain areas receive somewhat superficial assessment (e.g., partner violence).

Primary Reference
Ammerman, Van Hasselt, and Hersen (1993).

Scale Availability

Robert T. Ammerman
Children's Hospital Medical Center
Division of Psychology
3333 Burnet Ave.
Cincinatti, OH 45229-3039
(513) 636-8209

Related References

Ammerman, Hersen, and Van Hasselt, (1988); Ammerman, Hersen, Van Hasselt, Lubetsky, and Sieck (1994).

General Comments and Recommendations for Practitioners and Researchers

The CANIS–R provides exploration of family violence across generations and covers a variety of topic areas in a semistructured interview format. The primary reference contains a succinct description of the interview and clear, easy-to-follow guidelines for flexible administration.

---

5. Childhood Experience of Care and Abuse (CECA; Bifulco, Brown, & Harris)

Development and Description of Assessment Method

The CECA was designed in part to examine childhood origins of depression. As such, two community samples of London women were selected for potentially high rates of depression—one based on childhood experience of parental loss and the other based on disadvantages stemming from inner-city residence and working-class status. A variety of measures was used to explore the consequences of loss of a parent with the first group, including family arrangements, relationship quality with parents, quality of care in childhood, and discord in the home. Only those that related to subsequent adult depression were used in the next phase. In the second survey, parental loss, resulting parental arrangements, and discord in the home, two quality-of-care measures (parental indifference and parental control), and a quality of relationship measure (antipathy) were covered. Measures of physical and sexual abuse were added in the third phase in the follow-ups with the second group.

The authors included a number of techniques likely to increase recall, based on research, in developing the interview. These included encouraging the respondent to recreate the context in which the events occurred, allowing continued attention to the topic with few distractions or interruptions, and allowing more retrieval attempts.

This is a semistructured, retrospective, investigator-based interview with questions concerning quality of care, relationship with parents (or parent substitutes), and physical and sexual abuse in the household up to age 16.

Target Population

Adults abused as children.

Format

This semistructured interview contains six core scales focusing on objective material (behavior that was observed or experienced) rather than subjective material (feelings) from when the respondent was a child. Bifulco, Brown, Lillie, and Jarvis (1997) revised the scale, increasing the capacity to trigger memory of relevant material and to discriminate between actual experiences and respondent's responses to those experiences. The core scales are

- *Parental Indifference:* This deals with the amount of neglect or disinterest in the child's welfare; questions regard material and emotional neglect.
- *Parental Control:* This reflects the level of supervision of the child and parental enforcement of rules and discipline (rated on a 3-point scale: 1 = high control; 2 = moderate control; 3 = lax control). Questions cover the extent the child played out of the house alone for lengthy periods of time, was left alone at night, and the presence and enforcement of rules about homework, manners, and curfew.
- *Antipathy:* This concerns the degree of dislike, criticism, hostility, or coldness shown by the parent. Questions include determination of scapegoating, rejection, and favoritism of siblings.
- *Discord in the Family:* This concerns the amount of conflict in the home in the form of arguments.
- *Physical Abuse:* This concerns violence by a household member toward the child, simply rated as "present" or "absent." Ques-

tions include being beaten, kicked, hit with objects, and threatened with weapons.

- *Sexual Abuse:* This reflects sexual contact before age 17 other than willing contact in teenage years with nonrelated peers, covers household and nonhousehold members, simply rated as "present" or "absent." Questions involve physical contact and include sexual intercourse, oral sex and touching of breasts or genitals with details collected about severity, frequency, and relationship to the perpetrator.

Administration and Scoring

Core scales are rated on a 4-point scale, with 1 = marked, 2 = moderate, 3 = some, and 4 = little/none unless otherwise indicated. The investigator, rather than the respondent, decides whether experiences meet criteria for inclusion (for example, as abusive). Interviewers are trained to make objective ratings based on relevant behavioral information rather than feelings. Rater training takes four days. The first few interviews are monitored for consensus with the team to ensure the objectivity of ratings.

The length of administration time varies according to the complexity of childhood arrangements and number of surrogate parents, but it tends to last a minimum of one hour. Respondents are asked about each family arrangement before the age of 17, characterized by parents in the home for at least one year. Respondents are guided by an extended list of questions and are encouraged to relate their experiences as "stories," with questioning continued until a clear picture emerges. Interviewers can be flexible in the order of questions asked should topics naturally arise in an order different from that in the interview.

The investigator-based format of the CECA refers to the fact that the investigator rather than the respondent decides whether the experiences reported meet criteria for neglect or abuse with an objective threshold, regardless of the respondents' definitions of them. The goal of having the investigator define abuse is to increase accuracy while decreasing bias from reporting style or emotional responses.

Psychometric Evaluation

Norms

None reported.

Reliability

Interrater reliabilities of scales were calculated on 20 interviews that were rated by an independent rater blind to the psychiatric status of the respondent. Reliabilities were satisfactory to excellent, with weighted Kappas as follows: responsibilities for running the home: .85, presence of step-siblings: .79, parental indifference: .78, parental control: .63, antipathy from other: .83, discord in the home: .96, sexual abuse: 1.00, relationship to perpetrator: .98, and presence of physical abuse: .82.

Validity

The validity of the CECA was determined by a high level of agreement between 20 sister pairs' independent accounts, indicating criterion validity. Weighted Kappas and Pearson correlations are listed in Table 4.1.

Advantages

The CECA collects detailed, descriptive accounts and objective material, addresses a wide range of childhood experiences (not limited to abusive ones), and allows for specific childhood experiences to be explored in relation to correlates and sequelae. It is the only childhood measure that documents the sequence of childhood experiences, leading to the possible development of effective causal models, and it is one of very few retrospective measures that use an interview rather than a paper-and-pencil self-report format.

Limitations

The CECA requires a lengthy administration time, interviewers need extensive training, and rating of information requires frequent consensus meetings to ensure against potential biases.

Table 4.1

Weighted Kappas and Pearson Correlations

	Kw	Pearson r
Discord/tension in the home	.75	.90
Parental control	.78	.82
Parental indifference	.77	.85
Antipathy from surrogate mother	.72	.79
Punitiveness of surrogate mother	.69	.73
Punitiveness of father/surrogate father	.67	.58
Physical abuse	yet to be examined	
Sexual abuse	yet to be examined	

Primary Reference

Bifulco, Brown, and Harris (1994).

Scale Availability

Antonia Bifulco
Department of Social Policy and Social Science
Royal Holloway College (University of London)
11 Bedford Sq.
London, UK WC1B 3RA

Related References

Bifulco et al. (1997).

General Comments and Recommendations for Practitioners and Researchers

The CECA is an excellent clinical screening device or research tool, with sufficient psychometric properties. It offers a useful blend of standardization and flexibility of format and provides a rich portrait of early family environment. Its assessment of objective behaviors and interviewer-based determination of abuse status reduce the potential for biased or overly subjective reporting. Note that all of the childhood factors addressing quality of care, discord, relationship with parents, and physical or sexual abuse were shown to relate to adult depression.

---

6. Childhood Maltreatment Interview Schedule (CMIS; Briere)

Development and Description of Assessment Method

The CMIS is a retrospective interview schedule assessing family environment and experiences of maltreatment, used for either clinical assessment or research on child abuse.

Target Population

Adults abused as children.

Format

This is a 46-item interview, with some items containing subquestions assessing a given abuse or neglect experience in greater detail. Respondents are asked about historical information occurring before the age of 17. There are nine separate categories divided by areas of maltreatment, with each area having specific questions that probe the age of onset, the relationship to the abuser, and the severity of the maltreatment.

The interview is organized according to the following nine sections with sample questions:

- *Parental Physical Availability* (8 items): This includes the number and time periods children spent with parents, step-parents, and foster-parents, as well as instances of institutional care. An examples is
  - "Did your natural (biological) mother live with you until you were at least 16?"
- *Parental Disorder* (5 items): This includes a history of inpatient or outpatient psychological treatment, alcoholism or drug abuse, and family violence. An example is
  - "Before age 17, did any parent, step-parent or foster-parent ever have problems with drugs or alcohol that led to medical problems, divorce or separation, being fired from work, or being arrested for intoxication in public or while driving?"
- *Parental Psychological Availability:* This includes an experience of love and caring by parents (4 items). An example is
  - "On average, from age 8 through age 16, how much did you feel that your father/step-father/foster-father loved and cared about you?" (on a scale of 1 = "not at all" to 4 = "very much").
- *Psychological Abuse:* This includes aspects of verbal arguments and punishment (7 items with frequency counts): An example is
  - "When you were 16 or younger how often did the following (insult you, try to make you feel guilty, embarrass you in front of others) happen to you in the average year? Answer for your parents or step-parents or foster-parents or other adult in charge of you as a child" (on a scale of 0 = never to 6 = over 20 times a year).
- *Physical Abuse:* This includes aspects of physical abuse and medical emergency (2 items with detailed additional subquestions): An example is

- "Before age 17 did a parent, step-parent, foster-parent or other adult in charge of you as a child ever do something on purpose to you (for example, hit or punch or cut you, or push you down) that gave you bruises or scratches, broke bones or teeth or made you bleed?"
- *Emotional Abuse:* This includes verbal threats and physical isolation (7 yes/no items plus subquestions on perpetrator and frequency): An example is
  - "Before age 17 did your parent threaten to hurt or kill your pet?"
- *Sexual Abuse:* This includes all aspects of sexual behavior initiated by another (3 items with detailed additional subquestions). An example is
  - "About how many times were you touched in a sexual way or made to touch someone else's sexual parts by someone 5 or more years older before age 17?"
- *Ritualistic Abuse:* This includes aspects of abuse as part of a ritual or cult gathering (1 item with several subquestions). An example is
  - "Were there ever times when you were 16 or younger when you were tortured, repeatedly hurt, or forced to do something sexual during some sort of meeting, ritual, cult gathering or religious activity?"
- *Perceptions of Abuse Status:* This includes the respondents' perceptions of their abuse history (2 yes/no items and 1 Likert-rated item): An example is
  - "Overall, how would you rate your childhood?" (rated from 1 = "very happy" to 7 = "very unhappy").

There is also a short form including 12 sections with 46 yes–no items, a 4-point Likert-type scale, and a 6-point Likert-type scale for frequency counts. However, it is less detailed and should be used for research purposes only. (Noted on CMIS appendix.)

Administration and Scoring

The CMIS is administered in a structured interview format. Questions may be paraphrased as needed, and there is space to write in additional information. Scoring varies by question and subsection. The interview takes approximately 45 to 60 minutes, but may take less or more time, depending on the amount of experiences affirmatively endorsed (leading to more probing subquestions).

Psychometric Evaluation

Norms
None reported.

Reliability
The psychological abuse subscale has demonstrated moderate internal consistency (alphas ranging from .75 to .87).

Validity
The psychological abuse subscale has been shown to predict various symptom scales.

Advantages
Extremely comprehensive interview covering all types of maltreatment experiences. A shorter form is under development and may soon be available.

Limitations
This has not yet been compared to other methods of assessment, so it is difficult to evaluate validity of the CMIS. Reliability and validity of subscales need to be determined as well.

Primary Reference

None available.

Scale Availability

> J. Briere
> Department of Psychiatry
> LAC-USC Medical Center
> 1934 Hospital Pl.
> Los Angeles, CA 90033

Related References

Briere (1992).

General Comments and Recommendations for Practitioners and Researchers

The CMIS is a concise, clear, easy-to-administer interview, practical for use in clinical and research settings. More psychometric evaluation is needed to enhance the scale's utility.

7. Childhood Post-Traumatic Stress Reaction Index (CPTS–RI; Frederick, Pynoos, & Nader)

Development and Description of Assessment Method

The CPTS–RI is a semistructured interview used with children or adolescents to obtain information on reactions to a traumatic experience.

Target Population

Children or adolescents exposed to a traumatic event, who are generally 8 years old and older. With younger children, rewording of questions is suggested. Parents may also be assessed using the associated parent measures (see general comments section).

Format

The CPTS–RI consists of interview sections that include basic information about the child and his or her family, experiences before the traumatic event, previous traumatic events, description of the current or most recent traumatic event, first few days after the traumatic event, and the child's ongoing response to the event, especially in the past month, and associated symptoms.

Questions regarding response to the traumatic event include some of the *DSM-IV* (American Psychiatric Association, 1994) diagnostic criteria for posttraumatic stress disorder (PTSD), including,

- *Criterion B:* Reexperiencing (intrusive distressing recollections, bad dreams, anticipation of recurrence).
- *Criterion C:* Numbing and avoidance.
- *Criterion D:* Increased arousal (jumpiness, sleep disturbance, difficulty concentrating).

The interview has 20 items.

Administration and Scoring

Most items are rated on 5-point Likert scale from "none" to "most of the time." Items are summed to determine the degree of disorder, ranging from doubtful to very severe. The interview takes between 20 and 45 minutes to administer, and is accompanied by a training manual (Nader, 1993). A score of greater than 60 is indicative of very severe PTSD, scores of 40 to 59 indicate severe PTSD, and scores of 25 to 39 indicate moderate PTSD.

Psychometric Evaluation

Scores below 12 indicate doubtful PTSD, 12 to 24 indicate a mild PTSD reaction.

Norms
None reported.

Reliability
Interrater reliability has been measured at .94, and internal consistency (using Cronbach's alpha) was established at .78.

Validity
Severity ratings on the CPTS–RI have corresponded with independent referrals for treatment and diagnosis of PTSD, supporting the scale's criterion-related validity.

Advantages
The interview is comprehensive and is accompanied by a useful training manual. Also, the questions from the adult and child's version correspond to one another so that similarity between parent–child views can be determined.

Limitations
Not all *DSM-IV* symptoms are assessed by the interview, making it a less viable tool for diagnosis.

Primary Reference

Frederick, Pynoos, and Nader (1992).

Scale Availability

Kathleen O. Nader
P.O. Box 2251
Laguna Hills, CA 92654
fax (714) 454-0628
e-mail: knader@twosuns.org

Related References

Dubner and Motta (1999); Nader (1997).

General Comments and Recommendations for Practitioners and Researchers

A translated version has been used with children ages 11 and older in Kuwait, and a war-exposure questionnaire is available in Arabic. Two parent questionnaires have been developed for use in conjunction with the CPTS–RI, one an interview eliciting premorbid personality and trauma-related information concerning their children and the other corresponding directly to questions on the CPTS–RI.

---

8. Childhood PTSD Interview–Parent Form (CPTSDI; Fletcher)

Development and Description of Assessment Method

The Childhood PTSD Interview–Parent Form (CPTSDI) was developed to directly parallel the diagnostic criteria found in the *DSM-IV* (American Psychiatric Association, 1994). Initial psychometric work was conducted with a very small population of 10 clinic-referred and 20 non-clinic parents.

The CPTSDI was developed as a structured interview to assess parents' perspectives on each criterion required for the diagnosis of PTSD in their children.

Target Population

Parents of children who have experienced a traumatic event.

Format

The CPTSDI is an interview in which parents are instructed first to describe the traumatic event that happened to the child. This is followed by a series of yes–no questions about the child's perceptions of the event, the child's reexperiencing of the event, and the child's avoidance of stimuli associated with the event. There are several probe questions for each of the diagnostic criteria found in the *DSM-IV* diagnosis. Sample probe questions include,

- "Does your child think about _____ when s/he doesn't want to?"
- "Does your child talk a lot about what happened?"

Additional questions probe the associated symptoms of anxiety, depression, guilt, denial, and dissociation.

Administration and Scoring

Each item is scored for either the presence or absence of the symptom. In addition, each item is scored on a Likert-type scale for frequency, intensity, or duration (usually 0 to 5). The measure yields a score indicating the presence or absence of PTSD. In addition, a total PTSD severity score can be calculated, and associated symptoms can be assessed.

Psychometric Evaluation

Norms
None reported.

Reliability
Internal consistency was evaluated by the Kuder-Richardson-20 Formula. The full scale reliability was .94, criterion A was .60, criterion B was .86, criterion C was .86, and criterion D was .83.

Validity
The CPTSDI was significantly correlated with three other measures of PTSD developed by the same author (a parent paper-and-pencil measure, a child paper-and-pencil measure, and a child interview—the Childhood PTSD Interview–Child Form; Fletcher, 1996), as well as with a PTSD subscale derived from the Child Behavior Checklist (CBCL; Achenbach, 1991). The interview was also significantly correlated with parents' reports of the number of lifetime stressors experienced by their

children, parents' ratings of their children's reactions to these life stressors, and interviewer judgments of the severity of the traumatizing events children reported.

Fletcher (1996) reported significant correlations between the interview and all subscales of the CBCL (Achenbach, 1991) and cites this as evidence for both convergent and discriminant validity. Relationships with subscales theoretically related to experiences of maltreatment (e.g., anxiety, somatic complaints, social problems) support the interview's convergent validity, whereas the fact that correlations between the interview and the CBCL subscales are lower than those between the interview and other direct PTSD measures support its discriminant validity.

Advantages

The interview parallels the child format so that correspondence between parent and child report can be examined (correlated $r = .69$, $p \leq .001$ with the child interview). Both dichotomous (presence or absence of PTSD) and continuous (severity) scores are provided.

Limitations

The interview focuses primarily on diagnosis rather than a clinical assessment of the parents' view of their child's functioning. There is somewhat limited psychometric evaluation thus far, relying primarily on non-validated measures developed by the author rather than standardized, preexisting measures of PTSD. In addition, the scale was evaluated on a very small sample.

Primary Reference

Fletcher (1996).

Scale Availability

Kenneth E. Fletcher
University of Massachusetts Medical Center
Psychiatry Department
55 Lake Ave. North
Worcester, MA 01655
(508) 856-3329

Related References

Stamm (1996).

General Comments and Recommendations for Practitioners and Researchers

According to the author, the scale continues to undergo revisions as well as psychometric evaluation. The interview provides a useful method for assessing PTSD diagnosis and severity from the vantage point of a parent.

---

9. Childhood PTSD Interview—Child Form (CPI—Child; Fletcher)

Development and Description of Assessment Method

This is a semistructured child interview with a built-in rating scale designed to help the rater assess the *DSM-III-R/DSM-IV* (American Psychiatric Association, 1987, 1994) criteria for a PTSD diagnosis, calculate a total PTSD severity score, and assess additional associated symptoms.

In the initial study, a sample of 30 children, 10 in clinical settings and 20 in the community (10 who were traumatized in the community and 10 who were nontraumatized in the community), ages 7 to 14 (mean age 10.3) was used. The clinical group was asked how they responded to an event or events identified by the therapist as traumatic. The community children were asked how they responded to the worst event that happened to them in the past five years.

Target Population

Children between the ages of 7 to 14 years who have been exposed to trauma.

Format

This assessment is an interview in which the front page of the interview protocol provides space for the child's description of the traumatic event(s). Ninety-three questions follow. Each specific symptom for each criterion is clearly stated. Below each specific symptom question is a series of two or more questions that assess and probe for that specific symptom and help the interviewer determine whether or not criterion are met. The specific criterion question corresponds to the parent interview question. There are also cues to the rater on how to assess each question as it relates to the symptom of interest. The completed criterion section is followed by a section on associated symptoms. Sample questions include, for criterion A,

- "Did the child perceive (the event) as markedly distressing?" (asked of parent)
- "Did you ever think you might get really hurt while (the event) was happening?" (asked of child)

And for criterion B,

- Was the stressful of traumatic event "persistently reexperienced by the child in at least one of the following ways?" (asked of parent)
- "Does the child have recurrent and intrusive recollections of (the event)?" (asked of parent)
- "Do you sometimes think about (the event) when you don't want to?" (asked of child)
- "Does the child report recurrent distressing dreams of (the event)?" (asked of parent)
- "Do you ever have bad dreams or nightmares about (the event)?" (asked of child)

And for criterion C,

- "Does the child persistently avoid stimuli associated with the stressful or traumatic events, or show evidence of numbing or general responsiveness (not present before the trauma) as indicated by at least three of the following?" (asked of parent)
- "Does the child try to avoid thoughts or feelings associated with (the event)?" (asked of parent)
- "Do you ever try to just forget all about (the event)?" (asked of child)
- "Does the child display or feel detachment or estrangement from others?" (asked of parent)
- "Do you have anyone to talk to when things bother you?" (asked of child)

And for criterion D,

- "Does the child show persistent symptoms of increased arousal (not present before the stressful or traumatic event as indicated by at least two of the following?" (asked of parent)
- "Is the child easily irritated or have outbursts of anger since (the event)?" (asked of parent)

- "Do you lose your temper more now than you used to before (the event) happened?" (asked of child)
- "Does child have difficulty concentrating?" (asked of parent)
- "Is it easy for you to pay attention to things that you have to do at home or at school?" (asked of child)

Eleven categories of associated symptoms corresponding to the *DSM-IV* (American Psychiatric Association, 1994) diagnosis are also assessed. Examples include,

- *Anxiety:* "Do you worry much since (the event) happened?"
- *Omens:* "Since (the event) happened, did you start to think you could tell the future?"
- *Survivor Guilt:* "Do you ever feel bad that others were hurt more than you because of (the event)?"
- *Self-Blame:* "Do you ever feel like what happened is your fault?"

Administration and Scoring

The interviews are designed to be conducted by professionals or paraprofessionals. Interviews are self-scoring. Each question is answered "yes," "no," or "don't know." Yes is scored as 1 and no and don't know are scored as 0.

In addition to the categorical scoring, it is possible to derive a continuous measure of the severity of the child's responses simply by summing all answers that are indicative of PTSD responses. Also, four questions are specifically asked of the rater for an in vivo assessment of the child's response to the interview: "How willing was the child to describe the event?" "Is there reason to believe the child described events that did not happen?" "Is there any reason to believe the child misperceived or described details incorrectly?" "How does the child's description compare to the parent–guardian's description of the event?"

Psychometric Evaluation

Norms
None reported.

Reliability
Internal consistency was measured using the Kuder-Richardson-20 formula and was found to be .91 (full scale), .52 (criterion A), .80 (crite-

rion B), .76 (criterion C), and .78 (criterion D). Criteria A is somewhat lower because it is designed to include extreme questions that would be expected to lower the interitem correlations and thus the measures of internal consistency. Thus, adequate to excellent internal consistency was demonstrated for total PTSD severity scores and for the *DSM-IV* criteria. In a study of 150 foster care children (Dubner & Motta, 1999), 89% agreement was obtained between scorers diagnosing PTSD on the CPI-Child.

Validity

The interview significantly differentiated the clinical group and non-traumatized community group and differentiated the traumatized community group from the nontraumatized community group.

The child interview also diagnosed more children exposed to higher levels of traumatization with PTSD than children exposed to lower levels of traumatization. These results were significant when the child interview was used for diagnostic purposes.

This interview is significantly correlated with the parent interview and child and parent paper-and-pencil tests (also developed by Fletcher) and is significantly correlated with the CBCL PTSD scale, evidencing convergent validity. The scale is also correlated with theoretically related scales on the CBCL.

The interview was also significantly associated with parental reports of the number of lifetime stressors their children were exposed to as well as their children's reactions to these stressors, evidencing convergent validity. However, it was not significantly associated with children's reports of the number of lifetime stressors they have been exposed to.

All of the correlations between the CPI–Child reports and CBCL subscales were lower than the correlations of interview reports with related PTSD measures developed by the same author and a PTSD subscale of the CBCL, providing evidence of discriminant validity.

Advantages

This interview offers a thorough overview and assessment of PTSD diagnostic criteria and most of the associated symptoms suggested by the literature and was written specifically to be understood by children and adolescents.

Limitations

This is a long interview to administer for the sole purpose of supporting a PTSD diagnosis. The series of questions that are alternatively posed to the parent (or adult familiar with the child) and then to the child makes the interview protocol somewhat confusing.

Primary Reference

Dubner and Motta (1999); Fletcher (1996).

Scale Availability

Kenneth Fletcher
University of Massachusetts Medical Center
Psychiatry Department
55 Lake Ave. North
Worcester, MA 01655
(508) 856-3329
e-mail: Kenneth.Fletcher@banyan.ummed.edu

Related References

Stamm (1996).

General Comments and Recommendations for Practitioners and Researchers

This interview offers a highly comprehensive assessment of PTSD and related symptoms. More psychometric development is needed, using a larger sample and standardized measures of PTSD.

10. Childhood Trauma Interview (CTI; Bernstein et al.)

Development and Description of Assessment Method

The CTI is a brief, retrospective structured interview designed to assess several areas of childhood trauma. The structured interview format was developed in an initial study of 66 individuals.

Target Population

Adults exposed to trauma in childhood.

Format

The CTI uses initial queries and follow-up probes to gather data on the nature, severity, frequency, duration, number, and type of perpetrators and age at the time of victimization. Areas of childhood trauma covered include physical, sexual, and emotional abuse; physical neglect; separation; and witnessing family violence.

Administration and Scoring

This interview takes 10 to 20 minutes to administer. Each traumatic experience is rated on a 7-point scale of frequency and severity. An accompanying manual provides objective scoring criteria and examples.

Psychometric Evaluation

Norms

None reported.

Reliability

Preliminary psychometric evaluation indicated high levels of interrater reliability for ratings of severity and frequency of physical and sexual abuse, with intraclass correlations ranging from .92 to .99.

Validity

The preliminary study indicated convergent validity with measures of PTSD, personality disorders, and the Childhood Trauma Questionnaire (CTQ; Bernstein et al., 1994). Specifically, 70 ratings of physical abuse on the interview were correlated at $r = .38$ ($p < .01$), with the physical and emotional abuse subscale of the CTQ and the severity ratings of sexual abuse were correlated at $r = .32$ ($p < .01$) and $r = .65$ ($p < .01$) for the physical and sexual abuse subscales of the CTQ, respectively.

Advantages

This is a brief yet reasonably thorough assessment strategy. An accompanying manual assists with and standardizes the relatively straightforward scoring procedure.

Limitations

The interview has been not been subject to sufficient psychometric evaluation. Existing psychometric evaluation has been mostly limited to the physical and sexual abuse sections of the interview.

Primary Reference

Bernstein et al. (1994).

Scale Availability

> David P. Bernstein
> Psychiatry Service
> VA Medical Center
> 130 West Kingsbridge Rd.
> Bronx, NY 10468

Related References

Fink et al. (1993).

General Comments and Recommendations for Practitioners and Researchers

The CTI is an especially useful clinical screening tool because of its brief administration time and ease of scoring. However, we would caution against its use as a research tool or as a sole clinical measure of abuse until further validation of the interview is reported.

---

11. Children's Attributions and Perceptions Scale (CAPS; Originally Semi-Structured Inventory for Children; Mannarino, Cohen, & Berman)

Development and Description of Assessment Method

The CAPS is an assessment of sexual abuse–related factors designed to evaluate how sexually abused children cognitively process their victimization experiences. Administered in an interview format, the interviewer records the responses of children on the inventory.

In the clinical experience of the authors and others, sexually abused children may develop unique attributions and perceptions related to their victimization experiences that are not addressed by existing symptom-oriented measures. The CAPS was designed to assess attributions and perceptions relevant to sexually abused children that are not measured by existing instruments. The scale was developed based on the authors' experience with evaluating and treating sexually abused children. Two of CAPS subscales (feeling different from peers and reduced interpersonal trust) correspond to two factors (stigmatization and betrayal) in Finkelhor's (1984) four-factor traumagenic dynamics model of child sexual abuse.

Target Population

Children who were sexually abused between the ages of 7 and 12 years old.

Format

The CAPS has 18 items across four subscales that address issues without reference to sexual abuse. The following are subscales and sample items:

- *Feeling Different From Peers* (4 items):
  - "Do you feel different from other girls your age?"
  - "Do you act different from other girls your age?"
- *Personal Attributions For Negative Events* (4 items):
  - "Do you feel that you make bad things happen to other people?"
  - "Do you blame yourself when things go wrong?"
- *Limited Perceived Credibility* (5 items):
  - "Do people ever doubt what you are telling them?"
  - "Do people ever accuse you of lying?"
- *Low Interpersonal Trust* (5 items):
  - "Do you ever feel that you can't count on anyone?"
  - "Do you ever feel that trusting people can be risky?"

Administration and Scoring

The CAPS is administered in an interview format. Children are told, "These are questions about some things that you may have felt in the last 6 months. There are no right or wrong answers." Items are rated on a 5-point Likert scale ranging from 1 = "never" to 5 = "always." Higher scores on each subscale reflect a greater sense of feeling different from peers, heightened self-blame for negative events, lower perceived credibility, and reduced interpersonal trust.

Psychometric Evaluation

Norms

The CAPS was normed on 50 sexually abused girls between the ages of 7 to 12 years and on a sample consisting of 40 sexually abused and 40 nonabused 7- to 12-year-old girls, with a mean age of 9.67 years. Norms are reported in the primary reference.

Reliability

Two-week test–retest reliability was $r = .82$ for feeling different from peers, $r = .60$ for personal attributions for negative events, $r = .70$ for limited perceived credibility, $r = .62$ for low interpersonal trust, and $r = .75$ for the total scale. Correlations for internal consistency were calculated to range from .64 for the interpersonal trust subscale to .73 for the perceived credibility subscale.

Validity

A sexually abused group scored significantly higher than a group of normal controls on the total CAPS and three of the four subscales, supporting known groups validity. The perceived credibility scale had a nonsignificant trend in the same direction.

Higher scorers on the CAPS reported significantly more depressive symptoms, trait anxiety, and self-esteem problems than lower scorers, supporting convergent validity. Also, for the two groups combined, the total CAPS, feeling different from peers subscale, and the interpersonal trust subscale were significantly correlated with the Child Sexual Behavior Inventory (CSBI; Friedrich et al., 1992) and all Child Behavior Checklist (Achenbach, 1991) factors. However, these findings were no longer apparent when each group was analyzed individually.

Advantages

Because of both interview format and the omission of references to actual sexual abuse, this assessment method may ease the anxiety of the experience for vulnerable children.

Limitations

The authors note that their scale development sample may be biased because of socioeconomic differentials and because there may have been some sexually abused girls in the control group because parents were not specifically asked about abuse. Also, because the items on the CAPS do not make reference to sexual abuse, this measure is not a specific measure of this construct.

Primary Reference

Mannarino, Cohen, and Berman (1994).

Scale Availability

The scale is available in primary reference or from
Anthony P. Mannarino
Medical College of Pennsylvania
Allegheny General Hospital
320 East North Ave.
Pittsburgh, PA 15212

Related References

Achenbach (1991).

General Comments and Recommendations for Practitioners and Researchers

The CAPS is not a diagnostic measure of the existence of sexual abuse and should not be used for that purpose. Note that although the CAPS was developed for sexually abused children, similar reactions are often found in physically abused children as well.

---

12. Children's Perception Questionnaire (CPQ; Miller-Perrin & Wurtele)

Development and Description of Assessment Method

The CPQ is an interview designed to assess children's perceptions of a victim, a perpetrator, and situational characteristics relating to a hypothetical abusive vignette.

A projective vignette describing a personal body-safety violation was read to 51 nonclinical population children, ages 4 to 12, grouped into three developmentally distinct age levels to assess for differences in the developmental characteristics of children's conceptions about personal body safety.

Target Population

Children between the ages of 4 and 12 years old.

Format

This assessment involves the reading (by an interviewer) of a vignette depicting a hypothetical personal body-safety situation using androgynous names to control for attributions based on gender. The interviewer then asks a standard list of questions to probe understanding of the incident. The questions pertain to the age and gender of the perpetrator and victim, how they knew each other, whether the victim should and would tell someone, whether the touch was inappropriate, and whether the perpetrator would try to offend the victim again. There are a total of 32 questions and 4 aspects–subscales: general conceptions about personal body safety (5 items), characteristics of violators (11 items), characteristics of victims (6 items), and consequences of safety violation for victim and perpetrator (10 items). The following introduction is given:

> I want to tell you about two people who have different names. The first person's name is Sinter, and the second person's name is Lockie. One day when Sinter and Lockie were alone, Sinter looked at and touched Lockie's private parts. Lockie went along with Sinter.

Following the vignette, the experimenter reads introductory comments and questions that probe for the first subscale, general conceptions about personal body safety: "Could something like this ever happen in real life?" Categories of response include yes, no, unsure: "Where would something like this happen?" Categories of response include unsure, vague, indoors, outdoors.

The experimenter next probes for characteristics of the violator and then characteristics of the victim: Sample questions include

- "How old is Sinter?" (Categories of response include ages 3–8, 9–12, teen/adult)
- "Is Sinter a boy/man or a girl/woman?"
- "What kind of person is Sinter?" (Categories of response include unsure/physical description, global terms, mental deviant)
- "Is there anything wrong with Lockie?" (Categories of response include unsure, yes, no)

Questions regarding consequences of safety violation for the victim and perpetrator are included in the previous sections. Sample questions include,

- "What should happen to Sinter?" (Categories of response include unsure/neutral, punishment, instruction/rehabilitation)
- "Can Sinter be helped?" (Categories of response include unsure, no, yes)

- "Will Lockie tell anyone about what happened?" (Categories of response include unsure, no, yes)

Administration and Scoring

Children's responses to each vignette question are coded based on categories established on review of subject responses. A copy of the scoring format is available from Miller-Perrin.

Psychometric Evaluation

Norms

The primary reference reports the percentage of respondents selecting each response category for three different age levels across all 32 questions.

Reliability

Children's responses to the vignette questions were independently coded by two raters with an interrater agreement of 95% over all items (Miller-Perrin & Wurtele, 1989).

In addition, using the CPQ in a pretest–posttest design, they obtained reliability by comparing alternative-treatment control of children's responses from time 1 and time 2 and found that responses did not change significantly on any CPQ items (Sarno & Wurtele, 1997).

Validity

The CPQ is able to discriminate between abused and nonabused children as well as between children from developmentally distinct age groups, evidencing concurrent validity.

Advantages

The projective format of the vignette allows for children to reveal their perceptions and attributions about abusive situations, as well as to possibly reveal painful or hidden secrets in a controlled setting. The story-like format might be particularly effective in engaging and eliciting responses from young children.

Limitations

The CPQ is lengthy to administer with young children, and young children may have difficulty verbalizing responses to many of the questions. The use of a standardized list of questions in which the interviewer merely asks children to describe the characteristics of the vignette situations without probing for how they arrived at their answers may limit findings.

Primary Reference

Miller-Perrin and Wurtele (1989).

Scale Availability

> Sandy K. Wurtele
> Department of Psychology
> 1420 Austin Bluffs Parkway
> P.O. Box 7150
> University of Colorado
> Colorado Springs, CO 80933-7150

Related References

Sarno and Wurtele (1997).

General Comments and Recommendations for Practitioners and Researchers

This projective yet guided interview assessment may be used with victimized children or as an outcome assessment in a sexual abuse prevention program. The interview assesses knowledge of body safety as well as cognitions concerning perpetrators, victims, and sexually abusive situations.

---

13. Clinician Administered PTSD Scale for Children and Adolescents for the *DSM-IV* (CAPS–CA; Nader et al.)

Development and Description of Assessment Method

Items written for the CAPS–CA were derived from *DSM-IV* (American Psychiatric Association, 1994) diagnostic criteria for PTSD, as well as additional childhood PTSD symptoms found in the literature, including those for complicated and ongoing traumas.

The CAPS–CA is a structured clinical interview designed to measure 17 signs and symptoms of PTSD plus associated features in children and adolescents. Specifically, the interview evaluates the frequency and intensity dimensions of individual symptoms, impact of the symptoms on the child's social and scholastic functioning, overall severity of the symptoms, child's global improvement since baseline (for repeated evaluation), and validity of the ratings obtained.

Target Population

Any child or adolescent suffering from PTSD or exposed to trauma. This assessment is best for children over the age of 6.

Format

This is a structured interview containing six components.

- I. *Stressor Worksheet:* This assesses for criterion A of *DSM*-based diagnosis of PTSD. Children are asked about exposure to things that are "very upsetting or scary or frightening." Based on the description of events, the interviewer determines in a yes–no format whether the child satisfies the minimum requirement for exposure to a traumatic event.
  - "What happened to you?"
  - "Were you afraid or scared?"
  - "Did you feel like you didn't know what to do?"
- II. *Lifetime Diagnosis Instructions:* This assesses for symptoms before the past month.
  - "Before the last month, has there been any time since (the traumatic event) that you were more troubled than at other times since (the event)?" If yes, ask about symptoms and their severity.
- III. *Ratings for PTSD Symptoms:* This assesses for criteria B, C, and D of *DSM*-based diagnosis of PTSD.
  - Criterion B: (5 questions): Recurrent and intrusive recollections of events or traumatic play, recurrent distressing dreams of the event, acting or feeling as if the traumatic event were reoccurring (traumatic reenactment), extensive psychological distress at exposure to internal or external cues that symbolize or resemble traumatic events, and physiological reactivity.
  - "Did you think about (EVENT) even when you didn't want to? Did you see pictures in your head (mind) or hear the sounds in your head (mind) from (EVENT)? What were they like?"
  - Criterion C: (7 questions): Efforts to avoid thoughts, feelings or conversations associated with the trauma, efforts to avoid

activities, places or people that arouse recollections of the trauma, inability to recall an important aspect of the trauma or regressive behaviors, markedly diminished interest or participation in activities, feelings of detachment or estrangement from others, restricted range of affect, and sense of foreshortened future.

- "Do you do things to keep yourself from thinking about what happened or to stop the feelings about what happened?"
- "Do you feel alone even when other people are around?"
- Criterion D: (5 questions): Difficulty falling or staying asleep, irritability or outbursts of anger, difficulty concentrating, hypervigilance, and exaggerated startle response.
- "Have you been getting angry more quickly than you used to?"
- "In the past month, how hard was it for you to pay attention?"
- IV. *CAPS–CA Global Ratings* (5 questions): Impact on social functioning and impact on scholastic functioning and global rating of symptom change over the past six months, validity rating based on a scale of 0 (excellent) to 4 (invalid responses) and global severity based on a scale of 0 (asymptomatic) to 4 (extreme symptoms, pervasive impairment).
  - "Is it harder for you to do as well in school as you used to?"
- V. *Ratings of Associated or Hypothesized Features*—Optional (13 questions): Guilt, homicidal aggression, disillusionment with previously esteemed authority figures, feelings of hopelessness, memory impairment, sadness and depression, feelings of being overwhelmed, self-harm, revictimization, worry about another, loss, and reminder of previous life experience.
  - "Is it harder for you to keep yourself from hurting someone else?"
- VI. *Impact and Coping* (3 questions): This is aimed at transferring the child's focus from negative effects of traumatic experience to methods of coping with the event.
  - "How do you think (EVENT) has affected your life?"

Space is provided for written descriptions of signs and symptoms.

Administration and Scoring

This interview is intended for use by mental health professionals experienced with clinical interviewing and the *DSM-IV* (American Psychiatric Association, 1994). Prompts and follow-up questions are used to gather information. Items are rated based on a child's verbal response to prompts–questions, and ratings are derived only from information obtained from the interview. However, the authors recommend using the CAPS–CA in conjunction with other self-report, behavioral, or physiological measures. Frequency and intensity ratings are obtained for each symptom. Responses thought to be invalid should be noted "questionable validity."

Ratings of symptom frequency are on a 5-point continuum from 0 = none of the time to 4 = most of the time, daily. Ratings of symptom intensity and degree of impairment are also on a 5-point continuum from 0 = not at all to 4 = a whole lot. Diagnosis is based on frequency and intensity ratings of present symptoms.

Psychometric Evaluation

Psychometric testing has not yet been conducted on this instrument. However, it has been used to measure childhood trauma in a clinical setting with success for children 8 years and older.

Norms
None reported.

Reliability
None reported

Validity
None reported.

Advantages
The CAPS–CA provides a tool for obtaining a *DSM-IV*-based diagnosis of PTSD. It supplies specific information regarding particular symptoms the child is suffering with as well as changes in the child's behavior since the last examination.

Limitations
The interview form is somewhat complicated and is lengthy to administer. Younger children may have difficulty with the 5-point scales. In addition, it is not yet established with regard to psychometric properties.

Primary Reference

Nader et al. (1996).

Scale Availability

> Elana Newman
> University of Tulsa
> Department of Psychology
> Lorton Hall
> 600 South College Ave.
> Tulsa, OK 74104-3189

Or

> Danny G. Kaloupek
> National Center for PTSD (116B-2)
> Boston VAMC
> 150 South Huntington Avenue
> Boston, MA 02130

Related References

Nader (1997).

General Comments and Recommendations for Practitioners and Researchers

This is a lengthy and comprehensive interview that allows for not only making a diagnosis of childhood PTSD but also for assessing the impact of PTSD symptoms on overall functioning, intensity of symptoms, improvement since the last evaluation, and validity of ratings. With establishment of psychometric integrity, the CAPS–CA will make an excellent tool for research and for clinical settings in which highly specific assessment of PTSD symptoms is desired.

14. Parent Impact Questionnaire (PIQ; Wolfe)

Development and Description of Assessment Method

The PIQ is a structured interview developed to assess parents' or caregivers' reactions to sex abuse disclosures by children.

Target Population

Parents of children who have disclosed sexual abuse.

Format

This assessment consists of a questionnaire for parents in which distinct sections include

- Brief account of the family-related problems that the parent experienced during childhood and as an adult;
- Parent's personal history of sexual abuse as a child;
- The impact of disclosure on the parent (assessed via the Impact of Events Scale; Horowitz, Wilner, & Alvarez, 1979) and family (assessed via a catalogue of various stressful life events that may accompany disclosure, such as arrests of family members, children being taken to shelters, strain on family relationships, involvement with a number of officials and agencies).

Administration and Scoring

All response options are objectified through checklists or Likert-type ratings.

Psychometric Evaluation

Norms
None reported.

Reliability
None reported.

Validity
None reported.

Advantages
This appears to be an excellent chance to assess the impact of disclosure. It could help clinicians to understand family dynamics.

Limitations
Psychometric properties have not been reported.

Primary Reference

Wolfe (1988).

Scale Availability

This scale is available from the authors.

Related References

Wolfe and Birt (1997).

General Comments and Recommendations for Clinicians and Researchers

This assessment approach focuses on an extremely important but often overlooked variable in child sexual abuse—"disclosure." Because anticipated negative consequences for disclosure often deters victims from revelations of abuse, this is a critical assessment target.

---

15. Self-Report of Childhood Abuse Physical (SRCAP; Widom & Shepard)

Development and Description of Assessment Method

The SRCAP is a retrospective, structured interview designed to assess for history of childhood physical abuse.

Target Population

Adults physically abused or possibly physically abused as children.

Format

The SRCAP is a brief structured interview that retrospectively assesses childhood experiences of physical abuse by asking whether a family member engaged in any of the following six childhood experience items: (a) "beat or really hurt you by hitting you with a bare hand or fist"; (b) "beat or hit you with something hard like a stick or baseball bat"; (c) "injured you with a knife, shot you with a gun, or used another weapon against you"; (d) "hurt you badly enough so that you needed a doctor or other medical treatment"; (e) "physically injured you so that you were admitted to a hospital"; or (f) "beat you when you didn't deserve it."

Administration and Scoring

The interview is simply scored dichotomously, reflecting whether the individual reported having had any of the childhood experiences or none.

Psychometric Evaluation

Norms
None reported.

Reliability
Cronbach's alpha for the six-item SRCAP was .75, reflecting adequate internal consistency.

Validity
In a study of 1,196 research participants divided by externally documented official case records into four groups, including a physical abuse group (n = 110), a neglect group (n = 520), sexual abuse group (n = 96), and a nonabused (n = 543) control group. Five out of six of the individual items on the SRCAP and the overall SRCAP score discriminated significantly among the groups, providing evidence of criterion-related validity. Criterion validity was also supported in that the SRCAP was found to be a significant predictor of self-reported violence, an outcome found in officially reported physical abuse cases.

Advantages
The SRCAP is extremely brief and easy to score (the overall interview yields one dichotomous rating indicating the presence or absence of physical abuse).

Limitations
A necessary cost of the brevity and scoring ease is richness or detail concerning the participant's experience.

Primary Reference

Widom and Shepard (1996).

Scale Availability

Cathy Spatz Widom
School of Criminal Justice
The University at Albany
State University of New York
135 Western Ave.
Albany, NY 12222

Related References

None available.

General Comments and Recommendations for Practitioners and Researchers

The SRCAP is an extremely concise and simple to score measure that is useful for the purpose of simple categorization of respondents as physically abused in childhood or not. The interview has reasonable evidence of criterion validity and predictive efficiency (Widom & Shepard, 1996).

---

16. Structured Interview of Symptoms Associated With Sexual Abuse (SASA; Wells, McCann, Adams, Voris, & Dahl)

Development and Description of Assessment Method

The SASA was developed based on information in the literature on children's responses to sexual abuse. The SASA is a 26-item structured parent interview inquiring about emotional, behavioral, and physical symptoms that help clinicians determine the likelihood that sexual abuse has occurred.

Target Population

Parents of children who may have been victims of sexual abuse.

Format

This assessment is a structured interview format in which parents are asked to respond to questions in five categories: sleep ("nightmares"), emotional functioning ("crying easily"), academic/social functioning ("change to poor school performance"), sexual functioning ("seductive toward classmates, teachers, or other adults"), and physical complaints ("frequent headaches"). There are 26 items.

Administration and Scoring

Parents are asked if they have ever noticed any of 26 specific symptoms in their child. For each symptom noted, parents are asked specific follow-up questions regarding duration, time of onset, and other clarifying details.

Psychometric Evaluation

Norms

The initial study examined results among three subsamples of age-matched boys: 22 abused, 47 possibly abused, and 52 nonabused, with an age range of 3 years 8 months to 15 years (mean age = 8 years, 4 months). A table presenting the percentage of participants in each group reporting each of the 26 symptoms can be found in Wells, McCann, Adams, Voris, and Dahl (1997).

Reliability

The internal consistency, determined using Cronbach's alpha, was .83, suggesting strong internal reliability.

Test–retest reliability was evaluated in a second study of 39 prepubescent females who were seen twice for sexual abuse evaluations. The interval between first and second administration, given by the same interviewer, ranged from 1 month to 5 years 2 months, with a median interval of 16 months. The percentage of agreement on individual items between the two administrations ranged from 48% to 94%, with a mean of 74% for the total measure.

Validity

In comparison with nonabused boys, sexually abused boys showed significant differences in emotional, behavioral, and physical symptoms. The nonabused group had a mean of 1.5 symptoms endorsed, the possibly abused group had a mean of 6.5 symptoms endorsed, and the definitely abused group had a mean of 9.1 symptoms endorsed, demonstrating known-groups validity.

Known-groups validity was also demonstrated in a second study of prepubescent females in which abused research participants had significantly larger numbers of symptoms than did nonabused control participants.

Scoring of an abbreviated 12-item scale (the 12 items that demonstrated statistically significant differences between groups) demonstrated a sensitivity of 90.9% and a specificity of 88.5%. The positive predictive value of a score of three or more was 77%, and the negative predictive value was 96%, indicating that a score of three or more will correctly classify an individual as abused 77% of the time and a score of less than three will correctly classify an individual as nonabused 96% of the time.

Advantages

The SASA offers easy administration in a symptom checklist format with the opportunity to gather more information. When parents answer affirmatively to items, follow-up questions can result in more specific information. Authors indicate that items are relevant to both male and female victims.

Limitations

This checklist–parent interview format needs to be compared with other data used in the assessment of sexual abuse and its effects. Published norms are on all-male samples, and these samples were not matched on demographics.

Primary Reference

Wells et al. (1997).

Scale Availability

Robert D. Wells
Department of Pediatrics
Valley Children's Hospital
3151 North Millbrook Ave.
Fresno, CA 93703

Related References

Wells (1992).

General Comments and Recommendations for Practitioners and Researchers

The SASA is one of the rare sexual abuse instruments to be developed with reference to an all-male sample. Thus, norms are available for symptom rates in boys (according to parents' report). Sensitivity and specificity data are also provided. The authors recommend using this interview and a physical examination.

17. Structured Interview for Disorders of Extreme Stress (SIDES; Pelcovitz et al.)

Development and Description of Assessment Method

A list of 27 criteria often seen in response to extreme traumas and not addressed by the *DSM-IV* (American Psychiatric Association, 1994) criteria for PTSD were generated based on a systematic review of the literature and a survey of 50 authorities on psychological reactions to extreme stress. Five-hundred and twenty research participants were administered the SIDES, which measures the presence of these criteria, as part of larger *DSM-IV* PTSD field trials. Interviewers were blind as to the hypothesized differences between trauma groups but not to the type and number of traumas endured by the participants.

The SIDES is a structured clinical interview designed to measure psychological alterations following exposure to extreme stress. It is designed to be given after the Structured Clinical Interview for *DSM-IV*, PTSD module.

Target Population

Adolescents and adults exposed to extreme stress–trauma.

Format

The SIDES interview includes 48 items measuring 27 symptoms that are arranged into seven categories. The individual categories and symptom descriptions are described as follows (sample items are included):

- I. *Regulation of Affect and Impulses* (6 items, including questions regarding affect regulation, modulation of anger, self-destructiveness, suicidal preoccupation, difficulty modulating sexual involvement, and excessive risk taking):
  - "Do you have (more) trouble letting go of things that upset you?"
  - "Do you find yourself careless about making sure that you are safe?"
- II. *Attention or Consciousness* (2 items, including questions regarding amnesia and transient dissociative episodes and depersonalization):
  - "To what extent do you have trouble clearly remembering important things that have happened to you?"

- "Do you sometimes feel so unreal that it is as if you were living in a dream, or not really there or behind a glass wall?"
- III. *Self-Perception* (6 items, including questions regarding ineffectiveness, permanent damage, guilt and responsibility, shame, nobody can understand, and minimizing):
  - "Do you have the feeling that you basically have no influence on what happens to you in your life?"
  - "Do you feel set apart and very different from other people?"
- IV. *Perception of the Perpetrator* (3 items, including questions regarding adopting distorted beliefs, idealization of perpetrator, and preoccupation with hurting perpetrator):
  - "Do you sometimes think that people have the right to hurt you?"
  - "Do you sometimes think that people who have hurt you are special?"
- V. *Relations With Others* (3 items, including questions regarding inability to trust, revictimization, and victimizing others):
  - "Do you find yourself unable to trust people?"
  - "Do you have difficulty working through conflicts in relationships?"
- VI. *Somatization* (5 items, including questions regarding digestive system, chronic pain, cardiopulmonary symptoms, conversion symptoms, and sexual symptoms:
  - "Since the trauma, have you had trouble with abdominal pain, intolerance of food?"
  - "Since the trauma have you suffered from shortness of breath, chest pain?"
- VII. *Systems of Meaning* (2 items, including questions regarding despair–hopelessness and loss of previously sustaining beliefs):
  - "Have you given up hope in being able to find happiness in love relationships?"
  - "Do you feel that life has lost its meaning?"

Administration and Scoring

The 48 items are scored dichotomously with yes or no answers. The interviewer is encouraged to probe for specific details to get the correct rating and then a total score. Clarifying questions that are useful to ask appear in italics next to the items. If the interviewee has had the experience during the month preceding the interview, the interviewer indicates a severity rating for that item from 1 (little problematic) to 3 (extremely problematic).

Psychometric Evaluation

Norms

Pelcovitz et al. (1997) presented the percent endorsement of each SIDES symptom by type of trauma for a sample of 520 participants across five national sites.

Reliability

Interrater reliability conducted on 50 interviews by 10 raters for whether or not disorders of extreme stress (DES) criteria were met for each participant was .81 as measured by the Kappa coefficient. Internal consistency using coefficient alpha was .90 for alteration in regulation of affect and impulses, .76 for alterations in attention or consciousness, .77 for alterations in self-perception, .53 for alterations in perception of the perpetrator, .77 for alterations in relations with others, .88 for somatization, .78 for alterations in systems of meaning, and .96 for total DES score.

Validity

Content validity was demonstrated in that a panel of 12 experts agreed on the final list of 27 symptoms arranged into seven categories. Face validity was also established by having a group of trauma experts (the first three authors) unanimously agree that each subscale was a critical component of trauma.

Advantages

This is a useful tool for the investigation of response to extreme stress and for identifying areas of psychological impairment that are essential for treatment planning. It offers a helpful supplement to the measurement of *DSM-IV* PTSD criteria, which do not address many symptoms often seen in response to extreme trauma.

Limitations

Construct validity needs to be established by comparing endorsement of DES symptoms across different types of trauma populations as well as examining the association between the SIDES and other, established instruments assessing related constructs.

Primary Reference

Pelcovitz et al. (1997).

Scale Availability

David Pelcovitz
Department of Psychiatry
North Shore University Hospital
400 Community Dr.
Manhasset, NY 11030

Related References

van der Kolk et al. (1992).

General Comments and Recommendations for Practitioners and Researchers

The SIDES is a highly useful interview for clinicians or researchers who wish to go beyond *DSM-IV* PTSD criteria in evaluating the impact of trauma. The interview is useful in treatment planning and covers critical areas of functioning, including affect regulation and altered cognitions. The measure was used as part of a *DSM-IV* field trial and was designed in part to test the viability of a supplemental *DSM* trauma diagnosis, the category of "disorders of extreme stress."

---

18. Traumatic Antecedents Interview (TAI; Perry, Herman, & van der Kolk)

Development and Description of Assessment Method

The TAI is a semistructured interview designed to elicit reports of child-hood trauma and related experiences.

Target Population

Adolescents and adults who have or may have experienced traumatic events.

Format

The TAI is a 100-item semistructured interview that covers descriptions of primary caretakers, important relationships in childhood and ado-

lescence, major separations, moves and losses, sibling and peer relationships, family discipline, conflict resolution, family alcoholism, family
violence, and physical and sexual abuse. It includes a number of
introductory questions that are ancillary to trauma (demographics, role
of religion in childhood or current life, social support) that are designed so that the participant becomes comfortable and relaxed. The
first 59 questions create an exploratory mindset for recalling childhood
experiences and get at major themes of family. Specific questions about
abuse, neglect, household chaos, separation, and loss begin with question 60. Final questions are important in helping the person recover
from the discussion of what may be very upsetting experiences. The
participant is encouraged to narrate his or her experiences in detail
rather than simply provide yes–no answers and to describe childhood
experiences as coherent vignettes. This elicits a greater level of description.

The interview covers four domains of childhood traumatic experiences:

- *Gross Abuse:* This includes variables of physical abuse, sexual
  abuse, and witnessing family violence. Sample questions include,
  - "Did you consider the rules generally fair?"
  - "What was the usual way of disciplining children?"
- *Gross Neglect:* This includes variables of physical neglect and emo-
  tional neglect. Sample questions include,
  - "Who in the family was affectionate to you?"
  - "Was there anyone who recognized you as a special person?"
- *Separation and Losses:* This includes variables of significant sepa-
  rations and losses of caretakers. Sample questions include,
  - "Were you ever separated from your primary caretaker for
    more than a few weeks?"
  - "Were there any deaths in the immediate family before you
    were 16?"
- *Chaos:* This includes variables of family disturbance and disor-
  ganization. Sample questions include,
  - "Who made rules and enforced discipline at home?"
  - "Can you give a description of family rules?"

Administration and Scoring

This interview takes one to two hours to administer, and the interviewer
must be experienced. The interviewer should not follow the structure

of the interview rigidly and is encouraged to follow up specific questions with comments and questions aimed at increasing elaboration of the participant's responses. The interviewer should not simply code answers but use verbatim quotes when possible.

For each of the four domains, the interviewer ascertains during which of three developmental periods (0–6, 7–12, 13–18 years of age) the events of interest occurred. The data are scored separately for each of these periods.

First, a score for each variable for each of the three developmental periods is tallied. Then for each domain the scores of each variable within each developmental period is added to yield the three developmental subtotal scores for the domain. A second subtotal may be obtained for each variable across all ages. Finally, the total score for each domain (the total gross abuse score) is calculated by summing the subtotals for the three developmental periods.

The number of perpetrators is counted separately for the three abuse variables at each of the three developmental periods.

Psychometric Evaluation

Norms
None reported.

Reliability
None reported.

Validity
None reported.

Advantages
Extremely thorough, and questions are ordered to assist the respondent in being comfortable and recalling possibly traumatic material.

Limitations
This is a lengthy, time-consuming interview with complicated scoring. The lack of psychometric development compromises its use as a standardized assessment method.

Primary Reference

Perry, Herman, and van der Kolk (1992).

Scale Availability

> J. Christopher Perry
> The Institute of Community and Family Psychiatry
> Sir Mortimer B. Davis—Jewish General Hospital
> 4333 Chemin de la Cote Ste.-Catherine
> Montreal, Quebec, Canada H3T 1E4
> (514) 340-8210

Related References

Herman, Perry, and van der Kolk (1989); van der Kolk, Perry, and Herman (1991).

General Comments and Recommendations for Practitioners and Researchers

This comprehensive interview assesses rich family background information in addition to the traumatic event(s), including family or origin demographics, childhood separations and caretakers, peer relations, and childhood strengths. It also has sections on demographics and health status. Although lengthy, it is sure to elicit a detailed depiction of early experiences and prove useful for a variety of research questions.

---

19. "What If" Situations Test (WIST—III; Wurtele, Kast, & Kondrick)

Development and Description of Assessment Method

The original WIST was developed to measure the three major objectives of personal safety programs: recognizing, resisting, and reporting sexual abuse. The authors report that the vignettes were rated by a panel of experts as being age-appropriate and representative of sexually abusive situations.

The WIST—III measures children's abilities to recognize and respond in hypothetical sexually abusive situations. In addition, it is designed to assess primary prevention skills taught in a personal safety program.

Target Population

Preschool children.

Format

The WIST–III is a semistructured interview containing six hypothetical vignettes designed to assess children's abilities to recognize, resist, and report inappropriate touching. Six response scales assess the skills believed to be important in protecting children from child sexual abuse: two recognition skills, including appropriate request recognition (ARR) and inappropriate request recognition (IRR), and four personal safety skills, including say, do, tell, and report.

There are two practice vignettes followed by six brief vignettes. Each vignette describes a hypothetical situation in which an adult asks to touch or look at the child's private parts (or have the child touch their private parts), with each request resulting in the child feeling either good, bad, or confused. Three of the vignettes describe appropriate requests (e.g., physician wanting to touch the child's injured private parts) and three describe inappropriate requests (e.g., neighbor wanting to take pictures of the child's private parts). Two additional vignettes assess knowledge about sexual abuse (whose fault it is and whether secret touches should be reported) and attitudes toward sexuality (does the child like his or her private parts and is it okay to touch oneself).

Sample vignettes include,

- *Appropriate/Good:* "What if you were riding your tricycle and you fell off and hurt your private parts. When you went home your parents wanted to look at your private parts. Would you feel good if mom or dad wanted to check your private parts?"
- *Inappropriate/Confused:* What if you were playing at the park and a man you like said to you, "Hey, [name of child], I'll go buy you an ice cream cone if you take off your pants and let me touch your private parts." Would you feel sure about what to do?

After each vignette children are asked a series of questions:

- *Appropriate/Inappropriate:*
  - "Would it be okay for [person in vignette] to [do activity requested]?"

For inappropriate request vignettes correctly identified, children are asked the following questions, assessing the personal safety skills:

- *SAY:* "What would you say to [person in vignette]?"
- *DO:* "What would you do?"

- *TELL:* "Would you tell anyone about [the situation]?", if so "Who would you tell?"
- *REPORT:* "What would you say to [person named in d]?"

Administration and Scoring

The WIST–III takes approximately 10 minutes to administer. The child being evaluated is instructed to imagine him- or herself in each situation and is then asked the series of questions to determine his or her ability to recognize the appropriateness–inappropriateness of the request along with his or her abilities to use the prevention skills taught in personal safety programs.

There are two request discrimination scores that reflect the child's ability to correctly identify appropriate and inappropriate requests; these receive one point if correct and yield two recognition scores: an appropriate request recognition score (range = 0 to 3) and an inappropriate request recognition score (range = 0 to 3). Children's scores on the four personal safety skills can reach a maximum of eight points per vignette, and are then summed across the three inappropriate-request vignettes for a total skill score of (up to) 24. These scores indicate the child's ability to verbalize which primary prevention skills they would use.

Scoring criteria are available on request.

Psychometric Evaluation

Children were pretested using the WIST–III one week before participation in a behavioral skills training program. Interviewers were blind to the hypotheses and children's group assignments. The WIST–III was administered to 406 preschoolers involved in several studies conducted over five years. Participants ranged in age from 41 to 68 months, with a mean age of 54.7 months.

Norms

As reported in Wurtele, Hughes, and Sarno-Owens (1999): Appropriate recognition scores were reported as (range 0 to 3) 2.47 ± .91, inappropriate recognition scores were reported as (range 0 to 3) 1.42 ± 1.34, say skill scores were reported as (range 0 to 6) 2.02 ± 2.38, do skill scores were reported as (range 0 to 6) 1.49 ± 2.18, tell skill scores were reported as (range 0 to 6) .90 ± 1.76, report skill scores were reported as (range 0 to 6) .47 ± 1.25, and total skill scores were reported as (range 0 to 24) 4.88 ± 6.23 for the 262 preschoolers assigned to the skills training program at pretreatment.

Reliability

Cronbach's alpha for the personal safety subscales were appropriate response (AR) scale = .75, the inappropriate response (IR) scale = .88, Say = .85, Do = .85, Tell = .84, Report = .79, and WIST–III total skills scale = .90, indicating adequate internal reliabilities. Furthermore, scores within the three inappropriate vignettes were summed to determine consistency of response. Pearson product-moment correlations at pretest ranged from .73 to .77 In an $N = 100$ study, the prevention skill score's internal consistency as measured by Cronbach's alpha was .84. One-month test–retest reliabilities using Pearson product-moment correlations for the two recognition scales were AR = .76 and IR = .81. Correlations for the four safety skill scales were Say = .84, Do = .71, Tell = .71, and Report = .60, and the total skill scale = .83. Finally, children's responses were scored by two independent raters. Interrater reliability as measured by Kappa was .87 (Wurtele, Hughes, & Sarno-Owens, in press).

Validity

The WIST–III has been shown to be sensitive to a personal safety program intervention and a behavioral skills training program and was moderately correlated with a measure of personal safety.

Advantages

The WIST–III can be used as an evaluation tool for safety prevention programs, and because it is not program-specific, it can be used to evaluate a variety of programs. The WIST–III also assesses for generalization of learning because children are required to apply prevention knowledge to situations not presented in educational programs; identifies children who need further assistance in recognizing, resisting, and reporting abuse; and, by measuring several different skills, can help determine whether certain skills are more difficult to learn compared with others. The WIST–III holds attention with the storytelling format and has a short administration time.

Limitations

Predictive validity of the WIST–III has not yet been determined. That is, it is unknown if a child who reports skills would actually apply them.

Primary Reference

Wurtele, Kast, and Kondrick (1988).

Scale Availability

> Sandy K. Wurtele
> Department of Psychology
> University of Colorado
> 1420 Austin Bluffs Pkwy.
> Colorado Springs, CO 80933-7150

Related References

Sarno and Wurtele (1997).

General Comments and Recommendations for Practitioners and Researchers

As always, ethical constraints prohibit the assessment of children's responses to the threats of sexual abuse in real-life situations. As such, clinicians are limited to the hypothesized responses, which limits the assessment of the transfer of skills.

---

20. Wyatt Sex History Questionnaire (WSHQ; Wyatt, Lawrence, Vodounon, & Mickey)

Development and Description of Assessment Method

Interview items were generated and phrased based on focus groups of community samples of women. Some questions were then deleted or revised based on previous data obtained with the WSHQ (Wyatt, 1985). The WSHQ is a semistructured interview designed to obtain specific information regarding a range of women's sexual experiences, including consensual and coercive incidents and the effects on their intimate relationships and psychological and sexual functioning.

Target Population

Female adolescents and adults abused as children.

Format

The WSHQ is a 398-item semistructured interview used to assess retrospective and current consensual and abusive sexual experiences from childhood to adulthood and the initial and lasting effects of these experiences. Data on sexual socialization, age of onset, frequency of sexual interaction, and the circumstances of both consensual and nonconsensual sexual behaviors is collected. There are also questions inquiring about history of human immunodeficiency virus (HIV) and sexually transmitted diseases (STDs). Questions about sexual abuse are asked at the end of the interview, and any affirmative response is followed by a series of more detailed questions about each incident. Sample items include,

- "Have you ever had a sexually transmitted disease?"
- "Have you ever had an abortion?"
- "How old were you when you first had sexual intercourse?"
- "Has anyone tried to put their penis in your vagina when you were younger than age 18?"

Administration and Scoring

Questions are arranged chronologically (assessing sexual experiences from childhood through adulthood), so that inconsistencies in data are apparent. If inconsistencies are noted, immediate clarification from the participant is possible. The semistructured interview format allows the research participant to rate the severity of abuse incidents while the circumstances of each incident are objectively assessed. Approximately half the items are constructed in an open-ended fashion, and the remaining items are scored with Likert-type response categories.

Psychometric Evaluation

Norms
None reported.

Reliability
Four interview questions were readministered later in the interview to sample reliability of reports within the interview. Three obtained perfect consistency and one resulted in some discrepancies ($r = .88$, $p < .001$). Demographic questions were asked in a telephone interview following the face-to-face interview, and Pearson correlations reflecting reliability across time and method ranged from .79 to 1.00

Validity
To evaluate convergent validity on a small subsample of items, the authors compared nine items from the Sexual Behavior Inventory (Bentler, 1968) with corresponding items on the WSHQ concerning intercourse, fellatio, and cunnilingus. These items, pertaining to whether or

not the research participant had engaged in the behaviors, correlated perfectly ($r = 1.00$).

Advantages

This assessment tool is a thorough method of gathering complete sexual history information.

Limitations

The interview is lengthy to administer and there are limited psychometric data to support this as a methodologically sound assessment tool.

Primary Reference

Wyatt, Lawrence, Vodounon, and Mickey (1992).

Scale Availability

Gail Elizabeth Wyatt
Department of Psychiatry and Biobehavioral Sciences
University of California, Los Angeles
760 Westwood Plaza
Los Angeles, CA 90024-1759

Related References

Bentler (1968); Wyatt (1985); Wyatt, Guthrie, and Notgrass (1992).

General Comments and Recommendations for Practitioners and Researchers

The WSHQ is unique in its assessment of both consensual sexual history and coercive–abusive sexual experiences. It thus permits the assessment of potential or sequelae of child sexual abuse, including sexual dysfunction, infection with STDs, early first intercourse, unintended pregnancies, and other patterns and high-risk sexual behaviors. Another unique facet of the WSHQ is that the interview was written to be relevant to multicultured populations. However, psychometric data reported are limited to brief sections of the interview (i.e., small groups of individual questions) and additional evaluation is needed before this can be considered a fully reliable or valid interview.

5

Self-Report Inventories for the Assessment of Children

---

21. Abusive Sexual Exposure Scale (ASES; Spaccarelli)

Development and Description of Assessment Method

The ASES is a self-report inventory in which items assess the occurrence of 14 types of sexual abuse and the identity (by relationship) of all perpetrators for each type of abuse.

Target Population

Children and adolescents who were sexually abused.

Format

This assessment consists of a self-report inventory containing 28 items in total. Two of the sexual abuse items are "noncontact" sexual victimization, including exposure and being photographed when nude. The other items address six types of sexual contact, including breast or genital fondling of victim or perpetrator, oral copulation of victim or perpetrator, digital penetration of the victim's anus or vagina, and genital penetration of the victim's anus or vagina. Sample items include,

- "Did someone ever stare at you when you were naked or take naked pictures of you when you didn't want them to?"
- "Did someone older than you by 5 years or more ever have you touch or rub their private parts or sexual parts?"

- "Did a young person (no more than four years older than you) ever put their finger(s) or an object inside your anal or vaginal opening when you didn't want them to?"

If child answers in the affirmative, they also respond to the following question: "What person or persons have done that to you?"

Administration and Scoring

Before the respondent completes the questionnaire, each type of abuse asked about is described using terms for body parts that are defined. The four terms used for body parts are penis, vaginal area, anal area, and other sex parts (defined as including the previous three parts and the chest area on the female). To be sure that each term is understood, participants are asked to identify the body parts on anatomically detailed dolls.

Responses to the 28 items are used to create three variables: (a) severity of sexual exposure including either noncontact or fondling or invasive, (b) total number of types of abuse reported (number of yes answers), and (c) closest perpetrator named (parent/stepparent, other family member, extrafamilial perpetrator).

Psychometric Evaluation

Norms
None reported.

Reliability
None reported.

Validity
Items on the ASES have high face validity in that they directly address whether or not different types of sexual contact occurred under the two conditions that are commonly used to define abuse. (These are the age difference between victim and perpetrator and the "unwanted" nature of sexual contact.) In a study of 48 sexually abused girls (Spaccarelli & Fuchs, 1997), multivariate analysis was used to examine predictors of different types of symptomatology. The ASES is used to categorize incest occurrence, and was not correlated with any of the self-reported predictor variables. For parent-reported internalizing problems, the only significant ($p < .05$) zero-order predictor was incestuous abuse and it explained 12% of the variance in parent-reported anxiety on the Child Behavior Checklist (CBCL; Achenbach, 1991).

Advantages

The ASES is a brief, easy to administer instrument with specific computer-scoring strategies.

Limitations

Sparse psychometric information limits its use. The sole focus on total exposure and incest coding limits conclusions about impact of events on the child.

Primary Reference

Spaccarelli (1995).

Scale Availability

> Steve Spaccarelli
> Institute for Juvenile Research
> Department of Psychiatry
> University of Illinois at Chicago
> 907 South Wolcott Ave.
> Chicago, IL 60612

Related References

Spaccarelli and Fuchs (1997).

General Comments and Recommendations for Practitioners and Researchers

A computer-coding system is available from the author as part of package that includes other instruments for the assessment of the sexually abused child. ASES has not yet been used with a male population.

---

22. Adolescent Dissociative Experience Survey (A–DES; Armstrong, Putnam, & Carlson)

Development and Description of Assessment Method

The A–DES was designed for examining the developmental trajectories of both normal and pathological dissociation during adolescence as well as for use as an efficient screen for pathological dissociation, with other commonly occurring comorbid disorders in disturbed adolescents in clinical settings. The A–DES includes multiple constructs under the global construct of dissociation. This multidimensional approach was used to capture both normal and pathological dissociative phenomena. Individual items were generated by the authors and a team of clinicians.

The A–DES is a self-report measure modeled on the adult version of the Dissociative Experiences Scale (Bernstein & Putnam, 1986) designed to examine normal and pathological dissociative phenomena in adolescents and to be used as a screening measure for pathological dissociation during adolescence.

Target Population

Adolescents (ages 11 to 18) with an appropriate Flesch-Kincaid reading grade level of 5.7.

Format

This assessment is a self-report in which a total of 30 items sample six domains that are widely considered to reflect basic aspects of dissociation:

- *Dissociative Amnesia* (7 items; examines the lapses in memory for experiences that reflect dissociative breaches in information processing): "People tell me I do or say things that I don't remember doing."
- *Absorption and Imaginative Involvement* (6 items; examines the ability to become so wrapped up in fantasy activities that reality falls away, and the confusions between fantasy and reality that can occur if such behavior becomes chronic): "I find that I can make physical pain go away."
- *Passive Influence* (5 items; examines experiences of not having volitional control over one's body and sensations): "I hear voices in my head that are not mine."
- *Depersonalization and Derealization* (12 items; examines the sense of feeling disconnected from one's body and the world. In addition, two subsets of items were specifically designed to examine the effects of depersonalization on the adolescent's developmental reworking of identity and relationships). Examples include, "If find myself standing outside of my body, watching myself as if I were another person."

- *Dissociated Identity* (4 items; examines the sense of being disconnected from parts of oneself, including feeling that one's emotions or behaviors are not one's own). Examples include, "People tell me that I sometimes act so differently that I seem like a different person."
- *Dissociative Relatedness* (3 items; examines the "sense that interpersonal relationships are unaccountably changeable and unreal.": "I don't recognize myself in the mirror."

Subscale items are worded to reflect experiences and coping skills rather than symptoms–disabilities.

Administration and Scoring

Directions are to focus on "different experiences that happen to people" and to direct the adolescent to answer when not under the influence of alcohol or drugs. The response format is a continuous 11-point Likert scale, with 0 = "never" to 10 = "always." The total A-DES score is equal to the mean of all item scores.

Psychometric Evaluation

Norms

Mean scores and standard deviations on the A–DES for the following groups are as follows: dissociative disorders (n = 13) 4.85 ± 1.14; psychotic disorders (n = 8) 3.76 ± 2.17; impulse control disorders (n = 14) 2.60 ± 2.05; substance abuse disorders (n = 18) 2.42 ± 1.29; nonpsychiatric (n = 60) 2.24 ± 1.38; affective disorders (n = 24) 2.19 ± 1.43; oppositional defiant disorders (n = 16) 2.06 ± 1.91; other (n = 9) 1.26 ± .72.

Reliability

The A–DES is reported to be internally consistent in terms of full scale and subscale reliability. Smith and Carlson (1996) in a normal sample of 60 junior and senior high school students, found the A–DES had high split-half (Spearman Brown r = .94) and two-week test–retest reliability (Pearson r = .77). Furthermore, in a clinical sample of 102 adolescents ages 12 to 18, the Spearman Brown split-half reliability was r = .92, the Cronbach alpha coefficient for the total scale was .93, and subscale alphas ranged from .72 (absorption) to .85 (amnesia; Armstrong et al., 1997).

Validity

Known-groups validity was demonstrated because the A–DES was able to distinguish dissociative-disordered adolescents from a "normal" sample and from a patient sample with a variety of diagnoses, with the mean of the "dissociative disorder" group significantly higher than those of the five other groups, although not higher for the "psychotic disorder" group. Also, adolescents were grouped into four general trauma groups: no known abuse ($n = 47$), physical abuse alone, sexual abuse alone, and both physical and sexual abuse ($n = 54$ for these three). The A–DES means significantly differed by abuse status (they were highest for the physical and sexual abuse group). In addition, all four subscales were able to differentiate the normal from the dissociative disordered group.

Advantages

The A–DES is a short, easy to administer questionnaire that can also be used to examine the role of dissociative symptoms in more common psychiatric disorders of adolescence.

Limitations

According to the authors, the A–DES does not include checks for denial or fabrication of dissociative symptoms. Furthermore, it did not distinguish between dissociative and psychotic groups (which may be a reflection of overlapping symptoms, a result of diagnostic inaccuracy, or a combination of both).

Primary Reference

Armstrong, Putnam, Carlson, Libero, and Smith (in press).

Scale Availability

Judith Armstrong
501 Santa Monica Blvd.
Suite 402
Santa Monica, CA 90401

Related References

Farrington, Waller, Smerden, and Faupel (2001); Friedrich, Gerber, Koplin, Davis, Giese, et al. (2001); Putnam (1997).

General Comments and Recommendations for Practitioners and Researchers

Designed to capture both normal and pathological dissociation in adolescents, the A–DES is a practical measure to include in an assessment battery for teenage survivors of sexual abuse.

23. Angie/Andy Child Rating Scale (A/A CRS; Praver, Pelcovitz, & DeGuiseppe)

Development and Description of Assessment Method

The A/A CRS is based on the Levonn (Richters & Martinez, 1993), a cartoon-based measure in which the central character has been exposed to community violence. Items were generated from a review of previous research on abuse and community violence. Item construction was reviewed by five child psychology experts. Face validity was obtained by consensus of four of the experts. Another revision is in progress and the scale is expected to be reduced to no more than 70 items.

The A/A CRS is a clinician-administered scale with the primary aim of evaluating children's reactions to violence exposure.

Target Population

Children and adolescents who are allegedly victims of various types of violence.

Format

The A/A CRS is a self-report consisting of 105 items, 99 of which are illustrated, in which either a girl (Angie) or boy (Andy) has been exposed to four forms of violence: sexual abuse, physical abuse, witnessing family violence, and community violence.

Cartoons are accompanied by a two- to four-sentence scenario to illustrate vividly for the child specific posttraumatic symptoms, which are arranged into seven categories: regulation of affect, attention and consciousness, self-perception, relations with others, somatization, systems of meaning, and posttraumatic stress disorder (PTSD).

Administration and Scoring

The child is first presented with five sample cartoons depicting one of four frequency ratings. Sample cartoons are repeated until the child responds correctly. In the introduction there are suggestions of methods of checking to see if the child understands and of encouraging the child's responses. Sixteen reverse-positive items are included to reduce negative valence and to act as a separate adaptive functioning scale.

The A/A CRS takes 30 to 45 minutes to administer and approximately 80 minutes for seriously disturbed children. Scoring uses a 4-point thermometer rating scale, from 1 = "never" to 4 = "a lot of the time." The "scoring guide" consists of the assignment of questions to the seven categories. Training takes approximately one hour.

Psychometric Evaluation

Norms

Trained interviewers administered the A/A CRS to 208 children ages 6 to 11 from four hospital sites, the general population surrounding the hospital, and one school. They were divided into four groups, including the intrafamilial violence group (IV), extrafamilial violence group (EV), combined violence trauma group (CV), and nontrauma group (NT).

Reliability

Internal consistency using coefficient alphas ranged from .70 to .95 (the latter for the total associated symptoms scale, .70 to .88 for the six scales and .88 to .95 for the three composite scales.

Validity

Construct validity was supported. IV, EV, and CV groups each had significantly higher scores than the NT group on the six scales (the seven scales, excluding the PTSD scale), the composite, and the PTSD scales. Also, the NT group scored higher on the Adaptive Functioning Scale than the IV and CT groups.

Known groups validity was also supported: The six scales, the composite, and PTSD scales all predicted membership in trauma and nontrauma groups. The scales correctly classified between 76% and 90% of trauma and nontrauma groups.

Convergent validity was supported by significant correlations between the A/A CRS and parent ratings of their children's behaviors (Nader, 1997).

Advantages

The cartoon format makes this measure child friendly. In addition, the A/A CRS included multiple forms of violence assessment, including community violence, in one measure.

Limitations

Pictures may limit scope of focus for younger children who interpret information more literally and concretely. Also, it does not include all PTSD subcriteria.

Primary Reference

Praver, Pelcovitz, and DiGiuseppe (1996).

Scale Availability

F. Praver
5 Marseilles Dr.
Locust Valley, NY 11560
Or
D. Pelcovitz
Department of Psychiatry
North Shore University Hospital
400 Community Dr.
Manhasset, NY 11030

Related References

Gries, Goh, Andrews, Gilbert, Praver, and Stelzer (2000); Nader (1997).

General Comments and Recommendations for Practitioners and Researchers

There is a corresponding parent questionnaire (A/A PRS) that refers to "some children" rather than Angie or Andy and does not use the cartoons. Also in progress is the Child Rating Scales of Exposure to Interpersonal Abuse (CRS–EIA; Praver, 1994), which assesses the frequency and severity of 6- to 11-year-old children's exposure to interpersonal abuse.

24. Assessing Environments Scale (AEIII; Berger & Knutson)

Development and Description of Assessment Method

The AEIII is a retrospective true–false questionnaire that targets punitive and abuse-related childhood histories by assessing a broad range of punitive childhood experiences and family characteristics associated with child abusing environments.

The development of the questionnaire followed the rational statistical approach. Most of the original items were written specifically for this questionnaire with attention to items addressing family background, discipline, and abuse. Additional items were taken from the Home Environment Questionnaire (Laing & Sines, 1982). A preliminary questionnaire and two follow-ups were administered to a nonclinical college student population. Based on interitem correlations, the questionnaire was revised and then readministered for additional item analysis as well as the addition, deletion, or reforming of several questions leading to the development of the AE–II. After administration to more than 2400 participants, further item revision resulted in the AEIII. The scales of the AEIII were designed to assess self-reported descriptors of childhood environments and to sample specific content domains and childhood environmental characteristics that have been associated with abuse in the clinical literature.

Target Population

Adolescents and adults.

Format

This assessment consists of a questionnaire in which the following 164 items are categorized into 15 subscales:

- *Physical Punishment* (12 items): Assesses the occurrence of specific events of physical discipline from mild discipline (spanking) to severe and potentially injurious punishment (punching, kicking, choking). Although not scored, this scale also includes conditional items to help obtain a more thorough description of the experience. This includes the respondent identifying types of injuries sustained, types of medical care needed, and types of objects struck with. Sample item: "When I was bad my parents used to lock me in a closet."

- *Perception of Discipline* (14 items): Assesses perception that childhood discipline had been inappropriate or harsh. Sample item: "My parents were inconsistent in their discipline of me. I never knew whether or not I would be punished for a particular behavior."
- *Negative Family Atmosphere* (8 items): Assesses verbal aggression among members of the family not specifically directed at the respondent. Sample item: "We had lots of arguments in our family."
- *Father* (10 items): Assesses irritable, aggressive, and antisocial behaviors of the respondent's father. Sample item: "My father has or has had a problem with the police."
- *Mother* (4 items): Assesses whether the respondent's mother is described as depressed, neurotic, or having received treatment for emotional problems. Sample item: "My mother is/was often depressed."
- *Marital Discord* (6 items): Assesses discordant interactions between the respondent's parents consistent with descriptors of marital relationships in abusive families. Sample item: "My parents used to argue a lot."
- *Isolation* (4 items): Assesses isolation from family and friends. Sample item: "My parents never seemed to have many friends."
- *Community Involvement* (7 items): Assesses the involvement of the parents in activities outside of the home and beyond the extended family. Sample item: "My mother belonged to a social, civic political, study, literary, or art club."
- *Potential Economic Stress* (10 items): Assesses childhood events and experiences that could be associated with stressful economic circumstances because of membership in lower economic strata and to acute economic reversals. Sample item: "I never had my own crayons as a child."
- *Poor Peer Relations* (3 items): Assesses teasing or victimizing associated with child friendships. Sample item: "Other children didn't seem to like me."
- *Absence of Shared Parenting* (7 items): Assesses an asymmetry in the responsibilities of parents in important family or parenting decisions. Sample item: "My father rarely helped make important family decisions."
- *Positive Orientation to Education* (10 items): Assesses the educational history of the family as well as the existence of activities

and objects in the home that could be indicative of an educationally oriented environment. Sample item: "Our home had more than one hundred books, excluding children's books."

- *Age Inappropriate Demands* (5 items): Assesses being left unattended, being required to be responsible for siblings, being required to provide emotional support for the parents, and the existence of unrealistic expectations. Sample item: "When I was a young child, my parents used to leave me (and my young brothers and sisters) alone when they went out."
- *Positive Parental Contact* (10 items): Assesses past and present positive contact with parents. Sample item: "My parents used to give me piggyback rides when I was small."
- *Feelings of Parental Rejection* (7 items): Assesses feelings of rejection by parents. Sample item: "I never felt that my parents really loved me."

Some items are represented on more than one scale. In addition, because premarital conception and unplanned pregnancies have been associated with marital stress and abuse, individual items are included to assess whether respondents described their birth as occurring under such circumstances.

Administration and Scoring

The respondent completes the questionnaire in a true–false format for each item. The inventory takes approximately 20 minutes to complete.

Psychometric Evaluation

Norms

The AEIII has been used in studies with three relatively large samples drawn from three different populations. The largest sample includes 10,103 college students, predominantly White and middle-class. The second sample consists of a sample of 169 women (mean age = 21) who were admitted to University Hospital's antepartum clinic for obstetrical services. This sample tended to be younger and poorer than samples usually obtained from general obstetrical facilities. Finally, the AEIII was administered to virtually all the literate parents (mean age = 35.6) of children consecutively referred for services at child psychiatry hospitals and clinics serving all of Iowa and Western Illinois. Normative data from these samples are presented in Berger and Knutson (1984).

Reliability

Test–retest correlations over a 60-day period for an $N = 138$ nonclinical sample of college students ranged from .61 (age inappropriate demands) to .89 (marital discord), with a median = .83 and only 4 scales below .75 (isolation, peer relations, shared parenting, age inappropriate demands). All correlations were significant.

Internal consistency coefficients measured using KR-20 in a sample of $N = 1182$ ranged from .65 to .79 for all but three scales (potential economic stress, age inappropriate demands, and poor peer relations, which ranged from .48 to .52), indicating modest levels of internal consistency.

Validity

In a sample of 34 adolescents, the AEIII discriminated between 21 abused and 13 nonabused adolescents on the physical punishment scale, demonstrating discriminant validity. The physical punishment scale also significantly correlated with home observations involving a subset of respondents who had been child research participants 10 years earlier. In a sample of 4,695 college students, all but one subscale (community involvement) significantly correlated with the physical punishment scale. These interscale correlations ranged from .14 (positive orientation to education) to .60 (perception of discipline).

Advantages

The AEIII provides a comprehensive assessment of variety of factors associated with abusive childhood environments. Very large samples were used in the development and application of this scale.

Limitations

This scale was normed on a predominantly White and upper-Midwest sample, which may limit the generalizability of results.

Primary Reference

Berger and Knutson (1984).

Scale Availability

John F. Knutson
Department of Psychology
The University of Iowa

11 Seashore Hall East
Iowa City, IA 52242-1407
(319) 335-2406

Related References

Berger, Knutson, Mehm, and Perkins (1988); DiTomasso and Routh (1993); Knutson and Selner (1994); Rausch and Knutson (1991); Rodriquez, Ryan, Vandekemp, and Foy (1997); Weerts-Whitmore, Kramer, and Knutson (1993).

General Comments and Recommendations for Practitioners and Researchers

This scale was not developed for clinical use or diagnostic services but rather for research purposes. The authors report that results of research with this scale support the importance of asking about specific, behavioral discipline events rather than the general experience of abuse, because most participants who met the strongest abuse criterion did not describe themselves as having been abused.

A variation of the AEIII is the AEIII–Form SD: This involved the addition and deletion of various items from currently used scales, making it a 170-item scale. The sibling physical punishment scale and the sibling perception of discipline scale sample the same acts as the original scales. Two completely new scales, the deserving punishment scale and the sibling deserving punishment scale, assess whether research participants believe their own and their sibling's punishment was deserved. Items on all these scales are identical with the exception of the person or sibling reference. Using a sample of $N = 421$, the indexes of internal consistency were shown comparable to the other AEIII scales, with KR-20 coefficients of the new scales ranging from .68 to .74.

---

25. Checklist of Sexual Abuse and Related Stressors (C–SARS; Spaccarelli)

Development and Description of Assessment Method

The authors conceptualized sexual abuse as a transitional event or major stress that tends to involve a complex series of stressful events. This set of events includes not only the episodes of abusive contact but also perpetrator behaviors that are part of or set the stage for the abuse, events that occur as a consequence of the abuse, and events that occur as a consequence of public disclosure of the abuse. Item development was guided by a review of the literature concerning the types of events that make sexual abuse stressful.

This checklist is designed to assess victims' reports of the occurrence of 70 stressful events related to their sexual abuse experiences as well as degrees of stress associated with negative life events that were part of or related to the abuse.

Target Population

Children and adolescents who were victims of sexual abuse.

Format

The C–SARS is a self-report that assesses three subtypes of stressful events related to abuse. The three subtypes of events and sample items follow:

- *Abuse-Specific Events:* This section includes 34 items across four different subscales.
  - A. Negative Coercion (10 items): "Punish you for not doing a sexual behavior as he/she wanted?" "Threaten to hurt you if you talked to anyone else about what happened."
  - B. Inducements (14 items):
    - Bribes/Rewards: "Give you extra attention"
    - Misrepresentation: "Tell you that sexual behaviors were a grown up thing to do."
    - Seduction: "Tell you that you were sexy."
  - C. Violations of Trust (4 items): "Break a promise not to hurt you in the sex behaviors," "Lie about his/her feelings for you, just to get sex."
  - D. Stigmatizing messages and victim denigration (6 items): "Tell you that sexual behaviors were bad or naughty?" "Call you bad names (e.g., worthless, no-good, whore, slut)."
- *Abuse-Related Events:* This section includes 20 items across three different subscales:
  - A. Family conflict/dysfunction (5 items): "Your parents started fighting more."
  - B. Loss of social contacts (8 items): "Your mother spent less time with you."

- • C. Nonsupportive responses to disclosure (7 items): "Some people in your family were angry at you when they found out what happened."
- • *Public Disclosure Events:* This section includes 16 items assessing issues related to repeated interviews and adjudication problems:
  - • A. Investigation difficulty (4 items): "A doctor or nurse examined you in a way that was uncomfortable or invaded your privacy."
  - • B. Dislocation/placement (5 items): "Your family had to move because the court or the social worker made you."
  - • C. Legal system difficulty (7 items): "One of your parents had to go to jail because of what happened."

Administration and Scoring

Questions begin, "For the next questions think about the older person you just identified _____ did that person _____" and "These changes are about what changes you think happened after _____ did _____." Each item is answered in a yes–no format, indicating whether each stressful event had ever occurred in relation to the child's sexually abusive experiences with a specific perpetrator. Total scores for stressors experienced can range from 0 to 70 as each "yes" is given a score of 1 and each "no" a score of 0.

Psychometric Evaluation

Norms

The study sample included girls ages 11 to 18 (mean age = 14) who were sexually abused and their nonoffending parents or guardians who were referred for therapy. The victimized girls in this study reported that negative coercion inducement, loss of social contact, and violation of trust were the most common stress events, whereas legal events and family dislocation were the least common.

Reliability

Internal consistency was evaluated for total C–SARS score (.93), and reliabilities for the three subcategories were .66 (total disclosure events), .73 (total related events) and .93 (total abuse events).

Alpha levels for the individual subscales were as follows: negative coercion (.89), inducements (.89), violations of trust (.74), victim denigration–secrecy (.57), family conflict–dysfunction (.66), loss of social contacts (.56), nonsupportive responses to disclosure (.70), dislocation (.65), legal events (.67), and investigation difficulty (.45).

Validity

Construct validity was supported by significant correlations of the C–SARS total event score with therapists' overall ratings of abuse stress ($r = .36$, $p < .05$) and with victim reports of the number of types of sexual abuse experienced ($r = .40$, $p < .05$). In addition, higher levels of stressful events on the C-SARS were significantly related to parent-reported aggressive behavior problems, sexual concerns, and total symptoms on the CBCL (Achenbach, 1991).

Advantages

With the focus on stressful events related to sexual abuse, this measure may help answer the question of how to account for variability in mental health outcomes among victims.

Limitations

Numerous symptomatology measures and subscales were examined in the validity study resulting in an elevation in the risk for Type 1 errors. Also, the population used suffered from severe abuse and multiple perpetrators, and research participants were not grouped by developmental level, possibly limiting generalizability of results.

Primary Reference

Spaccarelli (1995).

Scale Availability

> Steve Spaccarelli
> Institute for Juvenile Research
> Department of Psychiatry
> University of Illinois at Chicago
> 907 South Wolcott Ave.
> Chicago, IL 60612

Related References

Spaccarelli and Fuchs (1997).

General Comments and Recommendations for Practitioners and Researchers

According to the author, correlations across reporters were significant within each subcategory of stressor and were nonsignificant across stressor category, which is consistent with viewing abuse-specific stress and stress related to the abuse or its disclosure as distinct constructs. Furthermore, the regression analyses conducted with several other measures indicated that there were significant effects of negative appraisals on internalizing symptoms when controlling for the level of stressful events experienced, suggesting that negative life events and negative appraisals associated with sexual abuse are valid constructs that help account for variability in mental health outcomes among child victims.

26. Child Abuse and Trauma Scale (CAT; Sanders & Becker-Lausen)

Development and Description of Assessment Method

According to the authors, the CAT was created as a research measure to be used in testing hypotheses about childhood maltreatment outcomes, with the construct of psychological maltreatment conceptualized to underlie numerous forms of abuse and neglect. Acts judged to be psychologically damaging are those committed by individuals who by their characteristics (e.g., age, status, knowledge, organizational form) are in a position of differential power that renders the child vulnerable (for example, acts of rejecting, terrorizing, isolating, exploiting). Subscales were developed based on factor analysis.

The CAT is a retrospective assessment that yields a quantitative index of the frequency and extent of various types of negative experiences in childhood and adolescence as well as a measure of the present subjective perception of the degree of trauma or stress that was present in childhood.

Target Population

Adults with traumatic or stressful childhoods.

Format

The CAT scale consists of 38 items that are presented to the respondent as a home environment questionnaire. Questions are related to an individual's childhood or adolescent experiences of sexual mistreatment, physical mistreatment and punishment, psychological mistreatment, physical or emotional neglect, and negative home environment (e.g., parental substance abuse or fighting) and are categorized into three subscales as follows:

- *Sexual Abuse* (6 items): "Before you were 14, did you engage in any sexual activity with an adult?" "Did you ever witness the sexual mistreatment of another family member?"
- *Punishment* (6 items): "When you were punished as a child or teenager, did you understand the reason you were punished?" "Did your parents ever hit or beat you when you did not expect it?"
- *Neglect/Negative Home Atmosphere* (14 items): "As a child did you feel unwanted or emotionally neglected?" "Did you ever think seriously about running away from home?"

Administration and Scoring

Responses are coded according to a 0 to 4 Likert scale, with 0 = "never" and 4 = "always." Four items are reverse-scored. Subscale scores equal the mean of all the items in that subscale. The total score equals the mean of all items on subscales.

Psychometric Evaluation

Norms

The CAT was normed on two large samples of college students (N = 834; mean age = 18.2; and N = 301; mean age = 18.9). The means of these normative samples were total CAT score = .75 ± .42 and .73 ± .41 (female mean = .77, male mean = .73), negative home environment/neglect = .85 ± .63 and .80 ± .59, sexual abuse = .08 ± .28 and .11 ± .29 and punishment = 1.20 ± .54 and 1.16 ± .53.

Reliability

In the first college study the internal consistency using Cronbach's alphas for the overall scale was .90, negativity of home atmosphere/neglect scale was .86, sexual abuse was .76 and punishment was .63. Six- to eight-week test–retest reliability for the entire scale was .89, negativity of home atmosphere/neglect scale was .91, sexual abuse was .85, and punishment was .71 ($p < .001$). Split-half reliability in a pilot sample of adolescents in a psychiatric hospital of $r = .86$ also indicates good internal consistency.

Validity

The CAT significantly correlated with related constructs, including dissociation, depression, stressful life events, and impairment in interpersonal relationships. Validity is also attested to by research participants with multiple personality ($n = 17$) achieving extremely high scores.

Advantages

The CAT can be used for research when working with groups or in clinical assessment as an initial screening instrument.

Limitations

Further psychometric development needs to be completed before use as a clinical tool. In particular, it is not yet known whether or not the CAT will discriminate between clinical groups.

Primary Reference

Sanders and Becker-Lausen (1995).

Scale Availability

Available in the appendix of the original scale or:
> Barbara Sanders
> Department of Psychology
> U-20
> 406 Babbidge Rd.
> University of Connecticut
> Storrs, CT 06269-1020

Related References

None available.

General Comments and Recommendations for Practitioners and Researchers

The hospitalized adolescents had scores twice those of the college students and approximately half those of the multiple personality disorder (MPD) sample. The authors stated that although scores for college students were significantly related to outcomes previously associated with various types of maltreatment, they were unrelated to variables that would not be expected to be affected by abuse history, such as the death or illness of close family or friends.

27. Child Dissociative Checklist (CDC; Putnam)

Development and Description of Assessment Method

The CDC was developed to measure observable dissociative symptoms in children in response to lack of validated dissociation measures for children. Questions were derived from clinical experience with children with dissociative disorders and based on dissociative symptomatology reported in the psychiatric literature.

The CDC is a parent (or other adult) observer report measure that taps domains of dissociative behavior in children.

Target Population

Parents or other caretakers of children and adolescents 6 to 15 years old. (This assessment is best for children 12 and under.)

Format

This 20-item instrument assesses several dissociative symptoms, including imaginary friends, different identities, moodiness, forgetfulness, thought absorption, and "spaciness." Parents report dissociative symptoms over the past 12 months, tapping the following domains of dissociative behavior:

- Dissociative amnesia;
- Rapid shifts in demeanor, access to information, knowledge, abilities, and age appropriateness of behavior;
- Spontaneous trance states;
- Hallucinations;
- Identity alterations; and
- Aggressive and sexual behavior.

Sample items include,

- "Child does not remember or denies traumatic or painful experiences that are known to have occurred."

- "Child goes into a daze or trance-like state at times or often appears 'spaced out.' Teachers may report he or she daydreams frequently in school."
- "Child sleepwalks frequently."
- "Child frequently talks to him- or herself, may use a different voice, or argue with self at times."

Administration and Scoring

No training is required for administering the CDC, which takes approximately 5 minutes to complete. It is filled out by an adult who is in frequent contact with the child and has therefore observed the child over the preceding 12-month period and is familiar with the child's behavior over a number of contexts. Ratings are on a 3-point scale (2 = "very true"; 1 = "sometimes true"; 0 = "not true") that best describes the child's behavior on a given item over the past 12 months. Ratings of each item are summed to yield a total score ranging from 0 to 32.

Psychometric Evaluation

Norms

A score of 12 or more on the CDC indicates a clinical level of dissociation. Mean scores of various samples are presented in Nader (1997).

Reliability

The CDC has been demonstrated as internally consistent and stable across test populations. In a mixed group of sexually abused and nonabused girls, the one-year retest reliability Spearman coefficient was .69 ($p = .001$). Cronbach's alpha was .95 for the whole sample, .73 for control girls, .91 for sexually abused girls, .64 for girls with dissociative disorder not otherwise specified, and .80 for children with MPD (Putnam, Helmers, & Trickett, 1993). In another study of sexually abused and nonabused girls, the test–retest correlation was $r(60) = .732$ ($p < .001$); Cronbach's alpha was .784 ($p < .001$; Malinosky-Rummel & Hoier, 1991).

Validity

The CDC discriminated between a sample of psychiatric inpatients and nonabused children, but not specifically between the sexually abused inpatients and nonabused inpatients. It also discriminated between

MPD cases and cases diagnosed with dissociative disorder not otherwise specified.

Advantages

The CDC is a quick and simple screening instrument, which has been researched on a number of different clinical populations and has been shown to be both reliable and valid. Comparable parent–adult and child versions allow the clinician to examine correspondence between two sources of information.

Limitations

The CDC is not a diagnostic instrument and does not systematically assess *DSM* (American Psychiatric Association, 1994) criteria for dissociative disorders. A decline in CDC scores across age indicates a decreased sensitivity of the scale for dissociative symptoms and behaviors in older children.

Primary Reference

Putnam (1990).

Scale Availability

Scale is reprinted in Putnam (1990, 1997).

Related References

Malinosky-Rummel and Hoier (1991); Nader (1997); Putnam et al. (1993); Putnam and Peterson (1994).

General Comments and Recommendations for Practitioners and Researchers

The CDC is intended as a clinical screening instrument and a research measure. It is not designed to be used as a diagnostic instrument. Reporting veracity may vary as a function of the accuracy of parents' perceptions of their children's behaviors.

Reliability and validity in children younger than 6 has not been systemically established yet. In general, high scores in younger children should be interpreted cautiously because these behaviors are normatively more common at younger ages.

28. Child Post-Traumatic Stress Reaction Index (CPTS–RI; Frederick, Pynoos, & Nader)

Development and Description of Assessment Method

This self-report inventory, which can also be administered as a direct, semistructured interview, is based on the criteria for PTSD. The purpose of this inventory is to assess the impact of the trauma after the trauma has been identified.

Target Population

Children and adolescents who were victims of trauma.

Format

The CPTS–RI is a self-report containing 20 items that include some of the *DSM-IV* PTSD symptoms from each of three main subscales and an associated feature. For the CPTS–RI, the *DSM-IV* criterion B of reexperiencing trauma includes fear or upset in response to reminders, fear or upset with thoughts of the event, intrusive thoughts, intrusive images, traumatic or bad dreams, thinking there will be a recurrence of the event, and somatic symptoms. The *DSM-IV* criterion C of numbing–avoidance includes numbing of affect, a sense of isolation, loss of interest in activities, avoidance of reminders (activities, places, people, thoughts, or conversations), and avoidance of feelings. The *DSM-IV* criterion D for physiological arousal includes jumpiness, sleep disturbance, difficulty concentrating, and difficulties in impulse control. Examples include, "Do you get scared, afraid, or upset when you think about (event)?" "Do you have good or bad dreams about (event) or other bad dreams?" "Do you sleep well?" and "Do you have more stomachaches, headaches, or other sick feelings since (event) than you did before?" Only direct self-report of symptoms still present are recorded.

Administration and Scoring

This takes 20 to 45 minutes to administer. The CPTS–RI is scored on a 5-point Likert frequency rating scale ranging from 0 = none to 4 = most of the time. Although the index does not provide a *DSM* PTSD diagnosis, there is a scoring system that establishes a level of PTSD. Items are summed and the raw score equals the degree of disorder. A total score of fewer than 12 = doubtful, 12 to 24 = a mild level of PTSD reaction, 25 to 39 = a moderate level, 40 to 59 = a severe level, and more than 60 = a very severe reaction. Training is recommended and is available on request from the authors.

Psychometric Evaluation

Norms
None reported.

Reliability
In a study by the scale's coauthors and their colleagues of children exposed to sniper attack, interrater reliability for this instrument was measured at .94 and interitem agreement by Cohen's kappa at .88. In a yet-unpublished study of children exposed to a tornado, interrater reliability was established at .97. In a study of Kuwait children following the Gulf War, internal consistency was established with a Cronbach's alpha = .78, and 16 of the 20 items were significantly correlated with the total score at $p < .01$.

Validity
None reported.

Advantages
This scale has been translated into Cambodian, Arabic, Croatian, Armenian, and Norwegian, and used extensively in research.

Limitations
Younger children may have difficulty with the 5-point scale and may require some minor rewording of terms. This scale does not assess for all *DSM* criteria. Also, there are three questions that are asked regarding the presence of healthy conditions rather than symptoms; the scoring of these questions does not always clearly indicate the extent of the symptom.

Primary Reference
Frederick et al. (1992).

Scale Availability
C. Frederick
760 Westwood Plaza
Los Angeles, CA 90024

Related References

Nader (1997).

General Comments and Recommendations for Practitioners and Researchers

There are two accompanying parent questionnaires. One is a more extensive clinical questionnaire used in a semistructured interview with parents eliciting premorbid personality and trauma-related information regarding their children. The other has been adapted to specific situations to match the CPTS–RI.

---

29. Child Sexual Behavior Inventory I (CSBI–I; Friedrich)

Development and Description of Assessment Method

According to the authors, the development of the CSBI–I was in response to the need for a measure to more comprehensively assess a much wider range of children's sexual behavior as well as to more objectively rate the frequency of these behaviors. An original 40-item measure was developed by adapting items from the Child Behavior Checklist insert (Achenbach, 1991) and including additional items related to sexual aggression, sexual inhibition, and gender behavior that had been elicited during interviews with mothers of sexually abused children. The initial 40-item measure was revised and various items were omitted, resulting in a 35-item measure that served as the basis for initial analysis.

The CSBI–I is a parent questionnaire that determines the presence and intensity of a wide variety of sexual behaviors in children related to self-stimulation, sexual aggression, gender-role behavior, and personal boundary violations and the child's response to sexual behavior, information, and materials in the home.

Target Population

Parents whose children (ages 2–12) may have been sexually abused.

Format

The current version of the CSBI–I is a self-report that contains 38 items that assess a wide range of sexual behaviors from normal behaviors to explicit sexual activity across nine dimensions: These include boundary issues, exhibitionism, gender role behavior, self-stimulation, sexual anxiety, sexual interest, sexual intrusiveness, sexual knowledge and voyeuristic behavior. Sample items include,

- "Undresses other people."
- "Shows sex parts to adults."
- "Dresses like opposite sex."
- "Masturbates with hand."
- "Asks to watch explicit TV."
- "Rubs body against people."
- "Tries to look at people undressing."

Administration and Scoring

The CSBI–I takes 10 to 13 minutes to administer and score. The primary (female) caregiver is asked how often she has observed each of the listed behaviors during the previous six months. Items are rated along a 4-point Likert scale related to frequency, from 0 = "never" to 4 = "at least 1×/week." The CSBI–I yields three clinical scales. The CSBI–I total scale indicates the overall level of sexual behavior the child exhibits, the developmentally related sexual behavior (DRSB) scale indicates sexual behaviors that can be considered normative for the child's age and gender, and the sexual abuse specific items (SASI) scale indicates sexual behaviors that can be viewed as relatively atypical for the child's age and gender (such behaviors raise the suspicion of possible sexual abuse). The CSBI–I test booklet contains a score summary box for recording raw scores and T-score conversions. There is a comprehensive manual available.

Psychometric Evaluation

Norms

Normative data for clinical and nonclinical samples are presented in Friedrich, Grambisch, Broughton, Kuiper, and Beilke (1991). In addition, T-score conversions for six age–gender groups are provided in the published CSBI–I manual.

Reliability

In a sample of 880 normal and 276 sexually abused children ages 2 to 12, reliability was established with an alpha coefficient of .82 for the normative sample and .93 for the clinical sample, indicating good internal consistency. Test–retest reliability after four weeks was calculated using 70 children from the normative sample and was .85. Three-month test–retest reliability for 24 sexually abused children was also significant at .47, although the majority of these children were in treatment and their behavior was expected to change.

Validity

Known-groups validity was shown in that the CSBI total score differed significantly between the sexually abused and nonabused groups, with sexually abused children showing a greater frequency of sexual behaviors than did the normative sample. Twenty-seven behaviors were found to differ significantly among the groups, with items endorsed significantly more often for the sexually abused than for the normative sample (Friedrich et al., 1991).

Advantages

The CSBI–I is the only available standardized measure designed to specifically assess sexual behavior problems that are a possible specific result of sexual abuse and to assess sexualized behavior in children. The CSBI–I has been translated into French, Spanish, German, and Swedish.

Limitations

The 276 clinical children in this sample are not a representative sample of the sexually abused population because many came from treatment settings. As a result, their behavior is likely more severe than that of sexually abused children not receiving treatments, which may limit generalizability of results. Also, there was a low frequency of non-Whites in the normative sample. Finally, there are no items related to sexual inhibition in the CSBI–I.

Primary Reference

Friedrich et al. (1991).

Scale Availability

Psychological Assessment Resources
800-899-8378

Or

William N. Friedrich
Section of Psychology

Mayo Clinic
Rochester, MN 55905

Related References

Friedrich et al. (1992).

General Comments and Recommendations for Practitioners and Researchers

The CSBI–I is directly related to specific features of sexual abuse, including severity, force, and number of perpetrators. Sexual abuse characteristics were shown to have a clear relationship to CSBI–I score. However, the authors noted that the CSBI–I should not be used in isolation as the primary indicator of sexual abuse.

---

30. Child's Reaction to Traumatic Events Scale (CRTES; Jones)

Development and Description of Assessment Method

A revision of the Impact of Events Scale for Children (Jones, 1992), this is a self-report measure that targets the intrusion and avoidance criteria of *DSM-III-R* and is designed to assess psychological responses to stressful life events.

Target Population

Children who were victims of a stressful life event.

Format

This assessment is a self-report in which there are 15 items containing 6 of the original items from the Adult Impact of Event Scale (Horowitz, Wilner, & Alvarez, 1979). Examples include

- *Avoidance Statements* (8 items): "I had a lot of feelings about it, but I didn't pay attention to them."
- *Intrusion Statements* (7 items): "I thought about it when I didn't mean to."

Administration and Scoring

The child is asked to "indicate how often the following comments were true for you in the past seven days." Administration is brief, 3 to 5 minutes. Scoring is on a 4-point frequency rating scale from 0 = "not at all" to 5 = "often," and scores are summed.

Psychometric Evaluation

Norms

A total score of less than 9 = low distress, 9 to 18 = moderate distress, and 19 and above = high distress.

Reliability

In a study following Hurricane Andrew (n = 213), Cronbach's alphas were .84 (intrusion), .72 (avoidance), and .85 (total). In a study of a high-crime, low-income area (n = 71), Cronbach's alphas were .68 (intrusion), .53 (avoidance), and .73 (total). Interrater reliability on a study of adolescents exposed to a fire with interviewers having undergone 51 hours of training averaged .91.

Validity

None reported.

Advantages

This is simply worded for children, brief, and easy to use.

Limitations

Asking if a child stays away from reminders rather than if he or she wishes to avoid them may almost always elicit a negative response. Thus, this may lead to apparent higher levels of intrusive reexperiencing symptoms and fewer avoidance symptoms.

Primary Reference

Jones (1994).

Scale Availability

Russell T. Jones
Virginia Polytechnic Institute and State University
Department of Psychology
Stress and Coping Lab

4102 Derring Hall
Blacksburg, VA 24060

Related References

Horowitz et al. (1979); Jones (1992); Nader (1997).

General Comments and Recommendations for Practitioners and Researchers

This is not a measure of PTSD because not all categories/criteria are included. Female children demonstrated the most intrusive symptoms. The authors recommend that interviewers are best trained by clinicians with a child psychopathology background.

31. Child Dissociative Predictor Scale (CDPS; Branscomb & Fagan)

Development and Description of Assessment Method

Because no standardized retrospective measure of dissociation proneness existed, the authors developed this retrospective measure of childhood abuse and dissociation proneness. Items were derived from the literature on predictors of childhood dissociation and multiple personality disorder. Particular questions on sexual trauma were adapted from research described by Finkelhor (1984). The authors described a pilot study in which inpatients were administered all items to determine their reactions.

The CDPS is a self-report scale with items relating to child abuse and childhood dissociative behaviors.

Target Population

Adults abused as children who are at risk for dissociation.

Format

The CDPS is a self-report consisting of 14 scored items and 3 research items within the two subscales of abuse and dissociation. The items on the dissociation subscale reflect the patient's report of subjective internal experiences of a dissociative nature. The items on the abuse subscale describe external aspects of the childhood environment and parental abuse or neglect.

Sample items from the abuse subscale include,

- "How often did your parents 'talk things out' instead of punishing you, so you understood why they were concerned?"
- "How often were you hurt (any kind of bruise, cut, or mark) when punished?"
- "Before you were 13, did anyone ever make you have sex or do anything sexual in a way that felt bad, shameful, or hurtful to you?"

Sample items from the dissociation subscale include,

- "Did you ever think or feel you had separate names?"
- "Did you have an imaginary playmate or friend?"
- "How often did you talk to yourself out loud?"

Administration and Scoring

The CDPS takes 5 minutes to administer and 5 minutes to score. Questions are answered on a yes or no basis for presence or absence or on a 5-point scale based on frequency. Ratings range from 0 = "never" to 4 = "very often/almost every day." The scale yields a total score as well as subscale scores on dissociation items and abuse items. Each subscale has seven items scored 0 to 4, yielding subscale scores from 0 to 28, and a total score range of 0 to 56.

Psychometric Evaluation

Norms

The CDPS was normed on 161 research participants consisting of 66 control participants, both men and women, and 95 psychiatric participants, consisting of men with various diagnoses and a mean age of 41.1 years. Mean for the normal group was 10.12 + 6.86. Means for various diagnostic subgroups of the psychiatric patients are presented in the primary reference and ranged from 11.85 ± 8.15 (subacute PTSD group) to 36.50 ± 6.37 (multiple personality disorder group).

Reliability

None reported.

Validity

The CDPS discriminated between psychiatric patients and normal controls and discriminated diagnostic subgroups of psychiatric patients from one another. In particular, the multiple personality disorder (MPD) group scored significantly higher than "normals" on all three scales and significantly higher than all other psychiatric groups on total score and dissociation. PTSD participants also scored significantly higher than "normals" on all three scales.

Advantages

The CDPS is easy to administer and score, is nonthreatening and easily understood by respondents, and can be used as a clinical screening tool. In addition, it offers a norm-referenced score on child abuse and dissociation.

Limitations

There are no reports related to temporal stability of the measure.

Primary Reference

Branscomb and Fagan (1992).

Scale Availability

In appendix of original article

Or

Louisa P. Branscomb
1834 Clairmont Rd.
Decatur, GA 30033

Related References

None available.

General Comments and Recommendations for Practitioners and Researchers

This is a promising quick screening tool that requires further psychometric development as well as comparisons to other retrospective child abuse measures. The scale allows for assessment of dissociative responses and child abuse on two separate dimensions, providing a basis to examine the relationship between these factors in various populations.

32. Childhood Trauma Questionnaire (CTQ; Bernstein et al.)

Development and Description of Assessment Method

The CTQ was developed to provide brief, reliable, and valid assessment of a broad range of traumatic experiences in childhood. Items were written by Bernstein and Fink based on an extensive review of the literature. CTQ factors were derived empirically with a principal-components analysis with a varimax rotation yielded four rotated orthogonal factors accounting for more than 50% of variance: physical and emotional abuse, emotional neglect, sexual abuse, and physical neglect.

This is a retrospective, self-report measure that assess experiences of abuse and neglect in childhood, including physical, emotional, and sexual abuse and physical and emotional neglect as well as related aspects of the child-rearing environment.

Target Population

Adolescents and adults who report childhood trauma. Items are readily understood by anyone with a high school background.

Format

The CTQ inventory contains 70 items arranged according to four factors: physical and emotional abuse, emotional neglect, and sexual abuse (6 items), and physical neglect (11 items). Sample items and subscales include,

- *Physical and Emotional Abuse* (23 items):
  - "When I was growing up, people in my family hit me so hard that it left me with bruises or marks."
  - "When I was growing up, the punishments I received seemed cruel."
  - "When I was growing up, someone in my family yelled and screamed at me."
  - "When I was growing up, people in my family said hurtful or insulting things to me."
- *Emotional Neglect* (16 items): Note that most of the items on this factor are reverse-scored). Examples include,
  - "When I was growing up, my family was a source of strength and support."

- "When I was growing up, someone in my family believed in me."
- "When I was growing up, I rarely got the love or attention that I needed."
- "When I was growing up, I felt that I was loved."
- *Sexual Abuse* (6 items). Examples include,
  - "When I was growing up, someone molested me."
  - "When I was growing up, someone tried to touch me in a sexual way or tried to make me touch them."
- *Physical Neglect* (11 items):
  - "When I was growing up, there was enough food in the house for everyone."
  - "When I was growing up I had to wear dirty clothes."
- *Validity Scale* (3 items), intended to detect a response bias toward minimization or denial of childhood maltreatment or dysfunction.

Administration and Scoring

The CTQ requires 10 to 15 minutes to administer and can be administered in individual or group sessions. Responses are quantified on a 5-point Likert-type scale according to the frequency with which experiences occurred, with 1 = "never true" and 5 = "very often true." Several items are reverse-scored. Item scores are summed to produce unweighted factor scores. A formula for computing the weighted total CTQ score, with each factor given equal weight, is provided.

Psychometric Evaluation

Norms

Drug- or alcohol-dependent patients ($N = 286$), ages 24 to 68 years (mean age 40.2), were given the CTQ as part of a larger test battery. Mean item sums (raw scores) for each factor were as follows:

Physical and emotional abuse:	48.3 ± 18.6
Emotional neglect:	35.7 ± 12.5
Sexual abuse:	8.8 ± 5.3
Physical neglect:	17.5 ± 6.2

Reliability

In the first study, the CTQ demonstrated a Cronbach's alpha of .95 for the total scale, with the following alphas for each factor: physical and emotional abuse (PEA) = .94, emotional neglect (EN) = .91, sexual abuse (SA) = .92, and physical neglect (PN) = .79, indicating high internal consistency. The CTQ also demonstrated good test–retest reliability for a subgroup of $n = 40$ over a 2- to 6-month interval (mean interval 3.6 months), with intraclass correlations for the total scale = .88 and intraclass correlations for each factor as follows: PEA = .82, EN = .83, SA = .81, and PN = .80.

Validity

Sixty-eight of the patients were also given a structured interview for child abuse and neglect, the Childhood Trauma Interview (CTI; Bernstein et al., 1994), also developed by the authors. The CTQ demonstrated convergence with the CTI, indicating that patients' reports of child abuse and neglect based on the CTQ were highly stable, both over time and across types of instruments. Discriminant validity was supported as the CTQ factors and total score were unrelated to measures of verbal intelligence and social desirability.

Advantages

The CTQ is an appropriate screening instrument for clinical and research purposes, especially in large-scale correlational studies. It is easy to administer, relatively noninvasive, less time-consuming, and offers continuous rather than dichotomous (present–absent) ratings of trauma and assessment of multiple content areas. Furthermore, reports of reliability and validity indicate that patient's reports of child abuse and neglect based on the CTQ are highly stable, both over time and across types of instruments.

Limitations

Validation was conducted using a bootstrap method, in that the authors demonstrated convergence with an unvalidated measure of their own construction (the CTI). The CTQ does not inquire about certain aspects of the trauma such as age of onset and relationship of perpetrator to victim that have been shown to have an impact on later psychopathology. Also, there is currently no normative data available other than results from the substance abuse sample.

Primary Reference

Bernstein et al. (1994).

Scale Availability

David Bernstein
Psychiatry Service
VA Medical Center
130 West Kingsbridge Rd.
Bronx, NY 10468

Related References

Fink et al. (1993).

General Comments and Recommendations for Practitioners and Researchers

Authors recommend embedding the CTQ in a battery of other self-report measures and using weighted scoring procedure because of intercorrelations between measures.

33. Children's Impact of Traumatic Events Scale B Revised (CITES–R; Wolfe, Wolfe, Gentile, & LaRose, Original; Wolfe & Gentile, Revised)

Development and Description of Assessment Method

The authors developed the original 54-item CITES as a standardized interview with objective response options as a method of assessing the impact of sexual abuse from the child's perspective. The original CITES was based on four conceptual models regarding the impact of child sexual abuse. These included the PTSD model (which adapted items from the Impact of Events Scale), the traumatogenic factors model, the eroticization model, and the revised learned helplessness theory/attributional theory model. A factor analysis was conducted that resulted in a 12-factor solution. Based on both the factor analysis and further refinement of theoretical positions regarding the impact of child sexual abuse, nine scales were formalized from the original CITES items, and a tenth scale was added to reflect the *DSM-III-R* (American Psychiatric Association, 1987) criteria for diagnosis of PTSD. Because the factor solution revealed some scales with relatively few items, new items were generated to increase the stability of those scales. As a result, the 78-

item CITES–R was developed, yielding 11 scales among the four dimensions.

The CITES–R uses self-report or an optional semistructured interview format to measure the impact of child sexual abuse by assessing children's sexual abuse-related perceptions and attributions across four dimensions, including PTSD, abuse attributions, social reactions, and eroticism.

Target Population

Children and adolescents ages 8 to 16 who have reported a sexual abuse experience. The report is worded for children with age-appropriate reading skills; when these are lacking, it may be administered as an interview.

Format

The CITES–R is a self-report that has 78 items that yield 11 scales in the following four dimensions:

- *Posttraumatic Stress:* Scales include,
  - *Intrusive Thoughts* (7 items): "I have dreams or nightmares about what happened."
  - *Avoidance* (8 items): "I try not to think about what happened."
  - *Hyperarousal* (6 items): "I often feel irritable for no reason at all."
  - *Sexual Anxiety* (5 items): "I wish there was no such thing as sex."
- *Abuse Attributions:* Scales include,
  - *Self-Blame/Guilt* (13 items): "This happened to me because I acted in a way that caused it to happen."
  - *Empowerment* (6 items): "If something like this happens again, I think I know what to do to stop it."
  - *Personal Vulnerability* (8 items): "Something like this might happen to me again."
  - *Dangerous World* (5 items): "People often take advantage of children."
- *Social Reactions:* Scales include,
  - *Social Support* (6 items): "Most people who know what happened are nice and understanding."
  - *Negative Reactions From Others* (9 items): "People who know what happened think bad thoughts about me."

• *Eroticization* (5 items): "I have more sexual feelings than my friends."

Administration and Scoring

The CITES–R takes between 20 to 40 minutes to administer and is recommended for use by professionals trained in the field of trauma. Although older children with good reading skills can complete the form in a self-report manner, a structured interview format is the preferred method for administration. The interviewer records information regarding the victimizing event, including the perpetrator, what happened and when and where the event took place. The following is then read to the child: "I am not going to ask you to describe what happened; instead, I want to know your thoughts and feelings about what happened. There are no right or wrong answers." Items are written as first person statements, with response options scored on a 3-point scale ranging from "very true" to "not true."

Psychometric Evaluation

Norms

The authors conducted an analysis using the 78-item CITES–R with 350 sexually abused children and adolescents, with an age range 8 to 16 (mean age = 11.72), with 71% of the sample female. Scale means are reported in the primary reference.

Reliability

Cronbach's alpha values were total scale = .89, PTSD = .88, social reactions = .87, attributions = .78, and eroticism = .57. The authors report individual subscale alpha coefficients from .68 (personal vulnerability) to .89 (negative reaction from others). The PTSD composite score had an alpha value of .91 and subscale alphas of .86 intrusive thoughts, .71 avoidance, .73 hyperarousal, .86 sexual anxiety, .81 social support, .84 self-blame/guilt, .83 empowerment, .82 dangerous world, and .85 eroticization.

Validity

Convergent and discriminant validity were demonstrated by significant associations between the CITES–R subscales and measures of related constructs, and a lack of association between the CITES–R subscales and measures assessing different constructs.

CITES–R taps all *DSM-IV* (American Psychiatric Association, 1994) criteria required for a PTSD diagnosis. Based on these criteria, 75% of the 350 sexually abused children and adolescents met PTSD diagnostic criteria, when "somewhat or sometimes true" served as the standard for symptom endorsement, supporting the CITES–R criterion validity. When "very true" served as the criteria for symptom endorsement, 32% met *DSM-IV* PTSD symptom criteria for diagnosis.

Advantages

The CITES–R measures the impact of sexual abuse as well as permits the examination of trauma factors, social reactions, and other subjective responses common to traumatized children in general. It is particularly useful for identifying areas of dysfunctional thoughts regarding the abuse. Further, the CITES–R is helpful as a clinical and research tool for quantifying PTSD. It is worded simply for children.

Limitations

Because the CITES–R was designed for assessment of sexually abused children, it does not include all of the symptoms required for PTSD diagnosis. In addition, because children are given the opportunity to endorse certain items several times over (i.e., intrusive thoughts), this gives the item more weight than other items and must be taken into account when interpreting results. Also, although significant convergent and discriminant validity was found, significant method variance and a substantial level of error variance was also revealed. Method variance was evidenced by relatively high correlations among scores, reflecting different traits assessed by the same method (e.g., CITES–R PTSD and social reactions scores).

Primary Reference

Wolfe, Gentile, Michienzi, Sas, and Wolfe (1991).

Scale Availability

Vicky Veitch Wolfe
Department of Psychology
Children's Hospital of Western Ontario
800 Commissioners Rd. East
London, Ontario, Canada N6A 4G5
(519) 685-8144

Related References

Wolfe and Birt (1997).

General Comments and Recommendations for Practitioners and Researchers

The CITES–AF (altered form) has been developed and is appropriate for nonsexually abused children. Children respond to questions regarding an event they report as having been stressful.

The CITES–FVF (Family Violence Form) is another alternative in which the wording of each item is changed to reflect the child witness experience rather than the child sexual abuse experience.

For a fee of $20, a computer-scoring diskette is available. The score program lists the items for the 10 scales along with the child's responses, the raw score for the scale, and a standard score as compared to the author's sample of sexually abused children. (However, as noted by the author, several of the scales have undergone revision and thus the standard scores are subject to change with additional psychometric evaluations).

---

34. Conflicts in Relationships Questionnaire (CIRQ; Wolfe, Reitzel-Jaffe, Gough, & Werkele)

Development and Description of Assessment Method

The CIRQ was developed specifically to assess the overt and covert forms of violence and abuse both expressed and experienced by youth in their daily relationships with the same and opposite sex, and constructed to reflect aspects of physical and sexual coercion, psychological abuse, and positive communication strategies. Nine items were adapted from the Conflict Tactics Scale (Straus, 1979), and the remaining items were developed based on the literature on emotional abuse and sexual assault. Factor analysis was used to determine the three scales. Three reliable factors emerged for the 38 items making up Part A and two reliable factors emerged for Part B.

The CIRQ is a measure of positive and negative conflict resolution–communication patterns and verbal and physical violence and abuse in reference to social dating situations. It measures the frequency of physically, sexually, and emotionally abusive and nonabusive behaviors committed by or experienced by the respondent.

Target Population

Adolescents involved in dating relationships.

Format

The CIRQ is a 76-item self-report in which there are identical inventories for males and females, except for pronoun changes and the elimination of two items of sexual coercion that would not apply to females. To separate victimization from offending behaviors, items are repeated in two sections: Part A reflects behaviors shown toward a dating partner (i.e., offending behaviors, such as "did something to make her feel jealous"), and Part B reflects behaviors a dating partner has shown toward the respondent—in other words, victimization experiences. Part A contains three subscales with items reflecting behaviors the respondent has shown toward a dating partner:

- *Abuse/Coercion* (13 items, comprising primarily items of physical and sexual force and threats to harm physically). Examples include,
  - "Pushed, shoved, or shook partner."
  - "Slapped or pulled partner's hair."
- *Negative Communication* (15 items comprising primarily items of verbal behaviors indicative of insults, jealousy, anger, and blame, as well as physical behaviors intended to intimidate—e.g. hit, kicked, or punched something—or destroy something the partner valued). Examples include,
  - "Gave partner the 'silent treatment' or 'cold shoulder.'"
  - "Said partner was being selfish."
- *Positive Communication* (10 items reflecting problem-solving attempts as well as statements intended to express feelings or beliefs). Examples include,
  - "Told partner how upset I was."
  - "Discussed the issue calmly."

Part B contains two subscales with items reflecting behaviors a dating partner has shown toward the respondent:

- *Abuse/Blame* (28 items, essentially an aggregate of the two negative scales in Part A: abuse–coercion and negative communication). Examples include,
  - "Threw something at me."
  - "Gave in, but brought it up later."

- *Positive Communication* (10 items identical to Part A except for one item—"Left the room to cool down."). Examples include,
  - "Left the room to cool down."
  - "Agreed that I was partly right."

Administration and Scoring

The CIRQ measures the frequency of physically, sexually, and emotionally abusive and nonabusive behaviors experienced by the respondent. It is scored on a 4-point scale ranging from 0 = "never" to 3 = "often" that best describes how frequently each of the items has happened over the past six months during a conflict or argument with a member of the opposite sex.

Psychometric Evaluation

Norms

Norms were based on a school-based sample of (n = 132) self-reported maltreated and (n = 227) self-reported nonmaltreated 15-year-olds. The norms for each scale for maltreated and nonmaltreated youth are reported in the primary reference.

Reliability

Alpha scores were .80 for abuse–coercion, .79 for positive communication, and .79 for negative communication in Part A and .90 abuse/blame and .84 positive communication in Part B.

Validity

Principal component analysis established factor validity. Three reliable factors emerged for the 38 items that made up Part A and two reliable factors emerged for Part B. The pattern of endorsed items relating to victim experiences in Part B fits easily into two dimensions of negative and positive conflict experiences. Item-loading on each of these five factors were combined in an additive fashion to form reliable subscales of conflict in relationships.

Maltreated youths reported use of significantly more abuse–coercion and negative communications strategies during a conflict with a partner than the nonmaltreated comparisons and reported significantly more positive communication methods as well. Across groups girls are significantly more likely than boys to report using forms of negative communication during a conflict. Youths in the maltreated group also reported that their partners engaged in significantly more abuse/blame behaviors toward them than their nonmaltreated counterparts.

Advantages

The CIRQ is one of the few measures available assessing abusive behavior in teenage dating relationships.

Limitations

The scale development study had several shortcomings, including that the high school sample used was nonrandom and relatively homogeneous, half the males declined to participate, and respondents were not asked to distinguish between a dating partner and an opposite-sex friend. This may limit the generalizability of the norms reported.

Primary Reference

Wolfe, Werkele, Reitzel-Jaffe, and Lefebvre (1998).

Scale Availability

David Wolfe
Department of Psychology
The University of Western Ontario
London, Western Ontario, Canada N6A 5C2

Related References

Wolfe and McEachran (1997).

General Comments and Recommendations for Practitioners and Researchers

Similar to the Conflict Tactics Scale (Straus, 1979), the CIRQ assesses specific behavioral exemplars of abuse in relationships. The CIRQ focuses specifically on teenage dating relationships and includes behaviors engaged in by the respondent as well as those engaged in by the respondent's partner.

35. Emotional and Physical Abuse Questionnaire (EPAB; Carlin)

Development and Description of Assessment Method

The EPAB is an instrument that describes childhood experiences of discipline and abuse.

A physical abuse subscale (PAB) was drawn from 14 EPAB items. If research participants endorsed an occurrence of any of nine major assault items (e.g., broken bones, teeth knocked out, being purposefully burned) or endorsed five other items as occurring with a frequency of three or greater (pinched, hit with a board, stick, or wire, or being shaken), they are characterized as objectively abused. Thus, participants' responses to the questionnaire allow them to be classified as physically abused on the basis of objective criteria, or on the basis of their own subjective characterization.

Target Population

Adults 18 years of age and older who were or may have been physically or emotionally abused.

Format

This assessment consists of a self-report containing 32 items that describe childhood experiences of discipline and abuse. An additional item asks participants to characterize themselves as physically abused or not. Sample items include broken bones, teeth knocked out, purposefully burned, pinched, hit with a board, stick, or wire, or being shaken.

Administration and Scoring

Participants respond on a 6-point Likert-type scale of frequency of occurrence ranging from "never" to "very frequently." Total EPAB and PAB scores are available as the sum of the frequency of occurrence of discipline and abuse items. Participants' responses to the questionnaire allow them to be classified as physically abused on the basis of objective criteria or on the basis of their own subjective characterization.

Psychometric Evaluation

Norms

In a study of 280 women (mean age = 35.92, range 18 to 90, 88% Caucasian) attending a family medicine clinic, 28.2% met objective criteria for being considered physically abused as a child, although only 11.4% considered themselves as such. Only 1% of the sample considered themselves abused but endorsed no PAB items. Means and standard deviations on the PAB were 23.97 ± 14.15 for n = 30 women who were objectively defined as abused and who defined themselves as such and 61.46 ± 25.15 on the EPAB for n = 28 women who were objectively defined as abused and who defined themselves as such. Means and standard deviations were 10.04 ± 5.37 on the PAB and 26.43 ± 13.39 for the EPAB for n = 49 women who were objectively defined as abused but did not characterize themselves as such. Finally, means and standard deviations were 2.44 ± 1.92 on the PAB and 7.47 ± 7.09 on the EPAB for n = 192 and n = 188 women, respectively, who did not meet criteria for abuse and also denied being abused.

Reliability

The EPAB has demonstrated good internal consistency reliability, with a Cronbach's alpha of .86.

Validity

Scores on the EPAB and PAB discriminated between three groups of women: those who were objectively defined as abused and who defined themselves as such scored higher than those who were objectively defined as abused but did not characterize themselves as such, who in turn scored higher that those who did not meet criteria for abuse and also denied being abused.

Furthermore, those who were objectively defined as abused and who defined themselves as such were likely to have experienced a major depression (83%), whereas an intermediate prevalence of depression was found for those who were objectively defined as abused but did not characterize themselves as such (56%). Those who did not meet criteria for abuse and also denied being abused experienced the lowest rate of lifetime depression (35%). In addition, those who were objectively defined as abused and who defined themselves as such were also more likely to have sought psychotherapy, to have received psychoactive medication, to have been hospitalized for depression, and to have made a suicide attempt than those who did not meet criteria for abuse and also denied being abused. Those who were objectively defined as abused but did not characterize themselves as such were intermediate in the occurrence of these correlates of psychopathology. Intentional, nonsuicidal self-hurt was more prevalent for those who were objectively defined as abused but did not characterize themselves as such.

Advantages

The EPAB was normed on an older, diverse, nonclinical sample.

Limitations

No men were used in the research sample, thus limiting generalizability of results.

Primary Reference

Carlin et al. (1994).

Scale Availability

Albert Carlin
Department of Psychiatry and Behavioral Sciences
XD-45
University of Washington
Seattle, WA 98195

Related References

None available.

General Comments and Recommendations for Practitioners and Researchers

The EPAB allows respondents to be classified as abused based either on objective criteria or on their subjective perceptions. The scale has good normative data and solid psychometric characteristics.

---

36. Exposure to Abuse and Supportive Environments—Parenting Inventory (EASE–PI; Nicholas & Bieber)

Development and Description of Assessment Method

According to the authors, the EASE–PI was developed in response to an awareness of the frequency of child abuse and the lack of a single instrument to assess the extent of exposure to both the abusive and supportive environments provided by parents. The rationale for development was to assess important parts of the parent–child environment, including behaviors deemed to be abusive but that may not have been experienced as abuse and to explore the effects of less severe parental behaviors on adult functioning. Item development was based on a rational/intuitive approach stemming from literature reviews, clinical experience, and knowledge of family abuse. A large number of items that represented examples of abusive or negative and supportive or positive parenting behaviors were generated by a research group. One-hundred-thirty negative parenting items and 64 positive parenting items were selected to be used in scale development based on face validity. Data from 271 research participants and then 518 participants were collected, and initial and follow-up factor analysis produced seven factors (the six listed previously along with a seventh factor: overprotectiveness). To include items that varied in degree of abusiveness or supportiveness, the 110 items were administered to 292 participants with an 11-point scale (0 = "not being abusive or supportive at all" to 10 = "being extremely abusive"). Items for the final inventory were then selected based on three considerations: Strength of relationship of the item with one or more of the factors (the item had to have a factor loading of .50 or greater), a test–retest reliability coefficient higher than .70, and the degree of abusiveness–supportiveness of the item had to be 6.5 or greater. Several items and the overprotectiveness scale as a whole were eliminated.

The EASE–PI is a self-report retrospective inventory that assesses how both mother and father treated the respondent, and includes both abusive and supportive parental behaviors.

Target Population

Young adults.

Format

The EASE–PI consists of 70 items divided into six scales, three scales (42 items) reflecting abusive behaviors and three scales (28 items) reflecting supportive behaviors.

The Abusive/Negative subscales include,

- *Emotional Abusiveness* (EA; 19 items). Sample items include,
  - "Made you want revenge."
  - "Said she/he hated you."
  - "Was cold or rejecting."
- *Physical Abusiveness* (PA; 13 items). Sample items include,
  - "Pulled your hair."
  - "Beat you."

- "Threatened to kill you."
- *Sexual Abusiveness* (SA; 10 items). Sample items include,
  - "Touched you sexually."
  - "Hugged or held you in a way that seemed sexual."
  - "Belittled or made fun of your masculinity or femininity."

The Supportive/Positive subscales include,

- *Love/Support* (L/S; 16 items). Sample items include,
  - "Believed in you."
  - "Was physically affectionate."
  - "Respected your feelings."
- *Promotion of Independence* (I; 6 items). Examples include,
  - "Let you feel you were in control of your own life."
  - "Allowed you to explore your own feelings."
- *Positive Modeling/Fairness* (M/F; 6 items). Examples include,
  - "Provided a good example."
  - "Taught you good values."

Administration and Scoring

Each item is rated on Likert scale, reflecting frequency ranging from 0 = "never" to 4 = "very often." Respondents are asked to rate the frequency of each item for mother and father separately.

Psychometric Evaluation

Norms

To give the scores a common context, each scale was standardized to have a minimum score of 0 and a maximum score of 100. Mean scores and standard deviations are as follows: EA mother = 13.02 + 16.95, EA father = 15.61 + 17.55, PA mother = 6.02 + 9.34, PA father = 6.22 + 9.67, SA mother = 2.54 + 5.18, SA father = 4.66 + 12.20, L/S mother = 77.17 + 20.47, L/S father = 67.19 + 23.47, I mother = 72.24 + 19.73, I father = 69.77 + 22.77, F/M mother = 80.49 + 17.79, F/M father = 75.21 + 22.03.

Reliability

Mean test–retest reliability coefficients for 216 participants tested 10 weeks apart were high: EA = .84, PA = .92, SA = .96, O = .75, L/S = .83, I = .79, and M/F = .87. Confirmatory factor analysis using a varimax rotation produced seven factors that were present regardless of the gender of the parent or the respondent, indicating internal consistency.

Validity

Parts of other instruments were considered conceptually similar to scales on the EASE–PI. In a validation study of 51 college students, the PA and EA scales had positive correlations with the Conflicts Tactics Scale (Straus, 1979), Family Environment Questionnaire (Briere & Runtz, 1988), and Parent–Child Relations Questionnaire (Roe & Siegelman, 1963), and L/S had a positive correlations with the Parent–Child Relations Questionnaire and the Parental Bonding Instrument (Parker et al., 1979), and, as expected, the I scale correlated negatively with the Parental Bonding Instrument, providing evidence for convergent validity.

Advantages

The EASE–PI considers both paternal and maternal treatment, includes positive parenting behaviors, is sensitive to subtleties, and measures not only highly abusive behaviors but behaviors not on the extreme end of the continuum.

Limitations

The EASE–PI was developed using college students who were primarily White, young adults with middle-class backgrounds. It has not been tested on abuse victims and clinical samples.

Primary Reference

Nicholas and Bieber (1997).

Scale Availability

Karen B. Nicholas
University of Wyoming
Department of Psychology
Box 3415
University Station
Laramie, WY 82071

Related References

Hoglund and Nicholas (1995).

General Comments and Recommendations for Practitioners and Researchers

The EASE–PI assesses both different types of abusive parenting behaviors and supportive behaviors that may mitigate potentially deleterious outcomes. The scale addresses perceptions of both parents by sons and daughters.

---

37. Family Environment Questionnaire (FEQ; Briere & Runtz)

Development and Description of Assessment Method

This is a self-report measure containing two subscales (psychological maltreatment and physical maltreatment) designed to assess adult retrospective reports of family maltreatment experiences. Scales were created based on a rational–intuitive approach. The authors indicate that a broader criterion for recollection of psychological maltreatment (average year) was based on the assumption that this form of abuse is more pervasive and less event-related and thus might be harder to specify in terms of a discrete time interval.

Target Population

Adults who were physically or psychologically abused as children.

Format

This 12-item self-report inventory includes,

- *Psychological Maltreatment Subscale* (PSY; 7 items that are primarily verbal in nature). Sample items include,
  - "Yell at you."
  - "Insult you."
  - "Try to make you feel guilty."
- *Physical Maltreatment Subscale* (PHY; 5 items that are primarily nonverbal parental behaviors associated with physical pain or fear of injury. Sample items include,
  - "Slap you."
  - "Punch you."
  - "Kick you."

Administration and Scoring

Respondents are asked to report on the "worst year" for physical abuse and the "average year" for psychological abuse occurring on or before age 14. Each of the 12 items are scored separately for maternal and paternal behaviors on a 6-point Likert scale corresponding to frequency. Scores range from 0 = "never" to 3 = "3 to 5 times per year" to 5 = "more than 20 times per year."

Psychometric Evaluation

Norms
None reported.

Reliability
In a study on 251 female undergraduates, acceptable internal consistency was achieved with alphas of .87 on the psychological maltreatment scale (PSY) for both mother and father, .78 on the physical maltreatment scale (PHY) for mother, and .75 PHY for father.

Validity
Known-groups validity participants with above median scores on PSYm, PSYf, and PHYm had (on average) scores that matched or exceeded a clinical group for depression, interpersonal sensitivity, and obsession–compulsion, whereas their below-median peers did not.

General parental abusiveness correlated highly with all subscales of Hopkins Symptom Checklist and history of suicidal ideation and dissociation checklist, evidencing convergent validity.

Multivariate analysis, multiple regression analysis, and the second canonical variate suggest that certain types of maltreatment are uniquely associated with later psychological difficulties, demonstrating predictive validity.

Advantages
The FEQ is a short and easy to complete instrument. Because respondent rates both mother and father, instrument helps to discriminate between family relationships.

Limitations
The FEQ was not tested on a clinical population. The focus on frequencies during an "average" or "worst year" may cause the respondent some confusion. Authors need to determine test–retest reliability.

Primary Reference

Briere and Runtz (1988).

Scale Availability

Available in original article

Or

John Briere
Assistant Professor of Psychiatry (Psychology)
LAC-USC Medical Center
1934 Hospital Place
Los Angeles, CA 90033

Related References

None available.

General Comments and Recommendations for Practitioners and Researchers

This has not yet been examined in persons from maltreating families, so generalizability is currently limited. Focus is simply on an estimation of frequency, which does not allow for conclusions about severity or impact.

---

38. Feelings and Emotions Experienced During Sexual Abuse (FEEDSA; Wolfe & Birt)

Development and Description of Assessment Method

The FEEDSA was developed to assess children's emotional reactions to their sexual abuse experience. The original format had 78 items. Factor analysis on data from 62 abused girls revealed the two subscales. Items reflecting positive reactions to the abuse were rarely endorsed and as such were deleted from the item pool, resulting in the present 54-item measure.

The FEEDSA assesses children's emotional reactions to their sexual abuse experience.

Target Population

Children who were sexually abused.

Format

The FEEDSA inventory consists of 54 items categorized into the two subscales—trauma (48 items) and dissociation (6 items)—that reflect negative emotions (e.g., anger, terror), perceptions that the event was uncontrollable (e.g., "Like I had no control," "Like I had to do it"), and dissociation during the event (e.g., "Like I disappeared," "Like I left my body").

Administration and Scoring

Children rate each of the items on a 3-point Likert rating scale ranging from 0 = "none" to 3 = "a lot." Instructions state, "I will read you each item and you can tell me whether or not you had that feeling 'none,' 'some,' or 'a lot.' Remember, tell about the feelings you had during the sexual abuse."

Psychometric Evaluation

Norms
None reported.

Reliability
The trauma subscale had an alpha of .95 and the dissociation subscale had an alpha of .80.

Validity
Birt et al. (1995) found that high FEEDSA trauma scores predicted reports of dissociation during abusive experiences.

Advantages
Specific focus on emotional experiences helps to support the PTSD criteria in *DSM-IV* (American Psychiatric Association, 1994) of intense feelings during the traumatic event.

Limitations
Psychometric evaluation is limited; in particular temporal stability, convergent, and discriminant validity needs to be established.

Primary Reference

Wolfe and Birt (1993).

Scale Availability

V. V. Wolfe
Department of Psychology
Children's Hospital of Western Ontario
800 Commissioners Rd. East
London, Ontario, Canada 5C2N6A

Related References

Birt and Wolfe (1995); Wolfe and Birt (1997).

General Comments and Recommendations for Practitioners and Researchers

The FEEDSA is a promising new measure of the emotions experienced by children during sexual abuse trauma. The instrument needs to be compared with other assessments of children's emotional experience.

---

39. History of Victimization Form (HVF; Wolfe, Wolfe, Gentile, & Bourdeau)

Development and Description of Assessment Method

The HVF obtains detailed information from social workers or therapists regarding all forms of maltreatment, allowing for the objective assessment of the severity of various forms of maltreatment.

The sexual abuse subscale has undergone two factor analyses, each yielding two factors. Factor 1, the severity of abuse, includes the type of sexual acts, force or coercion, and number of perpetrators. Factor 2, the course of abuse, includes duration, frequency, and relationship to perpetrator.

Target Population

Children who were or possibly were actually maltreated.

Format

The HVF has five scales, including sexual abuse, physical abuse, neglect, exposure to family violence and psychological maltreatment. Each scale contains a Gutman-like checklist of several abusive behaviors, listed in order of escalating severity. Each scale taps issues related to the severity of maltreatment and its physical sequelae. In addition to these content items, each of the five scales also contains items concerning the relationship of the child to the perpetrator; the emotional closeness between the child and the perpetrator; and the time frame, frequency, and duration of the abuse. The sexual abuse scale also includes seven questions about the type and extent of force or coercion used to gain compliance. The respondent indicates if abuse is suspected (S) or confirmed (C), when it occurred, and when it was reported.

- *Sexual Abuse Subsection* (14 items, including types of sexual abuse and resulting physical symptoms from abuse and how (by/to whom) the abuse was discovered and disclosed). Examples include,
  - "Invitation for child to engage in sexual behavior."
  - "Open-mouthed kissing."
  - "Child instructed to have oral contact with adult's genitals."
- *Degree of Coercion Regarding Compliance and/or Secrecy* (7 items). Examples include,
  - "Abuse of authority."
  - "Threats of physical coercion/harm."
  - "Blackmail."
  - "Rewards/privileges."
- *Physical Abuse Subsection* (7 items, including types of physical abuse and physical symptoms as a result of physical abuse. There is also a description of nature of abuse—in other words, excessive use of physical punishment—and how—by/to whom—the abuse was discovered and disclosed). Examples include,
  - "Excessive shaking."
  - "Pinched or bit."
  - "Burned."
- *Neglectful Subsection* (8 items, including types of neglect, health/physical problems as a result of neglect, and how—by/to whom—neglect was discovered or disclosed). Examples include,
  - "Failed to dress child appropriately."
  - "Improper medical attention."
  - "Failed to protect from abusive adult."

- *Family Violence Witnessed by Child Subsection* (items taken from CTS, Straus, 1979; 9 items, including type of family violence witnessed and how—by/to whom—it was discovered or disclosed). Examples include,
  - "Threw, smashed, hit, or kicked something."
  - "Slapped the other one [other family member]."
  - "Used a gun or knife."
- *Psychological Abuse Subsection* (20 items, including types of psychological abuse and how—by/to whom—it was discovered or disclosed). Examples include,
  - "Emotionally rejecting."
  - "Excessively critical."
  - "Excessive physical isolation of child from others."
  - "Uses humiliating forms of punishment."

Administration and Scoring

Of the five possible sections, only the sections of the scale appropriate to the type of maltreatment the child received are completed. Items are rated on a 5-point Likert scale.

Psychometric Evaluation

Norms
None reported.

Reliability
None reported.

Validity
Weights assigned to different types of sexual abuse as measured by the HVF correspondent with global ratings of abuse severity made by the children's social workers.

Advantages
The extremely detailed format will help organize information typically obtained by support personnel or caseworkers.

Limitations
There is limited psychometric data available. Interrater reliability would be crucial in determining the soundness of this assessment tool.

Primary Reference

Wolfe, Gentile, and Bourdeau (1987).

Scale Availability

V. V. Wolfe
Department of Psychology
Children's Hospital of Western Ontario
800 Commissioners Rd. East
London, Ontario, Canada 5C2N6A

Related References

Wolfe and Birt (1997).

General Comments and Recommendations for Practitioners and Researchers

The HVF is an extremely comprehensive measure assessing forms of child maltreatment. It is a clinician-friendly instrument designed to be completed by social workers–therapists, and provides a way for clinicians to organize their data and ensure a thorough assessment.

---

40. Multidimensional Neglect Scale (MNS; Straus, Kinard, & Williams)

Development and Description of Assessment Method

The authors generated an initial pool of 46 items based on their knowledge and experiences in the field of child abuse and neglect. Previously developed measures of child maltreatment were then consulted and an additional 17 items were added, resulting in a total of 63 items. Then 10 items were selected to represent each of the four domains of child neglect, resulting in a preliminary instrument of 40 items. This scale was then administered to a sample ($N = 359$) male and female college students (96% of which were White and 72% of which were from two-parent families). Item analyses resulted in elimination of half of the items least highly correlated with the total scores of each of the subscales, and factor analyses supported the high loadings of each item on the four subscales.

The MNS is a self-report inventory designed to measure adolescent and adult recall of child neglect in four domains: physical needs, emotional needs, cognitive needs, and supervisory needs. Although scores on the MNS may not indicate conditions that meet a legal definition of neglect, the device may be useful as a clinical screening of developmental risk for children.

Target Population

Adolescents.

Format

The MNS can be used in either interview or questionnaire format. The assessment measure contains 20 items, with five items representing each of the following domains of neglect:

- *Physical needs,* such as food, clothing, shelter or medical care. Sample items include,
  - "Did not keep me clean."
  - "Did not give me enough to eat."
- *Emotional needs,* such as affection, companionship, and support. Sample items include,
  - "Did not praise me."
  - "Did not do things with me just for fun."
- *Supervision needs,* such as limit-setting, attending to misbehavior, knowing a child's whereabouts and friends. Sample items include,
  - "Did not make sure I went to school."
  - "Were not interested in the kind of friends I had."
- *Cognitive needs,* such as being played with or read to and assisting with homework. Sample items include,
  - "Did not help me do my best."
  - "Did not read books to me."

Administration and Scoring

The respondent rates each item on a Likert-type scale ranging from 1 = "strongly agree" to 4 = "strongly disagree" that each statement is a description of either or both of his or her parents. Instructions indicate that "strongly disagree" is to be used if the item does not describe them at all. Four items, one on each subscale, are reverse-scored. Total scores can range from 20 to 80.

Psychometric Evaluation

Norms

Data from a sample of 350 college students indicate that frequency distributions of items are extremely skewed. Means and percentile norms reported in Straus, Kinard, et al. (1995) indicate greater emotional and cognitive neglect than physical or supervisory neglect, although the authors caution that the norms should be regarded with caution.

Reliability

For the college student sample ($N = 359$), alpha coefficients were .93 for the total MNS score and ranged from 180 (physical needs) to .89 (emotional needs) for the subscales. Test–retest reliability was not reported.

Alpha coefficients were also computed on two short forms of the MNS. The 8-item version of Form A (based on selections of two items in each subscale, with the highest item total correlation) and a 4-item version (based on the item in each subscale with the highest item-total correlation) resulted in alpha coefficients of .89 and .81, respectively.

Validity

Construct validity was examined via correlations between the MNS scale and demographic variables associated with a history of neglect. Significant correlations were found with variables of parental income and education, lower levels of social integration, and greater amount of parent violence between the parents as determined by the Conflict Tactics Scale (Straus, 1979).

Advantages

Good preliminary evidence for the psychometric properties of this brief inventory has been obtained. Alternative short forms seem to be as reliable and valid as the 20-item measure, thus making the MNS a practical instrument to use in research.

Limitations

Use of the college sample to develop the device limits its use because university students rarely come from impoverished families. In addition, the retrospective approach has limitations based on the recall of information and is not corroborated by any home observation data.

Primary Reference

Straus, Kinard, and Williams (1995).

Scale Availability

Murry A. Strauss
Family Research Laboratory
University of New Hampshire
Durham, NH 03824
murray.straus@unh.edu

Related References

None available.

General Comments and Recommendations for Practitioners and Researchers

Research on child neglect has been sorely limited by the lack of psychometrically sound assessment tools. The authors report on current efforts to develop parallel versions for use with parents and children to describe current levels of neglect and for use by clinicians as a means of standardizing and quantifying the results of their investigation of a case. In addition, instruction can be altered to examine individual parents or other caregivers with whom the respondent lived with the longest. The child version under development will be a picture version designed to be administered as an interview with children as young as 6.

---

41. Negative Appraisals of Sexual Abuse Scale (NASAS; Spaccarelli)

Development and Description of Assessment Method

The NASAS is a self-report measure that assesses victim's negative cognitive appraisals of threat, harm, or loss associated with sexual victimization to predict children's adjustment to sexual abuse.

The authors report using a rational intuitive method to generate items relevant to children's negative appraisals of sexual abuse and mental health outcomes.

Target Population

Children and adolescents who were victims of sexual abuse.

Format

The NASAS consists of rating scales in which there are 56 items categorized into eight subscales of different types of negative appraisals. Each item asks victims whether he or she had negative feelings or thoughts about what happened with the perpetrator. The following are subscales and sample items.

- *Physical Pain/Damage* (7 items): "You might get sick or catch a disease."
- *Negative Self-Evaluation: Global* (9 items): "You did something bad or wrong."
- *Negative Self-Evaluation: Sexuality* (8 items): "You were too sexy."
- *Negative Evaluation by Others* (5 items): "You might get yelled at or punished."
- *Loss of Desired Resources* (6 items): "You didn't get to do things you wanted."
- *Harm to Relationships/Security* (8 items): "Someone didn't love you anymore."
- *Harm to Others* (4 items): "Someone you care about got hurt."
- *Criticism of Others* (9 items): "Someone you care about was not trustworthy."

Administration and Scoring

Directions ask the victim to tell some of his or her feelings and thoughts about what happened with the person who involved them in sexual behaviors. Each item begins, "In relation to what happened with that person, did it make you think or feel that . . . ." The response format is on a 4-point Likert scale, from 1 = "not at all" to 4 = "a lot." Results are coded in the eight subscale scores and a total score for negative appraisals by summing up individual item scores.

Psychometric Evaluation

Norms

The authors report norms on a sample of 48 girls ages 11 to 18 (mean age = 14) who were sexually abused and referred for therapy related to sexual victimization; these norms are reported in the primary reference.

Reliability

Internal consistency reliability for the total scale score was .96. Internal consistency was also demonstrated with subscale alpha levels ranging from .78 for the negative self-evaluation/sexuality subscale to .90 for the negative self-evaluation/global and the harm to relationships subscales.

Validity

Convergent validity was demonstrated as total negative appraisals scores significantly correlated with therapist overall ratings of abuse stress. In addition, a significant correlation between the total negative appraisal score and number of stressful events reported on the C–SARS (Spaccarelli, 1995) and a significant correlation between total negative appraisals and the number of types of sexual abuse reported on the Abusive Sexual Exposure Scale (Spaccarelli, 1993) was found. Concurrent validity was also demonstrated because negative appraisals were significantly related to symptoms of depression and anxiety, and these effects were consistent across both parent reports of child behaviors and victim self-report measures, in addition to being significantly related to victim reports of posttraumatic stress and to parent reports of child sexual concerns (CBCL; Achenbach, 1991).

Advantages

This inventory helps to elicit the cognitive reactions that may be linked to particular internalizing symptomatology.

Limitations

Numerous symptomatology measures and subscales were examined in the validity study, resulting in an elevation in the risk for Type 1 errors. Also, the population studied suffered from severe abuse and multiple perpetrators, and participants were not grouped by developmental level, possibly limiting generalizability of results.

Primary Reference

Spaccarelli (1995).

Scale Availability

Steve Spaccarelli
Institute for Juvenile Research
Department of Psychiatry

University of Illinois at Chicago
907 South Wolcott Ave.
Chicago, IL 60612

Related References

Spaccarelli and Fuchs (1997); Spaccarelli and Kim (1995).

General Comments and Recommendations for Practitioners and Researchers

This focus on the specific reaction of negative appraisal will certainly help clinicians assess this cognitive aspect and may highlight particular cognitive interventions for more effective treatment planning.

42. Parent Perception Inventory (PPI; Hazzard, Christensen, & Margolin)

Development and Description of Assessment Method

The PPI is a measure of children's perceptions of positive and negative parental behavior.

The PPI was originally developed for evaluating behavioral family treatment, specifically for the assessment of children's perceptions of parent behaviors.

Target Population

Children 6 to 12 years old. (The PPI has been used with children from physically abusive families, families with a history of child behavior problems, and nondistressed families.)

Format

The PPI is composed of 18 parent behavior items. Half of the items are positive behaviors. They include positive reinforcement, comfort, talk time, involvement in decision making, time together, positive evaluation, allowing independence, assistance, and nonverbal affection. Half of the items reflect negative, although not necessarily inappropriate, parenting behaviors. They include privilege removal, criticism, commands, physical punishment, yelling, threatening, time-outs, nagging, and ignoring. Each item is answered separately for mother and father, yielding four subscales—mother positive, mother negative, father positive, and father negative—each with nine items. Sample items from subscales include,

- "How often does your mother (or father) . . . ."
- *Comfort Subscale:* "Talk to you when you feel bad and help you to feel better, help you with your problems, comfort you."
- *Yelling Subscale:* "Get mad at you, yell at you, holler at you, scream at you."
- *Allowing Independence Subscale:* "Let you do what other kids your age do, let you do things on your own."
- *Nagging Subscale:* "Nag you, tell you what to do over and over again, keep after you to do things."
- *Nonverbal Affection Subscale:* "Hug you, kiss you, tickle you, smile at you."
- *Ignoring Subscale:* "Ignore you, not pay attention to you, not talk to you or look at you."

Administration and Scoring

The inventory is administered to the child by reading descriptions and examples of each behavior class until the child understands the concept. For example, "How often does your mother (father) take away things when you misbehave (like not letting you watch TV or ride your bike or stay up late or eat dessert)?" The child responds by circling a phrase on a 5-point scale ranging from 0 = "never" to 4 = "a lot," which is enhanced by a visual aid of a progressively filled thermometer. Scores for each item can range from 0 to 4 points. Scores within subscales can range from 0 to 36 points. In addition, a negative subscore that reflects poor parenting practices can be derived by subtracting the three active parenting items (privilege removal, time-out, and ignoring) from the negative sum.

Psychometric Evaluation

Norms

Both the Hazzard, Christensen, and Margolin (1983) and the Glaser, Houre, and Myer (1995) studies report mean scores for several groups of children on their perceptions of their mothers' behavior. Means for mother positive subscale range from 23.5 for 12 participants from abusive families to 26.6 for 31 children in nondistressed families: The means for the mother negative subscale range from 10.9 for the nondistressed children in the 1983 study to 16.9 for children in the 1995 study.

Reliability

To analyze internal consistency, correlations were computed for each item and the PPI subscale in which the item is included. All of the positive items were significantly correlated with the mother positive subscale, with correlations ranging from .48 to .67, and all of the negative items were significantly correlated with the mother negative subscale, with correlations ranging from .44 to .70. In addition, Cronbach's alpha—.74 for mother positive subscale and .72 for mother negative subscale—was also used to demonstrate internal reliability.

Validity

In the Hazzard et al. (1983) study, correlations among PPI subscales, a measure of children's self-concept, and a parent measure of conduct were used to assess convergent validity. The results indicated that high positive behavior correlated with high self-esteem and high negative behavior correlated with high scores on the conduct disorder measure. Negative PPI scores were positively related to the conduct disorder measure. Discriminant validity was examined by correlating PPI subscales, with two measures not expected to be related to them: an achievement measure and an intellectual deficiency measure. Six of the eight correlations were as predicted. Also, positive PPI scores were unrelated to the measure of conduct problems.

In the 1995 study, convergent validity for the PPI was established by comparison to a parent report of child behavior (the Parent Daily Report [PDR]; Chamberlain & Reid, 1987). Small but significant correlations were found between the mother positive score as reported by the child on the PPI and the amount of positive child behavior as reported by the mother on the PDR ($r = .34$) and between the negative subscore as reported by the child on the PPI and the amount of negative child behavior as reported by the mother on the PDR ($r = .28$). Divergent validity was also established in that no correlation was found between the mother positive score as reported by the child on the PPI and the amount of negative child behavior as reported by the mother on the PDR and between the negative subscore as reported by the child on the PPI and the amount of positive child behavior as reported by the mother on the PDR.

Finally, following a 10-week group treatment for 48 child witnesses of family violence (Jaffee, Wilson, & Wolfe, 1988), significant increases in perceptions of both mothers and fathers were reported following the intervention program.

Advantages

The PPI includes specific concepts relevant for behavior treatment, such as time-out. Both father and mother items focus on positive as well as negative aspects.

Limitations

Only small populations of children have been used to provide psychometric data, and the father subscales have yet to be researched.

Primary Reference

Hazzard, Christensen, and Margolin (1983).

Scale Availability

All of the items and scoring information is available in Glaser et al. (1995).

Related References

Glaser et al. (1995); Jaffee et al. (1988).

General Comments and Recommendations for Practitioners and Researchers

Because both positive and negative behaviors are included in this brief inventory, clinicians can quickly assess a child's overall impressions of parental behavior. The separate mother and father subscale allows for easy comparisons as well.

---

43. Parent's Perceptions Questionnaire (PPQ) and Teacher's Perceptions Questionnaire (TPQ; Wurtele & Miller-Perrin)

Development and Description of Assessment Method

The PPQ is a parent questionnaire designed to assess the negative and positive effects of a sexual abuse prevention training program developed for young children. The TPQ is designed for teachers of the same preschool children.

Target Population

For PPQ: Parents of preschool-age children. For TPQ: teachers of these children.

Format

The PPQ and the TPQ consist of a checklist of 14 behaviors, which might indicate negative or positive emotional and behavioral reactions to prevention training. In addition, parents rate how afraid they believe their children are of nine various people and situations (including "strangers," "hug from mom or dad"). Parents also indicated whether their child made comments about the sexual abuse prevention program their child participated in or asked any questions about the topic, rated the global effect of the program on their child (good, bad, no effect), and indicated whether they would allow their child to participate in a similar program on safety.

- *Negative Behaviors* (10 items):
  - "Difficulty separating from parent."
  - "Refuses to obey."
  - "Inappropriate sexual behavior with peers, self, or toys."
  - "Withdrawn or aggressive."
- *Positive Behaviors* (4 items):
  - "Physically affectionate."
  - "Asks questions or talks about types of touching."
  - "Seems proud of own body."

In addition, the respondents are asked whether the target behavior has increased during the past two weeks and whether or not it is a problem.

Administration and Scoring

Parents and teachers rate each of the 14 target behaviors on a Likert-type scale, ranging from 1 = "never" to 7 = "often." In addition, parents rate their children's fears of the nine people and situations on a scale of 1 = "not at all afraid" to 7 = "terrified."

Psychometric Evaluation

Norms

None reported.

Reliability

In an investigation of the relative effectiveness of two educational programs for teaching personal safety skills ($N = 100$ children, $N = 10$ teachers), internal consistency reliability of the TPQ was .68 overall, .76 for negative behaviors and .15 for positive behaviors (Wurtele, Kast, Miller-Perrin, & Kondrick, 1989).

Validity

In the Wurtele et al. (1989) study, parents' ratings ($N = 42$) of fear levels were not significantly related to children's fear ratings. Parents tended to underestimate their children's fears, and thus the validity of this section of the PPQ is questionable.

In Wurtele (1990), results on the PPQ indicated no differences in parents' ratings of behavior associated with their child's program involvement from pre- to posttreatment, which again raises doubts about the usefulness of the PPQ.

Advantages

The PPQ and TPQ comprise parent and teacher forms, so there is comparison available of adults' ratings across informants and settings.

Limitations

Psychometric development of these two rating scales for adults is quite limited. Usefulness may be limited to a consumer satisfaction measure in a program evaluation.

Primary Reference

Wurtele and Miller-Perrin (1987).

Scale Availability

Sandy K. Wurtele
Department of Psychology
University of Colorado
1420 Austin Bluffs Pkwy.
Colorado Springs, CO 80933-7150

Related References

Wurtele (1990); Wurtele, Currier, Gillespie, and Franklin (1991); Wurtele et al. (1989).

General Comments and Recommendations for Practitioners and Researchers

Although the PPQ and TPQ offer clear utility in their present parent and teacher forms, more validation work is needed to support their use as screening or outcome measures.

44. Parent's Report on the Child's Reaction to Stress Scale (PRCS; Fletcher)

Development and Description of Assessment Method

The PRCS is a parent inventory of child's responses to a specific, stressful event. The PRCS covers all of the listed *DSM-IV* (American Psychiatric Association, 1994) symptoms with two or more questions designed to assess each symptom and allows for a PTSD diagnosis to be made, a total PTSD severity score to be calculated, and additional associated symptoms to be assessed.

Target Population

Parents with children who have experienced a stressful event.

Format

The PRCS is a rating scale that includes 79 items with a variety of different response formats, ranging from yes–no to a 5- or 6-point Likert scale. Parents are sometimes asked to elaborate on their answers to help the scorer decide if the answer qualifies as an indicator of symptomatic behavior. Most questions are followed by several lines in which parents can exactly describe or explain their child's behavior or feelings. Sample questions include,

- "How often does your child talk about the stressful event?"
- "How often do things remind your child of the stressful event?"
- "How often does your child act in new or unusual ways since the stressful event occurred?"

- "How often does your child try to avoid places or things that remind him/her of the stressful event?"
- "Compared to before the stressful event, how often does your child seem to be watchful or on guard for no reason?"
- "Compared to before the stressful event, how much does your child worry these days?"

Administration and Scoring

Parents are asked to fully describe the stressful event on the first page. Items are rated on either a 5- or a 6-point Likert scale and range from "not at all" to "always/completely."

Psychometric Evaluation

Norms

Norms are based on $N = 30$ children, 10 clinical and 20 community (10 traumatized and 10 nontraumatized), ages 7 to 14 (mean age 10.3). The clinical group was asked how they responded to an event or events identified by the therapist as traumatic. The community children were asked how they responded to the worst event that happened to them in the past five years.

Reliability

Good to excellent internal consistency was demonstrated for total PTSD severity score as well as for all the *DSM-IV* criteria. Cronbach's alphas were .89 (full scale), .81 (Criterion A), .86 (Criterion B), .70 (Criterion C), and .81 (Criterion D).

Validity

Evidence for convergent validity was provided in a correlational analysis completed for all four of Fletcher's PTSD assessment methods. The PRCS correlated at $r = .54$ ($p < .05$), with the children's self-report measures (When Bad Things Happen), $r = .60$ ($p < .001$) with the child PTSD interview, and $r = .93$ ($p < .001$) with the parent PTSD interview. In addition, the PRCS correlated $r = .82$ ($p < .001$) with the parent completed CBCL (Achenbach, 1991) PTSD subscale score.

In addition, the PRCS was significantly correlated with all other CBCL subscale scores, ranging from $r = .39$ for an association with the delinquent behavior subscale to $r = .77$ for somatic complaints. Unfortunately, these significant correlations do not support discriminant validity of the PRCS. Also, the PRCS did not adequately discriminate between children classified as clinically traumatized, community traumatized, and nontraumatized.

Advantages
Items are clearly worded and this instrument is easy to administer.

Limitations
Lack of discriminate validity compromises the use of this parent report. The interviews appear to provide more valid assessments of childhood PTSD, whereas this measure might serve best as a screening device. This scale does not parallel the other scales as closely because parents do not do as good a job reporting on their child's internal processes.

Primary Reference
Fletcher (1996).

Scale Availability
Kenneth E. Fletcher
University of Massachusetts Medical Center
Psychiatry Department
55 Lake Ave. North
Worcester, MA 01655
(508) 856-3329
e-mail: Kenneth.Fletcher@banyan.ummed.edu

Related References
Fletcher (1996); Stamm (1996).

General Comments and Recommendations for Practitioners and Researchers

The parent and child interviews described previously closely follow the wording of the parent and child self-report measures, respectively. Furthermore, the wording of the parent measures parallels that of the child measures.

Note that parental PTSD scores were generally more highly correlated with all CBCL (Achenbach, 1991) scales than were child PTSD scores, suggesting that parents may have been assessing their children's reactions to a stressful event in the light of general behavioral problems, in addition to the actual stressful experience of the child.

45. Personal Safety Questionnaire (PSQ; Wurtele, Kast, Miller-Perrin, & Kondrick)

Development and Description of Assessment Method

The PSQ assesses knowledge and attitudes about sexual behavior and sexual abuse. Questions cover various learning objectives of a prevention program.

Target Population

Preschoolers ages $3^1/_2$ to 5 years old.

Format

The PSQ is a self-report containing 12 questions to which the child simply responds yes or no. There are eight personal safety questions designed to assess children's knowledge about sexual abuse and four validity items.

In presenting items, children are told that "a big person touches a kid's private parts" and are then asked PSQ Question 1: "Has the kid done something wrong?" They are next told, "What if the big person says, don't tell anyone, let's keep it a secret" and asked PSQ Question 2: "Should the kid tell someone?"

To assess attitudes toward sexuality, children are presented with the vignette, "What if you were in the bathtub and you were washing your body?" and are asked two questions: PSQ Question 3: "Would it be okay for you to touch your own private parts?" and PSQ Question 4: "Do you like your private parts?" For these items, a positive attitude toward sexuality is indicated by a "yes" response. Other PSQ items include,

- "Are strangers the only people who try to touch a kid's private parts?"
- "Are you the boss of your body?"

Administration and Scoring

The PSQ is administered verbally. Children answer with a "yes," "no," or "I don't know" response. Correct responses receive 1 point; incorrect and "I don't know" responses receive 0 points. Scores can range from 0 to 8. At posttesting, children rate how much they liked their respective sexual abuse prevention programs and their private parts (as an additional measure of attitudes toward sexuality) by pointing to one of three faces ranging from a frowning to a smiling face.

Psychometric Evaluation

Norms
Results from several samples indicate the following preprogram norms: For 22 boys and girls ages 3.5 to 4.5 (mean age 49.3 months), PSQ mean scores and standard deviations were 6.21 ± 1.25 and 6.75 ± 1.67. For 30 boys and girls ages 4.5 to 5.5 (mean age 59.5 months), PSQ mean scores and standard deviations were 7.92 ± 1.71 and 7.59 ± 1.33.

Reliability
In Wurtele (1990), internal consistency was reported to be .78 and one-month test–retest reliability was .64, indicating adequate reliability for the PSQ. In Wurtele et al. (1989), internal consistency was .74 and one-month test–retest reliability was .53. Finally, in Wurtele et al. (1991), two-week test–retest reliability was .56.

Validity
The PSQ was sensitive to change following personal safety or behavioral skills training programs with preschoolers. The PSQ was also moderately correlated with the "What If" Situations Test (Wurtele, Kast, & Kondrick, 1988), a measure assessing children's abilities to recognize, resist, and report inappropriate sexual touching, supporting its convergent validity.

Advantages
This is a short, easy to administer screening tool that is sensitive to effects of various prevention skills training programs.

Limitations
Results from intervention programs suggest that younger children's scores on the PSQ reveal more posttest change than older children's scores. This may indicate that the cognitive development of younger children influences responding.

Primary Reference
Wurtele et al. (1989).

Scale Availability

Sandy K. Wurtele
Department of Psychology
University of Colorado
1420 Austin Bluffs Pkwy.
Colorado Springs, CO 80933-7150

Related References

Sarno and Wurtele (1997); Wurtele (1990); Wurtele et al. (1991).

General Comments and Recommendations for Practitioners and Researchers

This instrument is written for preschool-aged children, and may serve as a screening device for knowledge–attitudes about sexual behavior and abuse or as an outcome measure for prevention programs.

---

46. Responses to Childhood Incest Questionnaire (RCIQ; Donaldson & Gardner)

Development and Description of Assessment Method

Donaldson and Gardner developed the RCIQ to create an assessment measure for work with adult women who have experienced incest. In developing the scale, an initial 45-item version was administered to adult incest victims. Items were dropped if fewer than 40% of the research participants reported experiencing them. Additional items were developed based on stress response themes and *DSM-III-R* (American Psychiatric Association, 1987) PTSD criteria. The items were then grouped according to stress response themes and PTSD criteria. A principle-components analysis and screening test on the stress response themes items led to the retention of seven factors accounting for 61.2% of the total variance. A principal-components analysis on the PTSD items yielded four factors accounting for 57.9% of the variance.

The RCIQ is a self-report instrument that assesses a range of commonly reported symptoms experienced by adult survivors of incest, including the occurrence of PTSD and stress response themes.

Target Population

Adult survivors of incest.

Format

The RCIQ is a 52-item scale, divided into 11 subscales within the two sections of hypothesized stress response themes and the diagnostic criteria for PTSD. Seven factors correspond to hypothesized stress response themes and four factors correspond to the diagnostic criteria for PTSD. Hypothesized stress response themes include,

- *Vulnerability and Isolation* (6 items): This pertains to having difficulty trusting men or women, feeling vulnerability in relationships with women and men, feeling emptiness, and feeling that one could not trust oneself.
- *Fear and Anxiety* (6 items): This pertains to feeling frightened that one is "going crazy," feeling frightened and anxious when alone, and thinking about the incest and feeling frightened that one will be hurt sexually by someone again.
- *Guilt and Shame* (5 items): This pertains to feeling guilty that one had not stopped the incest, not liking oneself as a woman, feeling guilty that one had not told someone sooner, and blaming oneself for the incest.
- *Anger and Betrayal* (5 items): This pertains to feeling anger and blame toward one's mother, feeling angry that someone did not help sooner, and feeling like one could explode with anger.
- *Reaction to the Perpetrator* (4 items): This pertains to feeling so much anger and blame toward the perpetrator that one would like to hurt the abuser.
- *Sadness and Loss* (4 items): This pertains to feeling sad at the thought of the incest and about the fact that one's family life was not what one wanted it to be, difficulty trusting men, and a fear of losing one's identity if one got close in a relationship.
- *Powerless* (3 items): This pertains to feeling little control and much vulnerability with respect to work or school, with men, and a lack of confidence in oneself.

Sample items include,

- "I feel angry toward men."
- "I feel guilty that I didn't do something to stop the incest."

Diagnostic criteria for PTSD include,

- *Intrusive Thoughts* (5 items): All pertain to the experience of intrusive thoughts about the incest in numerous situations (e.g., at work, with men, in sexual situations).
- *Intrusive Behaviors and Emotions* (5 items): This pertains to experiencing strong emotional reactions to people or places that remind one of the incest and active avoidance of such situations.
- *Detachment* (3 items): This pertains to experiencing difficulty in expressing emotions and being unable to experience any feeling about the incest because these feelings are buried.
- *Emotional Control and Numbness* (4 items): This pertains to feeling numb inside, having others tell one they are "in control," and feeling detached from others.

Sample items include,

- "I have intrusive thoughts about the incest when I am alone."
- "I feel detached and estranged from others."

Administration and Scoring

Research participants are asked to read each item and to indicate on a 6-point scale how frequently they experience that symptom. The scale choices range from 0 = "never" to 5 = "always."

Psychometric Evaluation

Norms

Norms are based on a clinical population of 104 adult women, ranging in age from 17 to 54 with a mean age of 28.9 years, who had experienced childhood or adolescent incest. Mean subscale scores and standard deviations were as follows: stress response factors: vulnerability and isolation = 15.36 ± 6.42, fear and anxiety = 15.24 ± 5.77, guilt and shame = 9.60 ± 6.18, anger and betrayal = 12.08 ± 5.43, reaction to the abuser = 10.80 ± 5.21, sadness and loss = 12.90 ± 3.91, powerlessness = 7.43 ± 3.73; PTSD factors: intrusive thoughts = 11.33 ± 5.74, avoidance and intrusive emotions = 10.17 ± 5.36, detachment = 9.06 ± 3.09, and emotional control and numbness = 11.13 ± 4.26.

Reliability

Test–retest coefficients ranged from .58 to .88 (Edwards & Donaldson, 1989).

Validity

Results of the stress response themes factor analysis revealed factors that correspond with incest survivor symptom groupings reported in the sexual abuse literature, and results of the PTSD factor analysis produced factors that correspond with the major diagnostic criteria for the disorder, demonstrating criterion validity (Edwards & Donaldson, 1989). In a discriminant validity study, low to moderate correlations on measures of depression and anxiety with the RCIQ supported the notion that the RCIQ measures aspects of psychological functioning more specific to adult survivors of childhood sexual abuse (Edward & Donaldson, 1988). The RCIQ was also sensitive to change during a 20-week group therapy program for women survivors of childhood sexual abuse (Morgan & Cummings, 1999).

Advantages

The RCIQ can be useful as a pre- and posttreatment measure of symptomatology in incest survivors. It offers a comprehensive assessment of experimental incest sequelae.

Limitations

The RCIQ has no normed data on males or nontreated victims. Significant correlations between almost all subscales seems to indicate that symptoms are all interrelated, thus precluding the use of individual subscale scores.

Primary Reference

Donaldson and Gardner (1985).

Scale Availability

> Mary Ann Donaldson
> The Village Family Service Center
> 1201 25th St., SW
> Fargo, ND 58103

Related References

Edwards and Donaldson (1989); Morgan and Cummings (1999).

General Comments and Recommendations for Practitioners and Researchers

The RCIQ measures various thoughts, fears, and emotions experienced by adult survivors of incest in a comprehensive manner, and has been shown to be sensitive to change as a result of treatment. More work on construct validity is needed.

47. Sexual Abuse Exposure Questionnaire (SAEQ; Rowan, Foy, Rodriguez, & Ryan)

Development and Description of Assessment Method

The SAEQ was developed to assess the nature of sexual abuse experiences. The exposure items were based on Sgroi's (1982) spectrum of sexual abuse behaviors and modified in consultation with therapists who specialize in working with child victims of sexual abuse.

The SAEQ is a paper and pencil retrospective self-report instrument designed to systematically assess multiple aspects of childhood sexual abuse in adult survivors.

Target Population

Adult survivors of childhood sexual abuse.

Format

The SAEQ is a two-part self-report with rating scales. Part I identifies 10 categories of increasingly invasive sexual events and asks the participant to identify the relationship of the perpetrator for that particular act. Sexual events include,

- Adult exposed their genitals to child.
- Adult observed child's personal activities.
- Child disrobed or posed for adult.
- Child observed adult's sexual activities.
- Adult fondled child.
- Child manually stimulated adult's genitals.
- Adult manually or orally stimulated child's genitals.
- Child orally stimulated adult's genitals.
- Adult digital penetration of child.

- Adult penile penetration of child.

Sample items include,

- "Did a person ever expose his/her genitals to you or disrobe in front of you in a manner which made you uncomfortable?"
- "Did a person ever have you manually stimulate his or her genital area?"
- "Did a person ever insert his penis into your vagina or rectal opening?"

Part II assess other salient aspects of abuse, including a listing of each abuser by relationship; characteristics of the abuse, including frequency, duration, and coercion; memories; and reactions. The final question asks for a subjective, open-ended description of the overall effect of the abuse on the survivor's life.

Administration and Scoring

The SAEQ generally takes about 15 to 30 minutes to complete. Because many participants disclosed that the SAEQ evoked intense feelings and some required a significant debriefing to discuss feelings and memories evoked by the research, the authors suggest that the instrument be used by experienced clinicians on an individual basis.

For each of 10 exposure items (a measure of "overall exposure") scoring of each item is dichotomous, with 1 = "yes" and 0 = "no" or "not sure," resulting in a score that can range from 0 to 10. The highest or most invasive item endorsed "yes" is used as a "severity type" score. Score for age of onset of the abuse was the age at which the person indicated the abuse began. The duration score is the age at which the abuse was reported to have ended less the age of onset. The frequency score is on a 6-point rating scale from 1 = "once" to 6 = "more than weekly." There is also a score for number of perpetrators, ranging from 1 to 4. This score is the number reported if abuse involved one to three perpetrators and is "4" if four or more perpetrators are reported. A force variable is assessed by a yes or no response to a specific self-report question.

Psychometric Evaluation

Norms

In survivors of childhood sexual abuse (91% women, age range 20–51, mean age = 34), the mean score on "overall exposure" (the total score for the 10 SAEQ exposure items) was 6. The mean score on "severity type" (the number of the highest SAEQ item with a "yes" response) was 9. In another study of help-seeking adult survivors of childhood sexual abuse (94% women, mean age 35.3 years), the mean score for severity was 8. Finally, in a third study with adult female women, mean age 35.3, in outpatient treatment for childhood sexual abuse, the mean age of childhood sexual abuse onset was 5, and termination was 13. The mean duration of childhood sexual abuse was seven years.

Reliability

The SAEQ was first standardized on a clinical sample of $N = 123$ childhood sexual abuse survivors (mean age = 35.3, 94.3% female). Split half reliability of exposure items (first 10 items) for the entire group was .73. Two-week test–retest reliability ranged from .56 (perpetrator exposed/disrobed) to .86 (manual or oral stimulation of other's genitals; Ryan, 1993).

In a study by Ryan (1993), test–retest (two-week) reliability coefficients for the 10 exposure questions ranged from .73 to .94, age of abuse onset was .88, termination was .92, number of perpetrators was .96, and force was .82.

Validity

Correlations between the subscale scores of the SAEQ and PTSD scores from the SCID (Structured Clinical Interview for *DSM-III-R*; American Psychiatric Association, 1987) were examined. All correlations were significant and ranged from $r = .31$ ($p < .001$) for a correlation between number of perpetrators subscore and PTSD intensity scores to $r = -.61$ ($p < .001$) for age of onset subscore and duration scores on the SCID, demonstrating concurrent validity (Rodriquez, Ryan, Rowan, & Foy, 1996).

SAEQ scores were also significantly correlated with the Impact of Events Scale (Horowitz, Wilner, & Alvarez, 1979). Intrusion scores rated over the past week and the past year, demonstrating convergent validity (Rowan, Foy, Rodriguez, & Ryan, 1994).

Advantages

The SAEQ is a very comprehensive inventory with a short completion time.

Limitations

The SAEQ was tested mostly on women, thus limiting generalizability to men. Also, the majority of the studies used a clinical sample and thus the high incidence of PTSD may not necessarily be representative of childhood sexual abuse survivors not seeking help.

Primary Reference

Rowan et al. (1994).

Scale Availability

> Anderson B. Rowan
> Graduate School of Psychology
> Fuller Theological Seminary
> 180 N. Oakland Ave.
> Pasadena, CA 91101

Related References

Rodriguez et al. (1996); Rodriguez, Ryan, Vandenkemp, and Foy (1997); Ryan (1993).

General Comments and Recommendations for Practitioners and Researchers

The SAEQ assesses specific sexual events occurring in childhood as well as descriptive characteristics of those events. The measure produces a variety of scores representing specific items.

---

48. Sexual Abuse Fear Evaluation (SAFE; Wolfe & Wolfe)

Development and Description of Assessment Method

The SAFE is an extension of the 80-item Fear Survey Schedule for Children Revised (Ollendick, 1983). As reported in Wolfe, Gentile, and Klink (1988), factor analysis with SAFE with a sample of schoolchildren ($n = 171$) and sexually abused children ($n = 62$) revealed the two factors.

The SAFE assesses abuse-related fears believed to be common among sexually abused children as well as situations that sexually abused children may find particularly distressing.

Target Population

Children who have been sexually abused.

Format

The SAFE is a 27-item scale embedded into the 80-item Fear Survey Schedule for Children-Revised. It contains two factors/subscales:

- *Sexual Associated Fears* (11 items). Examples include,
  - "Watching people kiss on TV."
  - "Talking or thinking about sex."
  - "Someone kissing or hugging me."
  - "Taking my clothes off."
- *Interpersonal Discomfort* (13 items). Examples include,
  - "Saying no to an adult."
  - "Someone in my family getting into bad trouble."
  - "Going to court to talk to a judge."
  - "People not believing me."

Administration and Scoring

Responses to individual fears are scored on a 3-point scale, including "none," "some," or "a lot."

Psychometric Evaluation

Norms

All children endorse SAFE items at a high rate; the average sex-associated fear score was 16 for nonabused children, and the average interpersonal discomfort score was 27 for both abused and nonabused children.

Reliability

Internal consistency was demonstrated for both subscales: the sexual associated fears has an alpha value = .80 and interpersonal discomfort has an alpha value = .81.

Validity

Both sexually abused and nonabused children endorsed SAFE items at relatively high rates. Though abused and nonabused children differed only slightly on the sexual associated fear scale, the difference was significant. There was no difference on interpersonal discomfort. These findings suggest questionable scale validity.

Advantages

Because the SAFE scales are embedded in the Fear Survey Schedule, demand characteristics of responding to a series of sexual abuse-related items are minimized.

Limitations

The SAFE consists of a limited number of items describing potentially fearful situations that may be feared by most children whether or not they had experienced sexual abuse. Thus, both groups would be expected to fear many of the described situations. As such, the SAFE did not discriminate between 17 child victims of sexual abuse and a matched group of 17 nonabused nonreferred community children (Inderbitzen-Pisaruk, Shawchuck, & Hoier, 1992) in a sample of boys and girls, ages 5 to 15. Furthermore, the 3-point response continuum may not be sensitive enough to detect differences between groups (i.e., degree of fearfulness).

Primary Reference

Wolfe and Wolfe (1986).

Scale Availability

> V. V. Wolfe
> Department of Psychology
> Children's Hospital of Western Ontario
> 800 Commissioners Rd. East
> London, Ontario, Canada 5C2N6A

Related References

Inderbitzen-Pisaruk et al. (1992); Wolfe and Birt (1997); Wolfe et al. (1988).

General Comments and Recommendations for Practitioners and Researchers

Although useful in its embedded format within the Fear Survey Schedule for Children–Revised, more validation work is needed to test the scale's ability to discriminate children who have experienced sexual abuse.

49. Trauma Symptom Checklist for Children (TSCC; Briere)

Development and Description of Assessment Method

The TSCC, the child version of the adult Trauma Symptom Inventory (Briere, 1995), evaluates acute and chronic posttraumatic symptomatology and other symptom clusters found in some traumatized children who have experienced traumatic events. The clinical subscales are conceptually based.

Target Population

Children and adolescents ages 8 to 16 years old (17-year-olds can be evaluated using 16-year-old norms with minor adjustments).

Format

The TSCC consists of 54 items categorized into six clinical subscales. There are also two validity scales (underresponse and hyperresponse) and eight critical items. The clinical subscales are anger (9 items), anxiety (9 items), depression (9 items), dissociation (with overt and fantasy subscales; 10 items), posttraumatic stress (10 items), and sexual concerns (with sexual distress and sexual preoccupation subscales; 10 items). Some symptoms overlap scales. There is also an alternate form (TSCC–A) that has 44 items and only 7 critical items, with no sexual concerns scale or reference to sexual issues.

Administration and Scoring

The TSCC is suitable for group or individual administration. It can be completed in 15 to 20 minutes for all but the most traumatized or clinically impaired and scored and profiled in approximately 10 minutes. Items responses are rated according to frequency of occurrence over the past two months on a 4-point scale ranging from 0 = "never" to 3 = "almost all of the time." Scores are cumulative for each scale. There is a profile form that allows for conversion of raw scores to age- and sex-appropriate T-scores and graphing the results.

Psychometric Evaluation

Norms

The TSCC has been standardized on a group of more than 3,000 innercity, urban, and suburban nonclinical children and adolescents from the general population in addition to more than 500 sexually abused children and adolescents. Separate norms and T-scores are available according to sex and age (7–11 and 12–16) and are reported in the manual.

Reliability

Alphas have been reported by Lanktree, Briere, and Hernandez (1991) as .96 (total), .85 (anxiety), .89 (depression), .86 (post-traumatic stress), .83 (dissociation), .84 (anger), and .68 (sexual concerns), as well as by Singer, Anglen, Song, and Lunghofer (1995) as .95 (total), .82 (anxiety), .86 (depression), .87 (posttraumatic stress), .83 (dissociation), and .89 (anger); sexual concerns was omitted.

Validity

In a study of 105 sexually abused children ages 8 to 15, all TSCC scales except sexual concerns decreased after three months of therapy, and of these all but dissociation continued to decline at one or more assessment periods thereafter. At six months, those remaining in therapy continued to decrease on the anxiety, depression, posttraumatic stress, and sexual concerns scales of the TSCC (Lanktree & Briere, 1995).

In a study of 399 children between the ages of 8 and 15 who had either disclosed or not disclosed abuse, no differences were found on the TSCC between two subgroups of disclosing children (those who had partially disclosed and those with complete disclosure). Significant differences were found between nondisclosing abused groups (recanting children reported being more angry and depressed than never disclosing children). Finally, sexually abused children who disclosed abuse reported particularly high levels of symptomatology, nondisclosing (denying or recanting) abused children reported relatively low levels of distress, and nonabused children reported intermediate levels of symptomatology, which was generally consistent with the level found in a large normative sample. These findings indicated good known-groups validity (Elliott & Briere, 1994).

Based on samples of sexually abused children, the TSCC subscales correlate significantly with behavior problems, depression, dissociation, impact ratings of sexual abuse, and sexualized behaviors (Nader, 1997).

Advantages

The TSCC is simply worded and easy to administer. It is particularly useful with children who have experienced multiple types of abuse and appears to be sensitive to the effects of therapy for abused children. It does not orient respondents to their abuse experiences and is appropriate for children who have not disclosed abuse, as well as those who have.

Limitations

Some overlap between the PTSD and other subscales could influence the correlations between scales. Results of Elliott and Briere (1994) may not generalize to younger children. Furthermore, because disclosure interviews were conducted by a variety of staff, it is unclear how interview techniques may have influenced the results.

Primary Reference

Elliott and Briere (1994).

Scale Availability

John Briere
Psychiatry and Psychology Department
USC School of Medicine
1934 Hospital Pl.
Los Angeles, CA 90033
e-mail: Jbriere@hsc.usc.edu

Or

Psychological Assessment Resources, Inc.
P.O. Box 998
Odessa, FL 33556
(800) 331-TEST (x 8378)

Related References

Lanktree and Briere (1995); Nader (1997); Singer et al. (1995).

General Comments and Recommendations for Practitioners and Researchers

Subscales are not intended to provide a diagnosis of specific disorders. There is a comprehensive professional manual available that provides information on test materials, administration, scoring, interpretation, psychometric characteristics, and normative data. Also available are a TSCC-SP scoring program Windows Version 1 that automates scoring when the clients' responses to the TSCC or TSCC–A are entered and generates a four-page score summary report for the six clinical scales, the two validity scales, the critical items, and a graphic profile of the results.

50. Trauma Symptom Checklist 33 and 40 (TSC–33 and TSC–40; Briere & Runtz; Elliot & Briere)

Development and Description of Assessment Method

The TSC–33 is a revision and extension of the Crisis Symptom Checklist (CSC; Briere & Runtz, 1988) and meant to be a brief, abuse-oriented instrument that can be used in clinical research as a measure of long-term child abuse effects. Items were derived from the CSC and additional symptoms frequently reported in the literature on long-term child abuse effects. Based on potential shortcomings of the TSC–33, the TSC–40 was developed so that the extent and specific pattern of disturbance in trauma victims could be determined.

The TSC–40 is a research measure that evaluates symptomatology, including posttraumatic stress and other symptom clusters found in some traumatized adults arising from childhood or adult traumatic experiences.

Target Population

Adults who have experienced childhood or adulthood trauma.

Format

The TSC–40 has 40 items categorized into six subscales:

- *Anxiety* (8 items): "Headaches."
- *Depression* (9 items): "Sadness."
- *Dissociation* (6 items): "Flashbacks"—sudden, vivid distracting memories.
- *Sexual Abuse Trauma Index* (7 items): "Fear of men."
- *Sexual Problems* (6 items): "Low sex drive."
- *Sleep Disturbance* (8 items): "Insomnia."

Administration and Scoring

The TSC–40 requires approximately 10 to 15 minutes to administer and can be scored in approximately 5 to 10 minutes. Items may be read to the research participant or may be administered as a pencil and paper test. Item responses are rated according to frequency of occurrence over the previous two months on a 4-point scale ranging from 0 = "never" to 3 = "often." Items are summed to produce symptom subscales as well as a total score.

Psychometric Evaluation

Norms

The following mean subscale scores and standard deviations were obtained in a national sample of professional, nonclinical women, average age 41.7 years, with no history of sexual abuse (N = 2,072): anxiety = 3.80 ± 2.7, depression = 5.74 ± 3.3, dissociation = 2.35 ± 2.1, sexual abuse trauma index = 2.44 ± 2.1, sexual problems = 3.77 ± 3.0, sleep disturbance = 5.03 ± 3.0, TSC-33 total score = 16.75 ± 9.1, and TSC-40 total score = 20.91 ± 11.1. In a sample with a history of sexual abuse (N = 761), the following mean scores were obtained: anxiety = 4.74 ± 3.0, depression = 6.98 ± 3.4, dissociation = 3.05 ± 2.2, sexual abuse trauma index = 3.43 ± 2.5, sexual problems = 5.02 ± 3.4, sleep disturbance = 5.84 ± 3.1, TSC-33 total score = 20.80 ± 10.0, and TSC-40 total score = 26.02 ± 12.1.

Reliability

The subscales of the TSC–40 demonstrated reliability with the following alphas coefficients: anxiety = .66, depression = .70, dissociation = .64, sexual abuse trauma index alpha = .62 sexual problems = .73 and sleep disturbance = .77, alpha for the total scale = .90 (total scale alpha for TSC–33 = .88)

Validity

Anxiety, depression, dissociation, sexual abuse trauma index, sexual problems, and sleep disturbance subscale scores were each significantly higher for (self-reported) sexually abused women than for those with no sexual abuse history. The total TSC–40 score was significantly greater for abused than nonabused participants.

Advantages

The TSC–40 is a brief, easy to administer instrument tested with a large sample size.

Limitations

The TSC–40 was tested on a volunteer, nonclinical sample with a relatively high level of social and occupational functioning of the research participants. Thus, generalizability of results may be limited.

Primary Reference

Elliott and Briere (1992).

Scale Availability

> John Briere
> Psychiatry and Psychology Department
> USC School of Medicine
> 1934 Hospital Pl.
> Los Angeles, CA 90033
> Jbriere@hsc.usc.edu

Related References

Briere and Runtz (1988).

General Comments and Recommendations for Practitioners and Researchers

Because the TSC–33 and TSC–40 were validated on a sample of professional women, its utility as a clinical instrument remains questionable.

---

51. Trauma Symptom Inventory (TSI; Briere)

Development and Description of Assessment Method

The TSI was developed in response to the paucity of standardized, clinically useful measures of PTSD symptoms. A major revision and expansion of the TSC–33/40, the 10 clinical scales evaluate various forms of symptomatology, each of which are relevant to the psychological assessment of traumatized individuals.

The TSI evaluates acute and chronic posttraumatic symptomatology and other psychological sequelae of traumatic events, including intra- and interpersonal difficulties, often associated with psychological trauma.

Target Population

Adults ages 18 years and older and requires a 5th- to 7th-grade reading ability.

Format

The TSI consists of 100 items categorized into 10 clinical scales that measure the extent to which the respondent endorses trauma-related symptoms within three broad categories of distress (trauma, self, and dysphoria). The scales are as follows:

- *Anxious Arousal* (AA; symptoms of anxiety, including those associated with posttraumatic hyperarousal).
- *Depression* (D; depressive symptomatology, both in terms of mood state and depressive cognitive distortions).
- *Anger/Irritability* (AI; angry or irritable affect, as well as associated angry cognitions and behavior).
- *Intrusive Experiences* (IE; intrusive symptoms associated with posttraumatic stress, such as flashbacks, nightmares, and intrusive thoughts).
- *Defensive Avoidance* (DA; posttraumatic avoidance, both cognitive and behavioral).
- *Dissociation* (DIS; dissociative symptomatology such as depersonalization, out-of-body experiences, and psychic numbing).
- *Sexual Concerns* (SC; sexual distress, such as sexual dissatisfaction, sexual dysfunction, and unwanted sexual thoughts or feelings).
- *Dysfunctional Sexual Behavior* (DSB; sexual behavior that is in some way dysfunctional, either because of its indiscriminate quality its potential for self-harm or its inappropriate use to accomplish nonsexual goals).
- *Impaired Self-Reference* (ISR; problems in the "self" domain, such as identity confusion, self–other disturbance, and a relative lack of self-support).
- *Tension Reduction Behavior* (TRB; the respondent's tendency to turn to external methods of reducing internal tension or distress, such as self-mutilation, angry outbursts, and suicide threats).

The TSI also contains three validity scales:

- *Response Level* (measuring a tendency toward defensiveness, a general underendorsement response set, or a need to appear unusually symptom-free).
- *Atypical Response* (measuring psychosis or extreme distress, a general overendorsement response set, or an attempt to appear especially disturbed or dysfunctional).
- *Inconsistent Response* (measuring inconsistent responses to items, potentially because of random item endorsement, attention or concentration problems, or reading–language difficulties).

There are also 12 critical items that help identify potential problems such as suicidal ideation or behavior, substance abuse, psychosis, and self-mutilatory behavior that may require immediate follow-up.

Administration and Scoring

The TSI can be administered individually or in groups. Item responses are rated according to frequency of occurrence over the past six months on a 4-point scale ranging from 0 = "never" to 3 = "often." It requires approximately 20 minutes to complete for all but the most traumatized or clinically impaired individuals and can be scored and profiled in approximately 10 minutes.

The 10 clinical and 3 validity scales all yield sex- and age-normed T-scores. Profile forms for males and females allow conversion of raw scores to T-scores. A graph of the profile may be drawn to portray the respondents' scores relative to general population scores.

Psychometric Evaluation

Norms

Norms have been derived from a nationally representative sample of 828 adults from the general population and from 3,659 male and female Navy recruits. There are separate norms for males and females, ages 18 to 54 and 55+ years old. The norms for females and males with and without a victimization history are reported for each subscale in the manual.

Reliability

The 10 clinical scales had a mean alpha of .87 and a range of .74 (tension reduction behavior) to .90 (depression and intrusive experiences). Individual scale alpha reliabilities were AA = .87, D = .90, AI = .89, IE = .90, DA = .88, DIS = .88, SC = .89, DSB = .89, ISR = .87, and TRB =

.74. The mean scale alpha for all scales was .87. The mean intercorrelation between TSI scales was .54, with r's ranging from .28 to .79.

Validity

The TSI has demonstrated construct validity in that those with reported child or adult interpersonal victimization experiences scored higher on all scales of the TSI relative to those not reporting victimization. Also, psychiatric inpatients endorsed most TSI scales to a greater extent than did outpatients. The TSI also exhibited reasonable convergent, predictive, and incremental validity in standardized, clinical, university, and Navy samples. Validity scales covaried as expected with similar scales from other measures. In a subgroup of the standardization sample (n = 449), TSI scales predicted independently assessed PTSD status in more than 90% of cases, and in the psychiatric inpatient sample correctly identified 89% of those independently diagnosed with borderline personality disorder. Studies also indicate that specific TSI scale elevations are associated with a wide variety of traumatic experiences.

Advantages

The TSI is a well-developed, psychometrically sound assessment instrument with extensive norms. A computerized scoring system is available.

Limitations

The TSI does not generate a *DSM-IV* (American Psychiatric Association, 1994) diagnosis but evaluates the relative level of various forms of posttraumatic distress.

Primary Reference

Briere, Elliott, Harris, and Cofman (1995).

Scale Availability

> Psychological Assessment Resources, Inc.
> P.O. Box 998
> Odessa, FL 33556
> 800-331-TEST (x8378)

Related References

None available.

General Comments and Recommendations for Practitioners and Researchers

TSI scores vary slightly as a function of ethnicity (accounting for 2–3% of variance in most scales), and slight adjustments for validity scale cut-offs are suggested for certain racial groups.

The TSI professional manual provides comprehensive information on test materials, administration, scoring, interpretation, psychometric characteristics, and normative data. There is also a TSI-SP computer scoring program available. This program scores the test and produces a score summary report that includes raw scores and T-scores for each scale, as well as a profile of all 13 scales. It also provides three additional summary factor scales that indicate the relative extent to which the respondent is experiencing reduced or insufficient internal resources (self-factor scale), general posttraumatic distress (trauma factor scale), and dysphoric affect (dysphoria factor scale). Windows and DOS versions are available.

---

52. Traumatic Sexualization Survey (TSS; Matorin & Lynn)

Development and Description of Assessment Method

The first author wrote an initial pool of 60 items based on sequalae of childhood sexual abuse that were associated with the process of traumatic sexualization. Items measuring attitudes and cognitions about sexual behavior were geared toward heterosexual women. Items were rated by five experts in the field on a scale from 0 to 4, with 4 = "very good fit" with the construct of traumatic sexualization. Eight items receiving a mean expert rating of less than 3 were deleted, and the authors completed a factor analysis on the now 52-item TSS given to a sample of undergraduate females ($n = 540$). A varimax rotation facilitated interpretation of the factor analysis and based on the scree test, a four-factor solution fit the data the best. The four factors accounted for 42% of the variance, and items were retained if they had loadings of at least .50 on one factor and no more than .30 on any other factor. This resulted in a preliminary scale of 24 items. Additional items were added to further develop the scale and increase two of the factors. This resulted in a 55-item version from a second sample of female undergraduates ($n = 451$) in which 41% had experienced some form of childhood abuse. Items were analyzed using the alpha method of factor extraction and varimax rotation. The same item criteria were used to retain or delete items, and the result was the current 38-item final version of the TSS.

Target Population

Adolescent and adult women who have experienced sexual abuse in their childhood.

Format

The inventory includes 38 items divided among the following four sub-scales:

- *Avoidance and Fear of Sexual and Physical Intimacy* (16 items). Sample items include,
    - "I avoid being sexually intimate."
    - "I am afraid of acting sexual."
    - "I think sex is dirty."
- *Thoughts About Sex* (12 items). Sample items include,
    - "I daydream about sex."
    - "I can't get sex off my mind."
    - "I have unusual sexual thoughts."
- *Role of Sex in Relationships* (7 items). Sample items include,
    - "I use sex to avoid loneliness."
    - "I need sex to feel good about myself."
- *Attraction/Interest and Sexuality* (3 items). Sample items include,
    - "Men want to be with me because I am seductive."

Administration and Scoring

Respondents indicate how often each item was true for them on a 5-point Likert scale ranging from 1 = "never" to 5 = "almost always." Items for each subscale are summed and divided by the number of items in the subscale.

Psychometric Evaluation

Norms

Mean scores on each subscale were calculated for $n = 99$ women who reported no abuse history and were compared to other groups of women. The mean score and standard deviation for items on the avoidance and fear subscale was 2.51, ±69, for items on the thoughts about sex subscale was 2.19, ±.58, for items on the role of sex subscale was 1.22, ±.34, and for items on the attraction/interest subscale was 1.51, ±.60.

Reliability

Alpha coefficients for each subscale of the TSS and item-total correlations were computed to determine internal consistency in a sample of undergraduate females ($n = 451$). The coefficient alpha was equal to .92, .93, .85, and .80 for subscales 1 though 4, respectively. Item-total correlations ranged from .54 to .79, indicating good internal consistency. Test–retest reliability was calculated across a three-week time period for a portion of the sample ($n = 129$). The following Pearson correlations were calculated for each subscale score: $r = .88$ for avoidance and fear, $r = .87$ for thoughts about sex, $r = .89$ for the role of sex, and $r = .82$ for attraction/interest.

Validity

To assess convergent validity, each subscale of the TSS was correlated with other measures of aspects of traumatic sexualization with a sample of undergraduate females ($n = 451$). The results from these analyses indicated that 28 of the 32 correlations were significant at $p < .05$ and are reported in the primary reference. The avoidance and fear factor was positively correlated the sex guilt scale ($r = .54$, $p < .00$) and negatively correlated with the dysfunctional sexual behavior scale ($r = -.36$, $p < .01$). The thoughts about sex subscale was negatively correlated with sexual self-esteem ($r = -.32$, $p < .01$) and sex guilt ($r = -.36$, $p < .01$) and positively correlated with dysfunctional sexual behavior ($r = .46$, $p < .01$).

In support of discriminant validity, the TSS subscales did not correlate with general symptom distress, posttraumatic stress, or social desirability. Known-groups validity was examined by comparisons between women who reported sexual abuse ($n = 99$), women who reported physical abuse ($n = 44$), and women who reported no abuse ($n = 99$). The results from the one-way multivariate analysis of variance indicated that except for the avoidance and fear subscale, the abuse groups scored significantly higher than the control group ($F(8,474) = 4.21$, $p < .001$).

Advantages

This brief, easy to administer scale is well-developed from the psychometric viewpoint. Evidence for various types of reliability and validity is available for the restricted population of young, heterosexual women. Also, the items appear well-grounded in theories about the sequalae of traumatic sexualization.

Limitations

It is difficult to understand why none of the factors successfully discriminated between sexually and physically abused women. However, additional research on clinical samples of women with varying demographics is necessary for refinement of the TSS.

Primary Reference

Matorin and Lynn (1998).

Scale Availability

Steven Jan Lynn
Department of Psychology
Box 6000
SUNY at Binghamton
Binghamton, NY 13902-6000

Related References

None available.

General Comments and Recommendations for Practitioners and Researchers

These authors are to be commended for their careful development and evaluation of this inventory. Because they included the Child Sexual Victimization Questionnaire and the Family Environment Questionnaire (Briere & Runtz, 1988) in their assessment packet, they were able to examine differences between abuse and normal samples from a non-clinical population.

---

53. Weekly Behavior Report (WBR; Cohen & Mannarino)

Development and Description of Assessment Method

The WBR is a parent-report instrument that documents the frequency of 21 specific types of problematic preschool behaviors associated with sexual abuse.

Behaviors were selected based on available empirical data regarding abused preschooler symptomatology, the clinical literature, and consultation with recognized experts.

Target Population

Parents of sexually abused preschool children.

Format

The WBR is a 21-item checklist that tracks various types of problems in addition to the number of discrete episodes on items such as sleep difficulties; anxiety symptoms; inappropriate sexual behavior; and regressive, aggressive, and oppositional behaviors. Parents specifically record on a daily basis over the course of any one week whether a behavior occurred one or more times. Sample items include,

- "Refused or resisted going to sleep in own bed."
- "Cried at bedtime."
- "Clinging to you during the day."
- "Physical fighting."
- "Asked another child to get undressed."
- "Kissed with tongue."
- "Touched an adult's private parts."

Administration and Scoring

Parents complete the assessment on difficulties that their children have experienced. The WBR allows the parent to document the exact number of times the behavior has occurred by providing daily time blocks for recording each behavior. Thus, for each week the WBR tracks both the types and total number of discrete episodes of problematic behavior. The total score reflects the sum of all episodes independent of type. The type score reflects the number of different behaviors noted at least once.

Psychometric Evaluation

Norms

Norms are reported in the primary reference.

Reliability

Two-week test–retest reliability was shown to be $r = .81$ for types of behaviors and .88 for number of behaviors. Internal consistency was demonstrated at .80 for the sexually abused group and .76 for the control group.

Validity

Convergent validity was demonstrated as correlations with the Child Behavior Checklist (Achenbach, 1991) were very high for the sexually abused group and the normal control group. Correlations ranged from $r = .29$ (externalizing subscale for normals) to $r = .60$ [total CBCL (Achenbach, 1991) and total WBR scales for sexually abused children]. All correlations were statistically significant. Known-groups validity was supported by the significant differences found between the percentages of parents in the sexually abused and normal control groups who endorsed specific items and also by significant group differences in terms of the relative frequency of individual WBR behaviors. Known-groups validity was also demonstrated in that for 12 of the WBR behaviors, mean frequencies in the sexual abuse group were significantly greater than for the control group.

Advantages

The WBR is a more exact measure of the frequency of problematic preschool behaviors associated with sexual abuse than more global frequency scales.

Limitations

There was no consideration given to the relative severity of behavior. Also, too small a sample was used to provide reliable norms.

Primary Reference

Cohen and Mannarino (1996).

Scale Availability

The scale is available in the primary reference.

Related References

None available.

General Comments and Recommendations for Practitioners and Researchers

This instrument shows promise in measuring behaviors that may be particularly characteristic of sexually abused preschoolers. However, parent ratings are certainly influenced by parents' knowledge of and distress concerning known abuse.

54. "When Bad Things Happen" (WBTH; Fletcher)

Development and Description of Assessment Method

The WBTH is a self-report measure paralleling questions from the Childhood PTSD Interview (Fletcher, 1996) in which the child is asked to rate items according to a specific, presumably traumatic, event that happened. It covers all of the listed *DSM-IV* (American Psychiatric Association, 1994) symptoms with two or more questions designed to assess each symptom, and allows for a PTSD diagnosis to be made, a total PTSD severity score to be calculated, and additional associated symptoms to be assessed.

The 95 items are coded by a rating scale that groups items into the criteria requirements for PTSD diagnosis.

Target Population

Children and adolescents between the ages of 7 and 14 with a third-grade reading level or higher.

Format

The WBTH is a self-report measure in which symptoms for PTSD are assessed by 67 questions and are indicated by a "yes" answer on 47 and a "no" answer on 20 of the questions. Each item is directly related to a *DSM-III-R* or *DSM-IV* criterion symptom for PTSD, and each *DSM* criteria is assessed in two to six questions. Symptoms are considered present if the child endorses the symptom on two or more questions. Associated responses are assessed in 32 additional items and include anxiety (5 items), depression (3 items), possible dissociation (4 items), omens and future predictions (2 items), survivor guilt (2 items), guilt/self-blame (2 items), fantasy/denial (2 items), self-destructive behavior

(3 items), aggression (3 items), risk-taking (2 items), and changed eating habits (4 items). Sample questions include,

- "Was the bad thing scary?"
- "Were you afraid you might die?"
- "Do you try to forget about the bad thing?"
- "Is it easy for you to go to sleep at night?"
- "Do you worry much since the bad thing happened?"
- "Do you feel like what happened is your fault?"

Administration and Scoring

The first page asks the child to describe the event or "bad thing" that happened. The order of the following items should be mixed around because items tapping the same criteria following each other could pull for certain response set. Answers that are scored on a frequency rating include 0 = "never," 1 = "some," or 2 = "lots," and allow *DSM* criteria to be used to make diagnosis and provide continuous measures of the severity of the child's stress responses for *DSM* criteria and the associated symptoms. Symptoms are considered present if the child endorses the symptom on two or more questions.

Psychometric Evaluation

Norms
These are provided in the primary reference.

Reliability
Internal consistency was measured using Cronbach's alpha and ranged from .70 for criterion A (exposure to an upsetting event) and C (avoidance or denial of the experience and its consequences) to .92 (full scale). Criterion A was somewhat lower because it was designed to include extreme questions that would be expected to lower the interitem correlations and thus the measures of internal consistency.

Validity
Providing evidence for known-groups validity, all four of the PTSD measures developed by Fletcher (see Fletcher, 1996) significantly differentiated the 10 children seeking counseling for traumatic experiences from the 20 children recruited from the community. Also, all of the correlations between the childhood PTSD reports and the CBCL (Achenbach, 1991) scales were lower than the correlations of the child PTSD

reports with each other and with the parent PTSD report, providing evidence of discriminant validity. This was also the case for most of the correlations between parent PTSD reports and CBCL scales. Furthermore, when children were grouped according to Dimensions of Stressful Events Scale (DOSE) scores (Fletcher, 1996), differences emerged that provide additional evidence of the validity of the scale. The clinical group had the highest and the nontraumatized community group had the lowest scores on the WBTH.

Also, the WBTH diagnosed more children exposed to higher levels of traumatization (as measured by the DOSE) with PTSD than children exposed to lower levels of traumatization. These results were significant when the WBTH was used for diagnostic purposes.

All four of the child scales were significantly associated with parental reports of their children's reactions to lifetime exposure to stressors, although none of the PTSD scales was significantly associated with children's reports of the number of lifetime stressors they have been exposed to.

Advantages

Preliminary testing has shown that it may be easier to get a child to fill out this form than to answer questions in the parallel interview. This measure asks about each symptom more than once, permitting the endorsement of symptoms missed because of wording issues or state of mind. It is worded simply, has an easy format, and can be used in clinical and research settings. The WBTH is available in Hebrew and Armenian and is currently being translated into Spanish.

Limitations

Decision rules for diagnosing PTSD are not yet refined. Although the corresponding interviews developed by Fletcher appear to provide more valid assessments of childhood PTSD, the WBTH scale might serve best as a screening device.

Primary Reference

Fletcher (1996).

Scale Availability

Kenneth E. Fletcher
University of Massachusetts Medical Center

Psychiatry Department
55 Lake Ave. North
Worcester, MA 01655
(508) 856-3329
e-mail: Kenneth.Fletcher@banyan.umed.edu

Related References

Nader (1997).

General Comments and Recommendations for Practitioners and Researchers

Note that parental PTSD scores were generally more highly correlated with all CBCL scales than were child PTSD scores, suggesting that parents may have been assessing their children's reactions to a stressful event in the light of general behavioral problems, in addition to the actual stressful experience of the child.

Behavioral Observation and Analogue Methods

irect observation methods were introduced as a *sine qua non* of the behavioral assessment approach in that the quantification of overt behavior as it occurred in the naturalistic setting would provide the most objective information about children and families. However, the requirements of this direct measurement approach were impossible to achieve in the clinical setting, and behavioral assessors were forced to approximate the natural setting by developing analogue situations in which behavior could be observed and coded. What follows in this chapter is a variety of observational assessment methods used primarily in analogue situations to help in the assessment of at-risk families.

55. Assessment of Physiological Responses to Analogue Audiotaped Scripts (Orr et al.)

Development and Description of Assessment Method

This script-driven, psychophysiologic imagery technique was used to provide objective data on emotional responsiveness to cues of childhood sexual abuse experiences and the validity of the posttraumatic stress disorder (PTSD) diagnosis in a sexually victimized population. The technique was based on methods used in previous research (e.g., Pitman, Orr, Forgue, deJong, & Claiborn, 1987). Physiologic responses of adult women are measured during recollections of their sexual abuse and other life experiences.

Target Population

Women who report childhood sexual abuse.

Format

This is an assessment in which participants, with the help of a mental health professional, compose five 30-second scripts portraying past personal experiences. These comprise the two most stressful childhood sexual abuse experiences, the most stressful life experience unrelated to sexual abuse, the most positive life experience, and a personal neutral experience. All scripts are then taperecorded in a neutral voice to be played back for participants while physiologic responses are monitored. Six standard scripts (three neutral, two fear, and one action) are also played to the participants.

Administration and Scoring

Four physiologic responses were measured: heart rate (HR), skin conductance (SC), and electromyograms (EMGS) of two different facial muscles (the left lateral frontalis [LF] and the corrugator [C]). The participant has electrodes attached and listens to a three-minute relaxation instruction tape. Each script is then played, preceded by a baseline period and followed by a relaxation–recovery period. Participants are instructed to listen to each script and imagine it vividly, as though it were actually occurring. Following each recovery period, the participant rates emotional responses on 12-point Likert scales.

The presentation of the script recordings are controlled by a personal computer. This computer also stores participants' ratings of emotions and digitized physiologic signals.

A response score for each physiologic dependent variable is calculated by subtracting the baseline period mean from the corresponding imagery period mean.

Psychometric Evaluation

Norms
None reported.

Reliability
Each script (abuse and non–abuse-related) was rated by two experts who were unaware of the participant's diagnosis for its degree of trau-

matic impact on 1- to 12-point Likert scales. Interrater reliabilities were averaged for the two abuse experience scripts. Intraclass correlations were .70 (two abuse scripts averaged) and .46 (nonabuse stressful experience).

Validity

Physiologic responses during script-driven imagery of personal abuse experiences discriminated groups, such that survivors of childhood sexual abuse with a current PTSD diagnosis showed increased responses compared with survivors with no past or current PTSD. Those with a past (but not current) PTSD diagnosis fell between these two groups. During imagery of other stressful life experiences, there were no significant group differences in physiologic responding.

Advantages

Technique provides an assessment of PTSD responses (i.e., physiologic reactivity to traumatic cues) not based on self-report. The script-driven method allows for highly personalized assessment.

Limitations

This technique requires expensive and complicated equipment as well as complicated analyses. In addition, psychometric validation would require comparisons to other methods of PTSD symptomatology or other sexual abuse questionnaires.

Primary Reference

Orr et al. (1998).

Scale Availability

Scott P. Orr
Research Service
Veterans Affairs Medical Center
228 Maple St.
Second Floor
Manchester, NH 03103

Related References

Pitman et al. (1987).

General Comments and Recommendations for Practitioners and Researchers

In the primary reference, this method supported the validity of the PTSD diagnosis by demonstrating one of its defining features: physiological reactivity on exposure to internal cues evoking the traumatic event. In clinical settings, generating scripts for imagery evocation might be used as part of an exposure intervention.

---

56. Behavioral Observation of Abused Children (Haskett & Kistner)

Development and Description of Assessment Method

Naturalistic observation of children's behavior in a play setting.

Target Population

Young abused children or any other child population under the age of 6 years old.

Format

This is an assessment in which, to observe children's behavior in a free play setting, an abused child and matched peers are randomly chosen to play in a small, enclosed area of a day care center for a 10-minute free-play session. Blind observers watch for the following behaviors: social initiation, peer reciprocation, instrumental aggression, hostile aggression, negative verbalization, and rough play.

Administration and Scoring

Using a 10-second interval recording procedure, observed behavior is coded for each child. Children are given three scores: quality of social behavior, proportion of negative behaviors, and peer responses. Quality of social behavior is indexed by the number of initiations of positive interaction and the occurrence of the four negative behaviors (hostile aggression, instrumental aggression, negative verbalizations, and rough play). Proportion of negative behaviors is calculated by taking the sum of the number of intervals in which negative verbalizations, rough play, and aggression occurred and dividing by the total number of intervals in which a child engaged in any positive or negative peer interactions. Peer responses are indexed by the number of intervals in which research participants receive initiations of positive social interactions and the proportion of participant initiations reciprocated by peers with a positive or neutral response.

Psychometric Evaluation

Norms
None reported.

Reliability
Interrater reliability of child behavior was assessed for 70% of the observations, and reliability (Cohen's kappa) coefficients ranged from .66 (participants' positive interactions) to 1.00 (physical aggression), with a mean of .78

Validity
The naturalistic observation method discriminated between abused and nonabused children. In peer interactions, abused children appeared more withdrawn, made fewer attempts to interact, and exhibited negative behavior (particularly instrumental aggression) with an overall pattern of withdrawal and aggression.

Advantages
This technique allows for the direct observation and identification of behaviors in specific settings. It also allows for the collection of data on very young children who are unable to report on their own experiences.

Limitations
Naturalistic observations can be time-consuming and an observer can be disruptive to the naturalistic setting if not careful in being unobtrusive.

Primary Reference

Haskett and Kistner (1991).

Scale Availability

For coding system, contact
     Mary E. Haskett

Department of Psychology
North Carolina State University
Box 7801
Raleigh, NC 27695

Related References

Haskett (1990).

General Comments and Recommendations for Practitioners and Researchers

For clinicians, behavioral observations of young children in naturalistic settings may offer rich and unique information to a comprehensive assessment. Behavior categories such as those described herein may be used to guide and focus clinicians' observations.

---

57. Behavioral Observation of Shelter Children (Copping)

Development and Description of Assessment Method

In response to inconsistent results from research on child witnesses of family violence, the author developed clusters of behavior to code based on the literature on child witnesses to family violence.

The longitudinal naturalistic observation of children's behavior across daily activities is conducted using a standardized time schedule.

Target Population

Child witnesses of family violence, although any child shelter population or any other child population under the age of 6.

Format

This assessment consists of a naturalistic observation of children's behavior across daily activities using a standardized time schedule. Observations are held at women's shelters. One hundred-fifty-four behaviors are categorized into 10 specific clusters of behavior under the four main categories of physical, physiological, verbalized behavior, and feelings. The categories under physical include external (e.g., physical aggression), internal (lethargy), regressive (walking or crawling at age 4), and delayed (not walking at age 2). Physical behaviors are also categorized as other undercontrolled (overeating) or overcontrolled (refusal to eat more than one food item over time). Physiological includes external (teeth grinding) and internal (headaches) and verbal includes verbal abuse, excessive verbal behavior, and positive speech. Feelings expressed through "I" statements make up their own cluster. All of these categories are then characterized as either positive or negative.

Administration and Scoring

The categories of behavior, their frequencies, and the object of the behaviors are recorded over multiple hours of the day over a several week period.

Psychometric Evaluation

Norms
None reported.

Reliability
An interrater reliability of .86 was reported, but it was not indicated how this was assessed.

Validity
Most of the coding categories have high face validity in that they represent clearly specified behaviors. In addition, the coding system discriminated between male and female behaviors and among behaviors of children who witnessed family violence and were themselves abused and among behaviors of children who only witnessed abuse. Finally, an increase in problem behaviors over the first three weeks with steady decreases until discharge was shown.

Advantages
This technique allows for the direct observation and identification of behaviors of child witnesses. In addition, it allows for the collection of data on very young children who may not be able to verbalize their experiences or report on their own behavior. The use of participant observers minimizes reactivity of the observation procedure.

Limitations
Naturalistic observations are time-consuming and risk-intrusiveness to the naturalistic setting. Discrete behavior definitions are not always pro-

vided, and some of the behavioral categories are not readily observable (e.g., headaches).

Primary Reference

Copping (1996).

Scale Availability

For coding system, contact
    Valerie E. Copping
    Hamilton-Wentworth Regional Department
      of Public Health Services
    Child & Adolescent Services
    P.O. Box 897
    Hamilton, Ontario L8N3P6 Canada

Related References

None available.

General Comments and Recommendations for Practitioners and Researchers

The coding system and primary reference provide a model for conducting naturalistic observations with shelter children. The coding categories might be used as a basis for conducting behavioral observations of maltreated children in a variety of settings.

---

58. Behavioral Role-Play in Sex Abuse Prevention (BR–SAP; Harbeck, Peterson, & Starr)

Development and Description of Assessment Method

The BR–SAP "was designed to assess children's ability to appropriately identify abusive touches and to react behaviorally to abusive touches in an analogue situation" (Harbeck, Peterson, & Starr, 1992, p. 378).

This method involves observation of children through role-play to assess children's abilities to appropriately identify and react to abusive touches in an analogue situation.

Target Population

Children between the ages of 4 to 16 years who are to participate in a sexual abuse prevention program.

Format

The assessment strategy includes a warm-up role-play followed by five scenarios, with the child portraying him- or herself and the interviewer portraying five different male characters (an uncle, a babysitter, a family friend, a coach, and a father). The five role-plays include three with appropriate physical contact (hugging, stopping bleeding from a cut near the genitals, giving child two pats on the bottom) and two inappropriate–abusive touch situations (sexually stimulating touching game, taking the child swimming and asking the child to take off swimsuit for a picture).

Administration and Scoring

The administration of the role-play begins with a warm-up role-play in which the interviewer pretends to be a pitcher and the child pretends to bat (to increase comfort level and encourage behavioral responses rather than just verbal responses). Then the five role-plays are administered. The actual contact with the children is verbally described but the rest of the scene is acted out. For example, in a sexually stimulating card game, the person drawing the highest card gets to touch the other person "wherever he/she wants." Eventually the examiner will say, "Okay, I want to touch you under your underwear" but of course does not act out the inappropriate touch.

Points are given for both verbal and behavioral responses. Each role-play scores on a 7-point scale, with 1 point for each of the following: child verbalizes leaving the situation, child acts out leaving the situation, child describes saying "no," child actually says "no" in a loud–assertive voice, child describes telling someone about the touch, child acts out telling someone about the touch, child tells someone using appropriate and specific language. Where the child physically acts out the scenario he or she is also given credit for verbal responses.

The two abusive touch measures are summed and the nonabusive scenario is analyzed separately. Interviews are audiotaped and then transcribed on prepared answer sheets.

Psychometric Evaluation

Norms

None reported.

Reliability

Kappa coefficients on verbal response categories ranged from .28 to .87, with a mean of .65, and percent agreement ranged from 84 to 91%, with a mean of 89% for 20 (50%) randomly selected audiotapes. Because videotapes were not used, interrater reliability was not assessed on the two behavioral components: acting out leaving and acting out telling someone about the touch.

Validity

The data from the role-play test were moderately correlated with knowledge about sexual abuse and about personal safety regarding sexual abuse, which offers modest support for convergent validity.

Advantages

This role-play technique offers a rich source of data and provides a useful supplement to self-report data to be helpful in evaluating children's ability to discriminate abusive from nonabusive acts.

Limitations

Role-play assessments are time-consuming because they must be administered individually and then coded. In addition, behaviors demonstrated in role-plays may not generalize to an actual stressful situation of sexual abuse overtures. Finally, there is an ethical concern of causing unnecessary anxiety during the role-play scenarios.

Primary Reference

Harbeck et al. (1992).

Scale Availability

Cynthia Harbeck-Weber
Department of Psychology
Children's Hospital
700 Children's Dr.
Columbus, OH 43205

Related References

None available.

General Comments and Recommendations for Practitioners and Researchers

The generalizability of results from role-play tests to actual at-risk situations remains questionable, and thus predictive validity studies are needed. However, role-play assessments offer a promising supplement to self-report measures as part of a battery of screening or outcome measures.

59. Child Abuse Interview Interaction Coding System (CAIICS; Wood, Orsak, & Cross)

Development and Description of Assessment Method

This behavioral coding system describes both interviewer and child behaviors during a semistructured interview assessment with suspected child sexual abuse victims.

The coding system was designed following recommendations of Bakeman and Gottman (1986) to sample the interactive behaviors of an interviewer and child.

Target Population

Children suspected of being victims of sexual abuse.

Format

The CAIICS is designed to sample interviewer and child behaviors, which are rated for every 10-second interval of an entire videotaped interview assessing experiences of sexual abuse. Interviewer and child coding categories follow.

- *Interviewer Behavior Categories:*
  - Type of questions asked includes open-ended, closed, choice, complex, and no question.
  - Type of support provided includes attention/encouragement, general praise, praise for disclosure, physical reassurance, empathy, and no support.

- Type of information provided includes instruction on the use of aids, instruction on safety skills, explains purpose, non–abuse-related information, abuse-related information, commands, and no information.
- *Child Behavior Categories:*
  - Attention/on-task behaviors, which includes attentive/on-task, attentive/off-task, inattentive/on-task, and inattentive/off-task; observed emotions, which includes relaxed, angry, anxious, sad/hurt, guilt/shame, excited/happy.
  - Types of disclosures includes yes or no answer, one- or two-word answer, detailed abuse, related disclosure, acts out or draws abuse-related events, non–abuse-related narrative, says "I don't know"/"I don't remember," and no disclosure.

Administration and Scoring

The coding system codes behaviors during videotaped semistructured child sexual abuse interviews.

Interviewer and child behaviors are rated during 10-second intervals. For each interval, one or two interactions can be rated. Pairs of coders simultaneously code each interview. One coder rated interviewer behaviors while one rated child behaviors. Training to criterion in the CAIICS requires approximately 8 hours of training and supervision.

Psychometric Evaluation

Norms

The means, standard deviations, and percentages of each specific type of interviewer and child behavior are available from the author.

Reliability

Interrater reliability of behavioral ratings for child and interviewer behaviors was established using kappa. For child behaviors, kappas were .93 (attentive/on-task behaviors), .98 (type of disclosure), and .95 (observed emotions). For interviewer behaviors, kappas were .92 (type of question), .97 (support provided), and .87 (information provided).

Validity

None reported.

Advantages

Because the coding system looks at both interviewer and child behaviors, it offers the possibility of examining the influence of interviewer behaviors on children's responses. The coding system has excellent interrater reliability.

Limitations

Validation work is needed. There is a limited number of categories coded for interviewer and child behavior.

Primary Reference

Wood, Orsak, Murphy, and Cross (1996).

Scale Availability

> Barbara Wood
> P.O. Box 33239
> Seattle, WA 98133

Related References

Bakeman and Gottman (1986); Wood (1990).

General Comments and Recommendations for Practitioners and Researchers

CAIICS offers a novel assessment strategy in that it codes interviewer–child dyads and rates interviewer process variables that may affect child responses (e.g., disclosure patterns).

---

60. Mock Trial Role-Play (MTRP; Jaffee, Wilson, & Sas)

Development and Description of Assessment Method

To assess children's ability to testify and cope with the potential trauma in the courtroom, the authors conducted a case study of a 15-year-old who made allegations of sexual abuse against her father. A mock trial that did not focus on the sexual abuse incident but rather on an emotionally neutral topic was set up to provide the needed rehearsal and exposure to the courtroom process.

The MTRP is an in vivo mock trial used to demystify the courtroom for children by providing an opportunity for them to experience a courtroom setting as well as to provide a sense of mastery and desensitize anxieties about the courtroom situation.

Target Population

Potential sexual abuse victims who may need to appear in court to testify.

Format

The MTRP consists of an in vivo mock trial role play in which a child can be led through legal proceedings in an actual courtroom.

Administration and Scoring

A "trial" is conducted in an actual courtroom with a child being asked questions in front of a (safe) adult dressed in a judge's robe. Other adults act as prosecuting attorney, defense attorney, and courtroom spectators. The child is encouraged to pretend the trial is real and is evaluated in terms of ability to answer questions appropriately and serve as a reliable witness.

Psychometric Evaluation

Norms
None reported.

Reliability
None reported.

Validity
None reported.

Advantages
Although developed as a desensitization procedure for an adolescent girl scheduled to give courtroom testimony, this may be a promising procedure to use when assessing children's readiness/competency for this type of experience. The procedure provides a model for both assessment and intervention.

Limitations

The method was presented in a single case study format. No specific coding or scoring system exists for the evaluation.

Primary Reference

Jaffee, Wilson, and Sas (1987).

Scale Availability

Because this is not a scale per se, it is not available.

Related References

None available.

General Comments and Recommendations for Practitioners and Researchers

No specific scoring system has been developed; instead, the evaluation is based on the subjective judgments of experts. Although the MTRP offers an extremely promising assessment tool, scoring standardization is needed to evaluate and develop the methods reliability and validity.

---

61. Sexually Anatomically Detailed Dolls (Dawson, Vaughan, & Wagner)

Development and Description of Assessment Method

The structured interview protocol resembles that used by White, Strom, Santilli, and Halpin (1986). The authors attempted to build on previous research with a more refined coding procedure.

This is a structured, nonsuggestive extended interview to examine preschoolers' behaviors and verbalizations during interactions with sexually anatomically detailed dolls. The interview has discrete phases for allowing a range of interactions with the dolls.

Target Population

Children ages 3 years, eight months, to 6 years of age.

Format

This assessment consists of a structured, nonsuggestive interview with preschool boys and girls in which sexually anatomically detailed (SAD) dolls are examined (father, mother, boy, and girl dolls) and other play props are available. The interviews are videotaped for later coding.

There are five phases of the interview: warm-up free play (the average amount of time being 7.63 minutes for a child to appear comfortable), introduction of the SAD dolls by examiner and naming both neutral and sex body parts of undressed dolls by the child (the average amount of time = 9.02 minutes), interaction of the child with dressed SAD dolls and child showing what he or she does home alone with Daddy (average time 5.62 minutes), interaction of child with undressed SAD dolls and child showing what he or she does at home with mother and father (average time 7.72 minutes), and postsession free play (average time 5.37 minutes), for a total of 35 minutes of observation.

Administration and Scoring

Open-ended questions such as "show me what you did together" are used to prompt spontaneous responses of the children.

An interval recording method is used to code behaviors with an audiotape recorder used to signal time intervals for coding. Fifteen-second observation intervals with 5-second recording intervals are used. Only the first behavior or verbalization is coded in each 15-second-observation interval. Activities depicted by each child with the doll are recorded in narrative form (e.g., "takes a bath with father").

Behaviors are categorized as follows:

- BNSA: behavioral nonsexual aggression
- BSA: behavioral sexual aggression
- BSEP: behavioral sexual exploratory play
- BAA: behavioral active avoidance
- BA: behavioral affection

Verbalizations are categorized as follows:

- VNSA: verbal nonsexual aggression
- VSA: verbal sexual aggression
- VSEP: verbal sexual exploratory play
- VAA: verbal active avoidance
- VA: verbal affection

A sample definition of the behavioral category BSEP is as follows:

child investigates penis, breasts, vagina, or anus of the dolls. Examples include putting fingers into the vagina or anus and feeling the sex parts; nonexamples include demonstrating sexual intercourse and hitting. A complete list of definitions is available from the authors.

Psychometric Evaluation
Norms
This study was used to establish responses from a sample of nonsexually abused preschool girls and boys (mean age = 5 years). In frequencies across all phases, BSEP and VSEP combined represented the most responses (42 and 50%), although BNSA was also observed frequently. BSA, BA, VA, and VSA were displayed at a very low frequency. There were no instances in which children acted out or described sexual intercourse or sexual fondling, very few instances of sexual aggression, and a high incidence of VSEP, which is common among non (sexually) abused children. Exact rates of behaviors and verbalizations for each category are provided in the primary reference.

Reliability
Graduate students were trained to 90% agreement on four pilot videos. Interobserver agreement with a blind second observer who coded 30% of randomly selected observations demonstrated a percent agreement of occurrences of 77%, with a range of 60 to 89%, with the median for individual phases being 83%.

Validity
None reported.

Advantages
This method provides data on standardized or normal responses to SAD dolls, which can be used as a comparison basis in the assessment of children thought to have been sexually abused.

Limitations
The procedure is time-consuming and the primary study was conducted on a small, all-White middle-class sample, which limits the generalizability of results. The complex interval coding system may require extensive observer training and may not readily extend to the clinical situation.

Primary Reference

Dawson, Vaughan, and Wagner (1992).

Scale Availability

Brenda Dawson
Department of Psychology
University of Southern Mississippi
Southern Station Box 5025
Hattiesburg, MS 39406

Related References

Dawson, Geddie, and Wagner (1996); White, Strom, Santilli, and Halpin (1986).

General Comments and Recommendations for Practitioners and Researchers

The procedure allows for standardized assessment with SAD dolls, and the primary reference provides normative data for a nonabused sample of young children. However, validation studies are needed to allow for use of this method as part of routine sexual abuse evaluation.

Part III

Assessment of Parents and Caregivers

Introduction:
Assessment of Parents
and Caregivers

More than a decade has passed since Wolfe (1985) reviewed the empirical evidence on abusive parents' contributions to child maltreatment. The research and clinical literature highlighted abusive parent factors such as social isolation, low self-esteem and frustration tolerance, parenting-skills deficiencies, unrealistic expectations, an imbalance in the proportion of negative to positive parent–child interactions, as well as stress-related symptoms and health concerns (Wolfe, 1985). These characteristics that supported the bidirectional view of family behavior and emphasized contextual events that might precipitate and maintain child maltreatment broadened the long-standing psychiatric emphasis on the personality functioning of the abusive parent (Spinetta & Rigler, 1972). Few abusive parents are actually diagnosed with a psychiatric disorder (only 10 to 15%, Ammerman, 1990), and no clear abusive parent profile has emerged after decades of research.

More recent theoretical models have continued to emphasize the multideterminant nature of child maltreatment and have focused on multiple causative and protective factors. A brief review of these factors will help to understand the various parent variables targeted for clinical assessment. Within these process-oriented models, parenting behavior, parent affect, and the functional analysis of antecedent and consequent events continue to be a major focus. Milner's (1993) social information processing model focuses on the role of parent cognitions in child maltreatment. Included in his analysis are parent perceptions, interpretations, evaluations, and expectations of the child's behavior. The integration of this information and selection of a response to the child's behavior by the parent completes the process. Parents' attributions for children's behavior will have a direct effect on their emotional arousal and affective response (Dix, 1991). Researchers from a cognitive perspective who have focused on stable representations of relationships, conceptualized as schemas, have reported that parents who are most likely to view themselves as lacking power over their interactions with their children are most likely to make use of coercive control tactics (Bugental, Brown, & Reiss, 1996). In fact, abusive parents are more likely than nonabusive parents to see themselves as victims of their child's transgressions and to become highly reactive to caregiving challenges (Bugental, 1993a). Clearly, the study of cognitive processes that mediate parents' responses to their children has helped to identify both risk and protective factors in maltreating families.

In a model focused on the affective organization of parenting, Dix (1991) suggested that emotional arousal plays a key role in a parent's response to his or her child's behavior. In his review of research on affect in parenting, Dix (1991) concluded that parents' emotions reflect the health of parent–child relationships perhaps more than any other single variable. Heightened emotional reactivity will have a profound effect on the cognitive processes identified by Milner (1993) and on the situational appraisals identified by Hillson and Kuiper (1994). In addition, high arousal in the form of anger reflects an affective stress response (Novaco, 1985) that will affect not only cognitive mediational processes but perhaps behavior. Although the relationship between anger and reactive aggression is a complicated one, it is clear that for some parents anger arousal will compromise parenting behavior and may potentiate the use of aggression toward children. Rodriquez and Green (1997) as well as Holden and Banez (1996) reported data that support the links between anger expression and parenting stress and parental attitudes and characteristics associated with child abuse risk. Recent research on specific aspects of parental anger arousal (Sedlar & Hansen, 2001) indicates that this assessment focus is critical in the assessment of the parent. In addition, the intensity of a punishment strategy for perceived child misbehavior communicates information concerning the affective state of the parent (Gordon, Jones, & Nowicki, 1979). Dysfunctional attributions regarding the intentionality of the child's misbehavior as well as the parents' perceived lack of control over a discipline encounter may compound the emotional arousal the parent is already experiencing in response to aversive child behavior and increase the likelihood of harsh or overactive parenting (Smith &

O'Leary, 1995). In a cyclical pattern, distressed parents experience high levels of anger and dysphoria when their ineffective parenting skills fail to result in child compliance or cooperation (Dix, 1991). This emotional arousal then further affects parents' interpretation of interactions with their children.

Other factors that may influence parental behavior have been identified by clinical researchers. Azar (1991) clarified disturbed cognitive schema attributional biases and problem-solving deficits in abusive parents, and Hillson and Kuiper (1994) examined stress and coping factors in child maltreatment. In their model, the parents' primary appraisal of stress and secondary appraisal of resources, along with dispositional coping strategies, are influential in the occurrence of child maltreatment. In sum, elevated parental stress levels, dysfunctional appraisals, and negative coping responses will increase the probability of maltreatment (Hillson & Kuiper, 1994). Parenting-skills deficits in child management and effective communication, as well as marital dysfunction, are also likely to influence the risk for child maltreatment.

Finally, an often overlooked aspect of assessment of maltreating families is conditions considered to indicate child neglect. It may be hard to assess parent behaviors that are absent (such as failure to provide adequate supervision to prevent injury; see Petersen, Ewigman, & Kivlahan, 1993, or failure to provide adequate stimulation). However, because the largest proportion of termination of parental rights cases are neglect ones, a comprehensive assessment of parents' skills in ensuring their child's health and safety must be considered.

A critical issue pertaining to the assessment of parents in maltreating families is the definition and measurement of parenting competence (Budd & Holdsworth, 1996). Given the necessary decision making involved in risk assessment of child abuse cases, assessment of parenting skills, parental dysfunction and receptivity to treatment is often required. Azar, Benjet, Fuhrmann, and Cavallero (1995) suggested that the behavioral assessment emphasis on a functional analyses of family interaction within the natural context could be quite beneficial to forensic investigations. In an excellent review of clinical issues related to the assessment of parenting competence, Budd and Holdsworth (1996) suggested that the following eight dimensions be assessed to provide a comprehensive competency assessment: historical information, intellectual functioning, adaptive and social functioning, personality and emotional adjustment, parenting knowledge, attitudes and perceptions, parent–

child interactions, child functioning, and parental response to previous intervention efforts.

Although the clinician or researcher might be concerned that there are no standardized conceptualizations for assessing "minimal" parenting competence, Azar, Lauretti, and Loding (1998) provided one of the best models to use in guiding comprehensive assessment of parenting competence. They outlined five functional domains of parenting (parenting, social–cognitive, self-control, stress management, and social skills) and further define each domain into specific skill areas. Their functional–contextual framework helps to delineate parenting competence necessary for healthy child development and to identify deficit areas associated with increased risk for maltreatment. It is quite accepted in the field at this time that rather than focusing on diagnostic and trait-like qualities of parents, direct measurement of parenting behaviors, attitudes, perceptions, capabilities, and practices is a more constructive and valid approach (Budd, 2001).

An important issue related to the assessment of parents in maltreating or at-risk families is the reason for the assessment or how the information is to be used. Evaluating parents in the context of possible abuse or neglect to inform dispositional decisions such as placement, custody, or termination of parental rights poses particular difficulties for the clinician. The results of such an assessment may be used as forensic evidence in legal proceedings or may be used to predict future behavior (Budd, 2001). The assessment process then will be viewed by the parent as critical to retention of custody of his or her child and will certainly influence the parent's responses in a socially desirable fashion. Clearly, issues of reporting, the limits of confidentiality, and informed consent of parents who might be voluntarily completing assessment as part of a research study become paramount. In addition, the context of the assessment process may lead to a certain hostility or suspiciousness on the part of the parent respondent. Although the field of parent assessment has grown remarkably with many tools and methodologies available, Azar et al. (1998) urge extreme caution in conducting parenting competency evaluations because of the predictive limitations in our technology and the potential for biases to enter reports. Guidelines recommended by the American Psychological Association (1997) in the examination of parenting capacity focus on the current and potential functional capabilities of the parent to meet the needs of the child and the relationship between the parent and the child. Budd (2001) provided an excellent model for a parental fitness assessment with three core features and a focus on the interface between a parent's overall functioning, his or her child-rearing skills, and the child's development needs. The core features are (a) the focus on parenting qualities and the parent–child relationship; (b) the use of a functional approach to assessment that emphasizes behaviors and skills in everyday performance; and (c) the application of a minimal parenting standard, sufficient to protect the safety and well-being of the child (Budd, 2001). Discrete steps of the assessment process from identification of the referral question to the final written report are outlined, and underscored throughout is the need for multimethod assessment tools.

A comprehensive assessment of a parent involved in child maltreatment or a parent determined to be at risk for child maltreatment must include multiple targets for assessment. Parenting skills, expectations of child behavior, judgments, and attributions concerning discipline, stress, affective level and regulation, problem solving, and interactional style all represent significant targets for parent assessment. In addition, specific negative child qualities and misbehaviors that are salient and likely to add to the stress level, to undermine parenting abilities, and to increase the likelihood of abusive behavior have been identified (Ammerman & Patz, 1996). Therefore, parent assessment must also include a look at the interactions between child behavior and parent response. In fact, Azar et al. (1998) suggested that judgments regarding adequacy of parenting cannot be made solely on skills exhibited by parents but must include an evaluation of the "goodness of fit" between a particular parent or set of parents for a specific child. This will certainly require an examination of the child's functioning and needs, considered over time alongside the assessment of the parent's skills and responsivity. This section will examine a variety of structured interview, self-report, and analogue strategies that have been used in the assessment of parents, many of which may prove helpful in the identification of parents at risk for child maltreatment.

Interview Methods

There are several semistructured interviews that have been developed to examine discipline and interaction styles of parents. Although none of these has been used with abusive or at-risk parents, they are included as promising and creative methods for initial pretreatment assessment or as evaluations of parent interventions.

---

62. Child Conflict Index (CCI; Frankel & Weiner)

Development and Description of Assessment Method

Items reflected four clusters from the original Parent Daily Report developed by Patterson in 1975: aggression, immaturity, unsocialized, and retaliation. Authors added items reflecting conflicts and internalizing behaviors through a rational process.

The Child Conflict Index is a structured telephone interview of parents' recall of conflict with their child the previous day. Designed as a measure of problematic parent–child interaction in the home, its focus is on important negative characteristics of the interactions across an entire day.

Target Population

Parents of elementary schoolchildren.

Format

The Child Conflict Index is a structured interview format in which the parent is asked to respond to a checklist of 21 items about their son's behavior or 18 items about their daughter's behavior the previous day (12 items are the same for both genders). The two subscales based on identified factors and corresponding items are

- *Conflict/Attention Seeking* (14 items for boys version, 10 items for girls version): "Did _____ argue with peers or adults?" (boys' items)
- *Negativity/Withdrawal* (7 items for boys version, 8 items for girls version): "Did _____ show a negative attitude?" (boys' item); "Was _____ in a bad mood or easily annoyed yesterday?" (girls' item)

Administration and Scoring

For this interview, one hour is required to train telephone interviewers, 15 minutes to collect data, and 3 minutes to score the protocol.

Psychometric Evaluation

Norms
Not applicable.

Reliability
Interrater agreement was examined with two independent listeners rating a random sample of interviews; 99.9% reliability was obtained. Internal consistency was evaluated by comparing calls 2 through 5 with same respondent. Coefficient alphas ranged from .78 to .79 for mothers of boys and from .70 to .77 for mothers of girls. (In this initial research only mothers were examined, but fathers could be assessed as well.)

Validity
Convergent validity was examined via a comparison to a direct observation laboratory analogue of mother–child compliance task. Videotapes coded for mother commands and child compliance were compared to Child Conflict Index scores. A Mann-Whitney test was significant ($U = 6$, $p < .05$), indicating that the low-compliance group had a higher median percentile score on the Child Conflict Index (75.9) than the high-compliance group (53.8).

Convergent validity was also examined by comparing scores to mother-completed Child Behavior Checklist (CBCL; Achenbach, 1991) data. Correlations between the Child Conflict Index and the CBCL aggression and delinquency subscale scores were predominantly significant for boys across three age groups. For girls, however, none of the correlations reached significance. The authors do indicate the small number of girls in the study and propose alternative scoring for the CBCL (see Frankel & Weiner, 1990).

Advantages

The Child Conflict Index allows for low cost data collection and coding. Conducting an ongoing assessment with the Child Conflict Index evokes minimal parent–child reactivity and minimal constraints upon the setting. Versions are available for both boys and girls.

Limitations

Unfortunately, the Child Conflict Index condenses behavior across an entire day. Another limitation vis-à-vis comprehensiveness of data are that frequency and intensity data are not available; only occurrence or nonoccurrence of target behaviors are recorded. The Child Conflict Index focuses solely on child misbehavior and not on parental response, which is an important dimension.

Primary Reference

Frankel and Weiner (1990).

Scale Availability

Fred Frankel
Parent Training Program
UCLA Department of Psychiatry
300 UCLA Medical Plaza
Los Angeles, CA 90024

Related References

None available.

General Comments and Recommendations for Practitioners and Researchers

The clinician could add behaviors of particular concern to a certain family, making this interview an individualized assessment approach.

63. Concerns and Constraints Interview (CCI; Deater, Dodge, Bates, and Pettit)

Development and Description of Assessment Method

This is an open-ended interview format followed by a summary rating by the interviewer designed to assess mothers' use of physical discipline in response to hypothetical vignettes of child misbehavior. The Concerns and Constraints Interview also taps mothers' attributions and affect in response to misbehavior.

Target Population

Parents of elementary schoolchildren.

Format

The Concerns and Constraints Interview consists of five hypothetical vignettes involving child misbehavior—child losing a race and calling the winner a bad name, pushing a peer after being accidentally bumped, threatening to throw a ball into the sewer if peers don't let him or her join in, talking back, and teasing a peer—that are read to the parent. After each vignette is read, the parent describes discipline strategies with prompt questions such as "Why do you think the child behaved this way?", "How would you feel if your child behaved this way?", and "What would you do if your child behaved this way?"

Administration and Scoring

Mothers' free responses to each vignette were coded as to whether physical punishment was included (score of 1 given if physical punishment used and score of 2 given if no physical punishment used). Then, after hearing responses from the parent, the interviewer coded the interview on a 5-point, Likert-type scale with the following anchor points:

- 1 = nonrestrictive, mostly positive guidance;
- 3 = moderately restrictive, sometimes physical;
- 5 = severely strict, often physical.

A total physical punishment score is computed by averaging across the five vignettes; higher scores indicate a greater use of physical punishment.

Psychometric Evaluation

Norms
Based on a sample of 552 mothers, a mean rating of 2.6 would indicate that a moderate degree of physical discipline would be used.

Reliability
Good interrater agreement on the coding of 56 randomly selected interviews was reported as $r = .80$. Acceptable internal consistency was reported with an alpha of .42.

Validity
Not available.

Advantages
The format is flexible, allowing parents to fully describe their possible reactions and thus allows for cultural sensitivity.

Limitations
The coding of attribution and affect responses was not reported. The hypothetical vignettes were predominantly about peer interactions and may allow for generalization to family situations. Limited psychometric information is available.

Primary Reference

Deater-Deckard, Dodge, Bates, and Pettit (1996).

Scale Availability

> Kirby Deater-Deckard
> Institute of Psychiatry
> 113 Denmark Hill
> Denmark Hill, London, UK SE58AF

Related References

None available.

General Comments and Recommendations for Practitioners and Researchers

Format could be adapted for high-risk families by including vignettes typically occurring in their particular family context.

64. Daily Discipline Interview (DDI; Webster-Stratton)

Development and Description of Assessment Method

An extensive content analysis of 56 interviews randomly selected from 300 interviews was completed. The authors inductively derived an initial 66-item response code that captured the essence of all the types of disciplinary strategies. These 66 items were sorted and compiled into 6 categories based on the theoretical judgment of three psychologist/ experts and on previous research. Internal consistency scores were computed and categories refined by deleting items with low item–total correlations.

This is a semi-structured telephone interview designed to measure the variety, flexibility, and appropriateness of disciplinary strategies used by parents.

Target Population

Parents of young (3–7-year-old) children with conduct problems.

Format

The DDI includes 22 negative behavior patterns commonly engaged in by children. Parents' descriptions of their reactions to these behavior patterns are analyzed using a 43-item disciplinary response code reflecting six categories:

1. *Physical Force:* Negative physical responses such as spanking, slapping, hitting, kicking.
2. *Critical Verbal Force:* Negative verbal responses such as yelling, scolding, screaming, threatening.
3. *Limit Setting:* Time-out, withdrawal of privileges, logical consequences.
4. *Teaching:* Reasoning, explanations, giving alternatives, praise, attention.
5. *Empathy:* Parent identifying with child and responding warmly to feelings.
6. *Guilt Induction:* Humiliation, threats to tell father, expressions of disappointment.

Administration and Scoring

When a parent indicates a particular behavior problem occurred, the interviewer asks open-ended questions related to "How did you handle this problem?" The interviewer writes down the parent's verbal responses verbatim. The interview takes approximately 30 minutes to complete. From the verbatim transcript, each parental strategy is coded in terms of type and appropriateness using a 66-item coding system. Each parent receives a score for each of six discipline categories. Two additional scores were developed:

1. *Flexibility of Responses:* Computed based on the number of different responses used from each of six discipline categories, and
2. *Inappropriateness of Discipline Strategy:* A ratio score of number of inappropriate discipline strategies to the number of behavior problems.

Psychometric Evaluation

Norms
Not applicable.

Reliability
Interrater reliability was assessed on 20% of interviews (in $N = 122$ study) by independent scoring of a third rater. Coefficient alphas were .40 for empathy, .56 for guilt induction, .83 for teaching, .94 for physical force, .94 for verbal force, .97 for limit setting, .80 for flexibility, and .89 for inappropriateness. Mean percent agreement scores between the raters was 80% (ranging from 60% for teaching to 88% for limit setting and physical force).

Test–retest reliability obtained over a one-week interval ranged from $r = .45$ for physical force to $r = .75$ for empathy.

Internal consistency was analyzed via Spearman-Brown split half formula (Nunnaly & Bernstein, 1994). The scores ranging from $r = .59$ for limit setting to $r = .86$ for empathy show moderate internal consistency.

Validity
Convergent validity was examined via comparisons to the Child Behavior Checklist (Achenbach, 1991) and the Parenting Stress Index (Abidin, 1990). The DDI shows significant correlations with the Parenting Stress Index (Abidin, 1990) PSI child domain score ($r = .42$) and the

Child Behavior Checklist (Achenbach, 1991) total score ($r = .50$). In general, mothers' reports of discipline characterized by physical force and inappropriate and inflexible strategies are correlated with parents' report of deviant child behaviors.

Mothers' disciplinary strategies showed low but significant correlations with mothers' personal adjustment as measured by the Beck Depression Inventory (Beck, Ward, Mendelson, Mock, & Erbaugh, 1961; range $r = .16$ to $r = .24$), the State-Trait Anxiety Inventory (Spielberger, Gorsuch, Lushene, Vagg, & Jacobs, 1983; range $r = .25$ to $r = .27$), and the Parenting Stress Index: Adult Domain (Abidin, 1990; range $r = .22$ to $r = .30$). The more stressed or depressed the mother, the more critical verbal force and inappropriate and inflexible strategies were used.

Advantages

This assessment method is a low-cost data collection method that can be used reliably by telephone interviewers after training and that would seem to directly reflect changes in parent responding as a function of parent training interventions. The interview includes positive as well as negative categories of parent behavior.

Limitations

The authors determined which discipline strategies were appropriate according to type of misbehavior that may reflect their stereotypes and may not be culturally sensitive.

Primary Reference

Webster-Stratton and Spitzer (1991).

Scale Availability

Carolyn Webster-Stratton
Department of Parent and Child Nursing
SC-74
University of Washington
Seattle, WA 98195

Related References

None available.

General Comments and Recommendations for Practitioners and Researchers

The DDI is a good way to assess the range of parental responses that may be precursors to abuse.

---

65. Disciplinary Strategies Interview (DSI; Peterson)

Development and Description of Assessment Method

Vignettes were developed following a review of the literature on situations that parents found problematic.

This is a structured interview designed to examine anger and other variables known to be related to physical child abuse. Open-ended questioning about discipline style is included.

Target Population

Low-income mothers with children between the ages of 18 months and 5 years.

Format

This interview consists of four sections:

1. Background information about the mother and eligibility criteria for inclusion in the study;
2. General disciplinary procedures, including a description of common punishments used, reasons for their use, and frequency of use;
3. The occurrence of disciplinary response to and anger provoked by vignettes about four common child rearing challenges with children under five years of age—after the situation was described, the mother was asked if her child ever engaged in this behavior and, if so, she is asked to describe what she did about it and how angry she became; and
4. A description of the situations that provoke the most anger, the disciplinary response to these situations, and the level of anger provoked. Finally, the mothers were asked if they ever spank their child and, if so, how often.

Administration and Scoring

These individual interviews with 199 mothers in attendance at a community health clinic were conducted by research assistants. The disciplinary strategies outlined in parts 2 to 4 were subjected to empirically derived coding, which revealed eight major strategies: spanking, aggressive-physical/verbal, remove from situation (including time out and response prevention), instruction, reward alternative, situational consequences, allow misbehavior, and miscellaneous. Also, parents' descriptions of what behaviors made them angriest were coded into the following categories:

- *Disobedience:* Doing the opposite of what is asked.
- *Off-Limits Behavior:* Doing things the child knows is not allowed.
- *Defiance:* Saying "no you can't make me" or talking back.
- *Aggression:* Fighting with or hurting siblings or other children.
- *Tantrums:* Crying with force or displays.
- *Unsafe Behavior:* Touching stove, running into street.
- *Negative Affect:* Acting jealous, sulking.

Parental ratings of anger occurred via a 5-point Likert-type scale ranging from 1 = not angry at all to 5 = ready to explode.

Psychometric Evaluation

Norms
Not applicable.

Reliability
The disciplinary strategies outlined in Parts 2, 3, and 4 were coded by two independent raters with a Kappa coefficient of .74. Further, the descriptions of what behaviors made parents the angriest were also coded by a primary and a reliability coder. The Kappa coefficient of .75 indicates good interrater reliability.

Validity
Construct validity was assessed via comparisons between type of discipline and how much anger was evoked for each of the vignettes. These comparisons yielded low point biserial correlations (ranging from $r = .07$ to $r = .19$) for most vignettes. The extent to which mothers became angry was, however, related to their view of their child as assessed by the Eyberg Child Behavior Inventory (Eyberg & Ross, 1978). Significant correlations between anger ratings for throwing temper tantrums ($r =$

.38), disobedience ($r = .36$), and for the situation that made the parent angriest ($r = .46$) with ratings of child behavior problems indicated good concurrent validity.

Advantages

This interview seems to be an easily administered screening of situations provoking anger and commonly occurring parent discipline responses. Flexible format allows for assessment of idiosyncratic anger-provoking scenarios. Assessment of both affective and behavioral responses of the mother is a plus.

Limitations

The situations developed did not reflect the experiences of low-income parents; the authors found that behaviors that mothers felt undermined their authority with their child were more problematic. Further, cultural variables were not considered.

Primary Reference

Peterson, Ewigman, and Vandiver (1994).

Scale Availability

Lizette Peterson
Department of Psychology
210 McAlister Hall
University of Missouri-Columbia
Columbia, MO 65211

Related References

None available.

General Comments and Recommendations for Practitioners and Researchers

Although the four hypothetical vignettes selected for this study may not be relevant to all parent populations, further development of this interview might include vignettes described by maltreating families.

66. Parent Discipline Interview (PDI; Scarr, Pinkerton, & Eisenberg)

Development and Description of Assessment Method

The PDI is a structured interview in which parents respond to misbehavior scenarios designed to tap basic discipline issues.

Target Population

Parents of young children.

Format

In the PDI, parents are presented with five age-appropriate scenarios and are asked how they would respond the first time and what they would do if the behavior continued. Example vignettes include a child walking into the street (toddler), a child hitting a peer to get a toy (preschool), avoiding bedtime (school-age), ignoring directions to eat dinner (preschool). Although the vignettes vary in content across the age groups, they are designed to tap basic discipline issues such as violation of safety rules and noncompliance with parent demands.

Administration and Scoring

Interviews are audiotaped and scored by trained coders. Eighteen discipline categories are condensed into six variables. These variables include,

- *Physical Control,* defined as the parent's deliberate infliction of physical pain, including slapping, spanking, whipping, and so forth;
- *Coercive Verbal Control,* defined as reprimands such as "Stop it" or threats such as "If you do that again, I'll spank you";
- *Angry Interrogations,* for example, questions such as "Why do you keep coming out of your room?"; and
- *Disappointment and Withdrawal of Affection.*

Other variables include *physical restraint* (gently forcing a child's arm into a jacket sleeve if he or she was resisting) and *verbal reasoning* (explaining why the behavior is inappropriate). In one study (Deater-Deckard & Scarr, 1996), the use of reasoning was reverse scored and standardized and was summed with the standardized physical control score to produce an *authoritarian discipline score*. In another study (Deater-Deckard, Pinkerton, & Scarr, 1996), the frequency of mentioning physical punishment was summed across the five vignettes to produce a *harsh parental discipline score*.

Psychometric Evaluation

Norms
Not applicable.

Reliability
Interrater reliability of coders was reported to be $r = .86$. In one sample of Bermudan mothers, the use of physical punishment was reported to be stable over time (.49, $p < .001$; see Deater-Deckard, 1996). Internal consistency was examined when the 18 discipline categories were condensed into 6 variables. Correlations between these variables showed moderate internal consistency (.20 to $-.29$ range; Deater-Deckard & Scarr, 1996).

Validity
Convergent validity was examined through comparisons of PDI data with brief (20–30 min) observational measures of maternal control strategies used in a toy-sorting task. Modest correlations of $r = .20$ to $r = .30$ were obtained. Discriminant validity was examined in comparisons of PDI summed scores of physical control and coercive verbal control with the short form of the Parenting Stress Index (Abidin, 1990). None of these correlations was significant, indicating that the PDI is not a measurement of negative affect in the parent–child dyad.

Advantages
This interview helps to assess not only a parent's initial response to misbehavior, but also subsequent responses to child noncompliance. Discipline categories used in scoring seem comprehensive.

Limitations
Any assessment requiring parents to respond to hypothetical situations has a strong social desirability factor. Further research should examine parental correspondence between saying and doing. The use of only five scenarios may limit the interviewer's utility.

Primary Reference

Scarr, Pinkerton, and Eisenberg (1994).

Scale Availability

Sandra Scarr
Department of Psychology
University of Virginia
Charlottesville, VA

Related References

Deater-Deckard (1996); Deater-Deckard, Pinkerton, and Scarr (1996); Deater-Deckard and Scarr (1996).

General Comments and Recommendations for Practitioners and Researchers

Although this parent interview has been used extensively in development research on normal children, there are no data reported on its use with high-risk parents who may be under investigation for maltreatment risk.

---

67. Parental Problem-Solving Measure (PPSM; Hansen)

Development and Description of Assessment Method

This is a semistructured interview assessment of parents' problem-solving responses to hypothetical problems reflecting five domains: child behavior, interpersonal problems, anger/stress, financial problems, and child care problems.

The initial pool of 50 problematic situations was created by sampling the literature, giving the pilot problems questionnaire to eight abusive parents, and giving the pilot problems questionnaire to four mental health professionals.

The final 25 situations were randomly chosen (5 from each category). Items with item–total correlations less than $r = .33$ were deleted, resulting in this 15-item format.

Target Population

Parents of children under 18 years of age.

Format

In this assessment, three problem situations from each of the five domains are presented. Sample problem situations include,

- "Your child's teacher calls you and says that your child is misbehaving at school. Your child teases other children, is very disruptive in the classroom, and gets in fights on the playground. The teacher is very upset and you must do something."
- "You won't get paid for one week and you are out of money. You are almost out of groceries and do not have enough to feed your children for that week."

Administration and Scoring

Parents are read 15 brief problem vignettes and are then asked to describe what they could and would do in response and exactly how they would carry out the solution. Responses are audio recorded and later rated for (a) the number of alternative solutions generated, (b) the effectiveness of each solution on a 7-point Likert-type scale ranging from 1 = very effective to 7 = very ineffective, and (c) effectiveness of the best solution. The manual lists 176 sample responses (a mean of 11.7 per vignette) that were empirically developed for coding effectiveness.

Psychometric Evaluation

A psychometric study of 60 parents ($N = 27$ abusive parents, $N = 12$ clinic parents, and $N = 21$ control parents) was conducted.

Norms
Not available.

Reliability
Regarding interrater reliabilities, on a sample of 60 parents the mean Pearson correlation was $r = .93$ for number of solutions generated (range = $r = .82$ to $r = .96$) and $r = .88$ for effectiveness of best solution (range = $r = .83$ to $r = .94$).

Internal consistency scores computed via Cronbach's alpha were .91 for total score/number of solutions and .77 for total score/effectiveness of best solution. Alpha values for subscale domains ranged from .17 for effectiveness of best solution in child care domain to .79 for number of solutions in child behavior domain. Test–retest reliability examined across an average interval of 17 days indicated a mean correlation of $r = .71$ (range from .62 to .82) for number of solutions and a mean correlation of $r = .68$ (range from .58 to .74) for effectiveness of best solution.

Validity

Scores differentiated maltreating from nonmaltreating parents in that abusive parents scored significantly lower on all scales than community parents. Convergent validity was not found in that parental problem-solving responses were *not* correlated with the Eyberg Child Behavior Inventory (Eyberg & Ross, 1978), the Hassles Scale (Kanner, Coyne, Schaefer, & Lazarus, 1981) or the Parental Anger Inventory (MacMillan, Olson, & Hansen, 1988).

Advantages

The PPSM manual is extensive and provides 10 to 12 sample solutions and effectiveness ratings for each of the 15 problem situations. The PPSM is one of the few parent assessment measures actually used with abusive parents and is a good direct outcome assessment for parent training interventions.

Limitations

It is not clear to what degree these parent-reported solutions are socially desirable responses and how such reports are related to actual behavior. Additional psychometric work is needed to establish convergent and discriminant validity.

Primary Reference

Hansen, Pallotta, Christopher, Conaway, and Lundquist (1995).

Scale Availability

> David J. Hansen
> Department of Psychology
> University of Nebraska-Lincoln
> Lincoln, NE 68588-0308

Related References

Hansen, Pallotta, Tishelman, Conaway, and MacMillan (1989); Haskett, Myers, Pirillo, and Dombalis (1995).

General Comments and Recommendations for Practitioners and Researchers

Additional validation research is required to support convergent and construct validity. This type of assessment should be compared with analogue assessment of parent–child interaction on a compliance task to examine the correspondence between "saying" and "doing."

---

68. Parent Reaction to Abuse Disclosure Scale (PRADS; Everson)

Development and Description of Assessment Method

The PRADS is an interview-based clinician rating of the nonoffending parent's support of the victimized child in three areas: emotional support, belief of child, and action toward perpetrator.

Target Population

Parents of children who have disclosed sexual abuse.

Format

The PRADS consists of a series of structured questions asked of both the nonoffending parent and child. These questions relate to initial and subsequent reactions to the child's disclosure of alleged sexual abuse. The questions are assembled according to the following four subscales:

- Belief in the child's report,
- Emotional support offered to the child,
- Action toward perpetrator's behavior, and
- Use of professional services.

Administration and Scoring

Each subscale can be rated from −2 (least supportive) to +2 (most supportive) with a total scale score ranging from −8 to +8. One study (Cross, Martell, McDonald, & Ahl, 1999) reported on data from a principal component, analysis on a large data set ($N = 276$), which justifies the use of the total score above.

Psychometric Evaluation

Norms
None reported.

Reliability
None reported.

Validity
Intercorrelations of ratings between three subsections (omitting the use of professional services subscale) range from the mid $r = .60$s to the high $r = .70$s.

In one treatment study, data from the PRADS indicated an increase in clinician ratings of supportiveness following treatment.

In a large study examining child placement decisions following sexual abuse disclosure, Cross et al. (1999) concluded that lower maternal support as measured by the PRADS was significantly associated with the child's placement outside of the home. Results from their logistic regression analysis predicting child placement indicated that initial maternal support predicted improvement in child placement outcomes for both intrafamilial ($\chi^2(2) = 6.54$, $p = .03$) and extrafamilial ($\chi^2(2) = 6.2$, $p = .045$) cases. Interpretation is difficult because prosecution decisions also played an influential role.

Advantages
The PRADS offers a relatively straightforward method to assess an important family variable related to mother–child interactions.

Limitations
There has been limited psychometric study of the interview process and scaling, making it difficult to evaluate either reliability or validity issues. Face validity of questions may compromise integrity of respondents' answers in that mothers may give the socially desirable answer.

Primary Reference

Everson, Hunter, Runyon, Edelsohn, and Coulter (1989).

Scale Availability

Guidelines for interviewer's questions could not be located.

Related References

Celano, Hazzard, Webb, and McCall (1996); Cross et al. (1999).

General Comments and Recommendations for Practitioners and Researchers

The primary author of the assessment method has recently recommended doubling the emotional support rating, indicating its primacy in the assessment of parental support of the child.

Self-Report Assessment of Parents and Caregivers

By far the most frequently used method of assessment of parents in maltreating families is self-report. A number of measures exist that focus on parent attitudes, styles, discipline practices, and stress factors. Cognitive variables associated with parents' responses to their children have been emphasized in self-report measures of problem-solving abilities, attributional style, and expectations of child behavior. The affective component of parenting has also been targeted via self-report assessment of parent affect. The following review includes several devices developed specifically for the assessment of at-risk or maltreating parents (methods 69–76), as well as more general measure of parenting responses that may be appropriate to use in the assessment of family violence (methods 77–81).

---

69. Child Abuse Blame Scale–Physical Abuse (CABS–PA; Petretic-Jackson)

Development and Description of Assessment Method

An initial item pool was generated using the rational–empirical method from a review of literature in family violence domains. Some items resembled items on existing incest blame scales, whereas others focused on unique aspects of child physical abuse by parents. This initial scale version was administered to 350 young adults and was then subjected to a confirmatory factor analysis with varimax rotation. Four factors were revealed, and 37 items were retained. Scores from two other cross-validation samples were examined, and factor loadings of .40 or greater were used to select items.

The CABS–PA is a self-report inventory for parents or caretakers in maltreating families. The questionnaire focuses on attributions for physical abuse and assesses levels of blame assigned to the child, the parent, and the parent–child relationship, as well as situational variables and societal attitudes.

Target Population

Parents in maltreating families. This assessment can be used with non-abusive parents and nonparents as well.

Format

The CABS–PA consists of a questionnaire that includes 30 items across four independently derived factors:

1. *Child blame:* Nine items, including,
   - "By the way they act, certain children almost ask to be abused" and
   - "Children provoke a parent to commit abuse by acting willful and disrespectful";
2. *Situational Blame:* Eight items, including,
   - "Alcohol and drugs are significant factors in the occurrence of child abuse" and
   - "An abused child is the scapegoat in a disturbed family";
3. *Societal blame:* Seven items, including,
   - "The prevalence of child abuse is directly related to our societal values" and
   - "Societal acceptance of the use of physical force as discipline promotes child abuse"; and
4. *Parental blame:* Six items, including,
   - "Abusive parents could stop the abuse toward their children, but choose not to" and
   - "Given the right circumstances, all adults have the potential to be abusive toward children."

Taken together, the items emphasize either the child's role in contributing to the abuse by his or her misbehavior, the various environmental events that act as parental stressors, the social acceptance of corporal punishment, and parental control of angry impulses.

Administration and Scoring

Respondents rate each item on a 6-point Likert scale from 1 = strongly disagree to 6 = strongly agree. Because items do not overlap across the four factors, the sum of each item per scale indicates a blame score. The factor sums are then divided by the number of items in that scale to get a factor mean. Higher scores indicate higher blame on a particular factor.

When used for clinical purposes, the author suggests an individual item analysis in that four items on the child blame scale denote parent–child interaction subfactor items, and four items on the situational blame scale denote situation-specific parent behaviors that may be important to tease out.

Psychometric Evaluation

Norms

The author indicates that the scale has been administered to several adult samples, college students, parents, and nonparents, as well as adults who were abused themselves. The norms are available from the author.

Reliability

Results from reliability analysis of the primary standardization sample (N = 302) indicated that Cronbach's alpha ranged from .80 to .84 for the victim factor, .73 to .79 for the situational factor, .72 to .75 for the societal factor, and .53 to .54 for the parent perpetrator factor. These data indicate moderate to good internal consistency for the scale. No test–retest reliability was reported.

Validity

The author states that "given the face validity of the items, the absence of a 'lie' scale and the present lack of clinical norms for an abusive parent sample, the validity of using factor scores for predicting clients at risk of abuse ... is questionable" (Petretic-Jackson, 1992, p. 318). Results from validation samples, however, do indicate that respondents attribute the least amount of blame to children and that parents are capable of controlling themselves. The situational factor was attributed the most blame (M = 3.86 to 4.03). The author does not, however, compare these results across known groups, making it difficult to interpret these findings.

Advantages

The CABS–PA is a brief, easy-to-score screening measure that taps into an important cognitive dimension of parental explanation of and justification for abuse. Theoretically, attributions for blame play an important part in maintaining abusive behavior cycles and represent an important clinical target.

Limitations

Psychometric development needs to be continued so that concurrent and discriminant validity is established. High face validity of items may compromise its use with abusive parents.

Primary Reference

Petretic-Jackson (1992).

Scale Availability

> Patricia Petretic-Jackson
> Psychology Department
> University of Arkansas
> Fayetteville, AR 72701

Related References

None available.

General Comments and Recommendations for Practitioners and Researchers

The CABS–PA is an easy-to-administer inventory that could be included in a parent or caretaker assessment package. Individual item analysis of some subfactors may indicate that additional scales should be added to scoring procedures. It may be a helpful therapeutic tool to begin an analysis of parent perceptions and responsibility as well as parent stressors.

70. Child Abuse Potential Inventory—Form VI (CAPI; Milner)

Development and Description of Assessment Method

A well-established self-report measure designed to screen parents for physical child abuse risk, the CAPI focuses on attitudes and parent personality variables.

Target Population

Parents of children and adolescents. Items are written at a third-grade reading level.

Format

This assessment consists of 160 items on a forced choice screening questionnaire. The questionnaire has six factor scales: distress, rigidity, unhappiness, problems with child and self, problems with family, and problems with others. The physical child abuse subscale has 77 items such as "I do not trust most people," "Knives are dangerous for children," "People sometimes take advantage of me," "A crying child will never be happy," and "As a child I was abused." Examples of other items are, "You cannot depend on others," "Children are pests," "I am often worried inside," "A home should be spotless," and "I have a child who is slow." Two additional subscales, the ego strength and loneliness subscales, have also been developed.

The CAPI also contains three validity scales (i.e., random response and inconsistency) that are used in various combinations to produce the following induces: faking good, faking bad, and random response.

Administration and Scoring

Parents respond to each item on a 4-point, Likert-type scale (from 1 = agree to 4 = disagree).

With a range of scores from 0 to 486, standardized scoring yields three possible profiles: elevated, normal, and invalid. A valid, elevated abuse scale score (at or about 215) indicates the respondents' similarity to known, active physical child abusers. If any of the validity scales is elevated, the response distortion induces are computed to determine if the profile is valid and usable.

Psychometric Evaluation

Norms

Large normative sample comparisons are available (for example, $n = 2,062$) in the accompanying test manual. A cutoff score of 215 identifies high-risk parents.

Reliability

Internal consistency was evaluated by a split half, Kuder-Richardson 20 formula in many samples, all with $r = .90$ and above. In a sample of $N = 150$, test–retest reliability across a three-month interval was $r = .75$, and in another sample, one-week test–retest reliability was $r = .90$ for the abuse subscale.

Validity

Evidence for construct validity is strong. The CAPI significantly correlates with parental childhood history of abuse ($r = .29$), negative family interactions ($r = .41$) with the Family Environment scale (Moos & Moos, 1986), and $r = .41$ with the Conflict Tactics Scale (Straus, 1979). Known groups validity was demonstrated by correct identification of parents already categorized as abusive.

A recent study (Haskett, Scott, & Fann, 1995) examined the criterion-related validity by comparing scores on the CAPI with observed parenting behaviors for maltreating ($N = 25$), high-risk ($N = 7$), and neglectful ($N = 9$) parents. The Pearson product-moment correlation was highly significant ($r = .55$, $p < .001$). In a study of 75 adolescent mothers (Budd et al., 2000), slightly over half of the teens obtained CAPI abuse scores in the elevated range, and CAPI scores showed moderate correlations (for example, $\pm.41$ to $.44$, $p < .001$) with reading and math achievement, emotional distress, and social support satisfaction. Correlations with the Parent Opinion Questionnaire and the Home Observation for the Measurement of the Environment (HOME) Inventory were not significant, however.

Correlations with the Parenting Stress Index (Abidin, 1990; $r = .62$) and the Rotter's Internal–External Locus of Control Scale (Rotter, 1966; $r = .44$) have also been reported.

Advantages

An extensive psychometric evaluation and a Spanish version are both available. Validity scales are used in various combinations to form three response distortion indexes: faking good, faking bad, and random response. When parents were directly instructed to fake good, the CAPI validity indexes were successful in detecting more than 90% of the protocols as invalid. The random response index was also successful in labeling protocols as invalid.

Limitations

Because none of the items focuses on actual physical assault, the CAPI should only be used as an instrument for identification of at-risk parents and not for evaluation of interventions with abusive parents. The recent (Budd et al., 2002) study did not find significant correlations to other measures used in the assessment of maltreating parents.

Primary Reference

Milner (1986).

Scale Availability

> Joel S. Milner
> Department of Psychology
> Northern Illinois University
> DeKalb, IL 60115-2854

Related References

Budd, Heilman, and Kane (2000); Haskett et al. (1995); Kolko, Kazdin, Thomas, and Day (1993); Milner (1994); Milner and Crouch (1997).

General Comments and Recommendations for Practitioners and Researchers

The CAPI is an extremely well researched, psychometrically sound assessment device that is well suited for clinical use as a screening inventory or as a treatment outcome measure.

---

71. Conflicts and Problem-Solving Scale (CPSS; Kerig)

Development and Description of Assessment Method

The CPSS is a self-report inventory designed to assess parental perspectives on interparental violence to which their children have been exposed. Several dimensions of exposure shown to affect children, including frequency, severity, resolution, and efficacy of couples interactions are included.

The subscales reflecting conflict strategies were derived through factor analysis on a sample of 273 normative and distressed couples.

Target Population

Parents of children who have been exposed to family violence.

Format

The CPSS consists of a questionnaire on which the parent rates four dimensions related to engaging in major conflicts ("big blow ups") and minor conflicts ("spats, getting on each other's nerves") that occurred during last year. Frequency, severity, resolution, and efficacy ratings are made. Then, using a list of 44 tactics derived from the literature on marital and interpersonal conflict, parents rate a variety of conflict strategies grouped across six subscales:

1. *Physical aggression:* Seven items that measure the frequency of physically violent tactics, such as "slap" and "hit";
2. *Verbal aggression:* Eight items, such as "yell" and "insult";
3. *Child involvement:* Six items regarding ways in which parents might involve their children in interparental conflicts, such as "argue about the children" and "confide in children about marital problems";
4. *Collaboration:* Eight items, such as "try to reason with the other person" and "talk about the issue";
5. *Stalemate:* Seven items that reflect an impasse in attempts to end quarreling, including "Threaten to end the relationship" and "sulk, refuse to talk, give the 'silent treatment'"; and
6. *Avoidance–capitulation:* Eight items, such as "leave the house" and "change the subject."

Administration and Scoring

For the first part of the CPSS, each parent rates the frequency of each conflict on a 6-point ordinal scale ranging from "once a year or less" (scored 1 for minor conflicts and 2 for major conflicts) to "just about every day" (scored 6 for minor conflicts and 12 for major conflicts).

Scores for conflicts are summed resulting in possible scores ranging from 3 to 18. For ratings of the conflict strategies, each parent rates the frequency with which they and their partners used each strategy in the previous year. Separate self and partner conflict strategy subscales can be evaluated. Frequency ratings can also be summed over both scales to obtain a total conflict strategies score.

Psychometric Evaluation

Norms
In the large normative sample, men reported use of more capitulation and avoidance strategies, whereas women were more likely to use control-oriented strategies, such as verbal and physical aggression.

Reliability
Internal consistency assessed on the sample of 273 couples (Kerig, 1996) was reported as good, with alphas ranging from .75 to .98. Test–retest reliability over a 3-month period for a subsample of 48 couples was also good, with correlations ranging from $r = .53$ to $r = .87$, which were all significant at the $p < .01$ level.

Validity
Significant correlations were obtained between overlapping scales of the CPSS and other measures of marital conflict. Positive correlations were found between subscales of the Conflict Tactics Scale (Straus, 1979) and the CPSS. For example, the verbal aggression subscale of the CTS was significantly correlated with every dimension of the CPSS, indicating excellent convergent validity.

Advantages
The CPSS is a well-developed, psychometrically sound instrument designed to assess parents' perceptions of their conflict behaviors that may affect children who witness discord. This is a dynamic, often overlooked aspect of family functioning.

Limitations
The CPSS does not include the assessment of psychological strategies used by partners to intimidate each other, nor the extreme forms of physical abuse that characterize violent couples.

Primary Reference

Kerig (1996).

Scale Availability

> Patricia Kerig
> James Madison University
> School of Psychology
> Harrisonburg, VA 22807

Related References

Kerig (1998); Kerig and Fedorowicz (1999).

General Comments and Recommendations for Practitioners and Researchers

The child involvement subscale helps to assess the ways in which parents attempt to negotiate their conflicts by using their children. No other conflict measurement includes this factor. The variety of problem rating scales allow for a comprehensive assessment of dimensions of marital conflict that relate to marital happiness.

---

72. Conflict Tactics Scale: Parent to Child (CTSPC; Straus)

Development and Description of Assessment Method

The CTSPC parallels the Conflict Tactics Scale (CTS) used in the assessment of adult partner violence. Supplemental scales have been added to broaden measurement of maltreatment; these items do not reflect a conflict tactic, per se, reflect questions on neglect, corporal punishment, and sexual abuse, however. There is now a 22-item revision available.

The CTSPC is a self-report measure intended to measure the tactics or behaviors used by parents when they experience conflict or hostility toward their child. It measures the extent to which a parent has carried out specific acts of physical and psychological aggression in the last year, regardless of whether the child was injured.

Target Population

"At- risk" parents. Items are written at a sixth-grade level. The scale can be used with children as respondents in an interview format.

Format

The CTSPC includes the following subscales:

- *Nonviolent Discipline:* Four items reflecting the use of nonviolent discipline strategies, including, "explained why something was wrong" and "took away privileges or grounded him."
- *Psychological Aggression:* Five items that measure verbal and symbolic acts by the parent that cause the child fear or pain, including "swore or cursed at him/her" and "called him/her dumb or lazy or some other names like that."
- *Physical Assault:* Thirteen items reflecting physical discipline strategies from minor/corporal punishment, including, "slapped him/her on the face, head, or ears" and "threw or knocked him/her down," to very severe physical abuse, such as "grabbed him/her around the neck and choked him/her" and "burned or scolded him/her on purpose."
- Supplemental scales on *Neglect* (5 items, including failure to engage in behavior that is necessary to meet the developmental needs of the child) and *Sexual abuse* (four items about sexual assault, unwanted sexual touching, and forced sexual contact).

Administration and Scoring

Family members report on the frequency of the tactics listed during the 1-year period before the assessment. Responses were coded on a 6-point, Likert-type scale from 0 = did not occur to 6 = occurred more than once a month. Administration requires no more than 10 minutes, and scores are totals for each subscale. The test authors indicate that the referent time period can be changed to reflect specific situational variables.

Psychometric Evaluation

Psychometric evaluation was completed on a nationally representative sample of 1,000 U.S. parents interviewed by telephone. Gender of child and minority representation matched U.S. census information fairly closely.

Norms

The CTSPC found a prevalence rate for the severe physical assault subscale of 49 per 1,000 parents, whereas a rate of 614 per 1,000 was found for the corporal punishment subscale. Nonviolent discipline was reported by almost all parents (977 per 1,000), whereas psychological aggression was reported by 856 per 1,000. The most frequent mode of psychological aggression was shouting, yelling, or screaming at the child (847 per 1,000).

Reliability

Studies using the parent–child physical assault scale of the CTS showed internal consistency reported via alpha coefficients of .55 for the overall physical assault subscale, .60 for the psychological aggression subscale, .70 for the nonviolent discipline subscale, and .22 for the neglect subscale. Good test–retest reliability coefficients ranging from $r = .49$ to $r = .80$ over a 14-week interval were also reported.

Validity

Several studies have compared parents' and children's responses to the physical assault scale of the CTS and found that reports from mothers and children of fathers' aggressive behavior were significantly related (correlations ranged from $r = .30$ to $r = .46$). Validation work has not yet been reported using the CTSPC.

Intercorrelations between subscales indicate nonsignificant correlations for the supplemental sex abuse subscale and all other subscales, for the physical abuse and nonviolent discipline subscales, and for the minor corporal punishment and minor psychological aggression subscales, demonstrating discriminant validity for type of abuse. Significant correlations were found between nonviolent discipline and ordinary corporal punishment ($r = .39$) and severe corporal punishment ($r = .23$), as well as for ordinary psychological aggression ($r = .53$) and severe psychological aggression ($r = .22$). Further construct validity was demonstrated with significant correlations between the minor assault (corporal punishment) and psychological aggression subscales. In a study of abuse potential of mothers and maternal guardians, the reasoning subscale for both the child–sibling and child–mother versions discriminated between high and moderate potential groups and low potential group. Further, the children's responses to the reasoning subscale also discriminated between the three abuse potential subgroups (see Kolko, Kazdin, Thomas, & Day, 1993).

Advantages

The CTSPC includes an item on "shaking," which relates directly to responses to infants, an emphasis not usually included on parenting measures. Also included are supplemental questions on corporal punishment and other disciplinary practices used in the week before administration. The inventory is very brief and easy to administer. Improved items with greater operationalization of the distinction between minor and severe acts are also included. Items are interspersed in a random order of severity, which reduces potential response bias.

Limitations

Validity estimates are based on the parent–child physical assault scale of the original CTS and not on the current and improved version of the CTSPC.

Primary Reference

Straus, Hamby, Finkelhor, Moore, and Runyan (1998).

Scale Availability

> M. Straus
> Family Research Laboratory
> University of New Hampshire
> Durham, NH 03824
> (603) 862-2594

Related References

Straus and Hamby (1997).

General Comments and Recommendations for Practitioners and Researchers

Two new versions of the CTS were published in 1996—the CTS2, which is designed to measure partner aggression, and the CTSPC, which measures parent–child relationships. Much of psychometric data available for review are from the original CTS and may not be generalizable to the CTSPC. Evaluation of this measure alone is required. The CTSPC includes improved wording of items that make them more specific and provides a better operationalization of the distinction between minor and severe acts. Finally, the items are interspersed rather than being presented in hierarchial order of social acceptability, as in the CTS.

73. Maternal Characteristics Scale (MCS; Polansky, Gaudin, & Kilpatrick)

Development and Description of Assessment Method

Selection and phrasing of items on the MCS were based on psychoanalytic conceptions related to failures of maturation and dysfunctional maternal character traits. Subscales were derived via a principal components factor analysis with the relatedness subscale accounting for 55.5% of the variance, the impulse–control subscale accounting for 9.9% of the variance, the confidence subscale accounting for 7.7% of the variance, and the verbal accessibility subscale accounting for 6.4% of the variance.

This rating scale was developed to help case workers organize their observations of at-risk mothers according to various dimensions reflecting character traits. The case worker is prompted by each item to make an observation of a fairly specific behavior or attitude and to judge its presence or observe it in the mother who is interviewed.

Target Population

Mothers at risk for child neglect. The rating scale may be completed by clinicians as well as by child protective service workers.

Format

The MCS consists of 35 statements grouped according to four dimensions:

1. *Relatedness:* Twelve items indicating the absence of apathy and withdrawal, including "can laugh at herself," "shows interest in and knowledge of larger world scene," "takes pleasure in her children's adventures," and "discusses her children's behavior as if from the outside."

2. *Impulse control:* Ten items, including "has shown defiance toward authorities in word and deed," "sets and maintains control of her own behavior," "shows tolerance of routine," and "often buys things impulsively."

3. *Confidence:* Seven items indicating an absence of futility, including "has a sad expression or holds her body in dejected or despondent manner," "mentions she is aimless or getting nowhere," and "shows enthusiasm."

4. *Verbal Accessibility:* Five items, including "answers questions with single words or phrases," "shows warmth in tone when talking with her children," and "usually states opinion reasonably directly."

Administration and Scoring

Each item is rated true (yes) or not true (no) by a case worker following an extended interview with a target mother. If the item that reflects a personality facet thought to be positive is true, it is scored 1, and if not true, 0. A negative item earns a 0 if true, and a + if not true. The score is compiled by computing the percentage of pluses received out of all relevant ratings made for the subscale.

Psychometric Evaluation

Norms
A score of 1.00 would indicate all of the positive attributes affirmed and all of the negative attributes disconfirmed.

Reliability
Internal consistency was established in a sample of $N = 51$ neglectful and $N = 79$ non-neglectful mothers. Cronbach's alpha coefficients were .88 for the relatedness subscale, .77 for the impulse control subscale, .76 for the confidence subscale, and .63 for the verbal accessibility subscale. Although an article by Polansky, Gaudin, and Kilpatrick (1992) mentions training case workers in order to achieve interrater reliability, the exact data were not reported.

Validity
T-tests comparing groups of neglectful and non-neglectful mothers indicated significant differences on all four subscales, with neglectful mothers having much lower scores than control mothers. This provides good evidence for known groups validity.

Advantages
The MCS has strong psychodynamic, theoretical underpinnings such that the authors hope it will help to assess those who are vulnerable to the collapse of mothering leading to neglect. It may help clinicians to organize their observations about high-risk mothers.

Limitations

Much more research is needed to empirically validate this instrument. Of particular concern is the relationship between perceived maternal characteristics and actual behavior during mother–child interaction.

Primary Reference

Polansky, Chalmers, Buttenweiser, and Williams (1981).

Scale Availability

> James Gaudin
> School of Social Work
> University of Georgia
> Tucker Hall
> Athens, GA 30602–7016
> (706) 542-3364

Related References

Polansky, Gaudin, and Kilpatrick (1992).

General Comments and Recommendations for Practitioners and Researchers

Although the authors have included further clarification and examples for nine of the items (such as "says she enjoys living" = actual verbalization of pleasure with some aspect of her life or life in general), because items call for subjective judgments, the instrument may not prove reliable as an assessment tool.

---

74. Parent Attribution Scale (PAS; Celano, Webb, & Hazzard)

Development and Description of Assessment Method

This self-report measure is designed to assess a caretaker's attributions of responsibility for sexual abuse to the child, to herself, and to the perpetrator. It also includes a subscale designed to assess parents' perceptions of the event's impact on the child.

Target Population

Nonoffending parents or caretakers of children who have experienced sexual abuse.

Format

This is a 21-item, self-report inventory that includes the following subscales and sample items:

- *Self-Blame:* Five items, including "I feel guilty about what happened" and "What happened to my family after the abuse is not my fault."
- *Child Blame:* Five items, including "This happened to my child because she acted in a way that caused it to happen" and "My child was not to blame for what happened."
- *Perpetrator Blame:* Five items, including "It's not the perpetrator's fault that my family was so hurt by the abuse" and "If he could, the perpetrator would have continued to abuse my child."
- *Negative Impact:* Six items, including "My child will always feel afraid" and "My child's abuse will not affect her life when she is grown."

Administration and Scoring

Each item is rated on a 5-point, Likert-type scale from 1 = strongly disagree to 5 = strongly agree. Scores for the first three subscales range from 5 to 25, and scores for negative impact range from 6 to 30. A number of items are reverse keyed for scoring. Parents are instructed to answer according to what they believe and feel.

Psychometric Evaluation

Norms
None reported.

Reliability
Internal consistency of each of the subscales was examined in a sample of 48 girls who had experienced sexual abuse. The coefficient alphas were .66 for self-blame, .65 for child blame, .66 for perpetrator blame, and .71 for negative impact.

Validity
None reported.

Advantages
The PAS addresses an important aspect of family dynamics thought to mediate the consequences of child sexual abuse, namely parental attributions of blame.

Limitations
A lack of change in PAS data for one ($N = 32$) treatment study (for child blame and perpetrator blame) may reflect the limitations of this instrument in assessing the subtleties of caretakers' attributions of responsibility for abuse, especially for those already seeking treatment for their children.

Primary Reference

Celano, Webb, and Hazzard (1992).

Scale Availability

> Marianne Celano
> Department of Psychiatry
> Box 26064
> Grady Memorial Hospital
> 80 Butler St.
> Atlanta, GA 30335

Related References

Celano, Hazzard, Webb, and McCall (1996).

General Comments and Recommendations for Practitioners and Researchers

The PAS is a promising measure, but one that has only been used to evaluate small numbers of caretakers who are already seeking treatment for their children. This measure needs more extensive psychometric development, especially validity investigations vis-à-vis relationship with other parent assessments.

75. Screening for Problem Parenting (SPP; Avison, Turner, & Noh)

Development and Description of Assessment Method

The authors employed a three-stage strategy to select items for this parent screening. All 77 items from three previously used parent measures were entered into an orthogonal factor analysis. The items that loaded on each factor were then entered into a discriminate function analysis to determine which items could best distinguish maladaptive (sample of mothers from child protection case loads) from comparison mothers. Finally, those items with the greatest discriminating power in each factor were used in a final functional analysis to identify the best set of predictors. This process resulted in a set of eight items that were able to accurately classify subgroups of mothers with 86% accuracy. The authors added to these items to represent all relevant content domains and selected 12 additional items that also were efficient predictors in the discriminate function analysis.

The SPP is a 20-item self-report inventory composed of items from previously established parenting measures. The items were chosen based on their power in discriminating between maladapting and normal mothers. The inventory serves as a short screen for identifying women who may be at elevated risk for problems related to parenting attitudes and behaviors and social support.

Target Population

Mothers of children up to age 12.

Format

Items from already-established assessment instruments were included; the focus is on the following three areas, with item type variable according to content area:

- *Social Support:* Four items are adaptations of a story identification technique designed to measure the experience of social support. Each item is composed of three stories describing individuals with varying levels of support. The respondent is asked to choose which story is most representative of her on a 5-point scale. For example,

- "Phyllis is rarely admired and praised. There are very few people who think Phyllis is important and worthy."
- "Martha is sometimes admired and praised by some people. She is not always being reminded of her worth."
- "Tina is constantly admired by people. They always praise her and think that she is important and worthy."
- *Parenting Attitudes and Perceptions:* Six items were selected from the Michigan Profile of Parenting (Helfer, Hoffmeister, & Schneider, 1978). Sample items are rated on a 7-point Likert scale from "strongly agree" to "strongly disagree" and include, "No one has ever really listened to me," "As a child, I often felt like no one paid much attention to what I wanted or needed," and "Sometimes I just feel like running away." In addition, 10 items from the Parental Attitude Research Instrument (Schludermann & Schludermann, 1977) were added to the previous six to make up this subscale. Sample items include,
  - "A wise parent will teach a child early just who is the boss."
  - "Raising children is a nerve wracking job,"
  - "Loyalty to parents comes before anything else."
  - "A parent should never be made to look wrong in a child's eye."

These items are rated by the respondent on a 5-point Likert scale.

Administration and Scoring

Scores are computed for this 20-item instrument by simply summing scores for each item. A number of items are reverse keyed, such that high scores indicate greater social support and more adaptive parenting attitudes. Scores range from 20 to 100.

Psychometric Evaluation

Norms

The authors describe difficulties in determining cutoff scores from the research done with various samples. It seems that very small changes in raw scores result in sizable variations in the accuracy of known group classification. It seems, however, that a cut-point of less than 46 results in about 80% of maladaptive mothers being classified.

Reliability

None reported.

Validity

Data were obtained from separate samples. Assessment of normal mothers was done with 293 participants 2 to 4 weeks after they had given birth, and a second sample completed the inventory while their children took swimming lessons ($n = 100$). Two samples of maladapting mothers were obtained from child protective service case workers ($n = 78$ and, 2–3 years later, $n = 87$). All participants completed each of the three assessment measures in full in order to complete the factor analysis.

The final 20-item parent screening device correctly identified 95.6% of the comparison mothers and 90.1% of the maladaptive mothers for a total accuracy rate of 93.02%, indicating excellent known groups validity.

Advantages

This screening inventory with items culled from already-established parent assessment tools is a brief, easy-to-administer device that can accurately identify previously classified mothers.

Limitations

Although psychometric properties of the three measures used for item generation have already been established in previous research, there are no reliability and limited validity data available for this 20-item amalgam of items.

Primary Reference

Avison, Turner, and Noh (1996).

Scale Availability

R. Jay Turner
Health Care Research Unit
C.F.C. Building
University of Western Ontario
London, Ontario, Canada NGA-5B8

Related References

None available.

General Comments and Recommendations for Practitioners and Researchers

The SPP was developed based on numerous functional analyses and seems psychometrically sound and representative of the several domains hypothesized to relate to adaptive parenting. Much work needs to be done, however, in terms of establishing internal and external validity of the measure and in evaluating its potential as an instrument sensitive to therapeutic intervention.

76. Weekly Report of Abuse Indicators (WRAI; Kolko)

Development and Description of Assessment Method

The WRAI was developed by clinicians seeking to monitor the treatment course for maltreating families. Weekly information was necessary to assess risk of reabuse or reprisal. This is a short measure designed to evaluate high-risk parental behaviors occurring on a weekly basis.

Target Population

Maltreating parents who are in treatment. Older children can also complete the weekly reports about their views of their parents.

Format

The WRAI consists of three subsections to be completed by parents:

1. *Anger:* Severity of anger arousal displayed by parents toward their children across the week, rated on a 5-point, Likert-type scale from 1 = not at all angry to 5 = extremely angry.
2. *Problems:* Family problems experienced, rated on a 3-point, Likert-type scale from 1 = none to 3 = major.
3. *Force:* Items pertaining to parental use of threats, physical force, or discipline, including, "Did you think about using any physical force or discipline?", "Did you threaten to use any physical force or discipline?", and "Did you actually use physical force or discipline like slapping, hitting by hand, or with an object?"

Administration and Scoring

Parents respond to the first two Likert scales by simply indicating a numerical response. The third section asks parents to respond in a yes/no format to each item.

Psychometric Evaluation

Norms

None reported.

Reliability

In a small treatment sample ($N = 38$), Pearson correlations (parental anger, family problems) or Cohen's kappas (discipline/force) were computed based on actual scores reported for each of two sets of adjacent sessions in order to determine temporal stability. Parent reports revealed moderate to high stability during early and late treatment periods for anger and problem ratings. A lower level of stability was found for physical force/discipline. Compared to child ratings using same format, moderate correlations were found for parental anger ($r = .41$) and family problems ($r = .21$), and the kappa coefficient for physical discipline/force was $k = .53$.

Validity

Criterion validity was examined via correlations between mean ratings on the WRAI throughout treatment and several measures completed by both parents and children at retreatment ($n = 38$; Kolko, 1996a). Significant associations were found with the cohesion subscale of the Family Environment Scale (Moos & Moos, 1986) and parent anger ($r = -.38$, $p < .05$) and force ($r = .32$, $p < .05$) weekly ratings. Correlations between the Conflict Tactics Scale/Parent-to-Child Violence (Straus, 1979) were found for parent ($r = .41$, $p < .01$) and child ($r = .43$, $p < .01$) problem ratings as well as for parent force ratings ($r = .48$, $p < .01$). Two additional correlations were formed between the Parenting Scale total score (Arnold, O'Leary, Wolff, & Acker, 1993) and the parental force rating ($r = .40$, $p < .05$), and finally between the general functioning subscale of the Family Assessment Device (Epstein, Baldwin, & Bishop, 1983) and the parent anger rating ($r = .46$, $p < .01$). All of these results indicate that criterion or concurrent validity has been established with acceptable paper-and-pencil measures of family functioning.

Predictive validity was demonstrated by examining parents reporting at least one incident of physical discipline or force during the early period of treatment. These parents also reported heightened anger and family problems and use of physical discipline late in treatment.

Advantages

The WRAI corresponds directly to the child version, which assesses the child's view of whether the parent engaged in the behaviors. It allows for this interrater comparison within the family. Parent reports were associated with pretreatment validity measures.

Limitations

The instrument only includes a circumscribed set of maltreatment behaviors and does not distinguish among behaviors varying in severity or seriousness.

Primary Reference

Kolko (1996a).

Scale Availability

David J. Kolko
Child and Parent Behavior Clinic
Western Psychiatric Institute
3811 O'Hara St.
Pittsburgh, PA 15213

Related References

Kolko (1996b).

General Comments and Recommendations for Practitioners and Researchers

The WRAI is useful for a weekly evaluation of a clinical intervention program.

---

77. Intensity of Parental Punishment Scale (IPPS; Gordon)

Development and Description of Assessment Method

The IPPS is a self-report measure designed to assess the intensity of parent affective and behavioral responses to hypothetical child misbehavior situations. It is based on the notion that, regardless of the form of punishment, it is the child's perception of intensity that affects the behavior of children.

Item development for the IPPS began with a list of 68 situations in which a child was misbehaving, devised by a group of parents, teachers, and clinical psychologists. In order to develop a response scale, mothers (n = 35) wrote brief descriptions of their punitive reactions to each of these situations. A 7-point intensity scale and a 10-point anger scale were developed. The response scale was then ranked by 20 clinicians for increases in intensity and deleted items (situations) that did not correlate with anger ratings.

Target Population

Parents of children between the ages of 4 and 14 years.

Format

The IPPS includes 33 situations depicting child misbehavior. Factor analysis indicated five subscales:

1. School misbehavior(hitting another child, using curse words);
2. Disobedience after a recent reminder (painting on carpet);
3. Public disobedience (throwing a cereal box in a store);
4. Crying or running after being refused a request; and
5. Destructiveness (pulling the hair of a neighbor's child, scribbling on a neighbor's walls).

Administration and Scoring

Parents are instructed to imagine one of their children as the one described in the situation and to indicate how they would respond behaviorally on a 7-point response scale (1 = no reaction/ignore; 2 = short explanation; 3 = mild reprimand, express disappointment, long lecture; 4 = moderate scolding; 5 = yelling; 6 = express strong anger, spanking, grounding; 7 = express severe anger intentionally, severe spanking, whipping). Parents are also asked to indicate how they would feel on a 7-point, Likert-type scale ranging from "not at all angry" to "extremely angry."

Psychometric Evaluation

Norms

Initial psychometric work was done on several different samples:

- Parents of 5- to 10-year-olds ($N = 301$),
- Upper-middle-class parents of 7- to 12-year-olds at camp ($N = 50$),
- Mothers of 6- to 9-year-olds ($N = 26$), and
- Mothers of 6- to 14-year-olds ($N = 40$).

This population included lower-class parents of developmentally disabled children. An extensive item development process is described in the original article. The current version of 33 situations was derived from an original sample of 65 child behavior situations.

Reliability

Split-half reliability coefficients yielded a mean of $r = .78$ ($p < .01$), indicating good internal consistency. It is not clear, however, if this estimate is for all of the samples studied. Test–retest reliability was $r = .85$ over a 2-month interval ($N = 19$) and $r = .56$ over a 7-month interval ($N = 50$). When analyzed as a function of age, however, test–retest coefficients were significantly different: for fourth-grade children ($n = 21$) $r = .75$, and for first-grade children ($n = 28$) $r = .41$.

Validity

None of the five situation factors was correlated as highly with each other ($r = .30$ to $.55$) as with total score ($r = .65$ to $.84$), indicating that factors were measuring distinct aspects of the global construct. Parental report of anger intensity (rated on a 10-point scale) was highly correlated with the rank ordering of punishment intensity ($r = .84$, $p < .05$) for a sample of 42 parents.

Observations of mothers and their children in the waiting room for a small sample ($n = 26$) were conducted, and interactions were coded according to a system developed by the authors. Correlations between mothers' IPPS scores and their observed behavior were calculated. High IPPS total scores were correlated with low warmth ratings ($r = -.57$, $p < .01$), fewer nondirective attending statements ($r = -.46$, $p < .05$), and more interferences with the child's play ($r = .44$, $p < .05$). Further, parents ($n = 49$) with high IPPS scores rated their children as more maladaptive on a school-adjusted scale (Cowen et al., 1973) than parents with low IPPS scores. Specifically, significant correlations were formed with parental ratings of their daughters as overactive ($r = .32$, p

< .05) and less withdrawn ($r = .28$, $p < .05$) and of their sons as less cheerful ($r = -.24$, $p < .05$).

Advantages

Situations in the IPPS include a wide range of behaviors for which children are commonly punished. The focus on intensity of punishment varies from the usual focus on frequency of parental discipline responses.

Limitations

The association between this parental assessment of hypothetical responding and actual behavior during parent child encounters has not yet been evaluated.

Primary Reference

Gordon, Jones, and Nowicki (1979).

Scale Availability

> Donald A. Gordon
> Department of Psychology
> Emory University
> Atlanta, GA 30322

Related References

None available.

General Comments and Recommendations for Practitioners and Researchers

The IPPS provides a means of measuring the parameter of punishment intensity in hypothetical parent–child interactions and helps to assess the role of affect in the disciplinary encounter.

---

78. Parent Affect Test (PAT; Linehan, Paul, & Egan)

Development and Description of Assessment Method

The Parent Affect Test is a self-report inventory designed to measure both positive and negative parental affect in response to both positive and negative child behaviors. The authors wanted to examine the role of anger in the etiology and maintenance of punitive, aggressive, and violent behavior directed at children.

The initial pool of 1,000 pleasing and 1,000 negative situations was developed by 244 fathers and 323 mothers. Situations were categorized according to similarity of content and were rewritten in general brief format. A total of 164 situations were administered to another sample of parents ($N = 92$) who were asked to rate their emotional responses, and, finally, a sample of parents ($N = 180$) were asked to report on how frequently their child exhibited the 164 behaviors during the previous 2 weeks. The authors selected those 40 items that occurred most frequently and had the most unambiguous affective loading.

Target Population

Parents of children between the ages of 2 and 11 years.

Format

This test consists of a questionnaire listing 40 child behaviors (20 anger-provoking and 20 pleasure-provoking) that are listed in a random order along with six bipolar response scales that are listed (in one of four random orders and balanced for directionality) below each item. Sample items include,

- "My child comes home dirty and messy."
- "My child criticizes me as a parent."
- "My child makes good decisions."
- "My child seems happy."

Sample responses include,

1. Feel angry —————→ Feel pleased.
2. Feel bad —————→ Feel good.
3. Feel tense —————→ Feel relaxed.
4. Want to hit/spank —————→ Want to hug/kiss.
5. Want to yell —————→ Want to praise.
6. Want to send child to room —————→ Want to be with my child.

Administration and Scoring

Parents rate their responses to each child behavior on each of the 7-point bipolar response scales, each of which has a positive and negative descriptive anchor. Two scores can be obtained: PATp = pleasure and is scored by summing the average ratings for the 20 pleasing items, and PATa = anger and is scored by summing the average ratings for the 20 anger items. Higher scores indicate higher pleasure or higher anger.

Psychometric Evaluation

Smaller samples were used to assess reliability and validity of the measure.

Norms
None reported.

Reliability
Reliability examined via Cronbach's alpha (N = 46 couples) revealed correlations of r = .92 for the anger subscale and r = .96 for pleasure subscale, indicating strong internal consistency.

Validity
The Parent Affect Test is not correlated with the Edwards Social Desirability Scale (Edwards, 1957). For mothers, the anger subscore is highly positively correlated with self (r = .76) and spouse (r = .64) reports of anger problems. For fathers, the pleasure subscore is negatively correlated (r = .51) with anger self-report. Significant differences were found on the anger subscore between 17 mothers attending a Parents Anonymous group and 17 mothers from the community, which supports the scales's ability to discriminate between groups.

Advantages
Careful item development led to the inclusion of child behaviors that are normative and typical. The scale contains both positive and negative affect items.

Limitations
Response categories are limited.

Primary Reference

Linehan, Paul, and Egan (1983).

Scale Availability

In Fischer and Corcoran (2000).

Related References

None available.

General Comments and Recommendations for Practitioners and Researchers

This is a carefully developed self-report inventory of both positive and negative affect states as well as parents' hypothetical responses to children's behaviors.

---

79. Parent Attribution Test (PAT; Bugental)

Development and Description of Assessment Method

The Parent Attribution Test is a self-report inventory developed to examine a relationship schema that is organized around the sense of control one has in interpersonal situations. More specifically, the measure emphasizes the perceived balance of control between the parent and the child and taps into the parent's causal beliefs about interactions with children.

Original construction of the Parent Attribution Test was based on maternal responses to open-ended attribution questions (questions that asked for causes of caregiving success and failure) and used theoretically based scoring of items. Scales are developed from multidimensional scaling analysis and factor analysis.

Target Population

Parents of young children.

Format

In the Parent Attribution Test there are 26 items categorized into four subscales:

1. *Child Controllable:* Eight items, including "child being rested" and "child being stubborn."
2. *Child Uncontrollable:* Six items, including "child having a bad day" and "child having an unprepared neighbor."
3. *Adult Controllable:* Seven items, including "adult getting along with children" and "adult having trouble with children."

4. *Adult Uncontrollable:* Five items, including "adult having bad luck" and "adult being in a good mood."

Administration and Scoring

Respondents rate the importance of causes of failure in a hypothetical caregiving situation. Scoring is based on a four-factor model that includes causes that are *more* controllable by adults and children, and causes that are *less* controllable by adults and children. There are three scores obtained.

1. Child control over failure (CCF),
2. Adult control over failure (ACF), and
3. Perceived control over failure (PCF, which is the CCF subtracted from the ACF).

Higher scores on the PCF indicate parental beliefs about their own control over interaction.

Psychometric Evaluation

Norms

None reported.

Reliability

Alpha coefficients for the four subscales were .66 for child controllable, .40 for child uncontrollable, .71 for adult controllable, and .85 for adult uncontrollable, indicating moderate to high internal consistency.

Validity

Weak support for convergent validity was obtained in comparisons with the Parental Locus of Control Scale (Campis, Lyman, & Prentice-Dunn, 1986; $r = -.20$, $p < .05$). Although other validity research has shown that the Parent Attribution Test predicts affect, physiological reactions, and coercive adult behavior across a variety of tasks and settings, research by Lovejoy, Verda, and Hays (1997) showed little relationship of the Parent Attribution Test to other measures of parenting control, satisfaction, or efficacy.

Advantages

The Parent Attribution Test will help to clarify parents' cognitive distortions that may mediate their response to child behavior. It is strongly linked to theory about the influence of cognitive representations of power in caregiving relationships.

Limitations

Unfortunately, there is limited psychometric information available. Poor association with the well-established Parent Locus of Control Scale (Campis et al., 1986) may indicate difficulty in establishing construct validity.

Primary Reference

Bugental (1993b).

Scale Availability

Daphne B. Bugental
Department of Psychology
University of California
Santa Barbara, CA 93106
e-mail: bugental@psych.ucsb.edu

Related References

Bugental, Brown, and Reiss (1996); Lovejoy et al. (1997).

General Comments and Recommendations for Practitioners and Researchers

Results from a series of investigations by the primary author indicate that perceived control over caregiving failure is related to social interaction and information processing in parent–child relationships. Although this measure has not yet been used with parents at risk for maltreatment, the assessment of perceived control and power over interactions with children seems quite relevant.

---

80. Parent Behavior Checklist/Parenting Inventory (PBC; Fox)

Development and Description of Assessment Method

This self-report measure is designed to assess developmental expectations and behaviors of parents of young children.

A review of the literature, published tests, and clinical experience led to the development of items that met the following criteria: (a) items reflected parent behaviors rather than attitudes, (b) items reflected developmental expectations of typical parents, and (c) items were written in simple, short sentences that were easy to understand. Sixteen experts in child development then rated the 232 items in terms of relevance and item construction on a three-point scale (poor = 1, good = 3).

Target Population

Parents of young children between the ages of 1 and 5 years. Items are written at a third-grade reading level.

Format

The PBC consists of a 100-item measure with three subscales:

1. *Expectations:* Fifty items, including "My child should use the toilet without help" and "My child should be able to ride a tricycle."
2. *Discipline:* Thirty items, including "I would spank my child in public for bad behavior" and "I yell at my child for whining."
3. *Nurturing:* Twenty items, including "I play make believe with my child" and "I praise my child for learning new things."

Administration and Scoring

Parents are asked to rate each item on a 4-point, Likert-type scale from 1 = almost never to 4 = almost always. The entire checklist (including a demographic section, instructions, the 100 items, a scoring grid, and an interpretational profile) is presented in a separate PBC record form. The measure requires 10 to 20 minutes to complete; six items are reverse keyed.

Psychometric Evaluation

Empirically derived descriptive classification system of specific parent behaviors and developmental expectations yielded an initial pool of 232 items. A factor analysis yielded the three main factors.

Norms

The initial norms were based on a sample of 1,140 mothers. Because each subscale has a mean T score of 50 and a standard deviation of 10, scores between 40 and 60 would represent the average range.

Reliability

Good test–retest reliability over a 1-week interval was demonstrated with Pearson coefficients of $r = .81$ (nurturing), $r = .87$ (discipline) and $r = .98$ (expectations) for a sample of 45 parents. Good internal consistency was determined via alpha coefficients of $r = .82$ for nurturing, $r = .91$ for discipline, and $r = .97$ for expectations.

Validity

Known groups validity was demonstrated in that the items discriminated among four chronological groups of children in different developmental phases. Discriminant validity was demonstrated by relatively low correlations of the expectations and nurturing subscales with the four subscales of the Adult-Adolescent Parenting Inventory (AAPI; Bavotek, 1984), which measures attitudes toward parenting. However, the discipline subscale and the AAPI punishment subscales were intercorrelated at $r = .59$, indicating good convergent validity.

Advantages

There is a Spanish version available. The authors suggest that such a parent screening device may assist in the early identification of parents at risk for abusive situations in that their expectations are inappropriate for the ages of their childrens.

Limitations

The degree to which this parenting inventory measures actual parenting behaviors experienced by the child still needs to be examined.

Primary Reference

Fox (1992).

Scale Availability

Clinical Psychology Publishing Co., Inc.
4 Conant Sq.
Brandon, CT 05733

Related References

Fox and Bentley (1992); Peters and Fox (1993); Solis-Camara and Fox (1996).

General Comments and Recommendations for Practitioners and Researchers

This instrument is easy to administer because it is brief and most parents can complete it with no assistance. It clearly targets the appropriateness of developmental expectations and discipline strategies, two important aspects of maltreatment.

81. Parent Behavior Inventory (PBI; Lovejoy, Weis, O'Hara, & Rubin)

Development and Description of Assessment Method

The PBI was carefully developed in accordance with current views on relevant parent behavior. An initial pool of 57 items, culled from existing self-report and observational measures of parenting behavior, were reduced through principal-components factor analyses. The resulting 31 items reflecting five dimensions of parenting behavior were further reduced via a series of confirmatory factor analyses that specified the two-factor structure of the instrument.

The final version of the PBI is a brief self-report inventory designed to assess two broad aspects of parenting behavior that have been identified as key targets for treatment of problematic families: support/engagement and hostility/coercion.

Target Population

Parents of preschool and young school-age children, others who are familiar with the parents or observers of parent–child interactions.

Format

The PBI includes a total of 20 items reflecting two domains:

- *Hostile/Coercive Subscale:* Ten items that assess specific parental control strategies including,
  - "I grab or handle my child roughly."

- "I demand that my child does something (or stops doing something) right away."
- *Supportive/Engages Subscale:* Ten items that assess parental warmth, affection, and acceptance, including,
  - "My child and I hug and/or kiss each other."
  - "I comfort my child when s/he seems scared, upset, or unsure."

Administration and Scoring

Parents are asked to complete the PBI in relation to a specific child and to rate how well each item describes the way they usually act with that child. Items are rated on a 6-point Likert scale ranging from 0 = not at all true (I do not do this) to 5 = very true (I often do this).

Psychometric Evaluation

Norms
None reported.

Reliability
The internal structure and internal consistency of the PBI was evaluated via a confirmatory factor analysis with 107 mothers of young children (mean age was 3.7 years). The two-factor model provided a moderate fit with the data and all factor loadings were significant. Cronbach's alpha was .81 for the hostile/coercive (HC) subscale and .83 for the supportive/engaged (SE) subscale. The average interitem correlation was .32 for the HC subscale, with a range from .09 to .52 and the average interitem correlation for the SE subscale was .36 with a range from 113 to .58.

Test–retest reliability was examined over a one-week time period in a subset of 46 mothers who agreed to participate. The test–retest reliability coefficients were $r = .69$ for the HC subscale and $r = .74$ for the SE subscale.

Interrater reliability was examined when the PBI was used as an observer rating scale of actual parent behaviors in a controlled 30-minute parent–child interaction session for 50 mothers and their pre-school children. Pairs of raters watched videotapes of these sessions following their own six sessions of rater training, and coded each session according to the PBI items. Interrater reliability coefficients were $r = .87$ for the HC subscale and $r = .90$ for the SE subscale.

Validity

The content validity of the final 20-item version of the PBI was examined via a survey of 72 clinical child or development psychologists. Respondents were asked to rate each item in terms of relevance and representativeness of the parenting domain on a 5-point Likert scale. The mean ratings for the degree to which the group of items reflected the designated domain were 4.28 for HC subscale and 4.51 for SE subscale.

Convergent validity was examined in a sample of 41 mothers of preschool children by comparisons between the mothers' ratings of their parenting behaviors and spouses' ratings of their wives' parenting behaviors on the PBI. Correlations between husbands' and wives' ratings were $r = .26$ ($p < .05$) for the SE subscale and $r = .42$ ($p < .01$) for the HC subscale.

In addition, construct validity was assessed through correlations between the PBI subscales and measures of related constructs in a sample of 107 mothers of preschool children. Significant correlations were found between the PBI and intensity ratings on the Eyberg Child Behavior Inventory (Eyberg & Ross, 1978): $r = -.40$ ($p < .01$) with the SE subscale and $r = .61$ ($p < .01$) with the HC subscale. Correlations between the PBI and the Parenting Stress Index (Abidin, 1990) were also significant: $r = .53$ ($p < .01$) for the total stress score of the PSI and the SE subscale and $r = .49$ ($p < .01$) for the total stress score and the HC subscale.

Finally, derivation accuracy was assessed in a comparison of mothers' self-reports of parenting and observer ratings (using the PB) of actual behavior during a high-stress (15-minute task session) and low-stress (15-minute play session) laboratory analogue parent–child interaction. The correlations between mother self-report and observer ratings on the PBI were $r = .30$ ($p < .05$) on the HC subscale for the play and $r = .54$ ($p < .01$) for the task sessions. Correlations on the SE subscale were only significant for the task session ($r = .50$, $p < .05$), indicating that observer ratings may be sensitive to context and that mothers' scores or the PBI reflect objective differences in parenting.

Advantages

This inventory is a short inventory that reflects actual parenting behaviors rather than beliefs or attitudes. The authors developed it in such a fashion that it could be used to rate parent behavior by others familiar with that parent (such as a spouse) or by observers of parent–child analogue interactions. It is useful as a reliable rating scale by observers with relatively short observer training.

Limitations

The psychometric development of the PBI was limited to parents of relatively young children, so the scale may not be applicable to parents of school-aged children.

Primary Reference

Lovejoy, Weis, O'Hare, and Rubin (1999).

Scale Availability

> Christine Lovejoy
> Department of Psychology
> Northern Illinois University
> DeKalb, IL 60115–2892
> (or in primary reference)

Related References

None available.

General Comments and Recommendations for Practitioners and Researchers

The authors of the PBI are to be commended not only on their careful development of the inventory but also for their aim to provide a tool that can be used both as a self-report and as a "ratings by others" method for parent assessment. They have provided an easy example of a multimodal assessment approach.

---

82. Parent Opinion Questionnaire (POQ; Azar)

Development and Description of Assessment Method

The POQ is a self-report measure that examines the developmental appropriateness of parental expectations for their child's behavior.

Target Population

Parents with children up to age 12. Items can be read to parents who are unable to read.

Format

The POQ includes a total 80 items reflecting 6 domains:

1. *Family Responsibility and Care of Siblings:* Ten items, including, "A 7-year-old is old enough to be expected to do the laundry for the family."
2. *Punishment:* Ten items, including, "When a 2-year-old bites the mother, it is all right for the mother to bite the child back to teach the child that biting isn't allowed."
3. *Self-Care:* Ten items, including, "A 1-year-old can usually feed him or herself" and "In most cases, a 6-year-old can get up, wash, dress, and go to school unassisted."
4. *Help and Affection to Parents:* Ten items, including, "A 5-year-old can be expected to help by feeding, dressing, and changing diapers for an infant" and "Parents can expect infants to always show them love and affection."
5. *Leaving Children Alone:* Ten items, including, "Generally, it would be all right to leave kids alone for a few days if they were as old as 12 or 13."
6. *Proper Behavior and Feelings:* Ten items, including, "Parents do not need to approve of everything a child does" and "It is natural for a parent to be upset if a child breaks something expensive."

Administration and Scoring

The POQ requires parents to rate whether they agree or disagree with the appropriateness of expecting various child behaviors on a 4-point, Likert-type scale.

Psychometric Evaluation
Norms
None reported.

Reliability
Test–retest reliability was demonstrated over a 12-week interval for a small ($N = 16$) sample of mothers with correlations of $r = .85$ for total score and correlations ranging from $r = .34$ to $r = .87$ for subscale scores (all but "leaving children alone" were greater than $r = .65$).

Validity

Criterion-related validity was demonstrated by comparisons to a sample of 16 mothers who had abused their children. These mothers had significantly higher unrealistic expectations for their children when compared to other mothers. The discriminant function of the POQ successfully classified 75% of abusive mothers and 93% of mothers whose spouse or boyfriend abused. Overall, 83% of mothers in the 1986 study were correctly classified.

Advantages

The POQ assesses an important aspect of cognitive responding that may influence parents' interactions with their children.

Limitations

Psychometric data need to be updated with larger samples.

Primary Reference

Azar, Robinson, Hekimian, and Twentyman (1984).

Scale Availability

> Sandra Azar
> Department of Psychology
> Clark University
> 950 Main St.
> Worcester, MA 01610

Related References

Azar and Rohrbeck (1986).

General Comments and Recommendations for Practitioners and Researchers

Early intervention work with abusive parents targeted unrealistic expectations such as those contained in this instrument. The face validity of the items and the obvious socially desirable answers may limit valid assessment of at-risk parents, however.

83. Parental Anger Inventory (PAI; MacMillan, Olson, & Hansen)

Development and Description of Assessment Method

The Parental Anger Inventory is a self-report measure designed to assess anger experienced by parents in response to child misbehavior and other child-related situations. This instrument may help to identify anger control problems or to evaluate anger management interventions for parents.

The initial version of the Parental Anger Inventory contained 81 items generated from child-related complaints of maltreating parents during therapy sessions (as indicated by raters coding audiotaped sessions), an extensive review of the literature, and other problematic child behaviors identified by experienced therapists. In a pilot study, 40 parents were administered items in order to refine internal consistency. Items with item–total correlations below $r = .30$ on problem and anger intensity were eliminated.

Target Population

Parents of children between the ages of 2 and 10 years old.

Format

The Parental Anger Inventory contains 50 antecedent misbehaviors of children, such as "Your child gets out of bed after being put in bed," "Your child makes a mess around the house," and "Your child spills food or a drink." Parents report on whether this behavior is a problem for them (problem dimension) and how angry this behavior makes them (anger intensity dimension).

Administration and Scoring

Parents indicate if the situation described is a problem on a 5-point, Likert-type scale from 1 = not at all to 5 = extremely. Parents also indicate how much the situation makes them angry on a 5-point, Likert-type scale from 1 = not at all to 5 = extremely. Scores are determined by summing the ratings for the problem dimension and the anger intensity dimension.

Psychometric Evaluation

The first psychometric study included 48 parents with at least one child between the ages of 2 and 10, whereas a second study included 166 community participants. A more recent study examined maltreating and nonmaltreating parents (n = 98) of children between 2 and 10 years of age.

Norms

Responses from a small sample (N = 166) indicated a mean anger severity score of 97.85 (SD = 25.42). A cutoff score of 148 for clinically significant levels of child-related anger was developed.

Reliability

Alpha coefficients computed for item–total score comparisons were .57 for the anger intensity dimension and .49 for the problem dimension, indicating good internal consistency. In a second study of 17 maltreating parents, 18 nonmaltreating parents seeking psychological treatment, and 13 control parents, internal consistency was greater with item–total correlations of .90 for the problem dimension and .96 for the anger intensity dimension. Split-half Spearman Brown correlations were r = .84 for the problem dimension and r = .91 for the anger intensity dimension. Test–retest reliability computed across 8 to 21 days for a subset of the sample (N = 21) resulted in correlations of r = .78 for the problem dimension and r = .86 for the anger intensity dimension.

In a 2001 study, parents determined to be maltreating (n = 44), help-seeking but not maltreating parents (n = 24), and nonmaltreating, non-help-seeking parents (n = 30) completed the Parental Anger Inventory as well as other parent measures. In this study, alpha coefficients for the problem and anger intensity subscales were .96 and .81, respectively, indicating good internal consistency. A subsample of 39 parents completed two administrations of the Parental Anger Inventory, and good temporal stability was indicated with correlation coefficients of .80 and .79 for the problem subscale and the anger severity subscale, respectively.

Validity

The problem and anger intensity dimensions were significantly correlated (r = .72 in one study and .68 in another; Sedlar & Hansen, 2001). These correlations indicate that the dimensions are related but are not redundant.

Convergent validity was examined by Pearson product moment correlations between the Parental Anger Inventory and other scales. The anger intensity subscale was significantly correlated with the Novaco Anger Control Scale (Novaco, 1985; $r = .38$, $p < .001$), the Hassles Scale (Kanner, Coyne, Schaefer, & Lazarus, 1981) for both number of problems ($r = .28$, $p < .05$) and severity of hassles ($r = .33$, $p < .01$), whereas the problem subscale of the Parental Anger Inventory was significantly correlated with the Hassle Scale number ($r = .41$, $p < .01$) and Hassles Scale severity ($r = .40$, $p < .01$). Both subscales of the Parental Anger Inventory were correlated with the Eyberg Child Behavior Inventory (Eyberg & Ross, 1978) as well. Discriminant analysis was conducted in the 2001 study to determine known groups validity. Analyses showed that both the Parental Anger Inventory problem subscale and income significantly contributed to the discrimination among groups. The maltreating parents had a significantly lower income and more problematic Parental Anger Inventory subscale scores than the other two parent groups.

Advantages

The Parental Anger Inventory focuses on a very important moderator of parent behavior. The authors have continued to examine its psychometric properties.

Limitations

The single focus on antecedents to parent anger does not allow for a full evaluation of the angry interaction sequence.

Primary Reference

MacMillan, Olson, and Hansen (1988).

Scale Availability

D. J. Hansen
Psychology Department
P.O. Box 880311
University of Nebraska
Lincoln, NE 68588

Related References

DeRoma and Hansen (1994); Sedlar and Hansen (2001).

General Comments and Recommendations for Practitioners and Researchers

The Parental Anger Inventory was previously called the MacMillan-Olson-Hansen Anger Control Scale (MOHAC), which would suggest a psychometric comparison with the State-Trait Anger Expression Scale (Spielberger, Jacobs, Russel, & Crane, 1983). Initial correlations with the Novaco Anger Control Scale are promising, however.

84. Parental Stress Scale (PSS; Berry & Jones)

Development and Description of Assessment Method

The PSS is a short self-report inventory designed to measure individual differences in the level of stress associated with raising young children in a nonclinical sample. The measure seeks to address the dichotomy of parenthood in that having and raising children are sources of both pleasure and strain.

The items in the PSS were generated by a review of empirical literature. An initial pool of 20 items thought to measure the construct of parental stress was generated. After administration to the first group of parents ($N = 125$), two items were eliminated because of poor internal consistency.

Target Population

Parents of young children.

Format

The PSS has 18 items that focus on three main themes:

1. Positive emotional benefits, such as love, joy, happiness and fun, including "I am happy in my role as a parent" and "I find my children enjoyable";
2. Sense of self-enrichment and personal fulfillment, including "I sometimes worry if I am doing enough for my child(ren)"; and
3. Negative components such as demands on time, energy, and financial resources or loss of self-esteem or control, including "Having children has been a financial burden."

Administration and Scoring

Parents respond to each item on a 5-point, Likert-type scale from 1 = strongly disagree to 5 = strongly agree. Half of the items are reverse keyed.

Psychometric Evaluation

Norms
Not available.

Reliability
Reliability was examined in a sample of 233 parents. Cronbach's alpha coefficient was .83 for the whole sample. The mean interitem correlation was .23, whereas the mean item–whole correlation was .43, demonstrating good internal consistency. Test–retest reliability, evaluated over a 6-week interval, was demonstrated with a significant correlation of .81.

Validity
Convergent validity was demonstrated by significant correlations with the Perceived Stress Scale (Cohen, Kamarck, & Mermelstein, 1983; a more global measure of stress) and the Parenting Stress Index (Abidin, 1990). Known-group validity was determined via a comparison of scores from mothers of a clinical group and a nonclinical group. Scores for the groups were significantly different.

Advantages
The PSS is a very brief assessment measure and is quick to administer. It may be used as a repeated measure to evaluate an intervention program. It also includes positive parent items.

Limitations
There is limited psychometric evaluation; generalizations to clinical or at-risk populations may not yet be possible.

Primary Reference

Berry and Jones (1995).

Scale Availability

Judy O. Berry
Department of Psychology

University of Tulsa
600 South College Ave.
Tulsa, OK 74104-3189

Related References

None available.

General Comments and Recommendations for Practitioners and Researchers

The PSS has a rare focus on the benefits as well as the costs of raising children. It would be interesting to compare with a bidirectional affect measure.

85. Parenting Alliance Inventory (PAI; Abidin)

Development and Description of Assessment Method

The Parenting Alliance Inventory is a self-report instrument designed to assess the parent's view of his or her alliance with the co-parent. The focus is on the desire to communicate and the respect for the judgment of the other parent, along with the co-parent's investment and involvement with the child. *Parenting alliance* is a concept that describes the part of the marital relationship that is concerned with parenthood and child rearing and that emphasizes the degree of commitment and cooperation between parents.

The initial pool of 80 items was written by a group of family therapists and psychologists. Items were then evaluated by a panel of 10 professionals, and 20 items were selected.

Target Population

Parents of children and adolescents. Items are written on a fifth- to sixth-grade level.

Format

The Parenting Alliance Inventory is a 20-item measure. Sample items include,

* "My child's other parent enjoys being alone with our child."

- "My child's other parent and I are a good team."
- "I believe my child's other parent is a good parent."

Administration and Scoring

Parents respond to each item on a 5-point, Likert-type scale from 1 = strongly agree to 5 = strongly disagree. The Parenting Alliance Inventory takes approximately 10 minutes to complete and 5 minutes to score.

Psychometric Evaluation

Norms

The Parenting Alliance Inventory was normed on an initial sample of 512 parents (321 mothers and 191 fathers). More recent norms are available in a manual on a sample of 1,224 parents of children and adolescents.

Reliability

The Parenting Alliance Inventory is reliable with an internal consistency of .97 and a test–retest reliability of .80 across a 4- to 6-week period.

Validity

Some evidence for convergent validity is provided by comparisons with the Lock-Wallace Revised Marital Adjustment Test (Locke & Wallace, 1959). Correlations were $r = .20$ ($p < .05$) for mothers and $r = .44$ ($p < .001$) for fathers. Significant negative correlations with certain subscales of the Parenting Stress Index (PSI; Abidin, 1990; total stress, $r = .26$; child reinforces parent, $r = .24$; relationship with spouse $r = .45$) indicates good convergent validity as well. Known group validity demonstrated that the Parenting Alliance Inventory discriminates among married, separated, and divorced couples.

Advantages

The Parenting Alliance Inventory has a creative focus on a specific aspect of the marital relationship that may have a direct influence on parenting. It may be sensitive to dysfunctional marital relationships and perhaps those that characterize maltreating families.

Limitations

The Parenting Alliance Inventory is a relatively new scale that has not yet been used with clinical populations. Some items are difficult to understand because of the relational nature of questions.

Primary Reference

Abidin and Brunner (1995).

Scale Availability

Parenting Alliance Measure
Psychological Assessment Resources, Inc.
P.O. Box 998
Odessa, FL 33556
(800) 727-9329

Related References

None available

General Comments and Recommendations for Practitioners and Researchers

The Parenting Alliance Inventory emphasizes an important dimension to examine in high-risk families with two parents or live-in partners.

---

86. Parenting Locus of Control Scale (PLCS; Campis)

Development and Description of Assessment Method

The PLCS is a self-report inventory designed to assess locus of control beliefs regarding parent perspectives of child rearing success and failure. These beliefs are assessed with regard to feelings of responsibility, efficacy, and a sense of control.

The initial sample for scale refinement included 147 parents (115 mothers and 32 fathers). A second group of 105 parents was used for validity work. An initial factor analysis yielded five factors (identified as subscales) that helped reduce the original 109 items to the current 47. The original item pool ($N = 200$) was generated from previous scales and new item creation. Judges then rated items, and disparities helped to eliminate many.

Target Population

Parents of children and adolescents.

Format

The PLCS consists of an inventory that includes 47 items across the following five subscales:

1. *Parental Efficacy:* Ten items, including "What I do has little effect on my child's behavior" and "Capable people who fail to become good parents have not followed through on their opportunities."
2. *Fate or Chance:* Ten items, including "I am just one of those lucky people who happen to have a good child" and "Without the right breaks, one cannot be an effective parent."
3. *Parental Responsibility:* Ten items, including "My child's behavior problems are no one's fault but my own" and "Neither my child nor myself is responsible for his or her behavior."
4. *Parental Control:* Ten items, including "Children's behavior problems are often due to mistakes their parents make" and "Sometimes I feel I do not have enough control over the direction my child's life is taking."
5. *Child Control:* Seven items, including "My life is chiefly controlled by my child" and "I find that my child can get me to do things I really did not want to do."

Administration and Scoring

Parents respond to each item on a 5-point, Likert-type scale from 1 = strongly disagree to 5 = strongly agree. A number of items are reverse keyed to reduce response bias.

Psychometric Evaluation

Norms
Not available.

Reliability
The overall mean Cronbach alpha coefficient was .92 for total score; subscales ranged from .62 to .79.

Validity
Convergent validity indicated by a positive correlation with the Internal–External Scale (Rotter, 1966; $r = .33$). Factors of parent responsibility ($r = .26$), child control ($r = .24$), and fate/chance ($r = .27$)

were each related to the Locus of Control Scale (Rotter, 1966), whereas efficacy and parent control were not.

Discriminant validity was demonstrated by weak negative correlation with the Marlow-Crowne Social Desirability Scale (Crowne & Marlowe, 1960; $r = -.27$).

Advantages

Items are easy to read and relevant to the problems that parents report in clinical settings.

Limitations

There are no temporal stability data available. The scale was developed and validated only with parents of elementary school children.

Primary Reference

Campis, Lyman, and Prentice-Dunn (1986).

Scale Availability

In Fischer and Corcoran (2000).

Related References

Lovejoy, Verda, and Hays (1997).

General Comments and Recommendations for Practitioners and Researchers

Although the research with this scale indicates that parents with an external locus of control experience generalized feelings of incompetence and report difficulties with child management, it cannot be assumed that such a control orientation causes parent–child conflict. Further research especially related to maltreatment of children and parents' control orientation is needed.

---

87. Parenting Scale (PS; Arnold & O'Leary)

Development and Description of Assessment Method

The content of this self-report instrument is designed to reflect the use of ineffective parental discipline and other inappropriate or angry responses of parents to child misbehavior.

Items were based on a literature review that identified common parental discipline mistakes. Revisions of the scale were based on samples of up to 100 mothers of preschool children. A 2001 revision using only 10 of the original items was completed with a larger sample ($n = 187$) of economically disadvantaged mothers.

Target Population

Parents of children under the age of 3. (A recent study—Irvine, Biglan, Smolkowski, & Ary, 1999—examined its use with mothers of young adolescents.) A sixth-grade reading level is required.

Format

The PS is a 30-item measure with three subscales:

1. *Laxness:* Eleven items related to permissive discipline;
2. *Overreaction:* Ten items reflecting mistakes and displays of anger or meanness; and
3. *Verbosity:* Seven items reflecting lengthy verbal responses and a reliance on talking even when talking is not effective.

Sample items include,

- "When my child misbehaves:"
  - I do something right away ⎯⎯⎯⎯→ I do something about it later.
- "If saying no doesn't work:"
  - I take some kind of action ⎯⎯⎯⎯→ I offer my child something nice so he or she will behave.
- "When my child misbehaves:"
  - I rarely use bad language ⎯⎯⎯⎯→ I almost always use bad language.

Administration and Scoring

Parents respond to each item on a 7-point, Likert-type scale where the anchor points reflect either a mistake or an effective strategy for handling the child misbehavior. Each item receives a score from 1 to 7, where 7 = the ineffective parent response. A total of 14 items are reverse keyed. There are three subscale scores, and the total score is the average response on all items. The PS takes only 10 to 15 minutes to complete.

Psychometric Evaluation

A factor analysis yielded the three subscales. Factor analyses completed in 1999 and 2001 yielded two factors resembling the original laxness and overreactivity factors, however, thus eliminating the verbosity factor.

Norms
None reported.

Reliability
Internal consistency was shown by alpha coefficients ranging from $r = .63$ for verbosity to $r = .84$ for total score. Test–retest reliability over a 2-week interval for a small sample ($N = 22$) was demonstrated by correlations of $r = .79$ for verbosity, $r = .82$ for overreaction, $r = .83$ for laxness, and $r = .84$ for the total score.

In a larger study ($n = 187$), the alpha coefficients for the full scale (.71) and the laxness (.77) and overreactivity (.72) subscales were adequate, whereas the alpha for the verbosity subscale was inadequate (.23), leading the authors to drop these items from further analyses. For a small subsample of these parents ($n = 18$), 1-month test–retest reliability correlations were acceptable at $r = .73$ for laxness, $r = .71$ for overreactivity, and $r = .75$ for the PS full scale.

Validity
Several small samples provided evidence for criterion-related validity. The scores were related to discipline mistakes and child behaviors coded during 15 home observations of mother–child interactions. A comparison of clinic ($N = 26$) and nonclinic ($N = 51$) mothers revealed significant differences between groups on laxness and overreactivity subscales as well as for total score. Clinic mothers scored higher on the Beck Depression Inventory (Beck, Ward, Mendelson, Mock, & Erbaugh, 1961) and rated their children as more problematic on the Child Behavior Checklist (CBCL; Achenbach, 1991) as well.

In the larger study with disadvantaged mothers (Rectman et al., 2001), convergent and discriminant validity were examined in correlations between the PS total score and two subscales of other parenting measures, educational level and social desirability. Correlations between the PS and subscales of the Parental Authority Questionnaire (PAQ; Buri, 1991) revealed significant relationships between the permissive subscale of the PAQ and the total PS score ($r = .31$, $p < .002$), as well as between the laxness subscale of the PAQ ($r = .24$, $p < .002$) and the overreactivity subscale of the PS ($r = .25$, $p < .002$). The authoritarian subscale of the PAQ was positively correlated with only the overreactivity subscale of the PS ($r = .24$, $p < .002$). Subscales of the Parent–Child Relationship Inventory (PCRI; Gerard, 1994) were negatively correlated with all three of the PS scores, indicating that high scores on the PS were associated with lower levels of parental involvement and limit setting on the PCRI. Further significant correlations were found between the PS total score and the short form of the Parenting Stress Inventory (PSI; Abidin, 1990; $r = .39$, $p < .002$) and between the overreactivity subscale of the PS and the PSI total score ($r = .43$, $p < .002$), indicating good convergent and concurrent validity.

Advantages

The items on the PS are specific enough to target for a parenting intervention. Because of the format, the items are not tied to the frequency of the child's misbehavior.

Limitations

The authors suggest caution with the use of this measure because observational data are based on a small sample of only 15 participants, and the discriminant validity sample included only 26 clinic mothers.

The recent revision of the PS to 10 items and a two-factor scale without the verbosity dimension calls into question the original psychometric development and requires further examination.

Primary Reference

Arnold, O'Leary, Wolff, and Acker (1993).

Scale Availability

> Susan G. O'Leary
> Department of Psychology
> State University of New York at Stony Brook
> Stony Brook, NY 11790

Related References

Irvine et al. (1999); Reitman et al. (2001); Smith and O'Leary (1995).

General Comments and Recommendations for Practitioners and Researchers

The PS offers a promising assessment focus for evaluating areas of parenting difficulty in abusive or at-risk parents. Clinicians and researchers should examine differences between ratings by mothers and fathers and between parents of boys and girls. The recent research by Reitman et al. (2001) suggests that the shorter version (10 items) developed after their factor analyses is briefer yet retains two of the original subscales.

88. Parenting Sense of Competence (PSOC; Gibaud-Wallston & Wandersman)

Development and Description of Assessment Method

The PSOC is a short self-report inventory designed to measure two dimensions related to parenting self-esteem: affective and instrumental responses.

Factor analysis of the initial item pool revealed two dimensions of parenting self-esteem: skill–knowledge (efficacy subscale) and value–comforting (satisfaction subscale).

Target Population

Parents of children under the age of 12 years.

Format

The PSOC includes 17 items across two rationally derived subscales:

1. *Satisfaction:* Nine items representing the affective dimension of parenting, including "Even though being a parent could be rewarding, I am frustrated now while my child is at his or her present age" and "Being a parent makes me tense and anxious."

2. *Efficacy:* Eight items that represent the instrumental dimension, including "Being a parent is manageable and any problems are easily solved" and "I meet my own personal expectations for expertise in caring for my child."

Administration and Scoring

Parents respond to each item on a 6-point, Likert-type scale from 1 = strongly agree to 6 = strongly disagree. Eight items are reverse keyed. For all items, the higher the score, the greater the sense of self-esteem.

Psychometric Evaluation

Norms

None reported.

Reliability

Internal consistency was assessed via Cronbach's alpha coefficient on a large sample (297 mothers and 215 fathers of children 4–9 years old). Coefficients were .75 for the satisfaction subscale, .76 for efficacy subscale, and .79 for total score.

Validity

The relationship between parenting self-esteem and perception of child behavior was examined by comparisons with the CBCL (Achenbach, 1991). The total PSOC was significantly related to the internalizing subscale ($r = -.21$, $p < .01$) and the externalizing subscale of the CBCL ($r = -.24$, $p < .01$). Further, the correlations between the satisfaction score and the CBCL subscales were all significant.

Advantages

Separate mother and father versions are available. The PSOC provides a good assessment of the affective dimension of parenting, which is particularly sensitive to the effects of child behavioral problems.

Limitations

The PSOC has only been examined with normal families. Replication with clinical populations is still needed.

Primary Reference

Gibared-Wallston and Wandersman (1978).

Scale Availability

Charlotte Johnston
Department of Psychology

University of British Columbia
Vancouver, British Columbia, Canada V6T1Y7

Related References

Johnston and Mash (1989).

General Comments and Recommendations for Practitioners and Researchers

An interesting modified version of the PSOC has been created to examine abuse potential of residential child care workers (Dodge-Reyone, 1995).

---

89. Parenting Stress Index (PSI; Abidin)

Development and Description of Assessment Method

The PSI is a screening and diagnostic self-report instrument designed to measure the magnitude of stress in the parent–child system.

Target Population

Parents of children up to 10 years of age. It is most useful for parents of children in their first three years of life. A fifth-grade reading level is required.

Format

The PSI is a 120-item measure of child-related stress, parent-related stress, and general life stress. The complete version includes six child-related subscales:

1. *Adaptability:* Eleven items, including "My child gets upset easily over the smallest things."
2. *Acceptability:* Seven items, including "My child is not able to do as much as I expected."
3. *Demandingness:* Nine items, including "My child is always hanging on me."
4. *Mood:* Five items, including "My child generally wakes up in a bad mood."

5. *Distractibility/Hyperactivity:* Nine items, including "My child is so active that it exhausts me."
6. *Reinforcement of Parent:* Six items, including "My child smiles at me much less than I expected."

Also included are seven parent personality and situational variable subscales:

1. *Depression:* Nine items, including "There are quite a few things that bother me about my life."
2. *Attachment:* Seven items, including "The number of children that I have now is too many."
3. *Restriction of Role:* Seven items, including "I feel trapped by my responsibilities as a parent."
4. *Sense of Competence:* Thirteen items, including "Being a parent is harder that I thought it would be."
5. *Social Isolation:* Six items, including "I feel alone and without friends."
6. *Relationship With Spouse:* Seven items, including "Since having my last child, I have had less interest in sex."
7. *Parent Health:* Five items, including "I don't enjoy things as I used to."

There is also an optional 19-item life stress subscale. The short form contains 36 items that yield a total stress score from three subscales: parental distress, parent–child dysfunctional interaction, and difficult child.

Administration and Scoring

Parents are asked to respond to each item on a 5-point, Likert-type scale from 1 = strongly agree to 5 = strongly disagree. Administration time is approximately 20 to 30 minutes for the long form (101 items) and 10 minutes for the short form (36 items). Three summary scores are available for the complete version (parent domain, child domain, and total stress) in addition to subscale scores. Scores range from 101 to 505, and total scores greater than 260 indicate significant stress.

Psychometric Evaluation

Norms

Extensive normative information is available for a variety of reference groups and is provided in the accompanying test manual. The normal range for the total score is 175 to 245.

Reliability

In a large reliability study of parents (N = 534), Cronbach's alpha coefficients were .89 for the child domain (subscales ranged from .62 to .70), .93 for the parent domain (subscales ranged from .55 to .80), and .95 for total stress score.

Test–retest reliability was demonstrated at a three-month interval by correlations of .63 for the child domain, .96 for the parent domain, and .96 for the total stress score.

Validity

In a separate validation investigation (Tam, Chan, & Wong, 1994), the PSI was compared with other global measures of stress in a sample of Chinese mothers in Hong Kong (N = 248). Significant correlations with the General Health Questionnaire (Shek, 1987; r = .60), the Langer Stress Scale (Langer, 1962; r = .66), and the Global Assessment of Recent Stress (Linn, 1985; r = .384) provide good evidence for convergent validity. Criterion-related validity was demonstrated by comparisons of clinical status groups with control groups. Significantly different PSI scores were demonstrated between the groups. In recent study of parents (N = 216) of Head Start children, the short form of the PSI indicated a correlation between the total score with the parenting scale (Arnold et al., 1993; r = .39; p < .002).

Advantages

An extensive manual is available that includes reference group profiles, case illustrations, Hispanic norms, norms by age group, and "at-risk" diagnostic information. The PSI has an easy to use, all-in-one answer, scoring, and profile form. Chinese (Cantonese), French Canadian, and Spanish versions are available. Computer software is available for administration, automatic scoring, and report writing. To detect response distortions, the PSI contains a defensive responding subscale.

Limitations

The PSI is not useful for parents of adolescents. A recent study of general population (N = 100) and at-risk (N = 70) parents, instructed to either fake good and bad, be honest, or respond randomly indicated that the defensive responding subscale had limited utility in detecting individual cases of faking good behavior.

Primary Reference

Abidin (1990).

Scale Availability

Psychological Assessment Resources, Inc.
P.O. Box 998
Odessa, FL 33556
(800) 331-8378

Related References

Abidin (1995); Reitman et al. (2001); Tam, Chan, and Wong (1994).

General Comments and Recommendations for Practitioners and Researchers

The author suggests that the PSI may be used in the assessment of child abuse risk, in forensic evaluation for child custody decisions, and intervention and treatment planning for high stress, dysfunctional families.

Behavioral Observation and Analogue Methods

A lthough naturalistic observation of parents interacting with their children would be the optimal assessment strategy for the clinician or researcher, practical and ethical problems make this time-consuming approach virtually unfeasible. Simulated or analogue assessment strategies have been developed as the next-best alternative to the assessment of behavior as it occurs. These techniques entail a replication in the lab or clinical setting of some critical part of the natural environment, with the expectation that behavior in this analogue setting will accurately reflect in vivo functioning. This allows for more objective measurement of clinical targets that would otherwise only be available through self-report. Further, the analogue strategy increases control over the assessment situation and enhances the probability of obtaining the behaviors and responses of interest. The assessment of parents' responses to their children can be enhanced by the inclusion of analogue methods, some of which are easily incorporated into the clinical setting.

90. Analogue Parenting Task (APT; Zaidi)

Development and Description of Assessment Method

The APT is a photographic depiction method designed to assess viewers' hypothesized disciplinary actions. It is based on earlier work by Larrance and Twentyman (1983).

Target Population

College students; however, the methodology is applicable to parent groups as well.

Format

The APT is an assessment method consisting of 20 slides showing different child behaviors. Each participant views these slides. The photographed situations range from normal but irritating (spilling grape juice on a carpet, standing on the hood of a polished car) to those that are unequivocally deviant (puncturing an auto tire with a knife, burning papers on a carpeted floor).

The presentation of each slide is accompanied by a set of identical questions designed to assess the emotional reaction of the viewer (anger, annoyance, amusement) and to determine if he or she would discipline the child and which disciplinary tactic would be used. Finally, the viewer is asked to identify the disciplinary tactic he or she would use if the child were to persist in the depicted behavior nine more times. Listed disciplinary responses ranged from ignoring and verbal reprimands to potentially injurious physical discipline, including striking with objects.

Administration and Scoring

Administration time for the APT is approximately 1 hour, including 1.5 minutes of viewing time per slide. Participant responses are coded on four variables:

1. *Physical abuse potential:* Frequency with which physical forms of discipline are elected by respondents when confronted with child behavior on the first occurrence;
2. *Escalated abuse potential:* Frequency with which these same physical disciplinary responses are endorsed when responding as if the depicted behavior were occurring for the tenth time;
3. *Verbal reprimands:* Frequency of endorsement of verbal responses; and
4. *Anger variable:* Total number of times a participant endorses angry reactions to the depicted behaviors.

Psychometric Evaluation

Norms
None reported.

Reliability
None reported.

Validity
Persons with more punitive backgrounds (as measured by responses to the physical punishment subscale of the Assessing Environments III Inventory; Berger & Knutson, 1984) were significantly more likely to endorse potentially injurious disciplinary responses.

Advantages
Visual depiction of hypothetical child misbehavior is a creative variation on the usual verbal description of such situations.

Limitations
The APT was developed on a limited sample ($N = 49$) of college students with no known parenting experience. Parents may not relate to pictures of other people's children.

Primary Reference

Zaidi, Knutson, and Mehm (1989).

Scale Availability

> John Knutson
> Department of Psychology
> The University of Iowa
> Iowa City, IA 52242

Related References

None available

General Comments and Recommendations for Practitioners and Researchers

Generalizations from this experimental study with college students may be limited. The work needs to be replicated with various parent populations. The assessment process is long and may not be adaptable to the clinical setting.

91. Home Simulation Assessment (HSA; MacMillan)

Development and Description of Assessment Method

The HSA is an analogue method used to measure a parent's ability to apply child management skills with actors playing child roles in more complex and realistic problem contexts than those often used in clinic parent training programs.

Home simulations were directly related to each of the child management skills included in the treatment program applied in MacMillan, Olson, and Hansen (1991).

Target Population

Physically abusive parents involved in parent training programs.

Format

In each HSA, the parent is provided with a series of 10 tasks through which the parent is to do his or her best to get the actors playing the child roles to perform certain behaviors. The parent is allowed 30 seconds to direct the completion of the task, which was announced on an intercom. Scenarios and tasks relate to specific activities, such as cleaning up a mess or preparing for a shopping trip.

Actors are prompted to either comply with the parent directives or display deviant responses according to an established script. Two possible scripts are low deviance (in which a single actor displays a low rate of deviant responses) and high deviance (in which the actor displays a high rate of deviant responses). Deviant responses of the actors were randomly chosen from a pool of responses and include verbal arguing without objectionable content, failure to attend to instructions, noncompliance, rule violations, foul language, aggressive behavior, and escape from time-out.

Administration and Scoring

Trained observers code parent–actor home simulations from videotapes. In the primary references, the videos were made in the playroom of a mental health center. The following specific parenting responses are coded: instruction, warning sequence, time-out, and timeout problem sequence.

Psychometric Evaluation

Norms
None reported.

Reliability
Three parents participated in this single-participant design in order to evaluate the effects of a parent training program across nine sessions. A percentage agreement formula was used to calculate interobserver reliability. A second observer independently rated 48% of all HSAs. Percent agreements ranged from 95% for the warnings sequence in the high deviance simulation to 100% for the time-out sequence in the low deviance simulation, showing clear evidence for interrater reliability.

Validity
Parent evaluations of the HSAs indicated that they viewed the problem scenarios as realistic, although the scenarios did not elicit strong affective reactions from parents. Parents reported increases in their ability to successfully manage problems at home, which corresponded to increased correct responding across sessions for the simulations. The authors also conducted free play and home observations; however, data from these different sources were not compared to home simulation data.

Advantages
The HAS offers a unique approach to assessment of parenting skills in high-demand, stressful situations and may help clinicians assess potential generalization to home environments. Repeated assessments allow for evaluation of varying phases of treatment and allow for "within-subject" comparisons, because parents serve as their own baseline level.

Limitations
Undergraduates served as "child" actors, which limited naturalistic variables. It is unlikely that the average clinician would have the personnel to conduct frequent simulations, and the assessment system was quite labor-intensive, given the small number of participants.

Primary Reference

MacMillan et al. (1991).

Scale Availability

David Hansen
Department of Psychology
University of Nebraska-Lincoln
Lincoln, NE 68588-0308

Related References

None available.

General Comments and Recommendations for Practitioners and Researchers

The HSA is a creative use of analogue assessment methodology in evaluating parents who participate in a treatment program. It would seem that the scenarios used could be altered to fit the presenting problems of specific families in a clinical setting.

---

92. Hypothetical Compliance Vignettes (HCV; Strassberg)

Development and Description of Assessment Method

This analogue assessment method using pictorial vignettes was developed to test hypotheses concerning relationships between mothers' disciplinary dysfunction and their descriptive versus inference-level interpretations of child noncompliance. The method affords an examination of parents' attributions for child misbehavior and hypothesized disciplinary response.

Stimulus situations were based on knowledge of parent–child compliance situations. Raters ($N = 5$) evaluated the fidelity of the materials as to the intended stimulus value of the pictorial vignettes. The authors report 100% agreement between raters as to the stimulus categories.

Target Population

Mothers of aggressive and nonaggressive boys enrolled in a preschool program.

Format

In the HCV, a total of 18 pictorial vignettes (illustrations with a male child) are followed by verbal descriptions of mother and child behavior. Each vignette consists of the child engaged in play activity, followed by a maternal directive to engage in one of three less desirable activities (going to bed, having to deal with the arrival of guests, accompanying the mother on an errand). Then the child responds in each of six ways (compliance, request, statement, complaining, ignoring, mild opposition). The mother is instructed to imagine that the child in the picture is her own son. Child stimulus prompts included, "Can I play some more?" and "But I like playing this" (stated pleasantly and matter-of-factly).

Administration and Scoring

Following the vignette presentation, mothers were asked to make two ratings on 7-point, Likert-type scales. The first subscale was the judgment rating, which was presented as follows:

Did your child do what you told him to do?

$-3 \quad -2 \quad -1 \quad 0 \quad +1 \quad +2 \quad +3$

On this subscale, -3 = "Doing the opposite of what you told him," and $+3$ = "Doing what you told him."

The second subscale was the attribution rating, which assessed the mothers' perspective of retaliatory intent. This subscale was presented as follows:

"How much do you agree or disagree that he was trying to show you he didn't have to do what you wanted?"

$-3 \quad -2 \quad -1 \quad 0 \quad +1 \quad +2 \quad +3$

On this subscale, -3 = "definitely not true," and $+3$ = "definitely true."

Psychometric Evaluation

Norms
None reported.

Reliability
Cronbach's alpha coefficients, computed for the 18 vignettes with varying child responses, ranged from .84 to .87, with a median of .87.

Validity

Responses to the vignettes were correlated with the Maternal Coercion Scale (Strassberg, 1997), which was based on the Conflict Tactics Scale (Straus, 1979) and was developed for this study. Mothers rated 10 discipline items indexing verbal and physical coercion (the most severe items were hitting with a hand or object and spanking). Correlations between the analogue task and this scale revealed that attributions of defiant intent for child noncompliance was a much more robust predictor of maternal disciplinary function than maternal ratings of severity.

Advantages

Pictures and verbal descriptions of noncompliance situations are easily incorporated into the clinical setting for a preassessment battery.

Limitations

A small number of situations, maternal directives, and child responses were used, with the assumption that they were typical for this age group. The attribution ratings are limited only to defiant intent.

Primary Reference

Strassberg (1997).

Scale Availability

Zri Strassberg
Department of Psychology
The State University of New York
Stony Brook, NY 11794-2500

Related References

None available.

General Comments and Recommendations for Practitioners and Researchers

It is not clear whether mothers did imagine that the child in the picture was their own. It would seem that the social desirability element of this assessment method would be strong.

93. Judgments in Moments of Anger (JMA; Dix)

Development and Description of Assessment Method

This JMA was based on the theory that parents who are angry may enter compliance situations with more negative expectations of children, may make more negative attributions of causality and responsibility for non-compliance if it occurs, and may evaluate more favorably those responses containing negative affect and disapproval. Determination of the mood rating procedure as well as the development of the rating scales was based on an attributions model that links parenting judgment to specific aspects of information processing (expectations, attributions, and responsibility).

For this study, an analogue videotape method was designed for data collection in the home. Mothers used self-monitoring to monitor particular mood states and intensities. They were then instructed to watch a short videotape of a mother–child interaction during their mood state and to rate behavioral characteristics of their own children. Thus, this method combines self-monitoring and analogue assessment via a standard video stimulus tape.

Target Population

Mothers of elementary-school-age children.

Format

There are two parts to the JMA. First, mothers complete a self-monitoring task in which they record natural episodes of strong mood states via a daily log, with 1- to 2-hour intervals. When their mood matches a target mood (happy, angry, or neutral), they are asked to complete four tasks:

1. They respond to several questions to ensure that their mood is the correct kind and intensity (on a 7-point, Likert-type scale).
2. If their mood is an appropriate match, they watch a 40-second videotape segment of a mother–child interaction and make a series of judgments.
3. They answer nine questions about problems, traits, and behavioral characteristics of their own 6- to 8-year-old children.
4. They answer questions about the cause and current intensity of their mood.

The second part of the JMA consists of a series of videotaped segments in which a mother asks her child to fulfill a request (put shoes on before going outside, hang up washcloth and towel before leaving the bathroom), and the child makes either an ambiguous or a noncompliant response.

Administration and Scoring

Following the videotapes, mothers are asked to respond to each of the following questions on 7-point, Likert-type scales:

- *Expected Behavior:* "Do you think the child will do what is asked?"
- *Expected Tone:* "How pleasant or unpleasant do you think the next 30 seconds will be as mother–child interact together?"
- *Disposition to Resist:* "How much do you think the child wants to do what is asked?"
- *Sternness:* "How much sternness do you think is needed to get the child to do what is asked in this situation?"

For the noncompliance videotape segments, mothers are asked four additional questions:

1. *Trait Choice:* Mothers select adjectives that described the noncompliant child (dispositional attribution).
2. *Attribution of Blame:* Mothers are asked, "How much would you hold this child responsible for (the noncompliant response)?"
3. *Mother Affect:* Mothers are asked, "As a parent, how upset would you be with this child for (the noncompliant response)?"
4. *Intention to Express Disapproval:* Mothers are asked, "If you were this child's mother, how much disapproval would you express toward the child for (the noncompliant response)?"

Psychometric Evaluation

Norms
None reported.

Reliability
None reported.

Validity
The study examined the use of the JMA in a sample of 48 mothers. Mothers' mood ratings at home were significantly correlated with the

Positive and Negative Affect Schedule (PANAS; Watson, Clark, & Tellegen) and the Profile of Mood States (POMS; McNair, Lorr, & Droppleman, 1971).

Advantages
The JMA is a very creative approach to the assessment of concurrent mood and cognitive response in a unique analogue, in-home situation.

Limitations
The JMA is a labor-intensive assessment procedure for mothers taking part in its use. It would be unlikely that a distressed parent would comply with sequence of assessment tasks.

Primary Reference

Dix, Reinhold, and Zambarano (1990).

Scale Availability

Theodore Dix
Department of Human Ecology
Mary Gearing Hall
University of Texas
Austin, TX 78712-1097

Related References

Dix (1991).

General Comments and Recommendations for Practitioners and Researchers

Results from Dix et al. (1990) using this method indicate that anger-induced cognitive biases may distort appraisals of parents' interactions with their children, as well as promote negative conceptions of their children and thereby stabilize or exacerbate negative interaction cycles that characterize maltreating families. Perhaps the assessment sequence could be modified as an in-session approach to understanding decision making.

94. Maternal Observation Matrix (MOM; Tutuer, Ewigman, Peterson, & Hosokawa)

Development and Description of Assessment Method

The MOM is a brief observational system designed to assess the qualitative aspects of how mothers interact with their children in the clinical setting during a structured task. Both positive and negative components of the interaction are included in the interval recording system.

The initial 15 behavior categories of the MOM were selected based on previous research as well as suggestions from an advisory panel of child abuse professionals convened for this research. The three general categories that were suggested were maternal verbalizations, physical and process behaviors, and a description of how the mother handled the situation overall.

Target Population

Mothers of preschool children; abusive and nonabusive dyads were included.

Format

The procedure requires mother and child to sit next to each other at a table with paper and a brown crayon. Although there are other toys available in the room, the mother is instructed to help her child draw as many circles on one piece of paper as she can in 10 minutes. Task rules are that neither mother nor child can touch the toys, and the mother cannot touch the crayon or paper.

Administration and Scoring

The assessment task lasts 10 minutes, during which the primary observer continuously rates the quality and intensity of maternal behavior, recording the data as occurrence or nonoccurrence in 30-second intervals.

A comprehensive behavioral coding system contains the following categories:

- *Verbal Variables:* The description of the child is coded as either positive, neutral, or negative; the description of the child's behavior is coded as either superlative, positive, neutral, or negative; the request is coded as either positive, neutral, or negative; affect of the mother is coded as either positive or negative; nonphysical promise is coded as either positive or negative; and the tone of the mother's verbalizations is coded as either positive or negative.

- *Physical Variables:* Intense head touch is coded as either superlative or positive; intense body touch is coded as positive; uncharged head touch is coded as positive; and uncharged body touch is coded as either positive, neutral, or negative.
- *Process Variables:* These are control coded as positive, negative, or neutral.

Definitions and examples of these behavior categories are provided in the primary reference. Of note as well is the fact that, in Tuteur, Ewigman, Peterson, and Hosokawn (1995), four behaviors *not* observed in any of the 32 observations were verbalizations of a physical threat, loudness, threatening physical gesture, or touch of an inanimate object.

Psychometric Evaluation

Norms
None reported.

Reliability
Interrater reliability was assessed with a second observer simultaneously coding 22% of the observations. Reliabilities ranged from 80% agreement for neutral maternal request to 100% for superlative descriptions of the child's behavior, positive affect, superlative intense head touch, positive intense body touch, and positive uncharged head touch.

Validity
The MOM was evaluated by using the three behavior codes that showed the highest mean frequency of occurrence in the total sample. The discriminant analysis using these variables (positive control, neutral request, and positive request) correctly classified 85% (17/20) of the nonabusers and 75% of the abusers ($F(2,29) = 10.02$, $p < .0005$). A total of 81.3% of all participants was correctly classified. Further group comparisons indicated three behaviors more common among abusive dyads (neutral request, negative request, negative control), and one behavior (positive control) more common in nonabusive dyads.

Advantages

The MOM constitutes a creative use of a brief task suitable for clinic use to produce behavioral data on mother–child interaction. The authors indicate that the assessment procedure is an inexpensive method for identifting at-risk mothers.

Limitations

Small sample size did not allow for more in-depth psychometric evaluation in the primary reference.

Primary Reference

Tuteur et al. (1995).

Scale Availability

Bernard E. Ewigman
Department of Family and Community Medicine
MA303HSC
University of Missouri-Columbia
Columbia, MO 65212

Related References

None available.

General Comments and Recommendations for Practitioners and Researchers

The MOM is relatively easy-to-administer compliance analogue for assessing mother–child interaction. It may be difficult to use in the clinical setting, but development of this mother–child interaction scale is promising.

---

95. Mother's Responses to Videotapes (MRV; Smith & O'Leary)

Development and Description of Assessment Method

The MRV is a laboratory analogue assessment designed to investigate the relationships between dysfunctional child-centered attributions, mother's level of arousal, and parenting responses. Mothers provide continuous ratings of affective arousal and monitor cognitive responses while watching videotaped mother–child interactions.

Target Population

Mothers of toddlers.

Format

In this assessment, mothers watch a series of videotaped mother–child discipline interactions, some of which contain negative child affect. There are eight 1-minute scenes of a mother interacting with her toddler; four scenes contain negative affect, whereas four scenes contain no negative affect.

Administration and Scoring

The assessment procedure lasts 16 minutes. Mothers provide continuous ratings of affective arousal by manipulating a dial on a 180-degree scale (0 = very negative, 90 = neutral, 180 = very positive). The average affect rating for each scene is calculated via computer. The mother then reviews the two negative affect scenes that caused her the greatest distress. She is asked to (a) write down any thoughts or feelings regarding the scene just watched and (b) write down reasons for the child's negative affect. The mother's responses, which are coded as attributions, are then categorized according to their locus (mother-centered, child-centered, or situational) and are then coded along five 6-point attributions scales: (a) trait/state, (b) stability, (c) globality, (d) voluntariness, and (e) intent. A dysfunctionality score is then computed for each attribution scale.

Psychometric Evaluation

Norms

None reported.

Reliability

Interrater reliability was assessed for the entire sample in the primary reference (N = 40 mothers). The kappa coefficient for the presence of attributions was .89, and the kappa coefficient was .98 for categorization of locus. Reliability for degree of dysfunction was assessed via intraclass correlations (ICCs). For mother-centered attributions, the ICC was .97, and for child-centered attributions, the ICC was .98.

Validity

Concurrent validity was assessed via comparisons with the Parenting Scale (PS; Arnold, O'Leary, Wolff, & Acker, 1993), a self-report assessment of parenting style. The dysfunctionality of child-centered attributions was positively correlated with mothers' arousal ($r = .31$) and the harsh parenting subscale of the PS ($r = .40$).

Advantages

The MRV's "dial-method" of continuous rating of arousal helps to monitor perceived fluctuations in affect across time. Expanded assessment of locus and type of attributions helps to clarify the sequence of cognitive responses to hypothetical mother–child interactions.

Limitations

The MRV's methodology is not easily transportable from the laboratory or research setting.

Primary Reference

Smith and O'Leary (1995).

Scale Availability

Susan G. O'Leary
Department of Psychology
State University of New York at Stony Brook
Stony Brook, NY 11794-2500
e-mail: soleary@ccmail.sunysb.edu

Related References

None available.

General Comments and Recommendations for Practitioners and Researchers

This method is identical to one used to rate continuous affect in problem-solving interactions of couples (Gottman & Levenson, 1985).

96. Parent Behavior Rating Scales (PBRS; King, Rogers, Walters, & Oldershaw)

Development and Description of Assessment Method

The authors of this study devised a set of rating scales based on a process of *judgmental observation,* in which the observer encodes and interprets information within a coding system that emphasizes control strategies used by mothers to gain their children's compliance. Two general control categories, power-assertive (use of threat, humiliation, disapproval) and positive (reasoning, bargaining, approval) were used in the development of rating scales used by the coders to rate videotapes of mother–son interactions. These rating scales were developed from the extensive direct observation coding strategy previously used by Oldershaw (Oldershaw et al., 1986).

Target Population

Abusive dyads (mothers and sons) referred from a related project. The mean age of sons was 2.7 years. Naive coders were used to rate parent behaviors from the videotaped interactions.

Format

Videotapes included a general sequence of activities including snack time, free play, and cleanup. Also interspersed were three tasks that the mother was to request of her child: to (a) bring her a toy telephone, (b) retrieve a doll and place it on a shelf, and (c) move a small chair to a table.

Based on the previous coding system by Oldershaw et al. (1986), seven rating scale items were developed to reflect maternal responses:

1. Approving,
2. Disapproving,
3. Commanding (intrusiveness determined by how the parent interferes with the child's activity),
4. Ignoring (which taps into maternal responsiveness),
5. Humiliating (denigration of the child),
6. Threatening (including physical acts or verbal threats that are aversive to the child), and
7. Cooperative.

Administration and Scoring

Raters viewed two 30-minute videotapes of mother–son interactions to test the judgmental observation method. These videotapes had been previously coded, and the mothers had been determined to be the intrusive type in that they exhibited a high frequency of command, threats, negative physical contact, and disapproval using a behavioral coding system. The naive raters used a 7-point, Likert-type scale (1 = extremely, 7 = not at all) to rate each of the seven scales. Training, viewing, rating, and aggregation of data for one mother–child videotape took approximately 4 hours.

Psychometric Evaluation

Norms
None reported.

Reliability
Interrater reliability for videotapes was examined via correlations between raters ($N = 46$ college students). Four correlation matrices were generated, one for each set of 16 raters who viewed the same tape. Mean correlations were $r = .33$ for abusive mother–child dyads and $r = .32$ for control dyads. Interrater reliability for the rating scale was computed via comparisons to the original behavioral coding system. Agreement was calculated via the percentage of total agreement method between judgments made on these seven rating scales and behavioral frequency data from a set of 29 tapes. Reliabilities for the seven behavior categories ranged from 85% to 97%, with a mean percent agreement of 95%.

Validity
Concurrent validity was demonstrated by comparisons between the rating scale and the behavioral coding approaches. Mean correlations were $r = .48$ for abusive dyad 1 and $r = .39$ for abusive dyad 2. Construct validity was evident, in that ratings for abusive mothers were different from those of control mothers (six of the seven scales discriminated between the mothers).

Advantages
Use of the PBRS to provide single judgments about observed parent–child interactions is more portable to the clinical setting and easier for the rater to use than traditional behavioral coding systems. Partial scripting of the interactions increases the probability of being able to capture

compliance sequences. The PBRS could be used as a repeated measure analogue assessment to evaluate a parent intervention.

Limitations

Training of raters is not described well enough to fully understand the process of judgmental observations.

Primary Reference

King, Rogers, Walters, and Oldershaw (1994).

Scale Availability

Gary Walters
Department of Psychology
University to Toronto
Toronto, Ontario, Canada M5SIAI

Related References

Oldershaw et al. (1986).

General Comments and Recommendations for Practitioners and Researchers

The authors indicate that it took approximately 124 hours to complete training and administration of the direct behavioral observation codings of interactions. The approach described here may be reliable enough for clinical evaluation and is certainly more cost efficient.

---

97. Parent/Child Interaction Observations (PCIO; Haskett)

Development and Description of Assessment Method

The authors suggest that the quality of parenting patterns is more closely associated with the social-emotional functioning of children than simple rates of specific parent behaviors. They developed the PCIO to represent the quality based on Baumrind's (1971) Conceptual Dimensions of Parenting. An index of authoritarian/restrictive parenting that represented dominance, restrictiveness, and lack of warmth was derived by adding the frequency of negative behavior and commands divided by this total plus rate of positive/neutral behavior.

The PCIO consists of videotaped observations of parent–child dyads in a laboratory-based play session. The 30-minute session is divided into three segments: free play, instructions, and puzzles, and allows for the assessment of parenting during situations of relatively low- and high-task demands.

Target Population

Mothers or fathers and their children ages 4 to 8 years old.

Format

The 30-minute observation session is divided into three parts: First, the parent and child are simply instructed to spend 10 minutes together as if they were at home. They are not specifically told to play together, although a standard set of materials (crayons, paper, building blocks) and toys are available. In the second situation, parents are asked to have their child clean up the area, draw a picture of a person, and then sit quietly while the parent completes a checklist. The dyad is observed until 10 additional minutes have elapsed. Then the parent and child work on puzzles for the remaining 10 minutes.

Administration and Scoring

The following three categories of parental behavior are recorded:

1. *Interactive Behavior:* Verbal or physical behavior directed to the child that affirms their action or statement, is supportive or interactive; includes neutral and positive behaviors such as praise, smiling, hugging, questions, and responding to the child's requests.
2. *Negative Behavior:* Verbal or physical behavior directed to the child that is demeaning, derogatory, or disparaging; includes taking something away from the child, frowning, rolling the eyes, chasing the child, hitting the child, and denying the child's requests.
3. *Commands:* These are recorded if the parent asks the child to do something (directive) or to stop doing something (command), even when stated in a positive tone of voice; examples

include "Come here now," "Put the toy down," and "Please clean up your mess."

A 15-second time sampling procedure is used to code the occurrence of three parent behaviors. Coders observe the parent for 10 seconds and record behavior for 5 seconds. An audiotape cues observers as to whether to observe or record.

Psychometric Evaluation

Norms
None reported.

Reliability
Reliability assessment was completed for each of the three behavioral categories for 25% of the observations. Rates of occurrence were calculated, and reliability coefficients were .83 for negative behavior, .78 for commands, and .95 for positive/neutral behavior.

Validity
Convergent validity was reported as good, with the observations of parenting style correlated with Child Abuse Potential Inventory scores (Milner, 1986; $N = 41$, $r = .547$, $p < .001$). Further, observed parenting behavior was related to parents' problem solving as measured by the Problems Questionnaire (Hansen et al., 1989: $r = .49$, $p < .001$ for effectiveness of problem solving, and $r = .38$, $p < .001$ for number of solutions). Interestingly, observed parenting behavior was neither correlated with nor related to parents' perceptions of behavioral adjustment as measured by the Child Behavior Checklist (CBCL; Achenbach, 1991), but was related to teacher perceptions.

Advantages
The PCIO manual includes three clearly described situations that are easy to set up and would transfer to any clinical setting.

Limitations
Behavior categories seem overinclusive and may obscure some information. Further, the use of interval recording requires a certain sophistication in behavioral assessment, which may not be readily obtained.

Primary Reference

Haskett, Myers, Pirillo, and Dombalis (1995).

Scale Availability

> Mary E. Haskett
> Department of Psychology
> North Carolina State University
> 640 Poe Hall
> Campus Box 7801
> Raleigh, NC 27695-7801
> (919) 515-2251

Related References

Haskett, Scott, and Fann (1995).

General Comments and Recommendations for Practitioners and Researchers

There is methodologically sound research on this straightforward observation of parenting behavior. Psychometric research that examined this method along with self-report and checklist methods was completed using a clinical sample.

---

98. Parent Daily Report (PDR; Trickett)

Development and Description of Assessment Method

The authors of the PDR followed a theoretical model of parental competence in discipline that focuses on an integration of methods of parental discipline.

In order to understand parental behavior in the natural environment, a self-monitoring instrument was developed to explore the sequence of parent and child responses occurring at home. The diary format enables parents to record affective reactions during discipline situations as well.

Target Population

Families with children between the ages of 4 and 11. The test population was 20 families recruited from child protective services.

Format

The PDR form instructs parents to review instances of discipline that have occurred during the day. They are then asked to choose at least three situations and record the following:

- Exactly what the child did to require discipline (examples of common misbehaviors are provided);
- Exactly what the parent said and did in the situation;
- What happened next, or how the situation turned out; and
- How the parent felt about the situation.

Administration and Scoring

Transcripts of discipline episodes are coded in terms of the following:

- *Type of Child Misbehavior:* Noncompliance, high arousal behavior, conventional social or rule violations, moral aggressiveness or unprovoked aggression, moral–psychological misbehavior.
- *Child's Reactions to Interventions:* Compliance, sample noncompliance (for example, ignore), oppositional noncompliance, submission to discipline.
- *Parental Strategies:* Requests or commands, forced appropriate behavior, reasoning, isolation of the child, tangible punishment, verbal punishment, physical punishment.
- *Parental Affect:* Anger, dysphoria, satisfaction.

Total scores are obtained for each category, and data can be analyzed vis-à-vis parental strategy and affect for each category of misbehavior. Operational definitions for each of the responses in the above list are provided in Trickett and Susman (1988).

Psychometric Evaluation

Norms

None reported.

Reliability

The PDR forms were independently coded by two raters for a sample of parents ($N = 22$). Estimates of intercoder reliability ranged from

80% agreement for child compliance to 94% for parental affective response.

Validity
Results from this study indicate that control parents had a greater frequency of commands and reasoning strategies and a reduced frequency of isolation, total punishment, and anger responses as compared to abusive parents. Abusive parents were twice as likely to feel angry.

Advantages
The PDR is a low-cost methodology that enables continuous assessment in the home setting. It may provide parents with an alternative or distracting strategy during conflict situations. Open-ended questions on the form allow parents to thoroughly describe aspects of interest to them. It is a potentially rich source of self-report data.

Limitations
The report is biased in that it is from the parent's perspective only and really only measures the parent's behavior and not the child's.

Primary Reference

Trickett and Susman (1988).

Scale Availability

> Penelope Trickett
> Lida Lee Tall Learning Resource Center
> Towson State University
> Towson, MD 21204

Related References

Trickett and Kaczymski (1986).

General Comments and Recommendations for Practitioners and Researchers

The diary format for parental self-monitoring is an excellent way to collect information across the course of an intervention. Clinicians could learn to score such an assessment and provide continuous evaluation of treatment effectiveness.

99. Video Assessment Task (VAT; Fagot)

Development and Description of Assessment Method

The VAT is a laboratory analogue assessment technique that was developed to augment the multimethod assessment of coercive discipline strategies used by parents. A stimulus videotape containing behavioral vignettes of young children is shown to a parent, who then chooses between five hypothetical discipline responses.

The scenes used in the stimulus videotapes were selected as typical activities of young children that occur frequently and are likely to elicit parental intervention. The author surveyed 20 parents and obtained 80 statements describing children's activities. These 80 scenes were rated, on 7-point scales, by a separate set of parents for frequency, risk involved, and level of annoyance. The author then chose 14 items that were rated as most annoying and most risky to create the videotaped scenes. A further well-developed empirical process was used to determine items on the Coercive Discipline Scale (Fagot, 1992).

Target Population

Parents with children under 3 years of age. The VAT may be used with parents at risk for abuse.

Format

In this assessment, each parent is shown a 13.5-minute videotape containing 14 separate clips of risky or annoying behaviors of young children. The video clips were filmed in the child's natural environment (school, home, and neighborhood). Examples of item clips include:

- Riding a tricycle along the sidewalk and into the street;
- Climbing up to a medicine chest and playing with medicine bottles; and
- Fighting with another child over blocks.

Parents are given the following instructions: "You are going to be shown a videotape with a child engaged in a number of behaviors. Pretend that you are alone with these children and that you are responsible for their care. You can make one of five responses:

1. You can do nothing and simply let the behavior go by.
2. You can warn the child but not intervene.

3. You can redirect or verbally intervene with explanations.
4. You can stop the behavior and reprimand the child verbally.
5. You can stop the behavior and physically punish the child.

In Fagot (1992), a computer program was developed that allowed the parents to punch in their responses with a number pad attached to an Apple II computer. The program recorded all responses to a video clip and recorded the time between responses.

Administration and Scoring

The procedure, including instructions, takes about 20 minutes to administer. The stimulus videotape is shown, and the parent is asked to respond. After the parent has responded to all 14 clips, the computer program summarizes the data into number of each type of first intervention, total number of each type of intervention, and average time until first intervention. The following scores result from these data:

- First intervention verbal;
- First intervention physical;
- Total verbal interventions;
- Total physical interventions; and
- Total score.

Psychometric Evaluation

Norms
None reported.

Reliability
Internal consistency was examined by applying the Kuder-Richardson 20 (K-R 20; Nunnaly & Bernstein, 1994) formula to the coercive discipline scores across 14 clips (responses to each clip were scored as coercive or not coercive). The resulting KR-20 of .51 suggests only moderate internal consistency. Test–retest reliability was examined by a readministration of the video-based assessment to a sample of 20 mothers at a 1-month interval. Percent agreement of first responses was very high, at 92% with a kappa of .76. The temporal stability of the total coercive discipline score was also high ($r(19) = .72$, $p < .001$).

Validity
The coercive discipline score was compared to other discipline measures in a validation sample of 100 mothers of toddlers. Convergent

validity was shown with significant positive correlations of this video assessment and parent interviews and home observations of mother–child interactions.

Advantages

This video-based assessment of discipline can be administered quickly, in one setting, while sampling child behavior across several natural environments. It is not as transparent an assessment technique as parent self-report, and it retains some of the active involvement of the parent that is the trademark of in vivo observational techniques.

Limitations

The video includes scenes from a very narrow age range of children. Although videotapes could be developed for all other developmental levels, risky or annoying behaviors broaden in range and scope, making them more difficult to sample. Also, parenting responses for children over the age of 3 are more diversified, thus making the five options presented here very restrictive.

Primary Reference

Fagot (1992).

Scale Availability

Beverly Fagot
Oregon Social Leaning Center
207 East 5th Ave.
Suite 202
Eugene, OR 97401

Related References

Fagot (1984).

General Comments and Recommendations for Practitioners and Researchers

This represents a flexible method of assessment in that different aged children displaying different problem behaviors across varying contexts could be standardized and used for both clinical and research purposes.

100. Video Mediated Recall Task (VMRT; Johnston, Reynolds, Freeman, & Geller)

Development and Description of Assessment Method

The VMRT is an analogue method designed to assess parents' spontaneous attributions regarding their own child's behavior viewed in a videotaped parent–child interaction. It employs both a thought listing technique as well as open-ended attributional questions.

The VMRT is based on a previous investigation of attributions and reactions of parents of children with attention deficit hyperactivity disorder (ADHD) using written vignettes, recalled incidents of child behavior, and videotaped clips of their own child's behavior (Johnston & Freeman, 1997). The coding systems were devised specifically for this study and were based on an initial review of the content of the parents' responses and on methods used in previous research.

Target Population

Parents of elementary-school-age children. This method is used for assessment research on parents of children with ADHD.

Format

The VMRT consists of a 20-minute videotaping of a parent interacting with his or her child in a laboratory playroom. Play situations and tasks (using a variety of toys, materials, and dress-up clothing) are designed to elicit inattentive-overactive (IO), oppositional-defiant (OD), and cooperative (PRO) child behaviors. Sample tasks include:

- *IO:* Requiring the child to sit still on a rolling chair in front of a mirror for 1 minute.
- *OD:* Arbitrary or unfair tasks such as having the child set up bowling pins for parents and not letting the child have a turn.
- *PRO:* Parent and child being asked to hang up a poster together.

The parent–child interaction is videotaped and simultaneously coded by an observer. Observers select two examples of each of the three child behavior categories. Immediately following the parent–child interaction, the parent is shown these segments in the order they occurred. After receiving a general explanation regarding causal attributions, parents are asked to think back to when the behavior occurred during their interaction with their child and to respond to an open-ended thought-listing question beginning with "What were you thinking when . . ." and to insert the specific child behavior to finish the sentence.

Following the thought-listing question, the parent is also asked an open-ended attributional question: "Why do you think your child (specific child behavior)?"

Administration and Scoring

The parent's responses to the open-ended thought-listing questions are transcribed, and each statement the parent makes regarding his or her cognitions during the parent–child interaction are coded according to the following 11 categories:

1. *Parent Cognitions*
   a. *Attributions:* This refers to whether the parent's response included a causal attribution for the child's behavior ("It's because he is so excited").
   b. *Processing:* This reflects whether the parent had been thinking about the child's behavior ("I was wondering if he could do it").
   c. *Child's Perspective:* This indicates whether the parent's response reflected the child's perspective ("He was feeling excited about the chance to play").
   d. *Typicality:* This consists of comments regarding whether the child's behavior was typical ("I thought that's just how he is").
2. *Target of Parent's Thoughts*
   e. *Child:* "Hang on kid, you're getting there."
   f. *Parent:* "I was bored."
   g. *Parent–Child Interaction:* "She's showing me her manners."
   h. *Negative Affect:* This assesses the tone of the parent's response ("I didn't like it").
3. *Type of Response*
   i. *Child's Behavior:* "He's waiting to see what will happen."
   j. *Child's Disposition:* "He's pretty confident about math."
   k. *Parent Reaction:* "I was surprised by what he did."

Parent responses to the open-ended attribution questions are coded according to the following categories, which reflect combinations of locus, control, and stability attributions:

1. *Internal-controllable-stable (ICS):* "It's something he always wants to do."
2. *Internal-controllable-unstable (ICU):* "He was just acting smart at that moment."
3. *Internal-uncontrollable-stable (IUS):* "It's just his temperament."
4. *Internal-uncontrollable-unstable (IUU):* "He was tired."
5. *External-situational (ES):* "It was an interesting task."
6. *External-parent-related (EP):* "Because I told him to do it."

Finally, the parent is asked to rate the child's behavior on several 10-point scales:

- Perceived intensity of the behavior;
- Locus, ranging from 1 (something about the child) to 10 (something about the situation);
- Control, ranging from 1 (completely within the child's control) to 10 (not at all within the child's control);
- Stability, ranging from 1 (not at all likely to change) to 10 (very likely to change); and
- Parent's responsibility for the child's behavior.

Psychometric Evaluation

Norms
None reported.

Reliability
A detailed manual, regular meetings, and group coding sessions were used to train coders and to maintain agreement. For the thought-listing categories, percent agreement among coders was calculated as the number of agreements divided by the total number of categories. The average interrater agreement was 85%, and kappa was .61. For the open-ended attributional questions, the percentage of agreement occurrence between coders was calculated as the number of agreements in categories checked for each behavior divided by the total number of categories checked across all behaviors. Across 110 transcripts, 7% had an interrater agreement below 70%, and these were recoded in group meetings. For the remaining transcripts, the average interrater agreement was 95%, and kappa was .84.

Validity
In comparing methods of assessment of parents of children with ADHD and parents of children without behavior disorders, the authors re-

ported that the VMRT was sensitive to group difference. During the task, the problem behaviors of children with ADHD were rated as more intense than those of children without behavioral disorders. Convergent validity was so supported in that the VMRT showed high positive correlations with a written measurement of parent attributions (ratings were of locus of control, stability, parent responsibility, affective response, and behavioral response to standardized child behavior scenarios). These correlations ranged from $r = .18$ to $r = .49$ (see Johnston, Reynolds, Freeman, & Geller, 1998, for a more detailed description of validity data).

Advantages

The VMRT is a systematic method for evaluating parents' cognitive processing of their own interactions with their children. It is based on strong theoretical conceptualizations regarding parent attributions as a mediator of parenting responses to children's misbehaviors. Videotaped parent–child interactions and video-mediated recall tasks seem adaptable to the clinical setting and would seem to be sensitive to cognitive changes resulting from parent training.

Limitations

The VMRT's coding system may be a bit too complex to incorporate in the clinical setting. Child behavior categories, as well as parent attributional responses that are more closely associated with aggressive or potentially abusive interactions, may need to be added.

Primary Reference

Johnston et al. (1998).

Scale Availability

Charlotte Johnson
Department of Psychology
University of British Columbia
Vancouver, British Columbia, Canada V6t124

Related References

Johnston and Freeman (1997).

General Comments and Recommendations for Practitioners and Researchers

The VMRT is an extremely important assessment strategy designed to measure the process of parental thought when confronted with children's behavior. The theoretical underpinnings for this assessment target are strong, and it would be worthwhile to extend this type of assessment to parents at risk for maltreatment or parents targeted for intervention.

Part IV

Assessment of Family Interaction

Introduction: Assessment of Family Interaction

Families provide a unique context for the assessment of adult and child interaction. The social–interactional approach to the understanding of maltreating families has stressed the interactional nature of the processes involved in the abusive family environment. Family violence, whether between parent and child or between adult partners, by definition occurs within the context of an intimate relationship (Feldman, 1997). Rather than focus solely on the individual level, clinicians must examine maltreatment in a more relational way. Research on family variables has indicated that maltreating families are characterized by greater amounts of marital discord, lower emphasis on family members' independence, more enmeshed family boundaries, less family cohesion, and greater family disorganization and isolation (Faust, Runyon, & Kenny, 1995). More specifically, studies of incestuous families have suggested that incest victims had experiences in their families of origin that contribute to ineffectual parenting in their own families, a lack of emotional intimacy with their spouse, and extremely rigid or diffuse subsystem boundaries (Carson, Gertz, Donaldson, & Wonderlich, 1990), which places children at risk for additional victimization. Also, research has documented the deleterious effects of exposure to family violence by child witnesses. Rossman and Ho (2000) suggested that exposed children need to be evaluated for posttraumatic symptoms and distress.

The intergenerational transmission of interpersonal aggression and violence is supported by reviews of childhood victimization and exposure to violence in the histories of adults who are abusive parents or domestically violent partners (Feldman, 1997). Clearly, any comprehensive assessment of children and parents in maltreating families must examine the quality, quantity, and bidirectional nature of parent–child interactions, the family members' perceptions of family process variables related to family structure, communication, and cohesion, as well as the effects of witnessing violence between other family members. This section will seek to outline various methodologies, including interview, self-report, and direct observation useful in the quantification of family variables influential in the etiology and maintenance of abusive family interactions.

To lay an adequate conceptual ground for the review of family interaction assessment methods, several theoretical models need mention. Family theorists have described problematic families as having significant dysfunction in processes such as cohesion, flexibility, and communication (Olson, 1993). Family cohesion, defined as the emotional bonding that family members have toward one another, can range from disengaged to enmeshed, and family flexibility, defined as the amount of change in its leadership, roles, and relationship rules, can range from rigid to chaotic. Family communication, considered the facilitating dimension, is defined by adequate listening, speaking, and self-disclosure skills. The systemic model of family functioning focuses on the balance of these dimensions across phases of the life cycle and on how families cope with and adapt to stressful events. These interactional qualities can be evaluated by either direct observation of family interaction in a naturalistic or analogue setting or by self-report of individual family members on measures assessing family process variables.

Research on family process in maltreating families has indicated that compared to nonvictims and single-perpetrator victims, multiple-perpetrator victims of sexual abuse report greater conflict and more rigid control with lowered cohesion, expressiveness, and organization in their families of origin (Long & Jackson, 1991). In addition, in a study of functional, distressed, and abusive families, Glaser, Sayger, and Horne (1993) found that the family environments of maltreating families were characterized by limited cohesiveness, low levels of expressiveness, limited support of personal growth, and greater levels of conflict. Other researchers have reported that members of abusive families report greater stress (Barton & Baglio, 1993) and engage in more critical, more coercive, and less agreeable responses to one another (Silber, Bermann, Henderson, & Lehman, 1993). Finally, in a study of family communication style, Madonna, Van Scoyle, and Jones (1991) reported that parents in families where incest had been documented had weaker coalitions and had dysfunctional dominance–submission patterns. In addition, family beliefs were incongruous and problem-solving communication was ineffective. Bugental (1993a) suggested that communication patterns within families often revolve around power and control issues and that these issues are influenced by interpersonal cognitive schemes and caregiving relationships. This suggests that not only are communication patterns relevant for assessment, but perceptions related to the relationships within the family are as well.

Although research on family process with maltreating families is limited, the assessment of system dynamics may help the clinician to develop treatment objectives for family treatment. The commonly used family assessment devices are reviewed in this section to encourage their inclusion in a comprehensive assessment package. In their review of research done in a retrospective fashion on survivors of incest, Faust et al. (1995) indicated that information on multisystemic relationships and interactions of all family members as they act and react in the present is crucial to treatment. The authors suggested that the assessment of individuals' perceptions of their intrafamilial relationships (including the often overlooked sibling dyad) as well as behavioral observations of family interactions during structured and unstructured tasks is critical in analyzing variables that account for maltreatment in a particular family.

The social learning theory model to the understanding of maltreatment of children rests heavily on both the family coercion theory of Patterson (1982) and on the modeling theory of Bandura (1977). Research on maladaptive parenting practices that lead to highly aversive and violent outcomes in caretaking behaviors has emphasized the development of coercion and reciprocity patterns in dysfunctional families. Reciprocity reflects mutual positive reinforcement between the family members. Coercion reflects an asymmetrical reinforcement pattern wherein one family member controls the other by escalating aversive stimuli and receiving in turn positive reinforcement (i.e., compliance). The family member providing that positive reinforcement is negatively reinforced by the cessation of the aversive stimuli. Cerezo (1997) proposed a similarity in family interaction between families of aggressive children studied by Patterson (1982) and maltreating families. In her review of interaction of families, it is clear that an escalating cycle of coercive behaviors characterizes the parent–child interactions. A lack of parenting skills in handling common childhood problems combines with interpersonal contingencies of highly aversive behavior that is reinforced in cycles of escalation and thus lays the foundation for interpersonal aggression (Cerezo, 1997). If these bidirectional and cyclical interaction patterns characterize interactions between members of maltreating families, then the assessment of this coercive process must be a part of comprehensive assessment and may offer clear treatment goals for the clinician. In fact, high-risk parents' responses to their child's noncompliance (Oldershaw, Walters, & Hall, 1986), as well as their ability to regulate their emotional arousal during discipline (Peterson, Ewigman, & Vandiver, 1994) become significant assessment targets for the treating clinician. Finally, these aversive interaction patterns may be verbal in nature and more easily observed in family interactions than the supposed higher intensity variants involving physical aggression.

Modeling theory indicates that individuals learn a variety of behaviors from viewing others interacting in a particular context. Children who view aggressive adults or who experience victimization by adults directly have early learning experiences about aggressive interaction. The accumulation of research assessing childhood family experiences retrospectively demonstrates that domestically violent men are most likely to have witnessed physical violence between their parents and were at greater risk of being abused as children (Feldman, 1997). Modeling appears to communicate the general acceptability of aggression between family members and may in particular teach children that interpersonal violence is an expected outcome of conflict, anger arousal, and stressful events. Children who are either currently at risk for abuse and those who are exposed to family violence need careful assessment in terms of their perceptions of and reactions to interparental conflict. In particular, children exposed to violence may have inappropriate views on the acceptability and utility of violence as a means to conflict resolution, may blame themselves for the violence, and may feel anxiety and responsibility for protecting their mothers and younger siblings (Graham-Berman, 1996).

Finally, the functionalist theory of emotion (Campos, Mumme, Kermoian, & Campos, 1994) highlights the importance of emotional understanding skills learned in the context of parent–child interactions in the development of children's socioemotional competence. As a result of family socialization experiences, children learn not only how to manage their own emotions but learn how to respond to the emotions of others. Exposure to atypical experiences within the parent–child relationship, which often characterize interactions in the maltreating family, will undoubtedly influence children's development of atypical or inappropriate responses to emotionally arousing situations (Shipman & Zeman, 1999). Research has indicated that maternal affect as well as verbal and physical control strategies not only effect a child's compliance but also influence a variety of mood states for her child, and this path for mothers in maltreating families may prove detrimental to the child (Koenig, Cicchetti, & Rogash, 2000). The assessment of emotion-based interactions would thus be another objective for comprehensive assessment of maltreating families.

There are several methods of assessment that may assist in the understanding of children's perceptions of and reactions to interparental conflict. Self-report rating scales and interview information on views of the marital dyad, the parent–child relationship, as well as the sibling, and the creative use of analogue conflicts in a controlled laboratory or clinic setting will help quantify children's responses to family interaction variables. Every clinician working with a maltreating family should take care to assess those perhaps not directly involved as victim or perpetrator of abuse but those in the family exposed to interpersonal aggression. As children attempt to understand the reasons for family conflict, blame themselves for the conflict, and generate ideas for their role in solving the conflict, their own psychological health may be compromised via repeated exposure over time (Kerig, 1998).

In summary, family interaction patterns as well as individual members' perceptions and responses to family dynamics are important variables in understanding the etiology and the occurrence of maltreatment. The assessment of the family system will help the clinician analyze the context in which exposure to family violence or victimization occurs. Because some states have moved to categorize exposure to family violence as a form of child abuse and neglect, the assessment of the child witness and their family becomes critical. In addition, as one considers the family variables associated with maltreatment, conditions considered to be critical to the health of the child will also include an assessment of the physical environment. Little research is available on aspects of child neglect, but all would agree that home conditions such as lack of supervision, lack of health care and adequate food, clothing, shelter, or appropriate developmental stimulation would be indicators of high-risk situations. In addition, homes in which an unclear or unsafe environment is prominent should be targets for a comprehensive assessment of these acts of omission because they might be targeted for decisions concerning child placement and for intervention. There are numerous family assessment measures, cognitive assessment analogues, and methods for behavioral observation that will assist the clinician or researcher in the comprehensive assessment of the maltreating family.

10 ■ Interview Methods

The interview method allows clinicians a one-on-one opportunity to assess a child's perceptions, attitudes, and beliefs about their families' interactions as well as to probe historical details. There are only a few reported structured interviews focused on aspects of family members' aggressive interactions, and these all focus on children's responses to family violence.

101. Children's Marital Conflict Coping Strategies Interview (CMCCSI; O'Brien)

Development and Description of Assessment Method

The authors developed the CMCCSI as a modification of previous measures of interpersonal cognitive problem solving. The coding system was based on a review of available research on children's adaptability and coping with stress.

This is a semistructured interview designed to assess the types of marital conflict children have viewed in their families and their strategies used for coping with the conflict.

Target Population

Children from families in which aggressive or conflictual interaction has occurred.

Format

This method consists of an interview in which children are asked to report about two types of arguments that they may have witnessed between their parents (verbal disagreements and physical aggression). After the child describes in detail what was witnessed, the interviewer uses a series of standard probes to elicit a complete description of the child's responses to the arguments. Children are encouraged to spontaneously describe their strategies for coping with the marital conflict.

Administration and Scoring

Interviews are recorded and later coded. Each distinct response given by the child as to how he or she reacted to the argument is assigned to 1 of 10 mutually exclusive categories. These categories are as follows:

- *Avoid:* This refers to the child's attempt to distance him- or herself from the conflict.
- *Self-Rely:* In this instance the child involves him- or herself in self-soothing activity or self-distraction.
- *Seek Peer/Sibling:* These are attempts to seek comfort from proximity with peers and siblings.
- *Seek Authority:* These are attempts to seek aid/attention from non-parental adult.
- *Verbal Intervention:* These are attempts to tell parents to stop fighting.
- *Self-Blame:* This refers to attempts to deflect marital conflict by calling attention to him- or herself or to clearly state self-responsibility for parents' marital conflict.
- *Physical Intervention:* This is the child's use of physical actions to stop conflict.
- *Question Parent:* This refers to attempts to process the conflict with a parent after the conflict ends.
- *Express Feelings:* This refers to direct expression of emotion, such as laughing, crying, hitting, and so forth.
- *Helpless:* This refers to the child's statement that there is nothing he or she can do in the situation.

Psychometric Evaluation

Norms
None reported.

Reliability

An average kappa intercoder reliability coefficient of .76 was obtained when the response categories were combined into an avoid coping scale (avoid and self-rely combined) and a self-involve scale (verbal intervention, physical intervention, and self-blame combined).

Validity

The two subscales (avoid coping and self-involve) were not significantly correlated with each other ($r = -.20$), indicating two distinct factors. However, in a study of mother–child dyads ($N = 49$) the CMCCSI was also not related to children's responses in a structured postconflict questionnaire. Examining the interview responses compared to mother report of marital conflict, a significant correlation was found with the self-involve subscale ($r = -.33$, $p < .05$), indicating that in families where the mother reports conflict, children report less involvement in the marital conflict. In a regression analysis to evaluate the contribution of child coping responses to the prediction of child adjustment, higher levels of avoid and self-involve coping were associated with higher levels of childhood depression but were not associated with child-reported self-worth or mother reports of behavior problems.

Advantages

This is a fairly straightforward, easy to administer interview process with a comprehensive and clear coding system for children's coping responses.

Limitations

Limited psychometric development restricts the value of this relatively new and comprehensive interview format.

Primary Reference

O'Brien et al. (1997).

Scale Availability

Mary O'Brien
6 Washington Pl., Rm. 483
Department of Psychology
New York University
New York, NY 10003

Related References

None available.

General Comments and Recommendations for Practitioners and Researchers

This semistructured interview provides a useful tool for assessing children's repertoire of coping skills in response to viewing familial conflict–aggression. It is useful as a research tool (e.g., for assessing correlates of various coping styles) and as a clinical assessment device for helping to focus interventions.

---

102. Child Witness to Violence Interview (CWVI; Jaffee, Wolfe, & Wilson)

Development and Description of Assessment Method

The CWVI was developed in response to problems concerning the definition of witnessing violence and observations that children's reports vary according to time, place, and impact. Clinical experience led the authors to create a flexible assessment tool sensitive to various problems in measurement of child witnesses.

Presented both in interview and questionnaire formats, this structured interview assesses children's knowledge of family violence in their homes, their sense of responsibility for the violence, their anger reactions, and their safety skills.

Target Population

Children over the age of 6 who have witnessed violence in their families.

Format

In the CWVI, both the interview and the questionnaire have three main components:

- *Attitudes and Responses to Anger:* The questionnaire version has 19 items, some open-ended and others with check-off answers. Items include, "What kinds of things make you mad?" "What do you do when you get mad?" "Do you think it's all right for a man to hit a woman?" Other items are structured in a checklist fashion:

- When you're really mad at something or someone, do you ever: (circle 0 = never, 1 = sometimes, and 2 = often)

yell, scream, swear	0	1	2
go to room	0	1	2

- If someone your age hits you, what do you usually do:

  ignore them _____   threaten them _____

  ask them to stop _____   hit them _____

- *Responsibility for Violence:* The next section focuses on the child's sense of responsibility for his or her parents and the violence. The questionnaire version has 12 items similar to the interview questions. Items include,
- "How does it make you feel to hear them fight about you?"
- "What could you have done to prevent mom and dad from fighting?"
  - What do you think mom and dad fight about? (How often? 0 = never, 1 = sometimes, 2 = often)

money	0	1	2
drinking	0	1	2
untidy house	0	1	2

- *Safety Skills:* The final section includes questions concerning the child's knowledge of support and safety skills (the questionnaire has 11 items in this section). Interview questions include, "What do you do if mom and dad are arguing?" ". . . if dad is hitting mom when you are in the same room?" ". . . when you are in a different room?" Children can indicate the following responses: stay in the same room, leave/hide, phone someone, run out/get someone. Written items include,
  - If you were hit by mom or dad, what would you do or what have you done?

    stay in the same room ___   go to older sibling _____

    leave/hide _____   ask parents to stop _____

    phone someone _____   act out _____

Administration and Scoring

Whether administered as an interview or written questionnaire, the child's responses are coded according to the previously described items. All scores are then converted to percentages, with 100% representing the most appropriate responses for each of the three subsections.

Psychometric Evaluation

Norms
None reported.

Reliability
None reported.

Validity

In assessing the validity of the CWVI, a small population of children in family violence shelters ($N = 28$) was compared to a matched control group. Children exposed to family violence had significantly more inappropriate responses and attitudes to anger and less knowledge about safety skills. There were no significant differences on the responsibility for violence subscale.

Advantages

This instrument targets the experience of children who witness family violence.

Limitations

Lack of psychometric evaluation makes it difficult to guarantee the accuracy and meaningfulness of the data obtained.

Primary Reference

Jaffee, Wilson, and Wolff (1988).

Scale Availability

Peter Jaffee
London Family Court Clinic
80 Dundas St.
Box 5600
Station A
London, Ontario NGA 2P3

Related References

Wager and Rodway (1995).

General Comments and Recommendations for Practitioners and Researchers

The assessment format and content seem clinically relevant and well-related to targets for intervention with child witnesses; however, more data are needed to support the reliability and validity of this measure.

---

103. Family Interaction Interview (FII; Salzinger)

Development and Description of Assessment Method

The development of specific interview questions was based on the current literature in the field of child maltreatment and child witnesses of family violence.

This is a structured interview for parents or caretakers that focuses on disagreements between various dyads in the family. Questions focus on frequency and content of disagreements as well as harsh discipline tactics used with children.

Target Population

Mothers of children between 8 and 12 years of age in families where abuse has either been documented or is suspected.

Format

The FII includes initial questions related to demographic information and substance abuse. The family interaction section focuses on abusive and discordant behavior in the child's household. Sixty-four questions, along with numerous subquestions, are designed to collect information about disagreements and fights between the mother and her spouse–boyfriend, between the mother and any other adult in the household, between the mother and the target child, between the current spouse–boyfriend and the target child, and so forth. Questions focus on every dyad in the family. Although some questions are specific—for example, "How old was (the target child) when screaming, yelling, or cursing first happened?" or "How often do or did disagreements involving you and target child's father lead to hitting, punching, or anything physical?"—other questions encourage narrative descriptions that are later coded. These open-ended questions include, "Please describe the worst disagreement or fight between you and (current spouse/boyfriend)." "Now, between you and (target child), around what issues do the worst fights and disagreements occur?" "What do you consider the worst thing that you ever did to (target child)?" "Tell me how (current spouse–boyfriend) spanks (target child)."

There is a section that also details past emergency–medical or dental treatment and five questions concerning pleasant events that occurred between household members.

Administration and Scoring

The complete interview lasts between $2\frac{1}{2}$ and 3 hours and is conducted either in English or Spanish. A detailed coding manual, provided by the authors, indicates that many of the items are coded in a yes–no format or according to specific ages and frequency estimates. Other questions are coded along a 4-point Likert scale, indicating an estimate of severity.

Psychometric Evaluation

Norms

None reported.

Reliability

A random sample of 20 interviews in a study of 87 pairs of abusive and control families were coded by two independent coders. The average intercoder agreement was 88% (Salzinger, Feldman, Hammer, & Rosario, 1993).

Validity

Known-groups validity was demonstrated in the comparison of 87 maltreatment families with 87 matched control families. Both partner abuse and family discord significantly differentiated between the families.

Advantages

The structured interview format is easy to administer; the questions are clear and follow a logical process. The coding manual and scoring system are well-developed for a computer summary (contact authors).

Limitations

There is an extremely lengthy interview process with limited psychometric investigation.

Primary Reference

Salzinger, Feldman, Hammer, & Rosario (1991).

Scale Availability

Suzanne Salzinger
New York State Psychiatric Institute Unit 114
722 West 168th St.
New York, NY 10032

Related References

Salzinger, Feldman, Hammer, and Rosario (1992, 1993).

General Comments and Recommendations for Practitioners and Researchers

Although this structured interview was developed for collecting demographic information and screening for maltreatment in a series of research studies, it provides specific questions useful for clinicians interested in children who have been exposed to violence in the home, abused themselves, or both.

---

104. Witness to Violence Child Interview (Pynoos & Eth)

Development and Description of Assessment Method

Extensive evidence supports the basis of the authors' interview format, and they contend that an open discussion of the trauma offers immediate relief rather than further distress to the child. The projective and play methods of the interview are designed to recapture the child's affective experience of the traumatic events. The interview outline is clearly based on research with traumatized children and seeks to probe intrapsychic consequences, intrusive and avoidant phenomena, and suggestions for mastering the traumatic material. Reliability and validity aspects were not evaluated because the interview represents an individualized clinical assessment.

This method is a three-stage, 90-minute initial interview for children traumatized by witnessing family violence. The format proceeds from a projective drawing and storytelling, to a discussion of the actual traumatic situation and the perceptual impact, to issues centered on the aftermath and its consequences for the child.

Target Population

Young children exposed to family violence.

Format

The authors suggest the following outline for the stages of the interview:

- *Stage I: Opening.* (a) Establish the focus of the interview; (b) free drawing and storytelling, which enables the child to express the traumatic experience through metaphor; and (c) traumatic reference, where the interviewer's task is to identify the traumatic reference in the metaphor and look for ways the child regulates his or her anxiety.
- *Stage II: Trauma Assessment.* This includes two main sections: (a) Reliving the experience—emotional release, reconstruction of the event, perceptual experiences, their worst moment, and images of violence–physical mutilation—and coping with the experience—issues of responsibility, inner plans of action, punishment or retaliation, fears of retaliation, the child's impulse control over intense emotions, previous trauma, concerns for the future, and other current stressors; (b) closure, which focuses on the child's cooperation and courage in the interview and his or her realistic fears and reactions that might be expected.

Administration and Scoring

The authors suggest a number of play strategies and interview questions to elicit information about each of these components. The interviewer is encouraged to obtain details about the traumatic event before the interview with the child. The entire interview requires approximately 90 minutes. The authors encourage the interviewer *not* to collude with the child's attempt to avoid the traumatic material and to obtain proper closure of the session. There are no specific scoring procedures.

Psychometric Evaluation

Norms
None reported.

Reliability
None reported.

Validity
None reported.

Advantages
Although described as an interview assessment, the authors suggest this approach as a crisis consultation that helps to identify immediately the effects of the traumatic witnessing and to help the child begin to master the traumatic experience. The interview is a generic technique that has been used with children who have witnessed murder, suicide, rape, accidental death, aggravated assault, kidnapping, and school–community violence.

Limitations
A comprehensive interview with a traumatized child would require an experienced interviewer who could be very flexible with the format, which would probably require extensive training. Psychometrics have not been evaluated, and there is no standardized scoring format.

Primary Reference

Pynoos and Eth (1986).

Scale Availability

R. Pynoos
Division of Child Psychiatry
Psychiatry and Biobehavioral Sciences
UCLA—Neuropsychiatric Institute
760 Westwood Plaza
Los Angeles, CA 90024

Related References

None available

General Comments and Recommendations for Practitioners and Researchers

This represents one of the earliest and most comprehensive assessment approaches for child witnesses to trauma. However, the process of the interview, including the drawings and the reenactment of the trauma, clearly are therapeutic endeavors to provide anxiety relief and support coping strategies. As such, pure assessment objectives would not be met.

Self-Report Inventories

---

105. Brother–Sister Questionnaire (BSQ; Graham-Bermann)

Development and Description of Assessment Method

The BSQ is a self-report measure designed to measure four qualities of a child's relationship with his or her brother or sister. These qualities are similarity, coercion, boundary maintenance, and empathy.

Items were generated from a large survey of college students with siblings ($N = 1,450$). A principal components analysis of the initial item pool revealed four factors that accounted for 48.6% of the variance.

Target Population

Children older than 7 years of age.

Format

The following subscales and sample items comprise the measure:

- *Empathy:* Fourteen items that assess the extent to which the siblings care about one another, feel close, and are emotionally connected and in tune with what the other is experiencing, for example, "I care a lot about what he or she thinks."
- *Boundary maintenance:* Six items that assess the degree to which siblings are able to maintain interpersonal boundaries vis-à-vis physical property and an individual's wishes, for example, "He/she takes my things without asking."

- *Similarity:* Nine items that examine ways in which siblings have common interests and experiences such as shared friends, hobbies, and the same sports or chores, for example, "We are very much alike."
- *Coercion:* Six items that reflect elements of power and control of one sibling over another, including questions about explorative behavior, rejection, and planned isolation, such as "We do a lot of arguing or fighting" and "He/she tries to keep me away from my friends."

Administration and Scoring

The 35 items are scored according to a 5-point Likert scale. Anchor points are 1 = never true to 5 = always true. Mean scores for each of the subscales are derived.

Psychometric Evaluation

Norms

None reported.

Reliability

Internal consistency was determined via Cronbach's alpha. The following coefficients revealed good internal consistency: .92 for empathy, .85 for boundary maintenance, .73 for similarity, and .69 for coercion. A 10-day test–retest reliability examination on a small sample of college students (N = 25) revealed subscale correlations ranging from r = .65 to r = .75, with a total scale test–retest reliability of r = .91.

Validity

A sample (N = 202) of college students, divided into four family conflict groups based on their responses on the Conflict Tactics Scale (Straus, 1979), was compared to a nonconflict group. Those in the conflict groups differed significantly on all four subscales from the nonconflict group. Further, results from a discriminant analysis correctly classified 82.1% of abused and 81% of nonabused college student sibling relationships (N = 50 college students who self-reported abuse in their families).

Advantages

The BSQ offers a very timely assessment of an important relationship reflecting family functioning. It will allow clinicians to easily identify those sibling relationships that are potentially abusive in order to develop treatment approaches for one of the most underreported aspects of family violence.

Limitations

Given that the measure development and psychometric work on this instrument has focused only on college students, generalizations toward younger siblings still living together and perhaps engaged in current rather that retrospective conflict may be limited.

Primary Reference

Graham-Bermann and Cutler (1994).

Scale Availability

> Sandra Graham-Bermann
> Department of Psychology
> 525 East University Ave.
> University of Michigan
> Ann Arbor, MI 48109-1109

Related References

Graham-Bermann, Cutler, Litzenberger, and Schwartz (1994).

General Comments and Recommendations for Practitioners and Researchers

The BSQ is a relatively new assessment measure of an often overlooked relationship. Future research using this measure will help us to understand how the sibling relationship contributes to family functioning.

---

106. Children's Perceptions of Interparental Conflict Scale (CPICS; Grych, Seid, & Fincham)

Development and Description of Assessment Method

The CPICS is a self-report inventory designed to assess children's internal reactions to conflict between their parents. Items tap thoughts and feelings in response to arguments seen and heard between parents.

Items were generated based on clinical knowledge and a review of other available scales. The initial pool of 90 items was examined by experts in the field, and 70 items were chosen to reflect the dimensions to be measured. These items were piloted on a group of 44 fourth and fifth graders, and items not well correlated within their subscales were dropped. The subscales were developed following a confirmatory factor analysis.

Target Population

Children from 9 to 12 years of age. The self report can be used with adolescents.

Format

The CPICS is a 48-item self-report inventory using a 3-point, Likert-type scale (T = True, ST = Sometimes True, F = False). The following are sample items from nine subscales.

1. *Frequency of Marital Conflict:* Six items, including "I never see my parents arguing or disagreeing."
2. *Intensity of Marital Conflict:* Seven items, including "My parents have pushed/shoved each other during an argument."
3. *Resolution of Marital Conflict:* Six items, including "When my parents argue, they usually make up right away."
4. *Perceived Threat:* Six items, including "When my parents argue, I'm afraid that something bad will happen."
5. *Coping Efficacy:* Six items, including "When my parents argue, there's nothing I can do to stop them."
6. *Content:* Four items, including "My parents' arguments are usually about me."
7. *Self-Blame:* Five items, including "It's usually my fault when my parents argue."
8. *Triangulation:* Four items, including "I feel caught in the middle when my parents argue."
9. *Stability:* Four items, including "My parents have arguments because they are not happy with one another."

Administration and Scoring

Items are scored either 0, 1, or 2 to create nine subscale scores. These can then be combined into three summary scores: conflict properties (frequency, intensity, and resolution subscales), threat (perceived threat, coping, and efficacy), and self-blame (content and self-blame). Fourteen items are reverse-keyed. Children are asked to respond to items with the following information: "We would like you to write what you think or feel when your parents argue." Further, if parents do not live in same house, children are instructed to respond to items based on when the parents lived together.

Psychometric Evaluation

Norms
None reported.

Reliability
In two samples (N = 222, N = 144), internal consistency for subscales was examined with alpha coefficients ranging from .61 to .83. For the three main scales, coefficients were .90 for conflict properties, .83 for threat, and .84 for self-blame.

Test–retest reliability scores across a two-week interval were r = .70 for conflict properties, r = .68 for threat, and r = .76 for self-blame.

Validity
As evidence for the validity of the scale, the authors report significant correlations with parental reports of marital conflict and significant associations with children's reports of their reactions to specific episodes of conflict. In addition, the CPIC predicted parents' reports of child aggression and depression as well as externalizing symptoms reported by children. A study by Cummings, Davis, and Simpson (1994) indicated some gender differences on subscale correlations with Child Behavior Checklist (CBCL; Achenbach, 1991) scores. For example, the threat subscale was highly correlated with the mothers' reports of child behavior problems for boys and was not at all correlated for girls. In fact, the conflict properties and self-blame subscales were highly correlated with the internalizing and total behavior subscales for girls and were not at all correlated for boys.

Advantages
There is good psychometric data supporting both the reliability and validity of the measure. Some authors (Roecker, Dubow, & Donaldson,

1996) have reported using only the 19-item conflict properties factor, which make this inventory much shorter to administer.

Limitations

The validation samples were predominantly white, middle-class children living with two parents. Thus, the results may not be generalizable to other populations or children of other ages.

Primary Reference

Grych, Seid, and Fincham (1992).

Scale Availability

John Grych
Psychology Department
Marquette University
Schroeder Health Complex
P.O. Box 1881
Milwaukee, WI 53201-1881

Related References

Cummings et al. (1994); Kerig (1998); Roecker et al. (1996).

General Comments and Recommendations for Practitioners and Researchers

Recent research on gender differences in the relationship between mediating cognitions related to parent conflict and behavioral adjustment should be kept in mind for both researchers and clinicians working with child witnesses.

---

107. Discord Control and Coping Questionnaire (DCCQ; Rossman & Rosenberg)

Development and Description of Assessment Method

This self-report measure is designed to assess children's beliefs about their behavioral and cognitive control during marital conflict. Items reflect both action and cognitive domains, as well as beliefs directed mainly at controlling self or at controlling a parent. Total score indicates amount of coping effort by children.

The DCCQ was created through pilot interviews with school-age children from interparentally violent and nonviolent families. The two subscales were empirically derived from a principal components analysis for the sample ($N = 115$).

Target Population

Children between 6 and 12 years of age. Children ages 8 and under should be read the individual items.

Format

The DCCQ includes 23 items grouped into two subscales:

1. *Direct Intervention:* Thirteen items, including "Other kids believe they could protect their parents during a fight" and "Some kids believe that if they pray hard enough, their parents won't fight."
2. *Self-Calming:* Ten items, including "Some kids think they can do something else while their parents fight" and "When parents fight, some kids say to themselves 'Things will be okay.'"

Administration and Scoring

All items use a structured alternative format such that children first decide which kids they are more like (which side of "but" they are on) and then decide whether it is "really true" or "sort of true" for them. All items have word stem: "some kids believe ... *but* other kids don't." Each item is scored on a 4-point Likert scale indicating lower (1) to higher (4) control beliefs.

Psychometric Evaluation
Norms
None reported.

Reliability

Internal consistency alpha coefficients and test–retest reliabilities were .79 and .74, respectively, for the direct intervention subscale, and .76 and .87, respectively, for the self-calming subscale.

Validity

In a study of 94 children aged 6 to 12 years and mothers from conflict families (Rossman & Rosenberg, 1992), intercorrelations between a number of measures of family stress and the subscales of the DCCQ were examined. The self-calming subscale was highly correlated with the WISC-R Verbal Comprehension subtest (Wechsler, 1974; $r = .54$, $p < .01$) and was negatively correlated with the Child Behavior Checklist (Achenbach, 1991; $r = -.30$, $p < .05$). The direct intervention subscale was also negatively correlated with the Life Events Questionnaire (Garmezy et al., 1984; $r = -.13$, $p < .05$). These relationships may indicate an overlap in constructs of stress and control beliefs but also indicates that conflict control beliefs and verbal comprehension predict fewer behavior problems and family stress.

Advantages

The DCCQ is a brief assessment of very important dimension of children's beliefs about their sense of control and coping strategies during marital conflict. It is very relevant for those working with child witnesses.

Limitations

The structured alternative format ("Some kids ... other kids") requires respondents to first decide which group of kids they identify with and then to respond to the item in terms of how true it is. This could be confusing for younger children; the authors read each item to the child during administration.

Primary Reference

Rossman and Rosenberg (1992).

Scale Availability

B. Robbie Rossman
Psychology Department
University of Denver

University Park
Denver, CO 80208

Related References

Kerig (1998); Roecker et al. (1996).

General Comments and Recommendations for Practitioners and Researchers

This measure developed for this study (Rossman & Rosenberg, 1992) was evaluated on four different groups of children; 25 were recruited from shelters for family violence, 18 were recruited from intact violent families, 22 were recruited from families with marital discord, and 29 were recruited from nondiscordant families. Thus, this scale is one of the few developed to assess children exposed to family violence.

---

108. Family Worries Scale (FWS; Graham-Bermann)

Development and Description of Assessment Method

This self-report device focuses on the target of worry and the types of behaviors that may worry a child from an at-risk family. Items focus on how much the child worries about a specific event or action happening to or by his or her mother, father, brother, sister, or self.

Items for the FWS were developed from lists generated by 250 children in a kids club (a 10-week group intervention program for 7- to 12-year-old children from families with domestic violence).

Target Population

Children under the age of 12 years.

Format

On the FWS, children rate 20 items that relate to either Factor 1, vulnerable, indicating that the person named would be hurt, hungry, sick, or afraid; or Factor 2, harmful, indicating that the person named would hurt someone else, lie, get arrested, or scare a child.

Sample items include,

- "I worry that _____ will get hurt."
- "I worry that _____ won't have a place to live."
- "I worry that _____ will be mad or angry."

Administration and Scoring

Items are rated on a 4-point Likert scale ranging from 1 = never to 4 = always. Scores range from 20 to 80; higher scores indicate greater worry.

Psychometric Evaluation

Norms

None reported.

Reliability

Coefficient alphas ranged from .77 to .88 for the vulnerable factor and from .81 to .87 for the harmful factor, indicating good internal consistency. Temporal stability was evaluated across a 1-week test–retest period for a small sample ($N = 15$), and correlations ranged from $r = .59$ to $r = .74$ and from $r = .62$ to $r = .84$. Each of these coefficients was computed across five family members.

Validity

Initial evidence indicates that the FWS distinguishes level of worry between children from violent ($N = 60$) and nonviolent ($N = 61$) families. Children from violent families have greater concern about vulnerability. Further, worry that a sister would cause harm was significantly correlated ($r = .56$, $p < .01$) with internalizing symptoms on the CBCL (Achenbach, 1991). Worry that a brother would cause harm was significantly correlated ($r = .58$, $p < .01$) with externalizing symptoms on the CBCL. Further comparison with CBCL subscales indicated that anxiety/depression was positively and significantly correlated with worry of harm by the father ($r = .31$, $p < .01$), brother ($r = .33$, $p < .01$), and sister ($r = .33$, $p < .01$). Worries about the vulnerability of family members were not associated with the anxiety/depression subscale. None of the FWS scores was significantly correlated with the CBCL's withdrawal subscale.

Advantages

Assessing internalized reactions of children who may have witnessed marital or child violence but have not themselves been victimized is interesting and relevant.

Limitations

There is not yet enough psychometric data available. A version suitable for older children and adolescents needs to be developed.

Primary Reference

Graham-Bermann (1996).

Scale Availability

Sandra Graham-Bermann
Department of Psychology
525 East University Ave.
University of Michigan
Ann Arbor, MI 48109-1109

Related References

None available.

General Comments and Recommendations for Practitioners and Researchers

The FWS needs further psychometric development, particularly concerning how it correlates with standardized measures of children's anxiety. It would also be interesting to compare data from siblings in the same families.

---

109. Potential Family Conflict Questionnaire (PFCQ; Margolin)

Development and Description of Assessment Method

The PFCQ is a self-report inventory for parents or caregivers that lists child behaviors that represent areas for potential conflict in the family.

Target Population

Parents or caregivers of children and adolescents.

Format

The PFCQ consists of a questionnaire that lists 30 child behaviors such as bad grades, stealing, and swearing that represent significant problem areas.

Administration and Scoring

For each item, parents are instructed to rate how upset he or she becomes with their child on a 5-point Likert scale ranging from 0 = not at all to 4 = a lot. Each respondent then uses the same 5-point scale to rate how much he or she disagrees with his or her spouse on how to handle the problem. The most conflictual or salient problem areas are then identified by multiplying the responses to the two questions per item. Higher products indicate the behavior problem areas the parent is most concerned about and those that produce the highest interparent disagreement.

Psychometric Evaluation

Norms
None reported.

Reliability
None reported.

Validity
None reported.

Advantages
The PFCQ is a brief, easy-to-administer checklist that clinicians can use quickly to identify problem areas for further assessment or to use in conducting an analogue assessment of family communication and problem-solving styles.

Limitations
The PFCQ's restricted list may not include family-specific behaviors that are problematic, nor does it allow for a rating of disagreement between parent and child, which would be critical with older children or adolescents. Psychometric properties were not assessible.

Primary Reference

Margolin (1992).

Scale Availability

Gayla Margolin
Department of Psychology
University of Southern California
Los Angeles, CA 90089-1061

Related References

Gordis, Margolin, and John (1997).

General Comments and Recommendations for Practitioners and Researchers

The PFCQ was used in the Gordis et al. (1997) study as a standardized way of selecting family discussion topics for their behavioral coding, analogue assessment task. The most conflictual and salient problem areas were determined by multiplying the responses to the two questions per item. This then identified top scoring issues selected for the discussion task. This approach is easily incorporated into the clinical setting and allows for repeated rating across time in order to evaluate treatment.

---

110. Children's Beliefs About Parental Divorce Scale (CBPDS; Berg & Kurdek)

Development and Description of Assessment Method

The current 36-item version of the CBPDS was developed through item analysis of a previous 70-item scale. A principal components analysis with Varimax rotation indicated the above six clusters/factors accounting for 50% of the total variance.

The resulting inventory is a self-report assessment of children's beliefs surrounding parental separation and divorce.

Target Population

Children under the age of 12.

Format

The CBPDS is a 36-item, self-report inventory that includes six subscales, each of which has six items. The subscales, along with sample items, are:

1. *Peer Ridicule and Avoidance:* "I like playing with my friends as much now as I used to."
2. *Paternal Blame:* "When my family was unhappy it was usually because of something my father said or did."
3. *Fear of Abandonment:* "It's possible that both my parents will never want to see me again" and "I feel my parents still like me."
4. *Maternal Blame:* "My mother is more good than bad."
5. *Hope of Reunification:* "My parents will always live apart."
6. *Self-Blame:* "My parents often argue with each other after I misbehave" and "My parents would probably still be living together if it weren't for me."

Administration and Scoring

Each item is scored as either a "yes" or "no" for each of the six subscales. Total scores range from 0 to 36, with a higher score indicating more problematic beliefs. A number of items are reverse-keyed to control for response set.

Psychometric Evaluation

Norms

The inventory was standardized on a nonclinical sample ($N = 170$) with a mean age of 11 years.

Reliability

Temporal stability was assessed via a test–retest reliability comparison across a 9-week interval. The correlations for the small ($N = 30$) sample ranged from $r = .41$ to $r = .72$ for the six subscales, with an overall correlation of $r = .65$ for the total score, indicating good temporal stability. Internal consistency, determined via the alpha coefficient, was .62 for peer ridicule, .78 for paternal blame, .73 for fear of abandonment,

.77 for maternal blame, .78 for hope of reunification, .54 for self-blame, and .80 for total score.

Validity
Significant correlations were found between children's scores on this inventory and the Children's Trait Anxiety Inventory (Spielberger, 1973), indicating that problematic beliefs regarding parental separation are related to self-reported maladjustment.

Advantages
The CBPDS is a simple, brief, easy-to-read rating scale that taps the range of children's beliefs and concerns about their parents' divorces. It is easy to administer and score.

Limitations
The small normative population does not reveal clinically useful cutoff scores for at-risk children.

Primary Reference

Kurdek and Berg (1987).

Scale Availability

Larry Kurdek
Department of Psychology
Wright State University
Dayton, OH 45435-0001

Related References

Fischer and Corcoran (2000).

General Comments and Recommendations for Practitioners and Researchers

It would be interesting to examine the responses of child witnesses to family violence using this scale. In those cases, a divorce might be viewed as a positive outcome and a termination of chronic conflict.

111. Family Environment Scale–Children's Version (FES–CV; Pino, Simons, & Slawinowski)

Development and Description of Assessment Method

The FES–CV is a self-report inventory designed to assess the young child's perceptions about his or her family environment, with particular emphasis on family relationship dynamics.

Target Population

Children between the ages of 5 and 12 years old.

Format

The FES–CV consists of a 30-item inventory that contains three items for each of the following subscales: cohesion, expressiveness, conflict, independence, achievement orientation, intellectual–cultural orientation, active–recreational orientation, moral–religious emphasis, organization, and control.

A sample item from the conflict subscale is shown in Figure 11.1; a sample item from the control subscale is shown in Figure 11.2.

Administration and Scoring

Items are listed in a text booklet and can be administered individually or in a group. Each item is presented as a pictorial multiple-choice response: each has three equivalent pictures of a four-member family enacting a scene. The child is instructed to select which family picture looks most like theirs. The pictures are drawn in a cartoon style, and each receives a score of either 1, 2 , or 3. The scorer totals each subscale and then converts these raw scores into standardized scores.

Psychometric Evaluation

Norms
The FE–CV was normed in 1982 on an elementary school population. These scores are available in the accompanying manual.

Reliability
Temporal stability was shown with high test–retest reliability coefficients of $r = .80$ over a 4-week interval for a small sample ($N = 158$).

Figure 11.1

7. Which picture looks like your family?

Sample item from FES–CV Conflict Subscale. From Pino, Simons, and Slawinowski (1984). Used by permission.

Validity

The authors conducted a small ($N = 56$) study examining content validity in which children were asked to write out the meaning of each picture to investigate the "stimulus pull." Two scorers (with interrater reliability of $r = .84$) then scored each scale as to whether the responses matched the scale dimension. Z values were calculated in order to determine hit rate; values ranged from $Z = .30$ to $.72$. Values from third graders ($N = 26$) were lower than seventh graders ($N = 30$), indicating that children's social comprehension will increase with age.

Advantages

The FES–CV corresponds directly with the subscales of its adolescent/adult version, allowing for independent assessment of all family members.

Limitations

The cartoon depictions represent only one type of family (a 4-member family) and may not be relevant to all children.

Figure 11.2

28. Which picture looks like your family?

Sample item from FES–CV Control Subscale. From Pino, Simons, and Slawinowski (1984). Used by permission.

Primary Reference

Pino, Simons, and Slawinowski (1984).

Scale Availability

Slosson Educational Publications
P.O. Box 280
East Aurora, NY 15052

Related References

None available.

General Comments and Recommendations for Practitioners and Researchers

See the description of the adolescent/adult version of the FES for a more complete description of the assessment device.

112. Conflict Behavior Questionnaire (CBQ; Prinz, Foster, Kent, & O'Leary)

Development and Description of Assessment Method

This self-report inventory is a measure of perceived communication and conflict in the families of adolescents. A general estimate of each family member's experience of conflict and negative communication, as well as the level of distress that results, are targets for assessment.

The authors report that the CBQ was based on an item pool originally generated by eighth-grade students, clinical psychologists, and research assistants. Mothers with teenagers and college students recalling their family relationships then completed pilot versions of the CBQ and helped to refine the item pool, which discriminated between positively and negatively rated relationships.

Target Population

Parents and adolescents who are experiencing family conflict.

Format

The CBQ consists of two inventories, one for parents and one for adolescents. The parent version of the inventory contains 75 statements categorized into two subscales:

1. *Appraisal of the Adolescents:* 53 items, including "My child sulks after an argument," "My child does things to purposely annoy me," and "My child compares me to other parents."
2. *Appraisal of the Dyad:* 22 items, including "We joke around often," "The talks we have are frustrating," and "We listen to each other, even when we argue."

The adolescent version contains 73 statements; 22 items are identical to the parent form, thereby tapping an appraisal of the dyadic interaction. Further, the adolescent version includes an additional subscale, appraisal of parent, which consists of 51 items, including "My mom doesn't understand me," "My mom expects too much of us," and "My mom and I compromise during arguments."

Overall, the items reflect both positive and negative interaction behaviors and are counterbalanced so that a true response at times corresponds to a negative perception and at other times corresponds to a positive perception of the parent–adolescent relationship.

There are two shorter versions available: The CBQ-44 and the CBQ-20, which retain items that maximally discriminate between distressed and nondistressed parent–adolescent dyads.

Administration and Scoring

The scoring key (Robin & Foster, 1989) indicates points given for either true or false items, and scores range from 0 to 53, with converted + values ranging from 21 (for distressed mother's appraisal of adolescent) to 156 (for nondistressed father's appraisal of the dyad) for the original version. Higher scores indicate more negative perceptions. Scoring information for the two shorter versions is also available. The CBQ-44 takes approximately 10 minutes to complete, whereas the CBQ-20 can be completed in about 5 minutes. The *T*-value tables allow the clinician to quickly determine how distressed the family is with respect to normative distressed or nondistressed families.

Psychometric Evaluation

Norms

Normative data from a sample of nondistressed families are available in a converted *T*-value table for comparison purposes. A cautionary note: These normative data were gathered from a predominantly lower-middle- to upper-middle-class white population.

Reliability

Coefficient alphas of .90 and above for mother and teen reports on each scale indicate good internal consistency. Test–retest reliability over a 6- to 8-week interval for a small sample of mothers ($N = 19$), fathers ($N = 15$), and teens ($N = 19$) was computed, and resulting correlations ranged from $r = .37$ for adolescent appraisal of mother to $r = .85$ for adolescent appraisal of the teen–father dyad.

Validity

In a comparison of distressed ($N = 137$) and nondistressed ($N = 68$) families, scores on all of the subscales were significantly different. Point–biserial correlations between subscales and group membership (distressed versus nondistressed) ranged from .38 for adolescent appraisal of father to .72 for maternal appraisal of adolescent, indicating good criterion-related validity. Further, CBQ scores correlated $-.52$ with problem-solving communication observed during triadic discussions of conflictual issues coded via the Modified Marital Interaction Coding System (Hops, Wills, Patterson, & Weiss, 1972).

Advantages

The CBQ is easy to read and administer, and the shortened versions are quite brief. The parallel forms for adults and teens enable assessors to examine similar items from differing perspectives. Normative data and tables for conversion to T scores make the CBQ scores easier to interpret.

Limitations

The forced true/false choice response format does not allow for any assessment of frequency, intensity, or impact of a particular parent or child behavior. To date, CBQ scores have not been compared to actual behavior during a naturalistic interaction, so generalization may be limited.

Primary Reference

Prinz, Foster, Kent, and O'Leary (1979).

Scale Availability

Ronald Prinz
Department of Psychology
University of South Carolina
Columbia, SC 29208
prinz@sc.edu

Related References

Robin and Foster (1989).

General Comments and Recommendations for Practitioners and Researchers

The CBQ is easily adapted into the clinical situation for all family members and will help to develop targets for treatment intervention.

113. Family Adaptability and Cohesion Scale III (FACES III; Olson, Portner, & Laree)

Development and Description of Assessment Method

This self-report inventory is based on the specific Family System Circumplex Model (Olson, 1993) and provides an assessment of the family as a whole, with each member completing a separate inventory.

The previous version (FACES II) had 30 items, with 16 on the cohesion subscale and 14 on the adaptability subscale, and had better psychometric development.

Target Population

Adult and adolescent family members.

Format

This assessment, in its most recent version, is an inventory that consists of 20 items, including the following two subscales and sample items:

1. *Cohesion:* Includes 10 items that assess the degree to which family members are separated from or connected to their family. These items tap into emotional bonding, family boundaries, coalitions, time, and space. Sample items include "Family members feel very close to each other," "In our family, everyone goes his or her own way," and "We have difficulty thinking of things to do as a family."
2. *Adaptability:* Includes 10 items that focus on the extent to which the family system is flexible and able to change. These items tap into the power structure, role relationship, and negotiation style. Sample items include "Family members say what they want," "It is hard to know what the rules are in our family," and "Discipline is fair in our family."

Administration and Scoring

Respondents rate each of the 20 items according to a 5-point Likert scale ranging from 1 = almost never to 5 = almost always. Each subscale score results in a family category designation. For cohesion, this would be very connected, connected, separated, or disengaged; for adaptability, this would be very flexible, flexible, structured, or rigid. A balanced family is determined to be more functional than one categorized in the extreme. Each family member completes the inventory twice; responses indicate both a present view of the family and an ideal description of family functioning. The discrepancy between the two provides an additional measure of satisfaction.

Psychometric Evaluation

Norms

Norms are available for a large sample of adults (N = 2,543) across various stages of the life cycle and 412 adolescents from the author.

Reliability

In a small sample (N = 124), temporal stability was reported for test–retest correlations on the FACES II across 4 to 5 weeks. The total score correlation was r = .84, whereas correlations of r = .83 for the cohesion subscale and r = .80 for the adaptability subscale were reported. Internal consistency estimates of r = .77 for the cohesion subscale and r = .62 for the adaptability subscale have been reported (Olson, Portner, & Lavee, 1985).

Validity

High convergent validity was reported in a small (N = 183) comparison of the FACES III and the control and cohesion subscales of the Family Environment Scale (Moos & Moos, 1986; r = .86 for the cohesion subscales of both, and r = .53 for adaptability and control comparisons). In a construct validity study, raters watched videotapes of family interactions and rated each family on the Clinical Rating Scale (CRS; Thomas & Olson, 1993), an 8-point Likert scale ranging from 1 = disengaged to 8 = enmeshed and 1 = rigid to 8 = chaotic. Raters had 6 to 8 hours of training watching video samples and trained to 90% agreement. Correlations between CRS and FACES III for a sample of families (N = 45) were r = .88 for cohesion and r = .84 for adaptability. Further, there was good discrimination between clinical and nonclinical families.

Advantages

The FACES III is a brief, easy-to-administer self-report of family interaction styles that are directly linked to a family systems model of intervention.

Limitations

Limited research on maltreating families makes generalization to this population questionable.

Primary Reference

Olson (1993).

Scale Availability

> David Olson
> Family Social Science/College of Human Ecology
> University of Minnesota
> 290 McNeal Hall
> 1985 Buford Ave.
> St. Paul, MN 55108
> (612) 625-7250

Related References

Trepper and Sprenkle (1988).

General Comments and Recommendations for Practitioners and Researchers

This relatively short inventory has been well researched and provides a psychometrically sound assessment of family dynamics theoretically related to healthy functioning.

---

114. Family Assessment Measure III (FAM III; Skinner, Steinhauer, & Santa-Barbara)

Development and Description of Assessment Method

The FAM III is a self-report instrument that provides qualitative indices of family strengths and weaknesses across domains typically emphasized in theoretical models of family functioning. It was developed according to a construct validation paradigm with an active interplay between the specification of a theoretical model of family functioning and the constraints of an instrument designed to measure concepts of the model. The authors defined each construct, generated a large pool of items for each, and then administered the best 30 items to a large sample of families ($N = 433$), including clinical families ($n = 182$).

Target Population

Children at or above a fifth-grade reading level, as well as adolescent and adult family members.

Format

This assessment is an inventory that has three versions:

1. *General Scale:* A 50-item scale that focuses on the family as a system.
2. *Dyadic Relationships Scale:* A 42-item scale that examines relationships between specific pairs of family members.
3. *Self-Rating Scale:* A 42-item scale that taps the individual's perceptions of his or her own functioning in the family.

Each of these versions is composed of the following seven clinical subscales:

1. Task accomplishment,
2. Role performance,
3. Communication,
4. Affective expression,
5. Involvement,
6. Control, and
7. Values/norms.

There are two additional subscales on the general scale: social desirability and defensiveness. Sample items include "My family knows what I mean when I say something," "My family doesn't let me be myself," "My family knows what to expect of me," "I take it out on my family when I am upset," "We sometimes hurt each other's feelings," and "We don't really trust each other."

Administration and Scoring

The decision on which version to administer depends on the person targeted for assessment. Each item is scored on a 4-point Likert scale ranging from 1 = strongly agree to 4 = strongly disagree. Scales may be completed in 30 to 40 minutes. Each of the three main scales is also available in a shorter version, which consists of 14 items for each scale and takes only 3 to 5 minutes to complete.

Psychometric Evaluation

Norms
Normative data are available in the inventory manual.

Reliability
Internal consistency was examined in a large sample ($N = 933$ adults and $N = 502$ children). High alpha correlations were found for the three main scales: .93 for general, .95 for dyadic, and .89 for self-rating. For the general scale, the subscale alphas ranged from .67 for task accomplishment to .87 for social desirability. For the dyadic scale, the subscales ranged from .59 for affective expression to .82 for role performance; for the self-rating scale, scores ranged from .39 for the control subscale to .67 for the communication subscale. In another smaller sample ($N = 138$ families with teenage children), temporal stability was examined across a 12-day interval. Correlations ranged from $r = .46$ to $r = .72$ across all subscales.

Validity
Numerous validation studies have been completed with this measure. Concurrent validity has been demonstrated with significant comparisons to expert clinician ratings and behavioral observations. Predictive validity has been examined via the prognostic value of the FAM III with respect to treatment outcome. Convergent validity has been demonstrated with significant correlations with the Parental Stress Index (Abidin, 1990), the cohesion subscale of the FACES (Olson, 1993), and five subscales of the Family Environment Scale (Moos & Moos, 1986).

Advantages
This inventory is easy to administer and score on carbon answer sheets. Extensive psychometric data attest to its reliability and validity. Its different formats allow for comparisons between self and other ratings on the same subscales.

Limitations
The FAM III is a fairly new family measure that has not yet been evaluated with maltreating families.

Primary Reference

Skinner, Steinhauer, and Santa-Barbara (1995).

Scale Availability

MultiHealth Systems, Inc.
908 Niagara Falls Blvd.
North Tonawanda, NY 14120-2060
(800) 456-3003

Related References

None available.

General Comments and Recommendations for Practitioners and Researchers

Multiple formats (general, dyadic, and self-rating) allow for a variety of intrafamily comparisons across the same subscales. This allows clinicians to examine discrepancies between a family member's self-perception and perceptions by others.

---

115. Family Beliefs Inventory (FBI; Roehling & Robin)

Development and Description of Assessment Method

The FBI is a self-report measure with parallel forms for parents and adolescents. It is designed to assess distorted family thinking and unrealistic beliefs among family members. Subscale development was based on behavioral–family systems theory, which suggests that a rigid adherence to extreme beliefs elicits angry affect, impedes problem solving, and leads to escalating chains of reciprocally negative communication.

Target Population

Adolescents and their parents.

Format

The FBI consists of an inventory of 10 vignettes depicting sources of conflict between parents and their teens such as curfew and choice of friends. Each vignette is written from either the parent or teen perspective to match the respondent. One item representing each of the belief subscales is then presented and rated by the respondent.

The following six belief subscales are rated by parents:

1. *Ruination:* With too much freedom, teenagers will ruin their futures.
2. *Obedience:* Parents deserve absolute respect and obedience as the ultimate authority for teenagers.
3. *Perfectionism:* Teenagers should instinctively behave in a flawless manner.
4. *Malicious Intent:* Adolescents intentionally misbehave to hurt their parents.
5. *Self-Blame:* Parents are at fault for adolescents' misbehavior.
6. *Approval:* Adolescent disapproval of parents' child-rearing actions will be catastrophic.

The following four belief subscales are rated by adolescents:

1. *Ruination:* Parental rules and restrictions will ruin their teenage years.
2. *Unfairness:* It is catastrophic when parents treat teenagers unfairly.
3. *Autonomy:* Parents should give adolescents complete freedom to make decisions concerning rules and responsibilities.
4. *Approval:* It is catastrophic if parents become angry with adolescents.

Administration and Scoring

Each belief item is rated on a 7-point Likert scale indicating agreement, ranging from 1 = completely disagree to 7 = completely agree. Scores range from 10 to 70 for each vignette, with the higher score representing a greater adherence to the belief for each family. The summary score is a total beliefs score.

Psychometric Evaluation

Intercorrelations between subscales suggest that for adolescents, autonomy, injustice, and ruination cluster together. For parents, rigid thinking about obedience, ruination, and perfectionism cluster together.

Norms
None reported.

Reliability

Internal consistency was examined in a sample of families (N = 30 distressed and N = 30 nondistressed families) with adolescents around the age of 14. Alpha coefficients were generally high, ranging from .65 to .84, except for the approval subscale, where alpha coefficients were .46 for fathers, .59 for mothers, and .72 for teens.

Validity

Criterion-related validity was established in this comparison between distressed and nondistressed family members in that distressed fathers displayed the most unrealistic thinking regarding demands for flawless, obedient behavior, worries about adverse consequences of adolescent autonomy, and personalization of the adolescents' motives for rebellious behavior. In addition, teens from distressed families are most concerned with injustice and adverse consequences of parental restriction of their freedom. The measure, however, discriminates between distressed and nondistressed mothers. Limited validity investigations indicate low correlations with measures such as the Issues Checklist (Robin & Foster, 1989) and the Conflict Behavior Questionnaire (Prinz et al., 1979) but strong positive correlations with the Parent–Adolescent Relationships Questionnaire (Robin, Koepke, & Moye, 1990).

Advantages

The FBI assesses an important dimension underlying family member interactions, namely core belief systems. The assessment measure is directly related to targets for clinical intervention from a behavioral–family systems orientation.

Limitations

Although a promising measure, the FBI's limited psychometric development calls for only cautious use for research purposes. It has not yet been extended to maltreating families.

Primary Reference

Roehling and Robin (1986).

Scale Availability

Arthur Robin
Department of Psychology and Psychiatry

Children's Hospital of Michigan
3901 Beaubrien Blvd.
Detroit, MI 48201

Related References

Robin & Foster (1989); Robin et al. (1990).

General Comments and Recommendations for Practitioners and Researchers

From a cognitive–behavioral perspective, dysfunctional belief systems directly influence interactive behaviors among family members. Abusive families may hold particular types of dysfunctional schemas that clinicians should assess and target for intervention and this assessment measure will assist in the categorization of these schemas.

116. Family Crisis Oriented Personal Evaluation Scales (F–COPES; McCubbin, Larsen, & Olson)

Development and Description of Assessment Method

The F–COPES is a self-report assessment designed to identify effective problem-solving and behavioral strategies used by families in difficult or problematic situations. The items focus on the interaction between (a) the individual to the family system and (b) the family to the social environment. The assessment measure examines the family as a reactor to stress and as a manager of resources.

Item development for the F–COPES was based on a review of the literature on family stress and coping, as well as a review of other available coping inventories. The authors generated an initial pool of 49 items, which were administered to a sample of community adults ($N = $ 119). A factor analysis then yielded eight subscales grouped into two dimensions: internal and external family coping. These subscales were regrouped into the current five.

Target Population

Adolescent and adult family members.

Format

The F–COPES consists of 30 items distributed among the following five subscales:

1. *Acquiring Social Support:* Nine items that measure a family's ability to actively engage in acquiring support from relatives, friends, neighbors, and extended family, including "Sharing concerns with close friends" and "Seeking encouragement and support from friends."
2. *Reframing:* Eight items that measure a family's capability to re-define stressful events in order to make them more manageable, including "Accepting stressful events as a fact of life" and "Knowing we have the power to solve major problems."
3. *Seeking Spiritual Support:* Four items that focus on a family's ability to acquire spiritual support, including "Seeking advice from a minister" and "Having faith in God."
4. *Mobilizing Family to Acquire and Accept Help:* Five items that assess a family's ability to seek out community resources and accept help from others, including "Seeking information and advice from the family doctor" and "Seeking assistance from community agencies and programs designed to help families in our situation."
5. *Passive Appraisal:* Four items that focus on a family's ability to accept problematic issues while minimizing reactivity, including "Believing if we wait long enough, the problem will go away" and "Watching television."

Administration and Scoring

Items are introduced with the following question: "When we face problems or difficulties in our family, we respond by...." Family members then respond to each item according to a 5-point Likert scale from 1 = strongly disagree to 5 = strongly agree. Four items on the passive appraisal subscale are reverse-keyed. Other scores are derived by summing all item scores.

Psychometric Evaluation

Norms

Norms are available in manual for large samples of male and female adults and adolescents.

Reliability

Temporal stability was examined in a test–retest comparison across a 4-week interval for 116 family members. The correlation for the total scale score was $r = .81$, whereas subscale correlations ranged from $r = .61$ for reframing to $r = .95$ for seeking spiritual support. Internal consistency, examined via Cronbach's alpha, was .86 for the total scale score in a large sample of community adults ($N = 2,582$). Subscale alphas ranged from .63 for passive appraisal to .83 for acquiring social support.

Validity

The authors report that the F–COPES has good factorial validity and good concurrent validity, with high correlations to other family assessment measures.

Advantages

The F–COPES is an easy-to-administer inventory that taps into a family's coping resources both within and outside the family.

Limitations

Item content seems to have a strong social desirability element; this needs to be examined.

Primary Reference

McCubbin and Thompston (1991).

Scale Availability

E. I. McCubbin
University of Michigan
Family Social Science
290 McNeal Hall
St. Paul, MN 55108

Related References

None available.

General Comments and Recommendations for Practitioners and Researchers

Research to date has not examined the use of this measure with mal-treating families, but it would seem to function best as a quick screening for social support, which has been shown to be a moderating variable for high-risk families.

117. Family Environment Scale (FES; Moos & Moos)

Development and Description of Assessment Method

The FES is a self-report inventory that assesses 10 different aspects of the family environment, with particular emphasis on the interpersonal relationships among family members.

The original FES was deductively developed and was not subjected to empirical factor analysis. The initial choice and wording of items were based on interviews and observations with families. Two hundred items were chosen for pilot testing. Subsequent research did not provide support for either a 10-factor (related to subscales) or 3-factor (related to dimensions) model. Shorter versions have been developed to address internal consistency issues.

Target Population

Adolescent and adult family members.

Format

The FES consists of a 90-item inventory that focuses on three family dimensions containing a total of 10 subscales:

Relationship Dimension

1. *Cohesion:* The extent to which family members are concerned and committed to the family and the degree to which family members are helpful to and supportive of each other.
2. *Expressiveness:* The extent to which family members are allowed and encouraged to act openly and to express their feelings directly.
3. *Conflict:* The extent to which the open expression of anger, aggression, and generally conflictual interactions are characteristic of the family.

Personal Growth Dimension

4. *Independence:* The extent to which family members are encour-

aged to be assertive and self-sufficient, to make their own decisions, and to think things out for themselves.

5. *Achievement:* The extent to which different types of activities (school and work) are cast into an achievement-oriented or competitive framework.
6. *Intellectual–Cultural:* The extent to which the family is concerned about political, social, intellectual, and cultural activities.
7. *Active–Recreational:* The extent to which the family participates actively in various kinds of recreational and sporting activities.
8. *Moral–Religious:* The extent to which the family actively discusses and emphasizes ethical emphasis and religious issues and values.

System Maintenance Dimension

9. *Organization:* How important order and organization are in the family in terms of structuring family activities, financial planning, and explicitness and clarity regarding family rules and responsibilities.
10. *Control:* The extent to which the family is organized in a hierarchical manner, the rigidity of family rules and procedures, and the extent to which family members order each other around.

Sample items include "We put a lot of energy into what we do at home," "It's hard to blow off steam at home without upsetting anyone," "In our family we are strongly encouraged to be independent," "How much money a person makes is not very important to us," "Learning about new and different things is very important in our family," and "There are set ways of doing things at home."

Administration and Scoring

Family members respond to each item in a true-or-false format. Raw scores range from 0 to 9 for each subscale; the higher the score, the more prevalent the characteristic. A summary score, the family relations index, is derived by summing scores from the cohesion and expressiveness subscales and subtracting the score from the conflict subscale. Greene and Plank (1994) developed a short form of the FES with 40 items (four items per subscale) and with a revised 4-point Likert scale format related to how representative each item is of the respondent's family. The authors suggest that family members respond to the inventory in an independent rather than a collaborative fashion.

Psychometric Evaluation

Norms

The FES was standardized in 1979 and 1981 on large samples of normal ($N = 1,125$) and distressed ($N = 500$) families. The FES manual contains a wealth of normative data for families of different sizes, families with one spouse over the age of 60, as well as single-parent, African American, and Hispanic families.

Reliability

The conflict subscale shows good internal consistency, with an alpha coefficient of .75, and good temporal stability, with a test–retest reliability coefficient of $r = .85$. The authors report good test–retest reliabilities ranging from $r = .68$ to .86 for subscales. For the 40-item version's internal consistency, alphas were modest, ranging from .35 for expression to .67 for conflict.

Validity

Studies with families of incest victims show significantly greater scores on dimensions of conflict and control, as well as lower scores on the expressiveness, intellectual–cultural, active–recreational, independence, and organization dimensions (Carson et al., 1990). Another study focused on differences in familial characteristics as risk factors for multiple sexual victimizations in a sample of college women (Long & Jackson, 1991). Surprisingly, single-perpetrator victims and nonvictims described their families in similar terms. Multiple-perpetrator victims, however, showed significantly elevated scores on conflict and control and significantly lower scores on cohesion, expressiveness, and organization.

In a study of 162 mothers–guardians (Glaser et al., 1993) who were classified as either low, moderate, or high in abuse potential, scores on a number of FES subscales discriminated among these known groups. Mothers with high abuse potential ($N = 50$) had significantly lower scores on the following subscales: cohesion, expressiveness, independence, intellectual–cultural, and active–recreational, as compared to respondents with moderate abuse ($N = 43$) and low abuse ($N = 20$) potential.

Advantages

The FES is an easy-to-administer family assessment with an extensive psychometric database. It allows for comparisons to a wide range of normative samples. The items reflect all of the family dimensions emphasized in clinical literature as representing healthy and distressed families. Although not designed for assessment of maltreating families, recent studies seem to indicate patterns of dysfunction in families involved with sexual abuse.

Limitations

The true-or-false format limits assessment of intensity of each dimension and may force a less characteristic answer. Further extensions to families experiencing other types of maltreatment need to be completed. Internal consistencies of subscales seem lower than would be expected, especially for the independence, expressiveness, achievement, and control subscales.

Primary Reference

Moos and Moos (1986).

Scale Availability

> Consulting Psychologists Press, Inc.
> 3803 East Bayshire Rd.
> Palo Alto, CA 94303
> 800-624-1765

Related References

Carson et al. (1990); Glaser et al. (1993); Kolko, Kazdin, Thomas, and Day (1993); Long and Jackson (1991, 1994).

General Comments and Recommendations for Practitioners and Researchers

The FES is one of the only respected measures of family dynamics that has been used in research with maltreating families. Clinicians will benefit from the use of this straightforward assessment of family variables at pretreatment and as a measurement of treatment outcome.

118. Family Inventory of Life Events (FILE; McCubbin & Patterson)

Development and Description of Assessment Method

The FILE is a self-report inventory designed to measure the pile-up of life events experienced by a family as an index of stress. The items are intended to reflect a change of sufficient magnitude to require some adjustment in the pattern of family interaction. The scale includes both nonnormative stressors and life cycle events.

Items comprising the FILE inventory were based on clinical and research experience with families undergoing stress. Initial items were based on other life change inventories used in psychobiological stress research.

Target Population

Adult family members.

Format

The FILE is a 71-item self-report inventory composed of nine subscales:

1. *Intrafamily Strains:* "Increase in conflict between husband and wife," "Increased difficulty in maintaining teenage children."
2. *Marital Strains:* "Spouse/parent separated or divorced," "Spouse/parent has an affair."
3. *Pregnancy and Childbearing Strains:* "Spouse had unwanted or difficult pregnancy," "Family member had an abortion."
4. *Financial and Business Strains:* "Went to welfare," "Purchased or built a home."
5. *Work–Family Transitions or Strains:* "Decreased satisfaction with job or career."
6. *Illness and Family Care Strains:* "Parent/spouse seriously ill or injured," "Increase in number of tasks or chores not getting done."
7. *Losses:* "Close relative or friend of family seriously ill," "A child member died."
8. *Transitions " In and Out:"* "A young adult member began college," "A member was married."
9. *Family Legal Violations:* "A member went to jail or juvenile detention," "A member was picked up or arrested by police."

Administration and Scoring

Items are answered in a yes-or-no format for experiences during the previous 12 months and before the previous 12 months. Any yes answer is scored as 1, and all scores are then summed for total score. Higher scores indicate a pileup of stress. The authors of FILE recommend only using the total score because psychometric data for subscales are weak.

Psychometric Evaluation

Norms

The normative sample included 1,140 couples across seven stages of the life cycle. These data are available in the FILE manual.

Reliability

Internal consistency was examined, and significant alpha coefficients ranged from .79 to .82 for subscales and the total score. A 4-week interval for test–retest reliability resulted in a significant correlation of r = .80, which indicates good temporal stability.

Validity

Good convergent validity was reported along with significant correlations with the Family Environment Scale (Moos & Moos, 1986). In a separate study (Barton & Baglio, 1993), the FILE was administered to 151 parents previously convicted for physical child abuse. A factor analysis demonstrated three factors unique to the abusing environment: trouble with teenagers, violence and separation, and public assistance.

Advantages

The FILE is a brief device that is easy to administer and score. It is well-suited as a pretreatment screening device for an assessment of families under stress.

Limitations

The FILE does not allow an assessment of the intensity of the impact of the life events listed, nor does it tap into effective or ineffective coping strategies.

Primary Reference

McCubbin, Patterson, and Wilson (1980).

Scale Availability

E. I. McCubbin
University of Minnesota
Family Social Science
290 McNeal Hall
St. Paul, MN 55108

Related References

Barton and Baglio (1993).

General Comments and Recommendations for Practitioners and Researchers

Insufficient data have been collected thus far on maltreating families. Further research could examine high-risk families as well as families in treatment for maltreating in order to determine the role of stressful life events in the functioning of these families.

---

119. Mother–Adolescent Attribution Questionnaire (MAAQ; Grace, Kelley, & McCain)

Development and Description of Assessment Method

The authors modeled the development of this measure on the Marital Attributional Style Questionnaire (Fincham, Beach, & Nelson, 1987), using the definitions of attributions represented in that scale. The specific conflict situations represented the eight most commonly discussed issues in the literature on parent–adolescent conflict. The authors chose negative behaviors in order to better assess attributions as well as relationship distress.

The MAAQ is a paper-and-pencil inventory that assesses attributions made by either an adolescent or his or her mother for eight hypothetical conflict situations. The adolescent version assesses beliefs about the causes of negative mother behaviors, and the corresponding version for mothers assesses attributions about negative teenage behavior.

Target Population

Mothers and their teenagers who are experiencing conflict in the family.

Format

The MAAQ has an adult and an adolescent inventory. Both the adult and adolescent versions contain eight hypothetical conflict situations, each followed by nine statements that assess attributions and reactions to the situation. The statements reflect the following types of attributions:

- *Externality:* The cause of the behavior is located either within the other person in the dyad or the self.
- *Globality:* The cause of the behavior is perceived to affect other areas of the relationship.
- *Stability:* The cause of the behavior is perceived to be enduring.
- *Intentionality:* The other person in the dyad is perceived to have intended the behavior.
- *Selfish Motivation:* The other person in the dyad's behavior is perceived to be selfishly motivated.
- *Blame:* The other person in the dyad is held accountable for the behavior.

Two additional statements reflect the respondent's estimate of the frequency of occurrence of the conflict situation and the respondent's anger reaction.

An example of a hypothetical conflict situation and statements to be endorsed follows:

Time spent on homework:

- "My mother makes me spend too much time on schoolwork because of something about her (the type of person she is, the mood she was in)."
- "My mother makes me spend too much time on schoolwork because of something about me (what I said or did, the kind of person I am, or because of other people or circumstances)."
- "The reason that my mother makes me spend too much time on schoolwork is not likely to change."
- "The reason that my mother makes me spend too much time on schoolwork is something that affects other areas of our relationship."
- "My mother makes me spend too much time on schoolwork 'on purpose' rather than not 'on purpose.'"
- "My mother's making me spend too much time on schoolwork shows that she thought mainly of her own needs."

- "I hold my mother responsible (at fault) for making me spend too much time on schoolwork."
- "When my mother makes me spend too much time on schoolwork, I become angry."
- "My mother often makes me spend too much time on schoolwork."

Examples of other conflict situations include "My mother doesn't like some of my friends," "My mother complains about the way I spend my free time," "My teenager comes home after curfew," and "My teenager sometimes chooses undesirable friends."

Administration and Scoring

Respondents rate the extent to which each of the attributional statements reflect their mother's or teen's behavior using a 6-point, Likert-type scale from 1 = disagree strongly to 6 = agree strongly. A total score for each of the six dimensions is obtained by summing responses to each dimension across the eight conflict situations. Each attribution dimension therefore is assessed by an eight-item measure. Further, a frequency of conflict and an anger reaction score are also computed using the last two statements for each situation.

Psychometric Evaluation

Norms
None reported.

Reliability
For teenagers ($n = 122$) and mothers ($n = 115$) in this initial study, internal consistencies of each of the six attribution dimensions ranged from alpha levels of .76 to .85 for teens and from .78 to .89 for mothers. Further, correlations between all six dimensions were computed, and all were significant at the $p < .01$ level. This indicates that all of the attributional dimensions are related to one another.

Validity
Correlations between the MAAQ and other parent–adolescent measures (Issues Checklist and Conflict Behavior Questionnaire; CBQ; see Robin & Foster, 1989) were calculated in order to determine convergent validity. For teenagers, the correlations between self-reported conflict and attribution dimensions regarding globality, externality, and selfish

motivation were highest, ranging from $r = .34$ to $r = .53$. For mothers, the global and selfish attributions were most highly correlated with self-reported conflict.

Further, a stepwise regression analysis was conducted to examine the predictive validity of the attribution dimensions. For teenagers, the external and global dimensions were the best predictors of self-reported conflict (22% of the variance for Issues Checklist scores), and globality, intentionality, and blame accounted for 37% of the variance on CBQ scores. For mothers, the globality and blame dimensions were the best predictors for self-reported conflict.

Advantages
The adult and teenage versions of the MAAQ allow for comparison of two viewpoints of the same conflict situations across the same attributional dimensions. This is an important assessment target in that attributions are often implicated in the maintenance of dysfunctional interaction styles and may be good targets for clinical interaction.

Limitations
The forced choice format does not allow for variations on the attributional statements given. The redundancy of the attributional statements may reduce the attention paid to each item, and the wording of several statements is somewhat complicated.

Primary Reference
Grace, Kelley, and McCain (1993).

Scale Availability
Mary Lou Kelly
Department of Psychology
Louisiana State University
Baton Rouge, LA 70803-5501
(504) 388-8745

Related References
None available.

General Comments and Recommendations for Practitioners and Researchers

The MAAQ is an interesting approach to the assessment of cognition related to dyadic interaction. No causal implications should be made, however, in that the attributional dimensions cited are only associated with self-reported conflict. It will be important to look at the relationship of responses on the MAAQ and interactions of mother–adolescent dyads discussing a hypothetical conflict in an analogue setting or interactions in the natural environment.

120. Parent–Adolescent Relationship Questionnaire (PARQ; Robin, Koepke, & Moye)

Development and Description of Assessment Method

The PARQ was designed to be a comprehensive family assessment device for both adolescent and parent respondents. Multiple domains of family functioning, including communication, problem-solving, beliefs, family structure, and conflict are assessed in one instrument.

Items were rationally derived from existing literature and assessment instruments and behavioral family systems theory (Robin & Foster, 1989). A factor analysis produced three primary factors: skills deficit–overt conflict, extreme beliefs, and structural problems.

Target Population

Parents and adolescents who are experiencing conflict in the family.

Format

The PARQ is a 428-item inventory rated according to a yes-or-no format. Items are grouped, based on content, into 13 scales: global distress, communication, problem-solving, beliefs, warmth–hostility, coalitions, triangulation, hierarchy reversal, cohesion, somatic concerns, conflict over school, conflict over siblings, and social desirability. Further, the general beliefs scale has particular subscales for parents (ruination, obedience, perfectionism, self-blame, and malicious intent) and for adolescents (ruination, unfairness, autonomy, perfectionism, and approval). The coalitions and triangulation scales can also be broken down according to who is involved (mother–father with the adolescent in the middle).

Administration and Scoring

The PARQ is a lengthy instrument that requires an average of 45 minutes to complete. There are separate parent and adolescent versions with comparable scales.

Psychometric Evaluation

Norms
None reported.

Reliability
The authors (as cited in Robin & Foster, 1989) indicate that the PARQ scales all show internal consistency coefficients above .75, but there is no report of test–retest reliability.

Validity
The authors report that all of the PARQ scales (except triangulation, coalitions, self-blame, and approval) discriminated between distressed and nondistressed parents and adolescents, indicating good known groups validity. Strong evidence also exists for the construct validity of many PARQ scales, which correlated with clinical interviews and behavioral observation data. Finally, strong convergent validity is supported via strong positive correlations between the PARQ and the Family Beliefs Inventory (Roehling & Robin, 1986).

Advantages
The PARQ combines both a behavioral skills model of family interaction (focusing on conflict resolution, problem-solving, and communication) and a family systems mode (cohesion, triangulation, and coalitions). Further, the assessment of underlying cognitive schemas that influence interaction behaviors is a worthwhile addition.

Limitations
There is limited psychometric or clinical research reported on the PARQ. The device is much too long for most chaotic or high-risk families to complete.

Primary Reference

Robin, Koepke, and Moye (1986).

Scale Availability

Arthur Robin
Department of Psychology and Psychiatry
Childrens' Hospital of Michigan
3901 Beaubrien Blvd.
Detroit, MI 48201

Related References

Robin and Foster (1990).

General Comments and Recommendations for Practitioners and Researchers

The PARQ is an extremely comprehensive assessment of many domains of family functioning usually targeted for intervention in family treatment. Only the length of the inventory detracts from its use in the clinical setting. Researchers are encouraged to explore the assessment of interaction in abusive families with this instrument.

12 Analogue Methods and Behavioral Coding

---

121. Articulated Thoughts During Simulated Situations (ATSS; O'Brien)

Development and Description of Assessment Method

This assessment method is based on work by Davison and colleagues (Davison, Robins, & Johnson, 1983), who developed the ATSS as a compromise between direct observation and structured assessment and to allow for quantification of nonobservable cognitive and emotional responses.

The ATSS has a simulated situation format that offers a compromise between naturalistic observation and structured assessment of cognitive and emotional reactions to family discussions as experienced by sons and mothers. It is designed for assessment of family members from physically aggressive, verbally aggressive, and low-conflict marital relationships. It is used for assessment of both adult and child responses.

Target Population

Mothers and their sons between the ages of 8 and 11 years.

Format

The ATSS contains three situations that reflect typical examples of family conflict:

1. *Marital Conflict:* Who should be in charge of finances.

2. *Parent Conflict Over Child Rearing:* A son's poor school performance.
3. *Mother–Son Conflict:* Related to household chores.

For each situation, there is a low and a high conflict version. In the low-intensity version, the dyad discusses the issues calmly and courteously with listening, not raising their voices and cooperating with each other. In the high-conflict version, the dyads participate in more heated and conflictual discussions (raising voices, criticizing, and cutting each other off in midsentence).

An example of a high conflict script is:

The mother yells, "That's it! I have asked you three times to clean up your room, and you haven't done anything about it." The son replies in angry tone, "Don't bug me! I'm going to do it. I told you I would!" Mom yells, "I would like it done NOW! You know that it's your responsibility to keep your room neat." The son replies, "You know, some kids don't have to do anything around the house. Their mothers do it for them." Mom replies in an angry tone, "Oh, that's a fine idea! Brilliant! I should take care of all of your responsibilities?" The son says, "I wasn't saying that! Geez! I wish you didn't get so crabby about it all the time. It doesn't look that bad!" Mom asks, "You think that if I didn't talk to you about it, that you would do it?" The son replies, "Of course. I'll do it after this TV show is over." Mom yells, "Just hold on! You'll do it now." The son yells, "OK, OK!"

Administration and Scoring

Each individual is placed in a room with headphones, a tape recorder, and two speakers. After the administration of a practice tape, the individual hears simulated family interactions (each situation has a high and low conflict version). When the tone indicates the end of a segment, the individual is prompted to tune into his or her own thoughts and feelings and indicate into the tape recorder (a) the reactions that he or she would feel, and (b) what the actors should have done.

The audiotaped responses are then transcribed into the following categories:

- *Self-Distraction:* Reflecting tangential statements or an inability to deal with conflict.
- *Self-Inference:* The son's reported attempts to verbally or physically intervene.
- *Negative Evaluation and Attribution of Blame:* Capturing the amount of criticism directed toward the actors.

- *Positive Evaluation and Support:* Reflecting praise of the actors.
- *Positive Outcome:* Belief in open communication, recognition that family members have rights and feelings, belief in cooperation, and belief in democratic lifestyles.
- *Autocracy:* Belief in compliance and assumption of responsibility.
- *Prescription:* How family life should or must proceed.

Categories are not mutually exclusive and are rated on a 4-point, Likert-type scale from 0 = not at all (individual mentioned nothing of relevance to the code) to 3 = a lot (individual's statements were very strong).

Further, after every tape, respondents are asked to evaluate their physiological arousal on a 5-point scale ranging from 0 = not at all to 4 = greatly. Respondents rate the extent to which they experienced the following: face felt hot or flushed, hands or body got sweaty, I was breathing faster, etc.

Psychometric Evaluation

Norms
None reported.

Reliability
Cronbach's alphas used to assess intercoder reliability ranged from .46 for democracy statements to .69 for positive evaluation statements given by mothers, and from .61 for positive outcome statements to .88 for democracy statements given by sons. The categories of self-distraction and self-interference were coded for sons only, and intercoder reliability was .71 and .74, respectively.

Validity
Data analysis revealed differences in sons from physically aggressive (N = 12) and low-conflict (N = 12) homes. Sons from high-conflict homes revealed more self-distracting strategies, made statements advocating self-interference, and evaluated high-intensity conflict tapes less negatively than sons from low-conflict homes. Sons from low-conflict homes made significantly more positive predictions of outcome, evaluations, and democratic ideas and prescriptions.

Advantages
The authors suggest the ATSS to arrange assessment of low-frequency situations and to assess internal cognitions. An advantage of this stan-

dardized testing format is that individuals can respond spontaneously to stimuli rather than report retrospectively on thoughts and behaviors in particular situations. It is suitable for children, as well as for those with limited reading and writing skills. It allows for assessment of each member of the dyad to the standardized script, and may be helpful in gauging children's reactions to witnessing marital disputes, as well as participation in parent–child conflict.

Limitations

The ATSS requires extensive training for coders, who must review exact definitions of coding items. The authors report that 22 hours of training is required, which would be impractical for most clinical settings. The reliance on only six situations may limit external validity.

Primary Reference

O'Brien, Margolin, John, and Krueger (1991).

Scale Availability

Mary O'Brien
6 Washington Pl., Room 483
Department of Psychology
New York University
New York, NY 10003

Related References

Davison et al. (1983).

General Comments and Recommendations for Practitioners and Researchers

According to Davison, Vogel, and Coffman (1997), the ATSS is a think-aloud approach to cognitive assessment that has the following advantages: (a) an unstructured production response format that allows for open-ended responding in great detail; (b) "on line" rather than retrospective assessment, which minimizes reactivity and self-presentation; (c) greater situational specificity and control; and (d) flexibility in choice of situations, including some that may be unethical or impractical to study in vivo.

122. Audiotaped Interparental Verbal Conflict (AIVC; Adamson & Thompson)

Development and Description of Assessment Method

This multicomponent assessment procedure includes an individual child interview to determine hypothetical responses to four short, semi-projective story scenarios of interparental interaction, audiotaped stories of verbal conflicts between a man and a woman, and an interview about coping strategies of children.

The audiotaped story format was developed specifically for this study. The response coding system was based on Brotman-Band and Weisz's (1988) classification of children's coping responses to everyday stress.

Target Population

Children between the ages of 5 and 12 who have witnessed physical violence between their parents.

Format

The AIVC consists of an initial interview to determine children's perceptions of the frequency of interparental conflict in their own homes, to ensure that children can accurately identify the emotions depicted in the drawings that later accompany the audiotapes, and to establish a rating scale for intensity of feelings.

Following an introduction, each child listens to four audiotaped stories. Three consist of a narrative describing verbal conflict between a man and woman while their child listens. The other story describes the parents engaged in pleasant conversation. The topics of each story include conflicts regarding money, child-rearing, support of a political candidate, and pleasurable conversation about work. Drawings of a man and woman posed as though they are engaged in an argument accompany each audiotape.

Administration and Scoring

Children are interviewed after each story to assess their reports of the quality and intensity of the emotional response of the child in the scenario. Children are asked, "How do you think Pat (the hypothetical child witness) felt in this story?" Then they were asked, "How much did Pat feel that way?" on a 5-point Likert scale from 1 = very little to 5 = a whole lot. In order to evaluate coping strategies, each child was then asked, "What could Pat do right then to feel better?" and "Why do you think that will work to make Pat feel better?" All of these responses are audiotaped for later coding. Coping strategies are coded according to the following:

- *Primary Control:* Attempts to change or otherwise influence circumstances, objects, or individuals in order to augment outcome by aligning objective conditions with the child's wishes, including direct problem-solving, problem-focused crying, aggression, or avoidance.
- *Secondary Control:* Attempts to change or influence the child's own subjective, psychological state (mood, attributions, expectations) by realizing comfortable adjustment or fit with present conditions, social–spiritual support, emotion-focused crying or aggression, cognitive avoidance, or pure cognition.
- *Relinquished Control:* No evidence of goal-directed behavior, and no obvious effort to augment outcomes or reduce aversion.

Psychometric Evaluation

Norms
None reported.

Reliability
All of the coping strategies were first coded for the principal control strategy and then for each subcategory by two independent raters. Overall interrater agreement was reported as 97%, with disagreements resolved by consensus.

Validity
Evidence for known groups validity was supported in that child witnesses of family violence report greater frequency of parental arguing, greater intensity of emotion, and greater intensity of anger than do control children. Further, children from nonviolent homes were more likely to propose direct problem-solving strategies than other forms. Children from violent homes were likely to propose becoming involved in parental disputes by acting aggressively as a way to end conflict.

Advantages
The audiotape format would be easy to administer in a clinical setting; scenarios could be individualized to reflect themes for a particular fam-

ily. The coding system is quite comprehensive regarding relevant dimensions in children's coping.

Limitations

Coping strategies of children to hypothetical scenarios will vary directly as a function of age, so it is difficult to assess dysfunctional coping without a normative categorization of coping strategies at various developmental levels.

Primary Reference

Adamson and Thompson (1998).

Scale Availability

> Jackie L. Adamson
> Department of Psychology
> University of Nebraska-Lincoln
> 209 Burnett Hall
> Lincoln, NE 68588-0308

Related References

Brotman-Band and Weisz (1988).

General Comments and Recommendations for Practitioners and Researchers

The next step would be to examine the relationship of this analogue assessment method with children's self-report measures of coping as well as responses to parent conflict.

---

123. Children's Response to Live Interadult Anger (CRLIA; El-Sheikh & Reiter)

Development and Description of Assessment Method

This analogue paradigm is based on developmental research regarding children's responses to adult interaction pioneered by E. M. Cummings (Davies & Cummings, 1994).

The CRLIA was developed to examine the relationship between

high levels of marital discord and children's maladjustment. The analogue format provides an assessment of multiple modes of responding to live or videotaped arguments. Both overt behavioral and verbal responses are assessed.

Target Population

Young children exposed to marital conflict.

Format

Following exposure to an argument between male and female actors, children are interviewed about their perceptions of the arguing adults, their own feelings during the argument, and their expectations for the outcome of the couple's conflict. Specifically, children are shown cards with facial expressions depicting various affective states and are asked (a) "How do the two people feel?" and (b) "How did you feel when the people were fighting?" Next, the children are shown a series of behavioral response cards (including depictions of "hit the people," "cry," "yell at the people," "stop the fight," "leave the room," and "ignore the people") and are asked (c) "What did you feel like doing when the people were fighting?" and "What do you think they will be doing next?" The arguments deal with mundane issues and problems in a male–female relationship.

Administration and Scoring

The preschool child and mother are seated in a room when two actors enter and enact various arguments about mundane issues. Some arguments are unresolved, whereas others are resolved (with an apology and a compromise solution). Then comes the 60-second assessment argument. Children's responses to the arguments and their interview answers are videotaped and coded according to the following categories: facial and postural distress, verbal concern, and proximity seeking toward mother. Negative affect is rated on a 5-point Likert scale from 0 = no distress to 4 = severe distress.

In addition to these behavioral ratings, children's affective and behavioral response cards are coded and receive a score for either harmonious or conflictual outcome prediction for the assessment argument.

Psychometric Evaluation

Norms
None reported.

Reliability
Interrater reliability for children's responses to interview questions (selection of affect and behavioral response cards and prediction of outcome) was calculated for 53% of the data and yielded a kappa coefficient of .92, which indicates excellent reliability. Interrater agreement between two coders who rated the child's overt distress and negative affect was calculated for 100% of the data. This resulted in a kappa coefficient of .83, indicating good reliability.

Validity
Results from El-Sheikh, Cummings, and Reiter (1996) indicated that preschoolers exposed first to resolved disputes were more likely to exhibit diminished overt behavioral stress in response to future arguments and predicted a lower likelihood of conflictual outcome. Further, girls exposed to resolved disputes showed a less negative perception of the arguing adults and were less likely to endorse intervention in conflict. There were no attempts to assess the relationship of data from this procedure with other assessments of the children.

Advantages
Although the children in the initial study were not a clinical sample exposed to family violence or victimized themselves, it is an interesting approach to the assessment of cognitive and affective reactions to conflict. It is useful for young children who may not be able to accurately report on how they react in their natural environment.

Limitations
Although the response ratings are simple and possibly easy to replicate, the use of actors for the assessment argument seems complicated and a severe threat to the external validity (generalizability) of the results. Using the child's own parents would seem a more valid approach.

Primary Reference

El-Sheikh and Reiter (1996).

Scale Availability

M. El-Sheikh
Department of Psychology
Auburn University
Auburn, AL 36849-5214

Related References

El-Sheikh et al. (1996).

General Comments and Recommendations for Practitioners and Researchers

Although the authors claim that live interactions present more ecologically valid stimuli for examining children's reactions to angry interactions, the experimental manipulations of this exposure do not represent prolonged or repeated exposure to dimensions of marital conflict in the home.

---

124. Checklist for Living Environments to Assess Neglect (CLEAN; Watson-Perczel, Lutzker, Greene, & McGimpsey)

Development and Description of Assessment Method

The development of this assessment device was based on pilot research done with Project 12-Ways, a multifaceted ecobehavioral treatment program providing in-home services to families. Definitions for aspects of the CLEAN coding system were based on in-home observations.

This home observation data collection system was designed to quantify neglectful home conditions that are related to negative developmental and health consequences for children. Pilot research identified specific characteristics that consistently contribute to poor conditions in the home.

Target Population

Family dwellings of those at risk or those under investigation by state child protective services for neglect.

Format

Each room was assessed at the time of the home visit. Rooms were divided into "item areas" (furnishings, surface areas, fixtures, appliances).

The data collection system provided information concerning three distinct dimensions:

1. Whether a specific item area was clean or dirty (presence of dirt, human or pet food, or other organic matter in direct contact with the area),
2. The number of clothes or linens in direct contact with the item area, and
3. The number of items not belonging with the particular area.

Administration and Scoring

Data collection throughout the dwelling took approximately 25 to 30 minutes by a trained observer. Each room was examined completely until the entire house had been scored.

The CLEAN produced a "composite percentage score" reflecting the condition of the home and ranging from 0 to 100, with higher scores indicating more cleanliness. Numerical values were assigned to each item area based on an assessment of a clean (10) to dirty (0) dimension; the number of clothes/linens, 0 = score of 5 to >20 = score of 0; and number of items not belonging, 0 = score of 5 to >20 = score of 0.

The scores for all item areas in a particular room were then added and divided by the number of item areas, yielding a mean score for all areas in that room. This number was divided by 20 (the highest possible score; all items clean, 0 clothes/linens, and 0 items not belonging) and then multiplied by 100, yielding a percentage composite score.

Psychometric Evaluation

Norms
None reported.

Reliability
Staff from the treatment program were trained to an 85% reliability criterion with a primary observer using analogue practice sessions.

In one study (Watson-Perczel, Lutzker, Greene, & McGimpsey,

1988), reliability checks were completed on three separate families. Reliability was computed by calculating agreements and disagreements between two observer responses for each room. Agreements were defined as exact matches on either condition (clean or dirty) or number range. Reliability checks were conducted on approximately 32% of all observation sessions, and overall percentage agreement scores were between 83% and 90%, indicating good interrater reliability.

Validity

Known groups validity was examined by comparing the three target families with four families nominated by child protective service workers as having maintained clean homes. Data from observations of these dwellings indicated mean composite scores for maintenance of the entire home at 80%, which was higher than pretreatment scores of the three families in treatment.

Social validity of the home observation assessment was examined by asking caseworkers to complete a questionnaire related to environmental neglect methods. Of documentation and contributing characteristics of the 14 caseworkers, 67% indicated that half of their caseload consisted of families unable to maintain adequate cleanliness of the home, and many provided narrative descriptions of these environments that coincided with items on the CLEAN.

Advantages

This home observation system attempts to quantify an unrepresented area of concern for maltreating families. The system requires simple judgments about conditions in specific areas and rooms and seems easily taught to those routinely involved with home visits.

Limitations

The scoring system may seem too cumbersome for visiting caseworkers. Further, there has been limited use of this method reported in the literature, so no further psychometric development has been done.

Primary Reference

Watson-Perczel et al. (1988).

Scale Availability

Brandon Green
Project 12-Ways

The Rehabilitation Institute
Southern Illinois University at Carbondale
Carbondale, IL 62901
(618) 536-7704
e-mail: bfgreene@siu.edu

Related References

None available.

General Comments and Recommendations for Practitioners and Researchers

We highly recommend those involved with home observations of families to take a look at this simple assessment of a crucial area related to maltreating families. The CLEAN seems well suited to assist caseworkers in the quantification of home variables across the course of an investigation.

---

125. Cleanup Coding Systems (CCS; Koenig, Cicchette, & Rogasch)

Development and Description of Assessment Method

This comprehensive coding system allows for quantification of numerous child compliance and noncompliance strategies as well as maternal, verbal, and physical control strategies likely to emerge during this free-play and cleanup paradigm. Further, instances of both maternal and child affective displays are included in order to assess affective differences in maltreating families.

The behavioral coding systems were developed by researchers examining the development of internalization of moral standards in young children. These developmental theorists (see Kochanska, Akasan, & Koenig, 1995) viewed compliance with maternal commands as an essential precursor to the development of internalization in young children.

Target Population

Mothers and their preschool children.

Format

The CCS is composed of four distinct coding systems:

1. *Child Internalization System:* Measures the following child compliance and noncompliance categories:
   - *Committed Compliance:* Child fully endorses cleanup situation and requires little control from mother.
   - *Situational Compliance:* Child complies with maternal demands, but if mother ceases to make requests, stops cleaning up.
   - *Overt Resistance:* Child does not comply with maternal directives either by refusal or negotiation.
   - *Defiance:* Child does not comply with maternal directives usually by refusal with uncontrolled affect.
2. *Maternal Verbal Control System:* Codes each maternal utterance as one of 16 categories. Present study only used eight categories that captured power-assertive and inductive techniques:
   - *Direct Do:* "Put that away."
   - *Polite Do:* "Could you put the ball away?"
   - *Hint Do:* "The toys need to go in the basket."
   - *Reasoning:* "You played with the toys, so you need to clean them up."
   - *Positive Evaluation:* "You are doing a great job."
   - *Bargaining:* "If you pick up some of the toys, then I'll help you with the rest."
   - *Negative Evaluation:* "I know that you don't want to pick up."
   - *Empathy:* "I know that picking up the toys is hard."
3. *Maternal Physical Control System:* Includes the following power-assertive and inductive categories:
   - *Distant Signals:* Pointing from a distance.
   - *Negative Touch:* Forcefully grabbing the child's arm, hitting, or spanking.
   - *Positive Touch:* Hugging, kissing.
4. *Maternal and Child Affect Code:* Includes the following categories:
   - *Tender/Affectionate:* Baby talk, caring tone of voice.
   - *Pleasure/Joy:* Smiling, laughing, singing, enthusiastic.
   - *Neutral:* None apparent.
   - *Slightly Negative:* Whining, impatient tone, embarrassment.
   - *Sad:* Crying.
   - *Irritable/Anger:* Yelling/scowling.

Administration and Scoring

The coding systems were used following a videotaped semistructured free-play and cleanup sequence. First, the mother and child were instructed to play for 30 minutes in a laboratory playroom furnished with both male and female age-appropriate toys. During the first and last 10-minute segments, the mother is instructed not to initiate interaction with the child but to follow the child's lead as she does at home. During the second segment, the mother is told to interact freely with her child. This cleanup segment is signaled by an observer behind the one-way mirror, and the mother is asked to initiate cleanup. Up to 6 minutes of observation is allowed for this period.

The behavioral coding systems are scored from videotaped interactions during the cleanup period. For each 15-second interval, the predominant compliance/noncompliance, physical control, and maternal and child affective responses are coded. For maternal verbal control strategies, each maternal utterance is coded.

Psychometric Evaluation

Norms
None reported.

Reliability
Previous research on normal samples established kappa coefficients for each category in each of the four systems. For the child internalization system, Kochanska et al. (1995) reported kappas between .63 to .78 and .76 for the maternal physical control system. For maternal verbal control strategies, coefficients ranged from .62 to .99, whereas kappas for maternal affect ranged from .76 to .81 and from .77 to .84 for child affect. These coefficients reflect good internal consistency.

Interrater reliability was established for this study of maltreating dyads on the basis of 20% of the cases. For each 15-second segment, the researchers compared the predominant coded category between raters to determine agreement. The following kappa coefficients were found: child internalization, $k = .80$, maternal physical strategies $k = .85$, maternal affect, $k = .76$, and child affect, $k = .77$, which are all considered substantial. For the maternal verbal coding system, alpha coefficients used on category totals ranged from .75 (negative evaluation) to .97 (polite do and bargaining), with a mean of .78.

Validity

Known groups validity was examined in comparisons between nonmal-treating dyads (n = 43) and preschoolers and their mothers randomly selected from caseloads of child protective service workers (n = 20 physically abused; n = 26 neglected). Analyses of variance indicated significant differences among the three groups for amount of committed compliance ($F(2.86)$ = 3.50, p = .04) and situational compliance ($F(2.86)$ = 3.02, p = .05), with physically abused children exhibiting more situational compliance and less committed compliance. In terms of affective expression, the three groups differed significantly ($F(2.86)$ = 3.61, p = .03), with the neglect group exhibiting significantly more negative child affect.

Advantages

This approach to a play and cleanup sequence will certainly allow for an in-vivo assessment of spontaneous mother–child interactions. Further, the comprehensive coding system includes both desirable and undesirable behaviors, thus making it sensitive to changes as a result of treatment. There is good examination of aspects of reliability.

Limitations

The exact behavioral coding methodology is not clear from description, and data may be hard to summarize and analyze for anyone outside of the laboratory setting.

Primary Reference

Koenig, Cicchette, and Rogasch (2000).

Scale Availability

Amy L. Koenig
Mt. Hope Family Center
University of Rochester
187 Edinburgh St.
Rochester, NY 14608

Related References

Kochanska et al. (1995).

General Comments and Recommendations for Practitioners and Researchers

These authors extended an already existing behavioral coding system used in developmental research and based on developmental theory to the assessment of variables not often examined in maltreating dyadic interactions. In particular, the examination of both mother–child affect and mother–child control strategies help to quantify aspects of the compliance situations typical for preschool children. Perhaps clinical research should examine further the vast developmental literature for other assessment methods.

126. Dyadic Parent–Child Interaction Coding System (DPICS; Eyberg & Robinson)

Development and Description of Assessment Method

The DPICS is a comprehensive observational coding system developed for analogue assessment of families with conduct-disordered children. It can be used for either structured or unstructured observations of parent and child in a clinic or naturalistic home setting.

The DPICS is based on the coding system used by Patterson (1982) for the assessment of family interactions.

Target Population

Parents and their young children, usually between ages of 2 and 10 years.

Format

The DPICS consists of a two-part observation session, including a 5-minute child-directed interaction in which the parent is instructed to allow the child to choose any activity and to play along with the child; and a parent-directed interaction in which the parent is instructed to select an activity and keep the child playing according to the parents' rules. The DPICS consists of 29 separate behavior categories that form five mother variables and two child variables. Behaviors included in the parent assessment are direct command, indirect command, labeled praise, unlabeled praise, positive physical, negative physical, critical statement, descriptive statement, descriptive question, acknowledgment, and irrelevant verbalization. A "changes activity" category is included to evaluate activity level. Further, the parent's response following a child's deviant behavior (ignores or responds) and the child's response to a parent's command (complies, noncomplies, or no opportunity) are coded in order to assess interaction sequences. Other child behaviors included in the coding system are whine, cry, smart talk, tell, destructive, and physical negative. Exact behavioral definitions are provided in the manual.

Administration and Scoring

Parents and their child are observed for two 5-minute interactions in a playroom. Behaviors in both the child-directed interaction and the parent-directed interaction are observed continuously and result in a score for total frequency of each behavior or behavioral sequence per 5-minute interval. Scoring variables created from the DPICS categories include: total praise (labeled praise + unlabeled praise), total deviant (whine + cry + physical negative + smart talk + yell + destructive), total commands (direct + indirect) command ratio, no opportunity ratio, compliance ratio, and noncompliance ratio (all with a common denominator of total commands).

Psychometric Evaluation

Norms
None reported.

Reliability
In a standardization and validation study, 42 clinic families and 22 control families were assessed for four 5-minute observation sessions. Inter-rater reliability was assessed by correlating the frequency of each behavior recorded by two independent observers for 244 sessions. The mean reliability coefficient for child behaviors was .92, with a range from .76 to 1.0, and the mean coefficient for parent behaviors was .91, with a range from .67 to 1.0 (Robinson & Eyberg, 1981).

In a subsequent study (Webster-Stratton, 1985), percent agreement reliability was calculated for segments of both home and clinic observations (N = 40) and was based on occurrences of behavior, not non-occurrences. Mean overall interrater reliability was 78.6%. The authors also calculated product–moment correlations for both types of visits. These coefficients ranged from .61 for the category of "no opportunity commands" in an unstructured clinic observation session to .99 for "critical statements" during a home visit and .99 for "total praise" in a clinic visit. These results combine to indicate excellent interrater reliabilities, both from videotaped interactions and in-vivo observation in the natural environment.

Validity

Know groups validity was examined by comparing DPICS data in normal and conduct problem families. Results indicated that parents of conduct problem children made more critical statements and direct commands and gave fewer descriptive questions than comparison parents. Further, conduct problem children exhibited more whining, yelling, and noncompliance than normal children. A discriminant function analysis of DPICS data correctly classifies 100% of normal families, 85% of treatment families, and 94% of all families.

Advantages

Brief interaction tasks afford a comprehensive assessment of discrete child and parent behaviors as well as interactional sequences. Setup of the analogue environment requires nothing different from that available in a clinical setting for young children.

Limitations

The number of behavior categories makes it necessary to structure a number of observer training sessions in order to provide accurate measurement.

Primary Reference

Eyberg and Robinson (1983).

Scale Availability

S. M. Eyberg
Department of Medical Psychology
University of Oregon Health Sciences Center
Portland, OR 97201

Related References

Robinson and Eyberg (1981); Webster-Stratton (1985).

General Comments and Recommendations for Practitioners and Researchers

Although it does not seem that this coding system has been used to evaluate maltreating families, we would recommend an extension to this population. It is a well-researched, comprehensive, and psychometrically sound system based on a strong theoretical view of family interaction.

---

127. Exposure to Interadult Anger (EIA; Hennessey)

Development and Description of Assessment Method

This is a videotaped analogue measure accompanied by interview questions to examine children's responses to interadult anger. Videotaped interactions between adults and all procedures are based on the paradigm developed by Cummings (Davies & Cummings, 1994).

Target Population

Children from 6 to 11 years old with a history of physical abuse and exposure to interspousal aggression.

Format

In this assessment, eight different 1-minute segments of videotaped interactions between a male and female adult are presented. The following thematic contents are presented: nonverbal anger, nonverbal friendliness, verbal anger, verbal friendliness, hostile anger (verbal and physical), affection (verbal and physical), unresolved anger (friendliness turned into anger), and resolved anger (anger turned into friendliness).

A sample vignette for hostile anger is: "Begins with actors arguing about attending a party. Each one accuses the other of flirting at the last party. Ends with each one making verbal threats about ending the relationship and then pushing each other."

A sample vignette for resolved anger is: "Begins with actors sitting near each other talking about where to take the kids for the day. At first they disagree about where to go and insult each other's choices (30 seconds). They then compromise on where to go and end with both expressing excitement about the plans (30 seconds).

Administration and Scoring

Children are asked a series of questions following each segment:

- *"How Do the Actors Feel?"* Explores the child's ability to identify emotional expressions in adult interactions. The child may choose among a series of photographs expressing five different emotions.
- *"How Much Do They Feel That Way?"* Assesses the child's perceptions of the relative intensity of the emotional display. Ratings are on a 5-point, Likert-type scale from 1 = very little to 5 = a whole lot.
- *"How Did You Feel Watching Them?"* Photographs of emotional displays are again given.
- *"How Much Did You Feel That Way?"* Rated on the same 5-point, Likert-type scale of intensity.

Psychometric Evaluation

Norms
None reported.

Reliability
None reported.

Validity
Physically abused children ($N = 44$) responded with greater fear than nonabused children exposed only to interparental aggression ($N = 44$) across all forms of anger reactions. Further, relative to nonabused children, the physically abused children appeared particularly sensitive to whether the adult conflicts were resolved.

Advantages
The majority of previous work on children's responses to interadult anger focused on very young children. This method was used with older children, and it was simple to administer.

Limitations
The forced choice nature of responding to each question limits the child to selecting only one dominant emotion. Conflicts between strangers may not elicit responses similar to those of witnessing parents in actual conflict. Generalization to the natural environment may also be limited.

Primary Reference

Hennessey, Rabideau, Cicchetti, and Cummings (1994).

Scale Availability

Dante Cicchetti
Mt. Hope Family Center
187 Edinburgh St.
Rochester, NY 14608

Related References

Cummings, Vogel, Cummings, and El-Sheikh (1989).

General Comments and Recommendations for Practitioners and Researchers

The EIA was developed for a research study, and children were assessed in groups of 6 to 8 while they were in summer camp. It is not yet clear whether the procedure could be adapted for use in the clinical setting, but certainly the videotaped scenarios and standard set of questions seem generalizable.

---

128. Family Intake Coding System (FICS; Stormshak & Speltz)

Development and Description of Assessment Method

The FICS is an observational system designed to quantify occurrences of specific interaction behaviors during an initial unstructured clinical interview with a family.

Target Population

Two-parent families of young children with disruptive behavior problems.

Format

A clinical intake interview is conducted with the family. A trained clinician asks the parents to discuss primary behavioral concerns regarding the child and to provide detailed information about the behavior, its antecedents, and its consequences. Toys are provided for the child, who is invited to participate in the interview if he or she wishes. This interview is videotaped and edited to delete initial questions regarding the referral process. The first 10 minutes of each interview is coded by undergraduate raters blind to the status of the family (Stormshak, Speltz, DeKlyen, & Greenberg, 1997).

Administration and Scoring

The coding system consists of 21 codes categorized according to child, mother, father, or general codes. All codes are scored on an ordinal 5-point scale:

- *Child Codes:* Eight items that measured frequency, including,
  - Positive elicitation of mother and of father, defined as positive communication, proximity seeking, or contact with the parent.
  - Negative elicitation of mother and of father, defined as negative communication or behavior directed toward the parent (hitting, yelling at the parent).
  - Negative responses to parents discussion of problems.
  - Quality of affect toward mother and toward father, rated for each occurrence of elicitation (0 = anger/crying to 4 = happy/warm).
- *Parent Codes:* Items rated for the mother, and the same items rated for the father, including,
  - Validation of spouse, coded for any action that supported the partner's behavior, such as smiling, eye contact, or verbal agreement.
  - Invalidation of spouse, or verbal and nonverbal behaviors such as disagreeing, orienting away, contradicting, and domineering.
  - Affect, rated on an ordinal scale from 0 = negative affect, hostility, or depression to 4 = positive affect, happiness, and humor.
  - Engagement with the interview process, assessing the amount of talking and involvement during the interview process, including eye contact with and physical orientation toward the clinician.
  - General affect in the marital interaction, scored from 0 = hostile/depressed to 4 = positive/warm.
- *Global Codes:* Based on their observations, items focused on the

parents' attitude, affect, insight, and relationship with their child are rated by observers and are combined to form a global summary of the quality of the parent–child relationship, rated from 0 = very poor to 4 = excellent.

Psychometric Evaluation

Norms
None reported.

Reliability
Videotape coders were trained by the first author and were required to code five tapes with 80% accuracy to complete training. Weekly reliability checks were conducted on 22% of the videotapes. For each behavioral category, correlations between coders and the author of the coding system were conducted. Because of the ordinal nature of the rating scales, correlations were used to assess the reliability of the measure. Average correlations ranged from $r = .79$ (engagement of mother) to $r = 1.00$ (child negative elicitation of mother and father; child positive elicitation of father).

Validity
Clinic-referred families were distinguished from comparison families on 10 of 18 FICS categories, including every rating of affect during the interview. Clinic families displayed a pattern of greater child orientation toward mothers and more negative child interaction with fathers. Few correlations between child behavior during the interview and parents' ratings of child aggression on the Child Behavior Checklist (CBCL; Achenbach, 1991) were significant. Maternal ratings of aggression were inversely related to ratings of the child's positive affect toward the father ($r = .77$), and fathers' CBCL ratings were positively related to the child's negative elicitations of the father ($r = .25$).

Only 2 of 8 correlations between parent quality of interaction during interview and self-reported measures of marital satisfaction and parenting involvement were significant. The fathers' scores on the Locke-Wallace Marital Adjustment Test (Locke & Wallace, 1959) correlated at $r = .30$ with interview interaction, whereas their parent involvement scores correlated at $r = .26$ with the mothers' display of positive interaction during the interview.

Advantages

The FICS allows for initial assessment of family interactions during an unstructured clinical interview. The brief videotape from which behavior was quantified showed some relationships to more traditional self-report inventories.

Limitations

Caution must be used with extending results to single-parent families. Limiting the videotaped interview to 10 minutes for coding purposes might reflect infrequent child interaction or unusual behavior patterns caused by the novelty of the situation.

Primary Reference

Stormshak et al. (1997).

Scale Availability

Elizabeth Stormshak
Counseling Psychology Program
5251 University of Oregon
Eugene, OR 97403

Related References

Stormshak and Greenberg (1996).

General Comments and Recommendations for Practitioners and Researchers

The codes for parent behavior were derived from the Marital Interaction Coding System-Global (Weiss & Tolman, 1990). Perhaps the FICS categories could be restructured as a checklist to be completed by the clinician/therapist after each session, thus making it more applicable to the clinical setting. It would be very interesting to extend this to work with maltreating families to examine both the dynamics and affects of all family members.

129. Family Interaction Task (FIT; Madonna, Van Scoyle, & Jones)

Development and Description of Assessment Method

This assessment approach is based on family systems theory and re-search, which suggests that families can be ordered along an infinite linear continuum with respect to their competence. At the low end, Beavers (Lewis, Beavers, Gossett, & Phillips, 1976) described leaderless, invasive, chaotic families with diffuse boundaries between members. A midpoint on the continuum reflects families with rigid interpersonal control, frequent distancing, projection, and little intimacy. Finally, at the high end, families were characterized by autonomous individuals who share intimacy and closeness but respect separateness.

The Family Interaction Task is a videotaped assessment method in which families are presented with two structured tasks: (a) give their understanding of the problems that brought them into treatment, and (b) discuss among themselves the problems they had identified. Based on both family systems and developmental theory, families are rated on the stylistic quality of their interactions and their degree of competent family functioning.

Target Population

Sixty families from an agency serving families that have been involved in incest from a child psychiatric clinic.

Format

The family interactions are rated using the Beavers-Timberlawn Family Evaluation Scale (Beavers, Hampson, & Hulgus, 1985), which assesses family functioning on a continuum of competence. The following di-mensions are rated:

- *Structure of the Family:*
  - Overt power (how the family dealt with influence and domi-nance);
  - Parental coalitions (strength of husband–wife alliance);
  - Closeness (presence or absence of distinct boundaries and de-grees of interpersonal distance); and
  - Power structure (ease in determining family "pecking order").

- *Mythology:* Degree to which a family's concept of itself was congruent with the rater's appraisal of family behavior.
- *Goal-Directed Negotiation:* The effectiveness of family negotiations.
- *Autonomy:*
  - Communication of self-concept (degree to which the family nourished or discouraged clear communication of feelings and thoughts);
  - Responsibility (degree to which the family system reflected members' acceptance of responsibility for their own feelings, thoughts, and actions);
  - Invasiveness (extent to which the family system tolerated or encouraged family members speaking for one another); and
  - Permeability (degree to which the family system encouraged the acknowledgment of the stated feelings, thoughts, and behavior of its members).
- *Family Affect:*
  - Expressiveness (extent to which the open communication of affect was encouraged within the family system);
  - Mood and tone (ranging from warm and affectionate to cynical and hopeless);
  - Conflict (degree of family conflict and its effect on family functioning); and
  - Empathy (degree to which the family system encouraged members to be sensitive to each other's feelings and to communicate this awareness).

Administration and Scoring

In addition to rating the family members on each of the 13 interactional variables, the rater must make a global assessment of family functioning on a 10-point scale. The two directed tasks comprised a 15- to 20-minute segment of a 1-hour, semistructured family interview. A sample rating scale is shown in Exhibit 12.1.

Psychometric Evaluation

Norms
None reported.

Reliability
Interrater reliability coefficients were calculated via Spearman correlations and ranged from $r = .43$ to $r = .83$, with all being significant.

Exhibit 12.1

Sample Rating Scale.

A. *Expressiveness:* Rate the degree to which this family system is characterized by open expression of feelings.

1	1.5	2	2.5	3	3.5	4	4.5	5
Open, direct expression of feelings		Direct expression of feelings despite some hesitation		Obvious restriction in the expression of some feelings		Although some feelings are expressed there is masking of most feelings		No expression of feelings

B. *Mood and Tone:* Rate the feeling tone of this family's interaction.

1	1.5	2	2.5	3	3.5	4	4.5	5
Unusually warm, affectionate, humorous		Polite, without impressive warmth or affection		Overtly hostile		Depressed		Cynical, hopeless, pessimistic

---

Validity

The researchers reported good known groups validity in that there were significant differences on 12 of the 13 interactional variables between incest and nonincest families (only the power rating was nonsignificant). Scores were used to predict membership for each of the study's 60 families: 97% of incest families were correctly classified. For incest families, parents were rated as exhibiting dominance–submission patterns; parental coalitions were rated as weaker and less effective; boundaries were indistinct between individuals; family beliefs were incongruous; problem solving was inefficient, etc.

Advantages

Directed tasks are broad and flexible enough to be relevant for a variety of family constellations across varying ages of children. The FICS allows for an assessment of naturalistic family communication style.

Limitations

No clear information is provided about how to rate families using the Beavers-Timberlawn scale. For this study, the raters were not blind as to whether they were viewing an incest family.

Primary Reference

Madonna, Van Scoyle, and Jones (1991).

Related References

Beavers et al. (1985).

General Comments and Recommendations for Practitioners and Researchers

Training observers to rate family interactions across the five major dimensions would need to be quite comprehensive in that the FICS subscales are not behaviorally defined and require a global Likert-type response from the observer. A complementary 36-item self-report inventory has been developed and has been reported to correspond highly with judgments made by observers.

---

130. Family Interaction Task (FIT; Silber, Bermann, Handerson, & Lehman)

Development and Description of Assessment Method

This assessment method is based on family systems theory, which assumes that family behavior has "coherence," is patterned and repetitive, and that these patterns can be discovered by observers who view the family interaction.

A videotaped analogue assessment method is used to quantify verbal behaviors of family members engaged in discussion. Both initiation and response dimensions are quantified.

Target Population

Two-parent families where the father is the primary abuser and children are old enough to participate in discussions.

Format

Family members are asked to spend 10 minutes deciding on an area of shared disagreement. The family discussion is videotaped for later coding.

Administration and Scoring

The following categories of verbal behavior are coded by raters viewing the videotaped discussion:

- *Influence:* Information-sharing, guiding interaction, and control; and
- *Response:* Agreement, criticism, and protest.

Psychometric Evaluation

Norms
None reported.

Reliability
Interrater reliability was computed by comparing 200 remarks from transcripts coded by two independent coders. Kappa coefficients ranged from .87 to .98.

Validity
None reported.

Advantages
This brief, easy-to-arrange family discussion task is readily adaptable to the clinical setting.

Limitations
A lack of psychometric evaluation limits the conclusions that can be drawn from this analogue assessment.

Primary Reference

Silber, Bermann, Handerson, and Lehman (1993).

Scale Availability

Eric Bermann
Department of Psychology
University of Michigan
Ann Arbor, MI 48109

Related References

None available.

General Comments and Recommendations for Practitioners and Researchers

The antecedents to child maltreatment as well as the maintaining variables are clearly embedded in the context of the family system. These authors have extended observational procedure to this analogue situation to help identify these contextual patterns of family behavior.

---

131. Home Accident Prevention Inventory (HAPI; Tertinger, Greene, & Lutzker)

Development and Description of Assessment Method

This home observation system was designed to be administered by observers making home visits to families at risk for child abuse and neglect. The coding system focuses on safety hazards that are common sources of injury or death to young children that parents could eliminate. The inventory was developed to measure the nature and quantity of hazardous items accessible to children.

Hazards included in the HAPI were those identified on safety checklists provided by several organizations, including *Accident Facts*, published by the National Safety Council, as well as hazard analyses reports published by the U.S. Consumer Product Safety Commission.

Target Population

Home environments of families at risk for abuse and neglect of children from birth to 4 years of age.

Format

The HAPI consists of the following five broad categories of hazardous items, each with subcategories:

- Fire and electrical (matches, electric cords with exposed wires),
- Suffocation by ingested objects,
- Suffocation by mechanical means (cords, plastic bags),
- Firearms, and
- Poisoning by solids and liquids (pills, medicine, insecticides).

The hazardous items on the HAPI were considered dangerous only if they were accessible to the child. Thus, "inaccessible" was defined as items being locked up and childproof, having child-resistant closures, or being out of the child's reach.

Administration and Scoring

Observers were trained via a discussion of the definitions for each category, satisfactory completion of a quiz pertaining to HAPI, and practice with the HAPI in nontarget homes. During home visits to target families, observers walked through the dwelling and recorded the following information for each hazardous category:

- Location of each accessible hazard,
- Which and how many subcategories of hazards were present, and
- The absolute number of accessible hazards across subcategories.

Results were summarized in terms of total numbers of hazardous materials for each category during each home observation. Data were examined to determine which categories required intervention and if any safety accessories were needed.

Psychometric Evaluation

Norms
None available.

Reliability
Interrater reliability checks were conducted during baseline and throughout intervention conditions. Although data from each observer are presented visually across the multiple baseline design used with six families, percent agreement scores are not reported. Visual inspection indicates acceptable reliability.

Validity
Content reliability of the HAPI was established by five individuals associated with pediatric departments, safety commissions, and accident prevention research who completed a questionnaire containing 19 of the 26 hazardous situations in the HAPI. Using a scale ranging from 1 = no threat to 5 = very serious threat, the experts were asked to rate the situations and to suggest additional items. Mean ratings ranged from 4.0 (accessible firearms in home) to 2.8 (accessible petroleum or flammable products). Virtually all items were considered at least a moderate threat.

Advantages

The HAPI is a brief, easy-to-use checklist that will assist those making home visits for at-risk families. The process of determining content validity of items should be used by others developing family violence assessment methods. Items are directly related to clinical intervention needs to protect children.

Limitations

There are no comparison data available for normal families. Further, because this is an old measure, the items may need to be updated based on current safety checklists and hazardous items.

Primary Reference

Tertinger, Greene, and Lutzker (1984).

Scale Availability

Brandon Greene
Project 12 Ways
The Rehabilitation Institute
Southern Illinois University at Carbondale
Carbondale, IL 62901
(618) 536-7704
e-mail: bfgreene@siu.edu

Related References

None available.

General Comments and Recommendations for Practitioners and Researchers

The HAPI is one of the only reported assessment methods for a critical area of child neglect and potential injury. It would seem to be an easily applicable method for caseworkers to use and to document aspects of risk for young children, and it certainly adds to the overall assessment of the home environment.

132. Home Interaction Scoring System (HISS; Jacob, Tennenbaum, Bargiel, & Seilhamer)

Development and Description of Assessment Method

The HISS is an observational coding system that allows for the systematic description and quantification of naturalistic family interaction. The coding system provides for the assessment of three major dimensions of interpersonal interactions: affect expression and solidarity, skill performance and problem solving, and system dynamics such as reciprocity, rigidity, and predictability.

The authors based the development of the HISS on other observational coding procedures used in the study of family interaction. In order to create a more standardized yet naturalistic setting, a recording of dinnertime conversation was selected. An integration of behavioral and systems theory guided the development of coding categories that would capture the pattern of whole-family interactions. The authors relied heavily on the Marital Interaction Coding System (MICS; Hops, Wills, Patterson, & Weiss, 1972) and the Couples Interaction Scoring System (CISS; Gottman, 1979) used in the study of marital communication and on the Family Affect–Content Coding System (FACCS; Tennenbaum, 1980). The HISS was first used in 1982, and the authors reported in 1995 that more than 500 dinner times had been coded with this system.

Target Population

All family members participating during dinnertime family interactions. (The HISS is most applicable to families with children between the ages of 10 and 15 years.)

Format

The HISS coding system is used to describe all family behaviors in the temporal order in which they occur. A complete coding unit contains multiple information, including the speaker and target of the communication, the content code, the context of the message, and whether one of several types of overlapping speech occurred.

The coding system includes 27 behavioral content codes that describe a variety of affective and instrumental behaviors. The following are seven major codes, their subcategories, and sample items:

1. *Direct Positive Behaviors:*
   - PE: Positive evaluation statements such as "You really did that well";
   - AG: Agree statements such as "That's for sure";
   - AT: Attend statements such as "Yeah" or "Mm-hmm"
   - CO: Comply statements such as "Okay" in response to "Stop that";
   - HM: Humor; and
   - LA: Laugh.
2. *Direct Negative Behaviors:*
   - DN: Direct negative statements such as "You're a slob";
   - GN: General negative statements such as "You knew this would happen" said in an angry tone;
   - DG: Disagree statements such as "I don't think so"; and
   - NC: Noncomply statements such as "No" following a command.
3. *Conversational Positive Behaviors:* Statements where affect is not directed to the target of communication:
   - PS: Positive self-statements such as "I did well in class today";
   - EP: Evaluate other positive statements such as "She's a great teacher"; and
   - SP: Positive subjective talk such as "Their dog is so cute."
4. *Conversational Negative Behaviors:* Statements where affect is not directed to the target of communication:
   - NS: Negative self-statements such as "I feel terrible";
   - EN: Evaluate other negative statements such as "My boss is an idiot"; and
   - SN: Subjective negative talk such as "There's nothing good on TV."
5. *Commands:*
   - CM: Command statements such as "Pass the peas";
   - CR: Command repeat statements; and
   - CS: Command stop statements such as "Don't talk to your mother like that."
6. *Sharing Information:*
   - TE: Teaching statements such as "Banks are closed on Columbus Day";
   - IN: Instruct statements such as "First you put the lettuce on and then the tomato";

- SO: Solution statements such as "You can eat mine—I'll find something else for dessert"; and
- PP: Planning permission statements such as "Can I go with him?"
7. *General Conversation:*
- TA: General talk, including comments such as "It's raining";
- QT: Questions such as "Did anyone call me today?";
- NV: nonverbal communication; and
- UN: unintelligible conversation.

A coding hierarchy clarifies which codes to use when more than one applies to a particular response and which codes (AS, DG, CO, NC, CM, CR, and QT) must be multiply coded.

Administration and Scoring

Audiorecorded tapes of dinnertime family interactions are transcribed according to who is speaking and the temporal order of their responses (it takes 24–30 minutes to transcribe 1 minute of tape). The HISS is then applied by highly trained raters who simultaneously use the transcript and the audiotape, to which has been added audio signals every 30 seconds.

Following the rating of each tape using HISS codes, the data are entered into a series of software programs that calculate rater reliabilities and format the data.

Psychometric Evaluation

Norms
Not applicable.

Reliability
Interrater reliability was assessed for each content code by means of product–moment correlations for 20% of the dinnertime conversations reported in the 1995 study. Correlations for 59% of all codes were greater than $r = .80$, whereas 37% of the remaining codes were between $r = .60$ to .79. Occurrence percent agreement ratings were 75% for target of communication, 97% for speaker, and 91% for topic. Kappa coefficients determined for summary categories were as follows: .66 for direct negative, .62 for conversational negative, .75 for direct positive, .69 for conversational positive, .58 for teach/instruct, .87 for command, and .86 for general conversational. For the entire matrix of seven sum-

mary codes, the percent agreement score was 81%, whereas the kappa coefficient was .67. All of these analyses revealed high levels of interrater reliability.

Validity

Only descriptions of research studies aimed at providing validity data have been reported. In particular, the authors report their intentions to compare fixed versus random recording of family interactions, to examine distressed families (alcoholics and depressed) and nondistressed control groups to compare laboratory-based and naturalistic observation settings and to compare the HISS with other coding systems such as the Third Party Intervention Coding System (TPICSS; Vuchinich, 1987). These data have not yet been reported.

Advantages

This coding system makes use of the naturalistic setting of dinnertime conversation with some structure implied but not constrained by the laboratory setting. The coding system allows for a rich, sequential analysis of a multitude of family communication behaviors.

Limitations

This extremely complex coding system requires a tremendous amount of time in both the making of transcripts from audiotape, the coding of the transcripts, and the training of raters (60 hours). These requirements make this system applicable only to the research setting.

Primary Reference

Jacob, Tennenbaum, Bargiel, and Seilhamer (1995).

Scale Availability

Theodore Jacob
Family Research Center
Palo Alto VA Medical Center
3801 Miranda Ave.
Mail Code 151J
Palo Alto, CA 94304

Related References

None reported.

General Comments and Recommendations for Practitioners and Researchers

The HISS is one of the few systems focused on verbal family interaction for families with older children. Those working with at-risk or maltreating families could easily record dinnertime conversation and perhaps use overall judgment scores for each of the 27 behavioral codes. Further data on clinical families would be needed in order to interpret results; however, the data may be used to establish baseline patterns of family communication.

---

133. Home Observation for Measurement of the Environment (HOME; Bradley & Caldwell)

Development and Description of Assessment Method

The HOME is an environmental process measure designed to sample certain aspects of the quantity and quality of social, emotional, and cognitive support available to children within their home. It is used primarily in the assessment of child neglect.

The authors report that item development for the original Caldwell Home Inventory was guided by empirical evidence of the importance of certain types of experiences for nourishing the behavioral development of children. Based on observations of mother–child interactions, a 55-item home inventory was developed. Items requiring interview data about the child's experiences outside of the home were added later.

Target Population

Children between the ages of 3 and 6 years.

Format

Following direct observation of the child interacting with parents in the naturalistic home setting, the observer responds to 55 items divided into the following eight subscales:

1. Stimulation through toys, games, and reading material (11 items);
2. Language stimulation (7 items);
3. Physical environment is safe, clean, and conducive to development (7 items);

4. Pride, affection, and warmth (7 items);
5. Stimulation of academic behavior (5 items);
6. Modeling and encouraging of social maturity (5 items);
7. Variety of stimulation (8 items); and
8. Physical punishment (4 items).

Sample items include:

- "Child is permitted to hit parents without reprisal,"
- "Mother usually responds verbally to child's talking,"
- "All visible rooms are reasonably clean and minimally cluttered,"
- "Child is encouraged to learn the alphabet," and
- "Mother neither slaps nor spanks child during visit."

Administration and Scoring

Length of observation varies according to the environmental context. The HOME is administered in the home when the child is present and awake; however, informality is stressed. Observers note a simple yes or no based on either direct observation of actual transactions between the major caregiver and the child or an assessment of the natural setting itself.

Psychometric Evaluation

Norms
None reported.

Reliability
The Kuder–Richardson 20 formula was used to examine internal consistency. Reliabilities ranged from .53 to .83 for the subscales and was .93 for the total score.

Temporal stability was examined for 33 of the 117 families, with an interval of 1.5 years (homes of 3-year-olds were revisited when they were 4.5 years of age). These coefficients ranged from .05 to .70.

Validity
Correlations with several socioeconomic-status variables indicated low correlations between the rating scale and mother/father occupation and moderate correlations between maternal/paternal education and crowding with the stimulation and physical environment subscales.

Advantages

The HOME is an easy-to-use screening device for developmental assessment of appropriate environmental variables for young children. It is widely used by both clinicians and researchers.

Limitations

The training of raters is not described. The binary response format may obscure important frequency or intensity information. The observation session itself is not well structured.

Primary Reference

Bradley and Caldwell (1979).

Scale Availability

Robert H. Bradley
University of Arkansas
Center for Research on Teaching and Learning
Little Rock, AR 72203

Related References

Bradley (1993); Harrington, Dubowitz, Black, and Binda (1995).

General Comments and Recommendations for Practitioners and Researchers

Although the use of nonparticipant observers results in reactivity for those in the natural setting, this type of in-vivo assessment is critical for gathering information about the child's environment. Items may need to be updated vis-à-vis enriched home environments in the twenty-first century.

---

134. Interaction Behavior Code (IBC; Prinz & Kent)

Development and Description of Assessment Method

The IBC is a global–inferential behavioral coding system used to assess parent–adolescent communication. Its procedure relies on multiple ratings of audiotaped family interaction.

The global rating system for the assessment of parent–adolescent communication was developed in response to the time-insensitive nature of sequential and interval coding systems and the need for a system requiring less observer training.

Target Population

Parents and adolescents in families experiencing communication and problem-solving difficulties. It is suggested for families presenting with high levels of interpersonal conflict.

Format

In this assessment, family members are asked to select an issue that they disagree about and then to engage in a discussion concerning the selected issue. In some investigations, parents and adolescents rated frequency and intensity of issues on a standard checklist, and the highest intensity by frequency issue was selected.

The IBC consists of 32 categories of positive and negative verbal behaviors such as negative exaggeration, yelling, making suggestions, compromise, threatening, mind-reading, sarcasm, or acquiescence. Each category is accompanied by a brief definition. For example:

- *Name-Calling:* Applying a name to the other person that connotes something negative; must be a noun.
- *Praising, Complimenting:* Expressing approval of the other person; to command, say something positive about the other.
- *Anger:* To be annoyed, disgusted, or enraged with the other person.
- *Criticism:* Finding fault with the other person's actions, statements, or beliefs.
- *Willingness to Listen:* Paying attention to what the other has to say; showing interest with questions and acknowledgments.

Four additional categories help to code the overall quality of the dyadic or triadic interaction:

1. Outcome, or the degree of resolution of the problems being discussed;
2. Putting each other down, or the degree of belittlement and criticism;
3. Friendliness; and
4. Effectiveness of the solution.

Administration and Scoring

The IBC relies on the consensus of several raters who listen to and rate the audiotapes of a family's interaction and discussion. A structured rating form with separate columns for fathers, mothers, sons, or daughters is provided to each of the observers/raters who listen to the tape. They then record whether each of 5 positive and 17 negative behaviors was present or absent in the discussion. "Yes" items are given a 1-point value, and "No" items are given a zero value. They then rate two additional positive and seven negative behaviors on a 3-point scale: 0 = "no," .5 = "a little," and 1 = "a lot." Points are totaled separately for positive and negative items and are then divided by the total number of positive and negative items, respectively. This yields a composite positive and negative interaction score for each family member.

The four global items reflecting the quality of the interaction are rated on 4-point, Likert-type scales, and the means for the raters are used as the dependent measure. The authors indicate that observers/raters require only 2 hours of training with the rating criteria and sample audiotapes.

Psychometric Evaluation

Norms

None reported.

Reliability

Separate investigations of the IBC have reported consistently high interobserver agreement using the Spearman-Brown correction for multiple raters. Agreement figures ranging from .83 to .97 are based on means of four raters; agreement between any two raters would be much lower.

Validity

Several clinical investigations have shown behavior change in various communication categories as a result of behavioral interventions. This supports the efficacy of the IBC as a measurement of treatment outcome. Several authors (see Robin & Foster, 1989) have examined the relationship of the IBC with a complex frequency-based coding system based on the Marital Interaction Coding System (MICS; Weiss & Summers, 1983) but modified for analysis of parent–adolescent patterns of communication. Correlations between the codes ranged from .52 to .82, indicating good convergent validity.

Advantages

The IBC rating form is easy to complete because it includes columns for each family member as well as individual item definitions. The system requires less rater/observer training than traditional coding systems. Perhaps the rating form could simply be administered by the clinician from an audiotape of a family discussion, thereby providing a simple, unobtrusive interaction assessment that is portable to the clinical setting.

Limitations

The authors fail to give guidelines on the minimum and maximum length of the family discussion. With such global, inferential categories, it would seem likely that each family member could exhibit each category eventually during a discussion, and such a rating form in its Yes/No format might not be sensitive to therapeutic change. Perhaps raters should limit the session to a 10- to 15-minute discussion task and suggest that raters rate a family member for a predominant pattern.

The IBC does not allow for sequential coding so that dominant patterns of family communication that may be indicative of particular dysfunctional structures (triangles, coalitions, splits) cannot be assessed.

Primary Reference

Prinz and Kent (1978).

Scale Availability

In Robin and Foster (1989).

Related References

Robin, Koepke, and Moye (1990).

General Comments and Recommendations for Practitioners and Researchers

The IBC seems well-suited for adaptation to a clinical setting; however, a 32-category rating system might prove overwhelming. It would be interesting to compare the responses of maltreating families to those of other families.

135. Laboratory Family Interaction Task (LFIT; Kavanagh, Youngblade, Reid, & Fagot)

Development and Description of Assessment Method

An analogue assessment of family interaction that requires parents and children to play together in a laboratory playroom and then clean up, the LFIT was developed as part of a longitudinal study of family processes conducted at the University of Oregon Child Research Laboratory.

Target Population

Families with children between the ages of 6 and 7 years old. In the initial study, 22 families were court-referred for treatment of physical child abuse.

Format

Parents and their children are led to a laboratory playroom containing a standard set of play materials (blocks, Legos, board games, cards, and other materials that promote interactive play). The experimenter returns in 6 to 7 minutes and informs the family that it is time to clean up. During free play and cleanup, the family is videotaped through a one-way mirror. Each family video, about 12 minutes long, is then coded by at least one coder.

Administration and Scoring

The LFIT (Fagot, 1984) used to quantify family interaction behavior had five components:

1. *Context Code:* This refers to what the child is doing or paying attention to, or what is happening in the vicinity. Included are 14 possible categories, such as large and small motor activities, dolls, fantasy play, eat, or receive care.
2. *Interactive Code:* There are 15 possible categories here that refer to the child's interactive behavior, including use language, ask questions, demand attention, try to take object, and verbal aggressions.
3. *Recipients:* These categories refer to whom the interaction is directed and

4. *Reactors:* These categories refer to who reacts to the child's interactive behavior. (The eight possible categories include no one, female adult, mixed adults and children, boy, or boys.)

5. *Reaction Code:* There are 14 possible categories here that refer to how the reactor responds, including directive, positive physical, verbal interaction, talk, and child is ignored.

Each coding sequence begins with the child behavior. The coding is done continuously so that all of the subcoders are strung together to form one 8-digit code that describes what is happening. Data collection was completed on an OS-3 microcomputer data bank. Each time a new child behavior is initiated, a new entry is required.

Psychometric Evaluation

Norms
None reported.

Reliability
In this study, 15 of the 45 videotapes were randomly selected to be coded by two coders. Before beginning the coding of tapes, each coder had trained to 94% agreement of each of the subcodes and to 89% agreement on the 8-digit code. Time in agreement was calculated by comparing two records and dividing the number of seconds in which they had identical entries by the total number of seconds. The item-by-item agreement scores ranged from 92% agreement on the 8-digit code to 97% agreement on context. Kappas were also computed and were all above .65.

Validity
Results from this comparative study support the known groups validity of the LFIT. Abusive parents spent significantly less time (49.8%) in positive parenting acts than control parents (64.9%) and spent more time in onlooker and nonattending tasks. Further, children from abusive families spent significantly less time in positive conversation than children from control families.

Advantages
The LFIT enables the coding of sequences of behaviors, which more fully captures the reciprocal nature of parent–child as well as parent–parent and child–child interactions.

Limitations

The research laboratory playroom is difficult to duplicate in a clinical setting. The complex behavioral coding system would require extensive training to obtain reliable recordings. The costly data collection system is not easily transferable to the clinical setting.

Primary Reference

Kavanagh, Youngblade, Reid, and Fagot (1988).

Scale Availability

> Beverly I. Fagot
> Oregon Social Learning Center
> 207 East 5th Ave., Suite 202
> Eugene, OR 97401

Related References

Fagot (1984, 1992).

General Comments and Recommendations for Practitioners and Researchers

Although not easily adapted to the clinical setting, the use of online data collection for behavioral coding may be an area of future emphasis for assessments made in a clinical setting. Computer-generated analysis of interactive sequences may assist clinicians in obtaining methodologically sound family assessments.

---

136. Mother–Child Interaction Task (MCIT; Shipman & Zeman)

Development and Description of Assessment Method

The MCIT is based on past research on emotional patterns between mothers and their children (Denham, Zoller, & Couchoud, 1994) and pilot testing.

This structured task analogue assessment was designed to examine verbal interactions about emotion-eliciting situations between mothers and children. Responses related to emotional understanding skills of happy, sad, anger, and fear situations were included.

Target Population

Mothers and their children ages 6 to 12 years old who are at risk for child maltreatment.

Format

Following a brief rapport-building period, observers present in the home environment are given instructions.

Children were instructed to "Talk with your mother about a time you felt _____ (emotion)," with emotion type (happy, sad, fearful, angry) administered in random order. Mothers were told to interact with their child as they would if their child started to tell them about the situations in the context of a typical day.

Administration and Scoring

The discussion was tape-recorded and transcribed in order to quantify each conversational response. Categories coded for the presence or absence responses reflective of emotional understanding included causes and consequences of emotion, constructive strategies for coping with emotionally arousing situations, questions that encourage emotional discussion, and mother's reflective or elaborative statements about emotional experience. Each verbal response is scored as either 1 (discussion reflective of emotional understanding) or 0 (absence of emotional understanding).

Total scores were obtained by summing the number of conversational turns for both mother and child separately. The situations generated by the children for each emotion were coded to determine the types of situations children associated with specific emotional experiences. A content analysis revealed nine categories of situations, including interpersonal conflict, loss, activity, activity thwarted, and instrumental positive.

Psychometric Evaluation

Norms
None reported.

Reliability
Reliability calculations were conducted on 30% of the 44 dyad protocols. Interrater reliability for this study was calculated using kappa co-

efficients and resulted in the following: .83 for mothers' discussion reflecting emotional understanding.

Validity

Known groups validity was examined by comparing results between maltreating ($n = 22$) and nonmaltreating ($n = 22$) mother–child discussion tapes. Results indicated that maltreating mothers engaged in less emotional discussion ($F(1,40) = 9.70$, $p < .01$). However, chi-square analyses revealed no significant differences between child groups in the types of situations discussed. For negative affect situations of anger and sadness, all children expressed interpersonal conflict and loss of relationship or object most frequently. Results from the MCIT were compared to the Expectations of Maternal Support Interview (EMSI; Zeman & Shipman, 1996) and the Emotional Understanding Interview (EUI; Cassidy, Parke, Butkousky, & Braungart, 1992), which were administered independently. A significant correlation between children's expectations concerning either a supportive or nonsupportive response to hypothetical vignettes and their emotional understanding reflected on the MCIT ($r = .44$, $p < .01$). Finally, there was a significant positive relation between the frequency of maternal discussion reflective of emotional understanding coded on the MCIT and children's performance on the five scales of the EUI ($r = .42$, $p < .05$).

Advantages

The MCIT is a simple-to-implement discussion task that can be conducted in the natural environment with a tape recorder. It taps into the emotional understandings within the context of the parent–child relationship, which may reflect the child's socioemotional development.

Limitations

Coding each discrete verbal response on a verbatim transcript is time-consuming.

Primary Reference

Shipman and Zeman (1999).

Scale Availability

Kimberly Shipman
Department of Psychology

University of Georgia
Athens, GA 30602-3013

Related References

Cassidy et al. (1992).

General Comments and Suggestions for Practitioners and Researchers

The MCIT is an interesting approach to the assessment of the emotional climate between mother and child. Children's abilities to understand causes and consequences of emotions and to generate appropriate responses to emotional experiences of self and others are known to be influenced by their relationships with caretakers. Much work is still needed concerning areas of deficit in emotional understanding and remediation of these deficits; perhaps this coding system will prove helpful.

---

137. Mother–Son Interaction Task (MSIT; Mahoney, Boggio, & Jouriles)

Development and Description of Assessment Method

The MSIT is an analogue process that was developed in order to study the effects of verbal marital conflict on subsequent interactions between mothers and their sons. Mothers are first exposed to either a conflictual or nonconflictual discussion with their husbands and then are asked to assist their sons in the cleanup of a mess in the clinic playroom. Interactions are coded using direct observation methods.

Target Population

Mothers and their 4- to 10-year-old sons. (The primary reference included 26 mothers and their clinic-referred, 4- to 10-year-old sons.)

Format

While mothers are involved in a separate marital discussions, a standard "mess" is created in a playroom while a research assistant interacts with the son. Then mothers are told to supervise their son's compliance to a 10-minute session to (a) get the son to pick up approximately 400 plastic toy pieces and sort them into 3 boxes by color and (b) help the son clean up the playroom by doing other tasks such as picking up crayons and blocks. Mothers were instructed not to help their sons pick up or sort pieces.

In the primary reference, couples rank-ordered a list of 17 topics (using a 5-point, Likert-type scale) according to likelihood of an argument occurring. Topics were chosen from the top three conflict or non-conflict topics, depending on the experimental condition to which the family was assigned.

Administration and Scoring

Six categories of behavior are coded in continuous 6-second intervals using an internal recording method. The coding categories are:

- *Approval statements:* Maternal statements that reflect positive evaluation of attributes, behaviors, or products;
- *Disapproval statements:* Negative maternal evaluation, including threats of punishment;
- *Empathic statements:* Verbalizations that foster an empathic, supportive climate between mother and son (paraphrasing the child's distress about the task, encouragements, appropriate explanations);
- *Vague or confusing commands:* Not clearly specifying child behavior to be initiated or modified;
- *General conversation:* Attempts to engage sons in conversation not related to cleaning up the room; and
- *Child noncompliance:* Includes a clear command by the mother and the child's failure to respond in a desired manner for 6 seconds.

Following the cleanup session, mothers view a videotape of their marital interaction while providing a continuous self-report of affect that they experienced. Mothers move a computer mouse along a rating scale from "very negative" to "very positive" representing a 9-point Likert scale.

Psychometric Evaluation

Norms

None reported.

Reliability

Interobserver agreement data were collected by an independent reliability checker on 25% of the interactions. Kappa coefficients indicated excellent reliability; coefficients ranged from .85 for empathic statements to .95 for general conversation and child noncompliance.

Validity

Results from this assessment indicated that mothers who experienced marital conflict delivered significantly more empathic statements to their sons. They acknowledged their son's distress and provided more explanations and encouragement.

Advantages

The MSIT is an interesting approach to studying the link between marital discord and parent–child interactions.

Limitations

It would be difficult to provide a feasible rationale that would succeed in gaining compliance with assessment tasks in a clinical setting. The process may seem too artificial to yield an approximation of real-life circumstances. Analogue marital conflict cannot be assumed to replicate what goes on in the natural environment. Unfortunately, the authors did not examine father–son interactions subsequent to the marital conflict.

Primary Reference

Mahoney, Boggio, and Jouriles (1996).

Scale Availability

Annette Mahoney
Department of Psychology
Bowling Green State University
Bowling Green, OH 43403

Related References

None available.

General Comments and Recommendations for Practitioners and Researchers

There is limited generalizability to child witnesses of domestic conflict in that most child witnesses are actually exposed to the marital dispute occurring in the home and may be more reactive than the boys in this research study. However, the MSIT may be a useful way to help mothers analyze the spillover reactions toward their children. Data from this study helps to support hypotheses that poor marital functioning is associated with increases in mothers' sensitivity, attention, and facilitative behaviors toward their children.

138. Observational Coding System for Triadic Interaction (OCSTI; Gordis, Margolin, & John)

Development and Description of Assessment Method

The OCSTI is an analogue assessment of a family discussion task that includes interparental, parent–child, and child behaviors and that incorporates an evaluation of family members' behaviors, affect, and verbal content.

The development of this observational coding system was based on the assessment of parent–child coercion patterns (Patterson, 1982) and on theories of marital interaction (Gottman, 1979).

Target Population

Two-parent families with a child between 9 and 13 years of age.

Format

In this assessment, the assessor selects a family conflict topic from the Potential Family Conflict Questionnaire (Margolin, 1992) and interviews the parents about the two behavioral issues selected as the ones associated with the strongest feelings. Following a 12-minute parent discussion of the topics, the assessor states:

> Now we are going to bring (child's name) in and the three of you will have a snack. While you eat, we would like you to spend the next 10 minutes having a family discussion about the two topics you have just discussed with one another. We would like you to discuss

these issues in the same way that you would if we weren't around. We will leave it up to you to present these topics to your child.

The parents can then decide which particular aspects of the issues they are comfortable with discussing.

The general parent behavior code of parent hostility is categorized according to the following sample items:

- *Frustration:* This included expressions of negative affect in the form of anger, contempt, or frustration. An example is "Don't be so stupid" (stated in a negative tone of voice).
- *Self-Defense:* This included argumentative or defensive statements. An example is "See, I told you he does. I told you."
- *Blame:* This is defined as putting the responsibility of blame on another person. An example is "I don't let him watch television. You are the one who always lets him watch when he is not supposed to."

The general child behavior code includes the following subcategories:

- *Withdrawal:* This is scored when the child makes him or herself inaccessible to the other participants in some way. Examples include the child looking down and making no eye contact.
- *Anxiety:* This is scored when the child acts uncomfortable, anxious, or embarrassed. An example is the child giggling nervously.
- *Distraction:* This is scored when the child engages in irrelevant behavior that draws attention away from the discussion. An example would be when the child shoots drink in the air through a straw by squeezing the drink box.

Administration and Scoring

Family members participated in the three-person videotaped discussion for 10 minutes, after the parents had discussed child-related topics alone for 12 minutes. The authors indicate that the format and dynamic of a triadic discussion necessitated developing a coding system designed to draw inferences about relationships between behaviors, affect, and verbal content of family participants. For example, in judging frustration-contempt, coders are directed to take into account voice tone, content, and nonverbal behavior, or in judging distraction to take into account irrelevant verbal content as well as silly behavior exhibited by the child. Scores for the codes are the number of minutes during which a participant exhibited a certain behavior. Mean scores were taken across codes and across parents to create three main scores: interparental hostility, parent–child hostility, and child behaviors. Coders were instructed to view each videotaped family discussion four times. The first time, the entire 10-minute tape was viewed. Each of the next three times, the videotape was viewed minute by minute for coding behavior of each family member.

Psychometric Evaluation

Norms
None reported.

Reliability
Each videotaped interaction was coded by two research assistants. Reliabilities between them were calculated as intraclass correlation coefficients and ranged from $r = .70$ for distraction and withdrawal (child behavior categories) to $r = .92$ for interparental hostility.

Validity
Intercorrelations between the three child behavior codes were examined. For girls, anxiety was highly correlated with both withdrawal ($r = .31$) and distraction ($r = .42$), whereas for boys the only significant correlation was between anxiety and distraction ($r = .48$). To determine convergent validity, correlations between adult-reported physical marital aggression, observed interparental hostility, observed parent–child hostility, and observed child behavior during the discussion task were examined. For boys ($n = 45$), marital aggression was significantly correlated with all three child behavior codes ($r = .47$ for withdrawal, $r = .39$ for anxiety, and $r = .40$ for distraction). For girls ($n = 45$), however, marital aggression was only related to the child category of distraction ($r = .34$). Further, observed parent–child hostility was related to the child category of anxiety ($r = .29$) only for boys. Observed interparental hostility was not related to any of the child behavior categories.

Advantages
The OCSTI allows for quantification of family interaction behaviors and for judgments concerning more quantitative variables, such as affect or intent. It is a brief and relevant task for high-risk families.

Limitations

The complicated coding system requires coders to view each family discussion numerous times. Generalization from this controlled, semi-public, and safe discussion may not correspond to family interaction in the natural environment.

Primary Reference

Gordis et al. (1997).

Scale Availability

Elana B. Gordis
Department of Psychology
University of Southern California
Los Angeles, CA 90089-1061

Related References

None available.

General Comments and Recommendations for Practitioners and Researchers

The OCSTI provides an interesting assessment of areas of potential conflict for high-risk or maltreating families. The presence of the child in the interaction allows for an analogue assessment of the parent as well as of the child's reaction in a context that could involve them. Reliance on coding of primarily verbal behavior may limit this assessment vis-à-vis families in which discussion or problem-solving may be a novel approach.

---

139. Psychological Maltreatment Scales (PMS; Brassard, Hart, & Hardy)

Development and Description of Assessment Method

An observational coding method was developed to assess psychological maltreatment in either live or videotaped mother–child interactions.

The authors of the PMS focused on observation of live interactions because (a) maltreating mothers lack the emotional and cognitive resources required to accurately respond on self-report inventories, (b) analysis of mother–child interactions have high predictive validity in developmental research, and (c) live interaction provides clinically relevant material that can facilitate intervention. The four distinct subtypes of psychological maltreatment were identified via a multidimensional scaling process by experts in the field.

Target Population

Parents of children ages 5 to 9 years.

Format

The PMS consists of four scales related to psychological abuse and neglect:

1. *Spurning:* Defined as verbal battering that combines rejection and hostile degradation. ("Are you tired and frustrated already?").
2. *Terrorizing:* Includes threatening to physically hurt, kill, or abandon the child. ("You'd better behave.").
3. *Corrupting/Exploiting:* Defined as modeling antisocial acts, unrealistic roles, or condoning deviance ("It doesn't matter how we do it, just get it done.").
4. *Denying Emotional Responsiveness:* Includes ignoring the child's attempts to interact.

The PMS also contains nine scales that assess prosocial parenting. These are:

1. Mother's quality of instruction,
2. Mother's supportive presence,
3. Mother's respect for child autonomy,
4. Touching,
5. Mother's strategies for maintaining task involvement,
6. Mother's emotional response to the task,
7. Mother's mental status,
8. Experience of mutual pleasure, and
9. Body harmonies.

Administration and Scoring

Parents and children interact during 15-minute sessions that are videotaped and later coded. Parents are directed to engage their child in tasks, including playing board games and making a paper construction project.

Psychometric Evaluation

Norms
None reported.

Reliability
The authors report interrater reliability correlations ranging from $r = .72$ to $r = .94$. Test–retest reliability was calculated for a sample of 20 mothers across a 2-week interval. Percent agreements ranged from 46% (denying) to 100% (terrorizing). Mothers in the sample were nonmaltreating, however.

Validity
A factor analysis yielded the following three main factors:

1. Facilitation of social and cognitive development,
2. Psychological abuse, and
3. Quality of emotional support.

The PMS correctly classified 82% of cases of maltreating parents.

Advantages
The PMS' observational measures were superior to maternal self-report measures in correct classification of abusive parents. This is an extremely important category of child abuse that has received little attention to date.

Limitations
Extensive training of raters is required given the observational categories and definitions, which require frequent inferential judgments. Psychometric development of the PMS is still needed.

Primary Reference

Brassard, Hart, and Hardy (1993).

Scale Availability

Marla R. Brassard
School and Counseling Psychology Program

University of Massachusetts
Amherst, MS 01003

Related References

None available.

General Comments and Recommendations for Practitioners and Researchers

Use of rating scales to quantify data obtained from videotaped mother–child interactions may be the most practical approach to assessment in the clinical setting. Although the accuracy of data on discrete behavioral responses may be compromised, clinicians are more likely to use global rating scales than complex direct observational coding systems.

---

140. Response-Class Matrix (RCM; Mash, Johnston, & Kovitz)

Development and Description of Assessment Method

The RCM is an observational coding system developed for quantifying interaction behaviors of parents and children during both free play and task situations.

Target Population

Parents and their young children.

Format

The general form of the recording procedure uses two matrices—one in which the behaviors of a member of the dyad are designated as antecedents and the behaviors of the other member are designated as consequences; and the other in which the antecedent–consequence relationship is reversed.

Exhibit 12.2 shows a matrix of one form of the recording procedure that has been used extensively in observing mother–child interactions. Six child behaviors are given in the vertical column, and six parent behaviors are given in the horizontal column. For the companion matrix (not shown), the column contents would be reversed.

Exhibit 12.2

Response-class matrix.

MOTHER'S CONSEQUENCES

Child's antecedent	Directiveness	Question	Praise	Negative	Interaction	No response
Compliance						
Independent Play						
Question						
Negative/Noncompliant						
Interaction						
No response						

Administration and Scoring

Using a time-sampling procedure, two recorders each make a single mark in one of the matrix cells every 10 seconds, recording only the first scorable behavior unit to occur during that interval. The two matrices taken together provide a three-term contingency record in that it is possible to look at the events that precede a behavior, the behavior, and the events that follow. Each category is summed in terms of percent occurrence across the total number of intervals observed.

Psychometric Evaluation

Norms
None reported.

Reliability
Interobserver agreements using the 6 × 6 matrices were calculated as the number of agreements/sum of agreements plus disagreements. The percent agreements have ranged from 78% to 96% following 4 to 6 hours of observer training.

Validity
In a comparison of preschool abused ($N = 18$) and nonabused ($N = 18$) children, there were no statistically significant differences in dyadic interactions during structured laboratory observations.

Advantages

The RCM allows for the quantification of patterns of social interaction between members of any adult–child dyad and an estimate of both antecedent and consequent stimulus control.

Limitations

A significant amount of training and coding experience is required to get reliable ratings. Psychometric data regarding validity is extremely limited.

Primary Reference

Mash, Johnston, and Kovitz (1983).

Scale Availability

> Eric J. Mash
> Department of Psychology
> University of Calgary
> Alberta, Canada T2N IN4

Related References

Mash, Terdal, and Anderson (1973).

General Comments and Recommendations for Practitioners and Researchers

The RCM provides an easy-to-administer and visually oriented screening of mother–child interactions that will help develop a functional analysis of specific behaviors to target for intervention.

---

141. Sibling Conflict Resolution Scale (SCRS; Roberts)

Development and Description of Assessment Method

This assessment scale was designed to assess the overt reactions of pre-adolescent children to scripted sibling conflicts in a behavioral analogue format. The method is an extended interaction role-play test of sibling conflict resolution.

In order to develop a relevant list of conflict scenarios, parents in an initial study by the author ($N = 81$) completed a questionnaire. Each parent (a) rated the frequency of the proposed conflict situations (including contents of testing, improper toy possession, noncompliance, and aggressive threat), (b) nominated socially competent reactions, (c) rated proposed conflict resolution skills, and (d) nominated additional conflict situations.

Target Population

Young children between the ages of 3 and 10 years of age who have siblings.

Format

In the SCRS, each of 13 conflict scenarios is presented to the target child by a narrator and actor. The narrator describes the sibling conflict and prompts the child to "show me what you would do or say." The actor holds a large "sibling doll" that presents the stimuli. All narrator and doll responses are standardized. The sibling doll provides three verbal prompts to the target child. The following conflict situations are represented in the scenarios:

- Sibling plays with shareable household toy set.
- Sibling requests to play with shareable toys.
- Sibling emits blatant error.
- Child wants to play with sibling's personal toy.
- Sibling breaks household rule.
- Sibling makes unreasonable request.
- Simultaneous interest in unshareable activity or material.
- Sibling breaks game rule.
- Sibling uses toy or room without permission.
- Sibling disobeys request to play.
- Sibling disobeys request to do required work.
- Sibling teases.
- Sibling threatens aggression.

The following is a sample conflict scenario:

"This time you get to play with the Big Wheel. . . . Let's pretend that the Big Wheel belongs to everyone in your family. . . . This time you get the Big Wheel first and you just started to play with it, just this minute . . . (sibling's name) wants to ride, too. Show me what you would say and do."

Administration and Scoring

The extended role-play measure requires 45 to 60 minutes to complete. The scenarios are videotaped and are later coded according to the following scale: 5 = sophisticated verbal coping, 4 = verbal coping, 3 = neutral, 2 = verbal coercion, 1 = motoric coercion. These basic categories are further defined by the following: 5 = indirect request plus reason, verbal assertion, ignore; 4 = indirect request only, reasons only, incomplete verbal assertion, partial ignore; 3 = runs away, does nothing, other verbalizations; 2 = negative evaluation, bossy talk, threat, cry, yell, tease, argue, involves adult; and 1 = aggression, motoric coercion. Each scenario provides response examples for coding in that context. The manual for the SCRS provides detailed operational definitions for each of the behaviors included in the coding system.

Psychometric Evaluation

Norms
None reported.

Reliability
In a small psychometric study, 30 nonclinic children between the ages of 3 and 10 years completed the SCRS. The reliability coefficient between coders of the videotape was $r = .96$. Internal consistency was examined and revealed an alpha coefficient of .84, whereas test–retest reliability with a 1-week interval was .81.

Validity
None reported.

Advantages
The SCRS is a creative and playful way to allow extended natural responding to a variety of typical sibling conflicts. It attempts to assess an often overlooked family dyad typically fraught with conflict and aggression.

Limitations
The SCRS relies on the target child's ability to "pretend" that the scenarios are approximations to actual sibling interactions. This may prove difficult for young children, even though many of the scenarios seem more appropriate for younger children. It consists of a relatively long process in which older children perform better than younger children.

This may simply reflect the developmental nature of conflict resolution skills and not actual differences between target group regarding reactions to sibling conflict.

Primary Reference

Roberts, Arnold, and Magnum (1992).

Scale Availability

M. Roberts
Psychology Department
Idaho State University
921 South Ave.
Pocatello, ID 83209

Related References

None available.

General Comments and Recommendations for Practitioners and Researchers

Unfortunately, little additional research and use of this scale could be located. It would be beneficial to examine this analogue-type assessment along with other measures of sibling relationships recently developed in families experiencing family violence.

142. Standardized Observation Codes (SOCIII; Cerezo, Keesler, Dunn, & Wahler)

Development and Description of Assessment Method

The SOCIII focuses on the study of family interaction in the natural home setting. The system permits continuous coding of interactions of mother and child in a sequential fashion. Maternal behaviors, child behaviors, and mother–child interaction sequences are coded.

The SOCIII was developed in 1986 for research examining coercive family processes. Since then, it has been used extensively, and there are a substantial number of studies supporting the reliability and validity of the coding system. Often the system adds an interactor code in addition to the behavior codes, which allows for observations of up to six different family members.

Target Population

Mothers and their elementary-school-age children.

Format

Observation of family interactions is conducted during 60-minute sessions in the home. The family members are told to behave as usual, with a few minimal guidelines established in order to obtain desired information. It is suggested that family activity should be limited to two rooms, that all family members should be present with the television turned off, and phone calls should be made short. Interaction between the family members and the observer is not allowed.

The SOCIII code includes the following categories:

- *Maternal Behavior:*
  - Neutral social approach, which reflected neutral approach behavior of the mother toward her child;
  - Neutral instruction, which reflected approach responses that had an instructional character with a neutral valence;
  - Positive response, which reflected maternal approaches and instructions with a positive valence; and
  - Aversive response, which reflected negative maternal approaches or aversive instructions.
- *Child Behavior:*
  - Interactional prosocial behavior, which included all child behaviors considered to have a positive or neutral valence; specific subcategories were neutral behavior, positive behavior, neutral obedience, positive obedience, and positive instruction;
  - Noninteractional prosocial behavior, which reflected the two subcategories of play and work;
  - Interactional deviant behavior, which reflected categories of child behavior considered deviant, including negative approach, neutral opposition, negative opposition, and negative instruction; and
  - Noninteractional deviant behavior, which reflected child behaviors such as complaints, crying, and rule violation.

- *Mother–Child Interaction Behavior:*
  - Maternal response to child prosocial behavior, which reflected responses that were inappropriate because of their valence or content or were not contingent with the child's prosocial behavior; defined as a sequence of two behaviors, child's, then mother's; and
  - Maternal response to child deviant behavior, which reflected responses that were inappropriate because of valence, content, or lack of contingency; also a sequence of two behaviors.

Administration and Scoring

The measurement of the maternal and child behavior codes was calculated in terms of rate per minute obtained by dividing the frequency of the behavior by the duration of the observation session. Averages across sessions were computed according to the number of family observation sessions. The variables relative to the mother–child interaction code were measured as proportions of the inappropriate or non-contingent maternal responses to the immediate child behavior over the total number of maternal responses (both appropriate and inappropriate). A statistical software package for the SOCIII, (ARINFA), was indicated by the authors for use in these computations.

Psychometric Evaluation

Norms
None reported.

Reliability
For a recent study of 47 families (23 abusive and 24 control) in Spain (Cerezo, D'Ocon, & Dolz, 1996), graduate student observers were trained on videotapes of complex family interactions and then conducted reliability rating sessions. Interrater reliability was determined using the kappa coefficient and 15-second time periods for a total of 240 intervals in an hour. Kappa coefficients ranged from .58 for the category of child deviant behavior in the control group to .80 for maternal neutral instruction in the control group as well. All other kappa coefficients fell within that range, indicating good reliability between observers.

For low-frequency categories, intraclass correlation coefficients were computed. Results obtained for maternal positive and aversive behavior ranged between .89 and .97, which are very satisfactory values.

Validity

Using a stepwise discriminant function analysis and three maternal behavior variables (neutral social approach, neutral instruction, and negative behavior) as predictors, 70.2% of the families were correctly classified. Only one child behavior predictor (interactional deviant behavior) resulted in correct classification of 74.5% of the cases. Finally, using the two interactive codes as predictors, 78.7% of cases were correctly classified. A final analysis used three subcategories (maternal response to prosocial behavior, maternal instruction, and interactional child deviant behavior), and 82% of the cases were correctly classified.

Advantages

A well-researched and comprehensive coding system that allows for coding of behavioral sequences by multiple family members, the SOCIII is an excellent approach to the quantification of interactive processes.

Limitations

The SOCIII is a complex system that will be costly to implement unless observers and their time are readily available. The authors reported an average observer training period of 20 hours. It is not clear how data obtained from the SOCIII relate to other methods of family interaction assessment.

Primary Reference

Cerezo, Keesler, Dunn, and Wahler (1986).

Scale Availability

M. Angeles Cerezo
Departamento de Psieologia Basica
Avda. Blasco Ibanez, 21
46010 Valencia, Spain

Related References

Cerezo et al. (1996).

General Comments and Recommendations for Practitioners and Researchers

Although the SOCIII may be too complex and labor-intensive to use outside of the research setting, it is one of the few systems to code mother–child interaction sequences in the natural home environment.

143. Structured Laboratory and Home Observation: Single Case Study (SLHO; Schellenbach, Trickett, & Susman)

Development and Description of Assessment Method

The SLHO is a continuous behavioral coding system used to record interactive sequences between parents and a target child in the naturalistic home setting.

Observers were trained by recording interactions from a videotaped training tape and then observing and recording volunteer families. However, standards for training criteria were not specified in the primary reference.

Target Population

High-risk parents of young children.

Format

For the home observation, the observers bring a novel toy and instruct first the mother to play with the child for 10 minutes, then the father for 10 minutes. The parents then engage in free interaction with their child for 20 minutes.

The following categories are coded by observers:

- Whether there is interaction between family members;
- Who initiates the interaction and with whom;
- The nature of the behavior: either noninteractive (passive, attentive, self-stimulating, play, or work) or interactive (physical, verbal, nonverbal);
- The goal of the interaction (five items, including sociability and nurturance seeking/providing);
- The style of the interaction (nine items, including affect/tone, for example, pleasant, irritable, passive, humorous, anxious, apathetic); and

- The intensity of that style, from mild to moderate to strong.

Definitions of all of these behavior codes are available from the authors.

Administration and Scoring

Behaviors were coded via a Datamyte electronic recorder used for continuous observation. The authors used conditional probability analysis to determine the sequences of interaction.

Psychometric Evaluation

Norms
None reported.

Reliability
Because elapsed time from the beginning of the coding session was recorded with each sequence of codes entered on the electronic recorder, interobserver agreement was defined as the same code entered by both coders within a 12-second interval (which was the average interval for all codes entered). The percent agreement for all codes ranged from 71 to 95%, with a mean percent agreement of 78%.

Validity
For this single case assessment, the data from the behavioral observations supported scores derived from the CBCL (Achenbach, 1991) but was discrepant with results from a formal assessment of motor development.

Advantages
Electronic coding enables the researcher to analyze sequences of affective interchanges within an unstructured family situation and allows for examination of the reciprocal nature of dyadic interaction.

Limitations
The complicated observational coding system is not easily incorporated into the clinical setting.

Primary Reference

Schellenbach, Trickett, and Susman (1991).

Scale Availability

Cynthia J. Schellenbach
Department of Psychology
University of Notre Dame
Notre Dame, IN 46556

Related References

None available.

General Comments and Recommendations for Practitioners and Researchers

The case study approach will appeal to clinicians who might see this type of naturalistic observation as relevant.

---

144. System for Coding Interactions and Family Functioning (SCIFF; Lindahl)

Development and Description of Assessment Method

The SCIFF is a comprehensive behavioral coding system used to quantify particular aspects of family communication and interaction during a structured observation of parents and children. Interaction, dyadic, and individual style variables are included in the assessment of the family members.

The categories included in the behavioral coding system were derived from both family systems and social learning theories of family interaction variables.

Target Population

Families with children older than 7 years of age.

Format

In the SCIFF, there are 17 main behavioral categories for coding. These are grouped according to family member or relationship dimension:

- *Family Codes*
  - *Cohesiveness:* Represents the level of unity, comfortableness, to-

getherness, and closeness observed among all members of the family.

- *Negativity and Family Conflict:* Focuses on the levels of tension, anger, irritation, and hostility expressed among family members.
- *Positive Affect:* Reflects the overall positive emotional tone in the family; captures the feelings associated with communication (tone of voice, facial expression, and body language).
- *Focus of the Problem:* Evaluates the focal point of the family discussion according to the way parents describe the problem as either child- or family-centered.
- *Parenting Style Observations*
  - *Parenting Style:* Coded when parents either fail to exert authority or exhibit clashing and contradictory parenting styles that undermine each other's efforts (lax–inconsistent) or when behaviors indicate that one or both parents unmistakably holds authority; during interactions, rules and punishment are dictated by authority and are not arrived at by consensus (authoritarian).
  - *Alliance Formation:* Assesses the nature of the different dyadic relationships in the family as either balanced, marital (detour–attacking), parent–child, disengaged, or weak alliances; based on which dyad appears stronger in terms of closeness, influence, and affection.

The remaining behavioral categories emphasize individual behaviors for each parent and for the child:

- *Parent Codes*
  - *Rejection:* Reflects the frequency and intensity with which the parent makes critical, blaming, unkind, or insensitive statements to the child.
  - *Coerciveness:* Includes behaviors such as threatening, shaming, manipulation, or bullying statements made to direct or control the child's behavior.
  - *Triangulation:* Focuses on family communication patterns in which the parents appear to be in conflict with one another or when one tries to obtain support or sympathy from the child.
  - *Emotional Support:* Includes parent behaviors indicating the level of emotional support, affective attunement, and sensitivity expressed toward the child.

- *Withdrawal:* Reflects the degree to which a parent removes him- or herself from the interaction or avoids the discussion; may include evasive or detached behaviors, both physical and verbal.
- *Child Codes*
  - *Anger and Frustration:* Assesses the overall level of negative affect (anger, tension, irritation) expressed by the child through tone of voice, facial expressions, and body language during the interaction.
  - *Sadness and Distress:* Reflects verbal and physical expressions of sadness, sorrow, anguish, pain, and regret or remorse; distinguished from withdrawal by the need to be visibly anguished.
  - *Withdrawal:* Assesses the degree to which a child removes him or herself from the discussion either by evading or shutting down.
  - *Opposition/Defiance:* Evaluates the degree to which the child displays oppositional, defiant, or belligerent behavior.
  - *Positive Affect:* Assesses the positiveness of the child's tone of voice, facial expressions, and body language (affection, laughter, smiling).

Administration and Scoring

Each behavioral category contains specific behavioral anchors on a global rating scale to be used by coders of the videotaped family interaction. A 5-point Likert scale ranging from 1 = very low to 5 = very high is used to code the interactions. Parental rejection and coercion categories are combined and averaged to create an overall score of parental rejection–coercion, which results in 16 scores for each family interaction. For each of the 17 codes, complete anchor points are given for each of the five rating possibilities. The anchor descriptions include examples related to frequency and intensity of the behaviors included in the codes.

Psychometric Evaluation

Norms
None reported.

Reliability
Interrater reliabilities were calculated by four independent coders for 40% of the family interaction using Cronbach's alpha coefficient. Scores

were .80 for cohesiveness, .78 for family conflict, .69 for lax–inconsistent parenting, .72 for authoritarianism, .91 for parental rejection, .83 for parental coerciveness, .75 for parental triangulation, .79 for parental support, and .92 for parental commands.

Validity

Demonstrating known groups validity, various behavioral categories of the SCIFF distinguished among families of children with oppositional defiant disorder, attention deficit-hyperactivity disorder, and control families. The majority of discriminating power, derived via a discriminant analysis, was accounted for by controlling/coercive parent–child interactions and harmonious family processes. Low family cohesiveness, lax–inconsistent parenting, and patterns of parent rejection–coercion distinguish clinical groups from control samples.

Advantages

The SCIFF behavior code includes a blend of parent and individual behavior as well as dyadic and family process variables that combine to provide a comprehensive analysis of interaction data. Global ratings for each category may be easier to administer than more complex interval coding for frequencies of behavior. The code definitions are easy to read, and the scoring sheet is simple to use.

Limitations

Extensive training of 15 hours for coders makes this an unlikely assessment tool for use in the clinical setting. Global ratings introduce possibilities of rater biases and reduce the accuracy of this system as a direct observation measure.

Primary Reference

Lindahl (1998).

Scale Availability

> Kristin M. Lindahl
> Department of Psychology, Psychology Annex
> P.O. Box 249229
> University of Miami
> Coral Gables, FL 33124-0721

Related References

None available.

General Comments and Recommendation for Practitioners and Researchers

Although this comprehensive approach to rating family interactions has never been used in the assessment of maltreating families, the use of rating scales to code analogue family discussions seems a practical approach to family assessment in the clinical situation. The authors do describe an intensive training regimen for the undergraduate coders used in their research study.

References

Abidin, R. R. (1990). *Parenting Stress Index manual.* Charlottesville, VA: Pediatric-Psychology Press.

Abidin, R. R. (1995). *Parenting Stress Index* (3rd ed.). Odessa, FL: Psychological Assessment Resources.

Abidin, R. R., & Brunner, J. F. (1995). Development of a Parenting Alliance Inventory. *Journal of Clinical Child Psychology, 24,* 31–40.

Achenbach, T. M. (1991). *Manual for the Child Behavior Checklist/4-18 and 1991 Profile.* Burlington: University of Vermont Department of Psychiatry.

Adamson, J. L., & Thompson, R. A. (1998). Coping with interparental verbal conflict by children exposed to spouse abuse and children from non-violent homes. *Journal of Family Violence, 13,* 213–232.

American Psychiatric Association. (1987). *Diagnostic and statistical manual of mental disorders* (3rd ed. rev.). Washington, DC: American Psychiatric Association.

American Psychiatric Association. (1994). *Diagnostic and statistical manual of mental disorders* (4th ed.). Washington, DC: American Psychiatric Association.

American Psychological Association (APA). (1997). Professional, ethical, and legal issues concerning interpersonal violence, maltreatment, and related trauma. Washington, DC: Author.

Ammerman, R. T. (1990). Ecological models of child maltreatment: A behavioral perspective. *Behavior Modification, 14,* 230–254.

Ammerman, R. T., Hersen, M., VanHasselt, V. B., Lubetsky, M. J., & Sieck, W. R. (1994). Maltreatment in psychiatrically hospitalized children and adolescents with developmental disabilities: Prevalence and correlates. *Journal of the American Academy of Children and Adolescent Psychiatry, 33,* 567–576.

Ammerman, R. T., & Patz, R. J. (1996). Determinants of child abuse potential: Contribution of parent and child factors. *Journal of Clinical Child Psychology, 25*(3), 300–307.

Ammerman, R. T., VanHasselt, V. P., & Hersen, M. (1988). Maltreatment of handicapped children: A critical review. *Journal of Family Violence, 3,* 53–72.

Ammerman, R. T., Van Hasselt, V. B., & Hersen, M. (1993). *The Child Abuse and Neglect Interview Schedule—Revised.* Unpublished manuscript. Western Pennsylvania School for Blind Children, Pittsburgh.

Andrews, B. (1995). Bodily shame as a mediator between abusive experiences and depression. *Journal of Abnormal Psychology, 104*(2), 277–285.

Armstrong, J. G., Putnam, F. W., Carlson, E. B., Libero, D. Z., & Smith, S. P. (1997).

Development and validation of a measure of adolescent dissociation: The Adolescent Dissociative Experiences Scale. *Journal of Nervous and Mental Disease, 185,* 491–497.

Arnold, D. S., O'Leary, S. G., Wolff, L. S., & Acker, M. M. (1993). The Parenting Scale: A measure of dysfunctional parenting in discipline situations. *Psychological Assessment, 5,* 137–144.

Avison, W. R., Turner, R. J., &., & Noh, S. (1986). Screening for problem parenting: Preliminary evidence on a promising instrument. *Child Abuse and Neglect, 10,* 157–170.

Azar, S. T. (1991). Models of child abuse. A metatheoretical analysis. *Criminal Justice and Behavior, 18,* 30–46.

Azar, S., Benjet, C., Fuhrmann, G., & Cavallero, L. (1995). Child maltreatment and termination of parental rights: Can behavioral research help Solomon? *Behavior Therapy, 26,* 599–623.

Azar, S. T., Lauretti, A. F., & Loding, B. V. (1998). The evaluation of parental fitness in termination of parental rights cases: A functional contextual perspective. *Clinical Child and Family Psychology Review, 1,* 77–100.

Azar, S. T., Robinson, D., Hekimian, E., & Twentyman, D. (1984). Unrealistic expectations and problem solving ability in maltreating and comparison mothers. *Journal of Consulting and Clinical Psychology, 52,* 687–691.

Azar, S. T., & Rohrbeck, C. A. (1986). Child abuse and unrealistic expectations: Further validation of the Parent Opinion Questionnaire. *Journal of Consulting and Clinical Psychology, 54,* 867–868.

Babiker, G., & Herbert, M. (1998). Critical issues in the assessment of child sexual abuse. *Clinical Child and Family Psychology Review, 1*(4), 231–252.

Bakeman, R., & Gottman, J. M. (1986). *Observing interaction: An introduction to sequential analysis.* Cambridge, England: Cambridge University Press.

Bandura, A. (1977). *Social learning theory.* Englewood Cliffs, NJ: Prentice-Hall.

Barton, K., & Baglio, C. (1993). The nature of stress in child-abusing families. *Psychological Reports, 73,* 1047–1055.

Baumrind, D. (1971). Current patterns of parental authority. *Developmental Psychology Monographs, 4* (2, Pt. 2).

Bavolek, S. J. (1984). *Handbook for the Adult-Adolescent Parenting Inventory.* Eau Claire, WI: Family Development Associates, Inc.

Beavers, W. R., Hampson, R. B., & Hulgus, Y. F. (1985). Commentary: The Beavers Systems approach to family assessment. *Family Process, 24,* 398–405.

Beck, A. T., Ward, C. H., Mendelson, M., Mock, J., & Erbaugh, J. (1961). An inventory for measuring depression. *Archives of General Psychiatry, 4,* 53–63.

Becker, J. V., & Hunter, J. A. (1992). Evaluation of treatment outcome for adult perpetrators of child sexual abuse. *Criminal Justice and Behavior, 19,* 74–92.

Bentler, P. M. (1968). Heterosexual behavior assessment—II. Females. *Behavior, Research and Therapy, 6,* 27–30.

Berger, A. M., & Knutson, J. F. (1984). *Assessing environments III.* Unpublished manuscript, Department of Psychology, University of Iowa, Iowa City.

Berger A. M., Knutson, J. F., Mehm, J. C., & Perkins, K. A. (1988). The self report of punitive childhood experiences of young adults and adolescents. *Child Abuse and Neglect, 12,* 251–262.

Berliner, L., & Saunders, B. E. (1996). Treating fear and anxiety in sexually abused children: Results of a controlled 2-year follow-up study. *Child Maltreatment, 4,* 294–309.

Bernstein, D. P., Fink, L., Handelsman, L., Foote, L., Lovejoy, M. C., et al. (1994). Initial reliability and validity of a new retrospective measure of child abuse and neglect. *American Journal of Psychiatry, 151,* 1132–1136.

Bernstein, E. M., & Putnam, F. W. (1986). Development, reliability and validity of a dissociation scale. *Journal of Nervous and Mental Disease, 174,* 727–735.

Berry, J. O., & Jones, W. H. (1995). The Parental Stress Scale: Initial psychometric evidence. *Journal of Social and Personal Relationships, 12,* 463–472.

Berry, J. W. (1994). An ecological perspective on cultural and ethnic psychology. In E. J. Trickett, R. J. Watts, & D. Birman (Eds.), Human diversity (pp. 115–141). San Francisco: Jossey-Bass.

Bieber, S. (1986). A hierarchical approach to multigroup factorial invariance. *Journal of Classification, 3,* 113–134.

Bifulco, A., Brown, G. W., & Harris, T. O. (1994). Childhood Experience of Care and Abuse (CECA): A retrospective interview measure. *Journal of Child Psychology and Psychiatry, 35,* 1419–1435.

Bifulco, A., Brown, G. W., Lillie, A., & Jarvis, J. (1997). Memories of childhood neglect and abuse: Corroboration in a series of sisters. *Journal of Child Psychology and Psychiatry, 38,* 365–374.

Birt, J., DiMito, A., & Wolfe, V. V. (1995, March). Origins of dissociation among sexually abused children. Poster presented at the biennial meeting of the Society for Research on Child Development, Indianapolis, Indiana.

Borum, R. (1996). Improving the clinical practice of violence risk assessment. *American Psychologist, 51,* 945–956.

Bradley, R. H. (1993). Children's home environments, health behavior and intervention efforts: A review using the HOME Inventory as a marker measure. *Genetic, Social and General Psychology Monographs, 119,* 437–490.

Bradley, R. H., & Caldwell, B. M. (1979). Home Observation for Measurement of the Environment: A revision of the preschool scale. *American Journal of Mental Deficiency, 84,* 235–244.

Branscomb, L. P., & Fagan, J. (1992). Development and validation of a scale measuring childhood dissociation in adults: The Childhood Dissociative Predictor Scale. *Dissociation, 2,* 80–86.

Brassard, M. R., Hart, S. N., & Hardy, D. B. (1993). The Psychological Maltreatment Rating Scale. *Child Abuse and Neglect, 17,* 715–729.

Briere, J. (1988). The long-term clinical correlates of childhood sexual victimization. *Annals of the New York Academy of Sciences, 528,* 327–335.

Briere, J. (1992). *Child abuse trauma: Theory and treatment of the lasting effects.* Newbury Park, CA: Sage.

Briere, J. (1995). *Trauma Symptom Inventory professional manual.* Odessa, FL. Psychological Assessment Resources.

Briere, J. (1996a). Methodological issues in the study of sexual abuse effects. *Journal of Consulting and Clinical Psychology, 60,* 196–203.

Briere, J. (1996b). *Professional manual for the Trauma Symptom Checklist for Children* (TSCC). Odessa, FL: Psychological Assessment Resources.

Briere, J. (1996c). Treatment outcome research with abused children: Methodological considerations in three studies. *Child Maltreatment, 1,* 348–352.

Briere, J., Elliott, D. M., Harris, K., & Coffman, S. G. (1995). Trauma Symptoms Inventory: Psychometrics and association with childhood and adult trauma in clinical samples. *Journal of Interpersonal Violence, 10,* 387–401.

Briere, J., & Runtz, M. (1988a). Multivariate correlates of childhood psychological and physical maltreatment among university women. *Child Abuse and Neglect, 12,* 331–341.

Briere, J., & Runtz, M. (1988b). Symptomatology associated with childhood sexual victimization in a non-clinical adult sample. *Child Abuse and Neglect, 12,* 51–59.

Briere, J., & Runtz, M. (1989). The trauma symptom checklist (TSC-33): Early data on a new scale. *Journal of Interpersonal Violence, 4,* 151–162.

Briere, J., & Runtz, M. (1993). Child sexual abuse: Long-term sequelae and implications for assessment. *Journal of Interpersonal Violence, 2,* 367–379.

Brotman-Band, E., & Weisz, J. (1988). How to feel better when it feels bad: Children's perspectives on coping with everyday stress. *Developmental Psychology, 24,* 247–253.

Bruck, M., Ceci, S., Francouer, E., & Renick, A. (1995). Anatomically detailed dolls do not facilitate preschoolers reports of a pediatric examination involving genital touch. *Journal of Experimental Psychology: Applied, 1,* 95–109.

Budd, K. S. (2001). Assessing parenting competence in child protection cases: A clinical practice model. *Clinical Child and Family Psychology Review, 4,* 1–18.

Budd, K. S., Heilman, N. E., & Kane, D. (2000). Psychosocial correlates of child abuse potential in multiply disadvantaged adolescent mothers. *Child Abuse and Neglect, 24,* 611–625.

Budd, K. S., & Holdsworth, M. J. (1996). Issues in clinical assessment of minimal parenting competence. *Journal of Clinical Child Psychology, 25,* 1–14.

Bugental, D. B. (1993a). Communication in abusive relationships: Cognitive constructions of interpersonal power. *American Behavioral Scientist, 36,* 288–308.

Bugental, D. B. (1993b). *Parent Attribution Test.* Unpublished manuscript, University of California, Santa Barbara.

Bugental, D. B., Brown, M., & Reiss, C. (1996). Cognitive representations of power in caregiving relationships: Biasing effects on interpersonal interaction and information processing. *Journal of Family Psychology, 10,* 397–407.

Buri, J. R. (1991). Parental Authority Questionnaire. *Journal of Personality Assessment, 57,* 110–119.

Campis, L. K., Lyman, R. D., & Prentice-Dunn, S. (1986). The Parental Locus of Control Scale: Development and validation. *Journal of Clinical Child Psychology, 15,* 260–267.

Campos, J., Mumme, D., Kermoian, R., & Campos, R. (1994). A functionalist perspective on the nature of emotion. *Monographs of the Society for Research in Child Development, 59,* 284–304.

Carlin, A. S., Kemper, K., Ward, N. G., Sowell, H., Gustafson, B., & Stevens, N. (1994). The effect of differences in objective and subjective definitions of childhood physical abuse on estimates of its incidence and relationship to psychopathology. *Child Abuse and Neglect, 18,* 393–399.

Carson, D. K., Gertz, L. M., Donaldson, M. A., & Wonderlich, S. A. (1990). Family of origin characteristics and current family relationships of female adult incest victims. *Journal of Family Violence, 5,* 153–171.

Cascardi, M., & Vivian, D. (1995). Context for specific episodes of marital violence: Gender and severity of violence differences. *Journal of Family Violence, 10,* 265–293.

Cascardi, M., Vivian, D., & Meyer, S. L. (1991, Nov.). *Context and attributions for marital violence in discordant couples.* Poster presented at the 25th annual Convention for the Association for the Advancement of Behavior Therapy, New York.

Cassidy, J., Parke, R. D., Butkovsky, L., & Braungart, J. M. (1992). Family-peer connections: The roles of emotional expressiveness within the family and children's understanding of emotion. *Child Development, 63,* 603–618.

Celano, M., Hazzard A., Webb, C., & McCall, C. (1996). Treatment of traumagenic beliefs among sexually abused girls and their mothers: An evaluation study. *Journal of Abnormal Child Psychology, 24,* 1–17.

Celano, M., Webb, C., & Hazzard, A. (1992, May). *Parental attributions of responsibility for child sexual abuse*. Paper presented at the National Symposium on Child Victimization, Washington, DC.

Cerezo, M. A. (1997). Abusive family interaction: A review. *Aggression and Violent Behavior, 2,* 215–240.

Cerezo, M. A., D'Ocon, A., & Dolz, L. (1996). Mother-child interactive patterns in abusive families versus nonabusive families: An observational study. *Child Abuse and Neglect, 7,* 573–587.

Cerezo, M. A., Keesler, T., Dunn, E., & Wahler, R. (1986). *Standardized observation codes: SOCIII.* Unpublished document. Child Behavior Institute, University of Tennessee.

Chamberlain, P., & Reid, J. B. (1987). Parent observation and report of child symptoms. *Behavioral Assessment, 9,* 97–109.

Cohen, J. (1960). A coefficient of agreement for nominal scales. *Educational and Psychological Measurement, 20,* 37–46.

Cohen, J., & Mannarino, A. (1996). The weekly behavior report: A parent-report instrument for sexually abused preschoolers. *Child Maltreatment, 1,* 353–360.

Cohen, S., Kamarck, T., & Mermelstein, R. (1983). A global measure of perceived stress. *Journal of Health and Social Behavior, 24,* 385–396.

Conti, J. R. (1993). Sexual abuse of children. In R. L. Hampton, T. P. Gullotta, G. R. Adams, E. H. Potter III, & R. P. Weissberg (Eds.), *Family violence: Prevention and treatment* (pp. 56–85). Newbury Park, CA: Sage.

Copping, V. E. (1996). Beyond over and under-control: Behavioral observations of shelter children. *Journal of Family Violence, 11,* 41–57.

Cowen, E. (1973). The AML: A quick screening device for early identification of school maladaptation. *American Journal of Community Psychology, 1,* 12–35.

Cronbach, L. J. (1951). Coefficient alpha and the internal structure of tests. *Psychometrika, 16,* 297–334.

Cross, T. P., Martell, D., McDonald, E., & Ahl, M. (1999). The criminal justice system and child placement in child sexual abuse cases. *Child Maltreatment, 4,* 32–44.

Crowne, D. P., & Marlow, D. (1960). A new scale of social desirability independent of psychopathology. *Journal of Consulting Psychology, 24,* 349–354.

Cummings, E. M., Davis, P. T., & Simpson, K. S. (1994). Marital conflict, gender and children's appraisals and coping efficacy as mediators of child adjustment. *Journal of Family Psychology, 8,* 141–149.

Cummings, E. M., Vogel, D., Cummings, J. S., & El-Sheikh, M. (1989). Children's responses to different forms of expression of anger between adults. *Child Development, 60,* 1392–1404.

Davies, P. T., & Cummings, E. M. (1994). Marital conflict and child adjustment: An emotional security hypothesis. *Psychological Bulletin, 116,* 387–411.

Davison, G. C., Robins, C., & Johnson, M. K. (1983). Articulated thoughts during simulated situations: A paradigm for studying cognition in emotion and behavior. *Cognitive Therapy and Research, 7,* 17–40.

Davison, G. C., Vogel, R. S., & Coffman, S. G. (1997). Think-aloud approaches to cognitive assessment and the articulated thoughts in simulated situations paradigm. *Journal of Consulting and Clinical Psychology, 65,* 950–958.

Dawson, B., Geddie, L., & Wagner, W. (1996). Low income preschoolers behavior with anatomically detailed dolls. *Journal of Family Violence, 11*(4), 363–378.

Dawson, B., Vaughan, A. R., & Wagner, W. G. (1992). Normal responses to sexually anatomically detailed dolls. *Journal of Family Violence, 7,* 135–152.

Deater-Deckard, K. (1996). Within family variability in parental negativity and control. *Journal of Applied Developmental Psychology, 17,* 407, 422.

Deater-Deckard, K. (1998). Parenting stress and child adjustment: Some old hypotheses and new questions. *Clinical Psychology; Science and Practice, 5,* 314–332.

Deater-Deckard, K., Dodge, K., Bates, J. E., & Pettit, G. S. (1996). Physical discipline among African-American and European-American mothers: Links to children's externalizing behaviors. *Developmental Psychology, 32,* 1065–1072.

Deater-Deckard, K., Pinkerton, R., & Scarr, S. (1996). Child care quality and children's behavioral adjustment: A four year longitudinal study. *Journal of Child Psychology and Psychiatry, 37,* 937–948.

Deater-Deckard, K., & Scarr, S. (1996). Parenting stress among dual-earner mothers and fathers: Are there gender differences. *Journal of Family Psychology, 10,* 45–59.

Deblinger, E., Lippmann, J., & Steer, R. (1996). Sexually abused children suffering from posttraumatic stress symptoms: Initial treatment outcome findings. *Child Maltreatment, 4,* 310–321.

DeLoache, J. S., & Maszolf, D. P. (1995). The use of dolls to interview young children: Issues of symbolic representation. *Journal of Experimental Child Psychology, 60,* 1–19.

Denham, S., Zoller, D., & Couchoud, E. (1994). Socialization of preschoolers' emotional understanding. *Developmental Psychology, 30,* 928–936.

Derogatis, L. R., Lipman, R. S., & Covi, L. (1973). SCL-90: An outpatient rating scale-preliminary report. *Psychopharmacology Bulletin, 24,* 454–464.

DeRoma, V. M., & Hansen, D. J. (1994, Nov.). *Development of the Parental Anger Inventory.* Presented at the Association for the Advancement of Behavior Therapy Convention, San Diego, CA.

DiTomasso, M. J., & Routh, D. K. (1993). Recall of abuse in childhood and three measures of dissociation. *Child Abuse and Neglect, 17,* 477–485.

Dix, T. (1991). The affective organization of parenting: Adaptive and maladaptive processes. *Psychological Bulletin, 110,* 3–25.

Dix, T., Reinhold, D. P., & Zambarano, R. J. (1990). Mothers judgments in moments of anger. *Merrill-Palmer Quarterly, 36,* 465–486.

Dodge, K. A., Pettit, G., Bates, J. E., & Valente, E. (1995). Social information-processing patterns partially mediate the effect of early physical abuse on later conduct problems. *Journal of Abnormal Psychology, 104,* 632–643.

Dodge-Reyone, N. (1995). Sense of competence and attitudes toward abusive interactions with adolescents in residential child care workers. *Journal of Child and Youth Care, 10,* 57–62.

Donaldson, M. A., & Gardner, R. (1985). Diagnosis and treatment of traumatic stress among women after childhood incest. In C. R. Figley (Ed.), *Trauma and its wake: The study and treatment of post-traumatic stress disorder.* New York: Brunner/Mazel.

Dubner, A., & Motta, R. (1999). Sexually and physically abused foster care children and post traumatic stress disorder. *Journal of Consulting and Clinical Psychology, 67,* 367–373.

Edelson, J. L., & Brygger, M. P. (1986). Gender differences in self-reporting of battering incidences. *Family Relations, 35,* 377–382.

Edwards, A. L. (1957). *The Social Desirability Variable in Personality Assessment and Research.* New York: Dryden Press.

Edwards, P. W., & Donaldson, M. A. (1989). Assessment of symptoms in adult survivors of incest: A factor analytic study of the Responses to Childhood Incest Questionnaire. *Child Abuse and Neglect, 13,* 101–110.

Elliott, D. M., & Briere, J. (1992). Sexual abuse trauma among professional women: Validating the Trauma Symptom Checklist-40 (TSC-40). *Child Abuse and Neglect, 16,* 391–398.

Elliott, D. M., & Briere, J. (1994). Forensic sexual abuse evaluations of older children: Disclosures and symptomatology. *Behavioral Sciences and the Law, 12,* 261–277.

El-Sheikh, M., Cummings, E. M., & Reiter, S. (1996). Preschoolers' responses to ongoing interadult conflict: The role of prior exposure to resolved versus unresolved arguments. *Journal of Abnormal Child Psychology, 24,* 665–679.

El-Sheikh, M., & Reiter, S. (1996). Children's responding to live interadult conflict: The role of form of anger expression. *Journal of Abnormal Child Psychology, 24,* 401–414.

Epstein, N. B., Baldwin, L. M., & Bishop, D. S. (1983). The McMaster Family Assessment Device. *Journal of Marital and Family Therapy, 9,* 171–180.

Everson, M. D. (1997). Understanding bizarre, improbable and fantastic elements in children's accounts of abuse. *Child Maltreatment, 2,* 134–149.

Everson, M. D., Hunter, W. M., Runyon, D. K., Eddsohn, G. A., & Coulter, M. L. (1989). Maternal support following disclosure of incest. *American Journal of Orthopsychiatry, 59,* 197–207.

Eyberg, S. M., & Robinson, E. A. (1983). Dyadic parent-child interaction coding system: A manual. *Psychological Documents, 13,* 24.

Eyberg, S. M., & Ross, A. W. (1978). Assessment of child behavior problems: The validation of a new inventory. *Journal of Clinical Child Psychology, 16,* 113–116.

Fagot, B. I. (1984). *A training manual for the Fagot Interactive Behavior Code.* Unpublished manuscript, Oregon Social Learning Institute, Eugene.

Fagot, B. (1992). Assessment of coercive parent discipline. *Behavioral Assessment, 14,* 387–406.

Fantuzzo, J. W. (1990). Behavioral treatment of victims of child abuse and neglect. *Behavior Modification, 14,* 316–339.

Farrington, A., Waller, G., Smerden, J., & Faupel, A. W. (2001). The Adolescent Dissociative Experience Scale: Psychometric properties and differences in scores across age groups. *Journal of Nervous and Mental Disease, 189,* 722–727.

Faust, J., Runyon, M. K., & Kenny, M. C. (1995). Family variables associated with the onset and impact of intrafamilial childhood sexual abuse. *Clinical Psychology Review, 15,* 443–456.

Feldman, C. M. (1997). Childhood precursors of adult interpartner violence. *Clinical Psychology; Science and Practice, 4,* 307–334.

Figley, C. R., & Kleber, R. J. (1995). Beyond the "victim": Secondary traumatic stress. In R. J. Kleber, C. R. Figley, & P. R. Bertold (Eds.), *Beyond trauma: Cultural and societal dynamics* (pp. 75–98). New York: Plenum Press.

Fincham, F. D., Beach, S. R., & Nelson, G. (1987). Attribution processes in distressed and nondistressed couples: 3. Causal and responsibility attributions for spouse behavior. *Cognitive Therapy and Research, 11,* 71–86.

Fink, L., Bernstein, D., Foote, J., Lovejoy, M., Ruggiero, J., & Handelsman, L. (1993). The Childhood Trauma Interview: Reliability, validity, and relationship to personality disorders. In *Proceedings of the Third International Congress on the Disorders of Personality.* Roskilde, Denmark: International Society for the Study of Personality Disorders.

Finklehor, D. (1984). *Child sexual abuse: New theory and research.* New York: Free Press.

Finkelhor, D., & Browne, A. (1985). The traumatic impact of child sexual abuse: A conceptualization. *American Journal of Orthopsychiatry, 55,* 536–541.

First, M. B., Spitzer, R. L., Gibbon, M., & Williams, J. B. W. (1995). *Structured clinical interview for DSM-IV axis I disorders—Patient edition* (SCID I/P, Version 2.0). New York: Biometrics Research Department, New York State Psychiatric Institute.

First, M. B., Spitzer, R. L., Gibbon, M., Williams, J. B. W., & Benjamin, L. (1994).

Structured clinical interview for DSM-IV axis I disorders—Patient edition (SCID-II) (Version 2. 0). New York: Biometrics Research Department, New York State Psychiatric Institute.

Fischer, J., & Corcoran, K. (Eds.). (2000). *Measures for clinical practice: A sourcebook* (Vol. 2, 3rd ed.). New York: Free Press.

Fletcher, K. E. (1996, Nov.). *Measuring school-aged children's PTSD: Preliminary psychometrics of four new measures.* Paper presented at 12th Annual Meeting of the International Society for Traumatic Stress Studies, San Francisco.

Fox, R. A. (1992). Development of an instrument to measure the behaviors and expectations of parents of young children. *Journal of Pediatric Psychology, 17*(2), 231–239.

Fox, R. A., & Bentley, K. S. (1992). Validity of the Parenting Inventory: Young children. *Psychology in the School, 29,* 101–107.

Frankel, F., & Weiner, H. (1990). *The Child Conflict Index:* Factor analysis reliability, and validity for clinic referred and non-referred children. *Journal of Clinical Child Psychology, 19,* 239–248.

Frederick, C., Pynoos, R., & Nader, K. (1992). *Childhood PTS Reaction Index (CPTS-RI).* Unpublished manuscript, Laguna Hills, CA.

Friedrich, W. N. (1993). Sexual victimization and sexual behavior in children: A review of recent literature. *Child Abuse and Neglect, 17,* 59–66.

Friedrich, W. N. (1996). Clinical considerations of empirical treatment studies of abused children. *Child Maltreatment, 1,* 343–347.

Friedrich, W. N., Gerber, P. N., Koplin, B., Davis, M., Giese, J., et al. (2001). Multimodal assessment of dissociation in adolescents. Inpatients and juvenile sex offenders. *Sexual Abuse: Journal of Research and Treatment, 13,* 167–177.

Friedrich, W. N., Grambasch, P., Broughton, D., Kuiper, J., & Beilke, R. (1991). Normative sexual behavior in children. *Pediatrics, 88,* 456–464.

Friedrich, W. N., Grambasch, P., Damon, L., Hewitt, S. K., Koverola, C., et al. (1992). Child Sexual Behavior Inventory: Normative and clinical comparisons. *Psychological Assessment, 4,* 303–311.

Gardner, R. A. (1987). *The parental alienation syndrome and the differences between fabricated and genuine child sexual abuse.* Cresskill, NJ: Creative Therapeutics.

Gardner, R. A. (1989). *Family evaluation in child custody mediation, arbitration, and litigation.* Cresskill, NJ: Creative Therapeutics.

Gerard, A. B. (1994). *Parent-child relationship inventory: Manual.* Los Angeles: Western Psychological Corporation.

Gibaud-Wallston, J., & Wandersman, L. P. (1978, Nov.). *Development and utility of the Parenting Sense of Competence Scale.* Paper presented at the meeting of the American Psychological Association, Toronto, Canada.

Glaser, B. A., Horne, A. M., & Myers, L. L. (1995). A cross validation of the Parent Perception Inventory. *Child and Family Behavior Therapy, 17,* 21–34.

Glaser, B. A., Sayger, T., & Horne, A. M. (1993). Three types of Family Environment Scale profiles: Functional, distressed and abusive families. *Journal of Family Violence, 8*(4), 303–311.

Golden, C. J., Sawicki, R. F., & Franzen, M. D. (1984). Test construction. In G. Golden & M. Hersen (Eds.), *Handbook of psychological assessment* (pp. 19–37). New York: Pergamon Press.

Gordis, E., Margolin, G., & John, R. (1997). Marital aggression, observed parent hostility and child behavior during triadic family interaction. *Journal of Family Psychology, 11,* 76–89

Gordon, B. N., Baker-Ward, L., & Ornstein, P. A. (2001). Children's testimony: A review of research on memory for post experiences. *Clinical Child and Family Psychology Review, 4,* 157–181.

Gordon, D. A., Jones, R. H., & Nowicki, S. (1979). A measure of intensity of parental punishment. *Journal of Personality Assessment, 43,* 485–496.

Gottman, J. M. (1979). *Marital interaction: Experimental investigations.* New York: Academic Press.

Gottman, J. M., & Levenson, R. W. (1985). A valid procedure for obtaining self-report of affect in marital interaction. *Journal of Consulting and Clinical Psychology, 53,* 151–160.

Grace, N. C., Kelley, M. L., & McCain, A. P. (1993). Attribution processes in mother-adolescent conflict. *Journal of Abnormal Child Psychology, 21,* 199–211.

Graham-Bermann, S. A. (1996). Family worries: Assessment of interpersonal anxiety in children from violent and non-violent families. *Journal of Clinical Child Psychology, 25*(3), 280–287.

Graham-Bermann, S. A., & Cutler, S. E. (1994). The brother–sister questionnaire: Psychometric assessment and discrimination of well-functioning from dysfunctional relationships. *Journal of Family Psychology, 8*(2), 224–238.

Graham-Bermann, S. A., Cutler, S. E., Litzenberger, B. W., & Schwartz, W. F. (1994). Perceived conflict and violence in childhood sibling relationships and later emotional adjustment. *Journal of Family Psychology, 8*(1), 85–97.

Graham-Bermann, S. A., & Levendesky, A. A. (1997). The social functioning of preschool age children whose mothers are emotionally and physically abused. *Journal of Emotional Abuse, 1*(1), 57–80.

Green, A. (1991). Child sexual abuse: Immediate and long-term effects and intervention. *Journal of the American Academy of Child and Adolescent Psychiatry, 32*(5), 890–902.

Greene, R. C., & Plank, R. E. (1994). The short-form Family Environment Scale: Testing a different response format. *Psychological Reports, 74,* 451–464.

Gries, L. T., Goh, D. S., Andrews, M., Gilbert, J., Praver, F., & Stelzer, D. (2000). Positive reaction to disclosure and recovery from child sexual abuse. *Journal of Child Sexual Abuse, 9,* 29–51.

Grych, J. H., Seid, M., & Fincham, F. D. (1992). Assessing marital conflict from the child's perspective: The Children's' Perception of Interparental Conflict Scale. *Child Development, 63,* 558–572.

Hamby, S. L., & Finkelhor, D. (2000). The victimization of children: Recommendations for assessment and instrument development. *Journal of the Academy of Child and Adolescent Psychiatry, 39,* 829–840.

Hampson, R. D., Hulgas, Y. F., & Beavers, W. R. (1991). Comparison of self report measures of the Beavers Systems Model and Olson's circumplex model. *Journal of Family Psychology, 4,* 326–340.

Hansen, D. J., Conway, L. P., & Christopher, J. S. (1990). Victims of child physical abuse. In R. T. Ammerman & M. Hersen (Eds.), *Treatment of family violence.* New York: John Wiley & Sons.

Hansen, D. J., Pallotta, G. M., Christopher, J. S., Conaway, R. L., & Lundquist, L. M. (1995). The Parental Problem Solving Measure: Further evaluation with maltreating and non-maltreating parents. *Journal of Family Violence, 10,* 319–336.

Hansen, D. J., Pallotta, G. M., Tishelman, A. C., Conaway, L. P., & MacMillan, V. M. (1989). Parental problem-solving skills and child behavior problems: A comparison of physically abusive, neglectful, clinic and community families. *Journal of Family Violence, 4,* 353–368.

Hansen, D. J., & Warner, J. E. (1992). Child physical abuse and neglect. In R. T. Ammerman & M. Hersen (Eds.), *Assessment of family violence: A clinical and legal source book.* New York: John Wiley and Sons.

Harbeck, D., Peterson, L., & Starr, L. (1992). Previously abused child victims' responses to a sexual abuse prevention program: A matter of measures. *Behavior Therapy, 23,* 375–387.

Harrington, D., Dubowitz, H., Black, M., & Binda, A. (1995). Maternal substance use and neglectful parenting: Relations with children's development. *Journal of Clinical Child Psychology, 24,* 258–263.

Haskett, M. E. (1990). Social problem-solving skills of young psychically abused children. *Child Psychiatry and Human Development, 21,* 109–118.

Haskett, M. E., & Kistner, J. A. (1991). Social interactions and peer perceptions of young physically abused children. *Child Development, 62,* 979–990.

Haskett, M. E., Myers, L. W., Pirrillo, V. E., & Dombalis, A. O. (1995). Parenting style as a mediating link between parental emotional health and adjustment of maltreated children. *Behavior Therapy, 26,* 625–642.

Haskett, M. E., Scott, S. S., & Fann, K. D. (1995). Child Abuse Potential Inventory and parenting behavior: Relationships with high risk correlates. *Child Abuse and Neglect, 19,* 1483–1495.

Hazzard, A., Christensen, A., & Margolin, G. (1983). Children's perceptions of parental behaviors. *Journal of Abnormal Child Psychology, 11,* 49–60.

Helfer, R. E., Hoffmeister, J. K., & Schneider, C. J. (1978). *MSPP: A manual for the use of the Michigan Screening Profile of Parenting: A 12-year study to develop and test a predictive questionnaire* (Grant Report 90-C-432). Washington, DC: Department of Health, Education and Welfare.

Hennessy, K. D., Rabideau, G. J., Cicchetti, D., & Cummings, E. M. (1994). Responses of physically abused and nonabused children to different forms of interadult anger. *Child Development, 65,* 815–828.

Herman, J. L., Perry, J. C., & van der Kolk, B. A. (1989). Childhood trauma in borderline personality disorder. *American Journal of Psychiatry, 146,* 490–495.

Hillson, J. M., & Kuiper, N. (1994). A stress and coping model of child maltreatment. *Clinical Psychology Review, 14,* 261–285.

Hoglund, C. L., & Nicholas, K. B. (1995). Shame, guilt and anger in college students exposed to abusive family environments. *Journal of Family Violence, 10,* 141–157.

Holden, E. W., & Banez, G. A. (1996). Child abuse potential and parenting stress within maltreating families. *Journal of Family Violence, 11,* 1–12.

Holtzworth-Munroe, A., Beatty, S. B., & Anglin, K. (1995). The assessment and treatment of marital violence: An introduction for the marital therapist. In N. S. Jacobson & A. S. Gurman (Eds.), *Clinical handbook of couple therapy* (pp. 317–339). New York: Guilford Press.

Hops, H., Wills, T. A., Patterson, G. R., & Weiss, R. L. (1972). *Marital Interaction Coding System.* Eugene: University of Oregon Research Institute.

Horowitz, M., Wilner, N., & Alvarez, W. (1979). Impact of Event Scale. A measure of subjective stress. *Psychosomatic Medicine, 41,* 209–218.

Hughes, D., Seidman, E., & Williams, N. (1993). Cultural phenomena and the research enterprise: Toward a culturally anchored methodology. *American Journal of Community Psychology, 21,* 687–703.

Hutchinson, S. A., Wilson, M. E., & Wilson, H. S. (1994). Benefits of participating in research interviews. *IMAGE: Journal of Nursing Scholarship, 26,* 161–164.

Inderbitzen-Pisaruk, H., Shawchuck, C. R., & Hoier, T. S. (1992). Behavioral characteristics of child victims of sexual abuse: A comparison study. *Journal of Clinical Child Psychology, 21,* 14–19.

Irvine, A. B., Biglan, A., Smolkowski, K., & Ary, D. V. (1999). The value of the Parenting

Scale for measuring the discipline practices of parents of middle school children. *Behavior, Research and Therapy, 37*, 127–142.

Jackson, D. N. (1970). A sequential system for personality scale development. In C. D. Spielberger (Ed.), *Current topics in clinical and community psychology* (Vol. 2; pp. 61–92). New York: Academic Press.

Jacob, T., Tennenbaum, D., Bargiel, K., & Seilhamer, R. (1995). Family interaction in the home: Development of a new coding system. *Behavior Modification, 19*, 147–169.

Jaffee, P., Wilson, S. K., & Wolfe, D. (1988). Specific assessment and intervention strategies for children exposed to wife battering: Preliminary empirical investigations. *Canadian Journal of Community Mental Health, 7*, 157–163.

Jaffee, P., Wilson, S. K., & Sas, L. (1987). Court testimony of child sexual abuse victims: Emerging issues in clinical assessments. *Canadian Psychology, 28*, 291–295.

Janoff-Bulman, R. (1989). Assumptive worlds and the stress of traumatic events: Application of the schema construct. *Social Cognition, 7*, 113–136.

Johnston, C., & Freeman, W. S. (1997). Attributions for child behavior in parents of nonproblem children and children with attention deficit hyperactivity disorder. *Journal of Consulting and Clinical Psychology, 65*, 636–645.

Johnston, C., & Mash, E. J. (1989). A measure of parenting satisfactions and efficacy. *Journal of Clinical Child Psychology, 18*, 167–175.

Johnston, C., Reynolds, S., Freeman, W. S., & Geller, J. (1998). Assessing parent attributions for child behavior using open-ended questions. *Journal of Clinical Child Psychology, 27*, 87–97.

Jones, R. T. (1992). *Impact of Event Scale for Children*. Unpublished manuscript.

Jones, R. T. (1994). *Child's Reaction to Traumatic Events Scale (CRTES): A self report traumatic stress measure*. Unpublished manuscript.

Jorgensen, S. R. (1977). Societal class heterogamy, status striving, and perception of marital conflict: A partial replication and revision of Pearlin's contingency hypothesis. *Journal of Marriage and the Family, 39*, 653–689.

Kanner, A. D., Coyne, J., Schaefer, C., & Lazarus, R. S. (1981). Comparison of two modes of stress measurement: Daily hassles and uplifts versus major events. *Journal of Behavioral Medicine, 4*, 1–39.

Kavanagh, K. A., Youngblade, L., Reid, J. B., & Fagot, B. (1988). Interactions between children and abusive versus control parents. *Journal of Clinical Child Psychology, 17*, 137–142.

Kazdin, A. (1998). *Research design in clinical psychology*. Needham Heights, MA: Allyn & Bacon.

Kendall-Tackett, K. A., Williams, L. M., & Finklehor, D. (1993). Impact of sexual abuse on children: A review and synthesis of recent empirical studies. *Psychological Bulletin, 113*, 164–180.

Kerig, P. K. (1996). Assessing the links between marital conflicts and child development: The Conflicts and Problem-Solving Scales. *Journal of Family Psychology, 10*, 454–473.

Kerig, P. K. (1998). Gender and appraisals as mediators of adjustment in children exposed to interparental violence. *Journal of Family Violence, 13*, 345–363.

Kerig, P. K., & Fedorowicz, A. E. (1999). Assessing maltreatment of children of battered women: Methodological and ethical concerns. *Child Maltreatment, 4*, 103–115.

King, G. A., Rogers, C., Walters, G. C., & Oldershaw, L. (1994). Parent behavior rating scales: Preliminary validation with intrusive, abusive mothers. *Child Abuse and Neglect, 18*, 247–259.

Knutson, J. F., & Selner, M. B. (1994). Punitive childhood experiences reported by young adults over a ten year period. *Child Abuse and Neglect, 18,* 43–54.

Kochanska, G., Akasan, N., & Koenig, A. (1995). A longitudinal study of the roots of preschoolers' conscience: Committed compliance and emerging internalization. *Child Development, 66,* 1752–1769.

Koenig, A. L., Cicchetti, D., & Rogosch, F. (2000). Child compliance/noncompliance and maternal contributors to internalization in maltreating and nonmaltreating dyads. *Child Development, 71,* 1018–1032.

Kolko, D. J. (1996a). Clinical monitoring of treatment course in child physical abuse: Child and parent reports. *Child Abuse and Neglect, 20,* 23–43.

Kolko, D. J. (1996b). Individual cognitive behavioral treatment and family therapy for physically abused children and their offending parents: A comparison of clinical outcomes. *Child Maltreatment, 1*(4)*,* 322–342.

Kolko, D. J., Kazdin, A. E., & Day, B. T. (1996). Children's perspectives in the assessment of family violence: Psychometric characteristics and comparisons to parent reports. *Child Maltreatment, 1*(2)*,* 156–167.

Kolko, D. J., Kazdin, A. E., Thomas, A. M., & Day, B. (1993). Heightened child physical abuse potential: Child, parent and family dysfunction. *Journal of Interpersonal Violence, 8,* 169–192.

Koocher, G. P., Goodman, G. S., White, C. S., Friedrich, W. N., Sivan, A. B., et al. (1995). Psychological science and the use of anatomically detailed dolls in child sexual abuse assessments. *Psychological Bulletin, 118*(2)*,* 199–222.

Kurdek, L. A., & Berg, B. (1987). The Children's Beliefs About Parental Divorce Scale: Psychometric characteristics and concurrent validity. *Journal of Consulting and Clinical Psychology, 55,* 712–718.

Laing, J. A., & Sines, J. O. (1982). The Home Environment Questionnaire: An instrument for assessing several behaviorally relevant dimensions of children's environments. *Journal of Pediatric Psychology, 7,* 425–449.

Lamb, M. E., Steinberg, K. J., & Esplin, P. W. (1994). Factors influencing the reliability and validity of statements made by young victims of sexual maltreatment. *Journal of Applied Developmental Psychology, 15,* 255–280.

Langer, T. S. (1962). A twenty-two item screening score of psychiatric symptoms indicating impairment. *Journal of Health and Human Behavior, 3,* 269–276.

Lanktree, C. B., & Briere, J. (1995). Outcome of therapy for sexually abused children: A repeated measures study. *Child Abuse and Neglect, 19,* 1145–1155.

Lanktree, C. B., Briere, J., Hernandez, P. (1991, Aug.). *Further data on the TSCC-Reliability, validity, and sensitivity to treatment.* Paper presented at the annual meeting of the American Psychological Association, San Francisco.

Larrance, D. T., & Twentyman, C. T. (1983). Maternal attributions and child abuse. *Journal of Abnormal Psychology, 92,* 449–457.

Levy, H. B., Markovic, J., Kalinowski, M. N., Ahart, S., & Torres, H. (1995). Child sexual abuse interviews: The use of anatomical dolls and the reliability of information. *Journal of Interpersonal Violence, 10,* 334–353.

Lewis, J. M., Beavers, W. R., Gossett, J. T., & Phillips, R. A. (1976). *No single thread: Psychological health in family systems.* New York: Brunner/Mazel.

Limandri, B. J., & Sheridan, D. J. (1995). Prediction of intentional interpersonal violence: An introduction. In J. C. Campbell (Ed.), *Assessing dangerousness: Violence by sexual offenders, batterers, and child abusers* (pp. 1–19). Thousand Oaks, CA: Sage.

Lindahl, K. M. (1998). Family process variables and children's disruptive behavior problems. *Journal of Family Psychology, 12,* 420–436.

Linehan, M. M. (1980). Content validity: Its relevance to behavioral assessment. *Behavioral Assessment, 2,* 147–159.

Linehan, M. M., Paul, E., & Egan, K. J. (1983). The Parent Affect Test: Development, validity and reliability. *Journal of Clinical Child Psychology, 12,* 161–166.

Linn, M. W. (1985). Global Assessment of Recent Stress (GARS) Scale. *International Journal of Psychiatry in Medicine, 15,* 47–59.

Locke, H. J., & Wallace, K. M. (1959). Short marital adjustment and prediction tests: Their reliability and validity. *Marriage and Family Living, 21,* 251–255.

Long, P. J., & Jackson, J. L. (1991). Children sexually abused by multiple perpetrators: Familial risk factors and abuse characteristics. *Journal of Interpersonal Violence, 6,* 147–159.

Long, P. J., & Jackson, J. L. (1994). Childhood sexual abuse: An examination of family functioning. *Journal of Interpersonal Violence, 9,* 270–277.

Lonner, W. J. (1994). Culture and human diversity. In E. J. Trickett, R. J. Watts, & D. Birman (Eds.), *Human diversity* (pp. 230–243). San Francisco: Jossey-Bass.

Lovejoy, M. C., Verda, M. R., & Hays, C. E. (1997). Convergent and discriminant validity of measures of parenting efficacy and control. *Journal of Clinical Child Psychology, 26,* 366–376.

Lovejoy, M. C., Weis, R., O'Hare, E., & Rubin, E. C. (1999). Development and initial validation of the Parent Behavior Inventory. *Psychological Assessment, 11,* 534–545.

MacMillan, V., Olson, R., & Hansen, D. J. (1988, Nov.). *The development of an anger inventory for use with maltreating parents.* Presented at the annual meeting of Association for Advancement of Behavior Therapy, New York.

MacMillan, V. M., Olson, R. L., & Hansen, D. J. (1991). Low and high stress analogue assessment of parent training with physically abusive parents. *Journal of Family Violence, 6,* 279–301.

Madonna, P. G., Van Scoyle, S., & Jones D. P. (1991). Family interaction with incest and nonincest families. *American Journal of Psychiatry, 148,* 46–49.

Mahoney, A., Boggio, R. M., & Jouriles, E. N. (1996). Effects of verbal marital conflict on subsequent mother-son interactions in a child clinical sample. *Journal of Clinical Child Psychology, 25,* 262–271.

Malinosky-Rummel, R. R., & Hoier, T. S. (1991). Validating measures of dissociation in sexually abused and nonabused children. *Behavioral Assessment, 13,* 341–357.

Mannarino, A. P., Cohen, J. A., & Berman, S. R. (1994). The Children's Attributions and Perceptions Scale: A new measure of sexual abuse-related factors. *Journal of Clinical Child Psychology, 23,* 204–211.

Margolin, G. (1992). *The Potential Family Conflict Questionnaire.* Unpublished instrument, University of Southern California, Los Angeles.

Mash, E. J., Johnston, D., & Kovitz, K. (1983). A comparison of the mother-child interactions of physically abused and nonabused children during play and task situations. *Journal of Clinical Child Psychology, 12,* 337–346.

Mash, E. J., Terdal, L., & Anderson, K. (1973). The Response-Class Matrix: A procedure for recording parent-child interactions. *Journal of Consulting and Clinical Psychology, 40,* 163–164.

Matorin, A., & Lynn, S. (1998). The development of a measure of correlates of child sexual abuse: The Traumatic Sexualization Survey. *Journal of Traumatic Stress, 11,* 261–280.

Matsumoto, D. (1994). *Cultural influences on research methods and statistics.* Pacific Grove, CA: Brooks/Cole.

McCubbin, E. I., Patterson, J. M., & Wilson, L. R. (1980). *Family Inventory of Life Events and Changes (FILE) Form A.* St. Paul: Family Social Science, University of Minnesota.

McCubbin, H., & Thompston, A. (1991). *Family assessment inventories for research and practice.* Madison: University of Wisconsin.

McGee, R. A., & Wolfe, D. A. (1990). *Development of a record of maltreatment experiences.* Unpublished manuscript, The Institute for the Prevention of Child Abuse, Toronto, Canada.

McGee, R. A., Wolfe, D. A., Yuen, S. A., Wilson, S. K., & Carnochan, J. (1995). The measurement of maltreatment: A comparison of approaches. *Child Abuse and Neglect, 19,* 233–249.

McLeer, S. V., Deblinger, E., Henry, D., & Orvaschel, H. (1992). Sexually abused children at high risk for PTSD. *Journal of the American Academy of Child and Adolescent Psychiatry, 31,* 875–879.

McNair, P. M., Lorr, M., & Droppleman, L. (1971). *Manual, Profile of Mood States.* San Diego, CA: Education and Industrial Testing Services.

Menzies, R. J., Webster, C. D., & Sepejak, D. S. (1985). Hitting the forensic sound barrier: Predictions of dangerousness in a pre-trial psychiatric clinic. In C. D. Webster, M. H. Ben-Aron, & S. J. Hucker (Eds.), *Dangerousness: Probability and prediction, psychiatry and public policy* (pp. 115–144). New York: Cambridge University Press.

Messman, T. L., & Long, P. J. (1996). Child sexual abuse and its relationship to revictimization in adult women: A review. *Clinical Psychology Review, 16,* 397–420.

Miller-Perrin, C. L., & Wurtele, S. K. (1989). Children's conceptions of personal body safety: A comparison across ages. *Journal of Clinical Child Psychology, 18,* 25–35.

Milner, J. S. (1986). *The Child Abuse Potential Inventory manual* (2nd ed.). Webster, NC: Psyctech.

Milner, J. S. (1991). Physical child abuse perpetrator screening and evaluation. *Criminal Justice and Behavior, 18,* 47–63.

Milner, J. S. (1993). Social information processing and physical child abuse. *Clinical Psychology Review, 13,* 275–294.

Milner, J. S. (1994). Assessing physical child abuse risk: The Child Abuse Potential Inventory. *Clinical Psychology Review, 14,* 547–583.

Milner, J. S., & Crouch, J. L. (1993). Physical child abuse. In R. L. Hampton, T. P. Gullotta, G. R. Adams, E. H. Potter III, & R. P. Weissberg (Eds.), *Family violence: Prevention and treatment* (pp. 25–55). Newbury Park, CA: Sage.

Milner, J. S., & Crouch, J. L. (1997). Impact and detection of response distortions on parenting measures used to assess risk for child physical abuse. *Journal of Personality Assessment, 69*(3), 633–650.

Moos, R. H., & Moos, B. S. (1986). *Family Environment Scale manual* (2nd ed.). Palo Alto, CA: Consulting Psychologists Press.

Morgan, T., & Cummings, A. L. (1999). Change experienced during group therapy by female survivors of childhood sexual abuse. *Journal of Consulting and Clinical Psychology, 67,* 28–36.

Nader, K. (1993). *Manual for the use of the CPTSD-RI; Introduction and item by item instructions for use of the Reaction Index.* Unpublished manuscript.

Nader, K. O. (1997). Assessing traumatic experiences in children. In J. P. Wilson & T. M. Keane (Eds.), *Assessing psychological trauma and PTSD* (pp. 291–348). New York: Guilford Press.

Nader, K., Kriegler, J., Blake, D., Pynoos, R., Newman, E., et al. (1996). *Clinician-administered PTSD Scale for Children and Adolescents for DSM IV.* Unpublished manuscript, National Center for PTSD and UCLA Trauma Psychiatry Program, Los Angeles.

Nannaly, J. C., & Bernstein, I. H. (1994). *Psychometric theory* (3rd ed.). New York: McGraw-Hill.

Nicholas, K. B., & Bieber, S. L. (1997). Assessment of perceived parenting behaviors: The exposure to Abusive and Supportive Environments Parenting Inventory (EASE-PI). *Journal of Family Violence, 12,* 275–291.

Novaco, R. W. (1985). Anger and its therapeutic regulation. In M. A. Chesney & R. H. Rosenman (Eds.), *Anger and hostility in cardiovascular and behavioral disorders* (pp. 203–226). Washington DC: Hemisphere.

Nunnally, J. C. (1978). *Psychometric theory.* New York: McGraw-Hill.

O'Brien, M., Bahadur, M. A., Gee, C., Balto, K., & Erber, S. (1997). Child exposure to marital conflict and child coping responses. *Cognitive Therapy and Research, 21*(1), 39–59.

O'Brien, M., Margolin, G., John, R. S., & Krueger, L. (1991). Mothers' and sons' cognitive and emotional reactions to simulated marital and family conflict. *Journal of Consulting and Clinical Psychology, 59,* 692–703.

O'Donohue, W., & Elliott, A. N. (1991). A model for the clinical assessment of the sexually abused child. *Behavioral Assessment, 13,* 325–339.

Oldershaw, L., Walters, G. C., & Hall, D. K. (1986). Control strategies and noncompliance in abusive mother-child dyads: An observational study. *Child Development, 57,* 722–732.

Oldershaw, L., Walters, G. C., & Hall, D. K. (1989). A behavioral approach to the classification of different types of physically abusive mothers. *Merill-Palmer Quarterly, 35,* 255–29.

Ollendick, T. (1983). Reliability and validity of the revised Fear Survey Schedule for Children (FSSC-R). *Behavior, Research and Therapy, 21,* 395–399.

Olson, D. H. (1988). *Clinical Rating Scale (CRS) for the Circumplex Model of Marital and Family Systems.* St. Paul: University of Minnesota, Department of Family, Social Sciences.

Olson, D. H. (1993). Circumplex model of marital and family systems: Assessing family functioning. In F. Walsh (Ed.), *Normal family process* (pp. 104–137). New York: Guilford Press.

Olson, E. H., Portner, J., & Lavee, Y. (1985). *FACES III.* St. Paul: Faculty of Social Sciences, University of Minnesota.

Orr, S. P., Lasko, N. B., Netzger, L. J., Berry, N. J., Ahern, C. E., & Pitman, R. K. (1998). Psychophysiologic assessment of women with posttraumatic stress disorder resulting from childhood sexual abuse. *Journal of Consulting and Clinical Psychology, 66,* 906–913.

Parker, G., Tupling, H., & Brown, L. B. (1979). A Parental Bonding Instrument. *British Journal of Medical Psychology, 52,* 1–10.

Patterson, G. R. (1982). *Coercive family process: A social learning approach* (Vol. 3). Eugene, OR: Castalia.

Patterson, G. R., Ray, R. S., Shaw, D. A., & Cobb, J. A. (1969). *Manual for coding of family interactions.* Unpublished manuscript, University of Oregon, Eugene.

Pearlman, L. A., & MacIan, P. S. (1995). Vicarious traumatization: An empirical study of the effects of trauma work on trauma therapists. *Professional Psychology: Research and Practice, 26*(6), 585–564.

Pelcovitz, D., & Kaplan, S. J. (1994). Child witnesses of violence between parents. *Child and Adolescent Psychiatric Clinics of North America, 3,* 745–758.

Pelcovitz, D., Vanderkolk, B., Roth, S., Kaplan, S., Mandel, F., et al. (1997). Development and validation of the structured interview for measurement of complex PTSD. *Journal of Traumatic Stress, 10,* 3–16.

Perry, J. C., Herman, J. L., & Van de Kolk, B. A. (1992). *Rating guidelines for the Traumatic Antecedents Interview (TAI)*. Unpublished manuscript, Montreal, Canada.

Peters, C. L., & Fox, R. A. (1993). Parenting inventory: Validity and social desirability. *Psychological Reports, 72*, 683–689.

Peterson, L., Ewigman, B., & Kivlahan, C. (1993). Judgements regarding appropriate child supervision to prevent injury: The role of environmental risk and child age. *Child Development, 64*, 934–950.

Peterson, L., Ewigman, B., & Vandiver, T. (1994). Role of parental anger in low income women: Discipline strategy, perceptions of behavior problems, and the need for control. *Journal of Clinical Child Psychology, 23*, 435–443.

Petretic-Jackson, P. A. (1992). The Child Abuse Blame Scale-Physical Abuse (CABS-PA): Assessing blame for physical child abuse. In L. Vandercreek, S. Knapp, & T. L. Jackson (Eds.), *Innovations in Clinical Practice* (pp. 315–324). Sarasota, FL: Professional Resource Exchange.

Petty, J. (1990). *Checklist for Child Abuse Evaluation*. Odessa, FL: Psychological Assessment Resources.

Pino, C. J., Simons, N., & Slawinowski, M. J. (1984). *Children's version: Family environment scale*. Palo Alto, CA: Consulting Psychologists Press.

Pitman, R. K., Orr, S. P., Forgue, D. F., deJong, J. B., & Claiborn, J. M. (1987). Psychophysiologic assessment of post traumatic stress disorder imagery in Vietnam combat veterans. *Archives of General Psychiatry, 44*, 970–975.

Polansky, N. A., Chalmers, M., Buttenwieser, E., & Williams, D. (1981). *Damaged parents: An anatomy of child neglect*. Chicago: University of Chicago Press.

Polansky, N. A., Gaudin, J. M., & Kilpatrick, A. C. (1992). The Maternal Characteristics Scale: A cross-validation. *Child Welfare League, 71*(3), 271–279.

Praver, F. (1994). *Child Rating Scales—Exposure to interpersonal abuse*. Unpublished copyrighted instrument, Locust Valley, NY.

Praver, F., Pelcovitz, D., & DiGuiseppe, R. (1996). *Angie/Andy Cartoon Scales*. North Tonawanda, NY: Multi-Health Systems.

Prinz, R. J., Foster, S. L., Kent, R. M., & O'Leary, K. D. (1979). Multivariate assessment of conflict in distressed and nondistressed mother-adolescent dyads. *Journal of Applied Behavior Analysis, 12*, 691–700.

Prinz, R. J., & Kent, R. N. (1978). Recording parent-adolescent interactions without the use of frequency or interval-by-interval coding. *Behavior Therapy, 9*, 602–604.

Putnam, F. W. (1990). *Child Dissociative Checklist* (Version 3. 0-2/90). Bethesda, MD: Laboratory of Developmental Psychology, National Institute of Mental Health.

Putnam, F. W. (1997). *Dissociation in children and adolescents: A developmental perspective*. New York: Guilford Press.

Putnam, F. W., Helmers, K., & Trickett, P. K. (1993). Development, reliability and validity of a child dissociation scale. *Child Abuse and Neglect, 17*, 731–741.

Putnam, F. W., & Peterson, G. (1994). Further validation of the Child Dissociative Checklist. *Dissociation, 4*, 204–211.

Pynoos, R. S., & Eth, S. (1986). Witness to violence: The child interview. *Journal of the American Academy of Child Psychiatry, 25*, 306–319.

Raskin, D. C., & Esplin, P. W. (1991). Statement validity assessment: Interview procedures and content analysis of children's statements of sexual abuse. *Behavioral Assessment, 13*, 265–291.

Rathus, J. H., & Feindler, E. L. (in press). *Handbook of assessment in partner violence*. Washington, DC: American Psychological Association.

Rausch, K., & Knutson, J. F. (1991). The self-report of personal punitive childhood experiences and those of siblings. *Child Abuse and Neglect, 15*, 29–36.

Reitman, D., Currier, R., Hupp, S., Rhode, P., Murphy, M., et al. (2001). Psychometric characteristics of the Parenting Scale in a Headstart population. *Journal of Clinical Child Psychology, 30,* 514–524.

Richters, J. E., & Martinez, P. (1993). The NIMH community violence project: I. Children as victims of and witnesses to violence. *Psychiatry, Interpersonal and Biological Processes, 56,* 7–21.

Rittner, B., & Wodarski, J. S. (1995). Clinical assessment instruments in the treatment of child abuse and neglect. *Early Child Development and Care, 106,* 43–58.

Roberts, M. W., Arnold, S. B., & Magnum, P. F. (1992). The Sibling Conflict Resolution Scale. *The Behavior Therapist, 15,* 254–256.

Robin, A. L., & Foster, S. L. (1989). *Negotiating parent-adolescent conflict: A behavioral family systems approach.* New York: Guilford Press.

Robin, A., Koepke, T., & Moye, A. (1990). Multidimensional assessment of parent-adolescent relations. *Psychological Assessment, 2,* 451–459.

Robin, A. L., & Weiss, J. G. (1980). Criterion related validity of behavioral and self report measures of problem-solving communication skills in distressed and non-distressed parent-adolescent dyads. *Behavioral Assessment, 2,* 339–352.

Robinson, E., & Eyberg, S. (1981). The Dyadic Parent-Child Interaction Coding System: Standardization and validation. *Journal of Consulting and Clinical Psychology, 49,* 245–250.

Rodriguez, C. M., & Green, A. J. (1997). Parenting stress and anger expression as predictors of child abuse potential. *Child Abuse and Neglect, 21,* 367–377.

Rodriquez, N., Ryan, S., Rowan, A. B., & Foy, D. W. (1996). Post traumatic stress disorder in a clinical sample of adult survivors of childhood sexual abuse. *Child Abuse and Neglect, 20,* 943–952.

Rodriquez, N., Ryan, S. W., Vandekemp, H., & Foy, D. (1997). Post traumatic stress disorder in adult female survivors of childhood sexual abuse: A comparison study. *Journal of Clinical and Consulting Psychology, 65,* 53–59.

Roe, A., & Siegelman, M. (1963). A parent-child relations questionnaire. *Child Development, 34,* 355–369.

Roecker, C. E., Dubow, E. I., & Donaldson, D. (1996). Cross-situational patterns in children's coping with observed interpersonal conflict. *Journal of Clinical Child Psychology, 25*(3), 288–299.

Roehling, P. V., & Robin, A. L. (1986). Development and validation of the Family Beliefs Inventory: A measure of unrealistic beliefs among parents and adolescents. *Journal of Consulting and Clinical Psychology, 54*(5), 693–697.

Rossman, B. B. R., & Ho, J. (2000). Posttraumatic response and children exposed to parental violence. *Journal of Aggression, Maltreatment, and Trauma, 3,* 85–106.

Rossman, B. B., & Rosenberg, M. S. (1992). Family stress and functioning in children: The moderating effects of children's beliefs about their control over parental conflict. *Journal of Child Psychology and Psychiatry, 33,* 699–715.

Rotter, J. B. (1966). Generalized expectancies for internal versus external control of reinforcement. *Psychological Monographs, 80*(1, Whole No. 609).

Rowan, A. B., Foy, D. W., Rodriguez, N., & Ryan, S. W. (1994). Posttraumatic stress disorder in a clinical sample of adults sexually abused as children. *Child Abuse and Neglect, 18,* 51–61.

Ryan, S. W. (1993). Psychometric analysis of the Sexual Abuse Exposure Questionnaire. *Dissertation Abstract International, 53*(11), 3709A (University Microfilms No. DFA93-23808).

Salzinger, S., Feldman, R. S., Hammer, M., & Rosario, M. (1991). Risk for physical child abuse and the personal consequences for its victims. *Criminal Justice and Behavior, 18,* 82–97.

Salzinger, S., Feldman, R. S., Hammer, M., & Rosario, M. (1992). Constellations of family violence and their differential effects on children's behavioral disturbance. *Child and Family Behavior Therapy, 14,* 23–41.

Salzinger, S., Feldman, R. S., Hammer, M., & Rosario, M. (1993). The effects of physical abuse on children's social relationships. *Child Development, 64,* 169–187.

Sanders, B., & Becker-Lausen, E. (1995). The measurement of psychological maltreatment: Early data on the Child Abuse and Trauma Scale. *Child Abuse and Neglect, 19*(3), 315–323.

Sarno, J. A., & Wurtele, C. K. (1997). Effects of a personal safety program on preschoolers knowledge, skills and perceptions of child sexual abuse. *Child Maltreatment, 2,* 35–45.

Sattler, J. M. (1997). *Clinical and forensic interviewing of children and families.* San Diego, CA: Author.

Saywitz, K. J., & Snyder, L. (1996). Narrative elaboration: Test of a new procedure for interviewing children. *Journal of Consulting and Clinical Psychology, 64,* 1347–1357.

Scarr, S., Pinkerton, R., & Eisenberg, M. (1994). *The parental discipline interview manual.* Charlottesville: University of Virginia.

Schellenbach, C. J., Trickett, P. K., & Susman, E. J. (1991). A multi method approach to the assessment of physical abuse. *Violence and Victims, 6,* 57–73.

Schludermann, S., & Schludermann, E. (1977). A methodological study of a revised maternal attitude research instrument: PARIQ. *Journal of Psychology, 95,* 77–86.

Sedlar, G., & Hansen, P. J. (2001). Anger, child behavior and family distress: Further evaluation of the Parental Anger Inventory. *Journal of Family Violence, 16,* 361–373.

Sgroi, S. (Ed.). (1982). *Handbook of clinical intervention in child sexual abuse.* Lexington, MA: Lexington Books.

Shek, D. T. L. (1987). Reliability and factorial structure of the Chinese version of the General Health Questionnaire. *Journal of Clinical Psychology, 43,* 683–691.

Shipman, K. L., & Zeman, J. (1999). Emotional understanding: A comparison of physically maltreating and nonmaltreating mother-child dyads. *Journal of Clinical Child Psychology, 28,* 407–417.

Shrout, P. E., & Fleiss, J. L. (1979). Intraclass correlations: Uses in assessing rater reliability. *Psychological Bulletin, 86,* 420–428.

Silber, S., Bermann, E., Henderson, M., & Lehman, A. (1993). Patterns of influence and response in abusing and nonabusing families. *Journal of Family Violence, 8,* 27–38.

Singer, M. I., Anglen, T. M., Song, L. Y., & Lunghofer, L. (1995). Adolescents' exposure to violence and associated symptoms of psychological trauma. *Journal of American Medical Association, 273*(6), 477–482.

Skinner, H. A., Steinhauer, P. D., & Santa Barbara, J. (1995). *Family Assessment Measure III—manual.* North Tonawanda, NY: Multi Health Systems.

Skinner, L. J., & Berry, K. K. (1993). Anatomically detailed dolls and the evaluation of child sexual abuse allegations: Psychometric considerations. *Law and Human Behavior, 17,* 399–421.

Skinner, L., & Giles, M. K. (1993). Sixteen reasons for not using anatomically detailed dolls in sexual abuse validation interviews. In L. Vandercreek, S. Knapp, & T. L. Jackson (Eds.), *Innovations in Clinical Practice* (Vol. 12, pp. 505–518). Sarasota, FL: Professional Resources Press.

Smith, A. M., & O'Leary, S. G. (1995). Attributions and arousal as predictors of maternal discipline. *Cognitive Therapy and Research, 19,* 459–471.

Smith, S., & Carlson, E. B. (1996). Unpublished manuscript, Menlo Park, CA.

Solis-Camara, P., & Fox, R. A. (1996). Parenting practices and expectations among Mexican mothers with young children. *Journal of Genetic Psychology, 157,* 465–476.

Spaccarelli, S. (1993). *Documentation of scales for the study of stress and coping in child sex abuse.* Unpublished manuscript, Arizona State University.

Spaccarelli, S. (1995). Measuring abuse, stress, and negative cognitive appraisals in child sexual abuse: Validity data on two new scales. *Journal of Abnormal Child Psychology, 23*(6), 703–725.

Spaccarelli, S. (1994). Stress, appraisal and coping in child sexual abuse. *Psychological Bulletin, 116,* 340–362.

Spaccarelli, S., & Fuchs, L. S. (1997). Variability in symptom expression among sexually abused girls: Developing multivariate models. *Journal of Clinical Child Psychology, 26,* 24–35.

Spaccarelli, S., & Kim, S. (1995). Resilience criteria and factors associated with resilience in sexually abused girls. *Child Abuse and Neglect, 19,* 1171–1182.

Spielberger, C. (1973). *Manual for the State-Trait Anxiety Inventory for Children.* Palo Alto, CA: Consulting Psychologists Press.

Speilberger, C., Gorsuch, R., Lushene, R., Vagg, P., & Jacobs, G. (1983). *Manual for the State-Trait Anxiety Inventory.* Palo Alto, CA; Consulting Psychologists Press.

Spielberger, C. D., Jacobs, G., Russel, S., & Crane, R. S. (1983). Assessment of anger: The State-Trait Anger Scale. In J. N. Butcher & C. D. Spielberger (Eds.), *Advances in personality assessment* (Vol. 2., pp. 159–187). Hillsdale, NJ: Erlbaum.

Spinetta, J. J., & Rigler, D. (1972). The child abusing parent: A psychological review. *Psycholgical Bulletin, 77,* 296–304.

Stamm, B. H. (1996). *Measurement of stress, trauma and adaptation.* Lutherville, MD: Sidran Press.

Stormshak, E. A., & Greenberg, M. T. (1996). *The Family Intake Coding System.* Unpublished manuscript, University of Washington.

Stormshak, E. A., Speltz, M. L., DeKlyen, M., & Greenberg, M. T. (1997). Observed family interaction during clinical interviews: A comparison of families containing preschool boys with and without disruptive behavior. *Journal of Abnormal Child Psychology, 25*(5), 345–357.

Strassberg, Z. (1997). Levels of analysis in cognitive bases of maternal disciplinary dysfunction. *Journal of Abnormal Child Psychology, 25,* 209–215.

Straus, M. (1979). Measuring intrafamily conflict and violence: The Conflict Tactics Scale. *Journal of Marriage and the Family, 41,* 75–88.

Straus, M., & Hamby, S. (1997). Measuring physical and psychological maltreatment of children with the Conflict Tactics Scale. In. G. Kaufman Kantor & J. L. Jasinski (Eds.), *Out of darkness: Contemporary research perspectives on family violence.* Thousand Oaks, CA: Sage.

Straus, M. A., Hamby, S. L., Finkelhor, D., Moore, D. W., & Runyan, D. (1998). Identification of child maltreatment with the Parent-Child Conflict Tactics Scales: Development and psychometric data for a national sample of American parents. *Child Abuse and Neglect, 22,* 249–270.

Straus, M. A., Hamby, S. L., Finkelhor, D., & Runyan, D. (1995). *Identification of child maltreatment with the Parent–Child Conflict Tactics Scale (CTSPC): Development and psychometric data for a national sample of American parents.* Durham: Family Research Laboratory, University of New Hampshire.

Straus, M. A., Kinard, E. M., & Williams, L. M. (1995). *The Multidimensional Neglect Scale, Form A: Adolescent and adult-recall version.* Presented at Fourth International Conference on Family Violence Research, Durham, NH.

Sue, S. (1999). Science, ethnicity, and bias. Where have we gone wrong? *American Psychologist, 54,* 1070–1077.

Tam, K., Chan, Y., Wong, C. M. (1994). Validation of the Parenting Stress Index among Chinese mothers in Hong Kong. *Journal of Community Psychology, 22,* 211–224.

Tennenbaum, D. L. (1980). *The effect of observer salience on family interaction in the home.* Unpublished masters thesis, University of Pittsburgh, PA.

Tertinger, D. A., Green, B. F., & Lutzker, J. R. (1984). Home safety: Development and validation of one component of an ecobehavioral treatment program for abused and neglected children. *Journal of Applied Behavior Analysis, 17,* 159–174.

Thomas, V., & Olson, D. H. (1993). Problem families and the circumplex model: Observational assessment using the Clinical Rating Scale. *Journal of Marital and Family Therapy, 19,* 159–175.

Thompson, R. (1999). Early attachment and later development. In J. Cassidy & P. R. Shaver (Eds.), *Handbook of attachment: Theory, research and clinical applications* (pp. 265–286). New York: Guilford Press.

Trepper, T. S., & Sprenkle, D. H. (1988). The clinical use of the Circumplex Model in the assessment and treatment of intrafamily child sexual abuse. *Journal of Psychotherapy and the Family, 4,* 93–111.

Trickett, P. K., & Kaczymski, L. (1986). Children's misbehaviors and parental discipline: Strategies in abusive and nonabusive families. *Developmental Psychology, 22,* 115–123.

Trickett, P. K., & Susman, E. J. (1988). Parental perceptions of child rearing practices in physically abusive and non-abusive families. *Developmental Psychology, 24,* 270–276.

Tuteur, J. M., Ewigman, B. E., Peterson, L., & Hosokawn, M. C. (1995). The Maternal-Observation Matrix and the Mother-Child Interaction Scale: Brief observational screening instruments for physically abusive mothers. *Journal of Clinical Child Psychology, 24,* 55–62.

van der Kolk, B., Pelcovitz, D., Herman, J., Roth, S., Kaplan, S., & Spitzer, R. (1992). *Structured Interview for Disorders of Extreme Stress.* Unpublished manuscript.

van der Kolk, B. A., Perry, J. C., & Herman, J. L. (1991). Childhood origins of self destructive behavior. *American Journal of Psychiatry, 148,* 1665–1671.

Velting, D. M., Rathus, J. H., & Asnis, G. M. (1998). Asking adolescents to explain discrepancies in self-reported suicidality. *Suicide and Life Threatening Behavior, 28,* 187–196.

Vivian, D., & Langhinrichsen-Rohling, J. (1994). Are bi-directionally violent couples mutually victimized? A gender sensitive comparison. *Violence and Victims, 9,* 107–124.

Vuchinich, S. (1987). Starting and stopping spontaneous family conflicts. *Journal of Marriage and the Family, 49,* 591–601.

Wager, J. M., & Rodway, M. R. (1995). An evaluation of a group treatment approach for children who have witnessed wife abuse. *Journal of Family Violence, 10*(3), 295–306.

Walker, C. E., Bonner, B. L., & Kaufman, K. L. (1988). *The physically and sexually abused child.* New York: Pergamon Press.

Walker, E. A., Newman, E., Koss, M., & Bernstein, D. (1997). Does the study of victimization revictimize the victims? *General Hospital Psychiatry, 19,* 403–410.

Watson, D., Clark, L. A., & Tellegen, A. (1988). Development and validation of brief measures of positive and negative affect: The PANAS scale. *Journal of Personality and Social Psychology, 54,* 1–63.

Watson-Perczel, M., Lutzker, J. R., Greene, B., & McGimpsey, B. J. (1988). Assessment and modification of home cleanliness among families adjudicated for child neglect. *Behavior Modification, 12,* 57–81.

Webster-Stratton, C. (1985). Comparisons of behavior transactions between conduct-disordered children and their mothers at the clinic and at home. *Journal of Abnormal Child Psychology, 13,* 169–184.

Webster-Stratton, C., & Spitzer, A. (1991). Development reliability and validity of the Daily Telephone Discipline Interview. *Behavioral Assessment, 13,* 221–239.

Wechsler, D. (1974). *Manual for the Wechsler Intelligence Scale for Children—Revised.* New York: Psychological Corporation.

Weerts-Whitmore, E., Kramer, J., & Knutson, J. (1993). The association between punitive childhood experiences and hyperactivity. *Child Abuse and Neglect, 17,* 357–366.

Weiss, R. L., & Summers, K. J. (1983). Marital Interaction Coding System-III. In E E. Filsinger (Ed.), *A sourcebook of marriage and family assessment* (pp. 8–115). Beverly Hills, CA: Sage.

Weiss, R. L., & Tolman, A. D. (1990). The Marital Interaction Coding System-Global (MICS-G): A global companion to the MICS. *Behavioral Assessment, 12,* 271–294.

Wells, R. D. (1992). *Test-retest reliability of the structured interview for symptoms associated with sexual abuse (SASA).* Unpublished manuscript, Department of Pediatrics, Valley Medical Center, Fresno, CA.

Wells, R., McCann, J., Adams, J., Voris, J., & Dahl, B. (1997). A validational study of the Structured Interview of Symptoms Associated with Sexual Abuse (SASA) using three samples of sexually abused, allegedly abused, and nonabused boys. *Child Abuse and Neglect, 21,* 1159–1167.

Werner, P. D., Rose, T. L., & Yesavage, J. A. (1990). Aspects of consensus in clinical predictions of imminent violence. *Journal of Clinical Psychology, 46*(4), 534–538.

White, S. (1993). Assessing child sexual abuse allegations in custody disputes. In L. Vandercreek (Ed.), *Innovations in clinical practice: A source book* (Vol. 12, pp. 15–34). Sarasota FL: Professional Resources.

White, S., Strom, G. A., Santilli, G., & Halpin, B. M. (1986). Interviewing young sexual abuse victims with anatomically correct dolls. *Child Abuse and Neglect, 10,* 519–529.

Widom, C. S., & Shepard, R. L. (1996). Accuracy of adult recollections of childhood victimization: Part 1. Childhood physical abuse. *Psychological Assessment, 8,* 412–421.

Wolfe, D. A. (1985). Child abusive parents: An empirical review and analysis. *Psychological Bulletin, 97,* 462–482.

Wolfe, D. A. (1988). Child abuse and neglect. In E. J. Mash & L. G. Terdal (Eds.), *Behavioral assessment of childhood disorders* (2nd ed., pp. 627–669), New York: Guilford Press.

Wolfe, D. A., & McEachran, A. (1997). Child physical abuse and neglect. In E. J. Mash & L. G. Terdal (Eds.), *Assessment of childhood disorders* (pp. 523–568). New York: Guilford Press.

Wolfe, D. A., Wekerle, C., Reitzel-Jaffe, D., & LeFebure, L. (1998). Factors associated with abusive relationships among maltreated and nonmaltreated youth. *Development and Psychopathology, 10,* 61–85.

Wolfe, V. V., & Birt, J. (1993). *The Feelings and Emotions Experienced During Sexual Abuse Scale.* Unpublished manuscript, London Health Sciences Centre, London, Ontario, Canada.

Wolfe, V. V., & Birt, J. (1997). Child sexual abuse. In E. J. Mash & L. G. Terdal (Eds.), *Assessment of childhood disorders* (pp. 569–623). New York: Guilford Press.

Wolfe, V. V., Gentile, C., & Bourdeau, P. (1987). Unpublished assessment instrument, London Health Sciences Centre, London, Ontario, Canada.

Wolfe, V. V., Gentile, C., & Klink, A. (1988). *Psychometric properties of the Sexual Abuse Fear Evaluation (SAFE).* Unpublished manuscript, University of Western Ontario, London, Ontario.

Wolfe, V. V., Gentile, C., Michienzi, T., Sas, L., & Wolfe, D. A. (1991). The Children's Impact of Traumatic Events Scale: A measure of post-sexual abuse PTSD symptoms. *Behavioral Assessment, 13*(4), 359–383.

Wolfe, V. V., & Wolfe, D. A. (1986). *The Sexual Abuse Fear Evaluation.* Unpublished manuscript, London Health Sciences Centre, London, Ontario, Canada.

Wood, B. J. (1990). The child abuse interaction coding system. Unpublished manuscript.

Wood, B., Orsak, C., Murphy, M., & Cross, H. J. (1996). Semistructured child sexual abuse interviews: Interview and child characteristics related to the credibility of disclosure. *Child Abuse and Neglect, 20,* 81–92.

Wurtele, S. K. (1990). Teaching personal safety skills to four-year-old children: A behavioral approach. *Behavior Therapy, 21,* 25–32.

Wurtele, S. K. (1998). Sexual abuse. In R. T. Ammerman & M. Hersen (Eds.), *Handbook of prevention and treatment with children and adolescents: Intervention in the real world context* (pp. 357–384). New York: Wiley.

Wurtele, S. K., Currier, L. L., Gillespie, E. I., & Franklin, C. F. (1991). The efficacy of a parent-implemented program for teaching preschoolers personal safety skills. *Behavior Therapy, 22,* 69–83.

Wurtele, S. K., Hughes, J., & Sarno-Owens, J. (in press). An examination of the reliability of the "What If" Situations Test: Brief report. *Journal of Child Sexual Abuse, 6.*

Wurtele, S. K., Kast, L. C., & Kondrick, P. A. (1988, Aug.). *Development of an instrument to evaluate sexual abuse prevention programs.* Paper presented at the convention of the American Psychological Association, Atlanta, GA.

Wurtele, S. K., Kast, L. C., Miller-Perrin, C. L., & Kondrick, P. A. (1989). A comparison of programs for teaching personal safety skills to preschoolers. *Journal of Consulting and Clinical Psychology, 57,* 99–112.

Wurtele, S. K., & Miller-Perrin, C. L. (1987). An evaluation of side effects associated with participation in a child sexual abuse prevention program. *Journal of School Health, 57,* 228–231.

Wyatt, G. (1985). The sexual abuse of Afro-American and White American women in childhood. *Child Abuse and Neglect, 9,* 507–519.

Wyatt, G. E., Guthrie, D., & Notgrass, C. M. (1992). Differential effects on women's child sexual abuse and subsequent sexual revictimization. *Journal of Consulting and Clinical Psychology, 60,* 167–173.

Wyatt, G. E., Lawrence, J., Vodounon, A., & Mickey, M. R. (1992). The Wyatt Sex History Questionnaire: A structured interview for female sexual history taking. *Journal of Child Sexual Abuse, 1,* 51–68.

Zaidi, L. Y., Knutson, J. F., & Mehm, J. X. (1989). Transgenerational patterns of abusive parenting: Analog and clinical tests. *Aggressive Behavior, 15,* 137–152.

Zeman, J., & Shipman, K. (1996). Children's expression of negative affect: Reasons and methods. *Developmental Psychology, 32,* 842–849.

Author Index

Numbers in italics refer to listings in reference sections.

A

Abidin, R. R., 261, 262, 267, 280, 311, 319, 320, 322, 327, 330, 332, 333, 412, *507*
Achenbach, T. M., 36, 87, 88, 97, 98, 126, 141, 150, 187, 195, 196, 223, 256, 261, 326, 329, 355, 391, 394, 396, 456, 500, *507*
Acker, M. M., 297, 327, 332, 350, *508*
Adams, J., 109, 110, 111, *527*
Adamson, J. L., 437, 439, *507*
Ahart, S., 63, 66, *518*
Ahern, C. E., 229, 231, *521*
Ahl, M., 271, 272, 273, *511*
Akasan, N., 445, 447, 448, *518*
Alvarez, W., 106, 153, 155, 205, *516*
Ammerman, R. T., 72, 75, 76, 249, 253, *507*
Anderson, K., 492, *519*
Andrews, B., 26, *507*
Andrews, M., 133, *515*
Anglen, T. M., 210, 211, *524*
Anglin, K., *516*
Armstrong, J. G., 127, 129, 130, *507*
Arnold, D. S., 297, 324, 327, 332, 350, *508*
Arnold, S. B., 495, *523*
Ary, D. V., 325, 327, *516*
Asnis, G. M., 20
Avison, W. R., 293, *508*
Azar, S. T., 251, 252, 253, 312, 314, *508*

B

Babiker, G., 61, 62, *508*
Baglio, C., 370, 424, 425, *508*
Bahadur, M. A., 377, *521*
Bakeman, R., 239, 241, *508*
Baker-Ward, L., 60, *514*
Baldwin, L. M., 297, *513*
Balto, K., 377, *521*
Bandura, A., 371, *508*
Banez, G. A., 250, *516*
Bargiel, K., 466, 469, *517*
Barton, K., 370, 424, 425, *508*
Bates, J. E., 55, 259, *512*
Baumrind, D., 353, *508*
Bavolek, S. J., *508*
Beach, S. R., 425, *513*
Beatty, S. B., *516*
Beavers, W. R., 458, 461, *508, 515, 518*
Beck, A. T., 262, *508*
Becker, J. V., 27, *508*
Becker-Lausen, E., 142, 144, *524*
Beilke, R., 151, 152, 153, *514*
Benjamin, L., 18, *513*
Benjet, C., 251, *508*
Bentler, P. M., 123, 124, *508*
Bentley, K. S., 309, *514*
Berg, B., 399, 401, *518*
Berger, A. M., 134, 136, 137, 138, 337, *508*
Berliner, L., 27, *508*
Berman, S. R., 95, 98, *519*
Bermann, E., 370, 461, 462, *524*

Bernstein, D. P., 47, 93, 94, 95, 158, 160, 161, *509, 513, 526*
Bernstein, E. M, 128, *509*
Bernstein, I. H., 43, 360, *521*
Berry, J. O., 318, 319, *509*
Berry, J. W., 15, *509*
Berry, K. K., 61, *524*
Berry, N. J., 229, 231, *521*
Bieber, S. L., 171, 174, *509, 521*
Bifulco, A., 76, 77, 80, *509*
Biglan, A., 325, 327, *516*
Binda, A., 472, *516*
Birt, J., 66, 107, 165, 177, 178, 179, 182, 208, *509, 527*
Bishop, D. S., 297, *513*
Black, M., 472, *516*
Blake, D., 101, 104, 147, *520*
Boggio, R. M., 481, 483, *519*
Bonner, B. L., 27, *526*
Borum, R., 31, *509*
Bourdeau, P., 179, 182, *527*
Bradley, R. H., 470, 472, *509*
Branscomb, L. P., 155, 157, *509*
Brassard, M. R., 487, 489, *509*
Braungart, J. M., 480, 481, *510*
Briere, J., 26, 35, 80, 83, 175, 209, 210, 211, 212, 214, 217, *509, 510, 512, 513, 518*
Brotman-Band, E., 437, 439, *510*
Broughton, D., 151, 152, 153, *514*
Brown, G. W., 76, 77, 80, *509*
Brown, L. B., 174, *521*
Brown, M., 250, 306, *510*
Browne, A., 26, *513*
Bruck, M., 61, *510*
Brunner, J. F., 322, *507*
Brygger, M. P., *512*
Budd, K. S., 251, 252, 253, 280, 281, *510*
Budkovsky, L., 480, 481, *510*
Bugental, D. B., 250, 304, 306, 371, *510*
Buri, J. R., *510*
Buttenwieser, E., *522*

C

Caldwell, B. M., 470, 472, *509*
Campis, L. K., 305, 306, 322, 324, 326, *510*
Campos, J., 372, *510*
Campos, R., 372, *510*
Carlin, A. S., 169, 171, *510*

Carlson, E. B., 129, 130, *507*
Carnochan, J., 53, 54, 58, 59, 68, 69, *520*
Carson, D. K., 369, 421, 422, *510*
Cascardi, M., 19, *510*
Cassidy, J., 480, 481, *510*
Cavallero, L., 251, *508*
Ceci, S., 61, *510*
Celano, M., 273, 290, 292, *510, 511*
Cerezo, M. A., 371, 372, 495, 497, 498, *511*
Chalmers, M., *522*
Chamberlain, P., 190, *511*
Chan, Y., 332, 333, *526*
Christensen, A., 188, 189, 190, 191, *516*
Christopher, J. S., 24, 270, *515*
Cicchetti, D., 373, 445, 448, 454, *516, 518*
Claiborn, J. M., 229, 231, *522*
Cobb, J. A., *521*
Coffman, S. G., 436, *511*
Cohen, J. A., 42, 95, 98, 221, 223, *511, 519*
Cohen, S., 319, *511*
Conaway, L. P., 270, 355, *515*
Conaway, R. L., 270, *515*
Conti, J. R., 24, *511*
Conway, L. P., 24, *515*
Copping, V. E., 234, 236, *511*
Corcoran, K., *514*
Cotman, A., 217, *509*
Couchoud, E., 478, *512*
Coulter, M. L., 272, *513*
Covi, L., *512*
Cowen, E., 300, *511*
Coyne, J., 270, 317, *517*
Crane, R. S., 318, *525*
Cronbach, L. J., 42, *511*
Cross, H. J., 239, 241, *528*
Cross, T. P., 271, 272, 273, *511*
Crouch, J. L., 24, 27, 281, *520*
Cummings, A. L., 26, 202, *520*
Cummings, E. M., 391, 392, 439, 441, 442, 452, 454, *511, 513, 516*
Cummings, J. S., 454, *511*
Currier, L. L., 194, 198, 199, *528*
Currier, R., 326, 327, 328, 333, *523*
Cutler, S. E., 389, *515*

D

Dahl, B., 109, 110, 111, *527*
Davies, P. T., 439, 452, *511*

Davis, M., 130, *514*
Davis, P. T., 391, 392, *511*
Davison, G. C., 433, 436, *511*
Dawson, B., 243, 246, *511*
Day, B. T., 58, 281, 286, 422, *518*
Deater-Deckard, K., 259, 266, 267, 268, *511, 512*
Deblinger, E., 24, 27, *512, 519*
deJong, J. B., 229, 231, *522*
DeKlyen, M., 455
DeLoache, J. S., 61, *512*
Denham, S., 478, *512*
Derogatis, L. R., *512*
DeRoma, V. M., 317, *512*
DiGiuseppe, R., 131, 133, *522*
DiMito, A., 178, 179, *509*
DiTomasso, M. J., 138, *512*
Dix, T., 250, 251, 343, 345, *512*
D'Ocon, A., 497, 498, *511*
Dodge, K. A., 55, 259, *512*
Dodge-Reyone, N., 330, *512*
Dolz, L., 497, 498, *511*
Dombalis, A. O., 270, 356, *516*
Donaldson, D., 391, 392, 395, *523*
Donaldson, M. A., 199, 201, 202, 369, 421, 422, *510, 512*
Dubner, A., 86, 92, 93, *512*
Dubow, E. I., 391, 392, 395, *523*
Dubowitz, H., 472, *516*
Dunn, E., 495, 498, *511*

E

Eddsohn, G. A., 272, *513*
Edelbrock, C. S., 36
Edelson, J. L., *512*
Edwards, A. L., 303, *512*
Edwards, P. W., 201, 202, *512*
Egan, K. J., 301, 303, *519*
Eisenberg, M., 266, 267, *524*
Elliott, A. N., 57, *521*
Elliott, D. M., 210, 211, 212, 214, 217, *509, 512, 513*
El-Sheikh, M., 439, 441, 442, 454, *511, 513*
Epstein, N. B., 297, *513*
Erbaugh, J., 262, *508*
Erber, S., 377, *521*
Esplin, P. W., 60, *518, 522*
Eth, S., 383, 385, *522*
Everson, M. D., 61, 271, 272, *513*

Ewigman, B. E., 251, 265, 346, 347, 348, 372, *522, 526*
Eyberg, S., 450, 451, *523*
Eyberg, S. M., 264, 270, 311, 317, 449, 451, *513*

F

Fagan, J., 155, 157, *509*
Fagot, B. I., 359, 360, 361, 476, 478, *513, 517*
Fann, K. D., 280, 281, 356, *516*
Fantuzzo, J. W., 24, *513*
Farrington, A., 130, *513*
Faupel, A. W., 130, *513*
Faust, J., 369, 371, *513*
Fedorowicz, A. E., 54, 55, 58, 59, 284, *517*
Feindler, E. L., 3, *522*
Feldman, C. M., 56, 57, 369, 372, *513*
Feldman, R. S., 55, 382, 383, *523, 524*
Figley, C. R., 27, *513*
Fincham, F. D., 9, 389, 392, 425, *513, 515*
Fink, L., 93, 94, 95, 158, 160, 161, *509, 513*
Finkelhor, D., 24, 26, 27, 50, 96, 184, 287, *513, 515, 517, 525*
First, M. B., 18, *513*
Fischer, J., *514*
Fleiss, J. L., 42, *524*
Fletcher, K. E., 87, 88, 89, 92, 93, 194, 195, 196, 224, 225, 226, *514*
Foote, J., 95, 161, *513*
Foote, L., 93, 94, 95, 158, 160, *509*
Forgue, D. F., 229, 231, *522*
Foster, S. L., 405, 406, 407, 415, 416, 427, 429, 430, 431, 474, 475, *522, 523*
Fox, R. A., 306, 308, 309, *514, 522, 524*
Foy, D. W., 138, 203, 205, 206, *523*
Francouer, E., 61, *510*
Frankel, F., 255, 257, *514*
Franklin, C. F., 194, 198, 199, *528*
Franzen, M. D., 40, *514*
Frederick, C., 84, 85, 148, 149, *514*
Freeman, W. S., 362, 365, *517*
Friedrich, W. N., 61, 97, 130, 150, 151, 152, 153, *514, 518*
Fuchs, L. S., 126, 127, 141, 188, *525*
Fuhrmann, G., 251, *508*

G

Gardner, R. A., 30, 199, 202, *512, 514*
Gaudin, J. M., 288, 289, 290, *522*
Geddie, L., 246, *511*
Gee, C., 377, *521*
Geller, J., 362, 365, *517*
Gentile, C., 161, 164, 179, 182, 206, 208, *528*
Gerard, A. B., 327, *514*
Gerber, P. N., 130, *514*
Gertz, L. M., 369, 421, 422, *510*
Gibaud-Wallston, J., 328, 329, *514*
Gibbon, M., 18, *513*
Giese, J., 130, *514*
Gilbert, J., 133, *515*
Giles, M. K., 61, *524*
Gillespie, E. I., 194, 198, 199, *528*
Glaser, B. A., 189, 191, 370, 421, 422, *514*
Goh, D. S., 133, *515*
Golden, C. J., 40, *514*
Goodman, G. S., 61, *518*
Gordis, E., 399, 484, 487, *514*
Gordon, B. N., 60, *514*
Gordon, D. A., 250, 298, 301, *515*
Gorsuch, R., 262, *525*
Gossett, J. T., 458, *518*
Gottman, J. M., 239, 241, 350, 466, 484, *508, 515*
Gough, R., 165
Grace, N. C., 425, 428, *515*
Graham-Bermann, S. A., 372, 387, 389, 395, 397, *515*
Grambisch, P., 151, 152, 153, *514*
Green, A. J., 24, 26, 250, *515, 523*
Green, B. F., 463, 465, *526*
Greenberg, M. T., 455, 457, *525*
Greene, B., 442, 443, 444, *526*
Greene, R. C., 420, *515*
Gries, L. T., 133, *515*
Grych, J. H., 9, 389, 392, *515*
Gustafson, B., 171, *510*
Guthrie, D., 124, *528*

H

Hall, D. K., 351, 353, 372, *521*
Halpin, B. M., 243, 246, *527*
Hamby, S. L., 50, 184, 287, *515, 525*
Hammer, M., 55, 382, 383, *523, 524*
Hampson, R. B., 458, 461, *508, 515*

Handelsman, L., 93, 94, 95, 158, 160, 161, *509, 513*
Hansen, D. J., 24, 54, 58, 250, 268, 270, 306, 315, 317, 338, 339, 355, *512, 515, 519, 524*
Harbeck, D., 236, 238, *516*
Hardy, D. B., 487, 489, *509*
Harrington, D., 472, *516*
Harris, K., 217, *509*
Harris, T. O., 76, 80, *509*
Hart, S. N., 487, 489, *509*
Haskett, M. E., 232, 233, 234, 270, 280, 281, 353, 356, *516*
Hays, C. E., 305, 306, 324, *519*
Hazzard, A., 188, 189, 190, 191, 273, 290, 292, *510, 511, 516*
Heilman, N. E., 280, 281, *510*
Hekimian, E., 314, *508*
Helfer, R. E., 294, *516*
Helmers, K., 146, 147, *522*
Henderson, M., 370, 461, 462, *524*
Hennessy, K. D., 452, 454, *516*
Henry, D., 24, *519*
Herbert, M., 61, 62, *508*
Herman, J. L., 115, 117, 118, *516, 522, 526*
Hernandez, P., 210, *518*
Hersen, M., 72, 75, 76, *507*
Hoffmeister, J. K., 294, *516*
Hoglund, C. L., 174, *516*
Hoier, T. S., 146, 147, 208, *516, 519*
Holden, E. W., 250, *516*
Holdsworth, M. J., 251, *510*
Holtzworth-Munroe, A. H., *516*
Hops, H., 407, 466, *516*
Horne, A. M., 189, 191, 370, 421, 422, *514*
Horowitz, M., 106, 153, 155, 205, *516*
Hosokawn, M. C., 346, 347, 348, *526*
Hughes, D., 17, *516*
Hughes, J., 120, 121, *528*
Hulgus, Y. F., 458, 461, *508, 515*
Hunter, J. A., 27, *508*
Hunter, W. M., 272, *513*
Hupp, S., 326, 327, 328, 333, *523*
Hutchinson, S. A., 47, *516*

I

Inderbitzen-Pisaruk, H., 208, *516*
Irvine, A. B., 325, 327, *516*

J

Jackson, D. N., 39, *517*
Jackson, J. L., 370, 421, 422, *519*
Jacob, T., 466, 469, *517*
Jacobs, G., 262, 318, *525*
Jaffee, P., 191, 243, 378, 380, *517*
Janoff-Bulman, R., 26, *517*
Jarvis, J., 77, 80, *509*
John, R. S., 399, 436, 484, 487, *514, 521*
Johnson, M. K., 433, 436, *511*
Johnston, C., 330, 362, 365, *517*
Johnston, D., 490, 492, *519*
Jones, D. P., 370, 458, 461, *519*
Jones, R. H., 250, 301, *515*
Jones, R. T., 153, 154, 155, *517*
Jones, W. H., 318, 319, *509*
Jorgensen, S. R., *517*
Jouriles, E. N., 481, 483, *519*

K

Kaczymski, L., 358, *526*
Kalinowski, M. N., 63, 66, *518*
Kamarck, T., 319, *511*
Kane, D., 280, 281, *510*
Kanner, A. D., 270, 317, *517*
Kaplan, S. J., 24, 111, 113, 114, 115, *521, 526*
Kast, L. C., 118, 121, 193, 194, 197, 198, *528*
Kaufman, K. L., 27, *526*
Kavanagh, K. A., 476, 478, *517*
Kazdin, A. E., 34, 35, 36, 48, 49, 58, 281, 286, 422, *517, 518*
Keesler, T., 495, 498, *511*
Kelley, M. L., 425, 428, *515*
Kemper, K., 171, *510*
Kendall-Tackett, K. A., 24, 27, *517*
Kenny, M. C., 369, 371, *513*
Kent, R. M., 405, 407, 415, *522*
Kent, R. N., 472, 475, *522*
Kerig, P. K., 54, 55, 58, 59, 281, 283, 284, 373, 392, 395, *517*
Kermoian, R., 372, *510*
Kilpatrick, A. C., 288, 289, 290, *522*
Kim, S., 188, *525*
Kinard, E. M., 182, 185, *525*
King, G. A., 351, 353, *517*
Kistner, J. A., 232, 233, *516*
Kivlahan, C., 251, *522*
Kleber, R. J., 27, *513*
Klink, A., 206, 208, *527*

Knutson, J. F., 134, 136, 137, 138, 337, *508, 518, 522, 527, 528*
Kochanska, G., 445, 447, 448, *518*
Koenig, A. L., 373, 445, 447, 448, *518*
Koepke, T., 415, 416, 429, 475, *523*
Kolko, D. J., 57, 58, 281, 286, 296, 297, 298, 422, *518*
Kondrick, P. A., 118, 121, 193, 194, 197, 198, *528*
Koocher, G. P., 61, *518*
Koplin, B., 130, *514*
Koss, M., 47, *526*
Kovitz, K., 490, 492, *519*
Kramer, J., 138, *527*
Kriegler, J., 101, 104, 147, *520*
Krueger, L., 436, *521*
Kuiper, J., 151, 152, 153, *514*
Kurdek, L. A., 399, 401, *518*

L

Laing, J. A., 134, *518*
Lamb, M. E., 60, *518*
Langer, T. S., 332, *518*
Langhinrichsen-Rohling, J., *526*
Lanktree, C. B., 210, 211, *518*
Larrance, D. T., 335, *518*
Lasko, N. B., 229, 231, *521*
Lauretti, A. F., 252, 253, *508*
Lavee, Y., 408, 409, *521*
Lawrence, J., 122, 124, *528*
Lazarus, R. S., 270, 317, *517*
Lefebvre, L., 168, *527*
Lehman, A., 370, 461, 462, *524*
Levendesky, A. A., *515*
Levenson, R. W., 350, *515*
Levy, H. B., 63, 66, *518*
Lewis, J. M., 458, *518*
Libero, D. Z., 129, 130, *507*
Lillie, A., 77, 80, *509*
Limandri, B. J., 31, *518*
Lindahl, K. M., 501, 504, *518*
Linehan, M. M., 41, 301, 303, *519*
Linn, M. W., 332, *519*
Lipman, R. S., *512*
Lippmann, J., 27, *512*
Litzenberger, B. W., 389, *515*
Locke, H. J., 321, 456, *519*
Loding, B. V., 252, 253, *508*
Long, P. J., 56, 370, 421, 422, *519, 520*
Lonner, W. J., 16, *519*

Lovejoy, M. C., 93, 94, 95, 158, 160, 161, 305, 306, 309, 312, 324, *509, 513, 519*

Lubetsky, M. J., 76, *507*

Lundquist, L. M., 270, *515*

Lunghofer, L., 210, 211, *524*

Lushene, R., 262, *525*

Lutzker, J. R., 442, 443, 444, 463, 465, *526*

Lyman, R. D., 305, 306, 324, 326, *510*

Lynn, S., 218, 221, *519*

M

MacIan, P. S., 27, *521*

MacMillan, V. M., 270, 315, 317, 338, 340, 355, *515, 519*

Madonna, P. G., 370, 458, 461, *519*

Magnum, P. F., 495, *523*

Mahoney, A., 481, 483, *519*

Malinosky-Rummel, R. R., 146, 147, *519*

Mandel, F., 111, 113, 114, *521*

Mannarino, A. P., 95, 98, 221, 223, *511, 519*

Margolin, G., 188, 189, 190, 191, 397, 398, 399, 436, 484, 487, *514, 516, 519, 521*

Markovic, J., 63, 66, *518*

Martell, D., 271, 272, 273, *511*

Martinez, P., 131, *523*

Mash, E. J., 330, 490, 492, *517, 519*

Maszolf, D. P., 61, *512*

Matorin, A., 218, 221, *519*

Matsumoto, D., 15, 16, 17, *519*

McCain, A. P., 425, 428, *515*

McCall, C., 273, 292, *510*

McCann, J., 109, 110, 111, *527*

McCubbin, H. I., 418, 423, 424, *519, 520*

McDonald, E., 271, 272, 273, *511*

McEachran, A., 55, 168, *527*

McGee, R. A., 53, 54, 58, 59, 67, 68, 69, *520*

McGimpsey, B. J., 442, 443, 444, *526*

McLeer, S. V., 24, *520*

Mehm, J. C., 138, *508*

Mehm, J. X., 337, *528*

Mendelson, M., 262, *508*

Menzies, R. J., 31, *520*

Mermelstein, R., 319, *511*

Messman, T. L., 56, *520*

Meyer, S. L., *510*

Michienzi, T., 164, *528*

Mickey, M. R., 122, 124, *528*

Miller-Perrin, C. L., 98, 100, 101, 191, 193, 194, 197, 198, *520, 528*

Milner, J. S., 24, 27, 75, 249, 250, 279, 281, 355, *520*

Mock, J., 262, *508*

Moore, D. W., 287, *525*

Moos, B. S., 280, 297, 409, 412, 419, 422, 424, *520*

Moos, R. H., 280, 297, 409, 412, 419, 422, 424, *520*

Morgan, T., 26, 202, *520*

Motta, R., 86, 92, 93, *512*

Moye, A., 415, 416, 429, 475, *523*

Mumme, D., 372, *510*

Murphy, M., 241, 326, 327, 328, 333, *523, 528*

Myers, L. L., 189, 191, *514*

Myers, L. W., 270, 356, *516*

N

Nader, K., 84, 85, 148, 149, *514*

Nader, K. O., 85, 86, 101, 104, 105, 132, 133, 146, 147, 150, 155, 210, 211, 227, *520*

Nelson, G., 425, *513*

Netzger, L. J., 229, 231, *521*

Newman, E., 47, 101, 104, 147, *520, 526*

Nicholas, K. B., 171, 174, *516, 521*

Noh, S., 293, *508*

Notgrass, C. M., 124, *528*

Novaco, R. W., 250, 317, *521*

Nowicki, S., 250, 301, *515*

Nunnally, J. C., 40, 43, 360, *521*

O

O'Brien, M., 375, 377, 433, 436, *521*

O'Donohue, W., 57, *521*

O'Hare, E., 309, 312, *519*

Oldershaw, L., 351, 353, 372, *517, 521*

O'Leary, K. D., 405, 407, 415, *522*

O'Leary, S. G., 250, 297, 327, 332, 348, 350, *508, 524*

Ollendick, T., 206, *521*

Olson, D. H., 370, 408, 409, 410, 412, *521, 526*

Olson, E. H., 408, 409, *521*

Olson, R. L., 270, 315, 317, 338, 339, *519*

Ornstein, P. A., 60, *514*

Orr, S. P., 229, 231, *521, 522*
Orsak, C., 239, 241, *528*
Orvaschel, H., 24, *519*

P

Pallotta, G. M., 270, 355, *515*
Parke, R. D., 480, 481, *510*
Parker, G., 174, *521*
Patterson, G. R., 371, 407, 449, 466, 484, *516, 521*
Patterson, J. M., 423, 424, *520*
Patz, R. J., 253, *507*
Paul, E., 301, 303, *519*
Pearlman, L. A., 27, *521*
Pelcovitz, D., 24, 111, 113, 114, 115, 131, 133, *521, 522, 526*
Perkins, K. A., 138, *508*
Perry, J. C., 115, 117, 118, *516, 522, 526*
Peters, C. L., 309, *522*
Peterson, G., 147, *522*
Peterson, L., 236, 238, 251, 263, 265, 346, 347, 348, 372, *516, 522, 526*
Petretic-Jackson, P. A., 275, 277, 278, *522*
Pettit, G. S., 55, 259, *512*
Petty, J., 69, 71, *522*
Phillips, R. A., 458, *518*
Pinkerton, R., 266, 267, 268, *512, 524*
Pino, C. J., 402, 404, *522*
Pirrillo, V. E., 270, 356, *516*
Pitman, R. K., 229, 231, *521, 522*
Plank, R. E., 420, *515*
Polansky, N. A., 288, 289, 290, *522*
Portner, J., 408, 409, *521*
Praver, F., 131, 133, *515, 522*
Prentice-Dunn, S., 305, 306, 324, 326, *510*
Prinz, R. J., 405, 407, 415, 472, 475, *522*
Putnam, F. W., 127, 128, 129, 130, 145, 146, 147, *507, 509, 522*
Pynoos, R. S., 84, 85, 101, 104, 147, 148, 149, 383, 385, *514, 520, 522*

R

Rabideau, G. J., 454, *516*
Raskin, D. C., 60, *522*
Rathus, J. H., 3, 20, *522*
Rausch, K., 138, *522*
Ray, R. S., *521*
Reid, J. B., 190, 476, 478, *511, 517*

Reinhold, D. P., 345, *512*
Reiss, C., 250, 306, *510*
Reiter, S., 439, 441, 442, *513*
Reitman, D., 326, 327, 328, 333, *523*
Reitzel-Jaffe, D., 165, 168, *527*
Renick, A., 61, *510*
Reynolds, S., 362, 365, *517*
Rhode, P., 326, 327, 328, 333, *523*
Richters, J. E., 131, *523*
Rigler, D., 249, *525*
Rittner, B., 55, 58, *523*
Roberts, M. W., 492, 495, *523*
Robin, A. L., 9, 392, 406, 407, 413, 415, 416, 427, 429, 430, 431, 474, 475, *523*
Robins, C., 433, 436, *511*
Robinson, D., 314, *508*
Robinson, E. A., 449, 450, 451, *513, 523*
Rodriguez, C. M., 250, *523*
Rodriguez, N., 138, 203, 205, 206, *523*
Rodway, M. R., 381, *526*
Roe, A., 174, *523*
Roecker, C. E., 391, 392, 395, *523*
Roehling, P. V., 9, 392, 413, 415, *523*
Rogers, C., 351, 353, *517*
Rogosch, F., 373, 445, 448, *518*
Rohrbeck, C. A., 314, *508*
Rosario, M., 55, 382, 383, *523, 524*
Rose, T. L., 31, *527*
Rosenberg, M. S., 392, 394, 395, *523*
Ross, A. W., 264, 270, 311, 317, *513*
Rossman, B. B., 392, 394, 395, *523*
Roth, S., 111, 113, 114, 115, *521, 526*
Rotter, J. B., 280, 323, 324, *523*
Routh, D. K., 138, *512*
Rowan, A. B., 203, 205, 206, *523*
Rubin, E. C., 309, 312, *519*
Ruggiero, J., 95, 161, *513*
Runtz, M., 26, *509, 510*
Runyan, D. K., 184, 272, 287, *513, 525*
Runyon, M. K., 369, 371, *513*
Russel, S., 318, *525*
Ryan, S. W., 138, 203, 205, 206, *523*

S

Salzinger, S., 55, 381, 382, 383, *523, 524*
Sanders, B., 142, 144, *524*
Santa-Barbara, J., 410, 413, *524*
Santilli, G., 243, 246, *527*

Sarno, J. A., 100, 101, 122, 199, *524*
Sarno-Owens, J., 120, 121, *528*
Sas, L., 164, 243, *517, 527*
Sattler, J. M., 13, 30, *524*
Saunders, B. E., 27, *508*
Sawicki, R. F., 40, *514*
Sayger, T., 370, 421, 422, *514*
Saywitz, K. J., 60, *524*
Scarr, S., 266, 267, 268, *512, 524*
Schaefer, C., 270, 317, *517*
Schellenbach, C. J., 499, 500, *524*
Schludermann, E., 294, *524*
Schludermann, S., 294, *524*
Schneider, C. J., 294, *516*
Schwartz, W. F., 389, *515*
Scott, S. S., 280, 281, 356, *516*
Sedlar, G., 250, 306, 317, *524*
Seid, M., 9, 389, 392, *515*
Seidman, E., 17, *516*
Seilhamer, R., 466, 469, *517*
Selner, M. B., 138, *518*
Sepejak, D. S., 31, *520*
Sgroi, S., 203, *524*
Shaw, D. A., *521*
Shawchuck, C. R., 208, *516*
Shek, D. T. L., 332, *524*
Shepard, R. L., 58, 59, 107, 108, 109, *527*
Sheridan, D. J., 31, *518*
Shipman, K. L., 372, 478, 480, *524, 528*
Shrout, P. E., 42, *524*
Sieck, W. R., 76, *507*
Siegelman, M., 174, *523*
Silber, S., 370, 461, 462, *524*
Simons, N., 402, 404, *522*
Simpson, K. S., 391, 392, *511*
Sines, J. O., 134, *518*
Singer, M. I., 210, 211, *524*
Sivan, A. B., 61, *518*
Skinner, H. A., 410, 413, *524*
Skinner, L. J., 61, *524*
Slawinowski, M. J., 402, 404, *522*
Smerden, J., 130, *513*
Smith, A. M., 250, 327, 348, 350, *524*
Smith, S. P., 129, 130, *507*
Smolkowski, K., 325, 327, *516*
Snyder, L., 60, *524*
Solis-Camara, P., 309, *524*
Song, L. Y., 210, 211, *524*
Sowell, H., 171, *510*

Spaccarelli, S., 125, 126, 127, 138, 141, 185, 187, 188, *525*
Speltz, M. L., 455
Spielberger, C. D., 262, 318, 401, *525*
Spinetta, J. J., 249, *525*
Spitzer, A., 8, 262, *526*
Spitzer, R. L., 18, 115, *513, 526*
Sprenkle, D. H., 410, *526*
Stamm, B. H., 88, 93, 196, *525*
Starr, L., 236, 238, *516*
Steer, R., 27, *512*
Steinberg, K. J., 60, *518*
Steinhauer, P. D., 410, 413, *524*
Stelzer, D., 133, *515*
Stevens, N., 171, *510*
Stormshak, E. A., 454, 455, 457, *525*
Strassberg, Z., 340, 342, *525*
Straus, M. A., 165, 168, 174, 182, 184, 185, 280, 283, 287, 297, 342, 388, *525*
Strom, G. A., 243, 246, *527*
Stuart, G. L., *516*
Sue, S., 50, *525*
Susman, E. J., 357, 358, 499, 500, *524, 526*

T

Tam, K., 332, 333, *526*
Tennenbaum, D. L., 466, 469, *517, 525*
Terdal, L., 492, *519*
Tertinger, D. A., 463, 465, *526*
Thomas, A. M., 281, 286, 422, *518*
Thomas, V., 409, *526*
Thompson, A., 418, *520*
Thompson, R. A., 56, 437, 439, *507, 526*
Tishelman, A. C., 270, 355, *515*
Tolman, A. D., 457, *527*
Torres, H., 63, 66, *518*
Trepper, T. S., 410, *526*
Trickett, P. K., 146, 147, 356, 357, 358, 499, 500, *522, 524, 526*
Tupling, H., 174, *521*
Turner, R. J., 293, *508*
Tuteur, J. M., 346, 347, 348, *526*
Twentyman, C. T., 335, *518*
Twentyman, D., 314, *508*

V

Vagg, P., 262, *525*
Valente, E., 55, *512*

Vandekemp, H., 138, *523*
van der Kolk, B. A., 111, 113, 114, 115, 117, 118, *516, 521, 522, 526*
Vandiver, T., 265, 372, *522*
VanHasselt, V. B., 72, 75, 76, *507*
Van Scoyle, S., 370, 458, 461, *519*
Vaughan, A. R., 243, 246, *511*
Velting, D. M., 20
Verda, M. R., 305, 306, 324, *519*
Vivian, D., 19, *510, 526*
Vodounon, A., 122, 124, *528*
Vogel, D., 454, *511*
Vogel, R. S., 436, *511*
Voris, J., 109, 110, 111, *527*
Vuchinich, S., 469, *526*

W

Wager, J. M., 381, *526*
Wagner, W. G., 243, 246, *511*
Wahler, R., 495, 498, *511*
Walker, C. E., 27, *526*
Walker, E. A., 47, *526*
Wallace, K. M., 321, 456, *519*
Waller, G., 130, *513*
Walters, G. C., 351, 353, 372, *517, 521*
Wandersman, L. P., 328, 329, *514*
Ward, C. H., 262, *508*
Ward, N. G., 171, *510*
Warner, J. E., 54, 58, *515*
Watson-Perczel, M., 442, 443, 444, *526*
Webb, C., 273, 290, 292, *510, 511*
Webster, C. D., 31, *520*
Webster-Stratton, C., 8, 262, 450, 451, *526*
Wechsler, D., 394, *527*
Weerts-Whitmore, E., 138, *527*
Weiner, H., 255, 257, *514*
Weis, R., 309, 312, *519*
Weiss, J. G., *523*
Weiss, R. L., 407, 457, 466, *516, 527*
Weisz, J., 437, 439, *510*
Wekerle, C., 165, 168, *527*
Wells, R. D., 109, 110, 111, *527*
Werner, P. D., 31, *527*

White, C. W., 61, *518*
White, S., 60, 243, 246, *527*
Widom, C. S., 58, 59, 107, 108, 109, *527*
Williams, D., *522*
Williams, J. B. W., 18, *513*
Williams, L. M., 24, 27, 182, 185, *517, 525*
Williams, N., 17, *516*
Wills, T. A., 407, 466, *516*
Wilner, N., 106, 153, 155, 205, *516*
Wilson, H. W., 47, *516*
Wilson, L. R., 424, *520*
Wilson, M. E., 47, *516*
Wilson, S. K., 53, 54, 58, 59, 68, 69, 191, 243, 378, 380, *517, 520*
Wodarski, J. S., 55, 58, *523*
Wolfe, D. A., 53, 54, 55, 58, 59, 67, 68, 69, 105, 106, 161, 164, 165, 168, 179, 191, 206, 249, 378, 380, *517, 520, 527, 528*
Wolfe, V. V., 66, 107, 161, 164, 165, 177, 178, 179, 182, 206, 208, *509, 527, 528*
Wolff, L. S., 297, 327, 332, 350, *508*
Wonderlich, S. A., 369, 421, 422, *510*
Wong, C. M., 332, 333, *526*
Wood, B. J., 239, 241, *528*
Wurtele, C. K., 100, 101, 122, 199, *524*
Wurtele, S. K., 54, 56, 98, 100, 101, 118, 120, 121, 191, 193, 194, 197, 198, 199, *520, 528*
Wyatt, G. E., 122, 124, *528*

Y

Yesavage, J. A., 31, *527*
Youngblade, L., 476, 478, *517*
Yuen, S. A., 53, 54, 58, 59, 68, 69, *520*

Z

Zaidi, L. Y., 335, 337, *528*
Zambarano, R. J., 345, *512*
Zeman, J., 372, 478, 480, *524, 528*
Zoller, D., 478, *512*

Subject Index

A

AAPI. *See* Adult-Adolescent Parenting Inventory

Abandonment fears. *See also* Separation and loss
  Children's Beliefs About Parental Divorce Scale (CBPDS), 400

Abusive Sexual Exposure Scale (ASES), 125–127, 187

Acceptability
  Parenting Stress Index (PSI), 330

Adaptability
  Family Adaptability and Cohesion Scale III (FACES III), 408–410
  Parenting Stress Index (PSI), 330

AD dolls. *See* Anatomically detailed (AD) dolls

Adolescent dating
  Conflicts in Relationships Questionnaire (CIRQ), 165–168

Adolescent maltreatment
  Angie/Andy Child Rating Scale (A/A CRS), 131–133
  Assessing Environments Scale (AEIII), 134–138
  Attributions for Maltreatment Interview (AFMI), 67–69
  Checklist for Child Abuse Evaluation (CCAE), 69–72
  Childhood Trauma Questionnaire (CTQ), 158–161
  Child Post-Traumatic Stress Reaction Index (CPTS-RI), 84–86, 148–150
  Clinician Administered PTSD Scale for Children and Adolescents for the *DSM-IV* (CAPS-CA), 101–105
  Conflicts in Relationships Questionnaire (CIRQ), 165–168
  Exposure to Abuse and Supportive Environments–Parenting Inventory (EASE–PI), 171–175
  Multidimensional Neglect Scale (MNS), 182–185
  Structured Interview for Disorders of Extreme Stress (SIDES), 111–115
  Trauma Symptom Checklist for Children (TSCC), 209–212
  Traumatic Antecedents Interview (TAI), 115–118

Adolescents
  abuse. *See* Adolescent maltreatment
  Adolescent Dissociative Experience Survey (A–DES), 127–131
  Child Dissociative Checklist (CDC), 145–147
  Children's Perceptions of Interparental Conflict Scale (CPICS), 389–392
  Exposure to Abuse and Supportive Environments–Parenting Inventory (EASE–PI), 171–175
  Family Adaptability and Cohesion Scale III (FACES III), 408–410

Adolescents (*Continued*)
  Family Assessment Measure III (FAM
    III), 410–413
  Family Beliefs Inventory (FBI), 413–
    416
  Family Crisis Oriented Personal Eval-
    uation Scales (F–COPES), 416–
    419
  Family Environment Scale (FES),
    419–422
  Interaction Behavior Code (IBC),
    472–475
  Mother–Adolescent Attribution Ques-
    tionnaire (MAAQ), 425–429
  Parent–Adolescent Relationship
    Questionnaire (PARQ), 429–431
  parents of. *See* Parents of adolescents
  sexual abuse. *See* Adolescent sexual
    abuse
  trauma experienced by. *See* Adoles-
    cents exposed to trauma
  "When Bad Things Happen"
    (WBTH), 224–227
Adolescents exposed to trauma
  Childhood Trauma Questionnaire
    (CTQ), 158–161
  Child Post-Traumatic Stress Reaction
    Index (CPTS–RI), 148–150
  Structured Interview for Disorders of
    Extreme Stress (SIDES), 111–
    115
  Trauma Symptom Checklist for Chil-
    dren (TSCC), 209–212
  Traumatic Antecedents Interview
    (TAI), 115–118
  "When Bad Things Happen"
    (WBTH), 224–227
Adolescent sexual abuse
  Abusive Sexual Exposure Scale
    (ASES), 125–127
  Adolescent Dissociative Experience
    Survey (A–DES), 127–131
  Checklist of Sexual Abuse and Re-
    lated Stressors (C-SARS), 138–
    142
  Children's Impact of Traumatic
    Events Scale B Revised
    (CITES–R), 161–165
  Conflicts in Relationships Question-
    naire (CIRQ), 165–168
  Negative Appraisals of Sexual Abuse
    Scale (NASAS), 185–188

Trauma Symptom Checklist for Chil-
    dren (TSCC), 209
  Traumatic Sexualization Survey
    (TSS), 218–221
  Wyatt Sex History Questionnaire
    (WSHQ), 122–124
Adolescents in family experiencing con-
    flict
  Conflict Behavior Questionnaire
    (CBQ), 405–407
Adolescent stress
  "When Bad Things Happen"
    (WBTH), 224–227
ADQ. *See* Anatomical Doll Question-
    naire
Adult–Adolescent Parenting Inventory
    (AAPI)
  Parent Behavior Checklist/Parenting
    Inventory (PBC), 308
Adult (non-parent) as source of com-
    fort
  Children's Marital Conflict Coping
    Strategies Interview (CMCCSI),
    376
Adult family members
  Family Assessment Measure III (FAM
    III), 410–413
  Family Crisis Oriented Personal Eval-
    uation Scales (F–COPES), 416–
    419
  Family Environment Scale (FES),
    419–422
  Family Inventory of Life Events
    (FILE), 423–425
Adult Impact of Event Scale, 153
Adult maltreatment
  Assessing Environments Scale
    (AEIII), 134–138
  Structured Interview for Disorders of
    Extreme Stress (SIDES), 111–
    115
  Traumatic Antecedents Interview
    (TAI), 115–118
Adults exposed to trauma
  Structured Interview for Disorders of
    Extreme Stress (SIDES), 111–
    115
  Trauma Symptom Inventory (TSI),
    214–218
  Traumatic Antecedents Interview
    (TAI), 115–118

Adult survivors of child abuse
  Child Abuse and Trauma Scale
    (CAT), 142–145
  Child Dissociative Predictive Scale
    (CDPS), 155–157
  Childhood Experience of Care and
    Abuse (CECA), 77
  Childhood Maltreatment Interview
    Schedule (CMIS), 80
  Childhood Trauma Interview (CTI),
    93–95
  Emotional and Physical Abuse Ques-
    tionnaire (EPAB), 169–171
  Family Environment Questionnaire
    (FEQ), 175–177
  Self-Report of Childhood Abuse Phys-
    ical (SRCAP), 107–109
  Trauma Symptom Checklist 33 and
    40 (TSC-33 and TSC-40), 212–
    214
Adult survivors of child emotional
  abuse
  Emotional and Physical Abuse Ques-
    tionnaire (EPAB), 169–171
Adult survivors of childhood trauma
  Child Abuse and Trauma Scale
    (CAT), 142–145
  Childhood Trauma Questionnaire
    (CTQ), 158–161
  Trauma Symptom Checklist 33 and
    40 (TSC–33 and TSC–40), 212–
    214
Adult survivors of child psychological
  abuse
  Family Environment Questionnaire
    (FEQ), 175–177
Adult survivors of child sexual abuse
  Assessment of Physiological Re-
    sponses to Analogue Audiotaped
    Scripts, 229–232
  Child Dissociative Predictive Scale
    (CDPS), 155–157
  Childhood Experience of Care and
    Abuse (CECA), 77, 78
  diagnostic disorders, 26
  family interaction assessment, 371
  Responses to Childhood Incest Ques-
    tionnaire (RCIQ), 199–203
  Sexual Abuse Exposure Question-
    naire (SAEQ), 203–206

Traumatic Sexualization Survey
    (TSS), 218–221
  Wyatt Sex History Questionnaire
    (WSHQ), 122–124
Adult trauma
  Trauma Symptom Checklist 33 and
    40 (TSC–33 and TSC–40), 212–
    214
  Trauma Symptom Inventory (TSI),
    214–218
AEIII-Form SD, 138
Affect
  Cleanup Coding Systems (CCS), 446
  Disciplinary Strategies Interview
    (DSI), 264
  Family Interaction Task (FIT), 459
  Mother's Responses to Videotapes
    (MRV), 348–350
  Parent Affect Test (PAT), 301–304
  Parent Daily Report (PDR), 357
  Structured Interview for Disorders of
    Extreme Stress (SIDES), 112
  System for Coding Interactions and
    Family Functioning (SCIFF),
    502, 503
Affection from child to parent
  Parent Opinion Questionnaire
    (POQ), 313
Affection from parent, withdrawal of.
    See Withdrawal of affection by
    parent
AFMI. See Attributions for Maltreatment
    Interview
Age inappropriate demands
  Assessing Environments Scale
    (AEIII), 136
Aggression. See also Physical abuse
  Conflicts and Problem-Solving Scales
    (CPSS), 282
  Disciplinary Strategies Interview
    (DSI), 264
  family interaction assessment, 372
  "When Bad Things Happen"
    (WBTH), 225
AIVC. See Audiotaped Interparental
    Verbal Conflict
Alliance formation
  parenting alliance, defined, 320
  Parenting Alliance Inventory (PAI),
    320–322

Alliance formation (*Continued*)
System for Coding Interactions and Family Functioning (SCIFF), 502
Alternate forms reliability, 43
American Psychiatric Association. *See DSM-III; DSM-III-R; DSM-IV*
American Psychological Association ethical guidelines, 24, 25–26
parenting competency evaluation guidelines, 252
Analogue measures, 20–21. *See also* Direct observation methods
and behavioral coding for family interaction assessment, 433–505. *See also* Family interaction analogue measures
parent or caregiver assessment, 335–366. *See also* Parent behavioral observation
Anatomical Doll Questionnaire (ADQ), 63–66
Anatomically detailed (AD) dolls, 243–246. *See also* Anatomical Doll Questionnaire (ADQ)
Abusive Sexual Exposure Scale (ASES), 126
Sexually Anatomically Detailed (SAD) Dolls, 243–246
use with children in sexual abuse interviews, 19, 61
Anger
Analogue Parenting Task (APT), 336
Child Witness to Violence Interview (CWVI), 378–379
Disciplinary Strategies Interview (DSI), 263–265
Exposure to Interadult Anger (EIA), 452–454
Judgments in Moments of Anger (JMA), 343–345
MacMillan–Olson–Hansen Anger Control Scale (MOHAC), 318
Parental Anger Inventory (PAI), 315–318
parental, in response to child's behavior, 250–251
Parent Discipline Interview (PDI), 266
Parenting Scale (PS), 324–328
Responses to Childhood Incest Questionnaire (RCIQ), 200

System for Coding Interactions and Family Functioning (SCIFF), 503
Trauma Symptom Checklist for Children (TSCC), 209
Trauma Symptom Inventory (TSI), 215
Weekly Report of Abuse Indicators (WRAI), 296
Anonymity of research, 48
Antipathy
Childhood Experience of Care and Abuse (CECA), 77
Anxiety
adult survivors of child sexual abuse, 26
Behavioral Role-Play in Sex Abuse Prevention (BR–SAP), 238
Childhood PTSD Interview–Child Form (CPI–Child), 91
Observational Coding System for Triadic Interaction (OCSTI), 485
Responses to Childhood Incest Questionnaire (RCIQ), 200
sexually abused children, 24
Trauma Symptom Checklist 33 and 40 (TSC–33 and TSC–40), 212–214
Trauma Symptom Checklist for Children (TSCC), 209
Trauma Symptom Inventory (TSI), 215
"When Bad Things Happen" (WBTH), 224
Approval seeking
Family Beliefs Inventory (FBI), 414
Mother–Son Interaction Task (MSIT), 482
Archival records, 22
Articulated Thoughts During Simulated Situations (ATSS), 433–437
ASES. *See* Abusive Sexual Exposure Scale
Assessing Environments III Inventory Analogue Parenting Task (APT), 337
Assessment of Physiological Responses to Analogue Audiotaped Scripts, 229–232
At-risk parents
Conflict Tactics Scale: Parent to Child (CTSPC), 284–287
family interaction assessment, 372

Family Worries Scale (FWS), 395–397
Parenting Scale (PS), 328
Structured Laboratory and Home
   Observation: Single Case Study
   (SLHO), 499–501
Video Assessment Task (VAT), 359–
   361
ATSS. *See* Articulated Thoughts During
   Simulated Situations
Attachment issues of parent
Parenting Stress Index (PSI), 331
Attachment security, 56
Attention-deficit hyperactivity disorder,
   24
Video Mediated Recall Task (VMRT),
   362–366
Attention or consciousness
Structured Interview for Disorders of
   Extreme Stress (SIDES), 112
Attributions for Maltreatment Interview
   (AFMI), 67–69
Audiotaped Interparental Verbal Con-
   flict (AIVC), 437–439
Autonomy
Family Beliefs Inventory (FBI), 414
Family Interaction Task (FIT), 459
Avoidance
Children's Marital Conflict Coping
   Strategies Interview (CMCCSI),
   376
Child's Impact of Traumatic Events
   Scale B Revised (CITES–R), 162
Conflicts and Problem-Solving Scales
   (CPSS), 282
Trauma Symptom Inventory (TSI),
   215
Traumatic Sexualization Survey
   (TSS), 219

B
Beavers–Timberlawn Family Evaluation
   Scale
Family Interaction Task (FIT), 458,
   460
Beck Depression Inventory
Daily Discipline Interview (DDI), 262
Parenting Scale (PS), 326
Behavioral assessment approach, 8–9
Behavioral Observation of Abused Chil-
   dren, 232–234

Behavioral Observation of Shelter Chil-
   dren, 234–236
Behavioral Role-Play in Sex Abuse Pre-
   vention (BR–SAP), 236–239
Beliefs. *See* Family beliefs
Betrayal
Responses to Childhood Incest Ques-
   tionnaire (RCIQ), 200
Blame. *See also* Self-blame
Child Abuse Blame Scale–Physical
   Abuse (CABS–PA), 275–278
Conflicts in Relationships Question-
   naire (CIRQ), 166
Mother–Adolescent Attribution Ques-
   tionnaire (MAAQ), 426
Observational Coding System for Tri-
   adic Interaction (OCSTI), 485
Parent Attribution Scale (PAS), 291
Borderline personality disorder (BPD),
   26
Boundary maintenance
Brother–Sister Questionnaire (BSQ),
   387
BPD. *See* Borderline personality disor-
   der
Brother–Sister Questionnaire (BSQ),
   387–389
Brotman-Band and Weisz classification
Audiotaped Interparental Verbal
   Conflict (AIVC), 437
BR-SAP. *See* Behavioral Role-Play in Sex
   Abuse Prevention
BSQ. *See* Brother–Sister Questionnaire

C
CABS-PA. *See* Child Abuse Blame
   Scale–Physical Abuse
CAIICS. *See* Child Abuse Interview In-
   teraction Coding System
CANIS-R. *See* Child Abuse and Neglect
   Interview Schedule–Revised
CAPI. *See* Child Abuse Potential
   Inventory–Form VI
CAPS. *See* Children's Attributions and
   Perceptions Scale
CAPS-CA. *See* Clinician Administered
   PTSD Scale for Children and
   Adolescents for the *DSM-IV*
Cartoons
Angie/Andy Child Rating Scale (A/A
   CRS), 131–133

Cartoons (*Continued*)
  Family Environment Scale–Children's
    Version (FES–CV), 402–404
CAT. *See* Child Abuse and Trauma
    Scale
CBCL. *See* Child Behavior Checklist
CBPDS. *See* Children's Beliefs About
    Parental Divorce Scale
CBQ. *See* Conflict Behavior Question-
    naire
CCAE. *See* Checklist for Child Abuse
    Evaluation
CCI. *See* Child Conflict Index; Con-
    cerns and Constraints Interview
CCS. *See* Cleanup Coding Systems
CDC. *See* Child Dissociative Checklist
CDPS. *See* Child Dissociative Predictive
    Scale
CECA. *See* Childhood Experience of
    Care and Abuse
Chaos
  Traumatic Antecedents Interview
    (TAI), 116
Checklist for Child Abuse Evaluation
    (CCAE), 69–72
Checklist for Living Environments to
    Assess Neglect (CLEAN), 442–
    445
Checklist of Sexual Abuse and Related
    Stressors (C–SARS), 138–142,
    187
Child abuse. *See* Child maltreatment;
    Child sexual abuse
Child Abuse and Neglect Interview
    Schedule–Revised (CANIS–R),
    72–76
Child Abuse and Trauma Scale (CAT),
    142–145
Child Abuse Blame Scale–Physical
    Abuse (CABS–PA), 275–278
Child Abuse Interview Interaction Cod-
    ing System (CAIICS), 239–241
Child Abuse Potential Inventory
  Parent/Child Interaction Observa-
    tions (PCIO), 355
Child Abuse Potential Inventory–Form
    VI (CAPI), 279–281
Child behavioral observation, 229–246
  Assessment of Physiological Re-
    sponses to Analogue Audiotaped
    Scripts, 229–232
  Behavioral Observation of Abused
    Children, 232–234

  Behavioral Observation of Shelter
    Children, 234–236
  Behavioral Role-Play in Sex Abuse
    Prevention (BR–SAP), 236–239
  Child Abuse Interview Interaction
    Coding System (CAIICS), 239–
    241
  Mock Trial Role-Play (MTRP), 241–
    243
  Sexually Anatomically Detailed
    (SAD) Dolls, 243–246
Child Behavior Checklist (CBCL), 36,
    87, 97
  Abusive Sexual Exposure Scale
    (ASES), 126
  Checklist of Sexual Abuse and Re-
    lated Stressors (C–SARS), 141
  Child Conflict Index (CCI), 256–257
  Children's Perceptions of Interparen-
    tal Conflict Scale (CPICS), 391
  Child Sexual Behavior Inventory
    (CSBI–I), 150
  Daily Discipline Interview (DDI), 261
  Discord Control and Coping Ques-
    tionnaire (DCCQ), 394
  Family Intake Coding System (FICS),
    456
  Family Worries Scale (FWS), 396
  Negative Appraisals of Sexual Abuse
    Scale (NASAS), 187
  Parenting Scale (PS), 326
  Parenting Sense of Competence
    (PSOC), 329
  Parent's Report on the Child's Reac-
    tion to Stress Scale (PRCS), 195,
    196
  Structured Laboratory and Home
    Observation: Single Case Study
    (SLHO), 500
  Weekly Behavior Report (WBR), 223
  "When Bad Things Happen"
    (WBTH), 225–226
Child Conflict Index (CCI), 255–257
Child Dissociative Checklist (CDC),
    145–147
Child Dissociative Predictive Scale
    (CDPS), 155–157
Childhood Experience of Care and
    Abuse (CECA), 76–80
Childhood Maltreatment Interview
    Schedule (CMIS), 80–84

Childhood PTSD Interview–Child
    Form (CPI–Child), 89–93
Childhood PTSD Interview–Parent
    Form (CPTSDI), 86–89
Childhood trauma. *See* Adult survivors
    of childhood trauma; Posttrau-
    matic stress disorder (PTSD)
Childhood Trauma Interview (CTI),
    93–95, 160
Childhood Trauma Questionnaire
    (CTQ), 94, 158–161
Child internalization system
  Cleanup Coding Systems (CCS), 446
Child involvement in interparental con-
    flict
  Conflicts and Problem-Solving Scales
    (CPSS), 282, 284
Child maltreatment, 51–246
  Angie/Andy Child Rating Scale (A/A
    CRS), 131–133
  antecedent events, 54–55
  at-risk situations, 55. *See also* At-risk
    parents
  attachment security and, 55
  Attributions for Maltreatment Inter-
    view (AFMI), 67–69
  behavioral observation, 229–246. *See
    also* Child behavioral observation
  characteristics of victimized children,
    55
  Checklist for Child Abuse Evaluation
    (CCAE), 69–72
  Child Abuse and Neglect Interview
    Schedule–Revised (CANIS–R),
    72–76
  Child Abuse Blame Scale–Physical
    Abuse (CABS–PA), 275–278
  Child Abuse Potential Inventory–
    Form VI (CAPI), 279–281
  Childhood Experience of Care and
    Abuse (CECA), 76–80
  Childhood Maltreatment Interview
    Schedule (CMIS), 80–84
  Childhood PTSD Interview–Child
    Form (CPI–Child), 89–93
  Childhood PTSD Interview–Parent
    Form (CPTSDI), 86–89
  Childhood Trauma Interview (CTI),
    93–95
  Child Post-Traumatic Stress Reaction

    Index (CPTS–RI), 84–86, 148–
    150
  Children's Perception Questionnaire
    (CPQ), 98–101
  Clinician Administered PTSD Scale
    for Children and Adolescents for
    the *DSM-IV* (CAPS–CA), 101–
    105
  consequences of maltreatment, 55
  definition of, 54
  developmental delays, 55–56
  effectiveness of interventions, 12
  Family Interaction Interview (FII),
    381–383
  Family Interaction Task (FIT), 461–
    463
  History of Victimization Form
    (HVF), 179–182
  interviews, 63–124. *See also* Child
    maltreatment interview methods
  issues, 53–57
  legal and ethical considerations, 59–
    62
  obstacles to reliability and complete-
    ness, 58–62
  parental anger in response to child's
    behavior, 250–251
  Parent Perception Inventory (PPI),
    188–191
  parent psychopathology and, 11
  physical–medical evidence, 11
  reporting discrepancies, 58–59
  reporting requirements, 28–30
  resiliency of children, 56–57
  self-report inventories, 125–227. *See
    also* Child self-report inventories
  Trauma Symptom Checklist for Chil-
    dren (TSCC), 209–212
  types of measures, 9
  veracity of allegations, 12, 13
  Weekly Report of Abuse Indicators
    (WRAI), 296–298
Child maltreatment interview methods
  Anatomical Doll Questionnaire
    (ADQ), 63–66
  Attributions for Maltreatment Inter-
    view (AFMI), 67–69
  Checklist for Child Abuse Evaluation
    (CCAE), 69–72
  Child Abuse and Neglect Interview
    Schedule–Revised (CANIS–R),
    72–76

Child maltreatment interview methods
  (*Continued*)
  Child Abuse Interview Interaction
    Coding System (CAIICS), 239–
    241
  Childhood Experience of Care and
    Abuse (CECA), 76–80
  Childhood Maltreatment Interview
    Schedule (CMIS), 80–84
  Childhood Post-Traumatic Stress Re-
    action Index (CPTS–RI), 84–86,
    148–150
  Childhood PTSD Interview–Child
    Form (CPI–Child), 89–93
  Childhood PTSD Interview–Parent
    Form (CPTSDI), 86–89
  Childhood Trauma Interview (CTI),
    93–95
  Children's Attributions and Percep-
    tions Scale (CAPS), 95–98
  Children's Perception Questionnaire
    (CPQ), 98–101
  Clinician Administered PTSD Scale
    for Children and Adolescents for
    the *DSM-IV* (CAPS-CA), 101–105
  Parent Impact Questionnaire (PIQ),
    105–107
  Self-Report of Childhood Abuse Phys-
    ical (SRCAP), 107–109
  Structured Interview for Disorders of
    Extreme Stress (SIDES), 111–
    115
  Structured Interview of Symptoms
    Associated with Sexual Abuse
    (SASA), 109–111
  Traumatic Antecedents Interview
    (TAI), 115–118
  "What If" Situations Test (WIST-III),
    118–122
Child neglect
  Checklist for Child Abuse Evaluation
    (CCAE), 69–72
  Checklist for Living Environments to
    Assess Neglect (CLEAN), 442–
    445
  Child Abuse and Trauma Scale
    (CAT), 143
  definition of, 54
  family interaction assessment, 373
  History of Victimization Form
    (HVF), 180
  Home Accident Prevention Inventory
    (HAPI), 463–465

Maternal Characteristics Scale
    (MCS), 288–290
  Multidimensional Neglect Scale
    (MNS), 182–185
  parent engaging in, 251
Child Post-Traumatic Stress Reaction
    Index (CPTS–RI), 84–86, 148–
    150
Child Rating Scales of Exposure to In-
    terpersonal Abuse (CRS–EIA),
    133
Children at or above fifth-grade read-
    ing level
  Family Assessment Measure III (FAM
    III), 410–413
Children between ages of 4 and 12
  Children's Perception Questionnaire
    (CPQ), 98–101
Children between ages of 4 and 16
  Behavioral Role-Play in Sex Abuse
    Prevention (BR-SAP), 236–239
Children between ages of 5 and 12
  Family Environment Scale–Children's
    Version (FES–CV), 402–404
Children between ages of 6 and 11
  Exposure to Interadult Anger (EIA),
    452–454
Children between ages of 6 and 12
  Discord Control and Coping Ques-
    tionnaire (DCCQ), 392–395
  Parent Perception Inventory (PPI),
    188–191
Children between ages of 7 and 12
  Children's Attributions and Percep-
    tions Scale (CAPS), 95–98
Children between ages of 9 and 12
  Children's Perceptions of Interparen-
    tal Conflict Scale (CPICS), 389–
    392
Children between ages of 10 and 15
  Home Interaction Scoring System
    (HISS), 466–470
Children exposed to violence. *See* Expo-
    sure of child to violence
Children over age 6
  Child Witness to Violence Interview
    (CWVI), 378–381
Children over age 7
  Brother–Sister Questionnaire (BSQ),
    387–389

Children's Attributions and Perceptions Scale (CAPS), 95–98

Children's Beliefs About Parental Divorce Scale (CBPDS), 399–401

Children's Impact of Traumatic Events Scale B Revised (CITES–R), 161–165

Children's Marital Conflict Coping Strategies Interview (CMCCSI), 375–378

Children's Perception Questionnaire (CPQ), 98–101

Children's Perceptions of Interparental Conflict Scale (CPICS), 9, 389–392

Children's Response to Live Interadult Anger (CRLIA), 439–442

Children under age of 12
  Children's Beliefs About Parental Divorce Scale (CBPDS), 399–401
  Family Worries Scale (FWS), 395–397

Child self-report inventories, 125–227
  Abusive Sexual Exposure Scale (ASES), 125–127
  Adolescent Dissociative Experience Survey (A–DES), 127–131
  Angie/Andy Child Rating Scale (A/A CRS), 131–133
  Assessing Environments Scale (AEIII), 134–138
  Checklist of Sexual Abuse and Related Stressors (C–SARS), 138–142
  Child Abuse and Trauma Scale (CAT), 142–145
  Child Dissociative Checklist (CDC), 145–147
  Child Dissociative Predictive Scale (CDPS), 155–157
  Childhood Trauma Questionnaire (CTQ), 158–161
  Child Post-Traumatic Stress Reaction Index (CPTS–RI), 148–150
  Child Rating Scales of Exposure to Interpersonal Abuse (CRS–EIA), 133
  Children's Impact of Traumatic Events Scale B Revised (CITES–R), 161–165
  Child Sexual Behavior Inventory (CSBI–I), 150–153

Child's Reaction to Traumatic Events Scale (CRTES), 153–155

Conflicts in Relationships Questionnaire (CIRQ), 165–168

Emotional and Physical Abuse Questionnaire (EPAB), 169–171

Exposure to Abuse and Supportive Environments–Parenting Inventory (EASE–PI), 171–175

Family Environment Questionnaire (FEQ), 175–177

Feelings and Emotions Experienced During Sexual Abuse (FEEDSA), 177–179

History of Victimization Form (HVF), 179–182

Multidimensional Neglect Scale (MNS), 182–185

Negative Appraisals of Sexual Abuse Scale (NASAS), 185–188

Parent Perception Inventory (PPI), 188–191

Parents Perceptions Questionnaire (PPQ), 191–194

Parent's Report on the Child's Reaction to Stress Scale (PRCS), 194–197

Personal Safety Questionnaire (PSQ), 197–199

Responses to Childhood Incest Questionnaire (RCIQ), 199–203

Sexual Abuse Exposure Questionnaire (SAEQ), 203–206

Sexual Abuse Fear Evaluation (SAFE), 206–208

Teacher's Perceptions Questionnaire (TPQ), 191–194

Trauma Symptom Checklist 33 and 40 (TSC–33 and TSC–40), 212–214

Trauma Symptom Checklist for Children (TSCC), 209–212

Trauma Symptom Inventory (TSI), 214–218

Traumatic Sexualization Survey (TSS), 218–221

Weekly Behavior Report (WBR), 221–224

"When Bad Things Happen" (WBTH), 224–227

Child sexual abuse
  Abusive Sexual Exposure Scale (ASES), 125–127
  adult survivors of. *See* Adult survivors of child sexual abuse
  Anatomical Doll Questionnaire (ADQ), 63–66
  Angie/Andy Child Rating Scale (A/A CRS), 131–133
  Attributions for Maltreatment Interview (AFMI), 67–69
  Behavioral Role-Play in Sex Abuse Prevention (BR–SAP), 236–239
  Checklist of Sexual Abuse and Related Stressors (C–SARS), 138–142
  Child Abuse and Neglect Interview Schedule–Revised (CANIS–R), 72–76, 74
  Child Abuse Interview Interaction Coding System (CAIICS), 239–241
  Childhood Experience of Care and Abuse (CECA), 78
  Childhood Trauma Questionnaire (CTQ), 159
  Children's Attributions and Perceptions Scale (CAPS), 95–98
  Children's Impact of Traumatic Events Scale B Revised (CITES–R), 161–165
  Child Sexual Behavior Inventory (CSBI–I), 150–153
  consequences of, 56
  definition of, 54
  diagnostic disorders of children, 24
  Exposure to Abuse and Supportive Environments–Parenting Inventory (EASE–PI), 173
  false allegations, keeping alert to, 30
  Family Environment Scale (FES), 421–422
  Feelings and Emotions Experienced During Sexual Abuse (FEEDSA), 177–179
  History of Victimization Form (HVF), 179–182
  Mock Trial Role-Play (MTRP), 241–243
  multiple-perpetrator victims, 370, 421
  Negative Appraisals of Sexual Abuse Scale (NASAS), 185–188
  obstacles to, 61–62
  Parent Attribution Scale (PAS), 290–292
  Parent Impact Questionnaire (PIQ), 105–107
  perpetrators of, 26–27
  Personal Safety Questionnaire (PSQ), 197–199
  Sexual Abuse Fear Evaluation (SAFE), 206–208
  Sexually Anatomically Detailed (SAD) Dolls, 243–246
  Structured Interview of Symptoms Associated with Sexual Abuse (SASA), 109–111
  supplemental aids for interviews, 19. *See also* Anatomically detailed (AD) dolls
  Trauma Symptom Checklist for Children (TSCC), 209
  Traumatic Sexualization Survey (TSS), 218–221
  Weekly Behavior Report (WBR), 221–224
  "What If" Situations Test (WIST-III), 118–122
Child Sexual Behavior Inventory (CSBI), 97, 150–153
Child Sexual Victimization Questionnaire, 221
Child's Reaction to Traumatic Events Scale (CRTES), 153–155
Child stress. *See* Stress
Chinese mothers in Hong Kong Parenting Stress Index (PSI), 332
CIRQ. *See* Conflicts in Relationships Questionnaire
CISS. *See* Couples Interaction Scoring System
CITES–AF (altered form), 165
CITES–FVF (Family Violence From), 165
CITES–R. *See* Children's Impact of Traumatic Events Scale B Revised
CLEAN. *See* Checklist for Living Environments to Assess Neglect (CLEAN)
Cleanup Coding Systems (CCS), 445–449
Clinical evaluation, 12–13

Clinical practice and use of assessment, 32–36
  defining and gaining description of problem, 33
  establishing rapport, 32–33
  multimodal assessment, 35–36
  pretreatment functioning, measurement of, 34
  targets for treatment, 33–34
  threats to internal validity, 35
  treatment outcome, measurement of, 34–35
  treatment progress, measurement of, 34
  treatment study design to deal with threats to internal validity, 35
Clinical Rating Scale (CRS)
  Family Adaptability and Cohesion Scale III (FACES III), 409
Clinician Administered PTSD Scale for Children and Adolescents for the *DSM-IV* (CAPS-CA), 101–105
CMCCSI. *See* Children's Marital Conflict Coping Strategies Interview
CMIS. *See* Childhood Maltreatment Interview Schedule
Coercion
  abusive families, 370, 371–372
  Conflicts in Relationships Questionnaire (CIRQ), 166
  History of Victimization Form (HVF), 180
  Parent Behavior Inventory (PBI), 309
  Parent Behavior Rating Scales (PBRS), 351
  Parent Discipline Interview (PDI), 266
  System for Coding Interactions and Family Functioning (SCIFF), 502
  Weekly Report of Abuse Indicators (WRAI), 296
Cognitive needs assessment
  Multidimensional Neglect Scale (MNS), 183
Cohen's kappa, 42
  Behavioral Observation of Abused Children, 233
  Child Post-Traumatic Stress Reaction Index (CPTS–RI), 149
  Weekly Report of Abuse Indicators (WRAI), 297

Cohesion. *See* Family cohesion
Collaboration
  Conflicts and Problem-Solving Scales (CPSS), 282
College students
  Analogue Parenting Task (APT), 335–337
  Brother–Sister Questionnaire (BSQ), 387–389
  Multidimensional Neglect Scale (MNS), 183
Commands of parent. *See also* Disobedience; Obedience
  Cleanup Coding Systems (CCS), 445–449
  Mother–Son Interaction Task (MSIT), 482
  Parent Behavior Rating Scales (PBRS), 351
  Parent/Child Interaction Observations (PCIO), 354
Committee on Legal and Ethical Issues in the Treatment of Interpersonal Violence (APA), 28, 29, 30
Communication. *See* Family communication; Positive communication
Community involvement
  Assessing Environments Scale (AEIII), 135
Conceptual Dimensions of Parenting
  Parent/Child Interaction Observations (PCIO), 353
Concerns and Constraints Interview (CCI), 258–259
Concurrent validity, 44
Conduct disorder, 24
Confidence of mother
  Maternal Characteristics Scale (MCS), 288
Confidentiality of research, 48
Conflict Behavior Questionnaire (CBQ), 405–407
  Family Beliefs Inventory (FBI), 415
  Mother–Adolescent Attribution Questionnaire (MAAQ), 427
Conflict, family. *See* Family conflict
Conflicts and Problem-Solving Scales (CPSS), 281–284
Conflicts in Relationships Questionnaire (CIRQ), 165–168

Conflicts Tactics Scale, 165, 168, 174
  Brother–Sister Questionnaire (BSQ),
    388
  Child Abuse Potential Inventory–
    Form VI (CAPI), 280
  Conflicts and Problem-Solving Scales
    (CPSS), 283
  Hypothetical Compliance Vignettes
    (HCV), 342
  Multidimensional Neglect Scale
    (MNS), 183
Conflict Tactics Scale/Parent-to-Child
    Violence
  Weekly Report of Abuse Indicators
    (WRAI), 297
Construct validity, 43–45
Consumer Product Safety Commission,
    463
Content validity, 45
Control
  Childhood Experience of Care and
    Abuse (CECA), 77
  Cleanup Coding Systems (CCS), 446
  Family Environment Scale (FES), 420
  Parent Attribution Test (PAT), 304–
    306
  Parent Behavior Rating Scales
    (PBRS), 351–353
  Parenting Locus of Control Scale
    (PLCS), 323
Convergent validity, 44, 45
Coping
  Audiotaped Interparental Verbal
    Conflict (AIVC), 437–439
  child abuse and parent's negative
    coping skills, 251
  Children's Marital Conflict Coping
    Strategies Interview (CMCCSI),
    375–378
  Children's Perceptions of Interparen-
    tal Conflict Scale (CPICS), 390
  Clinician Administered PTSD Scale
    for Children and Adolescents for
    the DSM-IV (CAPS–CA), 103
  Family Crisis Oriented Personal Eval-
    uation Scales (F–COPES), 416–
    419
Corrupting/Exploiting
  Psychological Maltreatment Scales
    (PMS), 488
Couples Interaction Scoring System
    (CISS)

Home Interaction Scoring System
    (HISS), 466
Courtroom preparation of child
  Mock Trial Role-Play (MTRP), 241–
    243
CPI–Child. See Childhood PTSD
    Interview–Child Form
CPICS. See Children's Perceptions of
    Interparental Conflict Scale
CPQ. See Children's Perception Ques-
    tionnaire
CPSS. See Conflicts and Problem-
    Solving Scales
CPTSDI. See Childhood PTSD
    Interview–Parent Form
CPTS–RI. See Child Post-Traumatic
    Stress Reaction Index
Credibility issues. See also Trust issues
  Children's Attributions and Percep-
    tions Scale (CAPS), 96
Crisis assessment and intervention, 12–
    13
Crisis Symptom Checklist (CSC), 212
Criteria for inclusion of measures, 8–10
Criterion-based content analysis
    (CBCA) of children's statements,
    60
Criterion-referenced scoring, 41
Criterion-related validity, 44
CRLIA. See Children's Response to Live
    Interadult Anger
Cronbach's alpha, 42, 43
  Adolescent Dissociative Experience
    Survey (A–DES), 129
  Articulated Thoughts During Simu-
    lated Situations (ATSS), 435
  Brother-Sister Questionnaire (BSQ),
    388
  Child Abuse and Trauma Scale
    (CAT), 143
  Child Abuse Blame Scale–Physical
    Abuse (CABS–PA), 277
  Child Dissociative Checklist (CDC),
    146
  Childhood Trauma Questionnaire
    (CTQ), 159
  Child Post-Traumatic Stress Reaction
    Index (CPTS–RI), 149
  Child's Impact of Traumatic Events
    Scale B Revised (CITES–R), 163

Child's Reaction to Traumatic Events Scale (CRTES), 154

Emotional and Physical Abuse Questionnaire (EPAB), 170

Hypothetical Compliance Vignettes (HCV), 341

Maternal Characteristics Scale (MCS), 289

Parental Problem-Solving Measure (PPSM), 269

Parental Stress Scale (PSS), 319

Parent Behavior Inventory (PBI), 310

Parenting Locus of Control Scale (PLCS), 323

Parenting Sense of Competence (PSOC), 329

Parenting Stress Index (PSI), 332

Parent Perception Inventory (PPI), 190

Parent's Report on the Child's Reaction to Stress Scale (PRCS), 195

Self-Report of Childhood Abuse Physical (SRCAP), 107

Structured Interview of Symptoms Associated with Sexual Abuse (SASA), 110

System for Coding Interactions and Family Functioning (SCIFF), 503

"What If" Situations Test (WIST–III), 120–121

"When Bad Things Happen" (WBTH), 225

Cross-cultural research, 15–17

CRS. See Clinical Rating Scale

CRS–EIA. See Child Rating Scales of Exposure to Interpersonal Abuse

CRTES. See Child's Reaction to Traumatic Events Scale

C-SARS. See Checklist of Sexual Abuse and Related Stressors

CSBI. See Child Sexual Behavior Inventory

CSC. See Crisis Symptom Checklist

CTI. See Childhood Trauma Interview

CTQ. See Childhood Trauma Questionnaire

Culture and diversity
  Concerns and Constraints Interview (CCI), 259
  Conflict Tactics Scale: Parent to Child (CTSPC), 285
  definition of culture, 16
  Family Environment Scale (FES), 421
  family violence assessment and, 15–17
  measurement problems, 17
  Parenting Stress Index (PSI), 332
  sampling, 16–17
  Wyatt Sex History Questionnaire (WSHQ), 124

D

Daily Discipline Interview (DDI), 260–263

Dangerousness, prediction of, 31–32

Dating by adolescents
  Conflicts in Relationships Questionnaire (CIRQ), 165–168

DCCQ. See Discord Control and Coping Questionnaire

DDI. See Daily Discipline Interview

Defiance
  Disciplinary Strategies Interview (DSI), 264
  System for Coding Interactions and Family Functioning (SCIFF), 503

Demandingness
  Parenting Stress Index (PSI), 330

Denial of child's emotional response
  Psychological Maltreatment Scales (PMS), 488

Depersonalization
  Adolescent Dissociative Experience Survey (A–DES), 128

Depressive disorders
  adult survivors of child sexual abuse, 26
  childhood origin of
    Childhood Experience of Care and Abuse to assess, 76
  Parenting Stress Index (PSI), 331
  perpetrators of child sexual abuse, 26
  sexually abused children, 24
  Structured Interview for Disorders of Extreme Stress (SIDES), 113
  Trauma Symptom Checklist 33 and 40 (TSC–33 and TSC–40), 212–214
  Trauma Symptom Checklist for Children (TSCC), 209

Depressive disorders (*Continued*)
Trauma Symptom Inventory (TSI), 215
"When Bad Things Happen" (WBTH), 224
Destructiveness of child
Intensity of Parental Punishment Scale (IPPS), 299
Detachment
Responses to Childhood Incest Questionnaire (RCIQ), 201
Diagnostic issues, 24–27
Difficult child
Parenting Stress Index (PSI), 331
Dimensions of Stressful Events Scale (DOSE), 226
Dinnertime interactions of family
Home Interaction Scoring System (HISS), 466–470
Direct observation methods, 21
analogue methods. *See* Analogue measures
children. *See* Child behavioral observation
family interaction, 433–505. *See also* Family interaction analogue measures
parent or caregiver. *See* Parent behavioral observation
Disappointment of parent
Parent Discipline Interview (PDI), 266
Disapproval of parent
Mother–Son Interaction Task (MSIT), 482
Parent Behavior Rating Scales (PBRS), 351
Disciplinary practices
Analogue Parenting Task (APT), 336
Assessing Environments Scale (AEIII), 134–135
Child Abuse and Neglect Interview Schedule–Revised (CANIS–R), 73
Child Abuse and Trauma Scale (CAT), 143
Child Dissociative Predictive Scale (CDPS), 156
Conflict Tactics Scale: Parent to Child (CTSPC), 285
Daily Discipline Interview (DDI), 260–263

Disciplinary Strategies Interview (DSI), 263–265
Intensity of Parental Punishment Scale (IPPS), 298–301
parental anger and, 250–251
Parent Behavior Checklist/Parenting Inventory (PBC), 307
Parent Daily Report (PDR), 356–358
Parent Discipline Interview (PDI), 266–268
Parenting Scale (PS), 324–328
Parent Opinion Questionnaire (POQ), 313
Parent Perception Inventory (PPI), 189
Disciplinary Strategies Interview (DSI), 263–265
Discord Control and Coping Questionnaire (DCCQ), 392–395
Discord in family
Childhood Experience of Care and Abuse (CECA), 77
Discriminant validity, 44
Disobedience
Mother–Son Interaction Task (MSIT), 482
Disobedience of child
Disciplinary Strategies Interview (DSI), 264
Intensity of Parental Punishment Scale (IPPS), 299
Mother–Son Interaction Task (MSIT), 482
Disorders of extreme distress
Structured Interview for Disorders of Extreme Stress (SIDES), 114, 115
Disruptive behavior problems of children
Family Intake Coding System (FICS), 454–457
Dissociation, 26
Adolescent Dissociative Experience Survey (A–DES), 127–128
Child Dissociative Checklist (CDC), 145–147
Child Dissociative Predictive Scale (CDPS), 155–157
Dissociative Experiences Scale, 128
Feelings and Emotions Experienced

During Sexual Abuse (FEEDSA), 178

sexually abused children and, 24

Trauma Symptom Checklist 33 and 40 (TSC–33 and TSC–40), 212–214

Trauma Symptom Checklist for Children (TSCC), 209

Trauma Symptom Inventory (TSI), 215

"When Bad Things Happen" (WBTH), 224

Dissociative amnesia

Adolescent Dissociative Experience Survey (A–DES), 128

Child Dissociative Checklist (CDC), 145

Dissociative Experiences Scale, 128

Distractibility of child

Observational Coding System for Triadic Interaction (OCSTI), 485

Parenting Stress Index (PSI), 331

Distress. See also Stress

Structured Interview for Disorders of Extreme Stress (SIDES), 114, 115

System for Coding Interactions and Family Functioning (SCIFF), 503

Diversity. See Culture and diversity

Divorced couples

Children's Beliefs About Parental Divorce Scale (CBPDS), 399–401

Parenting Alliance Inventory (PAI), 321

Dolls, anatomically detailed. See Anatomical Doll Questionnaire (ADQ); Anatomically detailed (AD) dolls

DOSE. See Dimensions of Stressful Events Scale

DPICS. See Dyadic Parent–Child Interaction Coding System

DSI. See Disciplinary Strategies Interview

DSM-III (American Psychiatric Association)

Responses to Childhood Incest Questionnaire (RCIQ), 199–203

DSM-III-R (American Psychiatric Association)

posttraumatic stress disorder (PTSD) criteria

Child's Impact of Traumatic Events Scale B Revised (CITES–R), 161

Child's Reaction to Traumatic Events Scale (CRTES), 150

"When Bad Things Happen" (WBTH), 224

Structured Clinical Interview for DSM-III-R (SCID), 205

DSM-IV (American Psychiatric Association)

Child Dissociative Checklist (CDC), 147

posttraumatic stress disorder (PTSD) criteria, 84, 86, 87, 89, 91, 92

Child Post-Traumatic Stress Reaction Index (CPTS–RI), 148

Child's Impact of Traumatic Events Scale B Revised (CITES–R), 164

Clinician Administered PTSD Scale for Children and Adolescents for the DSM-IV (CAPS–CA), 101–105

Feelings and Emotions Experienced During Sexual Abuse (FEEDSA), 178

Parent's Report on the Child's Reaction to Stress Scale (PRCS), 194–197

Structured Interview for Disorders of Extreme Stress (SIDES), 111–112

"When Bad Things Happen" (WBTH), 224–227

Duty to warn, 28

confidentiality issues, 48

Dyadic Parent–Child Interaction Coding System (DPICS), 449–452

Dysfunctional sexual behavior

Trauma Symptom Inventory (TSI), 215

Traumatic Sexualization Survey (TSS), 219

E

EASE–PI. See Exposure to Abuse and Supportive Environments–Parenting Inventory

Eating disorders

adult survivors of child sexual abuse, 26

Eating disorders (*Continued*)
  "When Bad Things Happen"
    (WBTH), 225
Economic stress
  Assessing Environments Scale
    (AEIII), 135
Educational history of family
  Assessing Environments Scale
    (AEIII), 135–136
Edwards Social Desirability Scale
  Parent Affect Test (PAT), 303
Effectiveness of interventions, 12
EIA. *See* Exposure to Interadult Anger
Elder abuse
  reporting requirements, 29
Elementary-school-age children
  Standardized Observation Codes
    (SOCIII), 495–499
Emergency medical or dental treatment
  Family Interaction Interview (FII),
    382
Emotional abuse. *See* Psychological
    abuse
Emotional and Physical Abuse Ques-
    tionnaire (EPAB), 169–171
Emotional arousal of parent in re-
    sponse to child's behavior
  family interaction assessment, 372
  parental or caregivers assessment,
    250
Emotional control
  Responses to Childhood Incest Ques-
    tionnaire (RCIQ), 201
Emotional needs
  Multidimensional Neglect Scale
    (MNS), 183
Emotional neglect
  Childhood Trauma Questionnaire
    (CTQ), 158–159
Emotional support
  System for Coding Interactions and
    Family Functioning (SCIFF), 502
Emotional understanding
  family interaction assessment, 372–
    373
  Mother–Child Interaction Task
    (MCIT), 478–481
Emotional Understanding Interview
    (EUI)
  Mother–Child Interaction Task
    (MCIT), 480

Empathy
  Brother–Sister Questionnaire (BSQ),
    387
  Daily Discipline Interview (DDI), 260
  Family Interaction Task (FIT), 459
  Mother–Son Interaction Task
    (MSIT), 482
Empirical criterion keying, 40
Empowerment
  Child's Impact of Traumatic Events
    Scale B Revised (CITES–R), 162
EMSI. *See* Expectations of Maternal
    Support Interview
EPAB. *See* Emotional and Physical
    Abuse Questionnaire
Eroticization
  Child's Impact of Traumatic Events
    Scale B Revised (CITES–R), 163
Ethical issues, 23–24
  APA ethical principles, 25–26
Ethnocentrism, 15
EUI. *See* Emotional Understanding In-
    terview
Evaluation of program, 13–14
Expectations of Maternal Support In-
    terview (EMSI)
  Mother–Child Interaction Task
    (MCIT), 480
Expectations of parents
  Parent Behavior Checklist/Parenting
    Inventory (PBC), 307
Exposure of child to trauma. *See also*
    Adolescents exposed to trauma
  Child's Reaction to Traumatic Events
    Scale (CRTES), 153–155
Exposure of child to violence
  Angie/Andy Child Rating Scale (A/A
    CRS), 131
  Audiotaped Interparental Verbal
    Conflict (AIVC), 437–439
  Behavioral Observation of Shelter
    Children, 234–236
  Child Abuse and Neglect Interview
    Schedule–Revised (CANIS–R),
    73–74
  Child Witness to Violence Interview
    (CWVI), 378–381
  Conflicts and Problem-Solving Scales
    (CPSS), 281–284
  Discord Control and Coping Ques-
    tionnaire (DCCQ), 392–395
  Exposure to Abuse and Supportive

Environments–Parenting Inventory (EASE–PI), 171–175
Exposure to Interadult Anger (EIA), 452–454
family interaction assessment, 369–370, 372
Family Interaction Interview (FII), 381–383
History of Victimization Form (HVF), 180
Witness to Violence Child Interview, 383–386
Exposure to Abuse and Supportive Environments–Parenting Inventory (EASE–PI), 171–175
Exposure to Interadult Anger (EIA), 452–454
Exposure to trauma
Structured Interview for Disorders of Extreme Stress (SIDES), 111–115
Traumatic Antecedents Interview (TAI), 115–118
Externality
Mother–Adolescent Attribution Questionnaire (MAAQ), 426
External validity, 49–50
Eyberg Child Behavior Inventory, 264
Parental Anger Inventory (PAI), 317
Parental Problem-Solving Measure (PPSM), 270
Parent Behavior Inventory (PBI), 311

F

FACES
Family Assessment Measure III (FAM III), 412
FACES II
Family Adaptability and Cohesion Scale III (FACES III), 409
FACES III. See Family Adaptability and Cohesion Scale III
Face validity, 45
FACSS. See Family Affect-Content Coding System
Factorial validity, 45
Faking good behavior by parents
Parenting Stress Index (PSI), 332
FAM III. See Family Assessment Measure III

Families with children between ages of 6 and 7 years
Laboratory Family Interaction Task (LFIT), 476–478
Families with children older than 7 years
System for Coding Interactions and Family Functioning (SCIFF), 501–505
Families with history of child abuse
Child Abuse and Neglect Interview Schedule–Revised (CANIS–R), 72–76
Laboratory Family Interaction Task (LFIT), 476–478
Family Adaptability and Cohesion Scale III (FACES III), 408–410
Family affect
Family Interaction Task (FIT), 459
System for Coding Interactions and Family Functioning (SCIFF), 502
Family Affect-Content Coding System (FACCS)
Home Interaction Scoring System (HISS), 466
Family Assessment Device
Weekly Report of Abuse Indicators (WRAI), 297
Family Assessment Measure III (FAM III), 410–413
Family at dinner time
Home Interaction Scoring System (HISS), 466–470
Family beliefs
Family Beliefs Inventory (FBI), 413–416
Family Crisis Oriented Personal Evaluation Scales (F–COPES), 417
Parent–Adolescent Relationship Questionnaire (PARQ), 429
Family Beliefs Inventory (FBI), 413–416
Parent–Adolescent Relationship Questionnaire (PARQ), 430
Family care strains
Family Inventory of Life Events (FILE), 423
Family cohesion
defined, 370
Family Adaptability and Cohesion Scale III (FACES III), 408–410

Family cohesion (*Continued*)
  Family Environment Scale (FES), 419
  family interaction assessment, 369, 370
  System for Coding Interactions and Family Functioning (SCIFF), 501
Family communication, 369, 370, 371
  defined, 370
  Family Interaction Task (FIT), 459
  Parent–Adolescent Relationship Questionnaire (PARQ), 429
Family conflict
  Articulated Thoughts During Simulated Situations (ATSS), 433–437
  Conflict Behavior Questionnaire (CBQ), 405–407
  Family Environment Scale (FES), 419
  Family Interaction Task (FIT), 459
  Parent–Adolescent Relationship Questionnaire (PARQ), 429
  Potential Family Conflict Questionnaire (PFCQ), 397–399
  System for Coding Interactions and Family Functioning (SCIFF), 502
Family Crisis Oriented Personal Evaluation Scales (F–COPES), 416–419
Family environment
  Assessing Environments Scale (AEIII), 134–135
  Exposure to Abuse and Supportive Environments–Parenting Inventory (EASE–PI), 174
  Family Environment Questionnaire (FEQ), 175–177
  Family Environment Scale (FES), 419–422
  Family Environment Scale–Children's Version (FES–CV), 402–404
Family Environment Questionnaire (FEQ), 174, 175–177, 221
Family Environment Scale (FES), 419–422
  Child Abuse Potential Inventory–Form VI (CAPI), 280
  Family Adaptability and Cohesion Scale III (FACES III), 409
  Family Assessment Measure III (FAM III), 412
  Family Inventory of Life Events (FILE), 424
  Weekly Report of Abuse Indicators (WRAI), 297

Family Environment Scale–Children's Version (FES–CV), 402–404
Family flexibility, defined, 370
Family interaction analogue measures, 433–505
  Articulated Thoughts During Simulated Situations (ATSS), 433–437
  Audiotaped Interparental Verbal Conflict (AIVC), 437–439
  Checklist for Living Environments to Assess Neglect (CLEAN), 442–445
  Children's Response to Live Interadult Anger (CRLIA), 439–442
  Cleanup Coding Systems (CCS), 445–449
  Dyadic Parent–Child Interaction Coding System (DPICS), 449–452
  Exposure to Interadult Anger (EIA), 452–454
  Family Intake Coding System (FICS), 454–457
  Family Interaction Task (FIT), 458–461, 461–463
  Home Accident Prevention Inventory (HAPI), 463–465
  Home Interaction Scoring System (HISS), 466–470
  Home Observation for Measurement of the Environment (HOME), 470–472
  Interaction Behavior Code (IBC), 472–475
  Laboratory Family Interaction Task (LFIT), 476–478
  Mother–Child Interaction Task (MCIT), 478–481
  Mother–Son Interaction Task (MSIT), 481–484
  Observational Coding System for Triadic Interaction (OCSTI), 484–487
  Psychological Maltreatment Scales (PMS), 487–490
  Response-Class Matrix (RCM), 490–492
  Sibling Conflict Resolution Scale (SCRS), 492–495
  Standardized Observation Codes (SOCIII), 495–499
  Structured Laboratory and Home

Observation: Single Case Study (SLHO), 499–501

System for Coding Interactions and Family Functioning (SCIFF), 501–505

Family interaction assessment, 369–505
analogue measures and behavioral coding, 433–505. *See also* Family interaction analogue measures
interview methods, 375–386. *See also* Family interviews
methods of assessment, 373
self-report inventories, 387–431. *See also* Family self-report inventories

Family Interaction Task (FIT), 458–461, 461–463

Family interviews, 375–386
Children's Marital Conflict Coping Strategies Interview (CMCCSI), 375–378
Child Witness to Violence Interview (CWVI), 378–381
Family Interaction Interview (FII), 381–383
Witness to Violence Child Interview, 383–386

Family Inventory of Life Events (FILE), 423–425

Family organization
Family Environment Scale (FES), 420

Family problems
Weekly Report of Abuse Indicators (WRAI), 296

Family responsibility of child
Parent Opinion Questionnaire (POQ), 313

Family self-report inventories, 387–431
Brother–Sister Questionnaire (BSQ), 387–389
Children's Beliefs About Parental Divorce Scale (CBPDS), 399–401
Children's Perceptions of Interparental Conflict Scale (CPICS), 389–392
Conflict Behavior Questionnaire (CBQ), 405–407
Discord Control and Coping Questionnaire (DCCQ), 392–395
Family Adaptability and Cohesion Scale III (FACES III), 408–410

Family Assessment Measure III (FAM III), 410–413
Family Beliefs Inventory (FBI), 413–416
Family Crisis Oriented Personal Evaluation Scales (F–COPES), 416–419
Family Environment Scale (FES), 419–422
Family Environment Scale–Children's Version (FES–CV), 402–404
Family Inventory of Life Events (FILE), 423–425
Family Worries Scale (FWS), 395–397
Mother–Adolescent Attribution Questionnaire (MAAQ), 425–429
Parent–Adolescent Relationship Questionnaire (PARQ), 429–431
Potential Family Conflict Questionnaire (PFCQ), 397–399

Family stress. *See also* Stress
Family Inventory of Life Events (FILE), 423

Family violence. *See also* Adolescent maltreatment; Child maltreatment; Exposure of child to violence
analogue measures. *See* Family interaction analogue measures
archival records, 22
Behavioral Observation of Shelter Children, 234–236
culture and diversity in, 15–17
interviews. *See* Family interviews
observation. *See* Child behavioral observation; Family interaction analogue measures; Parent behavioral observation
purposes of, 12–14
scope of, 3
self-reports. *See* Child self-report inventories; Family self-report inventories; Parent self-report inventories

Family Worries Scale (FWS), 395–397

Fantasy not separated from reality
Adolescent Dissociative Experience Survey (A–DES), 128
"When Bad Things Happen" (WBTH), 224

Fate
  Parenting Locus of Control Scale
    (PLCS), 323
Father as child abuser
  Family Interaction Task (FIT), 461–
    463
Father's behavior assessment. *See also
    entries starting with "Parent"*
  Assessing Environments Scale
    (AEIII), 135
  Parent Perception Inventory (PPI),
    188–191
FBI. *See* Family Beliefs Inventory
F–COPES. *See* Family Crisis Oriented
    Personal Evaluation Scales
Fear
  Fear Survey Schedule for Children–
    Revised, 206, 207, 208
  Responses to Childhood Incest Ques-
    tionnaire (RCIQ), 200
Fear Survey Schedule for Children-
    Revised, 206, 207, 208
Female samples (exclusive or majority).
    See also Mother's behavior assess-
    ment
  Abusive Sexual Exposure Scale
    (ASES), 127
  Assessment of Physiological Re-
    sponses to Analogue Audiotaped
    Scripts, 229–232
  Emotional and Physical Abuse Ques-
    tionnaire (EPAB), 171
  Sexual Abuse Exposure Question-
    naire (SAEQ), 205
  Traumatic Sexualization Survey
    (TSS), 218–221
  Wyatt Sex History Questionnaire
    (WSHQ), 122–124
FEQ. *See* Family Environment Question-
    naire
FES. *See* Family Environment Scale
FES–CV. *See* Family Environment
    Scale–Children's Version
FILE. *See* Family Inventory of Life
    Events
Financial and business strains
  Family Inventory of Life Events
    (FILE), 423
FIT. *See* Family Interaction Task
Force. *See* Coercion; Physical abuse
Foreign languages, translation into

Child Abuse Potential Inventory–
    Form VI (CAPI), 280
Child Post-Traumatic Stress Reaction
    Index (CPTS–RI), 86, 149
Child Sexual Behavior Inventory
    (CSBI–I), 152
Family Interaction Interview (FII),
    382
Parent Behavior Checklist/Parenting
    Inventory (PBC), 308
Parenting Stress Index (PSI), 332
"When Bad Things Happen"
    (WBTH), 226
Forensic medical exams, 11, 30–31
child abuse, 13
Frustration
  Observational Coding System for Tri-
    adic Interaction (OCSTI), 485
  System for Coding Interactions and
    Family Functioning (SCIFF), 503
FWS. *See* Family Worries Scale

G

Gender differences
  Children's Perceptions of Interparen-
    tal Conflict Scale (CPICS), 391
  Children's Response to Live Inter-
    adult Anger (CRLIA), 441
General Health Questionnaire
  Parenting Stress Index (PSI), 332
Global Assessment of Recent Stress
  Parenting Stress Index (PSI), 332
Globality
  Mother–Adolescent Attribution Ques-
    tionnaire (MAAQ), 426
  Parent–Adolescent Relationship
    Questionnaire (PARQ), 429
"Goodness of fit" between parent and
    child, 253
Gross abuse
  Traumatic Antecedents Interview
    (TAI), 116
Gross neglect
  Traumatic Antecedents Interview
    (TAI), 116
Guilt
  Child's Impact of Traumatic Events
    Scale B Revised (CITES–R), 162
  Daily Discipline Interview (DDI), 260
  Responses to Childhood Incest Ques-
    tionnaire (RCIQ), 200

"When Bad Things Happen"
(WBTH), 224
Guttman scale, 40

H

Hallucinations
Child Dissociative Checklist (CDC),
145
HAPI. *See* Home Accident Prevention
Inventory
Harm to relationships
Negative Appraisals of Sexual Abuse
Scale (NASAS), 186
Hassles Scale
Parental Anger Inventory (PAI), 317
Parental Problem-Solving Measure
(PPSM), 270
HCV. *See* Hypothetical Compliance
Vignettes
Head Start program
Parenting Stress Index (PSI), 332
Health care strains
Family Inventory of Life Events
(FILE), 423
Helplessness
Children's Marital Conflict Coping
Strategies Interview (CMCCSI),
376
HISS. *See* Home Interaction Scoring
System
Historical records, 22
History of family violence
Child Abuse and Neglect Interview
Schedule–Revised (CANIS–R),
73
History of Victimization Form (HVF),
179–182
HIV. *See* Human immunodifficiency vi-
rus
HOME. *See* Home Observation for
Measurement of the Environ-
ment
Home Accident Prevention Inventory
(HAPI), 463–465
Home Environment Questionnaire, 134
Home Interaction Scoring System
(HISS), 466–470
Home Observation for Measurement of
the Environment (HOME), 470–
472
Child Abuse Potential Inventory–
Form VI (CAPI), 280

Home observations, 21
homes at risk for abuse and neglect
Checklist for Living Environments
to Assess Neglect (CLEAN),
442–445
Home Accident Prevention Inven-
tory (HAPI), 463–465
Home Simulation Assessment (HSA),
338–340
Hopkins Symptom Checklist, 176
HSA. *See* Home Simulation Assessment
Human immunodifficiency virus (HIV)
Wyatt Sex History Questionnaire
(WSHQ), 123
Hurricane study
Child's Reaction to Traumatic Events
Scale (CRTES), 154
HVF. *See* History of Victimization Form
Hyperactivity of child. *See also*
Attention-deficit hyperactivity
disorder
Parenting Stress Index (PSI), 331
Hyperarousal
Child's Impact of Traumatic Events
Scale B Revised (CITES–R), 162
Hypothetical Compliance Vignettes
(HCV), 340–342
Hypotheticals, use of
Analogue Parenting Task (APT),
335–337
Children's Perception Questionnaire
(CPQ), 98–101
Concerns and Constraints Interview
(CCI), 258–259
Hypothetical Compliance Vignettes
(HCV), 340–342
Intensity of Parental Punishment
Scale (IPPS), 298–301
Mother–Adolescent Attribution Ques-
tionnaire (MAAQ), 425–429
"What If" Situations Test (WIST–
III), 118–119

I

IBC. *See* Interaction Behavior Code
ICCs, 42
Impact of Events Scale, 106, 161, 205
Impulse control of mother
Maternal Characteristics Scale
(MCS), 288

Incest
  Abusive Sexual Exposure Scale
    (ASES), 126, 127
  family interaction assessment, 369,
    370–371
  Family Interaction Task (FIT), 458–
    461
  Responses to Childhood Incest Ques-
    tionnaire (RCIQ), 199–203
Incremental validity, 45
Independence of family members
  Family Environment Scale (FES), 419
  family interaction assessment, 369
Informed consent, 48
Intensity of Parental Punishment Scale
    (IPPS), 298–301
Intentionality
  Mother–Adolescent Attribution Ques-
    tionnaire (MAAQ), 426
Interaction Behavior Code (IBC), 472–
    475
Interactive behavior between parent
    and child
  Parent/Child Interaction Observa-
    tions (PCIO), 354
Internal consistency reliability, 42–43
Internal–External Scale
  Parenting Locus of Control Scale
    (PLCS), 323
Internal validity, 35, 49–50
Interrater reliability, 42
Intervention by child
  Discord Control and Coping Ques-
    tionnaire (DCCQ), 393
Interview methods
  children, 60, 63–124. *See also* Child
    maltreatment interview methods
  sexual abuse, 61
  family interaction, 375–386. *See also*
    Family interviews
  parent, 255–273. *See also* Parent in-
    terviews
  use of, 15, 18–19
Intrusive thoughts
  Child's Impact of Traumatic Events
    Scale B Revised (CITES–R), 162
  Child's Reaction to Traumatic Events
    Scale (CRTES), 153–154
  Responses to Childhood Incest Ques-
    tionnaire (RCIQ), 201
  Trauma Symptom Inventory (TSI),
    215

IPPS. *See* Intensity of Parental Punish-
    ment Scale
Isolation
  Assessing Environments Scale
    (AEIII), 135
  family interaction assessment, 369
  Parenting Stress Index (PSI), 331
  Responses to Childhood Incest Ques-
    tionnaire (RCIQ), 200
Issues Checklist
  Family Beliefs Inventory (FBI), 415
  Mother–Adolescent Attribution Ques-
    tionnaire (MAAQ), 427, 428

J

JMA. *See* Judgments in Moments of An-
    ger
Judgmental observation
  Parent Behavior Rating Scales
    (PBRS), 351–353
Judgments in Moments of Anger
    (JMA), 343–345

K

Kappa statistic, 42
Known-groups validity, 44–45
KR–20. *See* Kuder–Richardson 20 For-
    mula
Kuder–Richardson 20 Formula (KR–
    20), 43
  Child Abuse Potential Inventory–
    Form VI (CAPI), 280
  Video Assessment Task (VAT), 360
Kuwait study
  Child Post-Traumatic Stress Reaction
    Index (CPTS–RI), 86, 149

L

Laboratory Family Interaction Task
    (LFIT), 476–478
Langers Stress Scale
  Parenting Stress Index (PSI), 332
Learning disabilities
  sexually abused children, 24
Leaving children alone
  Parent Opinion Questionnaire
    (POQ), 313
Legal issues, 27–32
  forensic evaluations, 30–31
  prediction of dangerousness, 31–32
  reporting requirements, 28–30, 59

risk management, 28
subpoenas for client records, 28
Legal violations
   Family Inventory of Life Events
      (FILE), 423
Levonn, 131
LFIT. *See* Laboratory Family Interaction
      Task
Life Events Questionnaire
   Discord Control and Coping Ques-
      tionnaire (DCCQ), 394
Likert scale
   Assessment of Physiological Re-
      sponses to Analogue Audiotaped
      Scripts, 230, 231
   Audiotaped Interparental Verbal
      Conflict (AIVC), 438
   Brother–Sister Questionnaire (BSQ),
      388
   Child Abuse and Trauma Scale
      (CAT), 143
   Child Abuse Blame Scale–Physical
      Abuse (CABS–PA), 277
   Child Post-Traumatic Stress Reaction
      Index (CPTS–RI), 85, 148
   Children's Response to Live Inter-
      adult Anger (CRLIA), 440
   Discord Control and Coping Ques-
      tionnaire (DCCQ), 393
   Exposure to Abuse and Supportive
      Environments–Parenting Inven-
      tory (EASE–PI), 173
   Family Adaptability and Cohesion
      Scale III (FACES III), 408, 409
   Family Assessment Measure III (FAM
      III), 411
   Family Beliefs Inventory (FBI), 414
   Family Crisis Oriented Personal Eval-
      uation Scales (F–COPES), 417
   Family Environment Questionnaire
      (FEQ), 176
   Family Environment Scale (FES), 420
   Family Interaction Interview (FII),
      382
   Family Worries Scale (FWS), 396
   Feelings and Emotions Experienced
      During Sexual Abuse (FEEDSA),
      178
   History of Victimization Form
      (HVF), 181

Mother–Son Interaction Task
      (MSIT), 482
Negative Appraisals of Sexual Abuse
      Scale (NASAS), 186
Parent Behavior Inventory (PBI), 311
Parent's Report on the Child's Reac-
      tion to Stress Scale (PRCS), 194,
      195
Potential Family Conflict Question-
      naire (PFCQ), 398
Screening for Problem Parenting
      (SPP), 294
System for Coding Interactions and
      Family Functioning (SCIFF), 503
Traumatic Sexualization Survey
      (TSS), 219
Likert-type scale, 40
   Articulated Thoughts During Simu-
      lated Situations (ATSS), 435
   Child Abuse Potential Inventory–
      Form VI (CAPI), 279
   Childhood Trauma Questionnaire
      (CTQ), 159
   Children's Perceptions of Interparen-
      tal Conflict Scale (CPICS), 390
   Concerns and Constraints Interview
      (CCI), 258
   Conflict Tactics Scale: Parent to
      Child (CTSPC), 285
   Emotional and Physical Abuse Ques-
      tionnaire (EPAB), 169
   Exposure to Interadult Anger (EIA),
      453
   Family Interaction Task (FIT), 461
   Hypothetical Compliance Vignettes
      (HCV), 341
   Intensity of Parental Punishment
      Scale (IPPS), 299
   Interaction Behavior Code (IBC),
      474
   Judgments in Moments of Anger
      (JMA), 344
   Mother–Adolescent Attribution Ques-
      tionnaire (MAAQ), 427
   Mother–Son Interaction Task
      (MSIT), 482
   Multidimensional Neglect Scale
      (MNS), 183
   Parental Problem-Solving Measure
      (PPSM), 269
   Parental Stress Scale (PSS), 319

Likert-type scale (*Continued*)
  Parent Attribution Scale (PAS), 291
  Parent Behavior Checklist/Parenting
    Inventory (PBC), 307
  Parent Behavior Rating Scales
    (PBRS), 352
  Parenting Alliance Inventory (PAI),
    321
  Parenting Scale (PS), 325
  Parenting Sense of Competence
    (PSOC), 329
  Parenting Stress Index (PSI), 331
  Parent Opinion Questionnaire
    (POQ), 313
  Parents Perceptions Questionnaire
    (PPQ), 192
  Teacher's Perceptions Questionnaire
    (TPQ), 192
  Weekly Report of Abuse Indicators
    (WRAI), 296
  Wyatt Sex History Questionnaire
    (WSHQ), 123
Limit setting by parent
  Daily Discipline Interview (DDI), 260
Locke–Wallace Marital Adjustment Test
  Family Intake Coding System (FICS),
    456
Lock-Wallace Revised Marital Adjust-
    ment Test
  Parenting Alliance Inventory (PAI),
    321
Locus of Control Scale
  Parenting Locus of Control Scale
    (PLCS), 323
Losses
  Family Inventory of Life Events
    (FILE), 423
Low-income mothers
  Disciplinary Strategies Interview
    (DSI), 263–265

M

MAAQ. *See* Mother–Adolescent Attribu-
    tion Questionnaire
MacMillan–Olson–Hansen Anger Con-
    trol Scale (MOHAC), 318
Male-only sample. *See also* Father's be-
    havior assessment
  Structured Interview of Symptoms
    Associated with Sexual Abuse
    (SASA) and all-male sample, 111

Malicious intent
  Family Beliefs Inventory (FBI), 414
  Parent–Adolescent Relationship
    Questionnaire (PARQ), 429
Maltreatment of adolescents. *See* Ado-
    lescent maltreatment
Maltreatment of children. *See* Child
    maltreatment
Mandated reporting of abuse, 28–30
Mann–Whitney test
  Child Conflict Index (CCI), 256
Marital Attributional Style Question-
    naire, 425
Marital discord, 369
  Assessing Environments Scale
    (AEIII), 135
  child abuse and, 251
  Children's Marital Conflict Coping
    Strategies Interview (CMCCSI),
    375–378
  Children's Perceptions of Interparen-
    tal Conflict Scale (CPICS), 389–
    392
  Children's Response to Live Inter-
    adult Anger (CRLIA), 439–442
  Discord Control and Coping Ques-
    tionnaire (DCCQ), 392–395
  Family Inventory of Life Events
    (FILE), 423
  Mother–Son Interaction Task
    (MSIT), 481–484
  Parenting Alliance Inventory (PAI),
    321
Marital Interaction Coding System
    (MICS)
  Home Interaction Scoring System
    (HISS), 466
  Interaction Behavior Code (IBC),
    474
Marital Interaction Coding System-
    Global
  Family Intake Coding System (FICS),
    457
Marlow–Crowne Social Desirability
    Scale
  Parenting Locus of Control Scale
    (PLCS), 324
Maternal blame
  Children's Beliefs About Parental Di-
    vorce Scale (CBPDS), 400

Maternal Characteristics Scale (MCS), 288–290
Maternal Coercion Scale
  Hypothetical Compliance Vignettes (HCV), 342
Maternal Observation Matrix (MOM), 346–348
MCIT. *See* Mother–Child Interaction Task
MCS. *See* Maternal Characteristics Scale
Meaningfulness of life
  Structured Interview for Disorders of Extreme Stress (SIDES), 113
Memory of young children, 60–61
MICS. *See* Marital Interaction Coding System
Mock Trial Role-Play (MTRP), 241–243
Modeling
  Exposure to Abuse and Supportive Environments–Parenting Inventory (EASE–PI), 173
  family interaction assessment, 372
Modified Marital Interaction Coding System
  Conflict Behavior Questionnaire (CBQ), 407
MOHAC. *See* MacMillan–Olson–Hansen Anger Control Scale
MOM. *See* Maternal Observation Matrix
Mood
  Family Interaction Task (FIT), 459
  Judgments in Moments of Anger (JMA), 343–345
  Parenting Stress Index (PSI), 330
Mother–Adolescent Attribution Questionnaire (MAAQ), 425–429
Mother–child interaction. *See also* Mother–son relationship
  Cleanup Coding Systems (CCS), 445–449
  Hypothetical Compliance Vignettes (HCV), 340–342
  Mother–Child Interaction Task (MCIT), 478–481
  Standardized Observation Codes (SOCIII), 495–499
Mother–Child Interaction Task (MCIT), 478–481
Mother's behavior assessment. *See also* entries starting with "Parent"

Assessing Environments Scale (AEIII), 135
Concerns and Constraints Interview (CCI), 258–259
Disciplinary Strategies Interview (DSI), 263–265
Family Interaction Interview (FII), 381–383
Hypothetical Compliance Vignettes (HCV), 340–342
Judgments in Moments of Anger (JMA), 343–345
Maternal Characteristics Scale (MCS), 288–290
Maternal Observation Matrix (MOM), 346–348
Mother–Adolescent Attribution Questionnaire (MAAQ), 425–429
Mother-to-child vs. child-to-mother violence reporting, 58
Parent Behavior Rating Scales (PBRS), 351–353
Parent Perception Inventory (PPI), 188–191
Screening for Problem Parenting (SPP), 293–296
Standardized Observation Codes (SOCIII), 495–499
Mothers of elementary-school-age children
  Standardized Observation Codes (SOCIII), 495–499
Mother–Son Interaction Task (MSIT), 481–484
Mother–son relationship. *See also* Mother–child interaction
  Articulated Thoughts During Simulated Situations (ATSS), 433–437
  in family with marital discord
    Mother–Son Interaction Task (MSIT), 481–484
Mother's Responses to Videotapes (MRV), 348–350
MRV. *See* Mother's Responses to Videotapes
MSIT. *See* Mother–Son Interaction Task
MTRP. *See* Mock Trial Role-Play
Multidisciplinary team approach, 8
Multimodal assessment, 35–36
Mythology
  Family Interaction Task (FIT), 459

N

National Safety Council, 463

Negative affect of child
Disciplinary Strategies Interview (DSI), 264

Negative behavior of parent toward child
Parent/Child Interaction Observations (PCIO), 354

Negative child behavior
Parents Perceptions Questionnaire (PPQ), 192
Teacher's Perceptions Questionnaire (TPQ), 192

Negative communication
Conflicts in Relationships Questionnaire (CIRQ), 166
Daily Discipline Interview (DDI), 260
Negative Appraisals of Sexual Abuse Scale (NASAS), 186
Parent Perception Inventory (PPI), 189

Negative impact
Parent Attribution Scale (PAS), 291

Negativity
System for Coding Interactions and Family Functioning (SCIFF), 502

Neglect. *See* Child neglect; Physical neglect

Negotiations
Family Interaction Task (FIT), 459

Norm-referenced scoring, 40–41

Novaco Anger Control Scale
Parental Anger Inventory (PAI), 317, 318

Nude photography
Abusive Sexual Exposure Scale (ASES), 125

Numbness
Responses to Childhood Incest Questionnaire (RCIQ), 201

Nurturing
Parent Behavior Checklist/Parenting Inventory (PBC), 307

O

Obedience
Cleanup Coding Systems (CCS), 445–449
Family Beliefs Inventory (FBI), 414

Parent–Adolescent Relationship Questionnaire (PARQ), 429

Observational Coding System for Triadic Interaction (OCSTI), 484–487

Observation methods
children. *See* Child behavioral observation
family interaction, 433–505. *See also* Family interaction analogue measures
parent or caregiver. *See* Parent behavioral observation

OCSTI. *See* Observational Coding System for Triadic Interaction

Off-limits behavior of child
Disciplinary Strategies Interview (DSI), 264

Omens
Childhood PTSD Interview–Child Form (CPI–Child), 91
"When Bad Things Happen" (WBTH), 224

Open-ended questioning
Disciplinary Strategies Interview (DSI), 263
Video Mediated Recall Task (VMRT), 363

Oppositional defiant disorder, 24

Overreaction of parent
Parenting Scale (PS), 325

P

PAI. *See* Parenting Alliance Inventory

Pain
Negative Appraisals of Sexual Abuse Scale (NASAS), 186

PANAS. *See* Positive and Negative Affect Schedule

PAQ. *See* Parental Authority Questionnaire

Parent–adolescent conflict
Interaction Behavior Code (IBC), 472–475
Mother–Adolescent Attribution Questionnaire (MAAQ), 425–429
Parent–Adolescent Relationship Questionnaire (PARQ), 429–431

Parent–Adolescent Relationship Questionnaire (PARQ), 429–431
Family Beliefs Inventory (FBI), 415

Parent Affect Test (PAT), 301–304
Parental affect
    Cleanup Coding Systems (CCS), 446
    Mother's Responses to Videotapes
        (MRV), 348–350
    Parent Affect Test (PAT), 301–304
    Parent Daily Report (PDR), 357
Parental alienation syndrome, 30
Parental Anger Inventory
    Parental Problem-Solving Measure
        (PPSM), 270
Parental Authority Questionnaire
        (PAQ)
    Parenting Scale (PS), 326–327
Parental behavior. *See* Father's behavior
        assessment; Mother's behavior
        assessment; Parenting behavior
Parental Bonding Instrument, 174
Parental disorders
    Childhood Maltreatment Interview
        Schedule (CMIS), 81
Parental indifference
    Childhood Experience of Care and
        Abuse (CECA), 77
Parental Locus of Control Scale
    Parent Attribution Test (PAT), 305,
        306
Parental or caregivers assessment, 249–
        253
    anger in response to child's behavior,
        250
    causative factors of child maltreat-
        ment, 249–250
    emotional arousal of parent in re-
        sponse to child's behavior, 250
    interview method, 254–274. *See also*
        Parent interviews
    observation. *See* Parent behavioral ob-
        servation
    psychiatric disorders of parents, 249
    self-report method, 275–333. *See also*
        Parent self-report inventories
Parental Problem-Solving Measure
        (PPSM), 268–271
Parental promotion of independence
    Exposure to Abuse and Supportive
        Environments–Parenting Inven-
        tory (EASE–PI), 173
Parental psychological availability
    Childhood Maltreatment Interview
        Schedule (CMIS), 81

Parental rejection
    Assessing Environments Scale
        (AEIII), 136
Parental responsibility
    Parenting Locus of Control Scale
        (PLCS), 323
Parental stress
    Parental Stress Scale (PSS), 318–320
    Parenting Stress Index (PSI), 330–
        333
    Parental Stress Scale (PSS), 318–320
Parental support
    Exposure to Abuse and Supportive
        Environments–Parenting Inven-
        tory (EASE–PI), 173
Parent as victim of sexual abuse as
        child
    Parent Impact Questionnaire (PIQ),
        106
Parent Attribution Scale (PAS), 290–
        292
Parent Attribution Test (PAT), 304–306
Parent behavioral observation, 335–366
    Analogue Parenting Task (APT),
        335–337
    Home Simulation Assessment (HSA),
        338–340
    Hypothetical Compliance Vignettes
        (HCV), 340–342
    Judgments in Moments of Anger
        (JMA), 343–345
    Maternal Observation Matrix
        (MOM), 346–348
    Mother's Responses to Videotapes
        (MRV), 348–350
    Parent Behavior Rating Scales
        (PBRS), 351–353
    Parent/Child Interaction Observa-
        tions (PCIO), 353–356
    Parent Daily Report (PDR), 356–358
    Video Assessment Task (VAT), 359–
        361
    Video Mediated Recall Task (VMRT),
        362–366
Parent Behavior Checklist/Parenting
        Inventory (PBC), 306–309
Parent Behavior Rating Scales (PBRS),
        351–353
Parent/Child Interaction Observations
        (PCIO), 353–356

Parent–Child Relationship Inventory
(PCRI)
Parenting Scale (PS), 327
Parent–Child Relations Questionnaire,
174
Parent Daily Report (PDR), 190, 255
Parent Discipline Interview (PDI), 266–
268
Parent health
Parenting Stress Index (PSI), 331
Parent Impact Questionnaire (PIQ),
105–107
Parenting alliance, defined, 320
Parenting Alliance Inventory (PAI),
320–322
Parenting behavior. *See also* Father's be-
havior assessment; Mother's be-
havior assessment
child abuse and, 249–253
Exposure to Abuse and Supportive
Environments–Parenting Inven-
tory (EASE–PI), 171–175
"goodness of fit" between parent
and child, 253
observation. *See* Parent behavioral ob-
servation
Parent/Child Interaction Observa-
tions (PCIO), 353–356
Parent Opinion Questionnaire
(POQ), 313
Parent Perception Inventory (PPI),
188–191
purpose of, 252
System for Coding Interactions and
Family Functioning (SCIFF), 502
Parenting efficacy
Parenting Locus of Control Scale
(PLCS), 323
Parenting Sense of Competence
(PSOC), 328
Parenting Locus of Control Scale
(PLCS), 322–324
Parenting Opinion Questionnaire
Child Abuse Potential Inventory–
Form VI (CAPI), 280
Parenting Scale (PS), 324–328
Mother's Responses to Videotapes
(MRV), 350
Parenting Stress Index (PSI), 330–333
Child Abuse Potential Inventory–
Form VI (CAPI), 280

Daily Discipline Interview (DDI),
261, 262
Family Assessment Measure III (FAM
III), 412
Parental Stress Scale (PSS), 319
Parent Behavior Inventory (PBI), 311
Parent Discipline Interview (PDI),
267
Parenting Alliance Inventory (PAI),
321
Parenting Scale (PS), 327
Parent interviews, 255–273
Child Abuse and Neglect Interview
Schedule–Revised (CANIS–R),
72–76
Child Conflict Index (CCI), 255–257
Childhood Post-Traumatic Stress Re-
action Index (CPTS–RI), 84, 86
Childhood PTSD Interview–Parent
Form (CPTSDI), 86–89
Concerns and Constraints Interview
(CCI), 258–259
Daily Discipline Interview (DDI),
260–263
Disciplinary Strategies Interview
(DSI), 263–265
parental competency evaluations,
255–273
Parental Problem-Solving Measure
(PPSM), 268–271
Parent Discipline Interview (PDI),
266–268
Parent Impact Questionnaire (PIQ),
105–107
Parent Reaction to Abuse Disclosure
Scale (PRADS), 271–273
Structured Interview of Symptoms
Associated with Sexual Abuse
(SASA), 109–111
Parent physical availability
Childhood Maltreatment Interview
Schedule (CMIS), 81
Parent psychopathology
and child abuse, 11
Parent Reaction to Abuse Disclosure
Scale (PRADS), 271–273
Parents (generally)
Analogue Parenting Task (APT),
335–337
Child Abuse Blame Scale–Physical
Abuse (CABS–PA), 275–278

Child Abuse Potential Inventory–
    Form VI (CAPI), 279–281
Parental Problem-Solving Measure
    (PPSM), 268–271
Parenting Alliance Inventory (PAI),
    320–322
Parenting Locus of Control Scale
    (PLCS), 322–324
Potential Family Conflict Question-
    naire (PFCQ), 397–399
Parents Anonymous
    Parent Affect Test (PAT), 303
Parents at-risk. *See* At-risk parents
Parent self-report inventories, 275–333
    Angie/Andy Child Rating Scale (A/A
        CRS), 133
    Child Abuse Blame Scale–Physical
        Abuse (CABS–PA), 275–278
    Child Abuse Potential Inventory–
        Form VI (CAPI), 279–281
    Child Dissociative Checklist (CDC),
        145–147
    Child Sexual Behavior Inventory
        (CSBI–I), 150–153
    Conflicts and Problem-Solving Scales
        (CPSS), 281–284
    Conflict Tactics Scale: Parent to
        Child (CTSPC), 284–287
    Intensity of Parental Punishment
        Scale (IPPS), 298–301
    MacMillan–Olson–Hansen Anger
        Control Scale (MOHAC), 318
    Maternal Characteristics Scale
        (MCS), 288–290
    Parent Affect Test (PAT), 301–304
    Parental Anger Inventory (PAI),
        315–318
    Parental Stress Scale (PSS), 318–320
    Parent Attribution Scale (PAS), 290–
        292
    Parent Attribution Test (PAT), 304–
        306
    Parent Behavior Checklist/Parenting
        Inventory (PBC), 306–309
    Parent Behavior Inventory (PBI),
        309–312
    Parenting Alliance Inventory (PAI),
        320–322
    Parenting Locus of Control Scale
        (PLCS), 322–324
    Parenting Scale (PS), 324–328

Parenting Sense of Competence
    (PSOC), 328–330
Parenting Stress Index (PSI), 330–
    333
Parent Opinion Questionnaire
    (POQ), 312–314
Parents Perceptions Questionnaire
    (PPQ), 191–194
Parent's Report on the Child's Reac-
    tion to Stress Scale (PRCS),
    194–197
Screening for Problem Parenting
    (SPP), 293–296
Weekly Behavior Report (WBR),
    221–224
Weekly Report of Abuse Indicators
    (WRAI), 296–298
Parents in family experiencing conflict
    Conflict Behavior Questionnaire
        (CBQ), 405–407
Parents of abused children
    Parent Impact Questionnaire (PIQ),
        105–107
    Weekly Report of Abuse Indicators
        (WRAI), 296–298
Parents of adolescents
    Family Beliefs Inventory (FBI), 413–
        416
    Parenting Alliance Inventory (PAI),
        320–322
    Parenting Locus of Control Scale
        (PLCS), 322–324
Parents of children between ages 2 and
    10. *See also* Parents of young chil-
    dren
    Parental Anger Inventory (PAI),
        315–318
Parents of children between ages 2 and
    11. *See also* Parents of young chil-
    dren
    Parent Affect Test (PAT), 301–304
Parents of children between ages 4 and
    8. *See also* Parents of young chil-
    dren
    Parent/Child Interaction Observa-
        tions (PCIO), 353–356
Parents of children between ages 4 and
    11. *See also* Parents of young chil-
    dren
    Parent Daily Report (PDR), 356–358

Parents of children between ages 4 and 14. *See also* Parents of young children
   Intensity of Parental Punishment Scale (IPPS), 298–301
Parents of children between ages 5 and 9. *See also* Parents of young children
   Psychological Maltreatment Scales (PMS), 487–490
Parents of children between ages 6 and 12
   Mother–Child Interaction Task (MCIT), 478–481
Parents of children between ages 8 and 12
   Family Interaction Interview (FII), 381–383
Parents of children under age 3. *See also* Parents of young children
   Parenting Scale (PS), 324–328
   Parent Stress Index (PSI), 330–333
   Video Assessment Task (VAT), 359–361
Parents of children under age 12
   Parent Daily Report (PDR), 356–358
   Parenting Sense of Competence (PSOC), 328–330
   Parent Opinion Questionnaire (POQ), 312–314
   Screening for Problem Parenting (SPP), 293–296
Parents of children who have experienced stressful events
   Parent's Report on the Child's Reaction to Stress Scale (PRCS), 194–197
Parents of elementary schoolchildren. *See also* Parents of young children
   Child Conflict Index (CCI), 255–257
   Concerns and Constraints Interview (CCI), 258–259
   Judgments in Moments of Anger (JMA), 343–345
   Parent Behavior Inventory (PBI), 309–312
   Video Mediated Recall Task (VMRT), 362–366
Parents of sexually abused children
   Child Sexual Behavior Inventory (CSBI–I), 150–153

Parent Attribution Scale (PAS), 290–292
Parent Reaction to Abuse Disclosure Scale (PRADS), 271–273
Structured Interview of Symptoms Associated with Sexual Abuse (SASA), 109–111
Weekly Behavior Report (WBR), 221–224
Parents of young children. *See also* Parents of elementary schoolchildren
   Cleanup Coding Systems (CCS), 445–449
   Daily Discipline Interview (DDI), 260–263
   Disciplinary Strategies Interview (DSI), 263–265
   Dyadic Parent–Child Interaction Coding System (DPICS), 449–452
   Family Intake Coding System (FICS), 454–457
   Hypothetical Compliance Vignettes (HCV), 340–342
   Judgments in Moments of Anger (JMA), 343–345
   Maternal Observation Matrix (MOM), 346–348
   Mother's Responses to Videotapes (MRV), 348–350
   Parental Stress Scale (PSS), 318–320
   Parent Attribution Test (PAT), 304–306
   Parent Behavior Checklist/Parenting Inventory (PBC), 306–309
   Parent Behavior Inventory (PBI), 309–312
   Parent Behavior Rating Scales (PBRS), 351–353
   Parent/Child Interaction Observations (PCIO), 353–356
   Parent Discipline Interview (PDI), 266–268
   Parenting Scale (PS), 324–328
   Parenting Stress Index (PSI), 330–333
   Response-Class Matrix (RCM), 490–492
   Video Assessment Task (VAT), 359–361

Video Mediated Recall Task (VMRT), 362–366

Parents Perceptions Questionnaire (PPQ), 191–194

Parent's Report on the Child's Reaction to Stress Scale (PRCS), 194–197

Parents who are physically abusive
Home Simulation Assessment (HSA), 338–340
Weekly Report of Abuse Indicators (WRAI), 296–298

Parent training programs
Home Simulation Assessment (HSA), 338–340

PARQ. *See* Parent–Adolescent Relationship Questionnaire

Partner relationship
Parenting Stress Index (PSI), 331

Partner violence
adult survivors of child abuse engaging in, 56
exposure of child to, 54, 56

PAS. *See* Parent Attribution Scale

Passive influence
Adolescent Dissociative Experience Survey (A–DES), 128
Family Crisis Oriented Personal Evaluation Scales (F-COPES), 417

PAT. *See* Parent Affect Test; Parent Attribution Test

Paternal blame
Children's Beliefs About Parental Divorce Scale (CBPDS), 400

PBC. *See* Parent Behavior Checklist/Parenting Inventory

PBRS. *See* Parent Behavior Rating Scales

PCIO. *See* Parent/Child Interaction Observations

PCRI. *See* Parent–Child Relationship Inventory

PDI. *See* Parent Discipline Interview

PDR. *See* Parent Daily Report

Pearson correlations, 42
Adolescent Dissociative Experience Survey (A–DES), 129
Child Abuse Potential Inventory– Form VI (CAPI), 280
Parental Anger Inventory (PAI), 317

Parent Behavior Checklist/Parenting Inventory (PBC), 308

Traumatic Sexualization Survey (TSS), 220

Weekly Report of Abuse Indicators (WRAI), 297

"What If" Situations Test (WIST–III), 121

Wyatt Sex History Questionnaire (WSHQ), 123

Peer as source of comfort
Children's Marital Conflict Coping Strategies Interview (CMCCSI), 376

Peer differences, feelings of
Children's Attributions and Perceptions Scale (CAPS), 96

Peer relations
Assessing Environments Scale (AEIII), 135
Behavioral Observation of Abused Children, 232–234
Children's Beliefs About Parental Divorce Scale (CBPDS), 400

Perceived Stress Scale
Parental Stress Scale (PSS), 319

Perceptions of abuse status
Childhood Maltreatment Interview Schedule (CMIS), 82
Structured Interview for Disorders of Extreme Stress (SIDES), 112

Perceptions of perpetrator
Structured Interview for Disorders of Extreme Stress (SIDES), 112–113

Perfectionism
Family Beliefs Inventory (FBI), 414
Parent–Adolescent Relationship Questionnaire (PARQ), 429

Perpetrators of child sexual abuse, 26, 27
multiple-perpetrator victims, 370, 421

Personal attribution for negative events. *See* Self-blame

Personal growth
Family Environment Scale (FES), 419–420

Personal Safety Questionnaire (PSQ), 197–199

PFCQ. *See* Potential Family Conflict Questionnaire

Physical abuse. *See also* Child maltreatment
  Analogue Parenting Task (APT), 336
  Child Abuse Blame Scale–Physical Abuse (CABS–PA), 275–278
  Childhood Experience of Care and Abuse (CECA), 77–78
  Childhood Maltreatment Interview Schedule (CMIS), 81–82
  Childhood Trauma Questionnaire (CTQ), 158
  Conflicts in Relationships Questionnaire (CIRQ), 166
  Conflict Tactics Scale: Parent to Child (CTSPC), 285
  definition of, 54
  Exposure to Abuse and Supportive Environments–Parenting Inventory (EASE–PI), 172
  Family Environment Questionnaire (FEQ), 175
  History of Victimization Form (HVF), 180
Physical control. *See also* Control
  Parent Discipline Interview (PDI), 266
Physical force. *See also* Coercion; Physical abuse
  Daily Discipline Interview (DDI), 260
  Weekly Report of Abuse Indicators (WRAI), 296
Physical intervention by child
  Children's Marital Conflict Coping Strategies Interview (CMCCSI), 376
Physical–medical evidence of child abuse, 11
Physical needs
  Multidimensional Neglect Scale (MNS), 183
Physical neglect. *See also* Child neglect
  Childhood Trauma Questionnaire (CTQ), 159
Physical restraint
  Parent Discipline Interview (PDI), 266
Physiological responses
  Assessment of Physiological Responses to Analogue Audiotaped Scripts, 229–232
Pictorials. *See* Cartoons

PIQ. *See* Parent Impact Questionnaire
Placing research participants at risk, 48–49
PLCS. *See* Parenting Locus of Control Scale
PMS. *See* Psychological Maltreatment Scales
POMS. *See* Profile of Mood States
Positive and Negative Affect Schedule (PANAS)
  Judgments in Moments of Anger (JMA), 344–345
Positive child behavior
  Parents Perceptions Questionnaire (PPQ), 192
  Teacher's Perceptions Questionnaire (TPQ), 192
Positive communication
  Conflicts in Relationships Questionnaire (CIRQ), 166, 167
  Parent Perception Inventory (PPI), 189
Posttraumatic stress disorder (PTSD), 26
  Child Dissociative Predictive Scale (CDPS), 156–157
  Childhood PTSD Interview–Child Form (CPI–Child), 89–93
  Child Post-Traumatic Stress Reaction Index (CPTS-RI), 84–86, 148–150
  Child's Impact of Traumatic Events Scale B Revised (CITES-R), 162, 163
  Clinician Administered PTSD Scale for Children and Adolescents for the *DSM-IV* (CAPS–CA), 101–105
  Parent's Report on the Child's Reaction to Stress Scale (PRCS), 194–197
  Responses to Childhood Incest Questionnaire (RCIQ), 199–203
  sexually abused children, 24
  therapists working with trauma victims, 27
  Trauma Symptom Checklist for Children (TSCC), 209–212
  Trauma Symptom Inventory (TSI), 214–218
  "When Bad Things Happen" (WBTH), 224–227

Potential Family Conflict Questionnaire (PFCQ), 397–399
  Observational Coding System for Triadic Interaction (OCSTI), 484
Powerlessness
  Responses to Childhood Incest Questionnaire (RCIQ), 200
PPQ. *See* Parents Perceptions Questionnaire
PPSM. *See* Parental Problem-Solving Measure
PRADS. *See* Parent Reaction to Abuse Disclosure Scale
Praise
  Dyadic Parent–Child Interaction Coding System (DPICS), 449
PRCS. *See* Parent's Report on the Child's Reaction to Stress Scale
Prediction of dangerousness, 31–32
Predictive validity, 44
Pregnancy and childbearing strains
  Family Inventory of Life Events (FILE), 423
Preschool children. *See* Young children
Prevention programs, 13
Problem solving
  Parent–Adolescent Relationship Questionnaire (PARQ), 429
  Parental Problem-Solving Measure (PPSM), 268–271
Professional liability insurance, 28
Profile of Mood States (POMS)
  Judgments in Moments of Anger (JMA), 345
Program evaluation, 13–14
Project 12-Ways
  Checklist for Living Environments to Assess Neglect (CLEAN), 442–445
PS. *See* Parenting Scale
PSI. *See* Parenting Stress Index
PSQ. *See* Personal Safety Questionnaire
PSS. *See* Parental Stress Scale
Psychological abuse
  Childhood Maltreatment Interview Schedule (CMIS), 81, 82
  Childhood Trauma Questionnaire (CTQ), 158
  Conflict Tactics Scale: Parent to Child (CTSPC), 285
  definition of emotional abuse, 54

Emotional and Physical Abuse Questionnaire (EPAB), 169–171
Exposure to Abuse and Supportive Environments–Parenting Inventory (EASE–PI), 172
Family Environment Questionnaire (FEQ), 175
History of Victimization Form (HVF), 180
Psychological Maltreatment Scales (PMS), 487–490
Psychological Maltreatment Scales (PMS), 487–490
Psychometric evaluation, 41–45
Psychometrics research problems, 46–47
PTSD. *See* Posttraumatic stress disorder
Public disclosure events
  Checklist of Sexual Abuse and Related Stressors (C–SARS), 140
Punishment. *See* Disciplinary practices

R
Rapport, establishing with client, 32–33
Rational and empirical approaches to scale development, 39–40
RCM. *See* Response-Class Matrix
Reaction to perpetrator
  Responses to Childhood Incest Questionnaire (RCIQ), 200
Reframing
  Family Crisis Oriented Personal Evaluation Scales (F–COPES), 417
Rejection
  System for Coding Interactions and Family Functioning (SCIFF), 502
Relationship problems
  Structured Interview for Disorders of Extreme Stress (SIDES), 113
Reliability, 41–43
  defined, 41
  split half. *See* Split-half reliability
  young children during evaluation process, 60
Reporting requirements, 28–30
Residential child care workers
  Parenting Sense of Competence (PSOC), 330
Resiliency of abused children, 56–57
Response-Class Matrix (RCM), 490–492

Restriction of parental role
  Parenting Stress Index (PSI), 331
Reunification hope of children
  Children's Beliefs About Parental Divorce Scale (CBPDS), 400
Revictimization by research, 47–48
Risk management, 28
Risk-taking
  "When Bad Things Happen" (WBTH), 225
Ritualistic abuse
  Childhood Maltreatment Interview Schedule (CMIS), 82
Role play
  Behavioral Role-Play in Sex Abuse Prevention (BR–SAP), 236–239
  Home Simulation Assessment (HSA), 338–340
  Mock Trial Role-Play (MTRP), 241–243
  Sibling Conflict Resolution Scale (SCRS), 492–495
Rotter's Internal–External Locus of Control Scale
  Child Abuse Potential Inventory–Form VI (CAPI), 280
Ruination
  Family Beliefs Inventory (FBI), 414
  Parent–Adolescent Relationship Questionnaire (PARQ), 429

S

Sadness and loss
  Responses to Childhood Incest Questionnaire (RCIQ), 200
  System for Coding Interactions and Family Functioning (SCIFF), 503
SAEQ. *See* Sexual Abuse Exposure Questionnaire
SAFE. *See* Sexual Abuse Fear Evaluation
Safety prevention programs
  Home Accident Prevention Inventory (HAPI), 463–465
  Personal Safety Questionnaire (PSQ), 197–199
  "What If" Situations Test (WIST–III), 121
Safety skills of children
  Child Witness to Violence Interview (CWVI), 378
Sampling
  cultural, 16–17

female. *See* Female samples (exclusive or majority)
  male-only, 111
  white and middle-class. *See* White and middle-class sampling
SASA. *See* Structured Interview of Symptoms Associated with Sexual Abuse
Schizophrenia
  perpetrators of child sexual abuse, 26, 27
School misbehavior
  Intensity of Parental Punishment Scale (IPPS), 299
School observations, 21
  Teacher's Perceptions Questionnaire (TPQ), 191–194
SCID. *See* Structured Clinical Interview for *DSM-III-R*
Scoring of the instrument, 40–41
Screening for Problem Parenting (SPP), 293–296
Scripts
  Assessment of Physiological Responses to Analogue Audiotaped Scripts, 229–232
SCRS. *See* Sibling Conflict Resolution Scale
Secondary traumatic stress, 27
Selection of assessment devices, 14
Self-blame
  Childhood PTSD Interview–Child Form (CPI–Child), 91
  Children's Attributions and Perceptions Scale (CAPS), 96
  Children's Beliefs About Parental Divorce Scale (CBPDS), 401
  Children's Marital Conflict Coping Strategies Interview (CMCCSI), 376
  Children's Perceptions of Interparental Conflict Scale (CPICS), 390
  Child's Impact of Traumatic Events Scale B Revised (CITES–R), 162
  Family Beliefs Inventory (FBI), 414
  family interaction assessment, 373
  Negative Appraisals of Sexual Abuse Scale (NASAS), 186
  Parent-Adolescent Relationship Questionnaire (PARQ), 429
  Parent Attribution Scale (PAS), 291

"When Bad Things Happen"
(WBTH), 224
Self-calming by child
Discord Control and Coping Questionnaire (DCCQ), 393
Self-care by child
Parent Opinion Questionnaire
(POQ), 313
Self-defense
Observational Coding System for Triadic Interaction (OCSTI), 485
Self-determination
ethical issues, 23–24
Self-esteem
Parenting Sense of Competence
(PSOC), 328–330
Self-hurt
Emotional and Physical Abuse Questionnaire (EPAB), 170
Trauma Symptom Inventory (TSI),
215–216
"When Bad Things Happen"
(WBTH), 224
Selfish motivation
Mother–Adolescent Attribution Questionnaire (MAAQ), 426
Self-perception
Structured Interview for Disorders of
Extreme Stress (SIDES), 112
Self-reference problems
Trauma Symptom Inventory (TSI),
215
Self-reliance of child
Children's Marital Conflict Coping
Strategies Interview (CMCCSI),
376
Self-report inventories, 19–20
child assessments, 125–227. *See also*
Child self-report inventories
family interaction, 387–431. *See also*
Family self-report inventories
parent or caregiver assessments, 275–
333. *See also* Parent self-report inventories
Self-Report of Childhood Abuse Physical (SRCAP), 107–109
SEM. *See* Standard error of measurement
Semi-Structured Inventory of Children.
See Children's Attributions and
Perceptions Scale (CAPS)

Sense of confidence of parent
Parenting Stress Index (PSI), 331
Separated couples
Children's Beliefs About Parental Divorce Scale (CBPDS), 399–401
Parenting Alliance Inventory (PAI),
321
Separation and loss
Traumatic Antecedents Interview
(TAI), 116
Separation anxiety disorder
sexually abused children, 24
Sexual abuse
adolescents. *See* Adolescent sexual
abuse
adult survivors. *See* Adult survivors of
child sexual abuse
children. *See* Child sexual abuse
parents of abused children. *See* Parents of sexually abused children
Sexual Abuse Exposure Questionnaire
(SAEQ), 203–206
Sexual Abuse Fear Evaluation (SAFE),
206–208
Sexual Behavior Inventory, 123
Sexual concerns
Child's Impact of Traumatic Events
Scale B Revised (CITES–R), 162
Trauma Symptom Checklist 33 and
40 (TSC–33 and TSC–40), 212–
214
Trauma Symptom Checklist for Children (TSCC), 209
Sexual disorders
adult survivors of child sexual abuse,
26
Sexually transmitted diseases (STDs)
Wyatt Sex History Questionnaire
(WSHQ), 123
Sexual victimization
diagnostic disorders, 26
Shaking of infants
Conflict Tactics Scale: Parent to
Child (CTSPC), 286
Shame
Responses to Childhood Incest Questionnaire (RCIQ), 200
Shelter children
Behavioral Observation of Shelter
Children, 234–236

Shelter children (*Continued*)
  Discord Control and Coping Questionnaire (DCCQ), 395
Sibling Conflict Resolution Scale (SCRS), 492–495
Sibling relationships
  Brother–Sister Questionnaire (BSQ), 387–389
  Children's Marital Conflict Coping Strategies Interview (CMCCSI), 376
  Parent Opinion Questionnaire (POQ), 313
  Sibling Conflict Resolution Scale (SCRS), 492–495
SIDES. *See* Structured Interview for Disorders of Extreme Stress
Sleep disturbance
  Trauma Symptom Checklist 33 and 40 (TSC–33 and TSC–40), 212–214
Sleepwalking
  Child Dissociative Checklist (CDC), 146
SLHO. *See* Structured Laboratory and Home Observation: Single Case Study
Social reactions
  Child's Impact of Traumatic Events Scale B Revised (CITES–R), 162
Social support
  Family Crisis Oriented Personal Evaluation Scales (F–COPES), 417
  Screening for Problem Parenting (SPP), 293
Social workers as reporters
  History of Victimization Form (HVF), 179–182
SOCIII. *See* Standardized Observation Codes
Somatization
  Structured Interview for Disorders of Extreme Stress (SIDES), 113
Somatoform disorders
  adult survivors of child sexual abuse, 26
  sexually abused children, 24
Sons. *See entries starting* "Mother-son"
Spain
  Standardized Observation Codes (SOCIII), 495–499
Spearman Brown correlations

Adolescent Dissociative Experience Survey (A–DES), 129
Daily Discipline Interview (DDI), 261
Interaction Behavior Code (IBC), 474
Parental Anger Inventory (PAI), 316
Spearman correlations
  Child Dissociative Checklist (CDC), 146
  Family Interaction Task (FIT), 459
Spiritual support
  Family Crisis Oriented Personal Evaluation Scales (F–COPES), 417
Split-half reliability, 43
  Daily Discipline Interview (DDI), 261
  Intensity of Parental Punishment Scale (IPPS), 300
  Parental Anger Inventory (PAI), 316
  Sexual Abuse Exposure Questionnaire (SAEQ), 205
SPP. *See* Screening for Problem Parenting
Spurning
  Psychological Maltreatment Scales (PMS), 488
SRCAP. *See* Self-Report of Childhood Abuse Physical
Stability
  Mother–Adolescent Attribution Questionnaire (MAAQ), 426
Stalemate
  Conflicts and Problem-Solving Scales (CPSS), 282
Standard error of measurement (SEM), 43
Standardized Observation Codes (SOCIII), 495–499
State protective services' investigations for neglect
  Checklist for Living Environments to Assess Neglect (CLEAN), 442–445
State-Trait Anger Expression Scale
  MacMillan–Olson–Hansen Anger Control Scale (MOHAC), 318
State-Trait Anxiety Inventory
  Daily Discipline Interview (DDI), 262
STDs. *See* Sexually transmitted diseases
Stimulation of research, 14–15
Stress. *See also* Posttraumatic stress disorder (PTSD)
  abusive families, 370

Assessing Environments Scale
(AEIII), 135
Checklist of Sexual Abuse and Re-
lated Stressors (C–SARS), 138–
142
Child's Reaction to Traumatic Events
Scale (CRTES), 153–155
Family Inventory of Life Events
(FILE), 423
Parental Stress Scale (PSS), 318–320
parent engaging in child abuse, 251
Parenting Stress Index (PSI), 330–
333
Parent's Report on the Child's Reac-
tion to Stress Scale (PRCS),
194–197
"When Bad Things Happen"
(WBTH), 224–227
Structured Clinical Interview for
DSM-III-R (SCID), 205
Structured Interview for Disorders of
Extreme Stress (SIDES), 112–
115
Structured Interview of Symptoms Asso-
ciated with Sexual Abuse
(SASA), 109–111
Structured Laboratory and Home Ob-
servation: Single Case Study
(SLHO), 499–501
Subpoenas for client records, 28
Substance abuse
adult survivors of child sexual abuse,
26
perpetrators of child sexual abuse,
26, 27
Suicidality, 26
Trauma Symptom Inventory (TSI),
215–216
Summer camp, children at
Exposure to Interadult Anger (EIA),
454
Supervision needs
Multidimensional Neglect Scale
(MNS), 183
Supportive environment
Exposure to Abuse and Supportive
Environments–Parenting Inven-
tory (EASE–PI), 171–175
Family Crisis Oriented Personal Eval-
uation Scales (F–COPES), 417
Parent Behavior Inventory (PBI), 310

Screening for Problem Parenting
(SPP), 293
Survivor guilt
Childhood PTSD Interview–Child
Form (CPI-Child), 91
"When Bad Things Happen"
(WBTH), 224
Survivors. *See* Adult survivors of child
abuse; Adult survivors of child
sexual abuse

T

TAI. *See* Traumatic Antecedents Inter-
view
Tantrums
Disciplinary Strategies Interview
(DSI), 264
Targets, 22–23
Teacher self-reporting inventories
Parents Perceptions Questionnaire
(PPQ), 191–194
Teacher's Perceptions Questionnaire
(TPQ), 191–194
Teacher's Perceptions Questionnaire
(TPQ), 191–194
Teaching by parent
Daily Discipline Interview (DDI), 260
Teenagers. *See* Adolescent *entries*
Tension reduction behavior
Trauma Symptom Inventory (TSI),
215
Terrorizing. *See also* Coercion; Fear
Psychological Maltreatment Scales
(PMS), 488
Test construction, 39–50
definitional problems of constructs,
46–49
difficulties in, 46–50
methods of, 39–41
placing participants at risk, 48–49
psychometric properties problems,
46–47
rational and empirical approaches to
scale development, 39–40
revictimization by research, 47–48
scoring of the instrument, 40–41
Test–retest reliability, 42
Therapists working with victims
History of Victimization Form
(HVF), 179–182
vicarious traumatization, 27

Third Party Intervention Coding System (TPICSS)
   Home Interaction Scoring System (HISS), 469
Thurstone scale, 40
Toddlers. *See* Young children
TPICSS. *See* Third Party Intervention Coding System
TPQ. *See* Teacher's Perceptions Questionnaire
Transitions
   Family Inventory of Life Events (FILE), 423
Translation of instrument. *See* Foreign languages, translation into
Trauma Symptom Checklist 33 and 40 (TSC–33 and TSC–40), 212–214
Trauma Symptom Checklist for Children (alternate form) (TSCC–A), 209
Trauma Symptom Checklist for Children (TSCC), 209–212
Trauma Symptom Inventory (TSI), 214–218
Traumatic Antecedents Interview (TAI), 115–118
Traumatic Sexualization Survey (TSS), 218–221
Treatment programs, 13
   types of, 27
Triangulation
   Children's Perceptions of Interparental Conflict Scale (CPICS), 390
   Parent–Adolescent Relationship Questionnaire (PARQ), 429
   System for Coding Interactions and Family Functioning (SCIFF), 502
Trust issues
   Children's Attributions and Perceptions Scale (CAPS), 96
   Negative Appraisals of Sexual Abuse Scale (NASAS), 186
   Structured Interview for Disorders of Extreme Stress (SIDES), 113
TSC–33 and TSC–40. *See* Trauma Symptom Checklist 33 and 40
TSCC. *See* Trauma Symptom Checklist for Children
TSI. *See* Trauma Symptom Inventory
TSS. *See* Traumatic Sexualization Survey
Two-parent families

Family Intake Coding System (FICS), 454–457
Family Interaction Task (FIT), 461–463
Observational Coding System for Triadic Interaction (OCSTI), 484–487
Types of assessment methods, 4

U

Unfairness
   Family Beliefs Inventory (FBI), 414
Unplanned pregnancy
   Assessing Environments Scale (AEIII), 136
Unsafe behavior of child
   Disciplinary Strategies Interview (DSI), 264
   Video Assessment Task (VAT), 359

V

Validity
   construct validity, 43–45
   defined, 41
   internal versus external, 49–50
VAT. *See* Video Assessment Task
Verbal accessibility of mother
   Maternal Characteristics Scale (MCS), 289
Verbal intervention by child
   Children's Marital Conflict Coping Strategies Interview (CMCCSI), 376
Verbal reasoning by parent
   Parent Behavior Rating Scales (PBRS), 351
   Parent Discipline Interview (PDI), 266
Verbal reprimands. *See also* Disciplinary practices
   Analogue Parenting Task (APT), 336
Verbosity of parent
   Dyadic Parent–Child Interaction Coding System (DPICS), 450
   Parenting Scale (PS), 325, 327
Vicarious traumatization, 27
Video Assessment Task (VAT), 359–361
Video Mediated Recall Task (VMRT), 362–366
VMRT. *See* Video Mediated Recall Task
Voices giving directions

Adolescent Dissociative Experience Survey (A–DES), 128
Vulnerability
    Child's Impact of Traumatic Events Scale B Revised (CITES–R), 162
    Responses to Childhood Incest Questionnaire (RCIQ), 200

W

WBR. *See* Weekly Behavior Report
WBTH. *See* "When Bad Things Happen"
Weekly Behavior Report (WBR), 221–224
Weekly Report of Abuse Indicators (WRAI), 296–298
"What If" Situations Test (WIST–III), 118–122, 198
"When Bad Things Happen" (WBTH), 224–227
White and middle-class sampling
    Assessing Environments Scale (AEIII), 137
    Children's Perceptions of Interparental Conflict Scale (CPICS), 392
    Sexually Anatomically Detailed (SAD) Dolls, 245
WISC–R Verbal Comprehension
    Discord Control and Coping Questionnaire (DCCQ), 394
WIST–III. *See* "What If" Situations Test
Withdrawal of affection by parent
    Maternal Characteristics Scale (MCS), 288
    Parent Discipline Interview (PDI), 266
    System for Coding Interactions and Family Functioning (SCIFF), 503
Withdrawal of child
    Observational Coding System for Triadic Interaction (OCSTI), 485
Witness to violence. *See* Exposure of child to violence

Witness to Violence Child Interview, 383–386
Work-family strains
    Family Inventory of Life Events (FILE), 423
WRAI. *See* Weekly Report of Abuse Indicators
WSHQ. *See* Wyatt Sex History Questionnaire
Wyatt Sex History Questionnaire (WSHQ), 122–124

Y

Young adults. *See* Adolescents
Young children (generally)
    Cleanup Coding Systems (CCS), 445–449
    Dyadic Parent–Child Interaction Coding System (DPICS), 449–452
    Home Observation for Measurement of the Environment (HOME), 470–472
    Personal Safety Questionnaire (PSQ), 197–199
    Response-Class Matrix (RCM), 490–492
    Sibling Conflict Resolution Scale (SCRS), 492–495
    "What If" Situations Test (WIST–III), 118–122
Young children abused. *See* Child maltreatment
Young children exposed to marital conflict
    Children's Response to Live Interadult Anger (CRLIA), 439–442
Young children exposed to violence. *See* Exposure of child to violence
Young children suspected of being sexually abused
    Anatomical Doll Questionnaire (ADQ), 63–66
    Sexually Anatomically Detailed (SAD) Dolls, 243–246

About the Authors

Eva L. Feindler, PhD, is a professor of psychology at the Long Island University (LIU)/CW Post Campus doctoral program in clinical psychology. As a faculty member of the Specialty Track in Family Violence department and as director of the Psychological Services Clinic, she is directly involved in programs to help children and families manage their anger and resolve conflict. She received her undergraduate degree in psychology from Mount Holyoke College and her master's and doctoral degrees from West Virginia University. Her clinical internship training was completed at the Children's Psychiatric Center in Eatontown, New Jersey. Before her position at LIU, she was an associate professor of psychology at Adelphi University, where she also directed the master's program in applied behavioral technology. She has authored several books *(Adolescent Anger Control: Cognitive–Behavioral Strategies; Handbook of Adolescent Behavior Therapy)* and numerous articles on parent and child anger and its assessment and treatment, and she has conducted professional training workshops across the United States and Canada. She has also served an appointed term on the New York State Board for Psychology and a term on the Board of the Nassau County Psychological Association, and she was the program coordinator for the Association for the Advancement of Behavior Therapy Conference in 1995. In addition, she served on the American Psychological Association (APA) Commission on Violence and Youth from 1992 to 1995 and on the APA Task Force on Violence and the Family.

Jill H. Rathus, PhD, is associate professor of psychology at Long Island University/CW Post Campus in Brookville, New York, where she is director of the Dialectical Behavioral Therapy (DBT) Program as well as the director of the Family Violence Program. After receiving her doctorate from the State University of New York at Stony Brook, she became research coordinator of the Adolescent Depression and Suicide Program at the Albert Einstein College of Medicine/Montefiore Medical Center in Bronx, New York. There, she received an Institutional Research Grant from the American Foundation for Suicide Prevention to study the treatment of suicidal adolescents. She codeveloped the adaptation of DBT for suicidal adolescents. In addition to training, consulting, and presenting her research nationally, she has published numerous articles and chapters on adolescent suicide as well as on marital discord/domestic violence, personality, and anxiety disorders. She is presently coauthoring her third book, *DBT for Suicidal Adolescents*. Finally, she maintains a clinical practice and is currently working on an adaptation of DBT for the treatment of partner violence.

Laura Beth Silver, PsyD, works as a project director at the Institute for Research on Youth at Risk at National Development and Research Institutes, Inc., in New York City. In this position she directs school-based research projects on violence, tobacco, and drugs. She completed her doctorate in clinical psychology at Long Island University/CW Post Campus, where she specialized in studies of family violence. Clinically she specializes in work with adolescents. She spent her internship working with children and adolescents with severe and chronic emotional, behavioral, and cognitive disturbances. She has collaborated on research studies assessing the characteristics of assaultive husbands and violent interactions within intimate relationships. She has presented at national conferences on topics including violence prevention, DBT, and battering.